*f***P**

*From*

# ARISTOTLE

*to*

# ZOROASTER

---

*An A-to-Z Companion
to the Classical World*

*ARTHUR COTTERELL*

THE FREE PRESS

NEW YORK · LONDON
TORONTO · SYDNEY · SINGAPORE

*f*P

THE FREE PRESS
A Division of Simon & Schuster Inc.
1230 Avenue of the Americas
New York, NY 10020

Copyright © 1998 by Arthur Cotterell
All rights reserved,
including the right of reproduction
in whole or in part in any form.

Originally published in Great Britain in 1998 by Pimlico as
*The Pimlico Dictionary of Classical Civilizations*
Published by arrangement with Random House UK Limited

THE FREE PRESS and colophon are trademarks
of Simon & Schuster Inc.

Manufactured in the United States of America

10   9   8   7   6   5   4   3   2   1

Library of Congress Cataloging-in-Publication Data

Cotterell, Arthur
    From Aristotle to Zoroaster : an A-to-Z companion to the classical
world / Arthur Cotterell.
        p.      cm.
    Includes bibliographical references and index.
    1. Civilization, Ancient—Encyclopedias.    I. Title.
CB311.C83      1998                98–21729       CIP
930'.03—dc21

ISBN 0–684–85596–8

# CONTENTS

## Preface

This dictionary is an attempt to embrace the classical era of the Old World, and not just the civilizations of Greece and Rome. For too long they have been dignified as the classical world and their study isolated from even the major powers that confronted them in Iran and India. Today we are more aware of the complex inter-relations that once existed between the Greeks and the Persians, the Macedonians and the Indians, the Romans and both the Parthians and the Sasanians.

Two examples of these old connections can be found in the development of philosophy and religion. The first concerns the influence of Indian asceticism on Greek philosophy. Pyrrhon of Elis (*c.* 365–270 BC) adopted an extreme scepticism, following a visit to northern India as a member of Alexander the Great's train. So impressed was he with the indifference shown by Indian ascetics to their surroundings that he subsequently held the view that judgement should be suspended because of the unreliability of the senses. Even though his friends had to protect him from all kinds of danger, Pyrrhon lived in a manner consistent with the view that no one thing was in itself more than another. When asked on his deathbed if he were still alive, he is supposed to have replied that he was not sure. Such imperturbability could not form the basis of a major philosophical school, but it introduced into the thought of the West a healthy scepticism.

The second example of an important transfer of ideas was the decision of the future St Augustine in AD 373 to temporarily abandon Christianity for Manichaeism. This gnostic belief derived from the teachings of Mani (AD 216–277), who had also been raised as a Christian in southern Babylon. Mani travelled to the Sasanian provinces in India so as to study Buddhism, and he also visited Rome as an envoy of Shapur I, his protector from the Zoroastrian priesthood. What infuriated these clerics were Mani's most obvious borrowings from

Zoroastrianism in the construction of an extreme dualism between the body and the spirit. The resurrection of the flesh was totally rejected in favour of a slow refining process for the soul. The essential knowledge granted to the chosen few of Mani chimed with Augustine's own sense of helplessness, which made him later believe that no one could be saved without grace. It was to inform his outlook after he became a bishop in Hippo, modern Bône in Algeria. There in AD 410 Augustine tried to make sense for Christians of the sack of Rome, an event which served to encourage his tendency towards predestination. For the collapse of the political order they took for granted could only be understood as part of divine providence, the gathering in of the saved.

The two-continent world of Hecataeus gave pride of place to Persia, around 500 BC.

The classical civilizations of Europe, West Asia, and Central and South Asia thus gradually became more knowledgeable about one another. For the classical Greeks the world was made up of two continents, Europe and Asia. A map reconstructed from the writings of Hecataeus of Miletus, an extensive traveller within the Persian empire, would give pride of place to that great power. This is hardly surprising when it is recalled how the Persian kings then ruled over the most populous state in the world. In 500 BC Hecataeus vainly advised the Ionian Greeks not to rebel against Persia. Some cities were forced to emigrate on the Persian counterattack, others were decimated in the revolt, including Miletus itself. It was Ionia's tragedy, and the good fortune of the Greek mainland, that over a decade elapsed before Persia was ready to resume its advance westwards. Though they failed to make headway in Europe, the Persians were untroubled themselves until in 334 BC the Macedonian king, Alexander the Great, invaded Asia intent upon establishing an empire of his own. Within eight years he was campaigning in northern India with an army of some 120,000 men, of whom the Macedonians were one-eighth, the Greeks above one-third, and the Balkan and Asian troops one-half. It would be incorrect to attribute Alexander's vision of a multiracial state, albeit based on Greek speech and Macedonian military tactics, to nothing more than manpower requirements. For the young conqueror was genuinely impressed by his own apparent destiny to reshape West Asia, once his Macedonian soldiers made it clear that further eastern conquests were ruled out. In 326 BC, they had refused to advance against the massive army of the Nanda dynasty, then the rulers of the Ganges valley.

Those, like the curious philosopher Pyrrhon, who travelled with the expeditionary force realized that Alexander had come nowhere near to 'the end of India', but they had a better notion of the world he had marched across.

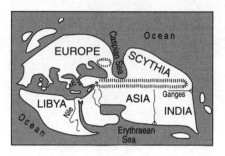

The world according to Eratosthenes, around 200 BC.

Their knowledge allowed Eratosthenes (275–194 BC) to provide a much better description of the earth, besides calculating at Alexandria its circumference. A reconstructed version of his map would give more space to India and Scythia, the steppelands of Central Asia. But the classical civilization of China is still missing. It does not appear in any Western map until another Alexandrian endeavoured to describe the world. In rejecting the ancient Greek idea of a circumfluent ocean, Ptolemy assumed in AD 150 the existence of a large subequatorial continent to balance an Asia enlarged by the addition of China. Possibly he imagined the Indian Ocean was another enclosed sea like the Mediterranean.

Familiarity with its northern waters was due to the discovery and exploitation of the monsoons and not to any improvements in Roman shipping. Only the Chinese had developed vessels capable of deep-ocean navigation, which during the classical era they used solely in eastern seas. For the Romans China was Seres, the source of silk, a commodity traded throughout the length of the Old World. The Kushana conquerors of Central Asia and northern India made determined efforts during the first century AD to divert this lucrative trade route away from Parthian Iran. Caravans from China descended through the Khyber Pass down to the Indus delta, whence their silk went by sea to Characene, a kingdom at the head of the Persian Gulf. Commerce between Rome and China was necessarily in the hands of middlemen, even though the Han dynasty imposed Chinese control over the so-called Western Regions, essentially the Tarim basin. The outflow of gold to pay for eastern luxuries such as silk, gems and spices worried the Roman authorities: some 12,000 pounds of gold were estimated to have been sent to India each year, almost enough to account for the high-quality gold coins issued by so many of its rulers.

Direct contact between Chinese and Roman officials may have occurred at Antioch in AD 97. That year a Chinese envoy was said to have been stopped by the Parthians from travelling farther west, and so it is now impossible to know if the Chinese and Roman

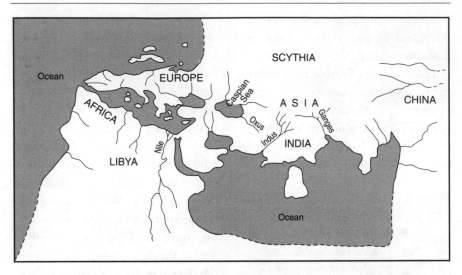

Ptolemy's map of the world included China for the first time in AD 150.

emperors ever exchanged gifts and messages. The silk trade appears to have been in the hands of Central Asian allies of the Chinese, who showed little interest in international trade themselves. It is indeed the persistent isolation of China, cut off by mountains and deserts from India, that makes the classical experience there so useful for comparison and contrast. The unimportance of slavery is but one cause for reflection. Early production of cast iron and steel provided efficient hoes, ploughshares, picks and axes: it may have allowed effective tillage without recourse to large-scale rural slavery, in striking contrast to Greece and Rome. Imperial unification in 221 BC was also intertwined with technical advance, but the ability of a dynasty to endure was also related to the acquiescence of the governed and the means by which they could effect political

changes. It happened in China that offensive weapons were always superior, the crossbow before the lifetime of Christ ruling out any armoured domination. For that reason Mencius (371–288 BC), the greatest follower of Confucius, could reasonably argue the right of the people to take up arms against tyrannical government. Yet the development of a highly educated imperial bureaucracy to govern the most populous of all classical states remains a feature of Chinese uniqueness. China alone subordinated the military to the control of civilians. It suffered war and foreign invasion as much as other parts of the Old World, but by the end of the classical period in AD 317 the Chinese had come to take for granted the necessity of strong central authority. Buddhism, China's greatest import, would never dislodge the emperor or his ministers from the

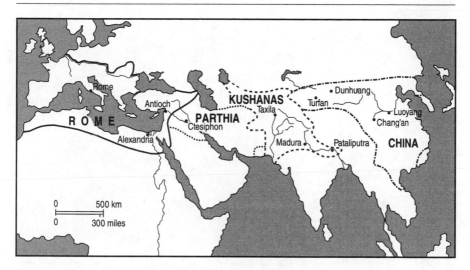

The four great powers at the beginning of the second century AD: Rome, Parthia, Kushana India and Han China.

apex of society, unlike the politically subversive influence of religion in India.

This dictionary cannot be more than an introduction to the classical age. But through looking at the ways in which the Greeks, the Macedonians, the Persians, the Romans, the Indians, the Kushanas and the Chinese dealt with the problems and opportunities their various civilizations threw up, it is hoped that a more general understanding of this fundamental period of the past will evolve. Cross references have been specially designed to assist this process, but in a way that aids freedom of movement within the text without impeding readability. Subjects and names listed at the end of each entry, in capitals, refer the reader to connected entries of further interest. An up-to-date recommendation of relevant books also follows the entries. After the

chronology and the section of maps there is also an index of names which do not appear as the titles of entries in the dictionary.

Special thanks, finally, are due to Professor John Crook, my old tutor, for his helpful suggestions about the Greek and Roman entries: I must bear sole responsibility, however, for the opinions expressed in them. And I also owe a great debt of gratitude to Ray Dunning for the quality of both the illustrations and the maps.

# A

**Achaean League** of city-states in the northern Peloponnese came into its own during the third century BC. It was a rare example of a successful confederation in classical Greece. Foreign policy, military matters and court cases were handled by a central government, while local affairs remained the preserve of individual member states. The Achaean League received support from Ptolemaic Egypt against Macedon but when, in the 220s BC, Sparta underwent a social revolution under King Cleomenes III and threatened to dominate the Peloponnese, it switched sides and helped the Macedonians defeat the Egypt-backed Spartans. Although an attempt was made to stay on good terms with Rome, it proved extremely difficult to maintain the league's independence as Roman armies moved against Macedon. After the final defeat of the Macedonians at Pydna in 168 BC, Roman envoys visited Achaea on a fact-finding mission: their purpose was to detect anti-Roman sentiment in spite of the league's declared willingness to put its forces at the disposal of Rome. The result of the visit was the deportation of 1,000 leading citizens to Italy, among whom was the historian Polybius (200–118 BC). Most of these hostages were kept clear of Rome, but Polybius was allowed to travel as he pleased. He owed this privilege to the influence of Scipio Aemilianus, son of Aemilius Paullus, the victor of Pydna. They had already met in Greece.

In 150 BC the Romans belatedly sent back home the 300 survivors of the hostages they had taken seventeen years earlier. Polybius, however, decided to remain as an adviser to Scipio Aemilianus (185–129 BC). Anti-Roman feeling was not long coming to the boil in the Achaean League, whose capital was then Corinth. When Roman envoys arrived to assess the situation, they were foolishly ill treated. Achaean hopes that the Romans were too heavily committed elsewhere to be able to retaliate proved misplaced, since in 146 BC the legions stationed in the Roman province of Macedonia marched south, destroyed Corinth, and sold its surviving citizens into slavery.

That same year Greece became just another province of the Roman empire.

See MACEDON; ROME; SCIPIOS

*P. Green, *Alexander to Actium: The Hellenistic Age* (London, 1990).

**Administration** was developed into an art by the classical civilizations of India and China. The Seleucid ambassador Megasthenes, who travelled to northern India several times between 302 and 291 BC, was impressed by the highly organized Mauryan bureaucracy. It consisted of three groups: district officials in charge of rural areas, town officials to govern the cities, including the capital Pataliputra, and officials to administer the armed forces. The large Mauryan army was organized under a committee of thirty, divided into subcommittees which controlled the infantry, chariots, elephants, navy and commissariat. The military class, who were numerically second only to the peasantry, led a life of great freedom and enjoyment, having only battles to fight. A parallel administrative arrangement is known to have existed for Pataliputra, where a committee of thirty members was supported by subcommittees responsible for welfare (along with the care of foreigners), manufacture, registration of births and deaths, commerce, and taxation. The law-abiding character of Mauryan India also struck Megasthenes. While he stayed with the emperor Candragupta (322–297 BC),

in an imperial camp numbering 400,000 people, the ambassador noted that daily thefts reported did not exceed 200 drachmas in value. Justice was personally dispensed by Candragupta in an open assembly.

Had another envoy journeyed farther east to China, he would have noted later on that Chinese administration was the most developed of all. In reaction to the authoritarianism of the brief Qin dynasty (221–207 BC), the government of the Han empire was based on the principle that no one person should have unlimited authority, and that all actions, including those of the emperor, should be open to scrutiny. Under Qin the newly unified empire was divided into thirty-six commanderies, each of which comprised several subprefectures. Each commandery was under the authority of a civil administrator and a military governor. The activities of the civil administrator were supervised by an inspector, who reported direct to the central administration. This new post seems to have been added to the provincial system of government in order to keep the capital informed about local affairs, and especially the enforcement of imperial edicts. At the head of each subprefecture was an official whose title is best rendered as prefect. This centralized bureaucracy left no place for feudalism, something even the cautious Han emperors were obliged to recognize as inheritors of the Qin unification. The removal of 120,000 noble families to the capital in

221 BC had effectively deprived the nobility of its territorial and hereditary privileges and made it subject to the law and a hierarchy of merit. Although the turmoil that accompanied the overthrow of Qin in 207 BC tore the empire apart and necessitated a compromise, the Han administration maintained a high level of control. Small fiefs awarded to old families, supporters of the first Han emperor Gaozu (202–195 BC), and his own relatives were carefully intertwined with territories controlled by imperial officials. A rebellion among the eastern domains in 154 BC upset the administrative balance, which was subsequently tilted towards a purely bureaucratic state under strong central control.

The structure of the classical Chinese empire has been likened to a pyramid, with the emperor at the apex, the officials immediately below, and the people at the base. The critical dividing line was literacy, because it marked the difference between the rulers and the ruled, between the educated gentry, from whom officials were drawn, and the peasants, who could neither read nor write.

Conscious efforts were made to recruit suitable candidates for office, the Han emperor Wu Di (140–87 BC) being the first to set examination questions. His interest extended to individual grades and he would revise the pass list whenever he spotted someone whose ideas he liked. Prior to the decline of the civil service in the second century AD, the system of

imperial examinations worked so well that it was bound to be revived as the method of filling the bureaucracy

Legendary foundation of the Chinese civil service in 1027 BC. Here officials of the defeated Shang dynasty are being enrolled in the new Zhou administration, a precedent that during subsequent changes of dynasty freed scholar-bureaucrats from slavish devotion to any particular royal lineage.

under the Tang emperors (AD 618–906). They inherited a reunified China that desperately required stable government, which only the continuity of a powerful civil service could provide.

In comparison with India and China the administrative arrangements of Rome were rudimentary. Although the Romans came to control a far-flung empire, they did not develop an imperial administration that matched

3

its dimensions. The chief concerns always remained the maintenance of order and the collection of taxes. Taxes were needed for wages, military expenses and to provide shows, buildings and handouts of food and cash in the capital. To achieve these limited aims the first Roman emperor Augustus (31 BC – AD 14) took the republican system of senatorial administration and expanded it, creating more posts for senators, but in addition employing for the first time in positions of public responsibility non-elected officials, men from the lesser aristocracy, and even freemen and slaves. But this expansion in the number of posts and diversification in the social background of officials did not give rise to a bureaucracy, not least because administration stayed local. To a great extent, local communities and local powerholders continued to manage their own affairs with relatively little interference from the centre of power at Rome or from Roman officials. That revolts were uncommon was in great part a result of the advantages that local magnates enjoyed under Roman rule. It was also foolhardy to challenge the power of Rome, as was pointed out to the Jews on the eve of their revolt in AD 66. For the cement which held the provinces together was the Roman army, whose strength was periodically renewed by the incorporation of foreigners. Loss of control over this formidable military machine occurred towards the close of the fourth century AD, when an acute

manpower shortage coincided with pressure from the Goths. Theodosius I (AD 379–395) was probably the last emperor to exercise effective military command.

Under the Persians (559–330 BC) virtually the whole of West Asia was administered in a manner looser than that adopted by Rome. Because of the diversity of the areas conquered – Asia Minor, Egypt, Syria, Mesopotamia and India – the Achaemenid kings encountered substantial difficulties during the setting up of their own administration. They were, therefore, obliged to assume a personal relationship with conquered peoples, crowning themselves according to local customs, and employing local administrators to rule for them. But the uprisings of 522–521 BC compelled Darius I to tighten control by means of Persian-nominated governors, who worked closely with local powerholders. Each Persian province, however, remained an independent socio-economic region with its own social institutions and internal structure. Subsequent dynasties, like the Greco-Macedonian Seleucids (312–64 BC), the Iranian Parthians (171 BC – AD 226) and Sasanians (AD 226–651), tended to follow the Achaemenid model at least until Zoroastrianism elevated a militant priesthood. Even then the Sasanian kings found themselves holding the balance of power between the nobility and the clergy.

In classical Greece, on the other hand, administration was almost always associated with elected office. Tyrannies and oligarchies aside, it was the custom of the city-state to share its administration between as many citizens as possible. At Athens the principle was first asserted by Solon in 594 BC that the law should be above any individual or group of individuals who might be granted or take upon themselves the right to interpret it. Despite a period of tyranny under the Pisistratids between 561 and 510 BC, the Athenians developed Solon's principle to such an extent that by the middle of the fifth century BC every male citizen had the same responsibility as any other for the administration of his society. No question seemed too important and very few too trivial to be exempt from popular decision, either directly in the assembly, or indirectly in a council chosen annually by lot from the whole citizen body. Executive power, civil as well as military, lay in the hands of ten elected officials, the generals. Pericles (c. 495–429 BC) held a generalship year after year, till in 430 BC he was removed from office and fined by an angry citizenry. All public officials underwent preliminary examinations and final audits: a panel of citizens elected by lot had final jurisdiction in all matters. But the law courts could also be used by political opponents unable to gain the advantage in the citizen assembly, and this seems to have occurred with the charge of corruption levelled against Pericles. For immediately after the trial a peace mission was sent to Sparta, in an abortive attempt to reverse his policy. But the shock of invasion did not last and in 429 BC Pericles was elected general once again.

See ATHENS; AUGUSTUS; DARIUS I; GOTHS; HAN DYNASTY; PERICLES; PERSIA; ROME; SELEUCIDS; TYRANTS

*H. Bielenstein, *The Bureaucracy of Han Times* (Cambridge, 1980); M. A. Dandamaev and V. G. Lukonin, *The Culture and Social Institutions of Ancient Iran* (Cambridge, 1989); J. K. Davies, *Democracy and Athens* (Glasgow, 1978); A. Lintott, *Imperium Romanum: Politics and Administration* (London, 1993).

**Aegina,** an island situated in the Saronic Gulf south of Athens, was an early Greek maritime power. Its highly profitable trade was facilitated by a mint which struck one of the earliest known coinages in Europe. A tortoise stamped on the reverse side of silver Aeginetan coins, like the owl on later Athenian issues, was recognized at trading ports throughout the length of the Mediterranean as a reliable medium of exchange.

Rivalry with the Athenians came to overshadow all other Aeginetan concerns. Without any declaration of war, the Aeginetans raided in 506 BC the Attic coast and burnt the Athenian port of Phaleron and other coastal settlements. Thus began a struggle which reached a climax in 431 BC, when in the first year of the Peloponnesian War between Athens and Sparta the Athenians expelled the Aeginetans from their island and in place of the original inhabitants decided to send their own settlers to Aegina. But early

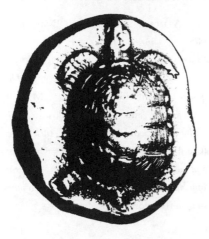

Silver Aeginetan coin, the first coinage to be struck in Europe.

in this long conflict Athens received unexpected support from Sparta, where King Cleomenes I (520–489 BC) overcame his dislike for the fledgling Athenian democracy and took hostages from Aegina so as to ensure it did not take advantage of the invading Persians to favourably settle the dispute. Yet the willingness of the Aeginetans in 491 BC to reach an accommodation with King Darius (521–486 BC) may have had as much to do with protecting their own trading interests in the extensive lands under Persian domination as any desire to do the Athenians down. Aegina traded with Egypt, Asia Minor and the Levant – all subject to Darius' rule.

There is no certainty as to whether Aegina ever formally joined either of the rival blocs headed by Sparta and Athens: the Peloponnesian League and the Delian League respectively. The historian Thucydides, however, tells us that one reason for the deportation of the Aeginetans in 431 BC was a firm belief on the part of Athenians that they bore a great responsibility for the outbreak of hostilities that year between the two leagues through their constant provocative actions against the Athenians at Sparta. Another reason for settling Athenians on Aegina was its strategic position next to the Peloponnesian coast. From the start of the Delian League in 478–477 BC the Athenians had planted colonies overseas for several reasons: they provided security against Persian threats, offered bases for launching attacks against defecting allies, and augmented the manpower resources upon which Athens could draw. In 405 BC, a year before Athens capitulated, the Spartan admiral Lysander restored the Aeginetans, but their freedom was limited by the imposition of a governor. The island remained a backwater right down till its bequest to Rome by Attalus III of Pergamum in 133 BC.

*See* ATHENS; CLEOMENES I; COINAGE; PELOPONNESIAN WAR; PERSIAN INVASIONS; ROME; SPARTA
★T. Figuera, *Aegina* (New York, 1981) and *Athens and Aigina in the Age of Imperial Colonialism* (Baltimore, 1991).

**Africa** was the name of the Roman province situated in present-day

Tunisia. Annexed after the destruction of Carthage in 146 BC, it was at first administered from nearby Utica. By the reign of the first emperor Augustus (31 BC – AD 14), the administration of a greatly enlarged Africa had been transferred to the newly founded Roman colony on the site of Carthage. Notwithstanding Roman sentiment about the defeated Carthaginians, this location was too attractive to remain long unoccupied. The wealth of the province was proverbial: the land was said to be so fertile that one grain would produce a stalk yielding 150 new grains. During the first century AD, Africa's cornfields provided two-thirds of the wheat required by the inhabitants of Rome. The other granaries were Sicily and Egypt. The continued importance of African corn made the imperial government very sensitive about rebellions in the province. When, in AD 312, the future emperor Constantine made his bid for supreme power, he was assisted not only by the vision of a cross before the decisive engagement at the Mulvian bridge near Rome; during the winter of AD 312–313 his position in Italy was also secured by the shipment of corn sent by African provincials who were grateful for the support which he had given to a revolt of their own. The anxiety felt in AD 429 is thus understandable. That year the Vandals crossed the Pillars of Hercules and began their conquest of the north African seaboard as far east as Tripolitania, today part of Libya. From

Carthage, which became their capital in AD 439, the Vandals raided the Mediterranean, even sacking the city of Rome in AD 455. They were not subdued until the eastern Roman emperor Justinian (AD 527–565) sent an expedition to Africa in AD 533–534. The reconquered province, or diocese, remained loyal to Constantinople and beat off earlier Muslim invasions, until captured in AD 697.

Throughout the period of Roman and Vandal rule Africa was a leading centre of Christianity. It is not unlikely that its local strength derived from nostalgia for a pre-Roman Carthaginian past, something the new faith seemed to offer in defiance of Rome. A group of seven men and five women were willing to accept martyrdom in AD 180 at the hands of the authorities because, as their spokesman succinctly put it, they did not 'recognize the empire of this world'. Most remarkable of the African martyrs, however, was Vibia Perpetua, a young married woman of good family with an infant son at her breast. The magistrate was furious with her pagan father for allowing Perpetua to embrace Christianity. It seemed incredible that she was prepared to defy him, the authorities, the world, and reject all the traditional pieties and loyalties in which she had been brought up. From the diary which she kept in prison, during AD 202, awaiting her martyrdom in the amphitheatre, it is clear that she regarded baptism as only a prelude to such a holy death. Even after she was badly hurt by a maddened bull, Perpetua found the strength to encourage her fellow martyrs. Voluntary martyrdom astonished pagans,

Carthaginian funerary pillar, third century BC. The Roman province of Africa never entirely eradicated the influence of Carthage.

much to the satisfaction of Carthage-born Tertullian (*c.* AD 160–240), a presbyter who believed that the end of the world was rapidly approaching. He eloquently warned the provincial governor that the rush to martyrdom constituted a serious danger to the Roman government. He asked: 'How will Carthage tolerate the decimation of its population?' The numbers caught up in the contemporary enthusiasm for martyrdom here are unknown, but both churchmen and imperial officials were evidently concerned. Cyprian, bishop of Carthage from AD 248, tried to reserve the ranks of martyrs for those who endured suffering and death in the face of periodic official persecutions. But as long as Christians believed that martyrs found a spiritual reward in death, then others still wished to emulate them.

In Tripolitania, unlike Africa and Mauretania, Christianity does not seem to have been so successful in making early converts. Possibly the Carthaginian population was more thinly spread to the east of Carthage. Tripolitania's first recorded bishopric was at Lepcis Magna, which the emperor Diocletian (AD 284–305) made into the capital of the newly created province around AD 303. The city already had the distinction of producing Rome's first African emperor in Septimius Severus (AD 193–211), who certainly had some Carthaginian blood in his veins. His family had moved to Italy and risen quickly to high office. Tripolitania succumbed to the Arabs in AD 645, well before the fall of Africa.

*See* CARTHAGE; CHRISTIANITY; CONSTANTINE; JUSTINIAN; ROME; SEVERAN DYNASTY; VANDALS

★S. Raven, *Rome in Africa* (London, 1969); D. J. Mattingly, *Tripolitania* (London, 1995).

**Agesilaus** (444–360 BC) in many ways typified the failure of Sparta after its defeat of Athens in 404 BC, at the end of the Peloponnesian War. Despite congenital lameness and not being in direct line of succession, Agesilaus became one of the two Spartan kings in 399 BC, largely through the influence of Lysander (died 395 BC), who wished to use him for his own political ends. Ambitious Lysander, the Spartan admiral who had destroyed the Athenian fleet at Aegospotami in 405 BC, seems to have wished to open up the dual kingship to others, including himself, rather than to members of the hereditary Agiad and Eurypontid royal houses. His plan miscarried, because after Agesilaus was appointed to command the Spartan expedition against the Persians in Asia Minor, the new king dispensed with Lysander. The Athenian exile Xenophon (428–354 BC) noted how the Spartan king was annoyed that 'there was always a great crowd of courtiers around Lysander wherever he went, so that it looked as if Agesilaus was an ordinary individual'. The campaign proved a failure and in 394 BC Agesilaus was recalled with his army to Greece: Sparta had to accept Persian rule over the Greek cities of Asia Minor. Already states in mainland Greece were growing weary of the Spartan hegemony, and especially Thebes and Athens.

Though Agesilaus overcame the Thebans at Coronea on his way home, the battle did not dent their resolve; and at Leuctra, in 371 BC, they introduced new tactics to inflict the first defeat ever on the Spartans and their allies, who were commanded by the other Spartan king, Cleombrotus. The decisive encounter was caused by

Agesilaus' own stubborn refusal to admit the claim of the Theban general Epaminondas (died 362 BC) to speak on behalf of all Boeotia, whose cities were federated under the leadership of Thebes. Sparta would tolerate no powerful opponents in Greece, but a growing manpower crisis was undermining its tradition of victory on the battlefield. Its citizenry had shrunk in the century following the Persian invasion of Greece in 480–479 BC from 8,000 to well under 2,000. After the loss of 400 men at Leuctra, Agesilaus was forced to arm 6,000 helots and promise their eventual liberation. Deserted by its Peloponnesian allies and with its own slave population of helots largely in revolt, Sparta just managed to fend off Epaminondas' winter invasion of 370–369 BC. What Agesilaus could not prevent, however, was the liberation of Messenia, upon whose servile labour the Spartan military system rested.

No longer could warfare be relied upon to settle all issues, although tyrants such as Dionysius II of Syracuse were willing to lend Sparta mercenaries. But without money to pay them there was nothing Agesilaus could do except become a mercenary general himself, first in the service of the Persians in Asia Minor, and then against them in Egypt. He died in 360 BC aged eighty-four at a place in Cyrenaica aptly called the Harbour of Menelaus, after the legendary Spartan king. His body was embalmed in wax, instead of the usual honey, and returned to Sparta for an elaborate funeral.

*See* ATHENS; EPAMINONDAS; LYSANDER; PELOPONNESIAN WAR; POPULATION

★P. Cartledge, *Agesilaos and the Crisis of Sparta* (London, 1987); C. D. Hamilton, *Agesilaus and the Failure of the Spartan Hegemony* (Ithaca, 1991).

**Agrippa** (*c.* 63–12 BC) was a staunch friend and supporter of the first Roman emperor Augustus (31 BC – AD 14). It was Agrippa's brilliance as an admiral which in 31 BC won the empire for Augustus at the battle of Actium, off the north-western coast of Greece. A defeated Antony and Cleopatra fled to Egypt with less than a quarter of their mangled fleet, and committed suicide there in the following year. In 21 BC Marcus Vipsanius Agrippa married Augustus' only daughter Julia, who bore him five children including Agrippina the Elder, the mother of the third emperor Caligula (AD 37–41). After Agrippa's death Julia married Tiberius, the second Roman emperor (AD 14–37), but her infidelities drove him from Rome in 6 BC. Eventually Augustus sent his wayward daughter to internal exile in southern Italy, where she died in AD 14. The historian Tacitus writes that her newly elevated husband 'let her waste away to death, exiled and disgraced, by slow starvation. Tiberius calculated that Julia had been banished for so long that her death would pass unnoticed.'

*See* ANTONY; AUGUSTUS; CALIGULA; CLEOPATRA; ROME; TIBERIUS

★J. M. Roddaz, *Marcus Agrippa* (Rome, 1984).

The Pantheon, originally built by Agrippa as part of a massive building programme in Rome, was rebuilt by the emperor Hadrian. In AD 608 it was consecrated as a church dedicated to St Mary and All Martyrs.

**Ajanta**, in present-day Maharastra, is the most impressive Buddhist monument to survive in India. Buddhist cave monasteries were common on the Deccan and regularly embellished with murals. Walls and ceilings depict scenes from the lives of the Buddha (many stories of his previous births as bird, animal and man are recorded), the celestial Buddhas and Bodhisattvas (the extended pantheon of the so-called Great Vehicle of Buddhism). At Ajanta the early caves were excavated at the centre of a curving scarp of rock, about 250 feet high, while later caves were added on each side. In total there are twenty-seven caves stretching over a distance of 600 yards; some of the smaller ones, however, are really adjuncts to their larger neighbours. Even though few of the caves are complete, the visitor today is not only overwhelmed by their artistic splendour, but by the feat of excavation itself. They are carved from living rock, reproducing architectural forms long lost. A single cave can be as much as 100 feet long and 40 feet wide. What makes Ajanta unique in the history of classical Indian art is the survival together of painting, sculpture and architecture.

A typical cave comprises a pillared entrance and vestibule; a pillared central court surrounded by monks' cells; and a small inner place of worship containing a figure of the Buddha. Inscriptions date the monastic complex to a period largely before AD 476. That year a southern Deccan king named Harisena is recorded in one of the later caves. He appears to have recently conquered the area.

*See* BUDDHISM

*★S. Dutt, *Buddhist Monks and Monasteries of India* (London, 1962); S. L. Weiner, *Ajanta: Its Place in Buddhist Art* (Berkeley, 1977).

Buddhas on the façade of cave XIX at Ajanta. The extended right arms signify generosity.

**Alcibiades** (*c.* 450–404 BC) attracted in almost equal proportions the admiration and the distrust of his fellow Athenians. Even his physical appearance, the historian Plutarch tells us, 'lent Alcibiades an extraordinary grace and charm, alike as a boy, a youth, and a man. A lisp suited his voice so well that it made his speech persuasive and pleasant to hear.' In his later life though, 'Alcibiades' character was to reveal many changes and inconsistencies, as one might expect in a career such as his, which was spent in the midst of great enterprises and shifts of fortune. He was a man of many passions, but none was stronger than the desire to challenge and gain the upper hand over his rivals.' It was an ambition that by turns caused Athens to celebrate and grieve.

Alcibiades was a kinsman of Pericles (c. 495–429 BC), in whose house he was raised. By 420 BC this young nobleman was able to assume the leadership of the extreme democrats. At his insistence the same year Athens concluded an alliance with Argos and other enemies of Sparta. The peace of 421 BC between Sparta and Athens after the first decade of the Peloponnesian War (431–404 BC) was not proving to be effective, as Sparta's allies disliked its terms. For Alcibiades the uncertainty offered an opportunity to weaken Spartan authority in the Peloponnese, but the Athenians were half-hearted in the support of his schemes with the result that Sparta brought them to an abrupt end at the battle of Mantinea in 418 BC. Undeterred by this setback, Alcibiades proposed in 415 BC an even greater scheme to the Athenian assembly. It was ostensibly an expedition against Syracuse but the real object was the conquest of Sicily. Nicias (c. 470–413

BC), a respected general and opponent of Alcibiades, spoke against the undertaking, but Alcibiades had judged the mood of his countrymen correctly, and they voted for the dispatch of an armada. Its three commanders were Nicias, Lamachus and himself.

Unfavourable omens marked the sailing of the expedition, which the historian Thucydides described as 'by a long way the most costly and the finest-looking force of Greek troops that up to that time had ever come from a single city'. That it was never to return from Sicily made it the greatest disaster ever to befall Athens, other than its surrender to Sparta in 404 BC. Arguably the loss of the expedition, and its reinforcement, in late 413 BC contributed to this final humiliation. Alcibiades may be blamed for assisting in its destruction, for he advised the Spartans to send an experienced general by the name of Gylippus to help Syracuse. Rather than return to Athens and face a charge of sacrilege, shortly after the expedition arrived in Sicily, Alcibiades had fled to Sparta where he gave his surprised hosts excellent military advice. Apart from urging assistance at Syracuse, he advised them to establish a fortified post at Decelea in northern Attica. The second suggestion was not immediately taken, but when in 413 BC the Spartans turned Decelea into a permanent base the Athenians found themselves hemmed in behind their city walls. With the formal renewal of hostilities, several of Athens' subject-allies sent delegations to Sparta to discuss the prospects of a revolt. So in 412 BC, Plutarch relates, 'Alcibiades himself sailed into the Aegean and succeeded in inciting almost all the Ionian cities to rebel, and as he worked closely with a Spartan admiral he did great harm to the Athenians.' But anxiety over his standing with the Spartans led Alcibiades to transfer his allegiance to the Persian governor of Sardis, Tissaphernes (died 395 BC). Though no friend of the Greeks, Tissaphernes was charmed by Alcibiades who persuaded him 'neither to help the Spartans whole-heartedly nor yet to finish off the Athenians'. Persian subsidies sustained the Spartan war effort at sea, where Athens was strongest. Quite likely Tissaphernes was willing to follow Alcibiades' advice in the hope of wearing down the strengths of both sides.

The real aim of Alcibiades was to secure his own recall to Athens. First, he tried to foster an oligarchic coup with the promise of Persian aid for a new form of government. When, in 411 BC, the oligarchy of the Four Hundred failed to impress Tissaphernes and he discarded Alcibiades, the desperate exile tried a second strategy of allying himself with the democrats in the Athenian fleet at Samos. It worked. In Samos Thrasybulus (died 388 BC) and Theramenes (died 403 BC) in Athens arranged for Alcibiades' reinstatement as a commander, and for several years he skilfully directed operations in Ionia and the Hellespont, winning a brilliant naval victory along

with them at Cyzicus in 410 BC. It restored Athenian morale and induced the Spartans to sue for peace. Unease in Athens, however, meant that neither the peace moves nor the military advantage were properly followed up. Alcibiades was politically compromised by involvement with the oligarchy, as were other commanders such as Theramenes. Because they were too strong and too successful to be deposed, they were left in command but without adequate reinforcements. In 407 BC Alcibiades finally returned to Athens, where a worried assembly once more entrusted him with the command of an expeditionary force. This time it was directed against a newly arrived Persian governor, Cyrus (died 401 BC), and the Spartan admiral Lysander (died 395 BC). The support Cyrus gave to Lysander won the Peloponnesian War for Sparta, once Alcibiades fell from Athenian favour again in 406 BC. He was blamed for allowing his second-in-command to lose the sea-battle of Notion, the port of Colophon, in Ionia. His enemies in Athens raised popular suspicions about tyrannical ambitions, and Alcibiades considered it prudent to abandon Athenian affairs altogether.

Plutarch recounts how Alcibiades recruited a force of mercenaries and campaigned on his own behalf in Thrace; how at Aegospotami in 405 BC he warned in vain the Athenian commanders of the danger of a surprise Spartan attack; and how the Thirty, another brief oligarchy at Athens, had him murdered in Phrygia a year later. The assassins were provided by Pharnabazus, the local Persian governor.

See ATHENS; CYRUS; LYSANDER; PELOPONNESIAN WAR; PERICLES; THERAMENES; THRASYBULUS; TISSAPHERNES
★W. M. Ellis, *Alcibiades* (London, 1989); D. Kagan, *The Peace of Nicias and the Sicilian Expedition* (Ithaca, 1981) and *The Fall of the Athenian Empire* (Ithaca, 1987).

**Alexander III**, king of Macedon, 336–323 BC. Called the Great on account of his conquest of Persia. He was born in 356 BC, son of Philip II and Olympias, a member of the Molossian royal family in Epirus. One of seven royal wives, Olympias' relations with Philip were strained, but there is no reason to suppose either she or her son had any connection with the king's assassination in 336 BC. Alexander inherited his mother's mystical interests as well as his father's practical approach to life. Tradition records that Philip once saw through a chink in the door a snake in bed with Olympias, and learned from the Delphic oracle that it was none other than Zeus. He was also told that he would lose the sacrilegious eye for spying on the king of the gods, whom Olympias informed Alexander was his real father. During the siege in 355 BC of the coastal city of Methone, Philip was duly struck by an arrow from a catapult, losing the sight of his right eye. Later at the oracle of Siwah in the Libyan desert, Alexander may have had all this confirmed, if he was literally called 'the son of Zeus Ammon'. On the other hand, the conquering Macedonian king could have been simply accorded the same divine courtesy as the Egyptian pharaoh.

Something of the determination of Alexander is preserved in this ivory head, found during the 1970s at the tomb of his father, King Philip II of Macedon.

Alexander was chosen king, however, in the customary Macedonian manner. The assembly of the Macedonians clashed their spears against their shields as a signal of his succession. His authority over the Greek city-states was confirmed by the Council of the Greek League, which also appointed him as commander of the forces then being assembled for the war against Persia. Having secured his European power-base, Alexander crossed to Asia Minor in 334 BC with an army of 32,000 infantry and 5,100 cavalry. The crossing was associated in Alexander's mind with the Trojan War, and before striking inland he visited Achilles' tomb close to Troy. His own claim was for the whole of Asia 'won by the spear', and not just the Persian empire. At the time few realized that he intended such a total conquest. Victories at nearby Granicus river (334 BC), Issus in Syria (333 BC), and Gaugamela in Assyria (331 BC) dealt with the Persians, whose last king, Darius III, was killed by his own followers in 330 BC on the shores of the Caspian Sea.

In his history of the campaign, Arrian tells us that Alexander learned of Darius' deposition from two Babylonian noblemen. Bessus, the Persian governor of Bactria, had replaced him as king because he was his only close relation who showed any desire to continue the fight. 'Darius' captors,' wrote Arrian, 'had determined to hand him over if they heard that Alexander was after them, and thus get favourable terms for themselves; if, on the other hand, there should be no pursuit, they proposed to gather as large a force as possible and together preserve what they could of their power.' But Alexander gave chase with such speed that he surprised the fugitives. He was too late to save Darius, though, since the deposed ruler was killed by his captors in panic. So the Macedonian king

sent Darius' body to Persepolis to be buried in the royal tombs there, like the Persian kings before him.

At the decisive Gaugamela battle the Macedonians comprised less than one-third of Alexander's army, which numbered about 47,000 men. Through subsequent recruitment of Asians its strength rose in India to 120,000, of whom the Macedonians were one-eighth and the Greeks one-third. This expansion was part of Alexander's policy to found a multiracial kingdom with a multiracial army in which every member was judged on merit. To underline the parity of esteem that he was sponsoring, Alexander and eighty of his closest followers married the daughters of Persian noble families. He also founded seventy new cities in Asia with mixed populations of Macedonians, Greeks and Asians. Their organization and language was Greek, for Alexander firmly believed in the value of the culture he represented. But his unprecedented victories gave him a sense of divine mission which worried some of his Macedonian and Greek followers. 'Alexander considered,' wrote the historian Plutarch, 'that he had come from the gods to be a governor and reconciler of the world. Using force of arms when he could not bring men together by reason, he employed everything for the same end, mixing lives, manners, marriages and customs, as it were, in a loving-cup.'

His eastern campaigns took him to Bactria, where he married in 327 BC Roxane, and into India, the scene of his last major battle against King Porus at Hydaspes river a year later. Dying in Babylon in the summer of 323 BC the young conqueror was asked to whom he left his vast realm. Because Roxane had still to give birth to an heir, this was no idle question. 'To the strongest,' Alexander replied, correctly anticipating the prolonged struggle between his generals.

See ANTIGONUS; CASSANDER; ORACLES; PERSIA; PHILIP II; PORUS; WARFARE
★N. G. L. Hammond, *Alexander the Great: King, Commander and Statesman* (London, 1981); P. Green, *Alexander of Macedon, 356–323 BC: A Historical Biography* (Berkeley, 1991); Arrian, *The Campaigns of Alexander*, trans. by A. de Sélincourt (Harmondsworth, 1971).

**Alexandria** was founded by Alexander the Great (356–323 BC), when, in 331 BC, he conquered the Persian province of Egypt. Unlike two late Persian kings, who had outraged the Egyptians by slaying Apis, the sacred bulls of their day, Alexander was careful to respect local religious sensibilities. As a result the Macedonian conqueror was accepted as pharaoh, perhaps even being named as a living god by the oracle of Ammon at the Siwah oasis. But communications were poor with Europe because the existing harbours were quite inadequate. To solve this problem, the historian Arrian tells us, Alexander 'in person laid down markers for the plan of the city of Alexandria, where the city-centre was

to be built within it, how many temples and to which gods, some being Greek but Isis being Egyptian, and where the circuit-wall was to be made. Then he made sacrifice, and the sacrifice proved favourable.'

Coins showing the deified Alexander. Issued by Ptolemy I as part of the Alexander cult he developed.

After his early death in Babylon, Alexander's embalmed body was placed on display at Alexandria in a golden coffin by Ptolemy, one of his generals. This was a very considerable propaganda triumph for Ptolemy, who probably bribed the commander of the funeral cortège to come to Egypt instead of going on to the royal burial ground in Macedon. Alexander's own ignored wish was to be buried at Siwah. The kingdom that in 305 BC Ptolemy I (305–282 BC) set up in Egypt was governed from Alexandria, although he and his successors always respected the native religious traditions. The city developed, nonetheless, into one of the greatest centres of

Greek learning, its famous Library housing the largest collection of books in the Mediterranean world. The mathematician Euclid taught there during the reign of Ptolemy I. For two centuries Alexandria drew talent like a magnet, its poets and philosophers eventually outstripping those living at Athens. The decline of the Ptolemaic dynasty, however, meant less generous subsidies for Alexandria's teaching institutions. The crisis could no longer be disguised when, in 87 BC, a later Ptolemy sold Alexander the Great's coffin to raise funds. Afterwards the great conqueror had to make do with an alabaster replacement. Finally Egypt itself was bequeathed to Rome in order that it could act as a pledge for Roman moneylenders. The last Ptolemaic ruler, Cleopatra VII, failed to survive the rivalry of Roman warlords, and in 30 BC the future emperor Augustus claimed the bequest at last. It was at this time that Alexander suffered another indignity. The Roman conqueror could not resist touching the preserved body, whereupon part of the nose broke off.

Alexandria was not granted any self-government by Augustus, although Alexandrian citizenship was allowed to continue. Local affairs were put back into the hands of its citizens by the Roman emperor Septimius Severus (AD 193–211). He also hailed from the north African coast, having been born at Lepcis Magna in nearby Libya. The large Jewish population at Alexandria seem to have had their own council throughout Roman and Byzantine times. The Jewish scholar Philo led a delegation to Rome in AD 39 to protest about the treatment of his community by Roman officials. Later on Clement (AD 150–215) continued the scholarly traditions of Alexandria by endeavouring to accommodate Christian doctrine with Greek philosophy.

The city really lost its importance after the Arab conquest, and the return of the political centre of gravity to inland Egypt. Yet the Pharos, Alexandria's famous lighthouse built on a rocky island of the same name, was not destroyed until 1326. One of the so-called seven wonders of the ancient world, this marble structure originally towered over 300 feet in height and was surmounted by a statue of Zeus, the supreme deity of Greeks and Macedonians. Today the site of the Pharos is covered by a fifteenth-century Muslim fort.

See ALEXANDER THE GREAT; CLEMENT; PHILO; PTOLEMIES

*P. M. Fraser, *Ptolemaic Alexandria* (Oxford, 1972); C. Haas, *Alexandria in Late Antiquity* (Baltimore, 1997).

**An Shihkao** (died *c.* AD 168) was an early translator of Buddhist texts into Chinese. A Parthian of royal lineage, he arrived in Luoyang from Central Asia in AD 148 and soon became head of the community of foreign monks already established there. His Chinese name refers to Parthia, or Anxi. Buddhist tradition even explains An

Shihkao's decision to travel eastwards as a reluctance to ascend the Parthian throne. Instead, he joined a monastery in order to prepare for a life as a missionary. In Luoyang An Shihkao effectively organized the original Buddhist monastery and translation school. To his own efforts are credited the translation of works on meditation, techniques of breath-control, and psychology. A fellow-countryman who was also engaged with translation at Luoyang then was the former merchant An Hsuan. Only one Indian is known to have been numbered in this essentially Central Asian community. Though there were a few Chinese monks, it was not until the arrival of the Chinese-speaking Fa Hu from Central Asia that translation could really progress. He brought numerous texts to Chang'an, where before his death around AD 310 he had translated over 100 himself. Fa Hu was the son of a Da Yuezhi family long resident at Dunhuang, an important Buddhist centre at the western terminus of the Great Wall.

See BUDDHISM; LIU YING

*E. Zurcher, *The Buddhist Conquest of China* (Leiden, 1959).

**Anaxagoras** (*c*. 500–428 BC) was the first Greek philosopher to reside in Athens. He arrived from Clazomenae in Asia Minor around 479 BC and became a close friend of the Athenian leader Pericles (*c*. 495–429 BC). The historian Plutarch relates how 'Pericles had an unbounded admiration for Anaxagoras, and his mind became steeped in the so-called higher philosophy and abstract speculation.' On one occasion, when a unicorn was brought to Pericles, the philosopher dissected the skull and explained the phenomenon rationally and scientifically. Pericles himself was not averse to accepting a favourable interpretation of this omen at the same time, however. Enemies of Pericles later brought a charge of impiety against Anaxagoras, but the case was never tried in court. The philosopher had already retired to the safety of Lampsacus on the Hellespont.

Anaxagoras took Empedocles' refutation of the ideas of Parmenides (born *c*. 515 BC) a stage further. He not only rejected the notion of an original unity of being but, without adopting the cyclicalism favoured by Empedocles (*c*. 492–433 BC), he proclaimed a plurality of substances filling the universe. These infinite and indestructible elements were moved by divine force, a kind of cosmic engine behind the movement of matter. The Athenian philosopher Socrates (469–399 BC) later expressed his disappointment at the way in which Anaxagoras relied on mechanistic explanation: he would have preferred the cosmic force to be recognized as an intelligent shaper of events. But Anaxagoras remained ambivalent, holding to a belief somewhere between the world as a product of natural forces and as a planned order of creation. Possibly he was influenced by his fellow Ionian Heraclitus (active 500 BC), who said everything was in a state of measured change.

See ATHENS; EMPEDOCLES; ORACLES; PERICLES

*G. S. Kirk, J. E. Raven and M. Schofield, *The Presocratic Philosophers* (Cambridge, 1983).

**Antigonus** (382–301 BC), a Macedonian nobleman, was born the same year as Philip II, Antigonus outliving that king by thirty-five years and enjoying his greatest and most prominent period after the death of Philip's son, Alexander the Great, in 323 BC. From 320 BC, when he was sixty-two, until his death aged eighty-one at the battle of Ipsus in 301 BC, Antigonus dominated the eastern Mediterranean and ensured that his descendants would be kings. They eventually formed the Antigonid dynasty of Macedon, inaugurated by Antigonus' son Demetrius (294–283 BC) but made secure by his grandson Antigonus Gonatas in 276 BC. During his own ascendancy Antigonus also established an administrative system in West Asia that was successfully taken over by the later Seleucid kingdom (312–64 BC).

Like King Philip earlier, Antigonus lost an eye during a siege in 339 BC, and gained the nickname the 'One-eyed'. After Philip's death he was given a command by Alexander the Great (356–323 BC) in Asia Minor, his future power base. The division of the spear-won realm of Alexander into virtually

autonomous kingdoms in 323 BC was not to the liking of Antigonus, who vainly endeavoured to keep the vast Asian empire intact. It was made an impossible task by the lack of an immediately acceptable successor to Alexander, and not even the energetic campaigning of Antigonus' son, Demetrius, could sway the balance of power in favour of this project for long. Separatist commanders worked against father and son, and in 301 BC at Ipsus (modern Sipsin in Turkey) they finally destroyed Antigonus, although Demetrius managed to escape to Greece. Thereafter the three main powers in the eastern Mediterranean were Antigonid Macedon, Seleucid Asia and Ptolemaic Egypt. These Macedonian dynasties survived till Roman times, albeit as shadows of Alexander the Great's former conquests.

See ALEXANDER THE GREAT; DEMETRIUS; LYSIMACHUS; MACEDON; PTOLEMIES; ROME; SELEUCUS

*R. A. Billows, *Antigonos the One-Eyed and the Creation of the Hellenistic State* (Berkeley, 1990); P. Green, *Alexander to Actium: The Hellenistic Age* (London, 1990).

**Antiochus III**, known as the Great, ruled the Seleucid kingdom of Asia from 223 to 187 BC. When he succeeded to the throne as a young man, following the assassination of his elder brother Seleucus III, he faced difficulties in securing his authority in the army and court, as well as from rebellious governors. His chief opponent

Coin of Antiochus III, struck at Ecbatana shortly after his successful Bactrian campaign. The elephant on the reverse side may refer to Euthydemus' gift of war elephants.

Achaeus, viceroy of Asia Minor, was besieged and captured at Sardis by Antiochus in 213 BC. He was punished in traditional style: having had his nose, ears and hands cut off, Achaeus' body was impaled on a stake in a public place. Though he suffered an initial reverse in Palestine at the hands of the Ptolemaic army, Antiochus was successful in the east, where he is said to have conquered Armenia and recovered Parthia and Bactria between 212 and 206 BC. It is not unlikely that he drove the Parthians out of former Seleucid provinces rather than occupying their mountainous homeland of Hyrcania or Parthyene, next to the Caspian Sea. Like the Bactrian ruler Euthydemus, King Arsaces I of Parthia may then have found it expedient to acknowledge Seleucid suzerainty. Apparently Euthydemus 'concluded a treaty with Antiochus and a sworn alliance'. The historian Polybius also records how the Seleucid king supplied 'his army with generous provisions and added to his forces the elephants which Euthydemus then owned'. Afterwards Antiochus spent some time in north-western India, where he extracted both treasure and additional elephants from Sophagasenus, whom Polybius calls 'king of the Indians'. He may have been a local chief taking advantage of the decline of the Mauryas (322–183 BC) to establish himself in the Kabul valley, or perhaps he was a Mauryan prince, in which case the alliance that was renewed could have been the original treaty of 303 BC between Seleucus I and Candragupta, or a later one with Ashoka (268–232 BC). The recent discovery of Greek translations of Ashoka's famous rock edicts, also cut in stone in what is now Afghanistan, shows Mauryan influence amongst Greeks settled there. Like Alexander the Great (356–323 BC), the Seleucids encouraged immigration from Europe and the Greek world generally by granting land and founding cities.

On his western frontiers, however,

Antiochus was slow to appreciate the growing power of Rome. While maintaining good relations with Macedon, he stripped the Ptolemies of their possessions in Syria, Palestine and Asia Minor. The Romans took alarm when in 196 BC Antiochus sought to conquer Thrace. At Thermopylae in Greece, then at Magnesia in Asia Minor, the Seleucid army was beaten in 190 or 189 BC. Despite a successful cavalry engagement and a heroic stand by Antiochus' infantrymen, the Roman legionaries decisively won the day at the second battle, with the aid of troops from Pergamum, an old enemy of the Seleucids. Stampeding elephants contributed materially to the rout. Though burdened by a heavy war indemnity and effectively barred from Europe by the loss of all territories west of the Taurus mountains, the Seleucid kingdom recovered after Antiochus' death in 187 BC. The main reason was the relatively undisturbed tenor of Seleucid rule in Syria and Mesopotamia before the rise of the Parthians, a resurgent Iranian dynasty (171 BC – AD 226).

See MACEDON; MAURYANS; PARTHIANS; PTOLEMIES; ROME; SELEUCIDS

*S. Sherwin-White and A. Kuhrt, *From Samarkhand to Sardis: A New Approach to the Seleucid Empire* (London, 1993).

**Antonine dynasty** ruled at Rome from AD 138 to 192. It was called into being by the unsatisfactory relations between the emperor Hadrian (AD 117–138) and his wife. First of all,

the childless ruler adopted Antoninus Pius (AD 138–161), who was in turn obliged to adopt as his sons Marcus Aurelius (AD 161–180) and Lucius Verus (AD 161–169). The last so-called Antonine emperor was Commodus (AD 180–192), Marcus Aurelius' own son.

Like his predecessor Hadrian, Titus Aurelius Fulvus Boionius Antoninus was of western provincial origin, his family coming from Nemausus (modern Nîmes) in southern Gaul. At first the senators were cool towards the emperor, but fear of army intervention, if the new regime suffered a setback, persuaded them of the wisdom of co-operation. Even though they regarded Antoninus as no better than themselves in origin and talents, their attitude changed when they appreciated his genuine respect for the senate, and upon the mild-mannered emperor they conferred the unusual title of Pius. Altogether a civilian, Antoninus Pius enjoyed a largely peaceful reign with the exception of Britain. There unrest caused a temporary advance north, and construction of another line of defences from the Firth of Forth to the Clyde. The 37-mile wall, half the length of Hadrian's Wall, was garrisoned by troops in small forts set at two-mile intervals. The so-called Antonine Wall was occupied from AD 143 till about 158, when it was abandoned and the garrison fell back to Hadrian's Wall. It was reoccupied again for a time and finally left to the mercy of raiding tribesmen sometime around AD 180.

When Antoninus Pius died in AD 161, he bequeathed the throne to Marcus Aurelius, his adopted son and son-in-law. But Marcus Aurelius promptly appointed Lucius Verus as a co-emperor. Trouble soon appeared on several frontiers. In the east the Parthians overran friendly Armenia and defeated two imperial armies. The dispatch of reinforcements under Lucius Verus in AD 163–164 not only restored the situation, but also led to the sacking of Ctesiphon once again. This second destruction visited upon the Parthian capital was not to be the last one. In AD 198 the Romans were provoked into another invasion of Mesopotamia. Lucius Verus probably fixed the Roman frontier at Dura, originally a Greek settlement on the Euphrates. Its defences were strengthened and a garrison was installed. Less easy to handle, were the German tribesmen on the northern frontier. Fighting there was more serious than anything of the kind that had occurred before, and it continued, under Marcus Aurelius' personal direction, for most of his reign. After the death of Lucius Verus in AD 169, he was compelled to shoulder the burden of defence alone, something the *Meditations* were obviously designed to assist; these Stoic reflections were written during the years in camp, and they offer a rare insight into an imperial mind. Marcus Aurelius' sorely tried detachment is evident in a saying such as that wisdom consists in being 'at the same time utterly impervious to all passions and full of natural affections'.

The basic problem on both the Rhine and Danube was the pressure then building up behind the German tribes settled opposite the Roman frontier. Notable among those harrying them were the Goths, then in the lower Vistula region. Gothic assaults on Dacia (present-day Romania) were to cause the Romans to abandon the province in AD 270. Marcus Aurelius adopted a twofold policy: he admitted large numbers of Germans into the empire as settlers, thereby reducing pressure on the frontier, bringing uncultivated land into use, and increasing potential military manpower; and he tried to annex what today is Slovakia in order to improve the line of the northern frontier. The policy of so-called barbarian settlement was not new, but henceforth the process became more systematic. Annexation proved impossible to achieve, however. It was put off in AD 175, first because of a serious rebellion in the eastern provinces, and then because of Marcus Aurelius' death. Quite likely a forward policy was already beyond the strength of Roman arms.

After the succession of his son Commodus in early AD 180, Marcus Aurelius was blamed for this reversion to the hereditary principle. But, unlike his predecessors from Nerva (AD 96–98) onwards, he was handicapped by the absence of any other generally acceptable candidate. Whatever their personal reservations, the friends of Marcus Aurelius had no choice but to accept the wishes of the dead emperor, and present Commodus to the army in the camp. The new emperor's desire to leave the northern frontier for Rome

The philosophical Antonine emperor Marcus Aurelius, who spent most of his reign fighting German tribesmen on the northern frontier.

fortunately meant the abandonment of a policy of conquest. The swiftness of the decision also revealed Commodus' desire to enjoy possession of the imperial palace, for once installed in its luxurious surroundings he was only too willing to let advisers take control of the government. Conspiracy became rife and relations between the senate and the throne reached an all-time low. Extravagance soon led to seizures of property as the emperor's whims became daily more outrageous. Commodus was particularly anxious to expand the annual programme of gladiatorial games, not least because of a belief that he was the greatest fighter

and hunter of wild game in the arena. The historian Dio Cassius records how the emperor delighted in spearing lions and decapitating ostriches in front of the senators, who had to stifle their laughter and dutifully shout: 'Hail to the victor!' Their patience eventually wore thin at the end of AD 192, when Commodus proposed to inaugurate the New Year by leading a procession from the gladiators' barracks to the Colosseum. The emperor had a cell in the barracks, as if he were a gladiator himself. Having assured themselves that the army would not bother to react unfavourably to a violent end to the Antonine dynasty, Dio Cassius tells us that on the last day of the year the conspirators 'administered poison to Commodus. But the immoderate use he made of wine caused the emperor to vomit up a great deal of the poisoned food, and so an athlete named Narcissus was sent to strangle him while he was taking a bath.' So died the would-be hero Hercules and Rome ceased to be officially known as Commodiana.

*See* GOTHS; HADRIAN; PARTHIA

*A. R. Birley, *Marcus Aurelius* (London, 1987); M. Grant, *The Antonines: The Roman Empire in Transition* (London, 1994); Marcus Aurelius, *Meditations*, trans. by M. Staniforth (Harmondsworth, 1964).

**Antony** (82–30 BC) was Julius Caesar's right-hand man. A natural soldier and capable politician, Marcus Antonius tried to hold on to supreme power himself after Caesar's assassination in 44 BC, but, with the encouragement of Cicero (106–43 BC), the young Octavian exploited his own adoption by the murdered Roman dictator to challenge this usurpation. In the will the four-year-old Caesarion, Caesar's son by Cleopatra (69–30 BC), received nothing; instead it was his great-nephew, Octavian (63 BC–AD 14), later the emperor Augustus, who was declared to be the heir. While Cleopatra and her son fled back to Egypt, Cicero turned the senate against Antony and secured the consulship for Octavian. The historian Plutarch reveals how the elder statesman was 'carried away with the words of a youth and utterly taken in by him . . . Once Octavian had established himself and gained his military command, he paid no further attention to Cicero. Instead he made friends with Antony and Lepidus, joined forces with them, and divided the government as though it were a piece of property.' He even acquiesced in Antony's elimination of Cicero in 43 BC. The Second Triumvirate between Antony, Octavian and Lepidus (89–12 BC) was made legal the same year. Their powers were practically absolute, and they used them to wipe out in 42 BC the last remnants of republicanism among the aristocracy, after the defeat of Caesar's assassins at Philippi in eastern Macedonia. The Triumvirate was later renewed for another five years, but Lepidus was deposed in 36 BC, and the division of

the Mediterranean world between Antony and Octavian finally broke down at the battle of Actium in 31 BC.

In the winter of 42–41 BC Octavian became so ill that his life was almost given up for lost. Antony, for a second time, was thus supreme, and Cleopatra decided that he must be bent to her will, something she swiftly accomplished. The show she put on – the gilded poop, silver oars, purple sails, and elegant crew of her barge – made such an immense impression that it survives today in one of Shakespeare's most celebrated passages. Although Antony succumbed to the spell, there is no evidence to suggest that he was ever as subservient to Cleopatra's wishes as Octavian liked to claim. Later imperial propaganda laid great emphasis on his passionate fall, in contrast to the single-minded pursuit of power exhibited by the future emperor Augustus. Marriage in 40 BC to Octavian's sister, Octavia, may have been an effort on Antony's

Silver coin with head of Marcus Antonius, dating from 34 BC. By then the Roman warlord was entirely dependent upon Cleopatra's financial support.

part to win a propaganda war in Italy. She bore him a daughter at about the same time as Cleopatra bore twins, another daughter and a son. Octavia did her utmost to patch up the deteriorating relations between her brother and her husband, but she could not prevent an open clash. If she had given birth to a son, things might have been different; but she had not, and Cleopatra had. Cleopatra also held the treasury of Ptolemaic Egypt, a war-chest Antony badly needed. The Parthians were threatening Syria once again, and there was trouble in the buffer-state of Armenia. In 36 BC the campaign against Parthia ended in a serious reverse, and Antony, in misfortune, became more dependent on Cleopatra than ever. After successfully intervening in Armenia a year later, he adopted Macedonian royal dress to match that of Cleopatra, and assigned Roman provinces to their children. Antony's grand gesture was enough to alienate opinion in Rome. Octavian could at last declare a national war against Cleopatra, rather than her misguided lover. A crushing naval victory at Actium, off north-western Greece, brought in 31 BC the Alexandrian dream to an end. Antony committed suicide before Cleopatra, who may have been stopped from following his example by Octavian. But she eventually found a means of suicide, and on Octavian's orders Caesarion quickly followed his mother to the grave. However, Octavia never wavered in her loyalty to Antony, and after his death she looked after all of his children. No wonder Cleopatra was always so anxious to keep Antony away from her.

*See* AUGUSTUS; CAESAR; CLEOPATRA; LEPIDUS; PTOLEMIES; ROME

*J. M. Carter, *The Battle of Actium: The Rise and Triumph of Augustus Caesar* (London, 1970); E. G. Huzar, *Mark Antony* (Minneapolis, 1978).

**Arabia** lay largely beyond the frontiers of the classical world. Occupation was restricted to the edges of the Arabian peninsula, notably the Sasanian holdings along the southern coast of the Persian Gulf and the Roman province of Arabia, part of modern Jordan. After Alexander the Great's conquest of the Persian empire (334–325 BC), Greek-style cities were established east of the River Jordan. To the Romans they were known as the 'ten cities', some of which seem to have entered into friendly relations with Rome when Syria was annexed in 64 BC. Their southern neighbours comprised two kingdoms: Judaea and Nabataea, the latter of which was ruled by an Arab dynasty. The capital of the Nabataean kingdom was Petra, a caravan-city now in southern Jordan. In AD 106 the emperor Trajan (AD 98–117) transformed this realm and the 'ten cities' into the Roman province of Arabia. A road was built through the middle of it linking Damascus in the north with Aela in the south, the present-day port of Aqaba on the Red Sea. Even though not chosen as the provincial capital,

Petra remained an important religious centre so that its rock-cut remains are among the most spectacular of classical ruins. A new city was built for this purpose well to the north at Bostra, next to a legionary fortress. In the AD 290s much of the southern part of Arabia, including Petra, was transferred to the province of Syria Palestine.

Judaea had been taken over by the Romans a century earlier than Nabataea. Its administration, however, was never as straightforward as that of Arabia. Jewish unrest, as well as the emperor Claudius' personal debt of gratitude to Agrippa, led in AD 41 to an unusual experiment in self-rule. This grandson of Herod the Great (37–4 BC) was allowed to administer Judaea and Samaria in place of a Roman governor. But Agrippa's death in AD 44, while his own son was still very young, caused Rome to reinstate direct rule. The Jewish revolt of AD 66–70 effectively ended Roman tolerance, leaving the Temple destroyed and Jerusalem occupied by a permanent garrison. Later uprisings, and especially the revolt of AD 132–135, merely confirmed the Jewish diaspora: the emperor Hadrian (AD 117–138) ordered the construction of a new city on the site of Jerusalem, into which no Jew was ever allowed to enter.

See ALEXANDER THE GREAT; HADRIAN; HEROD; JEWS; ROME
★G. W. Bowersock, *Roman Arabia* (Cambridge, Mass., 1993); F. Millar, *The Roman Near East, 31 BC–AD 337* (Cambridge, Mass., 1993).

**Archimedes** of Syracuse (287–212 BC) and his older contemporary Euclid in Alexandria were the greatest of the Greek mathematicians. Whereas Euclid was esteemed most for geometry, Archimedes ranked as an inventor because of the marvellous machines he devised in order to defend his city against the Romans. The siege of 213–211 BC was caused, according to the historian Polybius, by Syracuse siding with Carthage against Rome: at this time the Carthaginian general Hannibal (246–182 BC) was rampaging through Italy. But the besiegers, he tells us, 'failed to reckon with the talents of Archimedes or to foresee that in some cases the genius of one is far more effective than superiority in numbers'. For he 'had constructed artillery which could cover a whole variety of ranges . . . and so demoralized the Romans that their seaborne attack was brought to a standstill. In the end the Roman commander was reduced in despair to bringing up his ships under the cover of darkness. But when they were close to the shore, and were therefore too near to be struck by the catapults, Archimedes had devised yet another weapon to repel the marines, who were fighting from the decks. He had had the walls pierced with a large number of loopholes at the height of a man, which were about a palm's width wide at the outer surface of the walls. Through these loopholes were fired his scorpions, small catapults which shot down the marines with iron darts.'

To deal with the many siege towers

The early Hindu temple at Aihole. It contains all the features of classical construction, albeit in simplified form.

Archimedes deployed projecting beams capable of breaking ladders, while the ships they stood upon were often upended by means of iron grappling-hooks and chains. Abandoning the assault from the sea, the Romans turned their attention to the landward defences of Syracuse, but with no better result. In the end they were obliged to rely on starvation, cutting the city off from outside supply. For as long as 'one old man was there they did not dare to launch another attack'.

But all Archimedes was really concerned about were his theoretical discoveries in mathematics. It took the stimulus of the siege to make him apply his knowledge, in contrast to the very practical approach of contemporary Chinese scientists, and Archimedes was so absorbed with a problem on the fall of Syracuse that he hardly noticed the legionary who killed him. An excep-

tion to his preoccupation with theory was the so-called Archimedean screw, which is still used today to raise the level of water for irrigation.

*See* INVENTIONS; SYRACUSE

*Polybius, *The Rise of the Roman Empire*, trans. by I. Scott-Kilvert (Harmondsworth, 1979).

**Architecture** dating from classical times is found predominantly in the Mediterranean, in part because the Greeks and the Romans had easier access to durable building material. Stone was absent from the loess plains of northern China, while the abundance of hardwoods in India initially discouraged the use of stone for monumental buildings. The first imperial capital of India, Pataliputra (modern Patna), was surrounded by a timber pallisade. The description of Pata-

27

liputra left by the Seleucid ambassador Megasthenes, who first visited India in 302 BC, was later dismissed as fiction, but recently a section of its massive wooden fortifications have been excavated south of Bulandisbagh. Indian stone-cutting was nonetheless highly developed, its most conspicuous early form being the pillar edicts erected on the orders of the Mauryan emperor Ashoka (268–232 BC). Apart from spreading his own moral concern by means of these inscriptions, Ashoka also commemorated the mission of the Buddha through the construction of stupas, stone-covered mounds enclosing relics. Very often Buddhist monasteries were built in association with them. The original stupa at Sanchi, in present-day Madhya Pradesh, was built during Ashoka's reign. His patronage of Buddhism was doubtless critical in facilitating its growth, although the picture of Ashoka as an enthusiastic adherent found in Buddhist literature is exaggerated. But as a result of Mauryan favour, much of India's architectural effort was expended on Buddhist buildings; the greatest surviving monument is the series of rock-cut monasteries at Ajanta, in present-day Maharastra. Stretching over a distance of 600 yards, they preserve classical architectural forms long since lost. From inscriptions it would appear that work on the monastery complex ceased in the early fifth century AD. One of the earliest Hindu temples to survive dates from the following century; it stands at Aihole in the cen-

tral Deccan. This small stone building comprises a porch, a main hall, and an innermost sanctuary surmounted by a spire that is now in ruins. A pillared porch on two sides, running the length of the building, widens to a gallery that encircles the structure and is meant for the ritual of circumambulation. The pillars within are decorated with ornamental friezes representing chains of pearls and others representing dancing girls; these indicate that the temple was designed as a copy of the heavenly home of Durga, the beautiful warrior goddess whose mount was a tiger. Her rise to the head of the Hindu pantheon began with a titanic struggle against Mahisha, a monstrous buffalo demon.

The wholesale disappearance of classical buildings in northern India, as in northern China, was caused by foreign invasion. Wooden construction was particularly vulnerable to the deprivations of the Hunas, who accelerated the breakup of the Gupta empire (AD 320–550) in India, and the Tartars, who overran the northern provinces of China in AD 317. The loss of Chinese classical buildings, however, is less serious in understanding their use than at first appears. For the singular characteristic of Chinese architectural tradition is its basic uniformity and standardization in both construction and planning. There was always a sharp differentiation between the function of masonry and brickwork and that of timber. Besides a shortage of stone, the reason for such an unvarying approach was the incidence of earthquakes, an anxiety which led Zhang Heng (AD 78–139) to invent the first practical seismograph. Frequent earth tremors obliged the Chinese to develop timber-framed buildings: walls were not weight-bearing and, because they were often made of rammed earth, buildings were furnished with generously overhanging eaves. Even the Great Wall itself possessed a rammed-earth core, its sides and top having where possible a dressing of stone. The other surviving imperial monument consists of the underground sections of the First Emperor's tomb complex at Mount Li, in modern Shaanxi province. So far the burial chamber remains unexplored, but thousands of life-sized terracotta warriors have been discovered in several pits, where they were placed sometime before 207 BC.

Chinese pavilion showing the typical timber-frame construction.

Although Iran also suffered its share of destruction, including Alexander the Great's well-known decision to fire the great palace of the Achaemenids at Persepolis in 330 BC, there are sufficient remains to form a picture of its classical architecture. The Archaemenid rulers of Persia (559–330 BC)

built on a grand scale. The artists and materials they worked with were brought from practically all territories of what was then the largest state in the world. Pasargadae, founded in the 540s BC by Cyrus the Great, set the standard: it blended Egyptian, Mesopotamian and Greek forms in a city laid out in an extensive park, with bridges, gardens, colonnaded palaces and open columned pavilions. Pasargadae, along with Susa and Persepolis, forcefully expressed the authority of the King of Kings, the staircases of the latter recording in relief sculpture the vast extent of the imperial frontiers. Following the fall of Persia, the dominant style in West Asia for a couple of centuries not unsurprisingly was Greek, but with the Iranian revival under the Parthians (171 BC – AD 226) and the Sasanians (AD 226–651) there was an appearance of new forms. Architectural innovations begun under the Parthians flowered during the Sasanian period in massive barrel-vaulted chambers, solid masonry domes, and tall columns. Possibly owing something to Rome, since the Parthians and the Sasanians both used Roman prisoners on public works, the last phase of Iranian classical architecture was as impressive as the first under the Achaemenids. Parthian Ctesiphon and Sasanian Coche-Veh Ardeshir, both sited on the Tigris close to Greek Seleucia, were great cities.

The Greco-Roman heritage upon which Iran partly drew achieved its classical form in the sixth century BC.

Large-scale construction was common under the Roman emperors. This basilica at Trier was built for official use.

Above all at Athens public works transformed the acropolis into an exemplar for Greek architecture. The Parthenon, the main temple dedicated to the goddess Athena, was constructed between 447 and 432 BC, using revenues from Athens' maritime empire. The famous Parthenon frieze, over 3 feet high and 165 feet in length, ran around the top of the external walls. Depicted is a festive procession, the sole non-mythological scene known on a Greek temple. The sculptures on the west pediment, however, portray the struggle for control of Attica between Athena, the mind-born daughter of Zeus, head of the Greek pantheon, and his brother, the sea god Poseidon. The Romans, too, were deeply influenced by Greek architecture well before their annexation of Greece in 146 BC. The centre of Rome, its forum, was remodelled during the third century BC on a Greek pattern, most probably by workmen imported from the Greek cities of southern Italy and Sicily. A second influence on Roman architecture came from Etruria. The earliest temples had followed the Etruscan model, and throughout the classical period the blending of Greek and Etruscan elements can be discerned in Roman architecture. Where the Romans made their own distinctive contribution was in the enormous public buildings which arose under the emperors (31 BC – AD 476). Besides the imperial palaces themselves, these buildings included the Colosseum, opened in AD 80, the Pantheon, redesigned and rebuilt between AD 118 and 128, and the great baths. Those of Caracalla (AD 211–217) were truly grandiose, with a bathing capacity of 6,000 people at a time. The main hall of the baths was so large (185 feet by 80 feet) that its users were dwarfed by the size; they were no longer individuals but members of a mass citizenship, Caracalla having extended this status to all the inhabitants of the Roman empire, with the exception of slaves. The emperor's motive for ending Roman and Italian exclusiveness appears to have been financial, since he was concerned to increase the number of people liable to taxation.

See AJANTA; ASHOKA; ATHENS; PATALIPUTRA; PERSEPOLIS; PERSIA; QIN DYNASTY; ROME; SASANIANS

*A. Boyd, *Chinese Architecture* (London, 1962); P. Brown, *Indian Architecture: Buddhist and Hindu* (Bombay, 1956); A. W. Lawrence, *Greek Architecture* (Harmondsworth, 1984); W. L. MacDonald, *The Architecture of the Roman Empire* (New

Haven, 1976–82); E. Porada, *The Art of Ancient Iran* (New York, 1965).

**Ardashir I** (AD 226–240) was the founder of the Sasanian dynasty (AD 226–651), the third and last Iranian royal house of classical times. His successful rebellion against the Parthians (171 BC–AD 226), the second Iranian dynasty, was centred on Fars in the south of modern Iran. The revolt was started by a certain Papak, some two decades before the formal start of Sasanian rule. He may have been a Zoroastrian priest. Some traditions make Papak the father of Ardashir, others his grandfather: in the latter case, it was the early death of Sasan, Ardashir's father, which caused Papak to protect the future king as a boy. Yet another version of Ardashir's descent claims that his mother was the daughter of Papak. By marrying a shepherd descended from the Archaemenids (559–330 BC), the first Iranian dynasty, she was supposed to have brought royal blood into the line. This would seem to be a fabricated genealogy, rather like an earlier one broadcast by the Parthians as a way of establishing their right to rule Iran, not least because the Sasanian name clearly derives from that of Sasan. He must, therefore, have been regarded as the royal ancestor.

Coins struck by Ardashir show the different stages in his rise to ascendancy over all Iran. His first capital was at present-day Firuzabad in Fars, but he soon expanded his control in both easterly and westerly directions. At an unknown place on the Oxus, in Central Asia, around AD 228 Ardashir decisively defeated the Kushanas, then approaching the end of their supremacy in northern India. Ctesiphon, the Parthian capital, fell shortly afterwards, confirming Ardashir's authority in the Tigris-Euphrates valley. The new capital he had built nearby was called Veh Ardashir, which means 'Ardashir's good deed'. At the same time envoys were sent to the Romans, with the message that the Sasanian king expected

Gold coin of Ardashir I. On the reverse is a fire altar, a witness to the king's Zoroastrian orthodoxy.

them to evacuate the lands they occupied in northern Mesopotamia. Heavy losses were sustained on both sides, until the Sasanians got the upper hand following the assassination of the last Severan emperor, Severus Alexander, in early AD 235. Strongly fortified Carrhae and Nisibis, present-day Harran and Nusaybin in northern Syria, were captured by Ardashir. Yet these strategically situated cities were of less value to the Sasanians than the military anarchy into which Rome slipped between AD 235 and the accession of the emperor Aurelian in AD 270. So determined were the legionaries to have emperors of their own choosing that their squabbles raised and deposed fifteen rulers during this period. When Ardashir died himself in AD 240, he left his son, Shapur I (AD 241–272), a very powerful kingdom to rule.

See AURELIAN: KUSHANAS; PARTHIANS; ROME; SASANIANS; SEVERAN DYNASTY; SHAPUR

*G. Hermann, *The Iranian Revival* (Oxford, 1977).

**Argos** was in the Peloponnese the chief rival of Sparta, the most powerful state in classical Greece. The high tide of Argive fortunes was the decisive defeat of the Spartans at Hysiae in 669 BC, after which Sparta threw itself into an intensive programme of military training usually associated with the name of Lycurgus. It is not impossible that these legendary reforms were an attempt to match the improved military tactics of the Argives. According to the philosopher Aristotle (384–322 BC), the half-legendary Argive tyrant Pheidon first demonstrated the superiority of the phalanx over the much looser formation favoured by aristocratic fighters. Initially, the battlefield had been the exclusive domain of horse-riding nobles, but improvements in armour and weapons gave pride of place to armoured infantrymen who fought in disciplined ranks. The new equipment cost a great deal and in consequence the development of the phalanx, the close-packed formation in which infantrymen were deployed, cannot be regarded as the democratization of Greek armies. Only the Spartans received state aid for armour, a fact which ensured in most city-states that poor citizens were obliged to fight on land as lightly armed auxiliary troops.

Yet the phalanx obviously gave an enlarged military role to those with substantial means, and in time allowed them to exercise a similar one politically. Aristotle plainly underlines this when he states that the earliest Greek constitutions, immediately after the disappearance of kings, were narrowly based; whereas, once the military strength of a city-state came to rely on armoured infantry, the basis of the constitution was necessarily widened. The custom of referring to the infantry shield, the hoplon, as the Argive one does support the proposition that Pheidon owed his own unchallenged authority to military innovation. But the power of Argos died with him, checked perhaps by Corinth and a recovered Sparta. Thereafter the Argives sought to maintain a precarious neutrality which was punctuated each generation by a war with the Spartans.

During the Persian invasion of Greece in 480–479 BC Argos refused to take the field against the invaders, a calculated inactivity the Persians did not forget in the late 460s BC when the Argives successfully sought financial support against Sparta. Democracy had taken root at Argos by this period and so it was not surprising that the democrat politician Themistocles went to live there on his exile from Athens in 471 BC. His activities in the Peloponnese may have caused his eventual move to Persia at Spartan insistence. But the Spartans could not prevent the repeated alliances between Argos and Athens, one of which brought both of them to the battlefield at Mantinea in 418 BC. It was the timely support of the Athenian cavalry that prevented a disaster when the Spartans out-manoeuvred the impetuous Argives and Mantineans. The Athenians still lost 200 infantrymen in the engagement, however.

Although Argos joined further anti-Spartan alliances, its influence on Greek affairs progressively declined, even after the Thebans broke the power of Sparta at the battle of Leuctra in 371 BC. It had long ceased to count as a city-state when in 146 BC the Romans incorporated Greece into their empire.

*See* ATHENS; PERSIAN INVASIONS; SPARTA; TYRANTS; WARFARE

*R. A. Tomlinson, *Argos and the Argolid* (London, 1972).

**Aristides** (*c.* 525–467 BC) was one of the Athenian generals at the battle of Marathon. Like Miltiades (*c.* 550–489 BC), the prime mover of this Greek victory over the Persians, Aristides later found himself a target of democratic attack and in 482 BC he suffered ostracism. Aristides' political rival was Themistocles (*c.* 528–462 BC), who was then in the process of building up the strength of the Athenian navy. Whether or not he opposed this naval development is uncertain, for the specific reason for banishment is not recorded: Aristides was simply sent into exile for ten years on the grounds that his influence in public affairs had become too great. Along with other exiles he was recalled on the approach of the second Persian invasion of Greece in 480 BC, and Aristides gave good service at the battles of Salamis and Plataea; 8,000 Athenians were under his command at the second engagement in 479 BC.

After the defeat of the Persian expeditionary force at Plataea, in central Greece, the Greeks decided to follow up their great victory with an offensive throughout the Aegean. But the extravagant behaviour of the Spartan commander-in-chief, Pausanias, soon led to his recall and an opportunity for Aristides to take over the leadership of

Greek resistance to the Persians. Already Aristides had come to an understanding with Themistocles, backing the democratic leader's rebuilding of Athens' walls despite Spartan opposition. So it happened that the maritime Greeks came to see the Athenians, with their fleet and interest in the corn supply route from the Black Sea, as more likely to assist them than the Spartans in keeping their freedom from Persian domination. In 478–477 BC at a meeting held on the sacred island of Delos, Athens and allies from the Aegean founded a league, one of whose chief objects was, according to the historian Thucydides, 'to compensate themselves for their losses by ravaging the territory of the Persian king'. Aristides fixed the quota of each contributory state in this new organization, the so-called Delian League. Some states were required to contribute manned ships, others to pay tribute in money. Afterwards Aristides seems to have been content to let Cimon (510–450 BC), the son of his old colleague Miltiades, assume the role of military leader of the league. Apparently he was so impoverished on his death in 467 BC that the Athenians had to vote financial support for Aristides' children.

See ATHENS; CIMON; DELIAN LEAGUE; MILTIADES; OSTRACISM; PAUSANIAS; PERSIAN INVASIONS; THEMISTOCLES
*R. Meiggs, *The Athenian Empire* (Oxford, 1972); Plutarch, *The Rise and Fall of Athens: Nine Greek Lives*, trans. by I. Scott-Kilvert (Harmondsworth, 1960).

**Aristotle** (384–322 BC), second only to Plato as a Greek philosopher, was a native of Stagira in Chalcidice, but spent most of his life in Athens. He came to study there in the Academy at the age of eighteen and stayed until Plato's death in 347 BC. His departure from Athens that year may have had as much to do with politics as his teacher's death, because anti-Macedonian feeling would have made northerners such as Aristotle feel very uncomfortable in the city. His own attitude to the rising power of Macedon can be judged perhaps from acceptance in 343 BC of an invitation to act as the tutor of Alexander the Great (356–323 BC). In 335 BC, however, Aristotle returned to Athens and taught at the Lyceum, a philosophical school which he set up in rivalry to the Academy. This move must account for the apocryphal tradition preserved by the commentator Diogenes Laertius, which relates how he seceded from the Academy while Plato was still alive. Plato was supposed to have said: 'Aristotle spurns me, as colts kick out at the mother who bore them.' Aristotle's period at the Lyceum lasted till 323 BC when, following the early death of Alexander, once again Athens became a centre of anti-Macedonian feeling. The Athenians were aware of the huge sum of 800 talents which Alexander had sent to Aristotle from the captured Persian treasury. The philosopher had used the gift from his grateful pupil to found the classical world's first great library and first collection of specimens for teaching, notably in the field of zoology. Like Socrates in 399 BC, Aristotle was charged with impiety and rather than let the Athenians execute a second philosopher, he fled to the island of Euboea, where he died shortly afterwards.

The philosopher Aristotle, who was the tutor of Alexander the Great.

Aristotle's interests embraced every branch of knowledge, including several new ones that he invented himself. He lectured on logic, physics, astronomy, meteorology, biology, zoology, metaphysics, ethics, politics, rhetoric and poetics at the Lyceum. There at a grove sacred to Apollo Lyceius, Diogenes Laertius tells us, 'Aristotle would walk up and down discussing philosophy with his pupils. Hence the name Peripatetic given to his school. But others say that it was given to him

because, when Alexander was recovering from an illness and taking daily walks, the philosopher joined him and talked with him.' Aristotle would have had much to discuss because he amassed an immense amount of information on a variety of subjects. Politically his views were out of date, for by 343 BC the era of the autonomous city-state was almost over. But he was convinced that man was by nature a political animal and the free association of the villages of a hinterland with a larger settlement as a city-state was a natural phenomenon. For Aristotle the state should always be quite small because it was 'defined by nothing else so well as by participation in judicial functions and political office'. Its affairs were best run directly by its citizens. Of the three types of state he analysed – monarchy, oligarchy and democracy – Aristotle preferred a moderate democracy. This explains his admiration for Theramenes, who bravely tried to temper the oligarchic reactions at Athens in 411 and 404 BC. He goes on to say in the *Politics* that 'the view that the many, rather than a few good men, should be sovereign . . . would seem perhaps to be true. For although each of the many is not a good man, still it is possible that, when they come together, they should be better – not as individuals but collectively, just as communal dinners are better than those supplied at one man's expense.'

*See* ATHENS; PLATO; THERAMENES

*J. L. Ackrill, *Aristotle the Philosopher* (Oxford, 1981); J. P. Lynch, *Aristotle's School* (Berkeley, 1972); D. Keyt and F. D. Miller, *A Companion to Aristotle's Politics* (Oxford, 1991).

Coin of Tigranes the Great, struck in Syria during Armenia's short-lived supremacy during the 70s BC.

**Armenia,** in classical times, lay not in the Caucasus but near the headwaters of the Tigris. The Romans noted the close affinity of the Armenians to the Syrians and the Arabs. The first mention of the Armenians as a people occurs in an inscription of the Persian king Darius I (521–486 BC). Then Armenia was a province of the Persian empire, although its inhabitants enjoyed considerable freedom under tribal chiefs. Independent kings ruled after Alexander the Great's conquest of Persia, and in the reign of Artaxias (190–159 BC) a powerful new dynasty, the Artaxiad, made Armenia a player on the international stage. Situated on the borders of Rome and Parthia, the Armenian kingdom was to become important in the balance of power in northern Mesopotamia and Syria. Never strong enough to be a major state in its own right – despite the short-lived empire of Tigranes the Great (95–56 BC) – Armenia's attitude to rival eastern and western power blocs was often critical. The failure of Armenian cavalry to arrive during Crassus' campaign against the Parthians in 54–53 BC resulted in a humiliating defeat for Rome at Carrhae, in northern Mesopotamia. Rome's policy towards Armenia rested upon the view that the eastern frontier was safe only so long as an anti-Parthian monarch was on the throne. Military intervention occurred on occasions when Parthia gained the upper hand in Tigranocerta, the Armenian capital. Only the expansionist emperor Trajan (AD 98–117) tried to turn Armenia into a province between AD 115 and 117. Afterwards the Romans accepted the Euphrates as the border between themselves and the Parthians, but a more aggressive stance adopted by the Sasanians, who toppled the Parthians in AD 226, led eventually to a partition of Armenia in AD 387. By this time it had converted to Christianity, probably as early as AD 301, making the Armenians the oldest Christian nation to survive into modern times. The Arabs conquered classical Armenia in AD 653.

See CRASSUS; PARTHIANS; PERSIA; ROME; SASANIANS
*C. Burney and D. M. Lang, *The Peoples of the Hills: Ancient Ararat and Caucasus* (London, 1971).

Art from the classical period remains an incomplete legacy. With the notable exception of the Greco-Roman tradition, painting has almost completely disappeared and sculpture is often damaged. But enough works of art are extant for an appreciation of the unprecedented heights which creativity then scaled.

In China till 1974, however, there was no evidence of a classical tradition for sculpture. That year excavations at Mount Li, the site of the great tomb of the First Emperor (221–210 BC), revealed several thousand life-sized terracotta warriors and horses. Columns of foot-soldiers are modelled wearing iron mail-coats, even the heads of the rivets being shown. Although there are signs of mass-production methods having been used for the torsos, each detachable head is a personal portrait, and so far the excava-tors have not discovered two faces which are the same. Unlike the stereo-typed funerary statues of many other ancient rulers, the soldiers in the terra-cotta army are modelled on living men. Some bronze statuary has since been unearthed, but this metal seems to have been used primarily for the elaborate utensils required in ancestor worship, a unique Chinese devotion. The cook-ing of food in ritual cauldrons, some of which were 5 feet high, had long been regarded as a duty owed to the ancestral spirits. Other vessels were designed to prepare special dishes, dis-pense wine, and hold water. Painting was also well advanced by the time of the Qin unification of China in 221 BC. Paintings of mythological scenes on silk have recently been recovered from several tombs. But the earliest painting that can be attributed to an individual artist dates from the

Bronze statuary found in the 1980s near the tomb of the First Emperor of China.

Sogdians presenting tribute to the Persian king. One of the many subject peoples depicted in relief at Persepolis.

post–classical period.

Monumental architecture in India, and possibly sculpture, was influenced by Iran. Parts of north-western India had been annexed to the Persian empire by Darius I (521–486 BC), and the stone columns favoured by the Mauryans, who dominated the subcontinent from 322 to 183 BC, reveal typical Achaemenid capitals. The Mauryan emperor Ashoka (268–232 BC) supposedly erected hundreds of stone buildings, many of which were dedicated to the propagation of the Buddhist faith. None of the sculpture or painting associated with this enormous programme survives, and few of the buildings themselves can be identified with certainty because of later reconstruction. Where Mauryan art remains visible today is in rock-cut caves, the antecedents of the great Buddhist complex at Ajanta, in present-day Maharastra. This impressive monastery has caves embellished with sculptures and paintings depicting scenes from the lives of the Buddha and the Buddhist saints. Inscriptions date Ajanta to a period largely before AD 475. Indian and foreign dynasties, such as the Kushanas (AD 50–250), followed the Mauryan example of patronizing Buddhism. At modern Peshawar the Kushana king Kaniska (AD 78–102) constructed an enormous stupa, a circular mound enclosing relics of the Buddha. Its base was decorated with both sculpture and Indo-Greek columns. Already the so-called Gandharan school had begun to fuse Greco-

Roman and Indian traditions in a striking series of sculptures. For the craftsmen who served the Kushana religious establishments in Gandhara (present-day Pakistan) were probably at first Romans from the eastern Mediterranean, although Bactrian Greek remains probably kindled Kushana interest in the style. After the re-establishment of Indian dominion under the Gupta dynasty (AD 320–550), the resurgence of Hinduism inaugurated a building programme almost as extensive as Ashoka's. Unfortunately its major monuments, along with their sculpture and painting, have also disappeared so that what remains are provincial shrines from the southern fringes of the Gupta empire. A classic survival at present-day Udayagiri is the rock-cut depiction of Vishnu, as the boar incarnation, rescuing mother earth from the depths of a flood. As he rises from the waters, Vishnu remarks: 'Every time I carry you this way. . .' It is a reminder of the return of the great Hindu deities to prominence. Their recurring mythological actions are represented as a process of birth, death, and reincarnation that encompasses the individual, society, the planet, the gods, the universe: it is the time-scale of Nature herself.

The Achaemenid art which inspired the Mauryan emperors is one of the great legacies of West Asia. It is a blend of two elements: the artistic tradition of the Iranian plateau prior to the conquests of Cyrus the Great (559–530 BC), and the arts of Mesopotamia, Greece and, to a lesser extent, Egypt. One look at the relief sculpture of Persepolis, the royal city destroyed by Alexander the Great in 330 BC, is enough to reveal the extent to which foreign styles and motifs were borrowed. But the overall impression remains Persian, and a bold statement of the authority of the King of Kings. Here in monumental form is represented vast power: the depiction of the numerous peoples subject to the Persians underlines the fact that their empire was at the time the largest state in the classical world. Notwithstanding this very grand emphasis in both Achaemenid art and architecture, the most beautiful works to come down to us are metalwork and jewellery, a lesser Iranian tradition that continued to flourish under the Parthians (171 BC–AD 226) and the Sasanians (AD 226–651). But the imprint of the Macedonian conquest, and the subsequent Seleucid occupation (312–64 BC), cannot be missed under the Parthians, whose wealthy citizens commissioned lifelike sculptures of themselves. Gradually these figures cease to be idealized in the way Greek artists would have produced them, and the focus moves to the personal trappings of the individual rather than the beauty of the subject's form.

Their ultimate inspiration was classical Greek art. In sculpture the decisive step forward occurred in the mid-fifth century BC, when the stiffness of earlier statues was replaced by a growing sensitivity to the human body. The con-

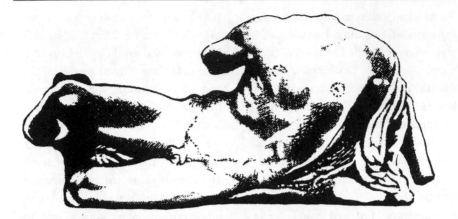

A river deity from the west pediment of the Parthenon, the most celebrated classical Greek temple.

struction of temples dedicated to Zeus at Olympia and Athena at Athens brought sculpture to the fore. On the Athenian acropolis Phidias (born 490 BC) set the standard in the friezes he carved for the Parthenon, since against them later sculptors' work was always judged, and their style was consciously recaptured by the artists of republican Rome. The first Roman emperor, Augustus (31 BC–AD 14), gave Greek sculpture its final boost by having Greek sculptors fashion a series of imperial portraits; these propaganda pieces were sent to every Roman province as a reminder of the universal authority he now claimed over their inhabitants. The portraiture ranges from the grim determination needed during the years of struggle against Mark Antony (82–30 BC), through the sober assumption of imperial responsibility, to the self-confidence that derives from becoming the sole ruler of the Mediterranean world. Whilst

painting clearly suffered as much from destruction and decay in Europe as elsewhere, the Greek delight in vase-painting has at least ensured that a rich legacy of small-scale images survives. Athens was the chief centre for the painting of pots, producing both black-figure and red-figure wares. Classical vase-painters tended to stick to well-known scenes from legend and mythology, and their skill lay in treating them in an original manner. As a result, many aspects of daily life are to be found in these lively compositions.

*See* AJANTA; ASHOKA; ATHENS; KANISKA; MOUNT LI; PERSEPOLIS; QIN DYNASTY; ROME

★J. Boardman, *Greek Sculpture: The Classical Period* (London, 1989); and *Athenian Red Figure Vases: The Classical Period* (London, 1989); A. W. Lawrence, *Greek and Roman Sculpture* (London, 1972); E. Porada, *The Art of Ancient Iran* (New York, 1965); B. Rowland, *The Art and Architecture of*

India (London, 1967). W. Watson, *Style in the Arts of China* (Harmondsworth, 1974).

**Ashoka**, the third Mauryan emperor (268–232 BC), was the grandson of Candragupta, who had founded the dynasty in northern India around 322 BC. He continued the policy of expansion begun by his grandfather, with the result that nearly the whole subcontinent came under Mauryan control. Even though Ashoka's own father Bindusara, who ruled from 297 to 272 BC, is supposed to have initially disliked his ungainly son, it was to Ashoka, not the heir-apparent, that he turned to deal with an emergency at Taxila, the chief city of Gandhara, an important province in what today is Pakistan. In 326 BC Taxila had welcomed the arrival of Alexander the Great and its Indian ruler had been confirmed as a Macedonian ally, with full sovereign rights. Following the departure of the Macedonians, though, Candragupta had incorporated it into the Mauryan empire, along with several neighbouring states. But under Bindusara there seems to have been such oppression by officials that Taxila rose in revolt, thereby endangering the security of the whole north-western frontier. Ashoka was dispatched to restore order: this he did so well that he was appointed afterwards as governor of Ujjain, a key position in the imperial administration. It was Ujjain, in present-day Madhya Pradesh, which provided Ashoka with the base he needed to bid for the throne on his father's death in 272 BC.

The struggle for succession among Bindusara's sons lasted four years. That Ashoka had blood on his hands cannot be doubted, though the Buddhist tradition that he secured the throne only after killing ninety-nine brothers is exaggerated. A younger brother by the name of Tissa appears to have been the sole survivor. Appointed to responsible posts, Tissa chose to neglect his duties for a life of pleasure until an exasperated Ashoka threatened him with death as well. According to a number of Buddhist texts, Tissa realized under threat of execution why monks, being conscious of eventual death, forsook pleasure. So he abandoned the palace and became a monk himself. Two different versions of Tissa's period as a holy man exist: one records his return to the Mauryan capital, Pataliputra, where an impressed Ashoka had a hill especially constructed for Tissa, so that even living in isolation he would still be close; the other ends with his execution as a heretic during a purge of monasteries on Ashoka's order. Even though the latter account says that Tissa was killed by mistake, the problem of being the younger brother of such an individualistic ruler as Ashoka cannot be entirely disguised. Tissa seems to have understood that becoming a monk and renouncing all claims to the throne was the only way he could hope to stay alive. After Ashoka's later conversion to the Buddhist faith, it is to be expected that commentators would credit the emperor with a desire to place his younger brother on the path to enlightenment.

One of seven surviving capitals from inscribed pillars set up by the order of the Mauryan emperor Ashoka. It dates from 244 BC.

From the moment he was crowned in 268 BC, however, Ashoka continued the dynastic policy of conquest, pushing the empire's frontiers southwards. But the campaign of 261–260 BC in Kalinga, a part of modern Orissa, proved to be a turning point. There the bloodshed seems to have been unprecedented, and Ashoka suffered a severe crisis of confidence in Mauryan aggression. To pull himself together, the shocked emperor embraced the Buddhist faith, and for the rest of his reign he endeavoured to conquer through righteousness rather than war-

fare. Ashoka's conversion to Buddhism took about two years to make him a zealot, but it did not persuade him to return conquered Kalinga to its former rulers. On the contrary, he came to believe it was his destiny to promote moral principles throughout India. Ashoka set out on provincial tours, visiting Buddhist monasteries in order to strengthen the faith; yet he also gave patronage to Jain and Hindu sects which sought 'mastery of the senses and purity of mind'. Ambassadors were sent abroad to spread the good news of Buddhism, a fact recorded on the inscribed pillars he erected, somewhat in the manner of modern motorway advertisements, at junctions of the empire's great highways. The so-called rock edicts were carved in the local script. Examples in Greek and Aramaic have recently been discovered in Afghanistan. This shows how seriously Ashoka took his duty as the first Buddhist ruler to ensure that Greeks and Persians, both inside and outside his empire, should be aware of the tenets of his newly adopted faith. The rock edicts were meant to be read by the population at large and explained by imperial officials. They covered a wide range of matters, starting with two edicts concerning the slaughter of animals and the provision of medical and welfare services, continuing with the moral principles and their application, and ending with a history of the Kalinga campaign and its effects.

Since suffering on earth is, according to Buddhism, the lot of every man, it is hardly surprising that tradition says even pious Ashoka had to undergo his due share of suffering. Towards the end of his long reign he began to lose control over the government of the empire, coming unduly under the influence of one of his queens. Once again officials became oppressive with the result that unrest caused a division of Mauryan territory after Ashoka's death in 232 BC. The eastern half had perhaps its capital at Ujjain in order to avoid pressure to the north from Bactrian Greeks, who had broken away from the Seleucids. Reunification was brought about in 223 BC by Samprati, who had come to power in the west and whom Jain texts regard as a great ruler, treating him as a patron of Jainism almost in the manner that Buddhist texts treat Ashoka.

See ALEXANDER THE GREAT; BACTRIA; BINDUSARA; BUDDHISM; CANDRA-GUPTA; JAINISM; MAURYAN DYNASTY; SELEUCIDS

*R. Thapar, *Asoka and the Decline of the Mauryas* (Oxford, 1961).

**Athens** was the most splendid of the classical Greek city-states, for not only did it develop in the fifth century BC into a major political and economic power, but more it acted as a magnet for creative talent in the Greek-speaking world even after its defeat by Sparta in 404 BC. Very many of those who came to live and work in Athens did not do so by choice, however. For a large group here, as in other city-states, comprised the slaves. The historian Thucydides tells us that, after the Spartans had established a fort at Decelea in 413 BC, the Athenians lost control of the Attic countryside and

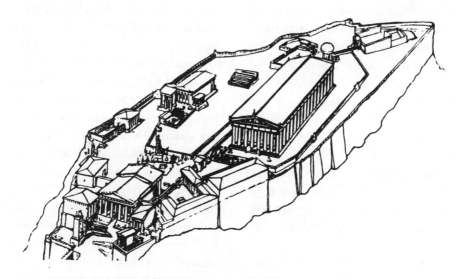

The Athenian acropolis, whose temples were built in the second half of the fifth century BC.

'more than 20,000 slaves ran away, most of them skilled workmen, and all sheep and beasts of burden were lost'. Argument about the real extent of Athenian dependence on slavery remains unsettled, but it was never so total as the state-owned slave population on which Spartan supremacy rested. So preoccupied were the Spartans with holding down slaves that they transformed their political institutions into something approaching a super military camp. In contrast, the Athenians went through a democratic revolution that still resonates with meaning today.

Athenian legend saw the unification of Attica by King Theseus as the key event. For acceptance of Athens as the political and, in consequence, religious centre of Attica created a large state in which no formal distinction can be said to have existed between city and countryside. Quite possibly the size of Attica provided an outlet which other city-states had to find abroad: the Athenians sponsored few colonies for its surplus citizens, who tended to seek their fortunes as individuals in others' foundations. A second safety-valve was mercantile trade, which culminated in an intense struggle with the neighbouring island of Aegina, the first known minter of coins in Europe. In 431 BC the Athenians expelled the Aeginetans from their island for nearly a generation.

Following the failure of Cylon's attempt in about 625 BC to set himself up as tyrant, a lawgiver named Draco formulated the first Athenian code. It removed the responsibility for revenge from the shoulders of the deceased's relatives, and made justice the property of every citizen, a right and a duty for rich and poor alike. But Draco's laws were not enough to deal with the growing social disorder and in 594 BC Solon was appointed as a mediator between the poor and the rich. A free peasantry seems to have been Solon's ideal, and the constitution he framed was intended to give these citizens a say in government without fundamentally weakening the leadership of the aristocracy. Solon could have made himself a tyrant, but, as he said: 'Tyranny is a very pretty position. The trouble is that there's no way out of it.' His reforms failed to end aristocratic squabbling and for a half-century there was intermittent tyranny. The last tyrant, Hippias, was only driven out with Spartan aid in 510 BC. Typical of his kind, Hippias guided the Persian invaders to Marathon in 490 BC as a means of personal restoration. By then, though, the Athenians had changed politically and backed the democratic measures of Cleisthenes, a nobleman whose family was associated with Solon's reforms.

What Cleisthenes gave Athens in 508 BC was a system of government that lasted for two centuries, till virtually all the Greek city-states lost their independence during the internecine wars fought by Alexander the Great's successors. Essentially it was local government without aristocratic interference, supplemented by larger administrative arrangements, all of which fell under the control of the assembly at Athens. It is calculated that, despite payment for attendance, the sovereign assembly rarely saw one-fifth of the citizenry on any of the forty days set aside for meetings each year. As the philosopher Plato (429–347 BC) was pleased to write of the ordinary citizens: 'They support themselves by their labour and do not care about politics; this is the largest and most important element in a democracy when it is assembled.' Plato's dislike of democratic government aside, the point being made is an interesting one. It is a reminder that the political revolution started by Cleisthenes was largely peaceful at Athens. The assassination of the democrat Ephialtes, in 461 BC, was an isolated event prior to the two short periods of reaction in 411 BC and 404 BC, political crises arising from the strain of the unexpectedly long Peloponnesian War, the bitter struggle between Athens and Sparta which lasted from 431 to 404 BC. Yet the much-criticized manoeuvring of the oligarch Theramenes (died 403 BC) in both these crises can be seen as going with the grain of Athenian politics. He was instrumental in setting up and pulling down the first tyranny, the so-called Four Hundred. His execution by the second one, the Thirty, was a result of his efforts to turn it into a moderate regime.

By the time of Ephialtes' murder the Athenians had come to believe that all questions should be decided by popular decision, either directly in the assembly, or indirectly in the council (chosen annually by lot from the whole citizenry), or in the lawcourts whose juries were again chosen by lot. Such was the context of Pericles' successful political career. A grand-nephew of Cleisthenes, Pericles (c. 495–429 BC) was elected as a general nearly every year from 443 BC onwards. He presided over the conversion of the Delian League into an Athenian empire, and the rebuilding of the city's public buildings, the most notable being the Parthenon, the temple of Athena on the Athenian acropolis. There was indeed a close connection between the conversion of the anti-Persian confederacy and a massive programme of public works because after 453 BC the league's treasury was removed to Athens, where it helped to finance Pericles' building schemes. Yet the energies released at Athens after the defeat of the Persian invasion of 480–479 BC were not confined to politics, imperial expansion, or architecture. They also embraced sculpture, painting, poetical drama, oratory, history and philosophy. Many of the famous names were indeed non-Athenian, but most of them visited Athens, or even chose to live there.

In drama five names stand out: the three tragedians Aeschylus (525–456 BC), Sophocles (496–406 BC) and Euripides (485–406 BC), as well as Aristophanes (450–385 BC) and Menander (342–289 BC) for comedy. At annual festivals these dramatists tackled the moral and political questions that exercised their audiences with a frankness less confident ages have found uncomfortable. History was likewise first transformed by Herodotus (484–425 BC), originally from Halicarnassus in Asia Minor, then by Thucydides (*c.* 455–400 BC), an Athenian aristocrat who was blamed in 424 BC for losing the city of Amphipolis in Thrace to the Spartan commander Brasidas. They endeavoured to make sense of the great conflicts of their times: the unsuccessful Persian attack on Greece (480–479 BC) and the bitter struggle for supremacy between Sparta and Athens respectively. A variety of philosophical schools also sought to explain the contemporary world. The Sophists, itinerant philosophers and teachers of oratory, were mostly non-Athenian, like Protagoras (*c.* 490–420 BC), a friend of Pericles who hailed from Thrace. Though Plato's disdain for their activities led to the coining of the pejorative term 'sophistry', the Sophists did much to enlarge traditional education in Athens, and elsewhere. Protagoras was responsible for the laws and constitution of the southern Italian colony of Thurii, which Pericles founded in 443 BC for the benefit of settlers from all of Greece. One of them was Herodotus.

Utterly different from Protagoras was Socrates (469–399 BC), an Athenian passionately devoted to his place of birth. He rarely left Athens, except on campaign as an infantryman

until no longer able to equip himself properly with armour. His distinctive idea was the equation of virtue with

A celebration of democracy dating from the 330s BC, the final decade of Athenian independence. Democracy is shown placing a wreath on the head of the people of Athens.

knowledge. Since wrongdoing arose from ignorance, Socrates held that it could be eradicated through enlightenment. After Socrates' execution in 399 BC, his admirer Plato (429–347 BC) gave written expression to Socrates' philosophy, which was included in the curriculum of the Academy, a centre of learning founded at Athens by Plato in 385 BC. A decade later Aristotle (384–322 BC) came from his birthplace, Stagira in Chalcidice, to the Academy and developed his ideas there. After acting as a tutor to Alexander the Great, Aristotle returned to Athens, where in 335 BC he founded his own school, the Lyceum. Other philosophers followed his example: Zeno of Citium arrived from Cyprus around 310 BC and founded Stoicism, while three years later Epicurus, a native of Samos, bought a house with a garden so as to gather together a group of like-minded people. Already Athens was well on its way to becoming the cultured university town so popular under Roman rule.

Defeat in 404 BC brought an abrupt end to Athens' imperial pretentions. Because the victorious Spartans feared the rising power of Thebes, they were prepared to let Athens survive as a city-state under the rule of the Thirty, oligarchs appointed by the Spartan admiral Lysander (died 395 BC). But the Athenian navy was destroyed along with the Long Walls, which joined the city to its port at Piraeus. Lysander's appointees were unable to prevent the restoration of democracy at Athens by Thrasybulus in 403 BC, and within a decade both its fortifications and fleet were restored as well. A second maritime league which the Athenians formed in 377 BC, however, was not really imperial in character despite some heavy handling of island allies. For Athens was preoccupied with keeping Macedon out of Greece, a subject very dear to the heart of Demosthenes (384–322 BC). It is somewhat ironic that another Athenian

orator, Isocrates (436–338 BC), gave the Macedonian king Philip II his programme for expansion, by calling for an expedition against Persia as a way of uniting the Greeks. The Macedonian seizure in the Hellespont of a convoy of merchant ships carrying grain to Piraeus caused the Athenians to declare war in 340 BC. A thrust by Philip into central Greece united Thebes and Athens, but at the battle of Chaeronea in 338 BC the Macedonians won the day. Athens, unlike Thebes, was spared destruction, possibly because of the value of its fleet in the forthcoming Persian expedition, and because of the admiration felt by the Macedonians for its cultural achievements.

Philip followed his victory by a political settlement more far-reaching than any which had preceded it. He established a confederation of Greek states, in which all were autonomous but at the same time lost the power of initiating action outside their own borders, since Philip alone could determine matters of war and peace. The new league met in Corinth, all the states except Sparta sending delegates. Even though there were defections on Philip's assassination in 336 BC, the fact that a league had been imposed on Greece by a Macedonian king announced the approaching end of the system of independent city-states. It effectively disappeared in the power struggle that erupted on the death of Philip's son, Alexander the Great, in 323 BC. Athens enjoyed a brief period of freedom as his generals strove to carve out kingdoms for themselves, but after 322 BC it was no longer a considerable military power. The city could no longer compete in wealth and prestige with the new capitals of the Seleucid and Ptolemaic kings. Ptolemaic Alexandria in Egypt, with its famous Museum and Library, even challenged Athens as a centre of learning.

In the second century BC a neutral Athens avoided the consequences of the wars which established Roman authority over Greece, but unwise support for Mithridates VI of Pontus led to its sack in 86 BC by the future Roman dictator Sulla (138–78 BC). Mithridates' commander, Archelaus, conducted a spirited defence, burning the siege engines that the Romans had built by the wholesale felling of woods, including the trees in the grounds of the Academy and the Lyceum. In the end Sulla's troops were denied total slaughter only by the pleas of Athenian exiles in the future dictator's retinue. As Sulla remarked, he was not in Athens to study but to punish rebellion. Afterwards the city settled down as a place of learning, overshadowed by the classical monuments of its glorious past.

See AEGINA; ARISTOTLE; CLEISTHENES; DELIAN LEAGUE; DEMOSTHENES; DRAMA; EPHIALTES; EPICURUS; LYSANDER; MACEDON; PELOPONNESIAN WAR; PERICLES; PERSIAN INVASIONS; PHILIP II; PLATO; PTOLEMIES; ROME; SELEUCIDS; SLAVERY; SOCRATES; SPARTA; STOICISM; SULLA; THEBES; THERAMENES; THRASYBULUS

*J. K. Davies, *Wealth and Power in Classical Athens* (New York, 1981); F. W. Ferguson, *Greek Imperialism* (Boston, 1913); C. Habicht, *Athens from Alexander to Antony* (Cambridge, Mass., 1997); M. H. Hansen, *The Athenian Assembly* (Oxford, 1987); A. H. M. Jones, *Athenian Democracy* (Oxford, 1957); J. Ober, *The Athenian Revolution: Essays on Ancient Greek Democracy and Political Theory* (Princeton, 1996); S. Hornblower, *The Greek World 479–323 BC* (London, 1983).

**Attalids**, a Macedonian dynasty based on the natural fortress of Pergamum in Asia Minor, was effectively founded by Attalus I (230–197 BC). Born in 269 BC, he only took the title of king after a decisive victory over the Galatians. These marauding Celts had crossed from Europe in 278 BC. Although driven into the interior by the Seleucids, the nominal rulers of Asia Minor, the Galatians continued raiding so that Attalus was also awarded the title of 'saviour' for their defeat. Two earlier rulers at Pergamum were Philetaerus and Eumenes: the former was appointed as commander of the fortress by Lysimachus (360–281 BC), but in the struggle between Alexander the Great's successors he switched to the Seleucids in 282 BC, after which he enjoyed a degree of local autonomy; the latter, his nephew, first tried to assert the independence of Pergamum from Seleucid control, with the aid of the Ptolemies. Attalus I was a cousin of Eumenes.

Under the Attalids Pergamum developed, eventually with Roman support, into a kingdom of almost equal status with those of the Antigonids in Macedon, the Seleucids in Asia, and the Ptolemies in Egypt. The historian Livy records in Rome that envoys of Attalus I explained 'how the king was assisting the Roman cause on land and sea with his fleet and with all his forces, and how he had carried out all the orders of the Roman consuls with energetic obedience; but they went on to say that they were afraid that he might not be free to continue this support because of the actions of King Antiochus; for that Seleucid monarch had invaded the kingdom of Attalus when it was bereft of its naval and military defences.' The subsequent Roman defeat of Antiochus III at the battle of Magnesia in 190 or 189 BC ensured Attalid freedom, but it also reduced the kingdom to little more than a pawn in Roman policy in the eastern Mediterranean.

All the Attalid kings were interested in learning, even though Pergamum never rivalled the brilliance of Ptolemaic Alexandria. Abroad they patronized in Athens Plato's school of philosophy, the famous Academy. The restored Stoa of Attalus, built in this city around 150 BC, shows today the extent of royal generosity. Pergamum's own gymnasium is the largest and most complete to survive from classical times. The independence of the king-

dom came to an end on the death of Attalus III in 133 BC, because his will bequeathed Pergamum to Rome. The reason for this bequest is unknown, although a number of possibilities suggest themselves. Despite their ostentatious patronage, the Attalid dynasty was by no means popular among the Greeks, who distrusted Pergamum's pro-Rome policy. At home, too, there was social unrest, a state of affairs that caused Attalus III to test out poison antidotes on condemned criminals. Quite possibly this ruler felt he was accepting the inevitable in accelerating the annexation of Pergamum as a Roman province of Asia.

See ANTIOCHUS III; PTOLEMIES; ROME; SELEUCIDS

*E. V. Hansen, *The Attalids of Pergamon* (Ithaca, 1971).

**Attila**, king of the Huns AD 434–453, was for a time the terror of the Roman world. According to the historian Ammianus Marcellinus, 'the nation of the Huns . . . dwelt beside the frozen ocean, and surpassed every extreme of ferocity'. Unaware of their Asian origins, he merely recorded the impact that they had upon other barbarian peoples living in eastern and northern Europe at the end of the fourth century. The Ostrogoths were subjugated by the Huns, while their cousins, the Visigoths, fled across the Danube into Roman territory, where in AD 378 at Adrianople they slew the emperor

Valens along with most of his army. The German problem, with which Rome had to contend henceforth, was exacerbated by Hunnish pressure.

Although Huns could be found bearing arms for Rome, like many Goths, the weakness of Roman emperors in the east and the west encouraged Attila to launch a series of devastating raids. In AD 434 he had inherited an enormous empire in eastern Europe, from which large forces could be raised. These were sent against the eastern provinces in AD 441, two years after the Vandals captured Carthage. Because the grain supply of the African provinces immediately around this city was as important to Constantinople as to Rome, the eastern emperor Theodosius II (AD 408–450) had dispatched an expeditionary force against the Vandals, leaving little to counter Attila's invasion across the Danube. The result was the collapse of frontier defences, the utter devastation of the Balkans, and in AD 443 a humiliating peace agreement. Constantinople had to make a heavy payment in gold each year to ensure Hunnish goodwill. But there was no real tranquillity and, five years later, Attila used a second invasion to dictate even harsher terms. It was fortunate for the east that in AD 451 the Huns turned the direction of their raids westwards. Bidding for control of half the western provinces, Attila marched into Gaul and met an unexpected reverse on the Catalaunian Fields, near modern Troyes. Frustrated in Gaul, the Huns moved into Italy

instead, where they even captured and sacked Mediolanum (modern Milan). This was an unusual success for the nomadic Huns, who drew upon the skills in siegecraft of their subject peoples. Rome itself would have been Attila's next target had not Pope Leo the Great (AD 440–461) somehow persuaded the Huns to quit Italy. That it was a churchman, and not an imperial official, who saved the day reflected the powerlessness of the western Roman emperors at Ravenna, from AD 404 till 476 the final seat of imperial government.

The departure of the Huns did not bring immediate relief, because their pillaging had left the countryside as well as the towns in ruins. Pestilence and famine stalked Italy and Gaul, but in AD 453 there was joy at the news of Attila's death, on the night of his marriage to a new wife. 'The Huns were dumbfounded,' relates a chronicler, 'they cut off their hair and slashed their faces with their swords, so that the greatest of all warriors should be mourned by no women's tears, but with the blood of men.'

See GOTHS; HUNS; ROME; THEODOSIUS II
*E. A. Thompson, *The Huns* (Oxford, 1996).

**Augustine** (AD 354–430), the Christian saint, was born at Thagaste (modern Souk Ahras in Algeria), the son of a pagan father and a Christian mother. Almost certainly of Berber stock,

Aurelius Augustinus was brought up a Christian, and his mother's moral influence was a decisive force in his life. Yet the influence of his father was not negligible because he insisted that the young Augustine receive a classical education. In his *Confessions*, written before AD 400, he says that he was never a brilliant scholar. He also admits to being a bad loser, a trait hardly suited to the future role of a bishop, whose primary task in an age dominated by theological argument was the maintenance of truth against error. Yet Augustine was always an idealist seeking after the perfect way of life, a quest which from AD 373 to 382 led him to become a Manichee. Long afterwards his own vision of the elect differed little from the chosen few of Mani, the austere Babylonian prophet who was martyred in AD 277 by the Zoroastrian priesthood. Because of a profound sense of his own personal worthlessness, Augustine believed that no one could be saved without grace, a view that could readily accommodate predestination. In the years following his reconversion to Christianity, however, he devoted immense energy writing refutations of Manichaean doctrines. In AD 388 Augustine established in his home town a monastic-style settlement with many of his friends, mainly former Manichaeans. The intention was not to influence Christian belief in north Africa, but rather to concentrate on their own salvation. The experiment may well have faltered prior to

Augustine's ordination several years later. It was a move which ended with his becoming in AD 395 the bishop of Hippo (modern Bône in Algeria), where he died while the city was being besieged by the Vandals.

A Christian symbol on a coin issued by Magnentius, who from AD 350 till 353 usurped power in the western provinces of the Roman empire.

Heresy was Augustine's main preoccupation as bishop, and he became increasingly intolerant during the long struggle against the local Donatists, who drew strength for their rigorous interpretation of the scripture from the example of earlier martyrs. They also regarded as diabolical the exploitation of the rural poor by great landowners. An Augustine who had once delighted in Roman freedom, albeit as narrowly propounded by Cicero (106–43 BC), found himself saying that liberty was being used only to commit sin. He even persuaded the western emperor Honorius (AD 395–423), whose government was bottled up at Ravenna, that the Donatists should be outlawed. Property was confiscated, heavy fines imposed, but there were no executions – no new martyrs were to be made. The fall of Rome in AD 410 to the Visigothic leader Alaric had shaken Augustine, whose most famous work, *City of God*, can be regarded as an attempt to make sense for Christians out of the collapse of Roman authority. Especially galling was the rumour that Rome's fall was a punishment inflicted by the non-Christian gods for the suppression of their worship. There is a fascinating parallel between Augustine and his contemporary Hui Yuan (AD 334–416), who lived immediately after the loss of the oldest provinces of the Chinese empire. Both men were devoted to their mothers, embraced heterodox creeds before reshaping Buddhism and Christianity respectively, and at the end of their lives they still remained deeply influenced by classical learning. In old age Hui Yuan believed that the Confucian classics contained the flower of Chinese thought, even though he was abbot of a monastery dedicated to the worship of Amida Buddha, in whose paradise of the Pure Land he hoped to be reborn.

*See* CHRISTIANITY; HONORIUS; MANICHAEISM; VANDALS

*P. Brown, *Augustine of Hippo* (London, 1967).

**Augustus** (31 BC – AD 14) was the first Roman emperor. Born in 63 BC, Gaius Octavius was the great-nephew of the dictator Julius Caesar (100–44 BC), who posthumously adopted him as his son and heir. In 44 BC Octavian rallied Caesar's veterans and used them to fight Mark Antony (82–30 BC), who had made a bid for supreme power himself; then in alliance with Antony and Lepidus (89–12 BC) he led them against the republicans, defeating Caesar's murderers in 42 BC at Philippi in Macedonia. Although the Romans had awarded Caesar divine honours, making Octavian in turn the 'son of a god', a serious illness obliged him to play a subordinate role to Antony immediately after the victory. By 40 BC, however, the Mediterranean world was divided between them: basing himself at Alexandria, Antony held the east, while at Rome Octavian controlled the west, except for Africa, the province to which Lepidus was relegated. When in 36 BC Octavian's admiral Agrippa (64–12 BC) overcame Sextus Pompeius, the son of Caesar's old rival Pompey (106–48 BC), Lepidus foolishly chose to challenge Octavian for control over Sextus Pompeius' base, the island of Sicily. He was swiftly disarmed and exiled internally to Italy.

With Agrippa's assistance, Octavian consolidated his position at Rome by starting an ambitious building programme. The first Pantheon, or 'temple of all the gods', formed part of an enormous layout of temples, baths and public gardens, completed shortly before 25 BC. Although the present building still has above its entrance the dedicatory inscription 'Marcus Agrippa, son of Lucius, consul for the third time, built this', the whole structure was rebuilt in the reign of Hadrian

The first Roman emperor Augustus, the sole ruler of the Mediterranean world after 31 BC.

(AD 117–138). Such was the later emperor's modesty (he never had his name inscribed on any of his buildings) and Agrippa's fame, that the original inscription was repeated on the new Pantheon. It is also likely that Hadrian was trying to revive the memory of Augustus' reign and associate his own with it. For the young Octavian set the imperial pattern, as visitors to Rome can trace in its surviving classical monuments today. He also did everything he could to stimulate public protest against Antony's involvement with Cleopatra, the Macedonian queen of Egypt. The assignment of eastern Roman territories to the children Cleopatra had borne Antony in 34 BC was almost the last straw. That

came two years later with Antony's divorce of Octavia, the long-suffering yet faithful sister of Octavian. So a national crusade against Cleopatra ended in a total naval victory for Octavian in 31 BC at Actium, off the north-western coast of Greece. With the shattered remnants of their fleet, Antony and Cleopatra fled to Egypt, where they committed suicide on Octavian's invasion of the country the following year.

Octavian then had put to death Cleopatra's son Caesarion, whose father she always claimed was Julius Caesar. He also annexed Egypt and preserved direct rule over the new province through his personal representatives. The capture of Cleopatra's treasury, which contained the residue of the fabled wealth of the Ptolemies, made it possible for Octavian to settle many veterans in colonies throughout the Mediterranean world. He reduced the number of legionaries to about 165,000 citizens, mostly Italians; they were supported by a larger number of auxiliary troops drawn from subject peoples resident within the imperial borders. After twenty-five years' service legionaries were to receive a lump sum from a military treasury maintained by special taxes. Auxiliaries, on retirement, were entitled to Roman citizenship. The fleet was reorganized, too, and Octavian replaced his Spanish bodyguard with a German unit. The practice of using mounted Germans for personal protection seems to have begun during the conquest of Gaul (58–50 BC): there Caesar recruited about 1,000 volunteers from beyond the Rhine. Whether or not Octavian's new bodyguard was indeed a continuation of the same force is impossible to tell, not least because he wanted to keep so monarchical an institution in the background.

But there could be no doubt that Octavian was now the master of the Mediterranean world, a fact the senate in Rome soon acknowledged with a series of titles such as 'first citizen' and Augustus. The constitutional settlement of 27 BC recognized him as an emperor rather than a king: but his personality was publicized through the so-called imperial cult, a complex of ceremonies making use of the forms of religion to express and instil loyalty to the ruler. At the same time Augustus voluntarily restricted his actions within the limits of various constitutional powers conferred by the senate, which in theory at least still had a role in the appointment of the emperor. His real support, however, came from the Roman army, now a professional force largely stationed in the frontier provinces. The only permanent force in Italy was the élite Praetorian Guard. To help with the administration of what was a very considerable empire, Augustus gathered together a group of 'friends' rather like the 'companions' of Macedonian kings. Because he was uninterested in interfering to any substantial degree with the lives of his subjects, he did not appoint many officials. The Roman empire was always undergoverned, certainly in comparison with the Chinese empire, which employed a large, permanent civil service. However, Augustus was lucky to have able yet reliable generals and admirals, most notably his friend Agrippa, and in later years his stepsons Drusus (38–9 BC) and Tiberius, who ruled as emperor after him from AD 14 to 37. These and others added the new provinces of Noricum and Raetia on the Danube frontier, completed the conquest of Spain, and restored the system of buffer-states facing Parthia. Great pride was taken in a peace agreement with the Parthians, who returned the legionary standards captured at Carrhae in 53 BC. Augustus was very conscious that the Greek east had joined the empire as defeated nations, and he deliberately associated its defence against Parthia with the historic expulsion of the Persians from Europe by the Greek city-states. It offered a potential for a second Antony to exploit a simmering discontent: so Augustus, Agrippa and Tiberius all conducted extensive tours there.

Roman expansion was halted by the Illyrian revolt (AD 6–9) and the loss of three legions east of the Rhine in AD 9. Fearing that they might turn against him after this defeat, Augustus dismissed his German bodyguard, but a similar unit was in Rome at the start of Tiberius' reign, and under Caligula (AD 37–41), the adopted grandson of Tiberius, the horse guard took centre stage. When Augustus died in AD 14, he bequeathed an unprecedented realm to the second Roman emperor, and one which – remarkably, for the classical world – was at peace. For the provincials, in particular, the Augustan period had come as something of a relief, for as the historian Tacitus points out, previously they had suffered from 'the feuds of dynasts and the greed of magistrates. The protection they received from the laws was feeble, since they were subverted by violence, intrigue and ultimately money.' The association of order and peace with Rome eventually became an indispensable element in the Christian view of its empire, which saw it as called into existence by divine providence in order to facilitate the birth and spread of Christianity.

See ADMINISTRATION; AGRIPPA; ANTONY; CHRISTIANITY; CLEOPATRA; ILLYRIANS; LEPIDUS; PARTHIA: PERSIAN INVASIONS; PTOLEMIES; ROME; TIBERIUS; WARFARE

*A. H. M. Jones, *Augustus* (London, 1970); F. Millar, *The Emperor in the Roman World* (Oxford, 1977); H. H. Scullard, *From the Gracchi to Nero* (London, 1982).

**Aurelian**, Roman emperor AD 270–275, was elevated by troops at Sirmium (modern Petrovic in Serbia). A local man of humble origins, the fifty-six-year-old Lucius Domitius Aurelianus appeared at first to be yet another military opportunist who seized the throne in the thirty-five years since the collapse of the Severan dynasty (AD 193–235). Foreign invasion and

The Roman emperor Aurelian, who did much to end the military anarchy of the third century AD.

plague would have weakened Rome without the added difficulty of civil war. But few of Aurelian's fifteen predecessors showed any real grasp of the crisis then threatening the empire, and one of them, Valerian (AD 253–260), even managed to become a prisoner of the Sasanians. In AD 260 he allowed himself to be tricked by the Persian king Shapur I into a parley without an adequate bodyguard. As a result, Shapur was able to use Valerian as a footstool when mounting his horse. Quite different was Aurelian, who both succeeded in reuniting the empire under a single ruler and restoring its borders with one exception, Dacia. This province (virtually modern Romania) was evacuated under Gothic pressure in AD 270, but energetic campaigning south of the Danube drove off all the German invaders. The Juthungi were severely mauled by Aurelian after a raid on Italy, the Vandals thrown back as soon as they attempted to move south, and the Goths completely routed in Moesia (present-day Serbia). The Visigoths

55

had been ravaging this province as well as Greece and Asia Minor for more than a year.

Aurelian's next target was Palmyra (modern Tadmor in Syria). This caravan-state was sponsored by Rome as a bulwark against the Sasanians, but weakness in the eastern Mediterranean had allowed it to absorb much Roman territory. The Palmyrene queen Zenobia, on behalf of her infant son Vaballathus, exercised a stranglehold over trade with India and China, something the Romans simply could not tolerate. By ensuring that his troops did not plunder the cities of recaptured eastern provinces, Aurelian was able to concentrate his forces against the Palmyrenes without anxiety about rebellion on his lines of supply. Two engagements were followed by the capture of Palmyra itself: renewed conflict with Rome in AD 273, however, forced Aurelian to destroy the city. Zenobia was compelled to parade in a magnificent triumph in Rome, although afterwards the former queen married a senator and settled down quietly in Italy.

To protect the city of Rome from barbarian attack Aurelian ordered the construction of a new wall, over 12 miles in length. Though less strong than the defences later built at Constantinople, the remains of its gateways and towers today testify to the new insecurity faced by the capital. For Aurelian's hasty defensive measures were an admission that Italy, like the other provinces, could expect to be the object of sudden raids. Another weakness he tackled was the coinage, whose debasement had contributed largely to the uncontrollable price inflation of the times. A shortage of precious metals prevented a return to true silver issues, but at least Aurelian's new base-silver coins assisted the renewal of commercial enterprise. Their values were fixed firmly in terms of gold. But Aurelian was not to witness the benefits his actions were to bring to Rome, for in AD 275 he was assassinated in Thrace by dissident officers. Six short-lived emperors emulated Aurelian in vain before Diocletian (AD 284–305) firmly grasped the reins of power once more. This equally hard-bitten soldier then began a thorough reorganization of the Roman empire.

*See* DIOCLETIAN; GOTHS; ROME; SASANIANS; SEVERAN DYNASTY; SHAPUR I; VANDALS; WARFARE

*H. M. D. Parker, *A History of the Roman World from AD 138 to 337* (London, 1958).

# B

Bactria was originally a province of the Persian empire in Central Asia. Today it would include northern Afghanistan, southern Uzbekistan and Tadjikistan. It was subdued with great difficulty by Alexander the Great in 329–327 BC. During this hard-fought struggle the Macedonian king was obliged to recruit, for the first time, local auxiliaries on a large scale. A mutiny of his Thessalian troops, tired of a campaign which had begun in 334 BC and brought them thousands of miles from home, forced this unexpected demobilization. Whilst the Thessalians marched away with good severance pay and bonuses, the newly recruited troops more than made good their loss, much to Alexander's relief. The conquest of Bactria was critical because its governor, Bessus, had proclaimed himself successor to the last Persian king Darius III, taking the title of Artaxerxes IV. Closely pursued by Alexander, Bessus had already killed Darius and sought to rally his forces beyond the Oxus. But the swift Macedonian crossing of this swollen river on floats made from tents stuffed with chaff surprised Bessus, who was taken prisoner. To show the distaste he felt for the regicide, Alexander punished him in Persian fashion: after being scourged, Bessus' nose and ears were cut off prior to a public execution in Ecbatana. The body of Darius, on the other hand, was borne back in state to Persepolis, and given a royal burial there, beside his Achaemenid forebears. During the Bactrian campaign Alexander also married Roxane, the daughter of a chieftain whose stronghold was a gigantic rock. This had been taken by a daring ruse, but the marriage gave the Macedonian king a valuable ally on his route to India.

Even before Alexander's death in 323 BC, the Greek settlers of Bactria had risen in revolt. Afterwards the Seleucids (312–64 BC) discovered that they could exercise authority there only by force of arms, a task beyond their strength by 250 BC. With the steady retreat of the Seleucid frontier westwards, and the revival of Iranian power under the Parthians, Bactria became a Greek enclave. Its first independent ruler was Diodotus, who like the Attalid kings of Pergamum still acknowledged Seleucid suzerainty on his coins. After Diodotus I's death, perhaps as early as 248 BC, his son of the same name succeeded him, and ruled till about 235 BC, when he was killed during a coup. Its leader was Euthydemus, who founded the second dynasty of Greco-Bactrian kings. His long reign and the shorter one of his son Demetrius I (200–190 BC) witnessed the expansion of Bactrian power right into north-western India. Taxila was annexed, and expeditions sent into both the Indus and Ganges valleys. Demetrius' determined son-in-law Menander even captured Mathura, and went on to threaten Pataliputra, the old Mauryan capital. The overthrow of the Mauryas gave the Greeks their brief chance of power in India. Against all the odds, they ruled for more than 150 years over parts of present-day Pakistan and north-western India. They maintained their culture, albeit by a degree of adaptation and compromise, in lands distant from a Greece already under Roman rule.

A city such as Ai Khanum, founded by Alexander on the bank of the Oxus in northern Afghanistan, was the model settlement. Refounded and laid out on a rectilinear pattern by the Seleucids before 250 BC, the city boasted strong fortifications, an arsenal, a palace, a theatre, and a gymnasium. Local temples, however, stood alongside ones dedicated to the gods of the Greek pantheon. This is hardly surprising when someone like King Menander (160–130 BC) is known to have been a Buddhist sympathizer. Indian tradition asserts that he built at Pataliputra a stupa, a tumulus-like structure which contained a Buddhist relic. Archaeological evidence for the earlier conversion of Greek settlers to Buddhism may be the recently discovered bilingual rock inscription at Kandahar in Afghanistan. Possibly dating from 258 BC, the inscription in Greek and Aramaic relates the massive

Demetrius I of Bactria, who in 200 BC struck coins in north-western India. On the reverse is shown the Greek hero Heracles.

effort made by the Mauryan king Ashoka to promote moral principles throughout his realm.

Bactria survived till about 140 BC when the Parthians annexed it. After the loss of Bactria, Greek kings continued to rule in southern Afghanistan and north-western India, despite prolonged internecine wars. The last rulers were swept away by the Sakas, Sythian people from Central Asia, sometime before 55 BC. A curious episode in the story of Bactria is the embassy of Zhang Qian, who returned to China in 126 BC. So as to obtain allies against the Xiongnu, probably the Huns who later invaded the Roman empire, Zhang Qian was dispatched westwards by the Han emperor Wu Di (140–87 BC) in order to find their enemies, the Da Yuezhi or Kushanas. They proved to be uninterested in an alliance, but Zhang Qian was amazed to find these former nomads living in a place where there were 'cities, mansions and houses as in China'. This was the first occasion on which the Chinese had encountered another civilization. It was in fact the northern part of Bactria, although Zhang Qian did not appreciate that the Da Yuezhi were settled on the fringes of the old Greco-Macedonian world. No cultural exchange occurred between China and the West: the Chinese became aware of other civilizations, but the only foreign influence during the classical period came from India, in the form of Buddhism.

*See* ALEXANDER THE GREAT; ATTALIDS; MAURYAN DYNASTY; MENANDER; PARTHIANS; PERSIA; SELEUCIDS; ZHANG QIAN

*S. Sherwin-White and A. Kuhrt, *From Samarkhand to Sardis: A New Approach to the Seleucid Empire* (London, 1993); A. K. Narain, *The Indo-Greeks* (Oxford, 1957); W. W. Tarn, *The Greeks in Bactria and India* (Cambridge, 1951); G. Woodcock, *The Greeks in India* (London, 1966).

**Ban Chao** (AD 31–101) was the younger brother of the historian Ban Gu. A distinguished general who reasserted Chinese influence in Central Asia, Ban Chao's future success on the battlefield was predicted as a young man by a physiognomist in Luoyang, then the capital of the Later Han emperors (AD 25–220). At this time he was too poor to keep a servant and had to earn extra money as a copyist. The physiognomist, however, assured him of fame through his swallow's beak and tiger's neck: these physical features were interpreted to mean that he would fly and eat meat miles away from the capital, a reference to his later enoblement as protector-governor of the Western Regions.

To this part of Central Asia, directly westwards from the Great Wall, Ban Chao was posted in the AD 70s. His resolute action against the Xiongnu impressed local rulers, and they once again swore allegiance to China. The Xiongnu, probably the Huns who later invaded the Roman empire, were the main rivals here, although in AD 90

Ban Chao was obliged to fight the Kushanas as well. This Da Yuezhi people had just carved out for themselves a great realm based on northwestern India. In Bactria Ban Chao routed the Kushanas, after which he marched on to the eastern shore of the Caspian Sea, the closest a Chinese army ever got to the Roman empire. It is not impossible, however, that earlier in 36 BC a group of former Roman legionaries was captured by a predecessor of Ban Chao at Turfan, for his brother Ban Gu records the use of a 'fish-scale formation', the locking of shields as a protection from arrows and spears. If these men were Romans in the service of a Xiongnu chieftain, then they may have been survivors from the battle of Carrhae in 53 BC. Afterwards the Parthians are known to have settled some of the 10,000 prisoners taken then on their eastern frontier.

Whatever the truth behind the story, the Chinese were equally adept in making use of foreign soldiers to defend exposed frontiers. Ban Chao raised local forces in the Western Regions, one excellent source being the oasis state of Khotan. After his retirement, and death in AD 101 or 102, Ban Chao's legacy of order there lasted for half a century.

See BAN GU; GREAT WALL; KUSHANAS; WESTERN REGIONS; XIONGNU

*Ying-shi Yu, *Trade and Expansion in Han China: A Study of the Structure of Sino-Barbarian Economic Relations* (Berkeley, 1967).

**Ban Gu** (died AD 92) lived in an age that was noted for the esteem accorded to scholarship. Even more remarkable then was the literary fame achieved by both Ban Gu and his sister Ban Zhao. It perfectly complemented the valorous deeds of their younger brother, the general Ban Chao (AD 31–101), who reasserted Chinese authority in Central Asia. Their father, Ban Biao, had been instrumental in the restoration of the Han dynasty, following the usurpation of Wang Mang (AD 9–23), and as a result the family was welcomed officially in Luoyang, then the capital. Whereas Ban Chao embarked on a diplomatic and military career, Ban Gu preferred a life of letters. It is somewhat ironic that Ban Gu should have died a prisoner of the Xiongnu, probably the Huns who later invaded the Roman empire. He had been sent on a military enterprise to Mongolia. Ban Gu's great work was *The History of the Former Han Dynasty*, which, like the earlier Han historian Sima Qian, he may have built upon his father's researches. The Han emperor He Di (AD 88–106) asked Ban Zhao to finish the history on her brother's death. That a woman could be considered good enough to accomplish such a task indicates the reputation for learning enjoyed by the Ban family. On publication it was found to be too difficult for most scholars.

See BAN CHAO; BAN ZHAO; HAN DYNASTY; SIMA QIAN

*H. H. Dubs, *The History of the Former Han Dynasty by Pan Ku* (Baltimore, 1938–55).

**Ban Zhao** was the sister of the historian Ban Gu (died AD 92) and the general Ban Chao (AD 31–101). She outlived both brothers and died around AD 120. A widow in early life, Ban Zhao devoted herself to learning and was asked by the Han emperor He Di to complete Ban Gu's work, *The History of the Former Han Dynasty*, which she did admirably. After the death of the emperor in AD 106, Empress Dowager Deng became regent and conferred with Ban Zhao on affairs of state. Though her infant son did not survive and his young cousin followed him soon, the dowager empress held on to power at court till her own death in AD 121. During these years Ban Zhao exercised considerable influence, for a chronicler noted how 'at one word from Mother Ban a whole family resigned from office'. Another book she wrote about AD 115 was entitled *Lessons for Women*. It sets out the proper path for women to follow, and in the process tells us much about family life in late classical China.

China's foremost woman scholar, Ban Zhao. She completed her brother's history of the early Han period.

According to *Lessons for Women*, subordination to men was the expected role for women, as they were obedient to their fathers when children, their husbands when they married, and their sons when they were widowed. The ideal age to marry was fifteen. Grounds for divorcing a wife included disobedience to parents-in-law, barrenness, adultery, incurable disease and jealousy. But it needs to be remembered, however, that a man could have only one wife. Concubines were not treated as full members of the family and the status of a concubine was always inferior to that of a wife. Unfortunately for women, Ban Zhao's recommendation that they should receive the same education that she had enjoyed was largely ignored.

*See* BAN CHAO; BAN GU; HAN DYNASTY; WOMEN

*N. L. Swann, *Pan Chao; Foremost Woman Scholar of China* (New York, 1960).

**Berossus** was the author of a history of Babylon dedicated to Antiochus I (281–261 BC), the second Seleucid monarch. According to his own testimony, Berossus was a priest, and most probably of Marduk, the chief Babylonian god. He certainly accepted the legitimacy of the Seleucid dynasty (312–64 BC) which was built upon the Asian component of Alexander the Great's vast empire. The Macedonian conquest, however, left poor Berossus suspended between two great cultures, Babylonian and Greek. Steeped in the traditions of Babylon and its priest-hood, he felt it incumbent on himself to explain them to the new rulers, so as to reduce cultural misunderstanding. He was likewise concerned to let King Antiochus know something of Babylon's own long and distinguished history. That Berossus eventually left Babylon for retirement on the Aegean island of Cos can mean two things: he may have decided to embrace Greek culture himself, abandoning his Babylonian heritage, or, more likely, he moved there because he was disap-pointed with Antiochus, despite that king's public adoption of Babylonian forms. Cos then belonged to Ptolemy II (283–246 BC), Antiochus' most bitter enemy.

The original history of Babylon is lost, but an abridgement of its Greek text has partly survived. What Berossus claimed he was making available to Greek readers was ancient Babylonian accounts of 'the histories of heaven, earth and sea and the first birth and kings and their deeds'. And he does indeed start with creation and the wisdom communicated to the Baby-lonians in a revelation 432,000 years before the Flood. This was very differ-ent indeed from the Greek approach to history, which saw civilization as a historical phenomenon, the product of human action over time rather than a single creation. For Berossus the civilization of Babylon resulted from the divine gift of law and order. The flood myth he recounts is an earlier parallel of the biblical story. After the

waters had gone down, the survivors 'sacrificed to the gods and proceeded to Babylon on foot'.

A similar task to that undertaken for the Seleucids by Berossus was the work of the Egyptian priest Manetho, who lived during the reigns of the first two Ptolemies. He wrote a history of the previous dynasties which had ruled Egypt.

See ALEXANDER THE GREAT; PTOLEMIES; SELEUCIDS

*A. Kuhrt and S. Sherwin-White, *Hellenism in the East* (London, 1987).

**Bindusara**, the second Mauryan emperor (297–272 BC), was the son of Candragupta, who founded the dynasty in northern India around 322 BC. Candragupta had witnessed the devastating impact of Alexander the Great's invasion of 327–325 BC on the states in the north-west, and afterwards he took advantage of the instability following the Macedonian withdrawal to establish an empire of his own, by annexing territories through a combination of war and diplomacy. Bindusara, on the other hand, extended Mauryan power largely by force of arms, earning for himself the nickname 'slayer of foes'. But his son Ashoka renounced the use of violence after conversion to Buddhism around 258 BC. However, he had succeeded to the throne in 268 BC only after a bloody struggle with his brothers. Buddhist traditions relate how Ashoka slew them all except Tissa, a younger brother. Bindusara showed little interest in Buddhism and favoured the Ajivikas, the followers of Maskarin Gosala, a contemporary of the Buddha (c. 563–479 BC). Gosala's teachings in fact drew the Buddha's most severe criticism because of their determinism. Gosala had argued that the attainment of enlightenment could not be hurried by means of virtue and asceticism, or delayed through vice: for the process took place in its own good time. It was likely to be spread over a span of countless rebirths. If the tradition of Candragupta abdicating and becoming a Jain ascetic is true, then Bindusara should be seen as the most this-worldly of the early Mauryan emperors. For his predecessor retired to India's far south in search of personal release from the cycle of rebirth, while his successor spent the majority of his long reign propagating moral principles derived from the Buddha's gentle teachings.

See ALEXANDER THE GREAT; ASHOKA; BUDDHISM; CANDRAGUPTA; GOSALA; JAINISM; MAURYAN DYNASTY
*H. Zimmer, *Philosophies of India* (Princeton, 1969).

**Boudicca**, better known today by the name of Boadicea, was the widow of Prasutagus, the ruler of the Iceni. This client-king of the Romans ruled a British people living in modern East Anglia. The Iceni had long been suffering from the exactions of tax-collectors and money-lenders, including the emperor Nero's tutor and adviser Seneca (4 BC – AD 65). When in AD 60 Prasutagus died without a son, Nero was persuaded to absorb the lands of the Iceni directly into the new Roman province, rather than recognize Boudicca as ruler. Coupled with the scourging of Boudicca and the rape of her daughters, the land seizure was enough to raise the Iceni in open revolt. Joined by the neighbouring Trinovantes, the rebels overran the Roman settlements of Camulodunum (Colchester), Verulamium (St Albans) and Londinium (London), putting 70,000 Romans or Romanized Britons to the sword. The historian Cassius Dio describes how Boudicca harangued her warriors, grasping a spear in her hand: 'In stature she was very tall, in appearance most terrifying, her glance was fierce, her voice harsh; a great mass of brown hair descended below her waist; around her neck hung a golden torc; she wore a coloured tunic over which a thick cloak was fastened with a brooch.'

Legionaries hastily sent against the insurgents from Lindum Colonia (Lincoln) were simply overwhelmed, and for a time southern Britain was at Boudicca's mercy. The Romans then concentrated most of their remaining forces near present-day Lichfield, where a crushing victory over the rebels caused Boudicca to take poison. Reprisals were halted only on the orders of Nero (AD 54–68). Even though a gentler approach subsequently kept the peace in the province, vacant lots in the three sacked cities still bore witness to the destruction wrought by the rebels for several decades afterwards. Not until after the visit of the emperor Hadrian in AD 121, or 122, did Britain begin to recover its previous prosperity.

*See* BRITAIN; CLAUDIUS; HADRIAN; NERO; ROME

*P. Salway, *Roman Britain* (Oxford, 1981); C. Webster, *Boudicca: The Roman Conquest of Britain* (London, 1993).

**Britain**, or Britannia as the Roman part of the British Isles was called, always represented an outpost, far from the Mediterranean core of Rome's empire. Yet its tin mines had attracted ships from the Mediterranean long before Julius Caesar landed his troops in 55 and 54 BC. The alleged reason for these two operations was that the Britons had been assisting their Gaulish cousins against him. More important, however, was the effect which successful campaigns would have at Rome: all

Gold coin celebrating the Roman emperor Claudius' conquest of southern Britain. It was struck at the birthplace of Claudius, Lugdunum, modern Lyon in France.

Caesar's actions need to be seen as part of the struggle for power in the capital. He desperately wanted to foster the impression of being a military genius so as to outshine his arch-rival Pompey (106–48 BC). Possibly the intention was to annex southern Britain, but nothing permanent was achieved with the result that the landings received no public notice at Rome.

The first Roman emperor, Augustus (31 BC – AD 14), exhibited no interest in following his great-uncle's example. Not until Caligula's reign (AD 37–41) was any attention given to Britain, and it is hard to understand exactly what lay behind the preparations of AD 40, other than the emperor's insanity. Instead of embarking for Britain, the historian Suetonius relates, troops were ordered to gather sea-shells on the beaches of Gaul: Caligula referred to them as 'plunder from the Ocean, due to the Capitol and the Palace', and made the soldiers fill their helmets with the shells. Perhaps the emperor had simply become involved with a military exercise, unlike his successor Claudius (AD 41–54), who accompanied a real expeditionary force in AD 43 across the Channel. Southern Britain was soon secured, although Caratacus gave the Romans cause for concern prior to his capture in AD 51. This chieftain was, however, granted an honourable retirement in Italy by Claudius. More serious was the major rebellion under Boudicca in East Anglia, which led to the destruction in AD 60 of Camulodunum, Verulamium and Londinium, modern Colchester, St Albans and London respectively. Excavations suggest that few buildings were not burnt to the ground, and many lots remained vacant for over a decade after the revolt. The next phase of Roman expansion in Britain occurred during the Flavian dynasty (AD 69–96), when the legions even advanced into Scotland. It was the policy of the emperor Hadrian (AD 117–138) which defined the northern frontier: he was concerned to rationalize the empire's defences and on a visit to Britain in AD 121, or 122, the line of the wall bearing his name was surveyed. It ran for some 70 miles between Wallsend and Bowness, with an extension in a chain of forts down the coast from the Solway Firth to prevent outflanking movements by sea. This diminutive Great Wall had a chequered history: in AD 159 it was temporarily abandoned for another defensive system farther north in Strathclyde; in AD 159 it was reoccupied, and repaired by the emperor Septimius Severus in AD 208, following a barbarian incursion; Theodosius I (AD 379–395) had to restore it after another attack, but its garrison was soon depleted by the usurpers who plunged the western provinces into civil wars.

Rebellions were a persistent problem in Britain. Combined with barbarian attacks by land and sea, the four provinces into which it was divided from AD 297 onwards struggled to maintain a reasonable level of prosperity. Saxon piracy was serious enough to require the building of forts along Britain's southern shore. Today the best-preserved example is at Portchester in Hampshire. The decision of the British usurper Constantine to invade Gaul in AD 407 effectively sealed the island's fate. Stripped of nearly all its soldiers, Britain faced an immediate Saxon attack, to which the western emperor Honorius (AD 395–423) could offer nothing except the advice to look after its own protection. The traditional date of the landing of the Saxons is AD 448, but some had certainly been allowed to settle earlier. Like the Visigoths, and the other German peoples settled in Gaul, they received land in return for military service. It was a stage in the barbarian take-over of Britain.

*See* BOUDICCA; CAESAR; CALIGULA; CARATACUS; CLAUDIUS; FLAVIAN DYNASTY; GOTHS; HADRIAN; HONORIUS; ROME; SEVERAN DYNASTY

*H. H. Scullard, *Roman Britain: Outpost of the Empire* (London, 1979); D. Perring, *Roman London* (London, 1991); G. Webster, *The Roman Invasion of Britain* (London, 1980).

**Buddhism** was not regarded by its founder, Guatama Siddartha (*c.* 563–479 BC), as a new religion. What he strove to do as the Buddha (the one who had attained enlightenment) was to expound an underlying fundamental order of the world in such a way that all could understand its workings. Only then would it be possible to overcome the sufferings necessarily involved in existence. Like his Jain contemporary Mahavira, the Buddha required his Indian followers to isolate themselves from worldly life. The saffron robe worn by the Buddhist monks was a badge which showed ordinary society that they had elected to leave its toils; the colour of this garment was the same as that used to dress condemned men on the day of execution. Jain ascetics, on the other hand, abandoned clothing altogether. Being liable to an endless round of rebirth and suffering because of the self, the Buddhist monk sought release into the bliss of the unborn by extinction of the ego. This goal was deemed possible through disciplined conduct in terms of vision, thought, speech, action, giving, striving, vigilance and concentration.

After his enlightenment at Bodh Gaya in Magadha (present-day Bihar) the Buddha spent his life teaching, travelling throughout the Ganges river valley. He even met King Bimbisara (c. 546–494 BC), the founder of the Nanda dynasty, but Buddhism did not impress any ruler enough to obtain official backing until the Mauryan emperor Ashoka was converted around 258 BC. By that time the religion had developed two distinct wings: one placed emphasis upon the ascetic ideal of the community of monks, whereas the other stood for a greater accommodation of the lay members and a broadening of the idea of the monastic community to include believers other than monks. The latter was to evolve into the so-called Great Vehicle, a form of Buddhism with an extensive pantheon. This was the version of the faith that was carried overland via Central Asian oasis-states to China. By the period of the Kushana domination of northern India (AD 50–250), there were eighteen Buddhist sects in India, a confused theological state of affairs that King Kaniska (AD 78–102) tried unsuccessfully to resolve at the Fourth Buddhist Council.

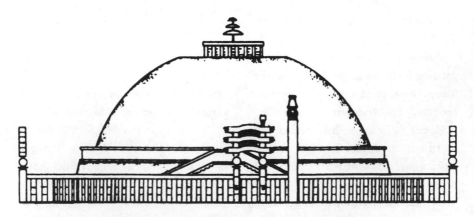

The original stupa at Sanchi, in present-day Madhya Pradesh, was built by Ashoka to house relics of the Buddha. This is a later enlargement.

A striking example of the Gandharan school. Sculpted under the Kushanas, this portrait of the Buddha uses Greco-Roman techniques of sculpture.

In China the phenomenal rise in the popularity of Buddhism took place after the end of the classical era. But the later religious fervour should not obscure the period of preparation that was essential for this remarkable event. Two complementary processes were at work from the second century AD onwards. One comprised the decline of imperial government and its ideology, in particular the Confucianism associated with the civil service and state-sponsored learning. The other process was the steady adaptation of Buddhism into a faith accessible to the Chinese. In these years of crisis, scholars turned to long-neglected works of Daoist philosophy and the new ideas found in the doctrines of Buddhism. The first translations of Buddhist texts were indeed so full of Daoist expressions that Buddhism was regarded as a sect of Daoism. The earliest Chinese reference to the imported faith typically mentions both: the Later Han emperor Ming Di addressed in AD 65 his half-brother Liu Ying as a prince who followed the ways of Lao Zi and the Buddha.

Daoist communities may have served to spread certain Buddhist symbols and cults, thus playing a role analogous to the Jewish communities which helped to spread news of early Christianity in the eastern provinces of the Roman empire. But eclecticism was born as much from the circumstances of the faith's arrival from India as the ability of the Chinese mind to hold a number of distinct propositions simultaneously without apparent discomfort. The first Buddhist converts had few texts, depended on the testimony of foreigners, and had scant knowledge of the society in which the Buddha had lived. Under the circumstances the task of translation proved very difficult. The first translators were of Central Asian origin, like the Parthian An Shihkao, who settled in Luoyang around AD 148. With the assistance of Central Asian and Chinese converts, An Shihkao translated works connected with meditation, techniques of breath-control, and psychology. Though within the imperial palace sacrifices were made in AD 166 to the Buddha, this worship was entwined with Daoism, as Lao Zi received honour at the same time. Not for another century would translations begin to free the imported faith from the Daoist embrace so as to allow Buddhism's central doctrine of emptiness to make a powerful challenge to the this-worldly approach of Confucianism.

Instrumental in the emancipation of Buddhist thought was Fa Hu, or Dharmaraksa, a man born of Da Yuezhi family long resident in Dunhuang, an important Buddhist centre at the western terminus of the Great Wall. As Fa Hu (died *c.* AD 310) had spoken Chinese from birth, he was able to translate over 100 sacred texts. Though the spread of the Buddhist faith among the peasantry was yet to occur, Fa Hu's translations ensured that scholars were fascinated by its ideas; they had only to await the voluminous writings of Hui Yuan (AD 334–416), the Chinese St Augustine, for their mature expression.

*See* AN SHIHKAO; ASHOKA; CONFUCIUS; DAOISM; HINDUISM; JAINISM; LIU YING; NANDA DYNASTY

*K. Chen, *Buddhism in China* (Princeton, 1973); T. Ling, *The Buddha: Buddhist Civilization in India and Ceylon* (London, 1973).

Julius Caesar, the winner of the civil war which
destroyed the Roman republic.

**Caesar** (100–44 BC) was the winner of
the civil war which effectively destroyed the Roman republic. Gaius
Julius Caesar was a most determined
aristocrat whose political ambitions
may have been originally financed by
Crassus (112–53 BC), reputedly the
richest man in Rome. In 60 BC he
joined Crassus and Pompey (106–
48 BC) to form an unofficial triumvirate, which lasted till Crassus' death on
an ill-fated campaign against Parthia in
53 BC. Part of the agreement was that
Caesar should be given command in
Gaul, which he held for ten years and
succeeded in subduing the whole
country. As military appointments
were the chief means to acquire the
funds necessary for prolonged political
success, he used this command to gain
the loyalty of a formidable army and
become a very wealthy man: one million Gauls had been enslaved by the
outbreak of the civil war in 49 BC.
Caesar's conquest of Gaul (approximately modern France and Belgium)
was a remarkable feat of arms. Its details
are outlined in his own memoirs,
which were published in 51 or 50 BC.
The Roman habit of providing a personal account of major events was
already well established, the dictator
Sulla (138–78 BC) having written
copious memoirs. But Caesar's war
commentaries, including the one on
the civil war itself, struck a new note.
Their plain and lucid style portrayed
Caesar as a committed patriot who was
simply fighting necessary wars. The
conquest of Gaul, however, was facili-

tated by the inability of its Celtic peoples to unite against Rome. Tribal animosities were not put aside until it was too late: the general revolt of 52 BC under Vercingetorix was a last, desperate attempt to mould the Gauls into an army capable of facing Caesar's legions. The failure of the rebels at Alesia, some 30 miles north-west of modern Dijon, left Rome with several new provinces: Aquitania, Lugdunensis and Belgica. Vercingetorix was executed after Caesar's triumph at Rome in 46 BC. In 55 and 54 BC there were advances across the Rhine and landings in southern England too. An unimpressed Pompey commented that the English Channel was just a mudflat.

Coin of Sextus Pompeius, struck in Sicily around 38 BC. The son of Caesar's great rival Pompey, Sextus managed to survive as a minor warlord till 35 BC, well after the assassination of Caesar himself.

Relations between Caesar and Pompey, the other great Roman general of the age, had broken down completely by 50 BC. As neither of them were prepared to relinquish their military commands, the senate had to choose between the two contestants, and Pompey won its backing since he was in control of Rome. When Mark Antony (83–30 BC) arrived there with a message from Caesar, the senators hardly paid him any attention: instead they confirmed Pompey as commander-in-chief of all Roman forces, leaving his opponent without any independent command. Stung by this rebuff, and contemptuous of constitutional forms, Caesar invaded Italy at the start of 49 BC. Pompey decided not to face him, but withdrew across the Adriatic and began to mobilize his forces in the Balkans. Thus Italy fell without a blow to Caesar, who entered Rome and seized the contents of the treasury. Having dealt with troops loyal to Pompey in northern Spain, Caesar crossed the Adriatic at the end of 49 BC for the final showdown, which occurred in the ensuing year at Pharsalus in Thessaly. A defeated Pompey fled to Egypt, where he expected to find support as a senate-appointed guardian of its ruler Ptolemy XIII, the younger brother of Cleopatra. But he was killed by a fellow Roman at Alexandria, where the Egyptians carefully saved his head for Caesar.

Cleopatra VII (51–30 BC) had already pushed Ptolemy into the background before Caesar arrived, made her his mistress, and intervened decisively in the dynastic feud. Had Pompey been victor it is more than likely that he would have fallen under

Cleopatra's spell as Caesar so patently did. There is even reason to believe that his own son, Sextus Pompeius (67–35 BC), had enjoyed her favours when in 49 BC he came to Alexandria looking for money, men and ships. Caesar installed Cleopatra and Ptolemy XIV, another of her brothers, as joint rulers: they were married in the pharaonic manner, but not before Cleopatra was pregnant with Caesar's son, Caesarion (47–30 BC). Whatever the state of his heart, Caesar was intelligent enough to appreciate the value of a sympathetic Ptolemaic dynasty. Egypt's accumulated resources would make a very useful contribution to his growing expenses.

Returning to Rome by way of Asia Minor, where in 47 BC he defeated Pharnaces, son of King Mithridates VI of Pontus, Caesar pardoned those who had sided with Pompey, including Cicero (106–43 BC). Even though he had failed to persuade this ardent republican to stay neutral in the conflict, there was no recrimination at all on Caesar's part. The historian Plutarch relates that 'when Caesar saw Cicero coming, he immediately got down from his conveyance and embraced him and then took him along with him for a considerable distance, talking to him privately. Afterwards, too, Caesar always honoured him and showed him kindness.' During his brief periods in Rome Caesar was responsible for many long-overdue reforms, from an overhaul of the calendar to legislation dealing with excessive interest rates, colonies, legionary pay, tax-farming, citizenship, senatorial recruitment, town-planning, bribery, and the corn supply. But the traditions of the republic died hard, and in 44 BC a group of senators struck him down. Since reducing his last opponents in southern Spain and Africa, Caesar had officially become dictator for life. An enlarged senate had heaped honours upon him, while passing over the rest of the aristocracy. Caesar was consul, censor, president of the senate, father of the fatherland, even the month in which he was born was renamed Julius, our July. Though always careful not to assume the title of king, despite Antony's public urgings, he was a monarch in all but name; divine honours were being contemplated prior to his assassination. With Cleopatra and Caesarion also resident in Rome, the sixty-six-year-old was a warlord who had gone too far. He probably knew it, but the cause of liberty was as dead as Caesar himself in 44 BC. Cicero enjoyed it for less than a year before falling victim in the final struggle to establish a lasting autocracy in Rome.

*See* Augustus; Cato; Cicero; Cleopatra; Crassus; Gaul; Mithridates; Parthia; Pompey; Vercingetorix

*M. Grant, *Julius Caesar* (London, 1974); R. Syme, *The Roman Revolution* (Oxford, 1939); *Julius Caesar: The Battle for Gaul*, trans. by A. and P. Wiseman (London, 1980).

**Caligula**, Roman emperor AD 37–41, was born in AD 12. Gaius Julius Caesar Germanicus was popularly known as Caligula, or 'Little Boots', because of the miniature military footware he wore as a baby on the German frontier. His father was one of Augustus' trusted generals, and adopted son of the second emperor Tiberius (AD 14–37). But his father's death in AD 19 left the young Caligula unexpectedly in line for the succession. A lack of preparation probably accounts for Caligula's indifference to the duties of office, and a preoccupation with pleasure that only scandalized Rome. Rumours about Tiberius' suffocation may have been true, but they are not really important because the ailing ruler was already terminally ill. What is notable in the historian Suetonius' account is the part played by praetorian officers, who thus launched their career as emperor-makers. With the backing of these guardsmen, Caligula was confirmed by the senate and began his brief but memorable reign. But the Praetorian Guard was not his only immediate support, for he was popular with the German horse guard, a formation first raised by Julius Caesar during the conquest of Gaul (58–50 BC). Caligula later appointed gladiators as its commanders, not least because with their fighting skills they could also train the German troopers. On the day Caligula was murdered, they went berserk and held hostage at sword point the theatre where he had been struck down.

Caligula's idea of imperial rule was

The Roman emperor Caligula, who once said: 'Remember that I can do anything to anybody.'

quite different from his two predecessors. Perhaps influenced by eastern Mediterranean practice, he was impatient with a disguised monarchy, and wished to rule openly as a king, even a deified one. For the pro-Roman Philo of Alexandria, who led a deputation of Jews to Rome in AD 39, the new emperor had given way to unbridled passions. Caligula had ceased to act as the shepherd of the flock, the steersman of the ship of mankind. Philo believed that the emperor's instability arose from the illness from which he suffered early in his reign as a result of over-indulgence. And the historian Suetonius came to a similar conclusion after listing among Caligula's sexual habits sadism, homosexuality and incest. His capricious behaviour indeed startled Roman society. On one occasion he seized the bride at a reception, holding her for his own pleasure on the wedding-night. Another time Caligula made a senator fulfil an oath to the effect that he would sacrifice his own life for the emperor's recovery from illness. The sacrifice was staged as a public event, with the hapless victim hurled from a high rock. About then Caligula also delivered his infamous remark: 'Remember that I can do anything to anybody.'

In AD 39 Caligula travelled to the northern frontier in order to prevent a military uprising. He spent the winter in camps on the Rhine and in northern Gaul. A planned expedition against Britain in AD 40 was never begun, although Suetonius says that the emperor ordered the legionaries to gather sea-shells instead. When he returned to Rome in self-declared triumph, Caligula was openly contemptuous of the senate and uninterested in matters of state. The end came when the Praetorian Guard turned against him. Caligula was stabbed to death on the last day of the Palatine Games, towards the end of January AD 41.

See AUGUSTUS; PHILO; ROME; TIBERIUS
*A. A. Barrett, *Caligula: The Corruption of Power* (London, 1989); Suetonius, *The Twelve Caesars*, trans. by R. Graves (Harmondsworth, 1956).

**Cambyses**, king of Persia 530–522 BC, was the eldest son of Cyrus the Great (559–530 BC). On the fall of Babylon to the Persians in 539 BC,

Cambyses was old enough to be appointed as its king, but the young man's reluctance to undergo the full ceremony involved in his installation offended the powerful Babylonian priesthood. On the fourth day of an eleven-day festival the king was due to don a special robe and wig and receive his sceptre in a manner which a Persian noble must have found degrading. Cambyses refused to change his clothes or lay down his arms. Finally he agreed to the latter, but Cyrus was obliged to call him in future the governor of Babylon, not its king. It was there in 530 BC that news reached him of his father's death in battle. The Scythian Massagete had massacred a Persian army on the Central Asian steppe.

But Cambyses ascended the Persian throne without incident, so it is not impossible that the stories about his early years in Babylon were deliberately hostile. Similar tales about a fit of insanity which struck Cambyses in Egypt do not square with the efforts he is known to have made after its conquest to place himself in a proper relationship to the Egyptian gods. Not to be overlooked, too, are the reasons his successor Darius I (521–486 BC) might himself have had to exaggerate Cambyses' weaknesses. It seems likely that Darius was privy to the plot which overthrew and killed Cambyses in 522 BC. Having conquered Egypt in 525 BC, Cambyses set about restoring order and protecting temple properties. The Egyptian official Udjahorresnet tells us that Cambyses did his utmost to conform to Egyptian traditions as Cyrus had done with Babylon. Shortly after the capture of Memphis, for instance, the sacred Apis bull died and according to custom was mourned for seventy days. It was given a magnificent burial in a fine granite coffin provided by Cambyses.

As a result of annexing Egypt, the Persians gained control of the island of Cyprus, which seems to have been an Egyptian possession for the previous half-century. They also received the voluntary submission of the Libyans and the Greek cities of Barka and Cyrene. Cambyses sent forces south towards Nubia and Ethiopia, which are both listed later as subject states. Possibly Cambyses had stayed too long in Egypt, for during these three years discontent became most pronounced in both Media and Persis, the Persian heartlands. In 522 BC an open rebellion broke out under the leadership of a man claiming to be Cambyses' brother. On his way to deal with the rebels the Persian king is supposed to have stabbed himself in the thigh, when hurriedly leaping onto his horse. Three weeks later he died in Syria.

It took Darius, his successor, over a year's hard fighting to put down this rebellion, and others which soon followed in Babylon, Armenia and Central Asia. They were as much signs of the strains that rapid territorial expansion had caused in Persian society as unfavourable reactions to Darius' seizure of the throne.

See CYRUS THE GREAT; DARIUS I; EGYPT; PERSIA

*M. A. Dandamaev, *A Political History of the Achaemenid Empire* (Leiden, 1989).

**Canakya** (sometimes rendered as Kantalya) was the legendary first minister and adviser of Candragupta, the founder in northern India of the Mauryan dynasty (322–183 BC). He was a brahmin, a member of the priestly class, but his life was devoted to laying the foundations of the first large state ever seen on the subcontinent. Eventually the Mauryan empire, during the reign of Candragupta's grandson Ashoka (268–232 BC), incorporated everything other than the far south and the far east. It was an achievement unrepeated until the Moguls reached the height of their power in the seventeenth century.

Although his famous treatise of statecraft may not have reached its final form until the third century AD, the work is clearly based on a Mauryan original written by Canakya himself. It gives detailed instructions on the control of the state and conduct of war, many of which reflect Mauryan conditions in spite of clear later features. The officers of state and the army were to be well paid, requiring a large state income. Such linking of taxation, administration and military power was crucial to the establishment of a centralized empire, which Candragupta (322–297 BC) first introduced into Indian politics. Canakya also pays close attention to foreign relations, not a surprising interest in the light of Candragupta's peace treaty of 303 BC, with Seleucus I, the main inheritor of Alexander the Great's conquests in Asia. It recognizes three types of ambassador: one with full powers to negotiate with a foreign ruler; one with definite instructions from which he could not deviate; and one who was nothing more than a messenger. The inviolability of diplomatic personnel was accepted, and indeed Bindusara (297–272 BC), the son of Candragupta, kept up a regular exchange of ambassadors with the Seleucids. He asked to be sent to him on one occasion sweet wine, dried figs and a philosopher.

See ASHOKA; BINDUSARA; CANDRAGUPTA; MAURYAN DYNASTY; SELEUCIDS
*Kautalya, *The Arthasastra*, trans. by R. Shamasastry (Mysore, 1956); S. Konow, *Kautalya Studies* (Oslo, 1945).

**Candragupta**, the first Mauryan emperor (322–297 BC), was in his twenties when India's north-west was shaken by Alexander the Great's abortive invasion of 327–325 BC. But the impact of the Macedonian incursion was profound on what had formerly been the most eastern provinces of the Persian empire; it indeed proved easy prey once Candragupta moved into the Punjab during the 320s BC. He had seized power in Magadha, a major state in the lower Ganges valley, in 322 BC. Guided by his mentor the brahmin Canakya, Candragupta used the acqui-

sition of Magadha as the first step in establishing a new native dynasty, the Mauryan (322–183 BC). Candragupta's origins are obscure. Alternatively he is presented as the son of the last Magadha king by a low-born woman, or as a successful adventurer of the warrior class.

This coin, issued around 300 BC by Seleucus I, refers to the war elephants received from Candragupta as part of the settlement of the Indian frontier.

The rapid rise of Mauryan power in northern India led to an accommodation in 303 BC with Seleucus, one of the successors to Alexander's Asian conquests. Seleucus I (312–281 BC) had tried to regain control of the easternmost territories and reached the Indus, but he was defeated by Candragupta and compelled to withdraw. The terms of the peace settlement awarded Aria, Arachosia and Paropamisadae (essentially modern Afghanistan and western Pakistan) to Candragupta in return for 500 war elephants, an armament which two years later Seleucus put to decisive use in Asia Minor at the battle of Ipsus. Inscriptions in Greek and Aramaic carved on the orders of Ashoka (268–232 BC), Candragupta's grandson, have been found recently in Afghanistan, indicating that Mauryan rule of the new territories was effective. Under Ashoka Indian influence spread far into Central Asia, in part because of the emperor's desire to propagate the teachings of the Buddha. Some of the oasis-states of the Tarim basin, like Khotan, were said to have been jointly founded by Indian and Chinese settlers.

Despite the conflict of 305–303 BC, relations between the Seleucid and the Mauryan realms were generally good. The peace treaty included a marriage alliance, of which unfortunately no details are given. This event has led to speculation about the mother of Bindusara, who succeeded Candragupta in 297 BC. There is no evidence, however, to suggest that this son had a Greek or Macedonian mother. But we do know that Seleucus' ambassador, Megasthenes, resided at the Mauryan capital of Pataliputra for a number of years between 302 and 291 BC, because he left an account of his stay. By the time Megasthenes returned home for good, Candragupta had abdicated in favour of Bindusara and become a Jain recluse at Sravana Belgola in the south of India. There today on a hillock, next to the main hill on which stands a giant statue of the Jain saviour Gommatesvara, is a record

in bas-relief of Candragupta's life. It shows how the Mauryan ruler, like Gommatesvara, came to see the vanity of worldly triumph, and as a result he sought release from the cycle of rebirth through meditation, prior to fasting to death. Possibly because Candragupta was such a new phenomenon in Indian politics – the usurper of power over an extensive area that had previously consisted of small kingdoms and republics – he could safely indulge his own preference for Jainism. Its tenets were located right at the impersonal end of the spectrum of classical belief, far removed from European notions about the survival of the personality. Only through a sustained act of self-renunciation could the soul make its own escape. Quite opposite was the outlook of Bindusara, who accepted the deterministic doctrines of the Ajivikas, another non-orthodox sect. As a dynasty, the Mauryas were very eclectic in their religious beliefs: Candragupta favoured Jainism, in reaction Bindusara clung to the this-worldly approach of the Ajivikas, while Ashoka became the world's first Buddhist ruler.

See ALEXANDER THE GREAT; ASHOKA; BINDUSARA; BUDDHISM; CANAKYA; JAINISM; MAURYAN DYNASTY; MEGASTHENES; SELEUCUS
*H. Zimmer, *Philosophies of India* (Princeton, 1969).

**Candragupta II**, the third or fourth Gupta emperor (*c.* AD 377–*c.* 412), was the grandson of Candragupta I, who founded the dynasty in AD 320. The name Candragupta was most probably adopted in order to associate the new imperial house with the Mauryans, who had ruled Magadha in northern India over half a millennium earlier. The accession of Candragupta II was accompanied by bloodshed. According to one tradition, his elder brother Ramagupta ascended the throne in AD 376. Within the year this weak emperor was forced to conclude a dishonourable peace with the Scythian Sakas, a Central Asian people then settled widely in north-western India. Ramagupta is even credited with a willingness to hand over his first wife to the Saka king. Candragupta opposed this appeasement, and may have slain the arrogant Saka ruler in his own camp. He is said to have gone there himself disguised as the empress. Whatever the truth of the story, Ramagupta was also killed and his younger brother became Candragupta II in late AD 376 or early 377.

A war of annihilation against the Sakas preoccupied Candragupta till AD 400. This reassertion of imperial control was fiercely resisted by the Sakas in a long-drawn-out struggle: only the death of the last Saka king, Rudrasena III, on the battlefield brought the conflict to a successful Gupta conclusion. The total absence of Saka coinage from the archaeological record afterwards is an indication of the completeness of Candragupta's triumph. The emperor's hereditary chief minister, Virasena Saba, commented

that 'the emperor set out to conquer the whole world'. Certainly the Gupta general Amrakardava is said to have won glory by winning many battles for Candragupta. Even though the Gupta empire did not equal the territories ruled by Ashoka (268–232 BC), the greatest Mauryan emperor, it encompassed the whole of northern India from the Arabian Sea to the Bay of Bengal. By the time of the arrival of the Chinese pilgrim Fa Xian, shortly after the final destruction of the Sakas, Candragupta ruled over a peaceful and prosperous land. 'The ruler governs without corporal punishments,' noted Fa Xian in amazement. 'Criminals are merely fined according to the gravity of their offences. Even for a second attempt at rebellion the punishment is only the loss of the right hand. The ruler's personal attendants, who guard him day and night, all have fixed salaries.' The implicit principle of non-violence, so very attractive to the Buddhist Fa Xian, drew its strength from the teachings of both Jainism and Buddhism; but in classical India it was always an ideal rather than a reality. Yet the general outlook of Gupta emperors was tolerant as regards religion: Candragupta recruited officials, and favoured hereditary office-holders, irrespective of their personal convictions. Amrakardava gave money to Buddhist monasteries, while Virasena Saba was an ardent follower of the Hindu deity Shiva. At this period the Buddhist faith had found a new lease of life through philosophical speculation and an extension of its pantheon to include Bodhisattvas, saint-like beings who had renounced bliss out of compassion for the sufferings of the world. Yet its popularity was already under pressure from a resurgent Hinduism. One of the baleful effects of the latter could already be discerned in untouchability, Fa Xian's bewilderment at this lack of humanity being the earliest datable reference to its practice. The untouchables were outcasts from the class system, and even accidental contact was believed to be a source of pollution that required ritual ablutions.

Candragupta had several wives, most of them the result of marriage alliances. It is transparent from inscriptions that he reinsured himself through such diplomatic means during the bitter conflict with the Sakas. Only one of his wives was designated empress, however. Candragupta's successor, Kumaragupta (c. AD 415–454) was the empress Dhruvadevi's son. He continued his father's patronage of all religions and the arts, with the result that the classical era in India entered its final stage. Sculpture flourished in the principal cities of the empire and reached a very high degree of excellence. But Kumaragupta did not share Candragupta's devotion to the Hindu deity Vishnu; instead he gave worship to his rival, the arch-ascetic Shiva.

*See* ASHOKA; BUDDHISM; GUPTA DYNASTY; JAINISM

★S. K. Maity, *The Imperial Guptas and their Times* (Delhi, 1975).

Cao Cao (AD 155–220) later became in Chinese tradition the archetypal warlord. His cynicism is best summed up in a favourite saying: 'I would rather betray the whole world than allow the world to betray me.' In stark contrast, one of his opponents, Guan Di (died AD 219), evolved into the Confucian god of war. Guan Di was portrayed neither as bloodthirsty and cowardly like the Greek deity Ares nor as an implacable foe like the Roman Mars; on the contrary, he was looked upon as the god who always sought to prevent conflict.

Cao Cao's father was the adopted son of the chief eunuch of the imperial palace under the Han emperor Lingdi (AD 168–189). During his reign the eunuchs formed such a powerful faction that all official appointments were in their gift. Their downfall in AD 189 was brought about through a general slaughter of eunuchs conducted by the enraged soldiers of a general whom the overconfident chief eunuch had dared to execute. The ultimate beneficiary of this action was Cao Cao, who from AD 196 onwards assumed authority in all but name.

Emperor Han Lingdi had inherited an empire already weakened by war. Four kinds of conflict threatened the security of the state: nomad incursions, which began again in earnest after AD 168; uprisings of foreign allies settled within the imperial frontiers; struggles between Chinese generals; and quasi-religious rebellions such as the Five Pecks of Grain movement.

This Daoist-inspired revolt was so popular in what today are the provinces of Shaanxi and Sichuan that, on its eventual defeat in AD 215, Cao Cao was obliged to spare the leaders, the Zhang family. Because of the strength of their local support Zhang Lu and his five sons received noble titles instead of punishment.

Shortly after the massacre of the eunuchs in AD 189 their imperial candidate was deposed by another general, who sponsored the last Han emperor, the eight-year-old Xiandi (AD 189–220). Thus the ruler became a creature of the warlords rather than the eunuchs. The tussle between the generals ended in AD 196, when Cao Cao took Xiandi into safe custody. Realizing the time was not right for his deposition, Cao Cao allowed the Han dynasty continue in existence, while he built up his own military position. The warlord did this by settling soldiers on agricultural land in exchange for regular payment of grain as taxes. Ostensibly a servant of the emperor, Cao Cao used the grain surplus to make himself master of north China. In AD 208 he was strong enough to move south against Sun Qian, a general whose power was centred on the lower Yangzi river valley. But at the battle of the Red Cliffs the superior nautical skills of the southerners won the day: Cao Cao's ships were burned and his soldiers defeated.

The reverse restricted the authority of Cao Cao, leaving the south in Sun Qian's hands and the south-west in those of Liu Bei, a member of the imperial house. When in AD 220, after Cao Cao's death, his son Cao Pi deposed Xiandi and founded the Wei dynasty (AD 220–265), both Sun Qian and Liu Bei declared themselves as independent kings of Wu and Shu respectively. The half-century of conflict between Wei, Wu and Shu is known as the period of the Three Kingdoms.

See HAN DYNASTY; THREE KINGDOMS
*W. Eberhard, *A History of China* (London, 1956).

**Caratacus**, the British chieftain who eventually surrendered to the Romans in AD 51, jointly ruled the Catuvellauni, a people who controlled present-day Hertfordshire, Middlesex, Buckinghamshire and Oxfordshire. The anti-Roman outlook of Caratacus became apparent shortly after AD 40, when he invaded the territories of Roman client-kings south of the Thames. It was usual Roman foreign policy to maintain a buffer zone of semi-dependencies just beyond the imperial frontiers. King Verica of the Atrebates, whose homeland comprised essentially modern Berkshire, fled on Caratacus' attack to Rome, where he asked for military aid from the emperor Claudius (AD 41–54). The plea for intervention was welcome, not least because the emperor's poor relations with the senate might be improved by an absence from the capital during the campaign. In AD 43

Claudius accompanied the expeditionary force of 40,000 men sent to restore Roman prestige in southern Britain. The main force landed at Rutupiae (present-day Richborough in eastern Kent) and marched to the Medway, where the Britons were massed. There the Romans won a decisive victory in which the future emperor Vespasian (AD 69–79) distinguished himself. Most of the defeated came to terms with Claudius, who restored Verica or his son as king of the Atrebates. But Caratacus was unwilling to accept that the struggle against

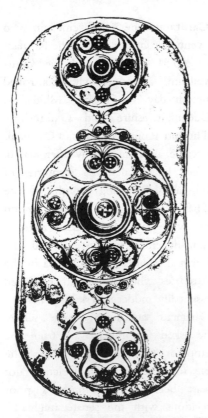

A bronze and enamel shield found in the Thames at Battersea. It is typical of the equipment used by Caratacus' followers.

Rome was over: he made a fighting retreat westwards and threw his lot in with the Silures, the dominant people of what is today South Wales.

According to the historian Tacitus, 'the Romans now moved against the Silures, whose natural spirit was reinforced by their faith in the power of Caratacus, whose many engagements with the Romans had raised him to a position of pre-eminence amongst the British chieftains. Since his strength lay not in military superiority but in the tactical advantages to be gained from knowing difficult country, he transferred the scene of the conflict to the lands of the Ordovices.' In mid-Wales, therefore, he selected a suitable battlefield and gathered 'those who dreaded the establishment of the Roman peace'. As the Romans formed up in AD 50 for this final encounter, Tacitus tells us that 'Caratacus rushed from place to place, telling the Britons how the battle would either mean the rebirth of liberty or the start of eternal servitude. He called upon his ancestors by name, those who had driven out Julius Caesar, the dictator. His words were greeted by voices of assent, as each man bound himself by the oath of his tribe that he would not yield before any weapons or any wounds.' Yet once again it was Roman discipline that told, and 'Caratacus himself was put in chains and handed over to the victor, although he had sought refuge with Cartimandua, queen of the Brigantes. It was the ninth year after the war in Britain had begun.'

A miserable death in Rome was probably Caratacus' expected fate, but the emperor had other ideas. Tacitus puts a heroic speech in the captured chieftain's mouth, resonant with the military virtues so cherished by the Romans. As a result Claudius is said to have spared Caratacus and his family, although the reason for clemency was more likely to have been the emperor's desire to share the undoubted fame of his most determined opponent. So Caratacus settled down to retirement in Italy, while southern Britain was as a province incorporated into the Roman empire.

See BRITAIN; CAESAR; CLAUDIUS

*G. Webster, *Rome against Caratacus: The Roman Campaigns in Britain AD 48–58* (London, 1981); Tacitus, *The Annals of Imperial Rome*, trans. by M. Grant (Harmondsworth, 1956).

**Carthage**, the great Phoenician colony in what today is Tunisia, became a problem for the Romans after their clash with the Epirote ruler Pyrrhus (319–272 BC). His admission of failure in halting the Roman advance southwards, when in 275 BC he withdrew his forces to Greece and left the Greek cities of southern Italy and Sicily to defend themselves, meant that for the first time Rome came face to face with Carthage, the other major power in the western Mediterranean.

Founded in 814 BC by colonists from Tyre, Carthage acted as an anchorage and place of supply for vessels plying the length of the Mediterranean in search of gold, silver and tin. Its foundation myth, however, suggests that the settlement was from the start unlike the other Phoenician colonies planted in either present-day Morocco or Spain. Elissa-Dido, the sister of the Tyrian king, had fled westwards on the murder of her husband. With her came not only a number of noble families but also the liturgical articles of the cult of the Phoenician god Melquart, whose name was once given to the Pillars of Hercules. Elissa-Dido's husband was most likely the priest of this potent sea deity.

Clearly Carthage had the makings of a state in itself, something the influx of settlers from Africa and other places soon turned into a reality. The lure of wealth here, as in Rome, supplemented the population and under its early kings Carthage became the dominant trading power in the western Mediterranean. Tradition tells us that Malchus, the very first ruler, was killed in the capture of Sardinia, a key island for control of the trade routes to Etruscan ports in north-western Italy. A bilingual inscription on sheets of gold, in Etruscan and Punic scripts, found in 1963 at Pyrgi, one of the several ports belonging to Caere (present-day Cerveteri), reveals the existence of an alliance between this Etruscan city-state and Carthage. The commercial prominence of the Carthaginians was recognized about the same time by the fledgeling republic of Rome. In a treaty of 507–506 BC, according to the historian Polybius, the Romans had to accept that their ships were not allowed to trade freely in Carthaginian waters around Sardinia, Sicily and Africa. 'No transaction,' the terms of the treaty state, 'may be conducted without the presence of a herald or clerk.' Polybius comments that the treaty showed 'how the Carthaginians considered Sardinia and Africa as belonging absolutely to them; in the case of Sicily they use different language to define their interests, and refer only to those parts of it which are under their rule. In the same way the Romans only make stipulations concerning Latium, and do not refer to the rest of Italy, since it was not then under their authority.'

Carthaginian coin struck in western Sicily, which was lost to the Romans in 241 BC.

That both the Etruscans and the Romans simultaneously acknowledged the naval power of Carthage signals its final emergence as an independent state. With the Phoenician homeland then under Persian rule, the leadership of its overseas colonies had fallen to Carthage, and especially the defence of those pressed by Greek attack in Sicily. One of its generals, Hamilcar, died in 480 BC at Himera on the northern coast of the island, by throwing himself onto a huge fire containing sacrificial animals when he saw his army fall back before the Greeks. Possibly he was offering himself to the gods for better fortune. Human sacrifice was practised by the Carthaginians, although the victims were usually children. An enclosure sacred to the goddess Tanit at Carthage is filled with thousands of urns containing the remains of small children burnt alive as offerings. This gruesome ritual derived from ancient West Asian practices: even the patriarch Abraham was prepared to sacrifice his first-born son until he received the divine instruction to substitute a sheep. Yet the Romans were not above sacrificing human beings, no matter the effort made to excise such events from their history. After the catastrophic defeat suffered at Cannae in 216 BC at the hands of the Carthaginian general Hannibal, we know that the Roman populace sacrificed six people: two Gauls, two Greeks and two Vestal Virgins. Whatever Hamilcar's intention in 480 BC, the defeat did not cause the loss of the Phoenician settlements in western Sicily, nor was the Carthaginian monarchy overthrown; but afterwards Carthage sought to consolidate its leading position among the Phoenician colonies in the west and avoid expansion except in northern Africa. Little information is available on Carthage's political arrangements. Kings were said to 'rule by virtue of laws', pointing to some form of electoral arrangement, which in the fourth century BC gave way to an oligarchy compared favourably by the philosopher Aristotle (384–322 BC) to the Spartan constitution.

Conflict with Rome began in 264 BC as a result of a Roman attempt to gain a foothold in Sicily by forming an alliance with Messana (modern Messina) against Syracuse, though the former Greek city had previously had a Carthaginian garrison. This First Punic War lasted till 241 BC and was said by Polybius to be the most destructive in terms of human life of any war up to that date. Largely fought in Sicily and its waters, the Romans endeavoured to end the military stalemate through an invasion of Africa in 256–255 BC. But the siege of Carthage was raised by the arrival of a force of Greek mercenaries under the command of a Spartan general named Xanthippus. He explained the dangers of meeting the Roman legions on uneven ground where their flexibility gave them the advantage over the less manoeuvrable Carthaginian phalanx. Adopting Xanthippus' advice, the Carthaginians defeated the Roman invaders and captured their commander. But peace terms had to be agreed by Carthage once the Roman fleet gained control of the sea. Sicily was immediately lost to Rome, and then Sardinia in 238 BC.

A funerary pillar in the sign of Tanit, the great Carthaginian goddess. From a cemetery near classical Carthage.

Polybius believed that Roman superiority rested with its legionaries, however. He noted how 'the Carthaginians largely neglect their infantry, though they do show some degree of interest in their cavalry. The reason for this is that they employ foreign and mercenary troops, whereas those of the Romans are citizens and natives of their own country ... The Carthaginians depend at all times on the courage of mercenaries to safeguard their prospects of freedom, but the Romans rely on the bravery of their own citizens and the help of their allies.' Yet it has to be said that Carthage only suffered one mercenary insurrection of any consequence, and

83

its foreign troops did not fail in their duties when Hannibal led an army across the Alps into Italy during the Second Punic War (218–201 BC). The renewal of conflict occurred because of competition with Rome in Spain, where Carthage had built up a new land empire. General Hannibal (246–182 BC) inflicted a series of disastrous defeats on the Romans, but his army was not large enough to launch an attack on Rome itself, and in the end Roman manpower told. Spain was lost to Carthage in 206 BC and Hannibal was recalled to Africa where another Roman expeditionary force under Scipio Africanus (236–184 BC) had landed. He was defeated there at Zama in 202 BC. Carthage was forced to surrender its fleet and all overseas territory, becoming in effect a Roman satellite. During the next fifty years Carthage survived as a commercial centre, till in the Third Punic War (149–146 BC) Rome decided to totally destroy the city.

See ETRUSCANS; HANNIBAL; ROME; SCIPIOS; SICILY; WARFARE

*M. A. Aubet, *The Phoenicians and the West* (Cambridge, 1993); S. Lancel, *Carthage: A History* (Oxford, 1995); Polybius, *The Rise of the Roman Empire*, trans. by I. Scott-Kilvert (Harmondsworth, 1979).

**Cassander** (*c.* 358–297 BC) was the son of Antipater, Alexander the Great's viceroy in Macedon and Greece during his long campaign in Asia (334–323 BC). Following the death of his father in 319 BC, Cassander took advantage of the loosening of ties between Alexander's successors to seize Macedon, and later Greece. He resisted the efforts made by Antigonus (382–301 BC) to hold the far-flung empire together. At the battle of Ipsus (modern Sipsin in Turkey) in 301 BC Cassander combined with Lysimachus (360–281 BC) and Seleucus (358–281 BC) to defeat Antigonus and his son Demetrius. In 310 BC Cassander had already tired of playing the royal guardian and executed Alexander's posthumous son and his Bactrian mother Roxane. As the historian Diodorus Siculus commented: 'All those who ruled nations or cities at this time nursed their own royal hopes.' As ruthless as his neighbour Lysimachus in Thrace, Cassander spent his final years trying to consolidate his dynastic position in Europe. But within a few years of his death, intrigue and murder opened the way to Demetrius, who founded in Macedon the Antigonid dynasty (294–168 BC). Although the war-weary Macedonians soon tired of Demetrius himself, they finally accepted the legitimacy of his son Antigonus Gonatas around 276 BC.

See ALEXANDER THE GREAT; ANTIGONUS; DEMETRIUS; LYSIMACHUS; MACEDON; SELEUCUS I

*P. Green, *Alexander to Actium: The Hellenistic Age* (London, 1990).

**Catiline** (108–62 BC) was a Roman conspirator. As an undischarged bankrupt, Lucius Sergius Catalina was debarred from standing for public office until 63 BC, when he put forward a programme of sweeping land redistribution and a general cancellation of debts. Cicero (106–43 BC), who regarded debt-cancellation as an attack on the sanctity of property, rallied the voters against Cataline, who retired to Tuscany to join forces with a group of discontented veterans. As consul, Cicero moved against the conspiracy which Cataline was hatching and, with the senate's approval, had him executed. The legality of this action was disputed, since it violated a Roman citizen's right to be tried, but Cicero always insisted that it had been necessary for the safety of the state.

See CICERO; ROME

*C. Habicht, *Cicero the Politician* (Baltimore, 1990).

**Cato the Elder** (234–148 BC) was regarded as a 'new man' because he lacked consuls among his ancestors. 'None of them,' the historian Plutarch tells us, 'made any mark in Roman history, but Cato himself praises his father Marcus as a man of courage and a capable soldier. He also mentions that his grandfather Cato was several times decorated for valour in battle, and was awarded by the state treasury for his gallantry the price of the five horses which had been killed under him.' Marcus Porcius Cato himself achieved the consulship in 195 BC; nine years later he was also elected as censor, a

part of whose duties was the supervision of public morals. A censor could remove a member of the senate, the council formed from those who had held public office. This office suited Cato admirably: it gave him a platform for his stern advocacy of traditional values, which in 184 BC he used to complete his attack on the personal reverence accorded to Scipio Africanus (236–183 BC), the victor over the Carthaginian general Hannibal. All the Scipios were temporarily driven from public life, an embittered Scipio Africanus dying soon afterwards in southern Italy. What Cato deplored was the Scipio fascination with Greece, and in particular their willingness to ape the personality cult of rulers such as the Seleucid monarch Antiochus III (223–187 BC), whom Scipio Asiaticus had defeated five years earlier.

Although he was not uninterested himself in Greek oratory, Cato considered that Roman culture was under threat from nearly all things Greek, and not least the luxurious tastes acquired by aristocrats as a result of Rome's expansion eastwards. They did not sit well with the gravity expected of a Roman, his careful gait, close-fitting toga, and undemonstrative form of speech. For Cato held that outward appearance must always conform with inner convictions. Equally austere was his approach to women, whose status had risen through the inheritance of property because of the heavy casualties taken by Rome in so many wars. He helped the passage of a bill insisting on the old limitation of women's rights to inherit. Wealth was a serious problem for contemporary Romans, as a political career involved the expenditure of vast sums of money, with officials outdoing the festivities and games put on for the public by their predecessors and rivals. An ambitious noble contracted debts that he sought to recoup eventually as a provincial governor, by means of crushing taxes on the provinces or the pillage of a city or people beyond its borders. Julius Caesar's ten-year campaign in Gaul was to rate as the supreme example of warlord plundering: by 49 BC he had acquired one million slaves. Even Cato adopted questionable methods to amass a fortune. Having failed to become rich through agriculture and industry, he turned to money-lending, a practice forbidden to senators. One of his freedmen organized a syndicate for him, financing merchant shipping at very little risk. It is not impossible that Cato's part in the final destruction of Carthage, his famous swan-song in the 150s BC, had some connection with its commercial revival.

So concerned was Cato about moral upbringing that he took personal charge of teaching his own son, although the boy also received some instruction from an accomplished slave. Plutarch relates how 'he composed his history of Rome, writing it out with his own hand and in large letters, so that his son should possess in his own home the means of learning about the events and traditions of his country'. The boy's health forced a relaxation of the harsh physical programme his father imposed, but it did not prevent him as a young man winning a reputation for bravery on the battlefield. After the victory over the Macedonians at Pydna in 168 BC, the Roman commander Aemilius Paullus wrote to the elder Cato praising the gallantry of his son. One incident towards the end of Cato's life throws a telling light on the relationship between father and son. Because Romans viewed any public display of affection as indecent, the widowed Cato caused embarrassment by falling in love with a young slave-girl, who visited his room every evening. 'The old man,' writes Plutarch, 'could not fail to notice that his son kept silent, glanced at the girl with intense dislike, and then turned away in disgust. As soon as Cato understood that his behaviour annoyed his children, he did not blame or find fault with them at all.' Tacitly acknowledging the justice of their criticism, he gave up the slave-girl but remarried a free-born girl instead, much to his son's consternation.

*See* CARTHAGE; ROME; SCIPIOS
*A. E. Astin, *Cato the Censor* (Oxford, 1978); Plutarch, *Makers of Rome*, trans. by I. Scott-Kilvert (Harmondsworth, 1965).

**Cato the Younger** (95–46 BC) became famous in later generations as the last Roman republican, not least because of his suicide at Utica in 46 BC. Marcus Porcius Cato Uticensis was the great-grandson of the elder Cato (234–148 BC), a stern upholder of traditional values during the period of Rome's expansion overseas. Although his own uncompromising opposition to all who appeared not to measure up to such standards did not endear him to everyone, the younger Cato had a wide circle of friends and admirers, including Cicero (106–43 BC). A disdain for Pompey (106–48 BC) did not prevent Cato from joining his forces at the outbreak of the civil war in 49 BC. He was disappointed, however, that Cicero chose not to act as mediator between Pompey and Julius Caesar (100–44 BC), the two warlords whose quarrel threatened to ruin once and for all the constitution.

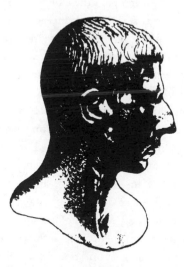

The younger Cato preferred in 46 BC to commit suicide rather than surrender to Julius Caesar.

After Pompey's defeat at Pharsalus in Thessaly in 48 BC, Cato went to the province of Africa, the last republican stronghold. There he governed the city of Utica for two years. At the approach of Caesar's army Cato reflected upon the Stoic proposition 'that only the good man is free, and all the evil be slaves'. He said now that liberty itself was about to be lost under Caesar's rule, life held no further meaning for him. Honour would remain the monopoly of a single man, and so he would rather die than live like a docile slave, attendant on his master's favours. But Cato's first attempt at suicide, the historian Plutarch tells us, failed because 'the sword thrust was somewhat feeble, owing to the inflammation of his hand ... A physician was summoned, and seeing that the entrails were unharmed, he tried to replace them and sew up the wound. However, when Cato became aware of what was happening, he pushed the physician away, tore at his entrails, widening the wound further and so died.'

News of his death was greeted by the people of Utica with the cry that Cato was 'the only man who was free, the only one unvanquished'. But Cato's motives remained competitive to the end; his pride was stimulated by the chance of his death wrenching from Caesar the honours he had refused him throughout his life. By the grand gesture of suicide, Cato would attain immortal fame as well as preventing Caesar from adding to his own through an act of clemency. Not for him the quiet retirement of a pardoned Cicero. That perpetual drive for fame and fortune, the gruelling life reserved for men such as Cato who belonged to the ruling class, thus reached a fitting climax and one which even brought distinction to the name of his illustrious great-grandfather. The sheer pressure to succeed politically among upper-class Romans was something that moulded behaviour at least till the foundation of the empire.

See CAESAR; CICERO; POMPEY; ROME
*R. Syme, *The Roman Revolution* (Oxford, 1939).

**Chang'an**, or 'Forever Safe', was in 202 BC founded as the imperial capital of China by the first Han emperor Gaozu (202–195 BC). Sited across the Wei river from the ruined Qin capital of Xianyang, Chang'an was built to face south, so that, when seated on the throne, the ruler faced in this auspicious direction too. Much of Chang'an was destroyed during the usurpation of Wang Mang (AD 9–23), who moved the seat of imperial power eastwards to Luoyang. In its heyday Chang'an was the premier Chinese city with a population of between a quarter and half a million. Particularly splendid was the reign of Emperor Han Wu Di (140–87 BC), who staged banquets, displays, and other forms of entertainment to impress visitors with the might and wealth of the empire. Some of these visitors, such as the nomad Jin Miti, were pleased to stay on and serve the Chinese empire. A mass surrender of the Hunnish Xiongnu in 121 BC had resulted in many of these tribesmen being settled on frontier lands. Because Jin Miti refused to lay down his arms, unlike the rest of the Xiongnu, he was not treated honourably but instead enslaved as a groom in the imperial stables. So delighted, however, was Wu Di with Jin Miti's service that he freed him from slavery. In due course the Xiongnu married a high official's daughter, before ending his own career in Chang'an as a minister.

Like all Chinese classical cities, Chang'an was laid out on a gridiron plan within a rammed-earth wall. Today its remains reveal a width of nearly 20 yards at the base. The exterior of the city wall (the same Chinese character is used for a city and a city wall) was once clad with bricks. Within the ramparts the city comprised 160 wards separated from each other with further gates and walls. At nights no free movement was allowed between wards. The orderliness of urban settlements in China derived from a tradition of strict official control predating imperial unification under the Qin dynasty in 221 BC. The city never succeeded through trade and industry in becoming sufficiently independent to challenge established political, legal and religious ideas. It always remained the focus of Chinese civilization, notwithstanding the periodic upsurges of rebellion amongst the peasantry.

See HAN WU DI; LUOYANG
*M. Loewe, *Everyday Life in Early Imperial China* (London, 1968).

**Chen Sheng** (died 209 BC) is celebrated in the People's Republic of China today as the original peasant rebel leader. A ploughman from the former state of Song, Chen Sheng led in 209 BC a group of conscript labourers in revolt. Heavy rain had prevented them from reaching their destination on time, a crime under the harsh law of Qin, the first imperial house, which was punishable by death. 'The common people have suffered enough,' said Chen Sheng, 'let us raise the standard of rebellion for them to answer like an echo.' So it was, the historian Sima Qian records, that rebels rose on all sides against the dispersed Qin garrisons, and Chen Sheng soon had a formidable following. A timely oracle certainly helped the humble leader, because his followers were reassured by the discovery of a piece of silk with blue characters in the belly of a fish. The message read 'Chen Sheng will be king.' And for several months the former ploughman acted as the king of a state called Zhang Chu, centred on modern Henan province.

The kingdom, however, was short-lived as a Qin army under Zhang Han crushed the rebels. Chen Sheng was murdered trying to escape the rout. But neither the death of the peasant king nor the continued successes of Zhang Han could quench the fires of rebellion. In 207 BC the Qin dynasty was overthrown and within five years another peasant leader, Liu Bang, came to mark the foundation of the Han dynasty.

*See* LIU BANG; ORACLES; QIN DYNASTY; XIANG YU; ZHANG HAN

★A. Cotterell, *The First Emperor of China* (London, 1981).

**Cheng Kuo** was a famous Chinese hydraulic engineer. In 246 BC, the year the future First Emperor became ruler of Qin, his canal was opened. Looking back on the triumph of Qin over the other feudal states, from the vantage point of the reign of the Han emperor Wu Di (140–87 BC), the historian Sima Qian appreciated the fundamental importance of the increase in agricultural productivity and the supply potential for maintaining military supremacy that derived from Cheng Kuo's canal. That this decisive edge was the result of a plot by the ruler of Han, a neighbouring state, only added to the disdain felt by Sima Qian for the Qin dynasty.

Han had sought to exhaust Qin with projects. An engineer was sent therefore to the Qin court, where he persuaded its king that a canal should be dug between the Jing and Luo rivers. The proposed canal would be several hundred miles long and used for irrigation. But the project was half finished when the plot was discovered. The Qin ruler was stopped from killing Cheng Kuo only by the engineer's own words. 'Even though this scheme was intended to injure you,' he said, 'if the canal is completed, it will be of great advantage to your state. Whilst Han has gained a few more years of independence, Qin has gained sustenance for ten thousand generations.' The work was then ordered to be completed. 'When finished,' Sima Qian noted, 'the output of the fields rose dramatically and Qin grew rich and strong until it finally conquered the whole of China. The canal was named after Cheng Kuo.'

That large-scale irrigation schemes were associated with Qin shows the extent to which Legalist policies, first introduced by Shang Yang (390–338 BC), had reshaped the outlook of this frontier state. It concentrated almost exclusively on agriculture and war. The extra 227,000 acres irrigated by Cheng Kuo's water-conservancy scheme turned Qin into the first key economic area, a place where agricultural productivity and facilities for transport facilitated a supply of tax-grain so superior to that of other places that the ruler who controlled it could control China. Not surprisingly, the imperial capital was situated there for most of the classical age.

See LEGALISM; QIN; QIN DYNASTY
*Ch'ao-ting Chi, *Key Economic Areas in Chinese History, as revealed in the Development of Public Works for Water-Control* (London, 1936).

**Choson** was the first Korean state. From Chinese sources we know that, after an unsuccessful rising against the first Han emperor Gaozu (202–195 BC), some of the defeated rebels sought refuge beyond the north-eastern imperial frontier. They were led by Wei Man, who took over the Korean state of Choson. He seems to have begun his career there as a mercenary commander, deploying his men along the border with China, but a coup quickly followed. Prudently adopting the Korean name of Wiman, the new king showed favour to existing officials in his administration. For Wiman was concerned to accommodate well-established native traditions, and not simply to pull Choson into the Chinese orbit.

Above all there was the question of language. The settlers of the Korean peninsula appear to have come originally from present-day Manchuria and Siberia. They spoke a polysyllabic and highly inflected language, in striking contrast to the monosyllabic and uninflected Chinese tongue. The Korean language, like Japanese, is now regarded as part of Altaic speech, a linguistic family named after the Altai mountains of Mongolia. Despite the obvious differences between Chinese and Korean, the Chinese script was adopted because it represented much more than the sole means of writing then available in East Asia. Its mastery allowed access to the Chinese classics, the contemporary standard for civilized living. The historical significance of sinicized Choson, and later settlements in Korea sponsored by the Han emperors, lay in their long-term cultural influence on Japan. In time the Korean peninsula became the main conduit through which Chinese culture flowed to the Japanese islands.

During the first half of the second century BC, however, the Han dynasty (202 BC – AD 220) was content to let Choson become the dominant power in Korea. Wiman's introduction of an iron industry gave his state a military and economic edge which allowed it to monopolize trade in the peninsula and enrich itself greatly. The Chinese emperors may not have approved entirely of the situation, but given the likelihood of ties between Choson and the Hunnish Xiongnu, they were disinclined to intervene as long as the nomads remained quiet. By the reign of Emperor Han Wu Di (140–87 BC), though, Xiongnu incursions from the steppe were so serious a threat that China was forced to take the offensive. In 128 BC a Chinese army failed to occupy the Yalu river valley and put pressure on Choson, but within twenty years the whole of northern Korea was taken into imperial control, and four commanderies were set up to administer the area. The defence of Choson was undermined by the murder of Ugo, Wiman's grandson, and conflict in the capital (modern Pyongyang). Following its surrender, the core of Choson was established as the chief commandery of Lolang, a census taken shortly afterwards recording a population of over 400,000. Lolang remained a centre of Chinese cultural influence for centuries after it ceased to be an actual colony in the fourth century AD. It was absorbed by the Korean state of

Koguryo, which asserted its own independence from China in AD 12.

*See* HAN DYNASTY; HAN WU DI; XIONGNU

*Ki-baik Lee, *A New History of Korea* (Cambridge, Mass., 1984).

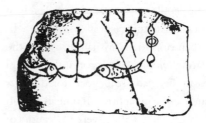

Fishes and anchors, Christian symbols from the catacomb of St Domitilla in Rome. Early fourth century AD.

**Christianity** was originally a Jewish sect, and as such was accorded the same degree of tolerance by Rome as Judaism. The great flare-up of Jewish nationalism in the first century AD, and the conflict which ensued with the Romans, changed the official attitude towards both Jews and Christians, however. Both chose to draw attention to themselves by believing in a single deity. They were also notable for being debarred from participation in numerous political, military and social activities of which pagan ritual was an integral part, and especially they could not hold public office. But the chief difference between Judaism and Christianity, as the latter developed under the influence of St Paul (died AD 65), was the claim by followers of Christianity that it was a universal religion unrelated to a particular people or place. Christian membership required a sustained act of personal commitment, since salvation required both faith and moral conduct. The influx of non-Jewish believers tended only to add to the suspicion of the Roman authorities, not least because people who took part in Christian congregational worship could come from any level of society. Conflict was inevitable. In urban riots the Christians provided the natural victims of pogroms: they could easily be made scapegoats for disasters such as the great fire at Rome in AD 64. Loyalty tests also were a cause of trouble, as Polycarp discovered to his cost at Smyrna. In either AD 155 or 165 this elderly bishop was burnt alive for failing to acknowledge the divinity of the Roman emperor, a formula that did not trouble non-Christian citizens. The persecutions of the emperors Decius (AD 249–251) and Diocletian (AD 284–305) were aimed at a subversive group felt to be threatening the unity of the empire itself.

Diocletian was concerned to reinstate the ancient gods of Rome, along with traditional forms of worship, as the foundation to a restored political order, following the military anarchy of the mid-third century AD. Only the emperor's political caution postponed the great persecution to the end of his reign and that of Galerius (AD 305–311). Imperial dislike of the Christian church was a measure of its nascent respectability and the threat it was seen to pose to a still-convalescent Rome. The death-bed decision of

Galerius to call off the persecution was credited to divine intervention by grateful Christians, but a more plausible explanation is that the dying

Although the apostle Mark was held to be the founder of Christianity in Alexandria, it was the healing shrine of St Menas which enjoyed great popularity in the late classical period. Here is depicted the martyrdom of Menas, around AD 304.

emperor knew it had failed. Far from creating a unified state by destroying Christianity, the persecution had only served to strengthen its followers' will to remain steadfast in the face of danger. As non-Christians were also unenthusiastic participants, Galerius had no choice but to grant Christians freedom of worship, legal tolerance, and the right to assemble for worship: in return, he asked them to pray for his health and the safety of the empire.

This act of toleration coincided with the emergence of an organized church, possessing a canonical literature of its own. The New Testament became distinguished from the Old Testament, the sacred text of Judaism. Correct interpretation was thought to be guaranteed by bishops of the apostolic sees, the linear descendants of Jesus' disciples. Even though heresies flourished, and competition remained intense with rival beliefs such as Gnosticism and Manichaeism, Christianity had evolved a coherent and homogeneous organization and a body of identifiable belief. Soon after he personally recognized the faith in AD 312, the emperor Constantine the Great (AD 306–337) gave official endorsement to Christianity in the foundation of a new capital at Constantinople (present-day Istanbul). There he built a great church to serve as a central place of worship and as his own mausoleum. Miraculously the Christian church had acquired a generous patron, but at the same time it took on a very powerful master indeed, for Constantine's subsequent efforts to settle theological disputes foreshadowed the role of the Byzantine emperor as a fount of Christian authority. Association between church and state was henceforth close, bishops remaining in regular contact with members of the imperial family and the court. All was thus accommodated within the existing social and political framework, which Christianity never sought to modify in any serious fashion. St Augustine (AD 354–430) could even use the defence of that order as a major argument for the suppression of heresy. It came as a shock to him in AD 410 that the Visigothic leader Alaric was able to sack Rome, while the Western emperor Honorius (AD 395–423) sought refuge behind

the marshes of Ravenna. His famous *City of God* can be seen, therefore, as Augustine's desperate attempt to make sense of barbarian invasion and triumph, for unlike in the east Roman, or Byzantine empire, western Christendom fragmented into a number of newly independent states.

See AFRICA; AUGUSTINE; CONSTANTINE THE GREAT; GNOSTICISM; JEWS; MANICHAEISM; POLYCARP; ROME

*H. Chadwick, *The Early Church* (Harmondsworth, 1986); W. H. C. Frend, *The Rise of Christianity* (London, 1984); R. Markus, *The End of Ancient Christianity* (Cambridge, 1990).

**Chu** was during the Warring States period (481–221 BC) the chief rival of Qin in the Middle Kingdom, as China was then called. Both of these feudal states were capable of putting into the field over one million soldiers. Battles had turned into massive infantry engagements, with armoured columns of foot-soldiers supported by cross-bowmen, spearmen, cavalry as well as chariots.

The intense struggle between Qin and Chu actually comprised the driving force behind the movement towards imperial unification, which eventually occurred in 221 BC. Of the two contenders, Qin was the better placed, since there was little unity of purpose amongst its northern neighbours (Qi, Yan, Zhao, Han, Wei, Song and Lu); while in the Yangzi estuary Chu had to deal with the belligerent powers of Yue and Wu. Not until 333 BC did Chu win a conclusive victory over these powers and secure its eastern flank, by which time Qin had thoroughly reorganized itself under the guidance of Shang Yang (390–338 BC) and was ready to take the offensive. In 330 BC Qin extended its eastern border to the Yellow river, at the expense of Wei, and in 316 BC a south-western thrust brought about the annexation of Shu, a large part of modern Sichuan province. Besides outflanking Chu, the Shu conquest added valuable resources to Qin once irrigation schemes were introduced on the Chengdu plain, thereafter known as 'sea-on-land'.

Military difficulties alone, though, cannot explain the falling behind of Chu in the race for supremacy. Although Chu itself was endowed with a mild climate suited to intensive agriculture, there was no determined exploitation of this critical resource, in contrast to its ruthless competitor, Qin. It is quite possible that the loess soil of the northern state, with the consequent importance of irrigation, comprised the lever by which the ruler of Qin could move his people as a unified force, whereas the ruler of Chu required less social cohesion in order to produce a reliable agricultural surplus. Another factor working against centralization may have been an apparent scarcity of cities. While town and city sites in Chu compare favourably with those excavated in the northern states, only a few have been located so far. From tomb finds, nevertheless, it is clear that the state possessed an advanced economy, which included bronze and iron manufacturing; the discovery of weapons amongst these funerary goods confirms the fear expressed in chronicles about the iron-tipped spears of Chu, 'sharp as a bee's sting'. A feudal order as shallowly founded as in Qin naturally inclined Chu towards Legalist doctrines, but no Shang Yang appeared to give the sprawling state an organization robust enough to withstand the storms raging at the time. Though not until after the conquest of Chu in 223 BC could Qin be certain of final victory, the growing strength of its forces was signalled in a series of defeats inflicted on the Chu army during the early campaigns of 280 and 278 BC, which resulted in the annexation of large tracts of the middle Yangzi valley.

In the great rebellion which overthrew Qin domination of China in 207 BC, not surprisingly one of the largest rebel forces was named the 'Avenging Army of Chu'; one of the most active rebel commanders was Xiang Yu, a 7-feet-tall aristocrat from the lower Yangzi river valley.

*See* QIN; QIN DYNASTY; WARRING STATES

*J. I. Crump, *Chan-kuo T'se* (Oxford, 1979).

**Cicero** (106–43 BC) was a 'new man' like the elder Cato (234–149 BC) and Marius (157–86 BC) because he lacked consuls among his ancestors. As concerned about the republican institutions of Rome as the elder Cato, and indeed his great-grandson the younger Cato (95–46 BC), Marcus Tullius Cicero was both a prolific author and an active politician. Typical was his approach to Greek philosophy, which many Romans feared might challenge and undermine society. For Cicero philosophy's chief role was to furnish the traditional order with secure intellectual foundations. Thus he could argue that proper conduct upheld the regime of property, privilege and power enjoyed by the Roman aristocracy. Quite overlooked were the endemic violence and corruption of its highly competitive political system. It might be said that Cicero himself contributed unnecessarily to the bloodshed in 63 BC, when as consul he insisted that the conspirator Catiline should be executed without trial. In the final senatorial debate the younger Cato supported Cicero's proposal and Julius Caesar (100–44 BC) spoke against it. Although a sentence of death was finally agreed, the conspiracy was not the tremendous crisis from which Cicero claimed to have saved the state, but a relatively minor upheaval. His motive was a burning desire to be recognized as first among his peers. Shortly afterwards Cicero was accused of assuming tyrannical airs, shorthand for a politician seeking to wield too much power for too long.

Publius Clodius (92–52 BC), a bitter opponent of Cicero, asked in 61 BC: 'How long are we going to put up with

this monarch?' The answer was not for very long, because Cicero's refusal to co-operate at all with Caesar, Crassus

The oratory of Cicero was not enough to save Rome from dictatorship.

(112–53 BC) and Pompey (106–48 BC) in what became known as the First Triumvirate effectively pushed him to the political margins. Their blatant use of force revealed how Rome, instead of being controlled by an oligarchy of nobles, was now in the hands of three ambitious men. And since Caesar relied on Clodius' street gangs to represent his interests during his absence from Rome, Cicero became an easy target and in 58 BC suffered exile for his handling of the Catiline conspiracy.

On his return to Rome a year later, at the insistence of Pompey, Cicero discovered that Clodius had demolished his house, scattered his statues and furniture, taken over part of his land, and built on the remainder a temple to Liberty. He tore down the temple and managed to rebuild his house, but not without the protection of gangs of gladiators loyal to Pompey. In 52 BC Clodius himself fell in a fight between these rival groups of supporters of Caesar and Pompey. The growing animosity of these two warlords, following the death of Crassus in 53 BC at the hands of the Parthians, placed Cicero in a political dilemma. Neither of them could claim to be guardians of republicanism, despite the senate's support for Pompey on the outbreak of civil war in early 49 BC. The clearer it became that Pompey would abandon Italy to Caesar, the more agitated Cicero became, troubled about what he should do and what was the right time for action. Possibly he still hoped for a compromise peace. Once he had gained control of Italy, Caesar endeavoured to win Cicero to his side or, at least, secure his neutrality. He failed in both aims when finally Cicero crossed the Adriatic to join Pompey. Cicero's late arrival did not impress everyone, but his reputation as a republican strengthened Pompey's cause. The younger Cato, however, said that he would have served the cause better by staying in Italy and trying to bring about peace.

After the defeat of Pompey at Pharsalus in 48 BC, Cicero refused Cato's invitation to assume command of the surviving republican forces and,

pardoned by Caesar, he returned to Italy. Rather than accept Caesar's mercy himself Cato chose suicide. The assassination of Caesar in 44 BC by a small group of senators shocked and delighted Cicero, who was himself not trusted enough to be included in the conspiracy. Cicero even suggested that Mark Antony, Caesar's chief lieutenant, should have been killed as well. This recommendation did not go unnoticed, for in 43 BC, on the formation of the Second Triumvirate between Octavian (63 BC – AD 14), Antony (82–30 BC) and Lepidus (89–12 BC), Cicero was marked down for elimination. The historian Plutarch relates how 'by Antony's orders his murderer cut off Cicero's head and hands'. Presumably the latter were also singled out for punishment because his writings as much as his speeches had caused offence to those who sought to usher in a new political order.

See ANTONY; CAESAR; CATALINE; CATO THE YOUNGER; POMPEY; ROME
*C. Habicht, Cicero the Politician (Baltimore, 1990); E. Rawson, Cicero: A Portrait (London, 1975).

**Cimon** (510–450 BC) was the son of Miltiades, an Athenian aristocrat and the general most responsible for the defeat of the invading Persians at Marathon in 490 BC. His mother was a Thracian princess. The historian Plutarch said of Cimon that 'he was not inferior in daring to Miltiades nor in intelligence to Themistocles [the democrat leader] and more just than both'.

On his father's death in 489 BC, Cimon paid the fine of 50 talents which had been imposed on Miltiades after an abortive attack on Paros. Frequently elected as one of the board of ten generals by the Athenian assembly, Cimon helped Aristides (c. 525–467 BC) to win the allegiance of the maritime Greeks, with the result that Athens, instead of Sparta, assumed the leadership of the league set up on Delos in 478–477 BC to continue the war against Persia. Around 474 BC he cleared Scyros of pirates, repopulated the island with Athenian settlers, and brought home the bones of Theseus, the legendary king of Athens who was credited with the unification of Attica as a single city-state. Four years later he reduced the island of Naxos to obedience, after this ally had tried to quit the Delian League. With the approval of other members, Cimon then converted the annual contribution of Naxos to the war against Persia from the provision of manned ships to the payment of money. Plutarch suggests that the energetic general also encouraged other allies to follow suit. Unwilling to be heavy-handed with defaulters, Cimon 'accepted money or empty ships from all those peoples who were unhappy to serve abroad. In this way he let the allies yield to the temptation of taking their ease and attending to nothing but private affairs, until they had lost all their military qualities and become unwarlike farmers and traders

through their own folly and love of comfort. On the other hand he forced a large part of the Athenian population to take turns in manning their ships and hardened them on his various expeditions, and so in a short period of time, using the funds the allies had contributed, he converted the Athenians into the masters of the very men who paid them.'

This centralizing tendency helped to make the league more effective militarily, but it led to a gradual but decisive change in the organization. Well before the outbreak of the Peloponnesian War between Athens and Sparta in 431 BC the Athenians ran the Delian League as an undisguised empire.

At Athens Cimon became the leader of the aristocratic party, the great landowning families opposed to the democratic programme of Themistocles. About 471 BC Themistocles (c. 528–462 BC) was ostracized, but he was replaced by Ephialtes, whose most significant constitutional success in 462–461 BC was the downgrading of the Areopagus, a council of aristocratic elders which claimed to be the guardian of the city's laws. Cimon appears to have been absent on campaign when the Athenian assembly reduced the council's powers and, Plutarch tells us, 'transformed the city into a thorough-going democracy with the help of Pericles, who had now risen to power and committed himself to the cause of the people. So it was that when Cimon returned and, in his disgust at the humiliation of the once revered Areopagus, tried to restore its judicial powers and revive the aristocratic approach of Cleisthenes, the democratic leaders combined to denounce him and stir up the people against him by accusing him of pro-Spartan sympathies.'

The moment was a turning-point in Athenian history: the generous, public-spirited but utterly conservative Cimon was faced by the ambitious Pericles (c. 495–429 BC), a young noble who sensed the shift of mood amongst ordinary citizens. Pericles possessed no military reputation to compare with Cimon's, nor could he match his fortune, enhanced as it was by booty. But he was presented with a lucky turn of events when Cimon persuaded the Athenians to send military aid to the Spartans, who were faced with a rebellion of their helots following an earthquake. These slaves had taken refuge on Mount Ithome in Messenia, and were still a threat. The democrats opposed helping the Spartans, so that Cimon suffered political humiliation when his force of 4,000 Athenians were quickly sent back home. Apparently the Spartans, according to the historian Thucydides, came to fear that the Athenians might be persuaded by the helots to take their side.

As a result of this embarrassment Cimon was ostracized in 461 BC. After his return from exile, he helped to negotiate a peace between Sparta and Athens in 450 BC. Cimon met his death the same year leading an expedition against the Persians in Cyprus. This heroic end allowed Plutarch to say that Cimon was the last Greek general to win a great victory over

Cimon's political career in Athens was ended by ostracism in 461 BC. This sherd records one of the votes cast against him that year.

Persia, prior to the invasion of Alexander the Great in 334 BC. 'Instead, a succession of demagogues and warmongers arose, who proceeded to turn the Greek states against one another, and nobody could be found to separate them and reconcile them before they met in the headlong collision of war.' Such a view is not without some truth, but Cimon was no less active than Pericles in opposing by force the succession of allies from the Delian League. Perhaps the ostracism of Cimon, rather than his death, should be seen as the moment of change, for it marked the transition of Cleisthenes' semi-aristocratic democracy into the full-blown version presided over by Pericles. So great was the hatred aroused by this event that Ephialtes was assassinated in the same year.

See ARISTIDES; ATHENS; CLEISTHENES; DELIAN LEAGUE; EPHIALTES; MILTIADES;

PERSIAN INVASIONS; SPARTA; THEMISTOCLES

*H. Hornblower, *The Greek World, 479–323 BC* (London, 1983); R. Meiggs, *The Athenian Empire* (Oxford, 1972); Plutarch, *The Rise and Fall of Athens: Nine Greek Lives*, trans. by I. Scott-Kilvert (Harmondsworth, 1960).

**Claudius**, Roman emperor AD 41–54, was born in 10 BC at Lugdunum (modern Lyon in France). After the death of Caligula, the first emperor to be assassinated, his fifty-one-year-old uncle Claudius was hailed as emperor by the Praetorian Guard. Tiberius Claudius Nero Germanicus had been found hiding behind curtains in the palace by some guardsmen, who took him to their barracks.

A bronze head of the Roman emperor Claudius, found in a Suffolk river. The emperor was present in AD 43 at the capture of Camulodunum, modern Colchester.

Officers from this élite corps were involved in Caligula's murder, but Claudius had little choice in accepting the guard's support. Ominously, he set a precedent for the future by rewarding the guardsmen with a large gift. An immediate problem for Claudius was popular outrage against the gladiator Sabinus, commander of the German horse guard; he had led his troopers on a rampage after Caligula's death. But Claudius was dissuaded from punishing Sabinus by his wife Messalina, whose lover the gladiator was. She was to overreach herself in AD 48, however, when she secretly married Gaius Silius, an ambitious nobleman. The imperial freedmen, in alarm, gathered evidence and forced a strangely reluctant emperor to act. The historian Tacitus relates how 'Silius asked only for a quick death', as did other lovers of Messalina. She tried to defend herself, but was killed before Claudius could forgive her. 'The vengeance on Messalina was just,' wrote Tacitus, 'but its consequences were grim,' not least because Claudius was easily controlled by his wives. His next wife Agrippina, Caligula's sister, proved the most manipulative of all, easily persuading Claudius to adopt her son Nero, the last and most disastrous of the Julio-Claudian emperors.

The senate had toyed with the possibility of restoring the republic in AD 41, but Claudius' forcible accession to the throne effectively ended senatorial influence. He was the emperor, the commander-in-chief, backed in Rome by the praetorians and the German horse guard. An abortive revolt the following year in Dalmatia cost thirty-five senators their lives. Perhaps to distract attention from this purge, Claudius personally took part in the invasion and annexation of southern Britain. He was present in AD 43 at the capture of Camulodunum (modern Colchester), which became the capital of the new province. Mauretania and Thrace were also taken from client rule and added to the empire, and colonies were established near the new frontiers. Claudius was unusual in refusing to see the empire as predominantly an Italian institution; ignoring all protests, he recruited new senators from Gaul. A provincial problem he settled from Caligula's reign was the bloody dispute between the Greek and Jewish residents of Alexandria. Both parties sent deputations to Rome, where Claudius admonished them to keep the peace. But he made it easier for the Jews by reversing Caligula's policy of demanding divine honours. His letter to the prefect of Egypt makes plain a dislike for such self-aggrandizement. 'I disapprove of a high-priest to me,' he wrote, 'and the erection of temples, for I do not wish to be offensive to my contemporaries, and I hold that sacred places and the like have by all ages been dedicated to the gods alone.'

Claudius died in AD 54, in his sixty-fourth year. Rumour even blamed Agrippina for poisoning him with mushrooms. Possibly she was anxious to get her seventeen-year-old son on the imperial throne in order to exercise greater influence herself.

See CALIGULA; NERO; ROME

*B. Levick, *Claudius* (London, 1990); Tacitus, *The Annals of Imperial Rome*, trans. by M. Grant (Harmondsworth, 1956).

**Cleisthenes** was held to be the creator of the Athenian democracy, even though the foundation had really been laid by the reforms of Solon almost a century earlier. An Athenian aristocrat, Cleisthenes was the son of Megacles and Agariste, daughter of the Sicyonian tyrant Cleisthenes. He persuaded the prophetess at Delphi, in return for the services of his family the Alcmaeonids in rebuilding the temple, to urge upon the Spartans the overthrow of the Athenian tyrant Hippias (527–510 BC). Taking advantage of the political vacuum thus created, Cleisthenes enlisted the support of the citizen-body to weaken further the power of noble families except his own. He achieved this by undermining the geographical basis of tribal loyalties. Within three main divisions – the city, the country, and the coast – wards were grouped to form so-called thirds. One third was selected from each area and the resulting three combined into a new tribe. In all, ten new tribes replaced the four previously in existence, and each elected 50 members to the council set up almost a century earlier by Solon. Its membership was thus increased from 400 to 500. While the old tribes continued as religious organizations, political consciousness focused upon the new tribes as the means of governing the city-state. The enlarged council functioned as the engine of democracy, for without its deliberative assistance the general assembly of citizens could never have exercised its sovereignty effectively.

The reason the councillors sitting on the council were unable to dominate Athens in the fifth century BC was due to annual elections by lot and the limitation of membership to two terms. The packing of the ancient Council of the Aeropagus with supporters of the tyranny had sullied its name, though during the crisis with Persia a temporary revival of its influence in state affairs took place. After 461 BC, the Council of the Areopagus was reduced to a minor, if venerated, part of the judicial system, as the court for cases of violent crime and arson. To protect the state from a recurrence of tyranny, Cleithenes is reputed to have introduced ostracism, the banishment of any citizen for a decade. If the assembly agreed to hold the annual ostracism, then the citizen against whom most votes were cast went into exile without loss of property. For though the Athenians wholeheartedly came to believe in democracy, they retained a healthy distrust for individuals in both the legislative and judicial spheres. The so-called 'writ of unconstitutionality' could also be invoked against any legislative proposal. This additional safeguard is usually attributed to Ephialtes in the 460s BC. Order was kept at meetings of the assembly by either members of the council, or Scythian archers. Except for an ostracism, the Athenians voted by a show of hands: the Spartans and the Macedonians used acclamation, the latter striking spears against shields.

The effect of Cleisthenes' constitutional reforms of 508 BC in distributing power more widely needs to be seen in historical context. While ownership of land ceased to be a qualification for citizenship in Athens, the size of the citizen-body remained strictly limited. Among others excluded from membership were allies, foreign residents, and slaves. And, as elsewhere in the classical world, women too were without any political rights. That the Greeks also took slavery for granted should never be forgotten. When in 413 BC the Spartans built a fort at Decelea in northern Attica, some 20,000 Athenian slaves are known to have run away. The total number of Athenian citizens at the time was probably 35,000.

See PERICLES; SOLON

★W. G. Forrest, *The Emergence of Greek Democracy* (London, 1966); C. G. Starr, *The Birth of Athenian Democracy: The Assembly in the Fifth Century BC* (Oxford, 1990).

**Clement** of Alexandria (AD 150–215) was a Greek convert to Christianity. He had been a wandering scholar who attached himself to an astonishing number of Christian teachers before settling in Alexandria. As he says himself: 'One was in Greece, the next in south Italy, others in the East, and in north Africa one was an Assyrian, another a Palestinian, a Hebrew by descent.' Apart from indicating the spread of Christianity in the eastern provinces of the Roman empire, Clement's travels show the growth of Christian centres for study. One of them was in Syria at Antioch, a city like Alexandria, with a large Jewish population. This Christian school, however, was famous for its disdain of Greek learning. Quite different in attitude was Clement himself, who valued the Hebrew legacy he found in Alexandria but tended to push it into the background in favour of the greatest possible accommodation with Greek philosophy. There he was drawing upon a tradition of thought that had started with the Jewish scholar Philo (20 BC – AD 50). Just as for Philo there was no incompatibility between Greek learning and Judaism, so for Clement it formed an essential part of a Greek convert's grounding. 'The law is for the Jew,' Clement insisted, 'what philosophy is for the Greek, a schoolmaster to bring them to Christ.' Clement's objection to Gnosticism, a contemporary Alexandrian heresy which taught a strict division between spirit and matter, was that it lay outside the Christian church and was offensive to human freedom of will and common sense. But like the Gnostics, his Christianity favoured the formation of an intellectual leadership, a latter-day parallel to Jesus' disciples. In AD 202 persecution drove Clement to flee to Cappadocia, where in this remote part of Asia Minor he died a saintly believer in a philosophic Christianity untouched by worldly events.

*See* CHRISTIANITY; GNOSTICISM; PHILO
*S. R. C. Lilla, *Clement of Alexandria* (Oxford, 1971).

**Cleomenes I**, king of Sparta 519–490 BC, was 'not quite right in the head', according to the historian Herodotus. His accession was marred by the voluntary exile of his younger half-brother Dorieus, who left with 'a body of men and took them off to found a settlement abroad, without previously consulting the Delphic oracle, or observing any of the usual formalities'. Whatever the reason for the quarrel, Cleomenes did not let it affect his actions as one of the two Spartan kings, for his assertive foreign policy was designed to weaken Argos, the traditional enemy of Sparta in the Peloponnese. In 510 BC he led an army to Athens and deposed the tyrant Hippias, a friend of the Argives. The last of the Pisistratid tyrants, Hippias eventually went to the court of King Darius of Persia (521–486 BC), returning as an old man with the Persian expeditionary force at Marathon in 490 BC. But civil strife in Athens caused three more Spartan interventions. The last one in 504 BC might have proved decisive had not Cleomenes' Corinthian allies withdrawn at the last moment, on the grounds that they were acting wrongly in invading Attica. What was more embarrassing still, the other Spartan king Demaratus also refused to go along with the plan, and returned home. As a direct result of this royal disagreement the Spartans passed a law to the effect that henceforth one king only was to go on campaign at any one time. Throughout the struggle against Athens Cleomenes seems to have behaved in an unconstitutional manner, since he alone decided on war, raised an army, and marched off without indicating any particular objective.

In 494 BC, however, he dealt Argos a devastating blow, even though his methods were controversial. At Sepeia Cleomenes routed the Argive army, and then killed the survivors by firing a sacred wood in which they had taken refuge. Argive power was thus crushed for a generation. Not surprisingly Argos remained neutral in 480 BC, when the Persian king Xerxes (486–465 BC) crossed with his expeditionary force from Asia Minor. The collapse of the Ionian revolt the same year as Sepeia had opened the way for a Persian advance into mainland Greece. Conscious of the growing danger, Cleomenes put aside his dislike for the fledgeling Athenian democracy and jointly planned for defence. From a wavering Aegina he took hostages; he also deposed his fellow king Demaratus, who fled to Persia. Back in Sparta Cleomenes' mental health broke down, and he beat every citizen he met with his staff: incarceration and suicide soon followed. Most Greeks believed that it was for the sacrilege at Sepeia

that the king was punished by insanity. The Spartans contested this view, saying that his brain had been destroyed by drinking wine unmixed with water, a habit he had learned from Scythian envoys. When it was later discovered that the Macedonians were similar to the Scythians in their taste for alcohol, some Greeks were only too willing to regard it as a confirmation of barbarism. There were even rumours about Alexander the Great's excessive drinking.

*See* Aegina; Alexander the Great; Argos; Athens; Darius; Ionian revolt; Tyrants; Xerxes
*G. L. Huxley, *Early Sparta* (London, 1962); P. Cartledge, *Sparta and Lakonia* (London, 1979).

**Cleon** (died 422 BC) was, during the early years of the Peloponnesian War (431–404 BC), a determined opponent of the Athenian leader Pericles, whose conduct of military operations he found insufficiently aggressive. The son of a wealthy tanner, Cleon was less gentle in his approach to Athens' enemies and subject-allies: after Pericles' death in 429 BC, when Cleon was in power, the Athenians were not only more active overseas, but they also sharply raised the imperial tribute. In 427 BC he persuaded the Athenian assembly to condemn to death all the men of Mytilene, the chief city of Lesbos, after the suppression of its revolt. According to the historian Thucydides, Cleon 'was remarkable among Athenians for the violence of his character, and at this time he exercised far the greatest influence over the people'. But Cleon's calculated policy of terror did not long hold sway in Athens, for the assembly rescinded the law next day and dispatched a second ship to cancel the order. The first vessel had a start of twenty-four hours, but the rowers chasing it were promised a reward if they got to the island of Lesbos first. They arrived in the nick of time, and just prevented a massacre. Instead, with the exception of the loyal city of Methymna, Lesbos was converted into an Athenian colony and the defeated rebels made to work the land as tenant-farmers.

Cleon's chance to rival Nicias (c. 470–413 BC) as a commander in the field occurred in 425 BC. A moderate leader opposed to the extreme democratic faction led by Cleon, Nicias offered to resign his command to him when criticized for inaction at Sphacteria, where a force of Spartans were trapped on this island near Pylos, in the south-western Peloponnese. Cleon was compelled to accept the challenge and, with aid from Demosthenes, the Athenian general on the spot, he forced the Spartans to surrender. With 120 Spartan citizens as prisoners of war, a significant number in terms of Sparta's diminishing citizenry, there were moves to conclude a peace. At Cleon's urging, Sparta's envoys were sent home with the warning that further ravaging of the Attic countryside would endanger the lives of the captives, while the Athenians prepared to continue the war. The war aims of Cleon harked back to a time in the mid-440s BC when Athens controlled Megara, Boeotia, and other parts of central Greece, as well as a number of Peloponnesian coastal cities. How far he wished to expand the imperial borders is unknown, although the popular dramatist Aristophanes (450–385 BC) has a character say that the Athenian assembly should rule over all Greeks. Already his topical humour had caused Cleon to accuse Aristophanes of demeaning the state. It is somewhat ironic that one of the honours awarded the victor of Sphacteria was front seats at the theatre.

Cleon's success led to his election as general in 424 BC along with others committed to the offensive. Nicias was re-elected as well. The year's first campaign was the capture by Nicias of Cythera, the island south of the Peloponnese. The Cythereans were enrolled as subjects and an Athenian garrison was installed. Later in the year civil strife in Megara, the tiny state on Athens' western frontier, would have delivered it into Athenian hands but for the timely arrival of the Spartan general Brasidas (died 422 BC). En route to Thrace, where his force was intended to threaten vital Athenian interests, energetic Brasidas prevented the fall of the city of Megara, though not its port. The impact of Brasidas' operations in Thrace, where the very important Athenian colony of Amphipolis was lost, soon forced

Cleon to lead in 424 BC an expedition there himself. While Brasidas enjoyed intermittent Macedonian support, Cleon could call upon both Macedonian and Thracian allies. Apparently awaiting their arrival at Amphipolis, Cleon was nonetheless forced into an action in which he died with about 600 Athenians. The Spartans lost only seven men, but one of them was Brasidas. It was the considered view of Thucydides, himself made an exile because of the loss of Amphipolis, that the incompetence of Cleon had decided the day. But the main result of the engagement, he concludes, was the removal of 'the men on each side most opposed to peace'. In Athens the arrangement of a peace treaty between Sparta and Athens was left to Nicias. Peace lasted much less than a decade because Pericles' kinsman, Alcibiades (c. 450–404 BC), took over the leadership of the extreme democrats, and initiated adventures overseas.

*See* ALCIBIADES; ATHENS; NICIAS; PELOPONNESIAN WAR; PERICLES
*D. Kagan, *The Archidamian War* (Ithaca, 1974).

**Cleopatra VII** (69–30 BC) was the last Ptolemaic ruler of Egypt. A passionate and intelligent Macedonian woman, she deployed sexuality in order to preserve her tottering dynasty from 51 to 30 BC. First Julius Caesar, then Mark Antony, fell under her spell. Blockaded in Alexandria in 48–47 BC by a Ptolemaic army opposed to Cleopatra,

Cleopatra VII, the last of the Ptolemies, who committed suicide in 30 BC.

Caesar (100–44 BC) had once to swim from the mole to save his life, leaving his purple general's cloak as a trophy for the enemy. After the city's relief, he confirmed Cleopatra on the Egyptian throne along with her eleven-year-old brother Ptolemy XIV. As a gesture towards pharaonic tradition, the sister and brother were married, but not before Cleopatra conceived Caesarion, the son of Caesar. On his triumphant return to Rome in 46 BC, Caesar even brought over Cleopatra and her entourage, much to the annoyance of conservative senators. Whilst the charms of the Egyptian queen were not lost on the Roman dictator, Caesar's interest in her kingdom was not unconnected with its very considerable wealth. By fathering Caesarion he probably intended to shore up the faltering Ptolemaic dynasty and prevent Egypt from becoming a Roman province under senatorial control. After Caesar's assassination in 44 BC, Cleopatra returned to Egypt, eliminated her brother, and had Caesarion declared co-ruler, with the title Ptolemy Caesar.

At Philippi in Macedon the slayers of Caesar were defeated in 42 BC by Antony (82–30 BC) and young Octavian (63 BC–AD 14), the future Roman emperor Augustus. With Octavian so ill that his life seemed lost and the third triumvir Lepidus (89–12 BC) relegated to the province of Africa, Antony appeared to be the new power in the Mediterranean world. So in 41 BC Cleopatra put on the famous show with her barge, and captivated the Roman general. She was never blind to his shortcomings as a commander or a man, but with Roman arms by then irresistible there was nothing else she could do but seek alliance with one of its chief warlords. Egyptian resources, therefore, backed Antony's military ventures, until in 31 BC, at the battle of Actium in north-eastern Greece,

Octavian won over him a decisive victory. Afterwards Cleopatra at the age of thirty-nine tried to captivate Octavian as well. According to the historian Cassius Dio, 'such were the subtle tones of speech and changes of expression with which she addressed him, casting sweet looks and murmuring tender words, that Octavian understood the passion with which she was speaking and the seductive power of her gestures'. But it was to no avail. He went on to become the righteous Augustus; she just managed to die by means of a self-inflicted snake-bite in 30 BC. Caesarion was killed on Octavian's orders shortly afterwards. Cassius Dio suggests that the reason for Octavian's coldness towards Cleopatra, and his refusal to let her end her own life, was 'a desire that she should make a brilliant spectacle at his triumph in Rome'. The war which he had won was declared against her alone: no declaration was ever passed against his rival Antony.

*See* ANTONY; CAESAR; EGYPT; PTOLEMIES; ROME

*Cassius Dio, *The Roman History: The Reign of Augustus*, trans. by I. Scott-Kilvert (Harmondsworth, 1987); R. D. Sullivan, *Near East Royalty and Rome, 100–30 BC* (Toronto, 1990); H. Volkmann, *Cleopatra: A Study in Politics and Propaganda* (London, 1958).

Coin of Julius Caesar, struck in 44 BC, the year of his assassination. Cleopatra, and their three-year-old son Caesarion, were in Rome at the time the dictator was killed.

**Coinage** was in general use during the classical period. There would seem to have been three distinct origins: Lydia

The sacred owl of Athena shown prominently on an Athenian silver coin, struck around 450 BC.

Zeus, the king of gods and men, depicted on a Rhodian coin dating from 200 BC.

in Asia Minor, northern India, and China. According to the Greeks, the first coins were struck in Lydia, a circumstance which did much to assist Aegean trade. Minting of silver coins then spread westwards via Aegina, the only mainland state to share in the eastern Greek foundation of Naucratis, a trading post in the Nile delta. There the Egyptians gave Aegina, Samos and Miletus separate concessions. Possibly large deposits of electrum, an alloy of gold and silver, allowed the earliest known coinage to emerge in Lydia at the end of the seventh century BC. Within the Persian empire, to which Lydia was added in 546 BC, coinage was at first restricted to Asia Minor. The Phoenicians struck no coins until the middle of the fifth century BC, shortly to be followed by their overseas cousins, the Carthaginians, at mints in Sicily. Even later were the Romans, whose first known coins date from mid-280s BC.

Coined money in India may have owed something to Persia, which under Darius I (521–486 BC) annexed its north-western approaches. But there is evidence of an indigenous tradition of minting prior to the arrival of foreign influence, which after the invasion of Alexander the Great (356–323 BC) was predominantly Greek. It can be said to have fused in the coinage of Bactria, many of whose issues were bilingual. The Indo-Greek kingdom of Bactria entered upon a period of expansion at the beginning of the second century BC, which led to conquests across north-western India. The coins of later invaders such as the Kushanas were even more cosmopolitan. King Kaniska (AD 78–102) was a convert to Buddhism, but his coins carried images of Zoroastrian, Hindu, Greek and Buddhist deities. Certainly Kaniska employed Greek craftsmen at his mints, just as Greco-Roman sculptors had a strong influence on the so-called Gandhara school, which was then enriching Buddhist art. The most beautiful classical coins anywhere are probably the gold issues of Samudra-

A coin celebrating progress in Spain under the Roman emperor Augustus, following the final conquest of the peninsula. Probably from a Spanish mint, 20-19 BC.

gupta (AD 335–376), who is shown as both a conqueror and a musician. The opportunity for Indian rulers to adopt a gold standard, from Kaniska onwards, was the massive outflow of coins from the Roman empire. In the AD 70s Pliny the Elder calculated that over 12,000 pounds of gold were sent to India each year to buy gems and spices. All eastern imports cost the Romans at least twice that sum.

An ultimate beneficiary of this international trade was China, the supplier of silk. But it is unlikely that Roman gold and silver ever reached the Han empire (202 BC – AD 220) in significant quantity, since the Chinese sought Central Asian and Indian products. Commerce between Rome and China was thus always in the hands of middlemen, even though Han armies imposed Chinese control over the so-called Western Regions, essentially the Tarim basin. Standardization of coinage, along with much else in China,

occurred during the brief Qin dynasty (221–207 BC). Imperial unification was accompanied by the sweeping away of currencies belonging to the old feudal states. Coins were restricted to those of gold of a fineness determined by colour, and of weight determined by a standard unit, and to those of copper of fixed weight. After the fall of Qin, the Han emperors added two other forms of money: silver coinage and 'deerskin notes'. Although the latter looked forward to the Chinese invention of printed, paper currency, treasury notes made from the skin of a white stag were a temporary measure to deal with financial problems. By 91 BC China was suffering economically from the long war against the Xiongnu, probably the Huns who later invaded the Roman empire. Mounting difficulties in production and distribution of basic commodities, the worsening condition of the peasant-farmers, the growing wealth of merchants, and inflation caused by the private minting of coin, demanded drastic action. To meet immediate financial commitments the Han emperor Wu Di (140–87 BC) sold titles and called in minted coins by issuing special 'deerskin notes'. Subsequent reductions in the weights of gold, silver and copper coins were intended to aid circulation in what was then becoming a money economy. The gold unit, however, was permanently fixed at the value of 10,000 copper coins.

Apart from Wu Di's early experiment with monetarism, China was also untypical in overlooking the propaganda dimension of coinage. The first to realize its full potential were the Ptolemies (305–30 BC), the successors to Alexander the Great's conquest of Egypt. Royal portraits on Ptolemaic coins were adorned with divine attributes, Ptolemy I (305–282 BC) associating himself with Zeus, the chief god of the Greeks and Macedonians. The Ptolemies also insisted upon a monopoly coinage, for visitors bringing foreign gold coins into Egypt had to exchange them, or have them restruck into Ptolemaic coins at the royal mint. That Ptolemaic coins are now rarely unearthed outside Egypt suggests that the prime objective of the currency monopoly was the efficient collection of taxes.

*See* AEGINA; ALEXANDER THE GREAT; DARIUS I; HAN DYNASTY; KANISKA; PERSIA; PTOLEMIES; QIN DYNASTY

*J. K. Davies, *Wealth and Power in Classical Athens* (Salem, 1984); K. W. Harl, *Coinage in the Roman Economy, 300 BC to AD 700* (Baltimore, 1996); N. L. Swann, *Food and Money in Ancient China* (Princeton, 1950).

**Confucius,** or Kong Qiu (551–479 BC), was the uncrowned king of Chinese philosophy. Of the ancestry of Confucius nothing is known for certain, for it was not until long after his death that the widespread fame of his ideas led to admirers claiming for him noble forebears. It would appear that his family were impoverished members of the scholar-gentry resident in the

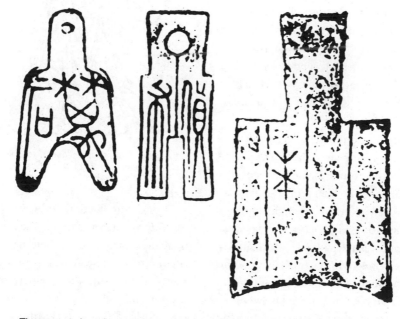

Three examples of coins circulating in China prior to its unification by the First Emperor in 221 BC.

eastern feudal state of Lu. His own official career was inconspicuous and brief. The two minor posts Confucius held were as keeper of the state granaries and director of state pastures. That he was unable to obtain any position of note may well have been due to a disinclination to flatter or conduct intrigues. Temperamentally a teacher rather than a politician, Confucius found that through his followers an influence could be exerted upon the feudal courts, once rulers appreciated the value of officials who prized loyalty to principles, not factions.

The students of Confucius were not chosen on grounds of birth. The only criteria for admission to the school were virtuous conduct, intelligence, and a willingness to study hard. Confucius commended in his teachings and his writings the renowned rulers of former days, kings and princes whose benevolence and propriety had led their subjects to perfect lives. The Chinese character for propriety tells us exactly what Confucius had in mind, since the strokes represent a vessel containing precious objects as a sacrifice to the ancestral spirits. The rite of ancestor worship thus became the focus of a moral code in which proper social relations were clearly defined: the loyalty a minister owed to a ruler was the same as that owed to a father by a son. Under the empire (which lasted, with some interruptions, from 221 BC till 1911) administrative requirements were to allow the service rendered by the scholar-bureaucrat to be a reality as

well as an ideal. Confucian scholars connected with the landowning class were one of the twin pillars of imperial society: the other was the great multitude of peasant-farmers, no longer tied to a feudal lord but liable to taxation, labour on public works, and military service.

Confucius, the most influential thinker in classical China, died in 479 BC.

During the lifetime of Confucius this future transformation could not be imagined. Indeed, the whole tenor of his thought is the recovery of a lost feudal ideal. 'I am a transmitter, not a creator,' he said. 'I believe in things of old and love them.' Referring to the Daoists, Confucius remarked: 'They dislike me because I want to reform society, but if we are not to live with our fellow men with whom can we live? We cannot live with animals. If society was as it ought to be, I should not be seeking to change it.' It was a point echoed by later Confucian thinkers whose outlook rested on a profound sense of personal responsibility for the welfare of mankind. Since they viewed the state as a large family, or a collection of families under the care of one leading family, the virtue of obedience also found a place amongst the characteristics that defined the relationship between the ruler and his subjects. When asked about government, Confucius said: 'Let the prince be a prince, the minister a minister, the father a father, and the son a son.' The cultivated man accepted the authority of his superiors because he cherished justice, unlike the selfish man who held nothing in respect except himself. 'When he sees a chance for gain, he stops to think whether to pursue it would be right; when he sees that his prince is in danger, he is ready to lay down his life; when he gives his word, no matter how long ago, he always keeps it.'

But harmonious social relations depended on a compassionate ruler, who instructed the people by his own example in following traditional usage. Confucius even warned progressive rulers that the setting down of laws was a dangerous practice for the nobility. Pointing out that a written law-code represented a break with tradition, he astutely predicted that the code of punishments inscribed on a tripod by the ruler of Qin in 513 BC would be learned and honoured by the people above all else. This was undesirable because, Confucius believed, the business of government was best left in the hands of those schooled for public service. In contrast to classical Greece, literacy in China did not take on at once a public purpose; it never disclosed to the people as a whole the workings of government. Only the learned could expect to enter the bureaucracy and wield power.

Not for a moment, however, was Confucius suggesting that arbitrary decisions were to be justified by reference to tradition. Without an understanding of propriety, a proper opinion could not be reached. Hence the value that he placed on scholarship. 'Love of humanity without love of learning,' said Confucius, 'becomes silliness. Love of wisdom without love of learning soon becomes lack of principle. Love of rectitude without love of learning soon becomes harshness. Love of courage without love of learning soon becomes chaos.' Another influential idea of Confucius concerns the supernatural, since his attitude to religion was purely practical. 'I stand in awe of the spirits,' he told his followers, 'but keep them at a distance.' This is neither the later scepticism of Xun Zi (c. 320–235 BC) nor the rationalism of Wang Chong (AD 27–100), but rather an intimation that Heaven was far above human comprehension:

something not easily plumed by omens. Because quite unlike Dong Zhongshu (c. 179–c. 104 BC), Confucius did not believe that floods and earthquakes could be readily interpreted as signs of divine disapproval.

See DAOISM; DONG ZHONGSHU; HUNDRED SCHOOLS; MENCIUS; XUN ZI
*D. H. Smith, Confucius (London, 1973); H. G. Creel, Confucius: the Man and the Myth (New York, 1949); A. Waley, The Analects of Confucius (London, 1938); V. A. Rubin, Individual and State in Ancient China (New York, 1976).

**Constantine the Great**, Roman emperor AD 306–337, was the son of Constantius I, one of the junior partners in Diocletian's college of rulers until AD 305, when he became co-emperor with Galerius (AD 305–311). In spring AD 305 the ailing Diocletian had abdicated along with his co-emperor Maximian at Nicomedia, after telling the troops assembled there that his reforms had saved the civilized world. He stepped down as a private citizen and his own junior partner, Galerius, was acclaimed as his successor. Then came the surprise. All eyes were then turned upon thirty-year-old Constantine, who was staying at the court of Diocletian. But he was thrust aside, and two friends of Galerius were appointed instead as Caesars. Dynastic arrangements which would have favoured him and Maximian's son, Maxentius, had been rejected in favour of others which might allow Galerius

to found a dynasty of his own. In AD 306, however, Constantius asked Galerius to allow Constantine to come to Britain, where the Picts had staged an invasion. With some reluctance it was agreed, and Constantine found himself proclaimed emperor by the soldiers stationed in the province, on his father's death at Eburacum (present-day York). Thus the scene was set for a power struggle that ended with Constantine (Flavius Valerius Constantinus) becoming co-emperor in AD 306 and sole emperor in AD 323.

Diocletian hoped to settle the succession in such a way that the frequent usurpations which had dogged the empire between the end of the Severan dynasty in AD 235 and his own seizure of power in AD 284 would be a thing of the past. But he underestimated the impact of his own powerful personality in making a collegiate system of government work. Now that Diocletian was gone it fell apart almost immediately under pressure from the ambitions of military leaders. After Constantine's elevation, Maxentius encouraged the troops in Italy to hail him as well. In AD 307 his father, Maximian, emerged from a retirement which he had not wanted and established himself in Gaul. The events of the next few years were chaotic. Sometimes there were as many as seven rulers, none of them recognized by all their colleagues. For Constantine, however, the unity of the empire was the ultimate goal. The death of Maximian in AD 310 added Gaul and

Spain to his British power-base, while Galerius' death a year later reduced the contenders to four: Constantine in the west, Maxentius in Italy, Licinius in the Balkans, and Maximinus in the east. In AD 312 Constantine invaded Italy, not to champion Christianity as legend soon claimed, but to remove a rival from power, which he did at an engagement close to Rome, at the Mulvian bridge. Afterwards he acquiesced in a Christian interpretation of the victory, so that by the AD 320s Christians living in Rome firmly believed that the emperor had seen a vision with a cross of light on the eve of the battle. The church historian Eusebius of Caesarea, drawing heavily on the writings of Jewish scholar Philo (20 BC – AD 50), went on to found the political philosophy of the Constantinian state, based on the unity of the church and empire under divine providence.

How far Constantine understood Christianity at this stage of his career is hard to tell. On coins Christ had to share the emperor's devotion with Sol, Mars, Jupiter and Hercules for over a decade, although he later said that his Christian faith was inspired by his father's example. Events during the winter of AD 312–313 favoured Constantine and the Christians. The province of Africa had not forgotten his support for its revolt against Maxentius, and by siding with him now assured Rome of its corn supplies, just as Constantine was about to meet Licinius for talks at Milan. The alliance

between the two rulers broke down following Licinius' defeat of Maximinus in AD 314, but another decade passed before Constantine finally overcame his last rival for supreme power. This victory made him become more and more convinced of his divine mission: he was the chosen one, led on by high destiny, and the commands which he was alone privileged to receive were to be obeyed unquestioningly. Thus the church miraculously acquired a generous patron, but at the same time took on a very powerful master, for Constantine's subsequent efforts to settle theological disputes foreshadowed the role of the Byzantine emperor as a latter-day high priest. At the Council of Nicaea in AD 325 he had to exert all his influence to get a creed agreed by the 220 bishops in attendance. Only two failed to accept

The head of the Roman emperor Constantine. A fragment of a gigantic statue once on display in the Basilica of Constantine at Rome.

that 'the Son of God . . . is of one substance with the Father', and were expelled for following Arius' view of the subordination of one to the other. The Libyan Arius (AD 260–366) was the most important of the early Christian heretics and his heterodox views through the missionary enterprise of his followers were to trouble the Catholic church after the loss of the western provinces. For though the Franks and the Anglo-Saxons were easier to convert as pagans, the Visigoths and the Vandals were more resistant because they subscribed to Arianism.

In AD 330 Constantine inaugurated a second capital on the site of the Greek city of Byzantium (modern Istanbul). Named Constantinople, the city was from the first wholly Christian, with no pagan cult sites at all. Constantine was buried in its chief church in AD 337, after a death-bed baptism. The Christian empire that he bequeathed to his sons was capable of defending itself, and especially its eastern provinces to which the political centre of gravity had now moved.

*See* CHRISTIANITY; CONSTANTINOPLE; DIOLETIAN; EUSEBIUS; PHILO; ROME; SEVERAN DYNASTY

*D. Bowder, *The Age of Constantine and Julian* (London, 1978); J. Holland Smith, *Constantine the Great* (New York, 1971).

**Constantinople** (present-day Istanbul) was inaugurated on the site of the classical Greek city of Byzantium in

AD 330. It was a direct result of the Roman emperor Constantine's decision to Christianize the empire. This New Rome was wholly Christian from the outset, with no pagan temples allowed at all. Initially, Constantine (AD 306–337) seems to have thought in terms of an eastern seat of government to complement rather than rival imperial Rome. But on what turned out to be the emperor's last visit to Rome in AD 326, a passionate loathing for paganism overcame him during the customary sacrifices on the Capitol. Rome no longer made him feel at ease, and so imperial officials were ordered to confiscate the assets of pagan temples in order to finance a new capital. The culmination was a splendid city ornamented with great churches, in the chief of which, the Holy Apostles, Constantine was laid to rest.

But the move eastwards was precipitated by much more than religious sentiment. The empire's political centre of gravity had already moved to the Greek-speaking eastern provinces, where its economic and cultural centre had long been. It was a process made transparent in the evoluton of Constantine himself into what might be termed an eastern sovereign. Just as he distanced himself physically from the senate and people of Rome, so he replaced the bay-leaves of his imperial predecessors with a jewel-encrusted diadem, and adopted an elaborate court ritual. His biographer, Eusebius of Caesarea, wrote at the Council of Nicaea in AD 325 how 'the emperor proceeded through the assembly of bishops like an Angel of God, clothed in a garment which glittered as though radiant with light, and adorned with the brilliant splendour of gold and precious stones'. The irresistible rise to supreme power, along with the triumph of Christianity, convinced Constantine of his position as a divinely appointed ruler. The city of Constantinople was thus the expression of the eternal authority which he claimed to wield for the benefit of mankind. It was Constantine's third son, Constantius II (AD 337–361), who gave the city the constitutional prerogatives of Rome: a senate and public offices. Over time the bishop of Constantinople acquired great prestige, in AD 381 being given 'primacy of honour after the bishop of Rome, because it is New Rome'. The new capital's defences were greatly strengthened during the reign of Theodosius II (AD 408–450), when the area enclosed almost doubled. They resisted all sieges and assaults till 1204, and remain impressive ruins today.

*See* Christianity; Constantine; Eusebius; Rome; Theodosius II
★J. E. N. Hearsey, *City of Constantine* (London, 1963); M. Maclagan, *The City of Constantinople* (London, 1968).

**Corinth** was an important city-state situated on the Isthmus, the neck of land joining the Peloponnese to central Greece. Its position encouraged trade and colonization. The second Corin-

thian tyrant Periander built sometime before his death in 585 BC a paved shipway across the Isthmus between the Gulf of Corinth and the Saronic Gulf. Vessels were hauled on a vehicle, the grooves in which its wheels ran still being visible today. In the fifth century BC Corinth suffered a loss of trade through the rise of the Athenian maritime empire, and a bitter dispute with Athens over its colonies at Potidaea in the Chalcidice and Corcyra in the Ionian Sea led to the outbreak of the Peloponnesian War (431–404 BC). Because the Spartans were hesitant about going to war with Athens, even though they considered that Athenian aggression had broken the peace, the Corinthians energetically advocated a declaration of war. The historian Thucydides records how 'the Corinthians, fearing that any further delay might cost them Potidaea, had already sent embassies on their own account to all the allies, urging them to vote for war. They, too, were present

Like Aegina and Athens, Corinth was one of the earliest city-states on mainland Greece to mint coins. Dating from 500 BC, this coin shows Pegasus, the winged steed of the Corinthian hero Bellerophon.

115

at the allied congress of 432 BC, and their representative made the final speech; . . . after which, the majority voted for war.' Much to the grief of Corinth, however, a year went by before serious hostilities started.

But it was the Athenian expedition sent in 415 BC to attack Syracuse that particularly enraged the Corinthians, since the Sicilian city-state was one of their earliest colonies. Yet following the defeat of Athens in 404 BC, Corinth was still prepared to join with Argos, Thebes and Athens in resisting Spartan high-handedness. Once Macedon became the predominant power in 338 BC, Corinth was chosen as the meeting-place of the Greek League, the collective security organization founded by the Macedonian King Philip II (359–336 BC) and continued by his son, Alexander the Great (356–323 BC). A diminished Corinth survived till 146 BC, when as the capital of the Achaean League it was destroyed by the Romans. The later Roman colony sited there in 44 BC had no connection with the old city-state, even though it was promoted as capital of the Roman province of Achaea. The emperor Nero visited it in AD 67, when he theatrically declared 'the freedom of Greece', and tried in vain to cut a canal through the Isthmus.

See ACHAEAN LEAGUE; ATHENS; MACEDON; PELOPONNESIAN WAR; ROME

*J. B. Salmon, *Wealthy Corinth* (Oxford, 1984).

**Crassus** (112–53 BC) was the richest man in late republican Rome. Born of a noble but relatively poor family, he improved his personal finances by becoming the city's greatest landlord. He bought up the property of people outlawed during Sulla's dictatorship (81–79 BC); tricked women into letting him have their land at less than its value; and paid arsonists to set fire discreetly to houses that interested him, while he waited round the corner with a team of firemen. As soon as the owner appeared, Crassus would offer to put out the fire, on condition that the owner agreed to sell him the building. If the owner refused, Crassus would stand back and watch the fire take hold, since Rome possessed no public fire-fighting service. The more damage the fire did, the lower Crassus would drop his price. The vast number of tenements he thus came to own were rented out to poor citizens.

Although he became notorious for his greed, Marcus Licinius Crassus had sober tastes and used his wealth entirely for political purposes. At this time in Rome it was almost impossible to remain rich and hold public office, such was the cost of the feasts and games expected by its citizens. Crassus' driving ambition was to achieve military fame, like a second Alexander the Great. He was, therefore, annoyed in 71 BC that Pompey (106–48 BC) tried to claim the credit for his defeat of the slave leader Spartacus. For the historian Plutarch relates how 'fugitives from the battle fell in with Pompey's troops and were destroyed, so that Pompey, in his dispatch to the senate, was able to say that, while Crassus certainly had overcome the slaves in open battle, he himself had dug up the root of the insurrection'. Not that Crassus could have expected to earn a triumph for his victory over an ignoble enemy like the slaves, no matter the devastation they had caused in southern Italy. But Pompey and Crassus settled their differences, and even combined together in early 60 BC with Julius Caesar (100–44 BC) to form the so-called First Triumvirate. Through this informal alliance they effectively controlled Rome, and in late 55 BC Crassus was given the governorship of the newly annexed province of Syria as well as the chance to lead a campaign against the Parthians. Intelligence of an internal struggle for control of Parthia may have allowed him to fantasize about a glorious conquest 'as far as the Bactrians and the Indians and the external sea', according to Plutarch. But Crassus' war aims were rudely shattered at Carrhae, a city lying between the Euphrates and Tigris rivers, in 53 BC. There the Parthian king Orodes II's brilliant general, Suren, utterly defeated the Roman legionaries and killed Crassus. The would-be conqueror's head was taken in triumph to Ctesiphon, the Parthian capital, where one of the works of the Athenian dramatist Euripides was then being performed in front of the kings of Parthia and Armenia.

Ten thousand Romans were captured at Carrhae. Some were put to work on public works, others settled on the eastern frontier of Parthia. A tantalizing sequel to the battle may have taken place near the Central Asian city of Turfan in 36 BC, when a Chinese general received the surrender of a mercenary force on the capture of a Hunnish Xiongnu chieftain. From the description of their drill, the mercenaries look suspiciously like former Roman legionaries: quite possibly they were survivors of the Carrhae disaster. If so, this was the only occasion in the classical era that Chinese and Roman soldiers met face to face in what was then known in China as the Western Regions.

See CAESAR; PARTHIANS; POMPEY; ROME; SPARTACUS; WARFARE; WESTERN REGIONS
*F. E. Adcock, *The Roman Art of War* (Cambridge, Mass., 1940); A. M. Ward, *Marcus Crassus and the Late Roman Republic* (Columbia, 1977).

**Croesus**, the last king of Lydia (560–546 BC), secured his position only after a struggle with a half-Greek half-brother, Pantaleon. The dynasty to which Croesus belonged, the Mermnads, also had a violent beginning around 685 BC, when Gyges, a member of the royal bodyguard, murdered his predecessor Kandaules, married his wife, and usurped the throne. From this seizure of power the Greeks coined the word tyranny.

Croesus' father, Alyattes (610–

560 BC), continued the expansionist policies first adopted by Gyges, although he was obliged to accept the independence of the city of Miletus. Most of the other Greek settlements of Asia Minor passed under Lydian control during the reigns of Alyattes and Croesus. For under the Mermnads, Lydia developed into a powerful commercial empire, rich in agricultural produce and mineral wealth. The land abounded in flocks and herds, and produced rich harvests of fruit and grain crops; and the mining of precious metals, especially gold and silver, greatly facilitated trade. Because the Lydians did not possess a fleet of their own, they left the moderately taxed overseas trade in the hands of the Greeks, who believed their transactions were made easier by the Lydian invention of coined money. By the sixth century BC the Lydian kings were issuing gold and silver coins, and by the end of the century, coinage was becoming widespread in the Aegean and mainland Greece.

Even though Lydian control had been imposed upon the Ionian Greeks by force, there seems to have been little resentment towards Croesus, who displayed considerable admiration for Greek culture. His court adopted many of the trappings of the Greek way of life, and the king himself made generous donations to Greek sanctuaries. 'Everything,' the historian Herodotus tells us, 'which Croesus sent to Delphi and to the shrine of the Amphiarus came from his own treasure and what

he had inherited from his father; other gifts were originally the property of an enemy, who had opposed him before his reign began and supported the claim of Pantaleon to the throne.' So generous was Croesus that Greeks flocked to his capital at Sardis, including the Athenian lawgiver Solon. Disaster struck Lydia in the form of the Persians, against whom Croesus chose to fight in 546 BC. The Lydian king had sent messengers to the temple of Apollo at Delphi, the sanctuary of Amon in Lybia, and to other holy places. The messengers carried with them many costly gifts, a large number of which were presented to Apollo. To the question whether or not the Lydians should start a war with the Persians the oracle of Apollo gave an ambiguous answer: for the Lydian king was told that he would destroy a mighty empire if he advanced eastwards. He was also advised to find himself a powerful ally, which he did in Sparta. It is quite likely the Spartans had never heard of the Persians before. Initial stalemate was broken by the sheer determination of King Cyrus (559–530 BC), who advanced his Persian and Median army unexpectedly on Sardis. After its capture, the fate of Croesus is uncertain, although a report of his suicide seems most plausible. One legend, however, says that Apollo saved him from a pyre and transported him to safety. Another tradition claims that he became a friend and counsellor of Cyrus. For his former Greek subjects the downfall of Croesus was always associated with the king's excessive self-confidence.

See CYRUS THE GREAT; COINAGE; DELPHI; ORACLES; PERSIA; SOLON; SPARTA; TYRANTS

*J. Boardman, *The Greeks Overseas* (London, 1980).

**Cynicism** was a Greek school of philosophy associated with Diogenes (400–325 BC), who moved to Athens from Sinope on the Black Sea sometime after 362 BC. It is said that this son of a banker was forced to leave his native city because he adulterated its coinage. Without helpful contacts in Athens, Diogenes dossed in a barrel and became known as the 'Dog' because of his total lack of shame: hence cynicism, from the Greek word *cynikos*, meaning 'like a dog'. According to the commentator Diogenes Laertius, he struck upon this simple means of survival by watching a mouse adapt to city life. Whether or not his dependence upon the Athenians fuelled his scorn for contemporary affairs is uncertain, but all Cynics faced the problem that they could loathe society only because it gave them licence to do so. 'The Athenians,' Diogenes admitted, 'have provided me with places to stay, like the portico of Zeus, the hall of processions, and public record office.' He even regarded law as essential to civic life, presumably for the good reason that it provided him with a degree of protection. Diogenes' own apparent anarchism can be seen as an assault on what he regarded as the artificial features of Greek society: manners, money, property, aristocracy, marriage, and intellectual pursuits.

One day the elderly Plato (429–347 BC) invited Diogenes to his house, where he trampled on the carpets and said: 'I trample on Plato's pride.' To which the other philosopher replied: 'Yes, Diogenes, with pride of another sort.' Once asked where in Greece he saw good men, Diogenes answered: 'Good men nowhere, but good boys at Sparta.' Yet the Athenians evidently relished his outrageous utterances, because when a youth broke his barrel, they flogged the culprit and presented Diogenes with another. The focus of attack for Cynics changed after the incorporation in 146 BC of Greece into the Roman empire. Afterwards the pretensions of Rome comprised their target, even though Cynicism soon became something of a counterculture attractive to wealthy young drop-outs. The shortcoming of the protest movement Diogenes started was that it never really developed into a proper philosophy; instead, it relied on moral criticism of a faulty but stable social system. Because of this fundamental weakness, Cynicism was soon outstripped by the teachings of the Stoics; although it could be argued that once Stoicism lost a cynical edge itself, this school also ceased to be radical and tended to interpret the individual's obligations in terms of the conventional expectations of society.

The Akkadian inscription cut on this cylinder records Cyrus' bloodless occupation of Babylon in 539 BC. The Persian troops, 'whose number was immeasurable like water, marched with their arms at their side.'

*See* PLATO; STOICISM

*D. R. Dudley, *A History of Cynicism* (Cambridge, 1937).

**Cyrus the Great** (559–530 BC) was the effective founder of the Persian empire. Starting as a client king of the Medes in Persis, the modern Iranian province of Fars, Cyrus or Kurush rose in revolt and defeated the Medes in 550 BC. A Babylonian chronicler relates how the Median king Astyages 'was taken prisoner and handed over to Cyrus. From the royal city of Ecbatana Cyrus carried off as booty silver, gold, goods and treasures.' As important as this influx of wealth to the Persians was the additional manpower the subject Medes were able to provide for their army. Possibly the clemency that Cyrus exhibited to Astyages was calculated, just as later in 539 BC he allowed the deposed Babylonian king Nabonidus to live out his life in quiet retirement

on a country estate. Quite exceptional was the end of King Croesus of Lydia in 546 BC: this defeated monarch seems to have committed suicide. Cyrus also subjugated the Greek cities of Asia Minor, whose citizens he regarded with some disdain. A feudal aristocrat himself, Cyrus despised the Greek addiction to trade and the free exchange of opinions that went with it. He expected absolute obedience as the King of Kings, the favourite of Ahura Mazda, the chief Iranian deity. For that reason Cyrus, and his immediate successors, always preferred to exercise authority through pro-Greek tyrants.

A quite unsolicited accolade was bestowed upon Cyrus by the Old Testament. His decision to return the Jews to their homeland ended the so-called Babylonian captivity: as their liberator, the Persian king was, according to the prophet Isaiah, Yahweh's anointed. In the Book of Ezra, too, there is preserved one of Cyrus' proclamations, the Hebrew version translates as follows: 'Thus says Cyrus the king of Persia: Yahweh, the God of Heaven, has given me all the kingdoms of the earth, and he has charged me to build him a house at Jerusalem.' Whilst Sheshbazzar, the appointed Jewish ruler, was expected to be loyal to Cyrus, the Persian respect for the religious sensibilities of a subject people shown in the edict contrasts sharply with the Hellenizing policies of the later Seleucid dynasty (312–64 BC), which gave rise to the Maccabean revolt.

One of the direct results of Cyrus' many conquests was the development of the Persian homeland. Cyrus founded the new royal city of Pasargadae, named after his own tribe. The new city drew craftsmen from the ends of the new empire and gave tangible form to Persian aspirations in ceremonial buildings. Yet Cyrus' own tomb was modest, a gabled structure set on a stepped platform after the style of Asia Minor. His death in 530 BC occurred during a campaign in Central Asia. The war against the nomadic Massagete, according to the historian Herodotus, was 'more violent than any other fought between foreign nations', not least because neither side were 'willing to give ground once battle was joined'. Daggers and spears soon replaced bows and arrows, till Cyrus fell with the bulk of his forces. His loss did not undermine Persian power, however. For his son Cambyses (530–522 BC) continued the policy of expansion, Egypt falling to Persian arms in 525 BC. Its conquest turned Persia into the classical world's first superpower.

See CAMBYSES; CROESUS; EGYPT; JEWS; PERSIA; SELEUCIDS

*J. M. Cook, *The Persian Empire* (London, 1983).

**Cyrus the Younger** (423–401 BC) was the second son of the Persian king Darius II (424–405 BC). It was customary for a new ruler to enter a temple dedicated to a potent war goddess at Pasargadae, the site of the elder Cyrus' tomb, the founder of the Persian empire. Inside the king would eat a simple meal and then put on a royal robe. When it was time for his elder brother Artaxerxes II (404–359 BC) to go through this coronation ritual, Cyrus concealed himself in the temple with a dagger, but he was denounced by one of the officiating priests. Only the pleas of his mother saved him from execution. His forgiving brother sent Cyrus back to Asia Minor as governor at Sardis, where in 401 BC he recruited a Greek mercenary force and marched eastwards in order to seize the throne. The Athenian soldier and author Xenophon (428–354 BC) was one of the so-called Ten Thousand who followed Cyrus until the battle of Cunaxa, where the would-be usurper was killed. In the action Cyrus broke through to his brother, whom he wounded and unhorsed. But his impetuosity carried him still deeper

into the enemy ranks, and in the confused fighting he fell. After the battle
Cyrus' head and right hand were cut
off. King Artaxerxes survived, as did
the undefeated Ten Thousand; they
marched back from Babylon to Asia
Minor via the Black Sea.

*See* XENOPHON

*Xenophon, *The Persian Expedition*, trans.
by R. Warner (Bristol, 1981).

# D

Daoism was in classical China both a philosophy and a popular religion, especially during the troubled times following the end of the Han dynasty (202 BC – AD 220). Casting doubt on man's place in society, Daoism looked upon social conventions as evil and called upon mankind to break loose from society's stifling embrace, shake off the fetters of man-made duties and obligations, and follow an unsullied and simple existence in harmony with the natural world. Its founder, Lao Zi, was an older contemporary and antagonist of Confucius (551–479 BC). For Lao Zi the whole edifice of feudalism was corrupting, and the actual cause of China's problems. A preoccupation with kinship and ceremony was all that Confucius seemed to be offering as a solution. 'Those that tell don't know,' complained Lao Zi, 'and those that know, don't tell.'

Daoist quietism was practised notably by Zhuang Zi (350–275 BC), who rejected the premiership of the huge, southern state of Chu. As he said at the time: 'A thief steals a purse and is hanged, while another steals a state and becomes a prince.' In the turmoil of the Warring States period (481–221 BC), the only sensible policy for the sage was to live the life of a recluse. Withdrawal from service in government, or becoming a hermit, did not of course develop Daoism as a practical philosophy. The only Daoists who attended feudal courts and, later, imperial ones, were experts in geomancy. They pursued the elixir of life, a will-o'-the-wisp peculiarly attractive to

A Doaist recluse. At times of disorder in China many scholars were drawn to Doaist quietism.

123

Chinese rulers. Prior to his early death in 210 BC, the First Emperor was to devote a fortune to this end, dispatching embassies to the tops of mountains in order to establish relations with the immortals as well as sending them overseas to find 'the three isles where the spirits live'. Absurd though this seems now, it has been plausibly argued that in Daoist observation of natural phenomena and experiments in alchemy are the dim beginnings of scientific method.

In Daoist religion, however, a revolutionary outlook flourished in the countryside, where the need for solace amongst the peasantry in the second and third centuries AD made its disdain for social conformity very popular. Chang Daoling, the first heavenly teacher of the Daoist church, even established for a time a small, semi-independent state. His organization of peasants in a quasi-religious, quasi-military movement was the first of many such ventures. It is reputed that Chang Daoling dramatically acquired immortality when in AD 156 he disappeared except for his clothes. In AD 215 the strength of Daoism in the countryside of north China caused the warlord Cao Cao (AD 155–220) to treat with dignity the defeated leader of the Five Pecks of Grain movement, another heavenly teacher.

See CONFUCIUS; HUNDRED SCHOOLS; LAO ZI; ZHUANG ZI

*A. Waley, *The Way and its Power: A Study of the Tao Teh Ching and its Place in Chinese Thought* (London, 1934).

**Darius I**, king of Persia 521–486 BC, was in all probability a regicide and usurper. For the circumstances of his predecessor's death have never been satisfactorily explained. Cambyses (530–522 BC) is said to have leaped onto his horse in a hurry and accidentally stabbed himself in the thigh, with fatal consequences. Whatever the truth, Darius had to face widespread rebellion on his accession to the throne. The great rock-face inscription at Behistun, in the modern Iranian province of Fars, is quite frank about the intensity of the struggle during 522–521 BC. It also makes clear Darius' personal debt to a handful of magnates, who commanded sizeable personal followings. 'My supporters,' reads the inscription, 'are Vindafarna, son of Vayaspara, a Persian; Utana, son of Thukhra, a Persian; Gaubaruva, son of Marduniya, a Persian; Vidarna, son of Bagabigna, a Persian; Bagabukhsha, son of Datuvahya, a Persian; Ardumanish, son of Vahauka, a Persian. Says Darius the king: You shall be king hereafter, protect well the families of these men.' Behind this convulsion must have been the political strains that unprecedented territorial expansion had placed on Persian society. Under Cyrus the Great (559–530 BC) and his son Cambyses the Persian empire had become a power without equal in the classical world.

Darius, the son of Hystaspes, belonged to another branch of the Achaemenids, the Persian royal family. He was on Cambyses' staff during the annexation of Egypt (525–522 BC), and with him on his death in Syria. That Darius was able to confront, and eventually overcome, so many opponents indicates that he had gained the loyalty of Cambyses' crack troops. Together with his Persian allies, he won the empire so convincingly that further foreign conquests were soon possible. North-western India was added, then some of the Aegean islands, and Thrace. Successes against the Scythians in Central Asia were not repeated in Europe, however. An expedition across the Danube in 512 BC ended in a stalemate, but it was becoming obvious that Persia meant business in Europe. For a start, it controlled all sea-traffic through the Bosporus, and thus the transport of Russian grain to mainland Greece. Egypt, the other great granary of the eastern Mediterranean, was already under Persian control, so the rising Greek population faced a real threat to its food-supply. How far westwards Darius originally intended to push the imperial frontier is impossible to guess, even though a Persian naval intelligence mission is known to have surveyed the coasts and harbours, not only of mainland Greece, but also of southern Italy. What provoked him into a westward move was the Ionian revolt (499–494 BC) during which the mainland states of Athens and Eretria sent some naval support to their rebellious cousins in Asia Minor. The rising amongst the Greek cities there took the Persians by surprise, and Darius'

authority was only re-established by hard fighting.

Afterwards the Persian king harboured a hatred for both the Athenians and the Eretrians. The historian Herodotus recalls that he maintained a servant whose sole job was to repeat the injunction 'Remember Athens'. By 490 BC a Persian expedition was ready to sail with orders to 'reduce Athens and Eretria to slavery and to bring the slaves before the king'. As a pro-Persian ruler at Athens it was intended to reinstall as tyrant the elderly Hippias, who had been expelled in 510 BC. It was he who suggested Marathon, on the northern coast of Attica, as a beach-head, after the Euboean city of Eretria was betrayed to the Persians. Marathon offered a suitable place to deploy cavalry, being a small plain situated

Darius I, carved in relief at Behistin. In 490 BC his attack on Greece was thwarted by the Athenians and their allies, the Plataeans, at Marathon.

125

between mountains and sea. Clever tactics, good discipline, and better body-armour gave the day to the Athenians and their Plataean allies, however. The Athenian aristocrat Miltiades (*c.* 550-489 BC) drew upon personal experience of Persian tactics to secure the stunning victory: 6,000 Persians were killed for a loss of 192 Greeks. Arriving too late to take part in the battle, the Spartans could only view the Persian dead and congratulate the victors.

Darius did not vent his anger at the repulse on the Eretrians, who were resettled near the royal city of Susa. The other great ceremonial centre was to the south at Persepolis. Building these cities was a preoccupation of Darius' final years, but the Greek refusal to give earth and water as a sign of submission to Persia rankled, as one Athenian knew it would. 'In Athens,' the historian Plutarch wrote, 'everyone except Themistocles believed that the Persian defeat at Marathon meant the end of the war. He alone realized that it was only the prelude to a far greater struggle, sensing the danger while it was still far away. So it was that he put his city into training to meet it.' The eventual showdown occurred during 480–479 BC, when Xerxes I (486–465 BC), Darius' son, failed just as decisively to subdue the Greek city-states. Although the Persian invasion became the 'great event' of classical history in Greece, for the Persians it was never more than a lost frontier war. Gold was soon discovered by the Persian kings to be an effective instrument for wearing down Greek strength: switching subsidies from one city-state to another helped to sustain those internecine wars which plagued classical Greece. In Persian history, therefore, Darius was regarded as a colossus, an all-powerful ruler, who was remembered for his saying: 'What was said to them by me, night and day it was done.'

*See* ATHENS; CAMBYSES; CYRUS THE GREAT; EGYPT; IONIAN REVOLT; MILTIADES; PERSIA; PERSIAN INVASIONS; SCYTHIANS
*M. A. Dandamaev, *A Political History of the Achaemenid Empire* (Leiden, 1989); Herodotus, *The Histories*, trans. by A. de Sélincourt (Harmondsworth, 1954).

**Delian League** is the modern name for the Greek alliance organized by the Athenians in 478–477 BC at a conference held on the sacred island of Delos. Its aim was to carry on the war against Persia after the defeat of King Xerxes' great invasion of mainland Greece in 480–479 BC. According to the historian Thucydides, the Spartans no longer wished to be burdened with fighting overseas, following the disgrace of their commander Pausanias: 'They regarded the Athenians as being perfectly capable of exercising the command and as being also at that time friendly to themselves. So Athenians took over the leadership, and the allies, because of their dislike of Pausanias' dictatorial manner, were pleased to see them do so. Then the Athenians assessed the various contributions to be made for the war against Persia, and decided which states should furnish money and which states should send ships: the object of this annual levy was to compensate themselves for their losses by ravaging the territories of the Persian king.'

The respected Athenian general Aristides (*c.* 525–467 BC) was responsible for fixing the quota of each contributory state. The financial contributions, initially fixed at 460 talents, were to be held under the care of twelve Athenian officials at Delos, where Thucydides adds 'representative meetings were held in the temple of Apollo'. The initial membership of the Delian League comprised 20 city-states from the Aegean islands, 36 from Ionia, 35 from the Hellespont, 34 from Caria, and 33 from Thrace. There were no Peloponnesian members at all because the league was primarily an organization for Greeks living on the coastline and islands of the Aegean. The oath that sealed the league's constitution reveals the leading role of Athens: on its behalf Aristides swore, while an Ionian swore for all the other members. But leadership was not immediately domination. In the early years of the league, the Athenians only exercised what Thucydides called a 'hegemony over autonomous allies who participated in representative meetings'. In these meetings each member, including Athens, could cast but a single vote.

Until 453 BC the treasury of the

A fragment from the tribute list for the year 440–439 BC. By then the league's treasury had been moved from Delos to Athens.

league remained on Delos; after that date it was transferred to the acropolis in Athens. Prior to this critical event the Athenians had become more despotic, according to Thucydides, through having to deal with attempted defections of league members. In 470 BC the island of Naxos was the first ally to be subjugated for rebelling from the league. Naxos was forbidden a navy and henceforth paid tribute only; a garrison may also have been installed. Though the league approved the swift Athenian action taken against Naxos, the compulsion rankled with some members, as did the insistence that there was to be no relaxation of obligations in the conflict against a now less threatening Persia. From the league's inauguration a distinction had been drawn between those states who pro-

127

vided ships and manned them and those who paid money instead. The burden of the ship-providers was usually heavier than those who were not and yet received protection. Heaviest of all was the burden borne by Athens, although its provision of the greatest number of ships in the league's fleet was not unpopular with poorer Athenian citizens who received regular payment as oarsmen. Booty obviously helped to meet some of the costs of campaigning, but it was not long before most of the allies allowed their annual assessments to be changed from ships to money. As the allied naval contribution dwindled, Athens' own position became ever more dominant until just before the outbreak of the Peloponnesian War in 431 BC it was obvious that the league had turned into an Athenian empire. This domination went largely unchallenged by the subject-allies till the Athenian expedition to Sicily met with disaster in 413 BC. Afterwards rebellion was widespread and the decline in imperial revenue for Athens, at a time when Sparta was receiving substantial Persian subsidies, meant an end to Athenian control of an overseas empire. The smaller league which Athens led in the fourth century BC was never really a thorough-going empire.

See ARISTIDES; ATHENS; CIMON; PELOPONNESIAN WAR; PERSIA; SICILIAN EXPEDITION

*S. Hornblower, The Greek World, 479–323 BC (London, 1983); R. Meiggs, The Athenian Empire (Oxford, 1972); J. K. Davies, Democracy and Classical Greece (London, 1978).

**Delos**, a tiny island in the central Aegean, was believed to be the birthplace of the twins Apollo and Artemis, the Greek god of music, archery and oracles and the Greek goddess of beasts and wild places respectively. Sacred to Apollo from earliest times, Delos attracted Athenian attention during the tyranny of Pisistratus (died 527 BC). Divine approbation in the guise of favourable oracles was important to tyrants, especially when their opponents in exile managed to effect the utterances themselves. Thus Pisistratus was forced to patronize Apollo's shrine on Delos because in the 530s BC his enemies were too well entrenched at Delphi, the chief oracle of the god. Having secured the neighbouring island of Naxos by supporting the local tyrant, Pisistratus exhumed the dead whose graves were in sight of the precinct, reburying them elsewhere on Delos, and then in the purified sanctuary he rebuilt the temple in Attic limestone. Though the task was also motivated by a desire to enhance Athens' political influence, the awe in which the classical Greeks held their gods was profound. Even the Persians, when in 490 BC they sailed across the Aegean on their way to attack Eretria and Athens, dared not pass Delos without sacrificing to both Apollo and Artemis and burnt upon the altar there an immense amount of frankincense. After their departure, the historian Herodotus notes, occurred the only earth tremor ever known on the sacred isle; he says that 'the shock was a divine sign to warn men of the troubles yet to come'. Not to be outdone by Pisistratus, the Samian tyrant Polycrates (c. 535–522 BC) captured the adjoining island of Rheneia and by a chain attached it to Delos as an offering to Apollo.

It is hardly surprising that the island was chosen in 478–477 BC for the first meeting of the anti-Persian league sponsored by Athens, following the defeat of King Xerxes' invasion of Greece. The Athenian general Aristides (c. 525–467 BC) was the architect of the new alliance, fixing the contribution of each member state. Oaths were sworn to have the same friends and the same enemies, and the league's permanence was symbolized by the dropping of iron weights into the sea: what we now term the Delian League was to last until the weights rose up again. Until 453 BC the league's treasury remained on Delos. But after the loss of a large expedition sent to aid the rebellious Persian province of Egypt, this financial reserve was moved to Athens for safe-keeping. Perhaps taking a leaf out of Pisistratus' book, the democratic leader Pericles (c. 495–429 BC) then placed emphasis on the sanctuary of the vegetation goddess Demeter at Eleusis, to the south-west of Athens. With the Athenians well on the way to convert-ing the league into an empire, they doubtless believed that they needed a major religious centre of their own.

Delos was not entirely forgotten. In 426 BC the Athenians undertook a second purification, and eight years later a festival was established to cele-brate a newly built temple for Apollo. When at the end of the Peloponnesian War in 404 BC Athens surrendered to Sparta, the administration of Delos reverted to a local official and the island became a miniature city-state. It flour-ished as a centre of the corn trade till the Romans accused the Delians of supporting the last Macedonian king Perseus (179–168 BC). Two years after his defeat at Pydna, Rome in 166 BC allowed its ally Athens to expel the island's inhabitants and replace them with Athenian settlers. For nearly a century Delos was one of the chief centres of international trade in the eastern Mediterranean, its speciality being slaves, some 10,000 being said to change hands daily. Even though this figure is exaggerated, the swiftness of the market at Delos is preserved in a popular saying: 'A merchant ship docks, a cargo is sold.' Commercial decline began with the struggle between Rome and Mithridates VI of Pontus (120–63 BC). By the time Corinth was refounded in 44 BC as a Roman colony and centre of trade, Delos was already off the main trade-routes; afterwards, it swiftly became a deserted ruin.

See ATHENS; DELIAN LEAGUE; DELPHI;

ORACLES; SLAVERY; TYRANTS
*E. Melas, *Temples and Sanctuaries of Ancient Greece* (London, 1973).

**Delphi**, situated on the slopes of Mount Parnassus in Phocis, central Greece, was originally a sanctuary dedicated to Python. This serpent sent up revelations through a fissure in the rock; a priestess, the Pythia, inhaling its potent breath, was thus inspired to give voice to cryptic utterances – the prophecies of the Delphic oracle. The Greek god Apollo killed Python and took its place. Another legend made the dispossessed creature a she-dragon named Delphyne, 'the womb-like'; hence the name of Delphi.

Unlike Olympia, where athletic contests were also staged, Delphi attracted musical contestants because Apollo was credited with the invention of the lyre. And unlike Olympia, which dozed between its famous games, Delphi was always busy, thanks to its oracle. By no means the only oracular shrine, it was the most respected one in classical Greece and consulted by individuals as well as states. Either in late 481 BC or early 480 BC the Athenians sent two envoys to Delphi to inquire what to do in the face of an imminent invasion by the Persian army under the command of King Xerxes. The situation was little short of desperate, since Athens could not be defended by land. The only viable course of action, according to

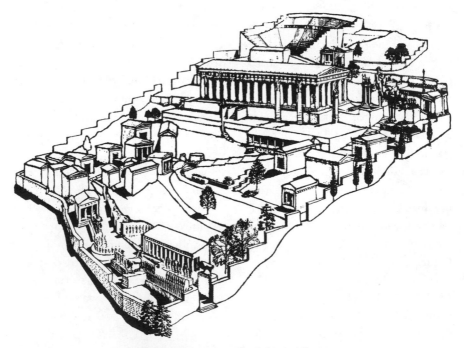

Delphi, the foremost oracle of classical Greece.

the democratic leader Themistocles (*c.* 528–462 BC), was to evacuate the entire population to the nearby island of Salamis and risk a naval engagement with its as yet untried fleet. According to the historian Plutarch, 'the majority of the Athenians felt that they did not want victory on these terms and that safety meant nothing to them if it required that they should abandon the temples of their gods and the tombs of their forefathers to the enemy'.

At this point Themistocles, seeing no hope of winning support for his plan by rational argument, endeavoured to influence public opinion through oracles and omens. 'He seized upon the episode of the sacred snake,' Plutarch tells us, 'in order to persuade the Athenians to leave the doomed city.' It had refused food and then disappeared from its enclosure on the acropolis. Themistocles also interpreted the oracle received from Delphi to mean that Athens' salvation lay in a 'wooden wall' of ships. Eventually the Athenians adopted Themistocles' plan and at the naval battle of Salamis defeated the Persian fleet in the autumn of 480 BC. After the Persians were thrown out of Europe a year later many statues, trophies and treasuries were set up as thank-offerings at Delphi. It became indeed something of a museum as the various treasuries belonging to the city-states were filled with booty. Inscriptions carefully explained to visitors the details of each victory, for a famous sanctuary like Delphi offered a place to prominently display a state's military achievements. Greek sanctuaries were a perfect arena for competition, both in terms of their games and their dedications.

Delphi was itself an object of military competition in the 350s BC. A Phocian general seized its treasury and hired 10,000 mercenaries to fight what was oddly entitled the Third Sacred War. In 352 BC King Philip of Macedon ended the seizure at an engagement where his men wore laurel wreaths as warriors of Apollo. In 279 BC a Celtic attack was repulsed, but despoliation began in earnest under the Romans. The Roman dictator Sulla plundered the sanctuary in 86 BC, the job being completed by the emperor Nero (AD 54–68). He had 500 statues removed to Rome. By the visit of the travel writer Pausanias, in the second century AD, the outward appearance of Delphi had been restored, but rather as a classical theme park than a sacred site. The oracle was hardly ever consulted, and Pausanias' guide was intended primarily for antiquarians.

*See* MUSIC; OLYMPIA; ORACLES; PERSIAN INVASIONS; SACRED WARS; THEMISTOCLES

*J. Fontenrose, *The Delphic Oracle* (Berkeley, 1978); C. Morgan, *Athletes and Oracles: The Transformation of Olympia and Delphi in the Eighth Century BC* (Cambridge, 1990).

**Demetrius I**, king of Macedon 294–283 BC. The son of Antigonus, one of Alexander the Great's commanders, Demetrius was born in 336 BC. Although his father's ambitious scheme to reunite the lands conquered by

One of the more flamboyant Macedonian kings, Demetrius was a better admiral than a general. This coin, minted on Cyprus in 290 BC, celebrates his naval victories with a reference to the sea god Poseidon.

Alexander (356–323 BC) came to nought, Demetrius conducted numerous campaigns for him, and later on his own behalf. A celebrated failure was the siege of Rhodes (305–304 BC), from which Demetrius gained the nickname of 'the besieger'. His father's stronghold comprised Asia Minor and Syria, although his sphere of influence included the Aegean islands except Rhodes and Crete, the Peloponnese and central Greece, the island of Cyprus, and Palestine. For the final showdown at Ipsus in 301 BC with the rivals of Antigonus, Demetrius was recalled from Athens, a city he was skilfully defending from Cassander (c. 358–297 BC). There Demetrius had behaved in flamboyant fashion. Taking over the rear chamber of the Parthenon as living quarters for himself and his harem, Demetrius spent his spare time partying. Athenian wits said that the goddess Athena received her guest in person.

But it was at the battle of Ipsus (modern Sipsin in Asia Minor) that Antigonus was finally defeated and killed. This engagement was decided through the manoeuvre of a corps of elephants, which had been given to Seleucus (358–281 BC), Antigonus' rival in Babylon, by the first Mauryan ruler Candragupta in return for renouncing any claim to north-western India. According to the historian Plutarch, the problem was the rashness of Demetrius, who commanded the cavalry: 'He fought brilliantly and put the enemy to flight, but by pressing the pursuit too far and too impulsively he threw away the victory. The enemy placed their elephants to block his return and he was prevented from rejoining the infantry: meanwhile Seleucus, seeing that his opponent's phalanx was unprotected by cavalry, altered his own tactics accordingly.'

132

Mounted archers came into action, and harassed Antigonus' infantry from a distance, as the Romans were later to do to Antiochus III, a descendant of Seleucus, at the battle of Magnesia in 190 or 189 BC. Under the constant harassment, the infantrymen lost their nerve, so that large numbers defected or fled. In the hope that Demetrius would come to the rescue, Antigonus fought to the last, 'until the enemy overwhelmed him with a cloud of javelins and he fell'.

After the battle the territories of Antigonus were divided among the victors – Lysimachus (360–281 BC) acquired Asia Minor, and Seleucus Syria. The Egyptian ruler Ptolemy I (367–282 BC) received nothing for the good reason that he had failed to participate in the decisive battle. Demetrius escaped to Greece, where he set about restoring his military fortunes. Intrigue and murder in Macedon gave him his chance, and in 294 BC he was acclaimed by the Macedonian army as king. But the dynasty which Demetrius founded, the Antigonids, was not secure till the reign of his son Antigonus Gonatas (276–239 BC). Because Demetrius remained a campaigner rather than a ruler, the war-weary Macedonians deserted him in 288 BC. An expedition he mounted in Asia shortly afterwards with a force of mercenaries went wrong, and the restless Demetrius found himself in 285 BC a prisoner of Seleucus. 'After living for three years in confinement,' Plutarch reports, 'he fell sick through inactivity and over-indulgence in food and wine and died in his fifty-fifth year.'

See ANTIGONUS; CASSANDER; LYSI-MACHUS; MACEDON; PTOLEMIES; RHODES

*Plutarch, *The Age of Alexander: Nine Greek Lives*, trans. by I. Scott-Kilvert (Harmondsworth, 1973).

**Demosthenes** (384–322 BC) was in Athens the outspoken opponent of Philip II of Macedon. He endeavoured to contrive an effective alliance against him without success, following Philip's move into Thrace in 352 BC. For the growing strength of Macedon and the perennial bickering of the Greek city-states doomed Demosthenes' efforts to failure. Just before Thebes and Athens jointly went to war with Philip in 340–339 BC, Demosthenes warned the Athenians about the dangers of complacency. 'On seeing the multitude of goods and the plentiful supplies in the market,' he protested, 'you let yourselves be beguiled as if the city were not exposed to any threat.' The Macedonian seizure of the fleet bringing grain to feed Athens from the Black Sea shortly afterwards confirmed his point exactly. But probably there was nothing Demosthenes could have done to save the Greek city-state, notwithstanding the view of the philosopher Aristotle (384–322 BC) that it was the best organization for civilized life. By this time his ideal of the free association of the villages of a hinterland with a larger settlement as a political entity was almost lost. Incessant warfare had impoverished many small states while enriching the large ones, and the appearance of mercenaries meant that the old link between voting as a citizen and fighting in the ranks was becoming tenuous. At the battle of Chaeronea in 338 BC even the Athenian contingent included at least 2,000 mercenaries.

Although this decisive defeat of Thebes and Athens left Philip master of Greece, Demosthenes did not abandon public life and held office during the period of Macedonian dominance. In 335 BC he was lucky not to be handed over to Philip's son, Alexander the Great, because of the aid he had given to the Thebans in their abortive rebellion. But Demosthenes soon became involved in anti-Macedon activities again and in 322 BC he was obliged to commit suicide. His collected speeches have been admired by orators for centuries.

See ALEXANDER THE GREAT; ATHENS; PHILIP II; THEBES

*R. Sealey, *Demosthenes and His Time: A Study in Defea*t (Oxford, 1993).

**Diocletian**, Roman emperor AD 284–305, was born around AD 240 of a poor Dalmatian family. Gaius Aurelius Valerius Diocletianus rose to power through the army, the sole arbiter of imperial power in the late Roman empire. His immediate problems were foreign invasions (German attacks across the Danube and an Arab inva-

sion of Syria), as well as widespread unrest in the western provinces. In Britain, for instance, a full-scale rebellion by the Roman naval commander of the Channel had led to the establishment of a separate kingdom (AD 287–296). To deal with these various threats and return the empire to stable government, Diocletian chose to rely on the collegiate exercise of authority by two senior emperors (Augusti) and two juniors (Caesars). He selected as his fellow Augustus the Dalmatian Maximian in AD 286, and seven years later the Dacian Galerius and the Danubian Constantius became their respective Caesars. Discounting propaganda later put out by Constantius' son, Constantine the Great (AD 306–337), that his family descended from noble ancestors, the uniformly humble origins of these northern provincials indicate just how far political power had shifted from Italy. It was understood that the juniors would automatically move up to the top positions on the death or abdication of their respective senior rulers. Adoption and marriage ties were intended to strengthen the bonds between the four imperial families. There was no territorial division of the empire: all four rulers had authority everywhere. By this new constitutional arrangement Diocletian hoped to avoid the civil wars which had dogged Rome since the fall of the Severan dynasty (AD 193–235). It was to prove a vain hope, although Diocletian's parallel simplification of provincial organization did much to expedite decision-making. What this radical reform introduced was greater local control through the reduction in the size but increase in the number of provinces, whilst at the same time grouping provinces into large administrative dioceses in order to facilitate a regional response to specific crises.

The Roman emperors Diocletian and Maximian, joint rulers who were supported by two deputies. Despite the show of co-operation, the empire remained under strain from personal ambition.

After Constantius reconquered Britain in AD 296, the Roman part of the island was divided into first two, then four provinces. A decade later Constantius returned as an Augustus to repulse an invasion by the Picts, and counterattacked to the far north of Scotland. The wall built by Hadrian across northern Britain was repaired, as well as the city-wall of Eburacum (present-day York). There Constantius died in the summer of AD 306, and his son Constantine was proclaimed as his successor by the troops, even though he was not a Caesar. Constantine soon had to leave Britain to fight for power, which he partly won at the battle of the Mulvian bridge near Rome in AD 312. Thus Diocletian's system broke down at its first test. Yet his administrative reforms left the empire much more tightly controlled and homogeneous than before. There was less tolerance for non-conforming groups in such a highly structured society, and so it was hardly surprising that the persecution of Christians which began in earnest in AD 303 should have been the most severe trial to afflict the early church. They had dared to challenge Diocletian's insistence upon the sanctity of the throne, and the divinely ordained order of the empire. 'Our laws protect nothing that is not holy,' ran an imperial edict, 'and thus Roman majesty has attained so great an extent by favour of the divine powers.' That in less than twenty years Constantine could invoke the same divine favour from the Christian deity merely underlines the current strength of autocracy. All were expected to perform their duties for the benefit of the empire, and not least to look after the needs of its army. A papyrus from Egypt offers an insight into the new degree of regulation: a woman who could not supply two animals for transport duty because one of them was sick had to write a formal report outlining the circumstances and asking to be excused.

From the start of the persecution Diocletian recognized the danger of making Christian martyrs. No blood, he insisted, must be shed. Instead, Christians were recalled to the worship of the Roman pantheon, while their churches and books suffered systematic destruction. Though no demand was made for public sacrifice to pagan deities, the loss of privileges, rights, and offices struck the Christian community hard. Had illness and old age not forced Diocletian to retire to his palace at Salonae (modern Split in Croatia), the growth of Christian influence might have been slowed. As it was, his Caesar and successor Galerius turned the persecution into an all-out war against the church, thereby bringing the religious issue to a head. Even this persecutor had to acknowledge, on his death-bed in AD 311, that the gods he worshipped could not restore his health, and in a vain hope of succour from the Christian deity Galerius ended the persecution. But the bitter division he had caused throughout the empire was not readily forgotten. In the end, it was Constantine who resolved the conflict by making Christianity the state religion. Politics as well as the strength of Christian conviction decided the issue.

See CHRISTIANITY; CONSTANTINE; ROME

★S. Williams, *Diocletian and the Roman Recovery* (London, 1985).

**Dionysius I** (*c.* 430–367 BC) was a tyrant of Syracuse, the chief Greek city of Sicily. His rise to absolute power was directly connected with the threat posed by Carthage, but conditions suited to a tyranny in part derived from the Athenian siege of the city between 415 and 413 BC. During this investment the whole population had concentrated within the city walls, and the military importance of the landless urban population and the poorer farmers became evident. There was a shift in the balance of political power away from the aristocrats, with a democratic constitution coming into force shortly after 412 BC. The fledgeling democracy, however, was quickly threatened by Carthaginian attack. Uncertainty also increased as a result of fighting between political factions, in which Dionysius was himself wounded. He seems to have set his mind on a tyranny in 406 BC, after serving with distinction against the Carthaginians. Playing on the prejudice and fears of his fellow citizens, Dionysius succeeded in being elected as a general with plenipotentiary power, a position which he was able to transform into an outright military dictatorship.

Having spread a rumour that his fellow generals were secretly negotiating with the enemy, Dionysius posed as the true defender of Syracusan freedom. When he threatened to resign in protest, the citizen assembly voted him the exceptional authority he desired. On manoeuvre at Leontini, a city to the north-west of Syracuse, Dionysius' friends shortly afterwards persuaded the army to provide him with a personal bodyguard of 600 soldiers. Away from his aristocratic opponents, he used the Syracusan army as an assembly, gaining ready support from its younger members. Then Dionysius returned to Syracuse and in its harbour took over Ortygia, or Quail Island, as a stronghold. But lack of success against the Carthaginians in 405 BC almost cost Dionysius his newly acquired power, for the Syracusans resented the unfavourable peace that he had made, and besieged him on Ortygia. Only the resolution of his closest followers appears to have steadied his nerve, since Dionysius is reported to have talked of ending his brief reign in a blaze of glory. 'Tyranny,' he said, 'is a noble winding-sheet.' In the event Dionysius survived through the arrival of mercenaries by sea, probably from the Peloponnese. Ambitious Lysander (died 395 BC) almost certainly spoke for Dionysius in Sparta.

Thereafter Dionysius relied upon mercenaries, although citizens from Syracuse and allied Greek cities served in his army too. A second war with Carthage (397–392 BC) allowed the tyrant to make peace on better terms. By 390 BC Sicily was virtually divided into two spheres of influence – Carthage controlled the western end of the island, Syracuse the rest. For the first time the native Sicels in the interior came under Greek domination. Later Dionysius intervened in southern Italy, or Magna Graecia,

'Great Greece', as it was then known. Renewed fighting with Carthage (382–375 BC) ended in defeat and an unfavourable peace, much to the dismay of the Syracusans. There is little doubt that Dionysius' restless energy and ambition prolonged the conflict with Carthage. Except for the single moment of doubt recorded in 405 BC, Dionysius believed in his destiny as a ruler. The philosopher Plato (429–347 BC), who visited Syracuse, made the most serious criticism of his tyranny when he commented on a policy for ever stirring up war. In his personal relations with those who were loyal to him, Dionysius was always consistently generous. But he is supposed to have forcibly reminded his courtiers of their position when the flattery of Damocles once became excessive. The apocryphal story has Damocles feasting with a sword suspended just above his head.

See CARTHAGE; LYSANDER; SICELS; SYRACUSE; TYRANTS

*B. Caven, *Dionysius I: Warlord of Sicily* (New Haven, 1990).


**Dong Zhongshu** (*c.* 179–*c.* 104 BC) never attained high office under the Han emperors, but he affected Chinese political thought more significantly than most of those who served as ministers. For it was his reinterpretation of Confucian philosophy which linked the exercise of imperial rule with the structure of the universe, and which was destined to become the ideological mainstay of the Chinese empire. His chief work was entitled *Luxuriant Gems of the Spring and Autumn Annals*, a study of events connected with the decline of feudalism during the so-called Spring and Autumn period (770–481 BC). Appointed a 'scholar of wide learning' by Emperor Han Jing Di (157–141 BC), Dong Zhongshu developed his idea of a close correspondence between the natural world and mankind. This was particularly evident in his reassertion of the theory of the heavenly mandate. 'Heaven,' he wrote, 'bestowed a mandate to rule on the Han, for the reason that Qin had grown tyrannical. So Han was able to overthrow Qin. The one in possession of Heaven's favour smote the one lacking it.' Thus, Dong Zhongshu argued, a ruler's position was granted and taken away by Heaven, whose agents for affecting change could be humble men such as the first Han emperor Liu Bang, an illiterate but virtuous peasant supported by the mass of the people. Originally put forward as a theory of justified rebellion by Mencius (371–288 BC), Dong Zhongshu's notion of a heavenly limitation on the exercise of imperial power formed the basis of China's constitution until the end of the imperial system in 1911. Imperial power always rested, of course, upon technical efficiency, but the ability of a dynasty to endure also related to the acquiescence of the governed and the means by which they could effect political changes. It happened in China that offensive weapons were superior, the crossbow before the lifetime of

Christ having already ruled out any domination by armoured imperial troops.

A portrait of Dong Zhongshu, the great propagandist of Confucianism under the Han emperors.

The forceful Han emperor Wu Di (140–87 BC) was persuaded by Dong Zhongshu to proclaim the state cult of Confucius in 136 BC, even though he refused to wholly accept that heavenly disapproval of the throne was shown in natural phenomena such as floods and earthquakes. Wu Di understood, however, how delay in mounting adequate relief measures would inevitably encourage peasant rebellion. Just as agriculture needed to be sustained through the maintenance of extensive government-sponsored water-control schemes, so speculation in foodstuffs could not be allowed to disrupt the economy, and so in 115 BC public granaries were established to stabilize prices. Provincial officials were ordered to buy when prices were low and sell in times of shortage. This practical approach was nonetheless supplemented by elaborate imperial rituals. In addition to the costly cycle of sacrifices instituted in the capital, the emperor journeyed in great state three times to the sacred mountain of Taishan (in modern Shandong province) to engage in private worship of Heaven.

Essentially Dong Zhongshu held that since mankind possessed only the beginnings of goodness, society was saved from barbarism only through the institutions of kinship and education. He stressed three relationships – ruler and subject, father and son, husband and wife – and said that the ruler, the father and the husband corresponded with the yang element and were therefore dominant, whereas the subject, the son and the wife tended towards the submissive yin element. Disharmonies were seen as the result of an upset in the yin/yang balance. Dong Zhongshu's position on human nature was midway between that of Mencius and Xun Zi (c. 320–235 BC).

*See* CONFUCIUS; HAN DYNASTY; MENCIUS; MO ZI; XUN ZI

*Kung-chuan Hsiao, *A History of Chinese Political Thought. Volume One: From the Beginnings to the Sixth Century AD* (Princeton, 1979).

**Drama** In classical Greece the home of drama was Athens. There, around 534 BC, Thespis first added an actor, who delivered a prologue and set speeches, to the chorus which performed tragedies. He is also credited with the introduction of the masks worn by actors and chorus, although it is likely that these props descended from ones originally used in the worship of Dionysus, god of vegetation, wine and ecstasy. For the Athenians were accustomed to seeing plays during two annual festivals dedicated to this potent deity: the city Dionysia, which lasted for six days in March, and the Lenaia, a four-day event held possibly outside the city in January. The festivals included religious ceremonies, processions, and choral performances besides plays. By the lifetime of the comic playwright Aristophanes (450–385 BC) the plays for the Dionysia were performed in the theatre of Dionysus, situated on the eastern slope of the acropolis. Plays were given in a competition held during each festival: at the Dionysia there were nine tragedies, with three satyr-plays, plus a few comedies, whereas at the Lenaia the comedies always formed the majority. Satyr-plays were not tragic, but rather semi-comic parodies of myths and legends, the usual dramatic material of the tragedies themselves. Pictures survive of satyr-players wearing the tails and genitals of satyrs, the beast-like companions of Dionysus. They may well preserve something of the origins of Greek dramatic performance. Only one complete satyr-play survives, the *Cyclops* of Euripides (485–406 BC).

Tradition also points to Athens as the originator of comedy. The story goes that a drunken gang of farmers came to the city and sang rude songs outside their enemies' windows. The city-dwellers laughed so much that they asked them to return next year with their humorous antics. That countrymen were associated with the earliest performances of comedies suggests adaptation of a rural equivalent of the English mummers' play. Tragedy, on the contrary, was ever conscious of its connection with a heroic past. As the tragic playwright Aeschylus (525–456 BC) said: 'We are all eating crumbs from the table of Homer.' Both comedy and tragedy eventually spread throughout the Greek-speaking world by means of travelling players. In Sicily, where a separate comic tradition is known to have existed, some of the Athenians who were taken prisoner by the Syracusans in 413 BC owed their eventual release to Euripides. So keen were their captors on his poetry that anyone who could recite passages from his tragedies was spared the horror of working in the stone quarries of Syracuse. Such familiarity with drama is hardly surprising when Athenian audiences were numbered by the thousand. The figure of 30,000 mentioned by the philosopher Plato is an exaggeration, however. But a charge for admission did not deter poorer citizens once Pericles (c. 495–429 BC) made the state responsible for meeting its cost, even though some of them saved money by claiming the grant and then staying away from the theatre. Whether women ever attended plays is

unclear. Allies most certainly took the opportunity to see the plays during the Dionysia, since at this time envoys from city-states within the Delian League handed over their annual tribute in Athens.

The Athenian dramatist Aeschylus fought against the Persians at Marathon and Salamis. He always ascribed the Greek victory to divine will, not military prowess.

These maritime Greeks would have remembered how their plight had been raised in a play at the Dionysia a year after the Persians put down the Ionian revolt (499–494 BC). Called provocatively *The Fall of Miletus*, Phrynichus' tragedy annoyed those who feared a confrontation with Persia and the playwright was fined, the historian Herodotus tells us, 'for reminding the Athenians of a disaster which touched them so closely, and he was forbidden from staging the play again'. It was perhaps the first time that a subject from contemporary history had been used. The effect was tremendous: 'the audience in the theatre burst into tears'. No matter the official reason given for the fine, the unsaid fear was a wish to avoid annoying the Persian monarchy any further. In the event, it made no difference for King Darius (521–486 BC) had decided to punish the Athenians for the assistance they had given to the Ionian rebels. At Marathon in 490 BC the Athenians with their Plataean allies threw back a Persian expeditionary force, and Aeschylus was able to stage *The Persians* without any difficulty. But his play of 472 BC refers to the second defeat of the Persians during their invasion of 480–479 BC; the Athenians played a vital role in one of the actions, the naval victory at Salamis, an island off the southern coast of Attica. The tragic hero is, of course, King Xerxes (486–465 BC), son of Darius. What the audience also knew was that the ageing dramatist had himself fought as an infantryman at Marathon. The play was a personal reminder of how the might of the Persian empire had been halted by the resolution of free citizens, supported by their gods. Even after the initial victory, the Athenians could hardly believe their luck and much of the credit for the success was given to Pan, god of mountains and lonely rural places. A statue of the god was dedicated on the acropolis with the inscription 'goat-footed Pan, who at Marathon fought against the Persians and with the Athenians'.

But according to the philosopher Aristotle, tragedy reached perfection in the plays of Sophocles (496–406 BC), and particularly *Tyrant Oedipus*. That after becoming aware of his terrible deeds of patricide and incest, this legendary Theban ruler should have chosen to die in the grove of Colonus near Athens made his tragedy a subject of local fascination. For *Oedipus at Colonus* draws together the deepest feelings of the classical Greeks about crime, punishment and fate in the final release of the blind ex-king. The son of a wealthy merchant, Sophocles took an active part in public life, besides writing plays. He twice served as a general and was instrumental in establishing the cult of the medicine god Asclepius. Sophocles' own house was the first home of the sacred snake connected with the deity. Asclepius' sanctuary eventually came to be built on the southern slope of the acropolis.

Although there were more tragedies written after the death of Sophocles in 406 BC than in his lifetime, they were all judged to have been inferior. But in comedy a lively tradition of performance did descend from Aristophanes right down into Roman times. The extent to which Aristophanes addresses political questions should not surprise a modern audience because he wrote in a period when politics was a common experience. The sexual humour of *Lysistrata*, first performed at Athens in 411 BC, would not have diminished its plea for peace. The plot turns on a conspiracy of women to refuse sex with their men until the men agree to make peace throughout the Greek-speaking world. A characteristic mixture of laughter and tears carried over to the work of Menander (342–289 BC), who lived in an Athens no longer an independent city-state. Overshadowed by the kingdoms set up by Alexander the Great's generals, the city had been transformed into a major commercial and educational centre, a state of affairs suited to comedies of manners. In *Samia* Menander deals with the social aspirations of two Athenian families, ending the plot with a long-delayed betrothal.

Roman drama inherited the so-called New Comedy of Menander. But the translation and adaptation of his plays by Plautus (*c.* 254–184 BC) and Terence (*c.* 185–159 BC) never aimed at reconstructing for the Roman audience the original Greek dramatic experience: rather their new versions sought innovation within the conventions of an established tradition. Terence readily converted monologues into dialogues, whilst Plautus added a strong musical element. Titus Maccius Plautus may have been a stage-hand or actor before turning to a highly profitable career as a writer of comedies. Even more lowly was the background of Publius Terentius Afer, who was born in Carthage and brought to Rome as the slave of a senator. His first play, *Andria*, was performed in 166 BC at the festival of the Phrygian goddess Magna Mater, shortly after Terence had gained his freedom. Acknowledging that it drew on two of

Menander's plays, the prologue of *Andria* declares 'the plot may not be very different, but very different are the thought and the style'. The warm reception given to the play sent Terence off to Greece in search of other Menander scripts. Not until the first century BC was a permanent theatre constructed at Rome. The plays of both Plautus and Terence were first seen on a makeshift stage in the city centre. Tragedies also seem to have been popular with Roman audiences down till the death of the playwright and grammarian Lucius Accius in 85 BC. Later tragedies, such as those of the younger Seneca (*c.* 4 BC – AD 65), were never intended for the stage, being composed solely for recitation.

A Roman actor's mask.

In India the origins of drama remain obscure because comparatively few texts survive before the Gupta dynasty (AD 320–550). Plays written by Bhasa, possibly in the second century AD, indicate that a mature dramatic tradition was already in existence. That its primary audience was of the courts of various kings who then ruled over a divided northern India can be deduced from the earlier association of the Buddhist poet and philosopher Ashvaghosa with the Kushana ruler Kaniska (AD 78–102). One of the five clans of the Da Yuezhi, enemies of the Hunnish Xiongnu whom the Chinese envoy Zhang Qian had contacted some two centuries before in Central Asia, the Kushanas controlled a vast tract of land which included the valleys of the Oxus, Indus and Ganges rivers. Their descent upon the Indian subcontinent was but one episode in an age of invasions that began with the Greco-Bactrian advance of the 180s BC and ended in the restoration of a single empire under Gupta rule in AD 320.

During the Gupta dynasty Indian drama emerged as a sophisticated form of public entertainment, both inside and outside the court. The romances of Kalidasa, the greatest of classical India's poets, were written for the pleasure of Candragupta II (AD *c.* 376–*c.* 412). Kalidasa was renowned as one of the nine jewels of his court. Three types of drama were popular: heroic romance based on an epic story; secular romance, based on an invented plot and with a more worldly hero; and farce. Kalidasa's most famous play, *Sakuntala and the Ring of Recollection*, was written in the heroic mode, its plot coming direct from the *Mahabharata*, a Sanskrit epic composed not later than the fourth century BC. The story the dramatist selected from this long tale of war between two sets of cousins was the passionate love between a king named Duhsanta and Sakuntala, the semi-divine foster-daughter of a sage. The play opens with the monarch hunting in his chariot, and the discovery of the beautiful girl watering trees and plants in a remote grove. They become lovers and, when Duhsanta is recalled to his capital, he leaves Sakuntala his signet ring as a token of his undying affection. The plot is given dramatic tension when Sakuntala loses the ring, so that he fails to recognize her when under a curse she follows him to court. The eventual recovery of the ring breaks the curse and leads to the reunion of the lovers and their son, in part through the agency of the sky god Indra. He sends his charioteer to fetch Duhsanta to a celestial hermitage.

According to the legendary critic Bharata, whose ideas were probably recorded in the second century AD, drama arose at the end of the golden age when conflicts began to trouble society. What the dramatist did was to place these examples of malice, sadness, pride, deceit or whatever, in an ethical perspective. The audience was thus expected to gain insight and pleasure at the theatre, the first of which was supposed to have been built by divine command after demons tried to disrupt the performance of a play. The demons were said to have been shamed by its action. The hierarchical ordering of classical Indian society was always reflected in the convention that characters spoke different languages according to their status; the hero, his advisers and others of high status, including brahmins, spoke Sanskrit, while those of lower status or education used the vernacular Prakrit. Whereas Sanskrit had already been fixed in its final form, Prakrit was still evolving towards a number of literary languages such as Hindi, Gujarati and Nepali. Considerable effort went into the making of costumes and props, since Bharata refers to the presence in an acting troop of a crown maker, an ornament maker, a garland maker, a dyer, and a dresser. Obviously they were meant to denote a character's rank, occupation, and birthplace.

*See* ATHENS; GUPTA DYNASTY; IONIAN REVOLT; LITERATURE

*J. R. Green, *Theatre in Ancient Greek Society* (London, 1994); D. M. MacDowell, *Aristophanes and Athens* (Oxford, 1995); B. S. Miller, *Theatre of Memory: The Plays of Kalidasa* (New York, 1984); E. Segal, *Roman Laughter: The Comedy of Plautus* (Oxford, 1968); O. Taplin, *Greek Tragedy in Action* (London, 1978); N. Zagagi, *The Comedy of Menander* (London, 1994).

# E

Egypt was during the classical period almost entirely under foreign rule. The last effective pharaoh of the twenty-sixth dynasty, Amasis (570–526 BC), did what he could to build a defensive alliance against the growing power of Persia. But naval aid from the Samian tyrant Polycrates (c. 535–522 BC), for instance, was not equal to the task of defending Egypt once the Persians had created their own navy. The Persian king Cambyses (530–522 BC) built ships and recruited sailors from his maritime provinces in preparation for an all-out invasion. It occurred in 525 BC. The Egyptians met the Persians in battle on the easternmost branch of the Nile, but were routed and fell back on Memphis. When they foolishly killed Persian envoys, the city was besieged and taken after ten days. The historian Herodotus suggests that the new pharaoh might have been installed as governor of Egypt, since the Persians were in the habit of treating with honour even those who had rebelled against them. But 'he was caught trying to stir up trouble, and

was properly paid for it'. Some high Egyptian officials are known to have been given senior positions in the new administration. One of these men, Udjahorresnet, has left an inscription praising the religious tolerance of Cambyses, who at his request expelled 'all the foreigners occupying the temple Neith at Sais'. Neith was none other than the mother of the sun god Re, an Egyptian deity of the first importance. That the occupants were not Egyptians is a reminder of the changes that had taken place in the country prior to the arrival of the Persians. Large numbers of foreigners, particularly Greeks, had settled either as traders or mercenary troops, making Egypt far more cosmopolitan than ever before.

Although tradition made it a time of misery and oppression, Persian rule does seem to have been a period of relative prosperity. During the reign of Darius I (521–486 BC) a canal connecting the Nile with the Red Sea was completed and the same monarch instigated a codification of Egyptian laws — hardly the acts of an oppressor. But, for whatever reasons, there were serious rebellions in 486–485, 460–454 and 401–399 BC. The second revolt was actively supported by the Athenians, who lost an entire fleet. They and their allies were eventually trapped on an island in the Nile: they held out for eighteen months, until the Persians diverted the waters on one side of the island and advanced overland. The rebellion between 401 and 399 BC was the most successful of all because it resulted in the expulsion of the Persians. Thereafter regaining control over Egypt was a Persian preoccupation, with notable failures in 373 and 351 BC, before Artaxerxes III (358–338 BC) in 343 BC used Greek mercenaries to support a successful reconquest. The last ruler of an independent Egypt, the pharaoh Nekhtharehbe, escaped to Nubia where he ruled a diminished kingdom. Yet Persian domination again of Egypt was just an interlude, before the arrival in 332 BC of the Macedonian army under the command of Alexander the Great (356–323 BC).

This new conquest placed Egypt under Macedonian rule till annexation by Rome in 30 BC. For after the death of Alexander, one of his generals by the name of Ptolemy established in 305 BC a dynasty there. Ptolemaic Egypt represented an uneasy compromise between Greek and Egyptian cultural traditions, notwithstanding the care taken by the conquerors not to offend local sensibilities. Except in matters of religion, the influence of Egyptians on the affairs of their own country was negligible. There was no sweeping secularization of temple property, and grants of all kinds, including land, continued to be made by the Ptolemies. Just as Christianity under the Romans was to be a succour for the indigenous population, so now the temples acted as a focus of hope under an essentially alien regime. The patent lack of interest in Egypt, other than its wealth, was evident in the location of the Ptolemaic capital at Alexandria, on the Mediterranean coast. Here royal patronage turned Alexander's foundation into an international seat of learning as well as centre of trade and industry. Something of a resurgence in Egyptian influence can be discerned in the second century BC, but the lot of the hard-pressed peasantry remained close to desperation. At the mercy of foreign tax-collectors, they increasingly sought the protection of powerful landowners, even though they were surrendering what little independence

This Roman coin, minted around 28 BC, refers to the annexation of Egypt two years before.

they had. It was apt that the last Ptolemy, Cleopatra VII, should be the first ruler to learn the Egyptian language. Though from the start of her reign in 51 BC she participated in Egyptian religious festivals, and was compared favourably to the goddess Isis, Cleopatra was no more than the plaything of successive Roman warlords. The Ptolemaic dynasty had become as impotent as the Egyptians themselves in the power politics of the Roman world.

From 30 BC until its conquest by the Arabs in AD 640, Egypt belonged to Rome, or the new eastern Roman capital of Constantinople. For the first emperor Augustus (31 BC – AD 14) appreciated fully its economic potential, and steps were taken to revitalize agriculture through the repair of neglected irrigation systems. Becoming one of the granaries of the Roman empire brought prosperity to Egypt, but it was not generally shared. Now more than ever the country was a vassal state, the possession of foreigners for whose benefit her natural resources were ruthlessly exploited, and the Egyptians themselves were merely the means by which this could be profitably achieved. The position of Jewish settlers in Alexandria also became problematic, with outbreaks of violence shaking the city at regular intervals. In AD 40 the Jewish philosopher Philo led a deputation of Jews to Rome in order to protest at their treatment. Whereas Philo could ignore the obvious shortcomings of the emperor

Caligula (AD 37–41) in order to maintain a pro-Roman outlook, the Egyptians later on were not prepared to compromise with Rome over their Christian beliefs. First brought to the Jewish inhabitants of Alexandria, Christianity soon spread throughout the country so that official persecutions claimed very many martyrs. Bishop Eusebius, an eyewitness of a persecution in AD 303, relates how most were volunteers, who, as soon as one of their number was condemned, leapt up one after another before the judgement seat to confess themselves to be Christians. But already some Egyptians had fled into the desert during previous persecutions, providing as an alternative the example of the ascetic life. One of these was Antony, who around AD 270 gave up his farm to form a community of hermits. Satan is supposed to have complained that wastelands, hitherto acknowledged as the preserve of demons, were now swarming with hermits. Although he survived Satan's famous assault on his faith, Antony made it plain that the Egyptian art of the embalmer, then becoming popular with Christians, was utterly superfluous. Of his own body, he said: 'In the day of resurrection I shall receive it incorruptible from the hands of Christ.'

See ALEXANDER; ALEXANDRIA; ATHENS; CHRISTIANITY; CLEOPATRA; PERSIA; PHILO; PTOLEMIES; ROME; SAMOS
*H. L. Bell, *Egypt from the Reign of Alexander the Great to the Arab Conquest* (Oxford, 1948).

**Empedocles** (492–433 BC) was born in Acragas (modern Agrigento) in south-western Sicily. This Greek philosopher and mystic became renowned for his success in curing diseases as well as his active support for democratic principles. Legend says he disappeared in the flames of Mount Aetna, his intention being to confirm the report that Empedocles was a god. This motive was later deduced when the volcano threw up a bronze fitting belonging to one of his sandals. Something similar happened in China five centuries later on the disappearance of Chang Daoling, the first heavenly teacher of the Daoist church. Only Chang Daoling's clothes were left behind.

Apocryphal tales aside, Empedocles was an important thinker about the nature of the universe. A follower of Pythagoras, who had settled in 531 BC at Croton in southern Italy, Empedocles seems to have written his two long poems *On Nature* and *Purifications* as a reply to the rigidly logical analysis being propounded by another Greek resident in Italy, Parmenides of Elea (born *c.* 515 BC), who claimed a goddess furnished his arguments. Parmenides concluded that what exists must be one, eternal, indivisible, motionless and changeless. While accepting the permanence of being, Empedocles denied its unity and immobility, substituting four elements of earth, air, fire and water which combined and separated in order to cause a cycle of the generation and dissolution for living things. This theory of four basic elements was to affect the thinking of Anaxagoras (*c.* 500–428 BC), Plato (429–347 BC), Aristotle (384–322 BC) and Zeno of Citium (335–263 BC), the founder of the Stoics. Even an atomist such as Democritus (born 460 BC) drew upon the idea of an endless reorganization of the constituents of matter.

*See* ANAXAGORAS; ARISTOTLE; PLATO; STOICISM

★G. S. Kirk, J. E. Raven and M. Schofield, *The Presocratic Philosophers* (Cambridge, 1983).

**Epaminondas** (died 362 BC), along with the other leading Theban general Pelopidas (died 364 BC), was responsible for ending the Spartan hegemony of Greece at the battle of Leuctra in 371 BC. A skilful use of cavalry, and a mass of infantrymen fifty shields deep on the left wing of their phalanx, were used to drive the Spartans backwards. Before the action Epaminondas had advised his men to crush the Spartan element in the Peloponnesian army as their only real enemy. Some 400 of the 700 Spartan citizens present on the battlefield fell in the fighting, plus Cleombrotus, one of the two Spartan kings. It was a loss that Sparta could not bear, and King Agesilaus (444–360 BC), the other Spartan king, was obliged to mount a makeshift defence when Epaminondas led his victorious army into the Peloponnese. The subsequent liberation of Messenia wrecked the Spartan military system, which relied on the food produced by its servile inhabitants, the helots.

After this successful invasion, Epaminondas was in 369 BC tried in Thebes for extending his military command beyond its time limit. Though he recognized the democratic validity of this restriction, the military advantage then enjoyed by Thebes and its Boeotian allies seemed too good to ignore. At the trial Epaminondas admitted his guilt and accepted the death penalty prescribed, only asking that a record of his deeds be inscribed on his tombstone: 'That the Greeks should know how he had compelled the unwilling Thebans to ravage Laconia, which has been free from devastation for 500 years, that he had caused Messenia to be resettled after 230 years, that he had gathered the Arcadians together and organized them into a league, and that he had given the Greeks their autonomy.' Upon hearing this request, the judges threw out the case amid laughter.

Re-elected year after year as one of seven generals who commanded the troops of the Boeotian confederacy, Epaminondas fell in 362 BC at the battle of Mantineia, just as the Theban infantry destroyed the Spartan battle-line. News of his death brought both the engagement and the Theban hegemony to an abrupt halt. Afterwards no single Greek state could reach such a height of military power that it could permanently subjugate the others. The result was a stalemate prior to the rise of Macedon, whose future king Philip II, the father of Alexander the Great, was a hostage at Thebes shortly after Leuctra. The tactical lessons he learned there undoubtedly influenced the military reforms he sponsored on ascending the throne in 359 BC. For the Macedonian conquest of Greece and Persia was achieved by means of a flexible deployment of horse and foot, although the core of the army remained a phalanx armed with a huge spear, the so-called sarissa.

See AGESILAUS; PHILIP II; THEBES; WARFARE

*J. Buckler, *The Theban Hegemony, 374–362 BC* (Cambridge, Mass., 1980); L. J. Worley, *Hippeis: The Cavalry of Ancient Greece* (Boulder, 1994)

**Ephialtes** (died 461 BC) is a man about whom hardly anything is known, despite his famous contribution to the development of democracy in Athens; namely, the downgrading of the ancient Council of the Areopagus, a bastion of aristocratic influence. Ephialtes' father was, like the Athenian general Aristides (c. 525–467 BC), described as poor and incorruptible. Following the ostracism in 471 BC of Themistocles, the democratic party in Athens had been on the defensive as the great landowning families had rallied their supporters behind Cimon (510–450 BC), the son of Miltiades. Both father and son were successful generals with personal fortunes in part derived from booty: it allowed Cimon especially to combine an active role on behalf of Athens with public generosity. Against this aristocratic predominance Ephialtes, with the aid of Pericles (*c.* 495–429 BC), used the changed temper of the times to attack the privileges and powers of the Areopagus. 'First of all,' the philosopher Aristotle noted, 'Ephialtes ruined many of its members by bringing actions against them in the courts. Then in 462–461 BC he stripped the council of all its prerogatives from which it derived its guardianship of the constitution, and assigned some of them to the council of 500 and others to the assembly and lawcourts.' Afterwards it was usual for laws passed in Athens to begin with the words: 'The council and the people decided . . .'

This removal of the last conservative brake on the Athenian constitution led to a period of radical democracy which lasted down to the outbreak of the Peloponnesian War in 431 BC. In order to counter the effects of aristocratic wealth, Pericles also introduced a payment equivalent to a day's wage for citizens who sat on juries, a precedent that eventually led to payment for office-holders, and even attendance at the assembly. The political change was not achieved without turmoil: Cimon was sent into exile in 461 BC, and Ephialtes was stabbed in the night by an unknown assassin. That murder of politicians was far less common in Athens than in Rome during the last century of the republic may have been connected with the safety-valve pro-

vided by ostracism; in the case of Ephialtes, however, violent passions were not so easily contained.

*See* ARISTIDES; ATHENS; CIMON; OSTRACISM; PERICLES

★J. K. Davies, *Democracy and Classical Greece* (London, 1978); C. G. Starr, *The Birth of Athenian Democracy: The Assembly in the Fifth Century BC* (Oxford, 1990); R. W. Wallace, *The Areopagus Council till 307 BC* (Baltimore, 1989).

The quiet philosophy of Epicurus never became wholly reputable: its hedonism was always looked upon as crude.

**Epicurus** (341–270 BC), a native of Samos, founded a Greek school of philosophy that caused much argument. About 307 BC he came to Athens and bought a house with a garden. There he and his followers formed a close community which, unusually, included women and slaves. Despite the austerity of their way of life, the doctrine of hedonism which Epicurus taught aroused a degree of suspicion and hostility, because for him pleasure was not sensual enjoyment but rather freedom from pain and mental anxiety, a goal to be achieved by sober reasoning and the considered rejection of anything liable to give rise to those evils. Pleasure consisted in having one's desires satisfied rather than in the act of satisfying them: the aim, like that of the Sceptics, was thus imperturbability. The Epicureans believed that there was no life after death, that the gods existed but were indifferent towards mankind, and that the universe ran on its own volition along the lines of the atomic theory of Democritus (born 460 BC). The latter had been known as the 'Laughing Philosopher' because the follies of his fellow men amused him so much. Democritus held that matter was composed of solid, invisibly small particles, which moved in infinite numbers through an infinite void.

Though the atomic theory was largely rejected by other schools of philosophy, its impersonal explanation of reality suited the inward-looking Epicureans, who preferred gentle friendship within a small group to any concern for the world of public affairs. Their withdrawal from political life seemed to make sense in the realities of late classical Greece: city-states were left with little scope for independent action when faced by the forces of Antigonid Macedon, Seleucid Asia or Ptolemaic Egypt. Even the Attalid dynasty of Pergamum, a conspicuous patron of learning, ended up as a pawn of Roman policy. But Epicureanism never quite became wholly reputable, although it briefly enjoyed a vogue in Italy towards the end of the first century BC. The Syrian Epicurean Philodemus (110–35 BC) flourished at Herculaneum: the remains of his extensive library reveal a wide range of rival philosophical texts which he used for systematic refutation of errors in his own writings. Despite the impassioned Latin poetry of his contemporary Lucretius, Epicureanism was in Italy outstripped by the teachings of the Stoics, who took their name from the painted hall in Athens, where Zeno of Citium (335–263 BC) taught sometime after 313 BC. Like Zeno, Epicurus was firmly convinced that by reason man could detect and choose the true path to follow: where he parted company with Zeno was in his lack of interest in social justice.

See LUCRETIUS; SCEPTICISM; STOICISM

★C. Bailey, *The Greek Atomists and Epicurus* (Oxford, 1928); J. Howard, *The Epicurean Tradition* (London, 1989); A. A. Long, *Hellenistic Philosophy: Stoics, Epicureans, Sceptics* (London, 1974).

**Epirus** (most of modern Albania and north-western Greece) was inhabited in classical times by Greek-speaking tribes, the most prominent being the Molossi. The first effective unification of Epirus was achieved by King

Alexander I (342–330 BC), who had been placed on the throne by his brother-in-law, Philip II of Macedon. He also crossed the Adriatic at the invitation of the Greek city-state of Tarentum (present-day Taranto) and gained control of much of southern Italy. Intervention on the Italian peninsula against Rome, and on Sicily against Carthage, became a marked feature of Epirote foreign policy under Pyrrhus, who seized control in the 290s BC. This expansionist king endeavoured to extend his realm with mixed success into Illyria, Macedon and Greece as well.

Around 232 BC the Epirote monarchy was replaced by a confederacy with a common citizenship. Involved on the losing side in the final war between Rome and Macedon, Epirus was severely punished on the orders of the Roman senate. Aemilius Paullus, the victor over the Macedonians at Pydna in 168 BC, gave his legionaries licence to rape and pillage before selling 150,000 Epirotes into slavery. These slaves, part of an enormous pool of manpower acquired by republican Rome as a result of war, were employed in agriculture, industry or the home. Epirus never recovered from the events of 167 BC, and became a neglected patch of the Roman empire.

See ILLYRIANS; MACEDON; PHILIP II; PYRRHUS; ROME; SLAVERY
*N. G. L. Hammond, *Epirus* (Oxford, 1967).

**Etruscans** were the dominant people of northern Italy till 300 BC. Either their culture developed as a result of contact with Greek traders or, as the historian Herodotus records, they migrated from Lydia in Asia Minor because of a famine. The Etruscans (from whose name Tuscany derives) were organized as a league of city-states, with a common religious centre at Volsinii (probably modern Orvieto). The Etruscan script formed the basis of the Latin alphabet: the Etruscans had borrowed from the Greeks, who in turn were themselves the beneficiaries of Phoenician writing. The Romans were also indebted to the Etruscans for divination, the reading of omens: these could be discerned in the behaviour of birds, or the livers of sacrificial animals. Roman armies took chickens on campaign in order to foretell the future. It was considered a good sign if they dropped food from their beaks while being fed. One thing popularly attributed to Etruscan influence was the gladiatorial contest, first staged publicly at Rome in 264 BC. This bloody event, however, seems more likely to owe something to Rome's southern neighbours, most likely the Campanians and Samnites. Both are known to have taken delight in games with armed opponents.

Etruscan interest in early Rome had nothing to do with its own attractions. Rather it was the city's strategic position on the road which the Etruscans built southwards to Campania, the fertile plain behind the Bay of Naples.

There in the south were sited a number of Etruscan colonies. Rome expelled its Etruscan kings around 507 BC, years before the power of the Etruscans was permanently crippled by the Carthaginians at the sea-battle off Cumae in 474 BC. The subsequent economic decline was severe enough to open the way for a Roman conquest of all the Etruscan city-states. The last to fall in 264 BC was Volsinii. Even though the Etruscans kept alive their own cultural traditions down into imperial times, their language gave way to Latin. The last Roman of any eminence who may have understood it was the emperor Claudius (AD 41–54), who as a young man wrote a history of Etruria.

*See* CARTHAGE; ORACLES; ROME
★M. Grant, *The Etruscans* (London, 1980).

**Eusebius** (AD 260–340) was born in Palestine and died there as bishop of Caesarea. His life, therefore, spanned the great transition from the pagan to the Christian Roman empire and he chronicled the main stages by which this revolution was accomplished. He hated the collegiate system of imperial government introduced by Diocletian

Bilingual gold sheets from Pyrgi, a port serving the Etruscan city of Caere, present-day Cerveteri. The text, Punic on the left and Etruscan on the right, reveals close relations with Carthage around 500 BC.

(AD 284–305), not least because it served to undermine one-man rule. As spokesman for Constantine (AD 306–337), Eusebius pushed the cause of unity by saying that nothing was so infuriating as divisions in the church: they were like cutting the body of Christ to pieces. His hero, after Constantine, was the first emperor Augustus, who in 31 BC had ended the republican civil wars and set up the empire. It was an admiration that he shared with the Jewish scholar Philo (20 BC – AD 50), upon whose writings Eusebius drew extensively. He pointed out that just as Christ was born into the world during Augustus' reign, so now the acceptance of the church as the state religion coincided with Constantine's rise to supreme power. Eusebius can be said to have formulated the political philosophy of the Constantinian state, based on the unity of the church and empire under divine providence.

Theological problems beset the early church, however, and Constantine discovered that doctrinal agreements tended not to last. The Council of Nicaea in AD 325 was sponsored by the emperor in an attempt to settle differences. There Eusebius had to accommodate his own beliefs to imperial impatience at the endless wrangling of the assembled bishops. A creed was duly declared sacrosanct, but it did not stop Constantine's third son, Constantius II (AD 337–361) from ignoring those parts he personally disliked. Ecclesiastical politics became party politics as different factions struggled to dislodge opponents from their sees. The turmoil may have given impetus to the abortive pagan restoration attempted by Julian (AD 361–363). This failed for the reason that, divided though the theologians might be about doctrine, Christian piety had already taken root in most sections of late Roman society.

*See* CHRISTIANITY; CONSTANTINE; DIOCLETIAN; JULIAN; PHILO; ROME
★T. D. Barnes, *Constantine and Eusebius* (Cambridge, Mass., 1981).

# F

**First Emperor** of China, who was sole ruler from 221 to 210 BC, sat first on the throne of Qin, a north-western state. He was crowned there as King Zheng in 246 BC at the age of eleven or twelve. Not until he had dismissed his regent in 237 BC could the future First Emperor exercise any control over policy. Thereafter he followed the advice of Li Si (died 208 BC), a Legalist scholar who became chief justice. Effectively chief minister, before and

The First Emperor of China, who died in 210 BC.

after the unification of China in 221 BC, Li Si helped Zheng direct his armies against one rival state after another. The last Zhou king, the nominal overlord of all the feudal monarchs, had already been dethroned by Qin forces in 256 BC. Even though Qin suffered reverses at the hands of Zhao in 228 BC and Wei in 225 BC, the decisive engagement did not occur till the year 223 BC when the great southern state of Chu was vanquished. The overrunning of Yan in 222 BC and the surrender of Qin without a fight a year later made the 'Tiger of Qin', as Zheng was then called, the ruler of all China.

Apart from being the king of a state virtually dedicated to war, Zheng possessed one other great advantage in the form of a massive agricultural surplus. It allowed more of his soldiers to remain on active service for longer periods of time than any of those belonging to his rivals. This advantage derived largely from the Chengkuo canal, an irrigation scheme completed the year he ascended the throne. The historian Ban Gu noted the strategic strength of Qin, which the subsequent Han dynasty kept as the seat of imperial power after 202 BC. 'In the abundance of flowering plants and fruits,' wrote Ban Gu, 'it is the most fertile of the nine provinces. In natural barriers for protection and defence it is the most impregnable refuge there is.'

As the only ruler left in 221 BC, King Zheng found himself in an unprecedented position. With some justification he could insist: 'We are the First Emperor, and Our Successors shall be known as the Second Emperor, and so on, for endless generations.' There is indeed a reference to divine favour, even divinity, in the new imperial title: First Sovereign Qin Emperor. Already a very old and complex word, emperor had been used by Daoist philosophers as a means of elevating the semi-divine figures they wished to claim for their own inspiration. Steadfast opponents of the Confucianists, the outspoken opponents of the First Emperor's rule, they looked back to a golden age which was said to have preceded the development of feudalism. Its great sage was the Yellow Emperor, Huang Di, who ascended into the sky as an immortal after an exemplary reign. Personal contact with Daoist magicians almost certainly encouraged the First Emperor's own superstitions, since he tried to communicate with the immortals first in 219 BC in order to acquire the elixir of life. Three assassination attempts also acted as a spur to this quest, which took

on bizarre forms. Embassies were sent up mountains and overseas in order to open up diplomatic relations with the immortals. The emperor's own divinity was protected on Daoist advice by secrecy, over 100 miles of enclosed walks being constructed in the capital alone so as to hide his movements. At Mount Li one of the most extensive imperial tombs ever built was started with a work-force of 700,000 conscripts. And last, but not least, the First Emperor's sudden death – most likely from pneumonia – was brought about in 210 BC by a similar anxiety. Having a dream of a sea god interpreted as an evil spirit blocking his contact with the immortals, the First Emperor roamed the shore of present-day Shandong province until he dispatched a stranded whale with a repeated crossbow.

The secrecy surrounding the throne gave two conspirators, Li Si and the eunuch Zhao Gao (died 207 BC), a chance to secure their own positions in 210 BC. Fearing the wrath of the crown prince Fu Su, whom they had contrived to exile from the court nearly eight years earlier, they devised a plot to install instead as the Second Emperor Hu Hai, his worthless younger brother. Li Si and Zhao Gao pretended the First Emperor was still alive until they were safely back in the capital. Edicts were issued from the imperial litter, which followed a cartload of mouldering fish. 'It was high summer,' the historian Sima Qian notes drily, 'and to disguise the stench of the corpse the escort was told to load a cart with salted fish.' As a result of the terror inspired by the title of the First Emperor, there was neither an onlooker to question these odd travel arrangements, nor on arrival in the capital an official to oppose the forged will the conspirators used to place Hu Hai on the throne.

Ignominious though this end was to the First Emperor's brief reign, its effect on Chinese history was profound. For the sweeping change the First Emperor began and Liu Bang, the founder of the subsequent Han dynasty (202 BC – AD 220), completed was nothing less than the permanent unification of China. Demonstrated once and for all was the value of unity. Since 221 BC the country has been united for a longer period than it has been disunited, making China an exception to the rule that in the pre-modern era large states do not endure. No other classical civilization can remotely match this continuity.

See LI SI; LIU BANG; MOUNT LI; QIN DYNASTY; ZHAO GAO

*A. Cotterell, *The First Emperor of China* (London, 1981).

**Flavian dynasty** (AD 69–96), the second imperial dynasty of Rome, was founded by Titus Flavius Vespasianus. He was born in AD 9 just north of Rome, the son of a tax-gatherer. The future emperor came to notice as a legionary commander during the conquest of southern Britain in AD 43–47. Later as governor of the province of Africa his administration was praised, for he did not use his position to make money. Vespasian was the governor of Judaea on Nero's death in AD 68, and he supported both Otho and Vitellius following the assassination of Galba, the successor to Nero chosen by the senate. But he was persuaded by the governors of Syria and Egypt to overthrow Vitellius, the commander of the legions stationed on the Rhine, and found a new imperial house because he possessed two able sons, Titus and Domitian. By the end of AD 69 the civil wars were over and Vespasian was

An account of an assassination attempt on the First Emperor's life in 227 BC. Because weapons were forbidden in the Qin court, the assassin on the left almost succeeded.

emperor: significantly, he chose to date the start of his reign (AD 69–79) not from the formal recognition of the senate, but from his acclamation by the troops. This was a frank admission that he owed his elevation to them, and a reminder to the senators that it was not themselves but the army which constituted the real basis of his power. Vespasian's policies were aimed at strengthening the imperial administration, which had suffered through the extravagance of Nero and the disruption of civil conflict. Provincial taxes were increased, frontiers pushed forward at strategic points in Germany and Asia Minor, revolts put down in Germany and Judaea, discipline was restored in the army, and to please the populace of Rome, work was started on the Colosseum, a truly gigantic amphitheatre designed to hold 50,000 spectators.

A coin struck in the third year of the emperor Vespasian's reign. It proclaims the re-establishment of public order.

Vespasian was the first emperor to be succeeded by his own son, Titus Flavius Vespasianus. His short reign (AD 79–81) was remembered with affection during that of his younger brother Domitian (AD 81–96). For Titus endeavoured to restore a more relaxed atmosphere at Rome: the activities of informers were discouraged, the charge of high treason was abolished, and money was lavished on public buildings and entertainments. The Colosseum was completed as well as baths which carry the emperor's name. Three disasters – the eruption of Mount Vesuvius in AD 79, the fire and the plague at Rome a year later – passed without unrest because of the obvious concern Titus exhibited over relief measures. His death at the age of fifty was genuinely mourned. Later it was rumoured that Titus died with one regret; namely, that his younger brother would succeed him.

Titus Flavius Domitianus, who came to the throne at the age of thirty, was certainly an embittered man. He believed that it was Vespasian's intention that he should have ruled jointly with his elder brother. Yet, unlike Titus, Domitian was never given any position of authority, nor allowed to pursue any military glory, during his father's reign. When Titus died, Domitian ensured his deification for the sake of the Flavian house, but the new emperor was determined to gain for himself the reputation of a great conqueror. Campaigns along the Rhine soon enabled him to assume the title Germanicus; in Britain his forces pushed into Wales and Scotland, although plans to annex the Scottish highlands were dropped around AD 85; but Domitian claimed in AD 89 a triumph for an invasion of Dacia, essentially the plateau of Transylvania, even though Roman authority there remained insecure. Having suppressed a mutiny among the legions in Upper Germany shortly after celebrating his triumph at Rome, Domitian campaigned successfully across the Danube frontier against German tribesmen. It was a foretaste of the crises on this frontier which the Germans would cause in the ensuing centuries.

The emperor Domitian was the second son of Vespasian, the founder of the Flavian dynasty. Domitian was killed in AD 96.

Domitian had proved his worth as a general and become popular with the army. But the rebellion of AD 88, among the legions stationed in Upper Germany increased his suspicions of the senate to the extent that he reintroduced treason trials, and executed a large number of leading Romans. There was indeed a terrifying correctness in his application of the law, which unluckily for the emperor spread at last to the commanders of the Praetorian Guard, the only regular unit stationed in Italy. In the autumn of AD 96, Domitian was murdered in a palace conspiracy and replaced at once by the sixty-six-year-old senator Marcus Cocceius Nerva. Dotitia Longina, the emperor's wife, was privy to the plot, since she appears to have been alienated by Domitian's blatant promiscuity. Senators could hardly hide their joy. Forgetting their dignity amidst a wave of recklessness, they voted that every one of Domitian's statues in Rome be smashed and his name erased from all inscriptions. The murder, however, caused such great anger in the army that Nerva was forced to hand over the assassins for execution. Immediately afterwards, to save his throne, he adopted Trajan, the governor of Upper Germany, as his son and heir. In AD 88 Trajan had been transferred there from Spain in order to quell legionary unrest. His own adoption inaugurated a period of over sixty years in which successions to the throne were determined by adoption. Nerva died in AD 98.

*See* GALBA; ROME; TRAJAN

*B. W. Jones, *The Emperor Titus* (London, 1984) and *The Emperor Domitian* (London, 1992).

# G

**Galatians** was the name given to a group of Celts who settled in the interior of Asia Minor. They were part of a larger number who invaded Macedon and Greece in 280-279 BC: estimates put the migration at between 150,000 and 300,000 people. In 278 BC some of them crossed to Asia Minor, where they raided the coastal areas before being restricted to Phrygia and Cappadocia. First the Seleucids, then the Attalids of Pergamum, kept them at bay, even though the Galatians remained formidable opponents down till their forcible incorporation in the Roman empire in 25 BC. The choice of Galatia for the new province's name reflects this reputation. An effective method of dealing with the Galatians was found to be stones and sling-shot. During the campaign of 189 BC the Romans used a vast quantity of such missiles, which the historian Livy explains did much to demoralize the naked Galatians, prior to battle taking place: 'Not one of them dared to run forward from their ranks for fear of exposing his body to shots from all sides; and as they stood immobile, they received all the more wounds for being so closely packed ... Then in utter confusion, and exhausted from their injuries, the Galatians fled on the first Roman assault.' Some 8,000 of these Celtic warriors fell at this engagement near the Halys river. Two senators, however, later objected to the Roman commander being awarded a triumph on the grounds that the enemy had been thrown into panic by missiles rather than the sword. Although stone throwers and slingers often played a decisive role in conflicts both on land and sea, there remained a lingering suspicion that somehow they spoilt the heroic aspect of war.

See ATTALIDS; GAULS; ROME; SELEUCIDS
*S. Mitchell, *Anatolia: Land, Men, and Gods in Asia Minor. Volume One: The Celts and the Impact of Roman Rule* (Oxford, 1993).

**Galba**, Roman emperor AD 68–69, was almost seventy years old when the senate invited him to succeed Nero (AD 54–68). At first Servius Sulpicius

Galba was content to watch the growing discontent in the provinces and among the Roman upper classes at Nero's erratic behaviour from Spain, where he governed a province. The collapse of an army mutiny in nearby Gaul did not worry him because it was soon followed by the suicide of Nero himself. When other commanders urged Galba to become emperor, he decided to make his move: supporters were given command over the legions stationed in Germany, and in Rome there was a purge of his opponents. But the historian Suetonius tells us Galba's 'power and prestige were far greater while he was assuming control of the empire than afterwards: though affording ample proof of his capacity to rule, he won less praise for his good acts than blame for his mistakes'. The problem seems to have been a marked reluctance on the part of Galba to spend money, with the result that even the soldiers were disappointed by his frugality. It was made worse by Galba's decision to establish a commission charged with recovering the lavish gifts distributed by Nero.

Galba survived as long as he did because, with the end of the Julio-Claudian dynasty on Nero's death, there was no obvious choice for the next emperor. Marcus Salvius Otho, another governor from Spain and one of Galba's earliest supporters, used the disaffected Praetorian Guard to seize power himself in AD 69. The head of Galba was paraded in Rome, stuck on a spear. The senate had no choice but to acknowledge the fact that Otho was now in control of the capital. Though he made history by being the first Roman emperor to reach office by killing his predecessor, Otho's reign lasted for less than four months. For the arrival in Italy of legions from Germany under the command of Aulus Vitellius gave Rome its third emperor of the year. But Vitellius was not to survive either, for in Palestine the legionaries had proclaimed Vespasian, who founded the Flavian dynasty (AD 69–96). Suetonius relates how at the end of AD 69 'Vespasian's advance guard had entered Rome without opposition, and at once began to loot the imperial palace, as was to be expected. They hauled Vitellius from his hiding-place and, not recognizing him, asked who he was and whether he knew of the emperor's whereabouts. Vitellius gave some lying answer, but was soon identified.' His execution, like that of Galba, occurred in public; only Otho enjoyed the dignity of suicide.

The events of AD 68 and 69 revealed the political power of the Roman army. When the third Roman emperor Caligula was assassinated in AD 41, Galba had been in Germany, and the action was in Rome. In AD 68, however, the centre of gravity had shifted to the provinces, where military discontent wiped out the last vestige of loyalty for the first imperial house. The only supporters Nero had left were his German bodyguards. So the succession of Galba was decided in Spain, just as in

AD 69 the final choice of Vespasian as the founder of a new dynasty was effectively made by soldiers in the eastern provinces. The empire had become no more than a military dictatorship, which taxed the provinces to feed the army and the inhabitants of Rome.

See FLAVIAN DYNASTY; NERO; ROME
★W. Wellesley, *The Long Year, AD 69* (London, 1975); Suetonius, *The Twelve Caesars*, trans. by R. Graves (Harmondsworth, 1957).

**Gauls** were, to the Romans, the Celtic peoples living in modern France, Belgium, Switzerland, northern Italy, and Austria. The Romans knew that the inhabitants of Britain were their cousins, in the same way that the Galatians in Asia Minor were obviously kinsmen too. The first known home of the Celts was the region between the Rhine and the Danube. From the fifth century BC onwards these fierce tribesmen expanded their control over much of Europe. In 278 BC one band crossed to Asia Minor and embarked on a campaign of destruction, which was eventually contained by the Seleucid king Antiochus I (281–261 BC). The Greeks were thoroughly scared of these intruders, even after they settled down in what became known as Galatia. This reaction was hardly surprising when the words of the historian Polybius are recalled. Many of the Gauls on the battlefield chose to 'throw off their clothes and

take up a position in front of the whole army naked and carrying nothing but their arms . . . The appearance of these naked warriors was a terrifying sight, for they were all men of splendid physique and in the prime of life.' Another war-band had sacked Rome in 390 BC, and it took the Romans a couple of centuries to become strong enough to conquer the lands which the Celts had populated. The Celts remained independent only in remote parts of Ireland, until recently thought to be unoccupied by Rome. The discovery of a fortress 15 miles north of Dublin, at Drumanagh, now reveals that the island may have been part of the imperial defences.

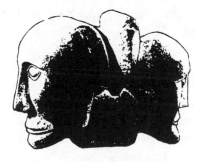

Heads were very important in Celtic culture. This double-headed statue may refer to head-hunting or wisdom.

Except in Ireland, Romanization led to the decline of Celtic religion. That it survived for so much longer there is one reason for the richness of Irish mythology. How typical the surviving Irish sagas were it is now impossible to tell. The Celts relied on the oral transmission of their religious beliefs, and so modern commentators are obliged to turn to the historical records of their Roman conquerors for assistance. These cannot be entirely relied upon for the good reason that Caesar's ten-year struggle to control Gaul, the Celtic heartland, left a vivid impression on Roman consciousness. A frustrated commander such as Julius Caesar (100–44 BC) was at pains to stress the barbarity of his opponents, in part to justify the one million slaves his own army took as booty during a hard-fought series of campaigns. Thus the blood-thirsty sacrifices of the 'superstitious' Gauls were contrasted with the civilized behaviour of the Romans, quite overlooking in his *Gallic Wars* a willingness on his own part to stage lavish gladiatorial games. Caesar had been the first to supply those condemned to fight in the arena with equipment made from silver. Resistance in Gaul ended with the failure of Vercingetorix's rebellion of 52 BC. The anti-Celtic tone is also obvious in the historian Livy's account of a Roman encounter with the Galatians in 189 BC which dwells on the effectiveness of stones against naked opponents. He mocks the boastfulness of warriors who disdain any form of bodily protection, not least because of his ignorance of Celtic beliefs concerning rebirth. It is not impossible that nakedness was regarded by the warriors as a guarantee of reincarnation in the event of death. More practical perhaps was the consideration of wounds: these could not be infected by a grubby jerkin.

Gaul itself developed under Roman rule into one of the rich parts of the empire through a thriving agriculture. It was famous for its foodstuffs and cuisine. Barbarian invasions and civil wars brought ruin during the fifth century AD, when imperial government in the western provinces broke down. Its Gaulish inhabitants had to make room for German settlers, such as the Visigoths, Burgundians and Franks. The latter went on under the Merovingian royal house to dominate what today is France.

*See* CAESAR; GALATIANS; ROME; SELEUCIDS; SLAVERY; WARFARE; VERCINGETORIX

*M. J. Green, *The World of the Celts* (London, 1995).

**Gnosticism** was, according to the Christian historian Eusebius, the work of the devil. 'Previously,' he wrote, 'Satan had used persecutions from without as his weapon against the church, but now he was no longer able to do this he used instead wicked men and sorcerers for his purpose.' These 'sorcerers' were the Gnostic thinkers, many of whom lived in Alexandria between AD 130 and 180. Their belief, though centred on Christ, accepted the scriptures as only one source of revelation, which might be supplemented and even superseded by ideas drawn from Greek, Persian, and Semitic mythology. The Palestinian sorcerer, Simon Magus, is usually regarded as the first Gnostic, or 'one with knowledge'. While in Jerusalem St Peter had to rebuke Simon for trying to purchase the magical powers with which he believed the Apostles were endowed; but the legendary encounter between the two men is supposed to have taken place in Rome, where the apocryphal Acts of Peter tell how Simon tried to fly heavenwards. When he soared and 'was lifted up on high, and all beheld him flying above Rome and its temples and hills', the faithful turned to Peter, who was disturbed by the impression that the aerobatics made of their minds. 'Hasten thy grace, O Lord,' implored the apostle, 'and let him fall from the height and be injured. Let him not die but be discomforted, and break his leg in three places.' And so it happened that Simon fell to the ground and injured only his leg, much to the annoyance of the crowd. Instead of becoming a martyr, the ultimate sacrifice reserved for Christians, Peter's prayer made certain that Simon instead suffered the indignity of a shower of stones from disappointed onlookers.

Notwithstanding this quite spectacular embarrassment, Gnosticism soon developed into a formidable movement during the second century AD. Its attempt to explain how a benevolent deity could coexist with the evils of the world proved attractive, especially when Gnostic teachers claimed to know of a spiritual resurrection that liberated the soul from all physical bonds. But Gnosticism could never have become such a threat to orthodox Christianity if it had been rooted in pagan worship. It was strong and persuasive because it was so steeped in Jewish and Greek thought. An early Alexandrian Gnostic by the name of Basilides probably quoted the philosopher Plato from memory when he said: 'God was not the cause of all things, but only of what is good.' The secret knowledge that the Gnostics believed they possessed gained a second lease of life in Manichaeism towards the end of the western Roman empire. For nine years (AD 373–382) Augustine was a Manichee, and long afterwards his own vision of the elect differed little from the chosen few of Mani (AD 216–277).

See CHRISTIANITY; MANICHAEISM

*G. Filoramo, *A History of Gnosticism* (Oxford, 1990).

**Gosala**, a contemporary of the Jain saviour Mahavira and the Buddha (*c.* 563–479 BC), took the Indian idea of almost endless rebirth in a vale of tears to its logical conclusion. Classical Hinduism held that an individual was reborn in happy or unhappy circumstances according to personal actions in a previous life, and therefore any suffering that had to be borne in the present one was a result of neither fate nor chance, but a just recompense for past behaviour. Even though this meant that the individual was always obliged to accept with resignation the situation in which he found himself, good conduct and the fulfilment of social duties would ensure a better lot in a future rebirth. Maskarin Gosala, however, took the view that no action had any consequence of good or ill. All one had to do was submit to the round of rebirth – possibly as much as 8,400,000 times – before naturally attaining perfection. Such determinism attracted strong criticism from Hindus, Buddhists and Jains. But his so-called Ajivika sect (the name refers to the soul's incomplete cycle of rebirths) proved attractive to at least one Mauryan emperor, Bindusara (297–272 BC). This forceful ruler had no time for his father's devotion to Jainism, nor did he share his son's later sympathy with the non-violent doctrines of Buddhism.

See BINDUSARA; BUDDHISM; HINDUISM; JAINISM

*H. Zimmer, *The Philosophies of India* (Princeton, 1969).

**Goths** troubled Rome from the late fourth century AD onwards. First the Visigoths in AD 378 dealt a body-blow to the eastern provinces at the battle of Adrianople (modern Erine in Bulgaria). Visigothic cavalry mowed down the Roman infantry and slew the emperor Valens, the brother of Valentinian (AD 364–375). Yet there were Visigoths and other Germans in the Roman ranks, because manpower shortages had already led to large-scale barbarian recruitment. From AD 360 onwards the Romans were obliged to recruit heavily among German peoples living directly across the northern frontier. There were set procedures for the recruitment, training, and station-

ing of such troops in order to ensure their loyalty and the stability of the regular units they joined. About AD 380 a clash occurred in Asia Minor between Visigothic recruits on their way to training and deployment in Egypt and the forces being transferred from there to the Balkans. The regulars came out of the scuffle on top, but it would not have taken long for the barbarian recruits to become an equally effective force on the Nile. What is significant about this episode is that it shows the old system in operation, perhaps for the last time. For on their arrival in the Balkans the soldiers from Egypt found the surviving legions in complete disarray and Visigoths freely loitering everywhere. The basic difficulty was the sheer numbers involved. Although the Roman emperor Theodosius I (AD 379–395) had managed to contain the Visigoths after their victory at Adrianople, he could make peace only through abandoning the usual recruitment arrangements. For the first time Rome had to accept as an ally a whole barbarian people, settled on land within the empire and yet living under its own laws and ruler.

This treaty meant that Visigoths settled in Thrace no longer served as individual recruits, but in units commanded by their own leaders. It was a policy which, as in classical China under the Western Jin dynasty (AD 265–316), led to disaster once barbarian peoples became engaged in civil wars. Theodosius himself never saw the barbarian problem as insoluble, and he might have judged correctly had not the western provinces been weakened by a series of usurpations and further migrations. His younger son Honorius, emperor in the west from AD 395 to 423, could do little more than watch from the safety of Ravenna as the various warlords struggled for supremacy. One of these was Alaric (died AD 410), who invaded Italy with an army of discontented Visigoths in AD 401. Frustrated by Honorius' refusal to reach an accommodation, Alaric let his men sack Rome for three days in AD 410. Later these Visigoths moved to Gaul and Spain, before in AD 418 receiving permission from Honorius to settle permanently on two-thirds of the land in south-western Gaul. Another first for Rome, the settlement in an interior province shifted barbarians into the very heart of the empire. It was to prove a fatal model for dealing with later migrations of German peoples, such as the Burgundians and the Franks.

After AD 418 the Visigothic kingdom in south-western Gaul gradually grew in strength and size. Campaigns undertaken by its king, Theodoric, were always in support of one Roman faction or another, but the net result was a steady extension of his virtually independent realm. While technically honouring his military commitments to the western Roman emperor, Theodoric consolidated Visigothic control of the original settlement area and expanded its borders as well. He continued in this fashion until his

death in AD 451, fighting alongside the Romans against Attila on the Catalaunian Fields, near present-day Troyes. At this period the most powerful barbarian allies of Rome in Gaul were the Burgundians, who in AD 413 had been allowed to settle inside the empire as part of the Rhine defences. Now they were able to demand the allocation of land in eastern and southern Gaul. Another barbarian kingdom was also being formed in the north by the Franks, a people used originally by the Romans along the lower Rhine frontier.

A second wave of Gothic migration comprised the Ostrogoths. Unlike their cousins the Visigoths, they did not respond to Hunnish pressure by crossing the Danube in the AD 370s. The Ostrogoths had remained instead beyond the Roman frontier, and eventually became part of the Hunnish empire. In AD 422 they participated in its first invasion of the Balkans; by AD 430 the imperial government had agreed to pay tribute to the Huns in return for peace. In AD 434 the new king of the Huns, Attila, demanded twice as much each year, and this burden was met with difficulty until the eastern emperor Marcian (AD 450–457) told him he could 'have iron in future, but no gold'. Part of a general tightening-up of public expenditure at Constantinople, the unexpected refusal to continue payments persuaded Attila to launch his famous assault on the feebler western provinces. There in AD 451, however, he met his only military setback, dying two years afterwards of a burst blood-vessel on his wedding night. The Hunnish empire abruptly fell apart and left the Ostrogoths as the dominant barbarian people in the Balkans. Hardly surprising, therefore, was the encouragement given by Constantinople in AD 488 to the Ostrogothic king to follow in the steps of Alaric, and invade Italy. There he overthrew Odoacer, the deposer of the last western Roman emperor Romulus Augustulus (AD 475–476), and established a powerful kingdom, which later on the eastern emperor Justinian (AD 527–565) had to fight very hard to overcome.

See ATTILA; HONORIUS; ROME; ROMULUS AUGUSTULUS; THEODOSIUS I; VALENTINIAN; WARFARE

★T. S. Burns, *Barbarians within the Gates of Rome* (Bloomington, 1994) and *A History of the Ostrogoths* (Bloomington, 1984).

**Gracchi** were two Roman noblemen who died for introducing much-needed agrarian reforms. The elder brother, Tiberius Sempronius Gracchus (163–133 BC), was interested in the radical doctrines of early Stoicism, a philosophy that at first regarded all forms of subordination as unjust. Later it split into two antagonistic bodies of thought, and the notions of reactionary exponents encouraged those who rallied against the younger brother, Gaius Sempronius Gracchus (154–121 BC).

What the Gracchi tried to address was the marked decline in the number of Roman citizens on the land, which went hand in hand with the increase in the slave population of Italy. Tiberius' proposal to the citizen assembly was to distribute illegally occupied public land to the landless poor. In reply the senate, the stronghold of the landowning aristocracy, arranged for his deposition from the office of tribune. When he tried to be elected again and revive the proposal, finance for which was to come from the revenues of the newly acquired province of Asia, the senators resorted to violence and Tiberius Gracchus was killed. Their followers, the historian Plutarch relates, 'were armed with clubs and staves, which they had brought from their homes. The senators themselves snatched up the legs and fragments of broken benches, and made straight for Tiberius, lashing out at those who were drawn up to protect him . . . The reformer was felled by a blow to the head, and more than a hundred of his supporters were killed with him, but none by the sword.' This first outbreak of civil strife in Rome, in 133 BC, not only marked the end of upper-class solidarity and the arrival of violent political confrontation; by Tiberius' use of the assembly, it also introduced a new factor into Rome's oligarchic constitution. The urban poor became through the assembly a rival to the wishes of senators, offering to unscrupulous politicians a new field for exploitation. The impoverished did not derive much benefit themselves, though, for the political uncertainty opened the way for military adventurers to seize power. Before leaving for his long campaign in Gaul, Julius Caesar (100–44 BC) even formed an alliance with a young popularist named Clodius, who he hoped would look after his interests in the capital. Clodius (92–52 BC) attempted this by means of his numerous and violent following.

When in 123 BC Gaius Gracchus endeavoured to extend the programme of reform such developments were still some years off. But his ideas were running along more radical lines than his older brother's, as Plutarch makes plain. 'He introduced a number of laws which he hoped would not only find favour with the people but would also undermine the authority of the senate.' These included measures to speed up the settlement of public land; provide clothing for conscripted citizens, a burden for those who had the minimal land qualification; introduce state-subsidized wheat rations for citizens resident in the capital; found colonies for poor citizens; extend the franchise to Italian allies; and establish juries which excluded senators to try cases of extortion in the provinces. The manpower crisis implicit in this programme was felt most acutely in army recruitment, by tradition the preserve of men who owned land. Prolonged campaigning overseas had impoverished many countrymen and land distribution seemed to offer the possibility of restoring some of them to the ranks. Yet the Gracchan reforms were not enough to solve the recruitment

problem on their own, and it was left to Marius (157–86 BC) to take the logical step in 107–106 BC, when he enlisted men in his army with no regard for property qualification whatsoever. The subsequent settlement of veterans as farmers, however, introduced yet another influence into Roman politics: generals of a progressively professional army. Thwarted in 121 BC, Gaius took the initiative when his armed supporters occupied the streets. This was exactly what Gaius' opponents were waiting for, and they forced the senate to declare a public emergency. In the riot which then ensued thousands of Gracchan loyalists were killed. The body of the reformer, like that of his brother just twelve years before, was thrown into the Tiber. A triumphant consul later had the cheek to dedicate a temple to Concordia, a goddess who personified good relations between all Roman citizens. One dark night someone wrote alongside its dedicatory inscription: 'Concordia's temple by mad Discord built'.

The land question remained a problem for Rome throughout the late republican period. The only solution, besides a programme of wholesale re-allocation like the one tried in China by the usurper Wang Mang (AD 9–23), was a huge extension of settlements for veterans, Italians and others, outside Italy, a policy the first Roman emperor Augustus (31 BC – AD 14) eventually adopted. In China the buying and selling of land as well as slaves was banned by Wang Mang, and small families in possession of large estates were forced to surrender part of their holdings for settlement of the landless. Government loans at low interest were offered to poor peasants for the purchase of tools and seed, the finance for this regeneration of the countryside coming from the profits of state monopolies over salt, iron, alcohol and gold.

*See* AUGUSTUS; MARIUS; ROME; STOICISM; WANG MANG

*A. E. Bernstein, *Tiberius Sempronius Gracchus: Tradition and Apostasy* (Ithaca, 1978); D. Stockton, *The Gracchi* (Oxford, 1979).

**Great Wall** of China, in its final form, extended nearly 2,000 miles from Shanhaiguan, 'the pass between the land and the sea', on the coast of the Yellow Sea to beyond Dunhuang, the huge Buddhist cave complex in the Gobi desert. Unequalled as a single line of defence, the Great Wall is the only work of man visible to orbiting space crews. Hadrian's Wall, built across the northern part of the Roman province of Britain, is a mere 76 miles in length.

When the First Emperor ordered the construction of the Great Wall in 214 BC, he intended to separate once and for all the ordered world of China from the attentions of the uncivilized peoples roaming the steppe. About 800 miles in length, this first Great Wall was a rationalization of the various rammed-earth walls already thrown up on their northern borders by the feudal states he had just conquered. The only

new section definitely built during the Qin dynasty (221–207 BC) was a northward extension to include the Ordos desert, a task overseen by Meng Tian. Argument still continues over the exact line this Qin general's new bastion took, and there is even a suggestion that he repaired an existing wall built by the state of Zhao. The remorse felt by Meng Tian himself in 210 BC, shortly before his death, for having injured the earth by his wall-building would suggest otherwise. Tricked into committing suicide by a court intrigue, following the First Emperor's sudden death, he accepted what he regarded as a just punishment for the Great Wall's construction. 'I have made walls and ditches,' Meng Tian said, 'over more than ten thousand li. In a work of this distance it is impossible not to have cut through the veins of the earth. This is my crime.'

The enormity of the task which

A model of a fortified farm, from a Later Han tomb. Such towers would have been constructed along the Great Wall.

Meng Tian accomplished was reckoned by the historian Sima Qian to be a factor in the successful popular rebellion against the Qin dynasty, China's first imperial house. According to Sima Qian, the general's death had less to do with upsetting natural forces than his 'utter disregard for the distress of the people'. As a compliant servant of the First Emperor, Meng Tian had shut his eyes to the suffering of the conscripted labourers who toiled and died in their thousands building the Great Wall.

Under the succeeding Han dynasty (202 BC – AD 220), the length of the Great Wall was virtually doubled, as Chinese arms pressed westwards into Central Asia. But against the aggressive Xiongnu, probably the Huns who later invaded the Roman empire, the Han emperors still found the northern defences inadequate. For most of the time there was little more than an armed truce along the Great Wall, with nomad leaders kept at bay more by annual subsidies than military might. But disunity amongst the Xiongnu largely removed the northern threat during the first century AD. Friendly nomads acted as buffer states immediately north of the Great Wall, and some of these tribesmen were even settled within the line of defences. When the Xianbei Tartars defeated the Xiongnu in AD 88, for instance, a memorial to the throne could congratulate the emperor for having won a war without losing a single Chinese soldier. Only towards the end of the Han dynasty did the system break down, with raids becoming a serious problem once again. After AD 168, a chronicler noted sadly, 'no year passed without a nomad invasion.'

Yet the northern defences held firm during the period of disunity following the fall of the Han in AD 220. The half a century of rivalry between the states of Wei, Wu and Shu known as the Three Kingdoms was centred well to the south of the Great Wall. That the northern state of Wei was the ultimate winner may in part explain the containment of the nomad threat. Pressure was also reduced by the westward movement of many Xiongnu tribes. But an internal threat was forming in the growing number of Xianbei and Xiongnu contingents employed by the Western Jin dynasty, which in AD 280 briefly reunified China. Its founder, Sima Yan, was a Wei general who drew upon the extra manpower of nomadic migrants who were allowed to settle in large numbers within the Great Wall. This policy of barbarian settlement had the same dire consequences for north China that it had for the western provinces of the Roman empire. Dynastic strife rendered the Great Wall redundant, when in AD 304 the Xiongnu backed one prince and the Xianbei were enlisted by another. In AD 311 Luoyang was sacked and the emperor captured; then in AD 316 the last Western Jin ruler was taken prisoner on the fall of Chang'an. The Chinese rallied in the southern provinces under the Eastern Jin dynasty (AD 317–420), but for almost three centuries Tartar houses ruled through-out in the north.

Apart from its obvious military func-tion, the Great Wall could be argued to have had in classical times a cultural and economic effect as well. The fun-damental division was always between the nomadic life of the northern steppe and the settled communities of farmers south of the line of the Great Wall. That is why for the First Emperor one of its intended purposes was to keep his subjects securely inside the imperial frontiers, lest they migrate northwards and strengthen the nomad economy.

See HADRIAN'S WALL; HAN WU DI; LI LING; MENG TIAN; WARFARE; XIONGNU
*A. Waldron, *The Great Wall of China: From History to Myth* (Cambridge, 1990); T. J. Barfield, *The Perilous Frontier: Nomadic Empires and China, 221 BC to AD 1757* (Oxford, 1989).

**Gupta dynasty** (AD 320–550) marked the return of large-scale native states to India. The period of disunity and foreign invasion, following the collapse of the Mauryan dynasty (322–183 BC), was ended in AD 320 when Candra-gupta I, the first important Gupta ruler, reasserted the hegemony of Magadha (present-day Bihar). Once again Pataliputra (modern Patna) became the capital of an Indian empire. During the preceding Kushana domination of northern India, the Guptas had been obscure vassals of these Central Asian conquerors. Only the name of Candragupta's immediate predecessor

is known with any certainty: he was Ghatotkachagupta, who ruled from AD 280 to 319. Ghatotkachagupta is termed a 'monarch' in surviving inscrip-tions, whereas his son Candragupta is always referred to as 'king of kings', a formula ultimately derived from the royal titles of the Persians, who had controlled north-western India from the late sixth century BC till the arrival of Alexander the Great in 327 BC.

Chandragupta I (AD 320–335) was clearly the first independent ruler of the Gupta dynasty. He strengthened his position in Magadha by means of marriage alliance as well as the pursuit of arms. Gold coins celebrate both political advances. Under Candra-gupta's son Samudragupta (AD 335–376), Gupta power spread far and wide. This energetic emperor was known as 'the toppler of kings' because of the drive for secure frontiers: the western bank of the Indus, the foothills of the Himalayas, the northern edge of the Deccan, and the sea. An inscription even claims Samudragupta 'extended his dominion to the four oceans'. There can be no doubt that he under-took a remarkable series of military campaigns, for his conquests included the western kingdoms based on Vidisa and Mathura; frontier powers in the north and the east; and in the south, twelve states such as Kosala (modern Raipur and Bilaspur), Kanci (Kon-jeeveram in Tamiland), and Eranda-palla (present-day Erandapalli, a town near Chicacole in Vizagapattam). But the southern thrust does not appear to have been without set back. On the Deccan Samudragupta found military domination difficult to achieve, and he may have suffered a serious reverse at the hands of the combined rulers of the eastern area. Also in the very far south, unlike the earlier Mauryan dynasty, the Guptas were never to enjoy lasting supremacy. They were obliged to rely upon alliances rather than annexation: Samudragupta set the pattern by reinstating defeated rulers and accepting gifts of treasure. Claims that the Sri Lanka king became his vassal are unfounded, since we know the purpose of the mission dispatched from the island to Pataliputra. The rich gifts sent to Samudragupta were intended to persuade him to look kindly upon a request to build a monastery and rest-house for Sinhalese pilgrims at Bodh Gaya, the place where the Buddha attained enlightenment. Evidently the Gupta emperor chose to regard this as paying tribute.

It would appear that the Guptas were anxious to match the territorial

Gold issue of the Gupta emperor Samudragupta, dating from the late fourth century AD.

achievements of the Mauryas, who at one time controlled almost the entire subcontinent. Samudragupta's father was probably called Candragupta in imitation of Candragupta Maurya (322–297 BC). During the reigns of the first two Guptas the whole of northern India enjoyed a peace and security which certainly helped the economy to revive through both internal and external trade. Roman demand for spices had already led Indian merchants to venture as middlemen to South-east Asia, where Indianized kingdoms were soon to form in what is now Burma, Cambodia and Indonesia. A brief period of disruption nevertheless came after Samudragupta's death in AD 376. Trouble with the Scythian Sakas was the specific cause, although Rama-gupta (*c.* AD 376–377) may have been a weak successor. One story relates how he was prepared to buy off the Sakas with the promise of his own wife, despite the opposition of his younger brother Candragupta II (*c.* AD 377–*c.* 412). In the event Candragupta went to the Saka camp disguised as the empress, and killed the Saka king. Sometime later Candragupta also did away with Ramagupta, whom some argue was never a historical ruler at all. Several coins ostensibly dating from his short reign have been discounted as late forgeries. Yet the second Candragupta was compelled to wage a long war of annihilation against Sakas settled in northern India. He was not free from it until almost AD 400. His own long reign, however, witnessed the culmination of classical Indian culture. The greatest sculpture was then produced and the finest literature written, in the poems and plays of Kalidasa. At Ajanta (in present-day Maharashtra) a series of Buddhist caves were cut and decorated with resplendent sculpture and murals. Today a visitor to the semi-circular gorge is still amazed at the feat of excavation itself: a single cave can be as much as 100 feet long and 40 feet wide.

Kumaragupta I (*c.* AD 412–455) continued his father's patronage of both religions and the arts, but none of his military campaigns are recorded. As he issued so-called rhinoceros-slayer coins, it has been suggested that Assam was annexed during his reign. What we can be sure about is the formidable adversary Kumaragupta faced in his final years: the Hunas, known in Europe as the White Huns. Hunnish invaders were eventually held in check by Skandagupta (AD 455–467), who was Kumaragupta's son by a secondary empress. The ability shown by Skandagupta on the battlefield secured his succession, because his defeats of the Hunas were praised throughout the Gupta empire 'by happy men, even down to the children'. Successful though his campaigns were as a prince and as an emperor, they taxed the resources of the state to the extent of debasing coinage. For the temporary reprieve from the Huns won by Skandagupta was the final phase of Indian classicism. The king himself worshipped Hindu gods and goddesses,

then returning to the fore, but he did not neglect other beliefs such as Jainism and Buddhism.

Skandagupta was the last Gupta ruler of real importance. Nothing is known about his sons, and the throne seems to have been contested by his nephews, Kumaragupta's grandsons. But Gupta authority was already in such decline that reliable information about the dynasty's last rulers is missing. Some sort of local revival in Magadha, the Gupta heartland, may have occurred under Buddhagupta (*c.* AD 477–495), but outlying territories were lost. A great defect of the administration was the reliance upon hereditary governors in distant provinces. These men took their chance for power once the Hunas broke into northern India around AD 460. One of their descendants by the name of Yasodharman rose to prominence in the AD 530s, when he claimed to rule over a large area of northern India. That the Hunas accelerated the breakup of the Gupta empire there is no doubt, although the dynasty was in difficulties prior to Skandagupta's death. Having lost direct control of so much territory, it was impossible to organize any form of national defence, and India remained a patchwork of antagonistic kingdoms until the Muslim invasion.

*See* BUDDHISM; CANDRAGUPTA II; DRAMA; HUNS; JAINISM; MAURYAN DYNASTY

*S. K. Maity, *The Imperial Guptas and their Times* (Delhi, 1975); R. K. Mookerji, *The Gupta Empire* (Delhi, 1969).

# H

**Hadrian**, Roman emperor AD 117–138, was born either in Spain or Rome around AD 76. Publius Aelius Hadrianus may never have been adopted by his childless predecessor Trajan (AD 98–117), who succumbed to a stroke. It was given out that the dying emperor had chosen Hadrian as his heir, and the support of Trajan's widow seems to have helped secure the succession. Though distantly related to Trajan, the new emperor was really able to rule for over twenty years because he gained the confidence of the Roman army, now the sole basis of imperial power. Perhaps the most notable aspect of his long reign was the fact that he spent more than half of it outside Italy, travelling throughout the provinces of the empire. His motives for all these journeys were varied. The chief aim was military, but Hadrian also ranks as the greatest imperial tourist ever. His concern over the effectiveness of the imperial defences came from a conviction that Trajan's conquests had badly overstretched the empire. So he reversed frontier policy

in the eastern Mediterranean, evacuated Mesopotamia, and reverted to the usual buffer zone of client-kingdoms. On the northern frontier, however, he confirmed the annexation of Dacia, a rich source of slaves and precious metals. But in Britain, which he visited in AD 121 or 122, Hadrian fixed a northern boundary by building the wall that bears his name. This policy of creating a permanent frontier involved removing soldiers from some of the forts in Wales to man the fortification, so that new centres had to be established for civilian administration there. A result of the emperor's interest in Britain was a provincial self-confidence soon evident in fresh building activity in many towns. Yet the Welsh town of Caerwent, in Gwent, still remained one of the smallest settlements, with an area of less than 44 acres. It was the tribal capital of the Silures, who were encouraged to manage their own affairs under the watchful eye of imperial officials. A consequence of Hadrian's revision of imperial foreign policy and his establishment of fixed frontiers was that it became increasingly rare for legions to be transferred from one province to another. Troops began to settle down in their bases and rely even more than before upon local recruitment. Perhaps in order to overcome any adverse effect such immobility might have on the army's performance in the field, Hadrian placed great emphasis on training and discipline, his inspections forming the basis of future Roman military regulations.

The Roman emperor Hadrian, perhaps the most travelled of all Rome's rulers.

Travel made Hadrian the first emperor to see the provinces from other than a Roman standpoint. He came to appreciate their distinct characters and aspirations, thereby giving full acknowledgement to the cultural diversity that was typical of the empire.

With only one people, the Jews, was Hadrian heavy-handed. Possibly his cosmopolitan outlook caused a lack of sympathy with Jewish separatism, for the imperial reaction to Bar Cochba's revolt of AD 132–135 in Judaea was untypically fierce. Hadrian may have even been present when the city of Jerusalem finally fell, because he certainly approved of the placing of a marble statue of a pig in front of the Bethlehem Gate: the animal happened to be the emblem of one of the legions involved in the siege. Not only did Hadrian renew the ban on circumcision, but he also sold large numbers of captured Jews into slavery. So many were put on sale that they fetched less per head than the price of a horse. Jerusalem was rebuilt as a Roman city, with temples to Jupiter and Venus placed on both Christian and Jewish sites. No Jew might henceforth enter. This final defeat of Jewish political and religious hopes, however, had a lasting effect on Christianity rather than Judaism. With less emphasis on messianism, the Christian church grew away from Judaism and began to absorb some of the ideas originated by Greek schools of philosophy. Had Hadrian been aware of this transformation, he would have been pleased, since in his mind civilization was deeply indebted to classical Greece: not for nothing was he nicknamed 'Greekling'. A keen writer and musician himself, the emperor patronized the arts and gave Rome its outstanding ancient building of today, the remodelled

Pantheon, first erected by Augustus' loyal supporter Agrippa (*c.* 63–12 BC). Other buildings are the Castel San Angelo, formerly the emperor's mausoleum, and the extensive villa laid out as his country retreat at nearby Tivoli.

One of the many portraits of Antinous, Hadrian's boyfriend. He became a god after drowning in AD 130.

The succession was Hadrian's worst problem. Relations with his wife were strained for the good reason that the emperor preferred the company of a Bithynian youth by the name of Antinous. This handsome boyfriend drowned in the Nile in AD 130, two years after Hadrian's wife had died childless. A distraught emperor was moved by a popular wave of religious feeling that elevated Antinous to divinity. Hardly surprising, therefore, were the Greek statues set up to Antinous shortly afterwards; those which survive manage to add to the beauty of a classical body a head laden with melancholy, an entirely new emotional intensity in sculpture. One tradition even asserts that Antinous had died so that Hadrian's life could be prolonged. The choice of successor eventually fell

on Antoninus Pius (AD 138–161), who was obliged to adopt two sons in turn: they were the future emperors Marcus Aurelius (AD 161–180) and Lucius Verus (AD 161–169).

*See* ANTONINE DYNASTY; BRITAIN; CHRISTIANITY; TRAJAN
★A. R. Birley, *Hadrian: The Restless Emperor* (London, 1977).

**Hadrian's Wall**, some 70 miles in length, closed the Solway-Tyne gap. Begun after the Roman emperor Hadrian's visit to Britain in AD 121 or 122, its western half from Wallsend was stone-built, while the eastern half to Bowness-on-Solway was constructed with turf. Some 15 feet high, excluding battlements, the wall was in places fronted by a defensive ditch, 26 feet wide and 15 feet deep. A series of forts acted as vantage points and gate-

A wooden writing-tablet discovered at Vindolanda, near Hadrian's Wall. It describes British military tactics.

ways through the wall, which was manned against the unconquered British peoples to the north, notably the Novantae and Selgovae. These had caused considerable disturbances in AD 118, but Hadrian chose to apply the same defensive policy in Britain as in the rest of the empire, where he abandoned most of the conquests made by his predecessor Trajan (AD 98–117).

Hadrian's Wall possessed a sentry walk, but it was not primarily intended as a line for static defence. Unlike the fighting platform provided by a town wall, its main function seems to have been a means of separating the Novantae, Selgovae and Votadini from their British cousins, the Brigantes, who dwelt to the south, within Roman territory. The existence of a ditch on the wall's southern side indicates rather a military zone, from which legionaries could launch attacks against enemies both inside and outside the frontier. Annoyance at continued resistance is evident from documents recovered from the pre-Hadrianic fort at Vindolanda in Northumberland. A memorandum written on a thin piece of wood relates how 'the Britons are unprotected by armour. There are very many cavalry. The cavalry do not use swords nor do the wretched Britons mount to throw javelins.' Soon after his succession, the emperor Antoninus Pius (AD 138–161) decided to move the frontier line northwards to the Forth-Clyde, and to modify Hadrian's defensive arrangements by removing the gates from the mile-castles, and by

building causeways across the outer ditch.

The building of the Antonine Wall may have drawn enough of the Roman army of occupation northwards to encourage the Brigantes to revolt in the AD 150s. Put down with some difficulty, this revolt seems to have led to a rethinking of the northern defences, which ended in the abandonment of the Forth-Clyde barrier for Hadrian's Solway-Tyne line. Even though the emperor Septimius Severus (AD 193–211) tried to push northwards once again, leading massive expeditions into Caledonia as far as the Moray Firth, Hadrian's Wall remained the effective Roman frontier. After Septimius' death in Eburacum (present-day York) no further attempt was made to change it by the Romans.

*See* BRITAIN; HADRIAN; TRAJAN; SEVERAN DYNASTY

*D. J. Breeze and B. Dobson, *Hadrian's Wall* (Harmondsworth, 1987); A. K. Bowman, *Life and Letters on the Roman Frontier: Vindolanda and its People* (London, 1994).


**Han dynasty** (202 BC – AD 220) was divided into two parts, the Former Han (202 BC – AD 9) and the Later Han (AD 25–220), by the usurpation of Wang Mang. The family of Wang Mang had been influential at the Chinese court through marriage to the imperial clan for two decades prior to his seizure of the throne. His brief dynasty, the Xin (AD 9–23), was closely bound up with recurring economic problems and the renewed activities of the Xiongnu, probably the Huns who later invaded the Roman empire.

The Former Han dynasty was founded in 202 BC by Liu Bang (247–195 BC), a man of the people. He emerged as the ultimate victor in the nationwide rebellion against Qin, the first imperial house (221–207 BC). Taking the title of Gaozu, or 'High Ancestor', this unusual peasant-emperor founded a new capital at Chang'an, across the Wei river from Xianyang, the Qin foundation which the rebels had burnt to the ground. Even though he was himself illiterate, Emperor Han Gaozu knew the value of learned and cultivated advisers, and he turned to those scholars uncontaminated by the excesses of Legalism, the philosophy behind Qin oppression. So it was that Confucianism gradually became the outlook of the officials who manned the bureaucratic empire. The early years of the Han were an inevitable compromise after the forcible unification of China under the First Emperor (221–210 BC). Certain feudal houses were restored, but their diminished holdings were intertwined with districts controlled by imperial officials. A rebellion among the eastern vassals in 154 BC was used to complete the downgrading of the old aristocracy.

Through his persistence and severity, it was the Han emperor Wu Di (140–87 BC) who ended all power-sharing with the nobility, and then bent to his own will the salaried officials who replaced it. Gaozu had summoned scholars to assist with administration, but Wu Di was the first emperor who set examinations for would-be officials. He would even revise the pass list personally when he spotted a candidate whose ideas he liked. The total bureaucracy, from ministers to minor officials, in 5 BC numbered about 135,000, a figure thought to be slightly higher than in Wu Di's reign. The political theories of the eminent Confucian thinker Dong Zhongshu (c. 179–c. 104 BC) were just beginning to take hold at this period, although the boundless energy of Wu Di effectively postponed any real limitation of imperial power. Wu Di was additionally troubled with economic difficulties exacerbated by a long war against the Xiongnu. A policy of appeasement adopted by Gaozu, following a decisive defeat on the battlefield at Pingcheng in 200 BC, no longer prevented nomad raids and a more robust approach was adopted by the Chinese. An envoy named Zhang Qian was sent to Central Asia in order to stir up the enemies of the Xiongnu there in 138 BC: by 101 BC military expeditions had established Chinese suzerainty over the Western Regions, as this important source of horses was called in Chang'an.

The arrival of Chinese arms in Central Asia disturbed the balance of nomad power, and for nearly half a century the Xiongnu were contained. In order to deny them supplies new colonies were also planted in the north-east as a protection for the overland route to Korea. All these victories made Wu Di famous, but by 91 BC he recognized that the strain of continuous campaigning was becoming intolerable. No Chinese emperor could wage a prolonged war and avoid rebellion, since imperial armies depended on a militia that supplemented small forces of professional soldiers. As Dong Zhongshu pointedly argued, a ruler's position of authority was granted and taken away by Heaven, whose agents for affecting change could be humble men such as Liu Bang. The radical policies Wu Di adopted to revive the ailing economy were debated, but not reversed, after his death in 87 BC. Confucianists remained uneasy about state monopolies declared over iron and salt, even though they supported discrimination against merchants. To counter speculation in foodstuffs Wu Di had established public granaries and ordered provincial officials to buy when prices were low and sell in times of shortage.

Wu Di himself ensured the smooth succession of his youngest son Zhao Di (87–74 BC), but court intrigue later undermined his successors and gave Wang Mang his brief chance of power. That Wang Mang felt obliged to outdo Wu Di in the extent of his own reforms indicates the gravity of the economic and political crisis then facing the empire. To curb the influence of the wealthy, he forbade the buying and selling of land as well as of slaves, and compelled small families with large estates to surrender land for distribution to those who had none. Low-interest government loans, funded by an extension of state monopolies over salt, iron, alcohol and gold, enabled poor peasants to buy tools and seed. Resistance to Wang Mang's radical measures was aided by the lukewarm attitude of officials, often themselves the relatives of important landowners. It became irresistible when floods, famine and mismanaged relief drove the northern provinces into a rebellion that coincided with large-scale operations against the Xiongnu. In AD 23 the severed head of the usurper was stoned in the marketplace of Chang'an.

An official seal belonging to a brother of the first Later Han emperor Gwangwu Di, who allowed his close relatives to rule small kingdoms within the imperial boundaries.

The Later Han restoration was not fully complete till AD 36, however. For Gwangwu Di (AD 25–57) faced many rivals without the popular support enjoyed earlier by Liu Bang. Because his chief supporters were the large landowners, there was never any scope for the restored dynasty to interfere with land tenure. As one of them commented: 'In present times, it is not only the sovereign who selects his subjects. The subjects select their sovereign too.' These are the words of Ma Yuan (14 BC – AD 49), whose generalship saved China from Tibetan attack and secured the far south through the pacification in AD 42 of northern Vietnam. The latter had rebelled two years before under two aristocratic sisters, Trung Trac and Trung Ni. With an army of 20,000 men, Ma Yuan dealt with the rebels and strengthened the administration in the three Vietnamese commanderies by means of fortified towns and irrigation schemes.

The transfer of the seat of imperial government a distance downstream from Chang'an to Luoyang was tacit acknowledgement on the part of the Later Han emperors that times were changing. The lower Yangzi and Huai river valleys had begun to overtake the northern provinces as the most developed region of the empire. The breakup of China during the Three Kingdoms period (AD 221–280) can be seen, therefore, as a continuation of this same process in that the southern kingdoms of Shu and Wu were sufficiently strong to challenge for many years the northern state of Wei, which was the rump of the Han empire.

In contrast with the Former Han capital, Luoyang appeared almost frugal. The splendours of Wu Di's reign were gone. With 500,000 inhabitants, Luoyang was about half as populous as Rome and without the high-rise tenement slums for which this western capital was so notorious. But it was destroyed soon after a massacre of the palace eunuchs in AD 189. Since the emperors had taken to using their eunuchs against powerful families, these conflicts tended only to make the eunuchs powerful in turn, until at last their plots drew the army into politics. The beneficiary of this particular coup was a general named Cao Cao (AD 155–220), who assumed authority in all but name: the dynasty was tolerated as long as Cao Cao considered it politically useful.

Despite imperial decline under the Later Han, a subject that exercised the philosopher Wang Chong (AD 27–100), Chinese arms were temporarily triumphant in Central Asia. General Ban Chao successfully contained the Kushanas, who had just carved out for themselves a great realm extending from northern India to Sogdia. And until AD 150 the balance of power on the steppe favoured China. That year the Xiongnu wrestled the Western Regions from Chinese control and raided south of the Great Wall. Other advances under the Later Han were significant inventions connected with imperial patronage. In AD 31 the state-owned iron industry took advantage of a water-powered metallurgical machine to move towards the production of steel. Another step forward in the imperial workshops was the perfection of paper-making around AD 105, a boon for a bureaucratic state.

See ADMINISTRATION; BAN CHAO; DONG ZHONGSHU; HAN WU DI; INVENTIONS; KUSHANAS; LIU BANG; MA YUAN; QIN DYNASTY; THREE KINGDOMS; WANG MANG; WESTERN REGIONS; XIONGNU

*M. Pirazzoti-t'Serstevens, *The Han Civilization of China* (Oxford, 1982); M. Loewe, *Everyday Life in Early Imperial China* (London, 1968); Yu Ying-shih, *Trade and Expansion in Han China* (Berkeley, 1967).

**Han Fei Zi** (*c.* 280–233 BC) and, earlier, Shang Yang (390–338 BC) propounded a theory of government that looked forward to the centralized order of the Chinese empire, which the Qin dynasty inaugurated in 221 BC. Of all the philosophers of the so-called Hundred Schools, Han Fei Zi was the only aristocrat, being a prince of the feudal state of Han. The others appear to have been members of the scholar-gentry and administrative class with one notable exception: Shen Buhai (*c.* 400–337 BC) may even have come from artisan or peasant stock.

Han Fei Zi was a firm Legalist. He believed that a combination of strict supervision and pitiless punishment was required for the security of a state. 'The ruler alone possesses power,' he insisted, 'wielding it like lightning or like thunder.' Obedience to the letter of the law was demanded, for 'if the law is weak, so is the kingdom'. As a result, the Confucian morals of daily life were termed the 'six lice'; along with Shang Yang, Han Fei Zi proscribed rites, compassion, generosity, virtue, good faith, and anti-militarism. 'Laws are enacted to lead people,' he added, 'but when scholars are revered, doubt arises among the people about following the law.' And again: 'When righteous conduct is publicized, the ruler's awe is divided; when kindness is heeded, the law and statutes are destroyed.'

It was a point of view that appealed to the future First Emperor, who met Han Fei Zi in 233 BC, a dozen years before the unification of China. But the encounter ended in the suicide of the philosopher at the instigation of the First Emperor's chief minister, Li Si (died 208 BC). Neither Li Si's motive nor the reason for Han Fei Zi's acquiescence has ever been satisfactorily explained. The most likely cause of the philosopher's death was the insecurity of Li Si, a personal trait cunningly exploited later by the eunuch Zhao Gao under the weak Second Emperor (210–207 BC). Quite possibly the minister was prepared to sacrifice a fellow Legalist because, in the cut and thrust of the Qin court, he could not cope with such an eminent competitor.

See CONFUCIUS; HUNDRED SCHOOLS; LEGALISM; LI SI; QIN DYNASTY; SHANG YANG

*B. Watson, *The Basic Writings of Mo Tzu, Hsun Tzu, and Han Fei Tzu* (New York,

1967); W. K. Liao, *The Complete Works of Han Fei Tzu* (London, 1959).

**Han Wu Di** (140–87 BC) was the fifth emperor of the Han dynasty, which ruled China from 202 BC till AD 220. Born in 156 BC, this energetic and forceful emperor was only sixteen when he began his reign of fifty-four years, one of the longest in Chinese imperial history. Although much of the initiative for the new policies introduced can be traced to his ministers, there is little doubt that Wu Di's own determination was the decisive factor behind the sweeping changes he presided over. To deal with the troublesome Xiongnu, probably the Huns who later invaded the Roman empire, Chinese armies went over to the offensive along the northern frontier. By 101 BC the greatest advances had been achieved: over the so-called Western Regions of Central Asia Chinese suzerainty was established, while in the east a number of commanderies were formed on the Korean peninsula.

Wu Di's envoy to the west, Zhang Qian, was indeed the first Chinese to encounter another classical civilization. He returned to Chang'an in 126 BC and reported to an amazed court that in what is now Afghanistan there were 'cities, mansions and houses as in China'. But the difficult overland journey via the oasis towns of the Western Regions kept outside contact down to the bare minimum, with the result that Wu Di was never made aware of the significance of Zhang Qian's encounter. The envoy had in fact visited the recently conquered Greco-Buddhist kingdom of Bactria.

Internally, Wu Di was faced with a pressing administrative problem. The empire still lacked a body of competent administrators, despite regular calls for the provinces to supply filially pious and incorrupt recruits for the civil service. From 135 BC onwards these scholars were expected to prove their abilities by answering questions which were set, in theory, by the emperor in person. Thus began the system of civil service examinations, the ultimate origin of present-day public testing. From the start candidates whose views reflected Legalist ideas suffered a disadvantage, for examiners were drawn from the ranks of Confucian scholars. These examiners also staffed the newly founded imperial university at Chang'an, whose first fifty students comprised the cleverest provincials and the sons of top officials. Student numbers steadily rose, however, so that by the time of Wang Mang's usurpation (AD 9–23) over 10,000 were enrolled.

Wu Di's interest in the examination system extended to individual grades and he would revise the pass list whenever he spotted someone whose ideas he liked. Such a candidate was Hong Gongsun, to whom he entrusted in 125 BC the reorganization of finance and education. Wu Di could not accept the low mark awarded to Hong Gongsun, who was so poor that he supported his family by breeding pigs.

The emperor's close involvement is hardly surprising in the context of his personal style of government which depended upon a reliable and subservient civil service. The popular hatred of the previous Qin dynasty (221–207 BC) ruled out any return to its Legalist outlook, however authoritarian his own character, while Daoism, to which he was attracted because of its expertise in supernatural matters, advocated too passive a role for the ruler: hence Wu Di's eventual support for an updated version of Confucianism largely derived from the thought of Dong Zhongshu (c. 179–c. 104 BC). Even though persuaded to proclaim in 136 BC the state cult of Confucius, Wu Di was often impatient at the traditional bias of the philosopher's followers.

A clash was inevitable over the running of the economy. Many of the Confucianists did not approve of the measures Wu Di sanctioned to deal with a severe economic crisis. In 119 BC new taxes were levied on trade, transport and land to supplement government revenues. Already steps had been taken to bring the salt and iron industries under state control. A state monopoly on the production of alcohol was in 98 BC only replaced by the payment of a tax. To counter speculation in foodstuffs public granaries were built and provincial officials received orders to buy when prices were low and sell in times of shortage. This 'levelling' system worked, and was copied by Koguryo, a Korean state which asserted its independence from China in AD 12. Koguryo also absorbed the commanderies Wu Di established in Korea, the greatest of which was Lolang with a population of nearly half a million inhabitants.

Yet on the death of Wu Di in 87 BC the Chinese empire was still impoverished by the long struggle against the Xiongnu. Even at the close of his life, though, the emperor was determined enough to ensure the smooth succession of Zhao Di, his youngest son. Political complications tended to arise in the imperial palace with plots centred on the consort family, the relations of the empress. The family of Wang Mang was influential at court through marriage to the imperial clan for two decades before his seizure of the throne in AD 9.

Although he did not direct the expensive military campaigns himself, the emperor was remembered by the title of Wu Di, or 'warrior ruler'. Later criticism of his reign failed to tarnish his reputation, for as the historian Ban Gu asked: 'If Wu Di, with his superior ability and his great plans, had not departed from the modesty and economy of his predecessors, and if, by means of his policies, he helped the common people, in what respects have any of these kings praised in the *Book of History* surpassed him?'

*See* ADMINISTRATION; BACTRIA; DAOISM; DONG ZHONGSHU; HAN DYNASTY; LEGALISM; QIN DYNASTY; WANG MANG; WESTERN REGIONS; ZHANG QIAN

*B. Watson, *Records of the Grand Historian of China* (New York, 1961); H. H. Dubs, *The History of the Former Han Dynasty by Pan Ku* (Baltimore, 1938–55).

**Hannibal** (246–182 BC), the great Carthaginian general, was the scourge of Rome. He was responsible for the start of the Second Punic War (218–201 BC), which subjected Italy to more than a decade of devastation. After losing Sicily and Sardinia to Rome as a result of the First Punic War (264–241 BC), Carthage was obliged to build an overseas empire in the far west, on the Iberian peninsula. There Hannibal married a Spanish princess and set about enlarging Carthaginian holdings. But his campaigns brought him into conflict with Rome's ally, Saguntum, a city near present-day Valencia. Possibly the oath of eternal hatred to Rome which his father had made him swear before leaving Carthage fuelled Hannibal's military ambitions, because in 219 BC he took Saguntum by siege knowing that its capture might lead to war again. The Romans immediately ordered the Carthaginians to hand Hannibal over to them, or face them in arms. Their overconfidence was soon deflated when Hannibal marched over the Alps into Italy and inflicted three major defeats on Roman forces in as many years; the worst ever suffered occurred in 216 BC at Cannae in southern Italy. There he encircled two armies and slew 80,000 men. 'The morning after the battle,' the historian Livy relates, 'the Carthaginians applied themselves to collecting the spoils and viewing the carnage, which even to an enemy's eye was a shocking spectacle. All over the field Roman soldiers lay dead in their thousands, horse and foot mingled together, as the shifting phases of the battle, or the attempt to escape, had brought them together.' Livy goes on to say that had Hannibal moved on the city of Rome itself straight away, the war would have been over. But he felt there was no immediate possibility of conducting a siege, and so a weakened Rome managed to adopt a war of attrition against the invaders and those Roman allies who defected to their side. Gradually it won most of the important ones back, Capua and Syracuse in 211 BC, and Tarentum in 209 BC.

Hannibal's military exploits are celebrated on a coin minted at New Carthage, modern Cartagena, in Spain.

Hannibal's problem was fighting far from home, without the possibility of regular supplies and reinforcements. Roman supremacy at sea meant he had to fend for himself, and especially after Scipio Africanus (236–184 BC) carried the counterattack to Spain in 209 BC. The end was in sight five years later on Scipio's invasion of Africa; Hannibal was recalled, but even he was unable to prevent a Carthaginian defeat at Zama in 202 BC, and humiliating peace terms that effectively marked the end of Carthage's status as a Mediterranean power. Prior to the final engagement, Livy tells us, 'exactly half-way between the opposing ranks of armed men, each attended by an interpreter, Hannibal and Scipio met ... For a moment mutual admiration struck them dumb, and they looked at each other in silence ... But at length the negotiations failed, and the two generals returned to their armies with the news that the issue must be settled by arms. Each side had to accept the fortune which the gods chose to give.' After the end of hostilities Hannibal settled down to a political career in Carthage, but Roman suspicions were aroused by his enemies, who told visiting envoys that he was scheming with the Seleucid ruler Antiochus III (223–187 BC). Whatever the truth of the accusation, Hannibal fled to Antiochus' court in Syria but played only a minor role in the struggle between Rome and Antiochus. After the Roman victory of 190 or 189 BC at Magnesia, in Asia Minor, the fugitive Carthaginian had to seek refuge in a number of places before taking his own life in 182 BC, in order to avoid a Roman extradition order.

See CARTHAGE; ROME; SCIPIOS; SYRACUSE

*Livy, *The War with Hannibal*, trans. by A. de Sélincourt (Harmondsworth, 1965); J. F. Lazenby, *Hannibal's War* (Warminster, 1978).

**Herod** the Great, king of Judaea 37–4 BC, was a Roman nominee. When his predecessor was carried off by Parthian invaders in 40 BC, he escaped to Rome and gained the support of Antony (82–30 BC), then the dominant warlord. But his throne was not secure until Roman troops forcibly installed Herod at Jerusalem in 37 BC. Considering Antony's passion for Cleopatra (69–30 BC), Herod did very well to maintain his independence in the face of the Egyptian queen's covetousness. He was equally fortunate in his confirmation by the first Roman emperor Augustus in 30 BC. Herod had reacted to the news of his victory over Antony and Cleopatra at Actium the year before, by setting off to meet Augustus on the island of Rhodes. Laying aside his royal diadem as a sign of submission, the Judaean king argued that his loyalty to Antony should be regarded as a sign of his prospective loyalty to himself. Augustus accepted Herod at face value, enjoying his lavish hospitality on his overland journey from Asia Minor to Egypt. Herod's generosity earned him additions to his kingdom around the Sea of Galilee and in Samaria.

In 9 BC Herod was at war again with

the Nabataean kingdom across the Jordan. Hostilities were long-standing, a major battle having been fought before Actium at Philadelphia (modern Amman). The renewed fighting was caused through the encouragement given by the Nabataeans to Judaean brigands. Such was the current weakness of Roman forces in the area that Herod was able to wage the war alone. His campaign proved successful and a certain amount of territory was gained. Afterwards Augustus nearly handed the whole of Nabataea to Herod and his sons, but he decided to leave both kingdoms intact. The emperor could already have been pondering changes in Judaea, however. Herod's rule was unpopular with the Jews, who disliked his sponsorship of Greco-Roman culture, including the imperial cult among his non-Jewish subjects. His power was based on a chain of fortresses, the strongest of which was actually situated at Jerusalem. Even before Herod's death in 4 BC, the Romans tightened their control and converted some areas into provincial territory. Minor roles were given to the sons of Herod, but it was only his grandson, Agrippa, who from AD 41 to 44 ruled anything approaching a kingdom. Because the emperor Caligula (AD 37–41) had aroused such anger by attempting to have his statue placed in the Temple, his successor Claudius (AD 41–54) thought it wise to put the province of Judaea under the rule of a client king.

See ARABIA; AUGUSTUS; CALIGULA; CLAUDIUS; JEWS

*F. Millar, *The Roman Near East, 31 BC–AD 337* (Cambridge, Mass., 1993).

**Herodotus** (484–425 BC) was the father of Greek history. Born in Asia Minor at Halicarnassus, a city with both Greek and Carian inhabitants, he was personally aware of the might of the Persian empire, and his *Histories* consist of an attempt to explain its defeat at the hands of the Greeks in 480–479 BC. Herodotus had travelled widely to gather material for this account of the struggle between the Greeks and the Persians. That many of the stories he relates may seem far-fetched would not have worried Herodotus, for he felt under no obligation to attempt an assessment of their truth, leaving to his readers' judgement what could or could not be believed. Sometimes he ventures an opinion of his own, but never in the manner of Thucydides (445–400 BC), who readily apportioned praise and blame in his account of the Peloponnesian War (431–404 BC). The fundamental reason that Herodotus cites for the allergy of the Greeks for Persian rule was a refusal to accept a despot in the form of the Persian king. This made the outnumbered Spartans stand at Thermopylae and the Athenians risk all in a sea-battle at Salamis in 480 BC.

See PERSIAN INVASIONS; THUCYDIDES

*J. Hart, *Herodotus and Greek History* (London, 1982); S. Usher, *The Historians of Greece and Rome* (London, 1969).

**Hinduism** reached its classical form under the powerful Gupta dynasty (AD 320–550). By then the age of religious fervour seemed long past: under the even stronger Mauryan dynasty (*c.* 322–183 BC), whose emperors the Guptas strove politically to emulate, the teachings of the Buddha had been instrumental in stirring up a profound spiritual movement which came to influence every aspect of life. For the conversion of the Mauryan emperor Ashoka shortly after 260 BC inaugurated nearly half a millennium of Buddhist domination in India. The new faith largely eclipsed Hinduism, the religion from which it sprang, and eventually forced Hindu scholars to reformulate the basis of their own belief. The law code of Manu, dating from the second or third century AD, was but a single example of this extensive reconstruction effort. What Manu prepared, however, was a model for a Hindu state in which every class had its divinely ordained place. No longer was there room for the spiritual individualism of the Buddha. Asceticism, Manu made clear, should be practised only in old age, after the fulfilment of social obligations. But the work of lawgivers such as Manu would have come to little without the upsurge of popular Hinduism associated with the puranas, vast collections of myths and legends. Whereas in Greece myth was abandoned as a valid interpretation of natural events, and traditional religious belief sat uneasily next to a rational outlook on the world, in India the

myth-making facility did not suffer a similar decline, but, on the contrary, it continued to refashion and reshape the sacred stories of Hinduism.

Shiva within the cosmic lingam, the sacred pillar of Hinduism.

The puranas, like the enormous Hindu epics, indicate that around the start of the Christian era the worship of Brahma was common. This creator deity formed part of a triad, whose other members were Vishnu the preserver and Shiva the destroyer. By the end of the Gupta dynasty, Brahma had lost his creative powers to the other two deities, and largely faded away. A myth concerning the origin of the lingam, the phallic-like post in the sanctum of every Hindu temple,

187

records this change of status. It concludes with Shiva settling an argument between Brahma and Vishnu as to who is the creator of the universe. Their quarrel is interrupted by a towering lingam crowned with flame, rising from the depths of the cosmic ocean. Brahma, as a gander, and Vishnu, as a boar, decide to investigate. Flying upwards, the gander is startled to observe the cosmic post burst asunder, and reveal in a cave-like sanctuary the hidden creator, Shiva, the supreme power in the universe. Puranic stories such as this helped to shape the construction of Hindu places of worship. The earliest shrines were just a four-square cell, but under the Guptas it was raised on a plinth and surmounted by a spire, intended to recall both the sacrificial flame and the world mountain. Carvings also referred to the stories found in the puranas.

*See* BUDDHISM; GUPTA DYNASTY; JAINISM
★S. Bhattacharji, *The Indian Theogony* (Cambridge, 1970); J. L. Brockington, *The Sacred Thread: Hinduism in its Continuity and Diversity* (Edinburgh, 1981).

**Hippias** was the second and last tyrant of Athens (527–510 BC). His father, Pisistratus, had first seized power in 561 BC through a bodyguard foolishly voted him by the Athenian assembly. Twice expelled by the Athenians, Pisistratus' final restoration in 546 BC followed the landing of a mercenary force at Marathon, the same spot on the northern coast of Attica to which

Hippias vainly directed the Persians in 490 BC. Pisistratus remained in power till he died of sickness in 527 BC, when his eldest son Hippias assumed the tyranny. Like his father in the last years of his rule, Hippias managed to remain on good terms with the aristocrats for over a decade. Then some of his supporters and discontented nobles turned against him, and the tyranny was badly shaken by the assassination of Hipparchus, Hippias' younger brother, in 514 BC. Two aristocratic lovers, Aristogiton and Harmodius, carried out the bungled attack. Harmodius was at once cut down by Hippias' guards, while Aristogiton was arrested and executed after torture.

Hippias was less inclined to gentle measures after this event, and exiled aristocrats seized a frontier post in Attica as a rallying-point for the growing opposition. Sensing a shift in public opinion at Athens, Hippias began to regard Persia as a possible supporter. His half-brother Hegesistratus, tyrant of Sigeum in the Troad, did homage to Darius I, when in 512 BC this Persian monarch crossed the Hellespont to campaign in Thrace. The marriage of his daughter to the tyrant of nearby Lampsacus can thus be seen as Hippias' attempt to ally himself with the pro-Persian tyrants of Asia Minor. Nothing of this political manoeuvre was missed by the Athenians, who were relieved at the intervention of the Spartan king Cleomenes I (519–490 BC). Prodded into action by the oracle at Delphi, where the Alcmaeonids, the family of the Athenian reformer Cleisthenes, had great influence, Cleomenes drove Hippias and his family from Athens in 510 BC. Fleeing to Sigeum, the deposed tyrant eventually made his way to the Persian court. From there he travelled in 490 BC with the expedition sent by Darius to punish Eretria and Athens for their intervention against Persia during the abortive Ionian revolt (499–494 BC).

Nearly eighty years old, Hippias was a political fossil utterly out of touch with Athens. It was twenty years since his expulsion and, faced with an invasion of the Greek mainland, even Sparta was prepared to overlook the democratic reforms of Cleisthenes in order to prevent foreign interference. Yet he believed that a restoration would be successful, the historian Herodotus tells us, because of an oracle which had announced that something of Hippias was destined to remain in Attica. It turned out to be the ex-tyrant's tooth. A violent fit of coughing shook the last one free and it was lost on the beach at Marathon. Thus disappointment was the probable cause of Hippias' death shortly after the defeated Persian expedition sailed back to Asia Minor.

See CLEISTHENES; CLEOMENES I; IONIAN REVOLT; ORACLES; PERSIAN INVASIONS; PISISTRATUS; TYRANTS
*Herodotus, *The Histories*, trans. by A. de Sélincourt (Harmondsworth, 1954).

**Honorius**, Roman emperor in the west AD 395–423, was the younger son of Theodosius the Great. Because of the acute manpower crisis facing Rome, after its defeat by the Visigoths at Adrianople in AD 378, Theodosius had been obliged to rely even more heavily on barbarian recruits to bring his forces up to strength. As a result, the Roman army now consisted largely of Germans, some of whom had risen to the highest ranks, such as the Romanized Vandal general Stilicho (died AD 408). It was indeed this man

The Romanized Vandal general Stilicho, in AD 395 the most powerful man in the Roman world.

who stood alone at the apex of the empire in AD 395, as the appointed guardian of twelve-year-old Honorius and probably of Arcadius, his elder brother, too. But the eighteen-year-old Arcadius (AD 395–408) soon fell under the influence of courtiers and commanders in Constantinople, while Stilicho endeavoured to secure Honorius' claim to rule the western provinces from Milan. The fundamental problem that Stilicho had to deal with was the fragility of the late Roman peace. Not only were there growing pressures along the Rhine frontier, as well as unrest among the military commanders, but in the Visigothic leader Alaric he also encountered a serious opponent.

Alaric (died AD 410) seems to have been one of the last to accept Roman employment in AD 391. His followers were not enlisted as individual recruits and assigned to regular units of the army like most of the other Visigoths; instead, for some unknown reason, they were allowed to remain as a separate force in the Balkans. On Theodosius' death Alaric marched his men without any opposition to Constantinople, and burned the countryside outside the walls. Having made his point about the weakness of Roman arms, Alaric accepted an official appointment in the east and took up a defensive position to check Stilicho's forays. The latter invaded Greece via the Peloponnese in AD 396 as part of his plan to take control of Arcadius as well as Honorius. Thwarted by Alaric, Stilicho returned to Italy in order to raise more troops, but he had already lost the initiative. For North Africa revolted and stopped the grain ships

destined for Rome. Fortunately for Stilicho the eastern provinces were also troubled by rebellion and court intrigue. In AD 400 the anti-German faction encouraged the citizens of Constantinople to slaughter Visigothic residents, including soldiers billeted there. The Visigoths were virtually defenceless, armed only with a few weapons smuggled into the eastern capital. Even though the massacre had no lasting effect on German-Roman relations, it did isolate Alaric because the new influence at court transferred a large part of his base-area to Honorius' territories.

Once again Alaric found himself no more than a Visigothic warlord, a demotion he may have sought to disguise by assuming the title of king. As far as he was concerned the emperor Arcadius had dismissed him without cause. By AD 401 Alaric's position had become so precarious that he invaded Italy, while Stilicho was busy north of the Alps recruiting soldiers. His invasion was helped by the weakness of the Alpine defences, undermanned since Theodosius I (AD 379–395) stripped them of soldiers during the civil wars near the end of his reign. The troops in Alaric's army were not, however, the same Visigoths who had overwhelmed the Romans at Adrianople. On the contrary, they were outcasts and refugees from upheavals in the Balkans and within the Roman army: they were malcontents who disliked the discipline of regular service. At most they numbered 12,000. That with such a small army Alaric could have fought Stilicho to a draw reveals the extent of the manpower shortage then being experienced by Rome. The stalemate suited Alaric for the good reason that he received another official appointment, this time with the western emperor Honorius, and with it access to Roman supplies.

Stilicho may not have intended this arrangement to last, but events forced him to look to the defence of Gaul. On the last day of AD 406 thousands of starving Germans crossed the frozen Rhine near Mogontiacum (present-day Mainz). The severity of the winter had driven Vandals, Sarmatians, Burgundians, Suevi and others to the Roman frontier in search of food, and provided in the thickness of the river ice a means for them to easily cross it. The Roman garrisons, in their winter quarters, could do no more than watch this greatest movement of people ever to enter the western provinces. The hungry invaders had to split up in order to find enough food to survive, but in the spring of AD 407 a concerted Roman counterattack failed to take advantage of this dispersal, because there were simply not enough troops available. Perhaps Stilicho also chose to reserve what strength he had left to meet the challenge of the usurper Constantine, a commander who had emerged triumphant in Britain and crossed the Channel with an army the same year. The removal of most of the legions from the island spelt the end of its attachment to Rome. By AD 408

the military situation had deteriorated so much that Stilicho fell to a court coup. He was executed for treason at Ravenna, since AD 404 the western capital of the Roman empire. Protected by marshes, and easy to escape from by sea, the city was to remain the imperial residence throughout the three-quarters of a century that remained before Italy passed under barbarian control.

Wishful thinking. The Roman emperor Honorius is shown trampling on a barbarian. In AD 404, however, the imperial government fled from Rome to Ravenna.

This new dignity for Ravenna turned Alaric's sack of Rome in AD 410 into something of a non-event, though it appeared at the time as a disaster to Christians and pagans alike. For a baffled St Augustine (AD 354–430) the three-day occupation raised the question of Christian destiny and the meaning of history. But in reality Roman authority in the west had already become a façade, behind which generals, barbarians, and great landowners attended solely to their own interests. Honorius never had the opportunity to rule: his own lack of vigour exactly suited the empty role in which a late western emperor was cast. Yet weak-kneed Honorius outlasted Alaric, who died in southern Italy shortly after the sack of Rome. He was trying to cross to Sicily and then to Africa, but storms smashed his ships. Alaric's plan was to seize the African grain supply and hold Honorius to ransom. The sacker of Rome was buried at the bottom of a river, with his share of the spoils, during a temporary diversion of its waters. The Visigoths turned to Alaric's brother-in-law, Athaulf, for leadership and he took over a considerable army: augmented by Stilicho's followers and runaway slaves, its total strength may have topped 30,000. Out of touch with military realities in the west, the court at Ravenna had foolishly tried a repeat of the Constantinople massacre in AD 408, but succeeded only in turning the barbarians loyal to Stilicho into bitter enemies.

The decision of Athaulf to move into Gaul in AD 412 resulted from Honorius' non-committal attitude towards the Visigoths. In that battle-scarred land they fought both for and against Rome, but made no attempt to round up the gangs of slaves then looting the countryside. In AD 415 Athaulf tired of the complicated struggle between Roman usurpers and agreed to move into Spain, ostensibly to fight the occupying Vandals on Rome's behalf. Athaulf's assassination in the same year was probably due to his failure to provide adequately for his followers. A new Visigothic king was prevented by the Roman fleet from crossing to Africa in order to solve the perennial problem of supplies. Stability of a kind, however, was achieved in the model settlement of AD 418, whereby the Visigoths were allowed to take up permanent residence in south-western Gaul. As a part of this agreement Galla Placidia, Honorius' sister, was released. Originally held as a hostage by Alaric, she had been married to Athaulf without the consent of Honorius, and bore him a son who soon died. From the safety of Ravenna it seemed that the Visigoths were no longer a cause for anxiety. They gave protection against Vandal raids from Spain, and acted as a reserve force for Gaul itself. But there was for the first time a barbarian people under their own government officially settled in an interior province of the Roman empire. When Honorius died in AD 423 the scene was already set for the emergence of a separate Visigothic kingdom, the first of several barbarian states. Under Theodosius II (AD 408–450) eastern armies tried to hold back the growth of their power in the west, but Italy, Gaul, Spain, Africa, and the frontier provinces, all passed out of Roman control. In AD 441 an eastern force had to occupy Sicily to prevent it falling to the Vandals.

*See* AUGUSTINE; GOTHS; ROME; THEODOSIUS I AND II; VANDALS

*T. S. Burns, *Barbarians within the Gates of Rome* (Bloomington, 1994).

**Hundred Schools** of Chinese philosophy coincided with the turmoil of the Warring States period (481–221 BC). Unprecedented in classical China was the intellectual ferment which accompanied the final collapse of feudalism and the imperial unification in 221 BC of the country under the Qin dynasty. The uncertainty of the age contrasted with an increasing prosperity as cities grew in size and number, technology made impressive advances, and commerce became important enough for merchants to suffer periodic government repression. Rulers seemed indifferent to anything but personal gain, so that only the glibbest advisers could expect to make official careers for themselves and avoid miserable ends. Even a successful policy-maker such as Shang Yang (390–338 BC) could find that death and dishonour awaited him at the close of his ministry in the state of Qin. The political troubles were lamented by scores of philosophers who keenly felt their own marginal influence on contemporary events. Their frustration produced an outpouring of ideas unmatched under the Confucian-dominated ideology of the Chinese empire. They were obliged to write books and found schools because rulers would rarely listen to their advice. Not until 221 BC was the king of Qin, the First Emperor of China (221–210 BC), able to win supremacy and impose a centralized bureaucratic regime that left room for neither feudal sentiment nor local variation. Then everything was standardized, including thought. The violent reaction toppled the first imperial house within half a generation and inaugurated the compromise of the Han dynasty (202 BC – AD 220).

The philosophers of the so-called Hundred Schools were, with the notable exception of Prince Han Fei Zi, members of the scholar-gentry and administrative class. They followed four main schools: Confucianism, Daoism, Moism and Legalism. Although the first two were to have a lasting importance in Chinese history, and especially Confucianism, the most heatedly debated philosophies before the Qin unification were the last two. It has been said that traditionally the Chinese were Daoist in private and Confucian in public, but it might be added that those who entered the imperial civil service always felt the lingering influence of the administrative concepts of Legalism. Only the doctrines of Mo Zi (c. 468–376 BC) permanently vanished from the Chinese mind when the First Emperor burnt the books and suppressed the Hundred Schools in 213 BC.

See CONFUCIUS; DAOISM; LEGALISM; MO ZI

*Kung-chuan Hsiao, *A History of Chinese Political Thought. Volume One: From the Beginnings to the Sixth Century AD* (Princeton, 1979); V. A. Rubin, *Individual* *and State in Ancient China* (New York, 1976).

**Huns** burst upon Europe at the end of the fourth century AD. Their formidable cavalry destroyed the Ostrogothic kingdom in the Ukraine, and drove the neighbouring Visigoths across the Danube into Roman territory. The historian of the upset the Huns caused then, Ammianus Marcellinus, was amazed at their ferocity and delight in raiding. He noted the gashes scored on Hunnish faces at birth, their small eyes, misshapen heads, thick necks, and powerful limbs. Though the Asian origins of the Huns are not specified, Ammianus placed their homeland correctly on the steppe, near 'the frozen ocean', in all probability the Sea of Azov. It is not unlikely the Huns were a group of nomads which had split earlier from a Central Asian people: their cousins were the Xiongnu tribesmen who roamed beyond the Great Wall of China, and the Hunas, the destroyers in India of the Gupta dynasty (AD 320–550). In Europe the Hunnish terror was associated most with Attila, who troubled the Roman empire till his death in AD 453.

*See* ATTILA; GUPTA DYNASTY; XIONGNU
*E. A. Thompson, *The Huns* (Oxford, 1986).

**Huo Qubing** (141–117 BC) was a distinguished Chinese general who inflicted unprecedented defeats on the Hunnish Xiongnu. The illegimate son of a singing-girl, who was taken into the imperial harem in 139 BC, Huo Qubing was so esteemed by the Han emperor Wu Di at the time of his death that he was awarded the highest possible honour – a state funeral within the imperial tomb complex, north of Chang'an. Wu Di (140–87 BC) ordered the general's tumulus to be like Mount Qilian, the site of one of his famous victories over the Xiongnu. It is recorded how this artificial mountain was covered with large boulders brought from afar and with strange stone animals and monsters. Their purpose was to obtain the continued support of the immortals, who were believed to live in mountains far to the west. Wu Di is known to have been advised by Daoist adepts that if he wished to communicate with the spirit world he must portray the strange forms taken by the gods on the public

One of the sculpted animals from the grave of Huo Qubing. This horse recalls his victories on the steppe.

works he commissioned.

Huo Qubing's successes came from adopting the mobile tactics of the Xiongnu. He positively refused to study the *Art of War* by Sun Zi, the traditional manual of generalship, and trusted solely in his own judgement. On his early death in 117 BC his mother's brother was President of the Board of War, a circumstance that may go some way to explain his splendid burial.

*See* DAOISM; HAN WU DI; LI LING; SUN ZI; WARFARE; XIONGNU

\*A. Paludan, *The Chinese Spirit Road: The Classical Tradition of Stone Tomb Statuary* (New Haven, 1991).

# I

**Illyrians** occupied a large part of the Balkans during classical times. The enemies of the Macedonians, they were decisively defeated by Philip II (359–336 BC), the father of Alexander the Great, after a bloody campaign in 358 BC. One source relates how 'Philip had inherited from his father a quarrel with the Illyrians and found no means of reconciling his disagreement. He therefore invaded Illyria with a large force, devastated the countryside, captured many towns and returned to Macedon laden with booty.' Another opponent of the Illyrians was Pyrrhus (319–272 BC), who built up in Epirus (much of present-day Albania) a power capable of challenging Rome for the control of southern Italy. With the decline of both Macedon and Epirus, however, the Illyrians pressed southwards by land and sea, becoming a major new power in the Adriatic. By 231 BC Illyrian ships were raiding the Peloponnese at will.

Even before their first war with Carthage (264–241 BC), from which they gained control of Sicily, the Romans had been alive to the danger to the Adriatic coast of Italy from seaborne attack. In 264 BC a colony of Roman citizens was settled at Brundisium (modern Brindisi) to keep watch on its southern waters. 'From time immemorial,' the historian Polybius tells us, 'Illyrians had attacked and robbed ships sailing from Italy.' So many were now taken by privateers that Rome decided something must be done. In 229 BC a Roman invasion caught the Illyrians completely off guard, as an attack was then being launched against the Greek cities on the island of Corcyra. The resulting peace was intended to curb Illyrian violence, but the invasion of Italy by Hannibal in early 218 BC so absorbed Roman energies that the Illyrians were able to resume large-scale raids. This might have gone unpunished by the Romans had the Illyrians not sided with the last king of an independent Macedon, Perseus (179–168 BC). A crushing defeat in 168 BC brought the Illyrian kingdom to an end, although it was not till the 30s BC that the area was finally subdued, and the Roman province of Illyricum came into existence.

*See* CARTHAGE; HANNIBAL; MACEDON; PHILIP II; PYRRHUS; ROME

\*J. Wilkes, *The Illyrians* (Oxford, 1995).

**Inventions** were best perfected in classical China. Indeed, the later part of the Han dynasty (AD 25–220) witnessed a number of significant technical advances that anticipated discoveries traditionally attributed to modern Europe. The talented Zhang Heng (AD 78–139) shone as a poet, a calligrapher and a scientist. Around AD 130 he invented the first practical seismograph, his 'earthquake weather-cock', which though not furnishing a scientific explanation for seismic disturbance, at least gave the emperor immediate notice of a disaster and its direction from the capital. The Chinese theory of the heavenly mandate to rule and the corresponding benevolence of Heaven made the throne sensitive to the interpretation of natural phenomena and marvels; hence the importance of the imperial observatory which Zhang Heng ran. Other inventions to his credit were an improved armillary sphere to trace the paths of the planets and the first known application of motive power to the rotation of astronomical instruments. Recognition of magnetism had already come from Daoist geomancy, the art of

The early perfection of iron and steel-making in China depended upon the invention of such water-powered blowing-engines.

adapting the abodes of the living and the dead so as to be in harmony with cosmic forces: it was achieved by means of a lodestone spoon. A passage written in AD 83 states: 'When the south-controlling spoon is thrown upon the ground, it comes to rest pointing south.' This is the earliest record of magnetism, and by Tang times (AD 618–906) a compass was in use, the original self-registering instrument.

A provincial official is said to have introduced a water-powered metallurgical blowing-machine in AD 31. The continuous blast thereby afforded was of inestimable value to the state-owned iron industry and may have led directly to the production of steel. There is no doubt that within a couple of centuries steel was being produced by a technique which foreshadowed the Siemens–Martin process of combining cast and wrought iron. Another invention of the imperial workshops was paper-making, announced in AD 105. A surviving fragment of paper reveals that a coarse version made of hemp fibres was available from the reign of the Former Han emperor Wu Di (140–87 BC), but after advances in production methods rolls of paper became commonplace, a bonus for a bureaucratic state. Although this remarkable example of Chinese inventiveness was an immediate aid to communication, it did not disturb a tradition which managed with few public documents. Quite typical was Confucius' concern in 513 BC over the publication of a law

code. He noted that the punishments inscribed on a bronze cauldron by a feudal lord would be learned and respected by the people above all else. Confucius (551–479 BC) held that the business of government was best left in the hands of those schooled for public service. In contrast to classical Greece, where laws were always displayed by stone inscriptions, literacy in China did not take on a public purpose; despite the availability of paper, it never disclosed to the people as a whole the workings of government. Only the learned could expect to enter the bureaucracy and exercise power. When later combined with block printing, however, paper did cause a fundamental revolution in communications that is still in progress throughout the modern world. The earliest known book, a Buddhist text, dates from AD 868 and was found in the immense complex of cave-temples at Dunhuang near the western end of the Great Wall. Paper-making also assisted the spread of hygienic habits throughout society: in lavatories toilet paper became available.

The state-owned salt industry, also nationalized along with iron in 119 BC, was able to exploit wells in western China because of the improvement in the manufacture of iron and steel bits. Bamboo tubes fitted with valves were lowered to a depth of over 1,200 feet in order to extract brine, which was evaporated with the aid of natural gas collected from the bore-holes. The ability to tap this source of salt so far from the sea expedited development of the western imperial borderlands. Besides its usefulness in salt mining, split bamboos could be used as irrigation flumes, thus providing a means of overcoming unsatisfactory surfaces for water. Vital as hydraulic engineering undoubtedly was to Chinese agriculture, the imperial programme of canal construction aimed at improving water transport, whose advantage in the shipment of heavy loads was not fully appreciated in Europe until the industrial revolution of the eighteenth century. The emperors were naturally interested in the movement of tax-grain to the capital, not in the development of trade. Navigation itself had been aided by the invention of the stern-post rudder by the first century BC. The steering oar, general elsewhere throughout the classical era, put a severe limitation on the size of a ship that could be safely constructed, besides giving the steersman a very hazardous task of control in rough weather. The stern-post rudder first appears in Europe about 1180, a time almost exactly simultaneous with the appearance and adoption of the magnetic compass there. In China the evolution of the stern-post rudder and the watertight compartment allowed junks to become deep-ocean craft.

On land several Chinese technical advances also contributed to better transportation. First, the 'wooden ox', or wheelbarrow, eased the lot of porters. A second improvement was the perfection of the equine collar har-

ness, first invented during the Warring States period (481–221 BC). Last but not least, the advent of the stirrup represented a decisive development in the use of the horse. Possibly stimulated by the Indian toe-stirrup, news of which could have been transmitted via Buddhism, the Chinese foot-stirrup made riding easier and in the process gave rise to the armoured cavalryman. Hardly surprising were the military inventions of the turbulent period prior to the Qin unification of China in 221 BC. The crossbow, the deadliest of all classical weapons, dates from the fifth century BC, when iron mail-coats started to replace padded jackets of treated sharkskin and animal hide as standard body armour. The heavy arrows fired by the crossbow would have turned into colanders the shields carried by contemporary Indian, Greek, Macedonian or Roman soldiers. Chinese infantrymen would seem to have thrown off their armoured coats as soon as the enemy was so close that continued crossbow fire became impossible for either side. In hand-to-hand fighting the favourite weapon was the halberd.

Another field of advance under the Han emperors was medicine. The Daoist quest for an elixir of life is evident from several tomb finds, as are the efforts made to understand the medicinal properties of foods. Typically Chinese is the myth of Shen Nung, who used his transparent stomach in order to investigate how plants affected his body. For cookery and medicine were always intertwined, the first pharmacopoeia having been written before the anxious First Emperor (221–210 BC) spent vast sums in his personal search for longevity, even immortality. Whilst medical theory was still permeated by the idea of universal balance, as expressed in the balance of yin/yang, doctors never rejected cures because of the fear of upsetting established principles. The first official dissection was carried out by order of the usurper Wang Mang (AD 9–23). This operation on the body of a criminal was conducted by a skilled butcher under the direction of the court physician: it involved 'measuring and weighing the five entrails and tracing the course of the cavities with the aid of fine bamboos to see where they begin and end, so that it would be possible to know how to cure illness'. The basic elements of contemporary therapy were medicines derived from plants and rocks, acupuncture and moxibustion, diet, massage, and small-scale incisions. While pills of deathlessness could be purchased from Daoist magicians, a practical approach to health was already in existence, and one founded on careful observation and diagnosis. The examination of the pulse was systematized, and in about AD 200 a work appeared that described infectious diseases including typhoid. It would seem that Hua Tuo (AD 190–265), an expert in physiotherapy, even devised a general anaesthesia by the use of a wine containing Indian hemp.

In classical Greece, too, medicine was emancipated from superstition, not least because the philosophers of Ionia, the major area of Greek settlement in Asia Minor, had already encouraged a rational approach. There Thales (625–547 BC) and his disciple Anaximander (610–540 BC) had set the pattern of Greek rationalism with their attempts to explain the perceptible world in the light of observation and reasoned theories rather than inherited assumptions. The impact of West Asian ideas upon them was critical, but their reliance on the intellect determined that they were never uncritical recipients. To the question of how the body worked, Hippocrates (460–380 BC), a native of the neighbouring island of Cos, tried to offer a balanced answer. The sixty or so treatises associated with his name are virtually free from magic and supernatural intervention. Medical schools were later established at Pergamum and Alexandria, where work was done on the eye, the brain, the liver and the reproductive organs. The outstanding physician was Galen (AD 129–204), who studied in both cities before becoming the medical adviser to three Roman emperors, Marcus Aurelius (AD 161–180), Commodus (AD 180–192), and Septimius Severus (AD 193–211), the founder of a new dynasty. Galen's first appointment, however, was as the doctor to the gladiators at Pergamum.

Also at Alexandria, a leading centre of learning through the patronage of the Ptolemies (305–30 BC), advances were made in astronomy, geometry and geography. Erastosthenes (275–194 BC), the head of its famous library, compared the shadows cast by sticks in two different places at midday to calculate the earth's circumference. Progress in applied sciences was no less impressive, including the invention of a pump and a water-clock. At Syracuse another inventor was busy applying his curiosity to a whole range of problems, till the Romans killed him in their sack of the city. This was the famous Archimedes (287–212 BC), who wrote extensively on optics, statics, hydrostatics, mathematics, astronomy and engineering. His defensive measures at Syracuse thwarted the Romans for several years. Yet there was slowness in the Greco-Roman world over applying technical knowledge to a practical context. This contrasts with China, where labour-saving devices were seized upon without any anxiety about their impact on society. Possibly the abundance of slaves in the Mediterranean had something to do with the gap between theory and practice. In the writings of the philosopher Aristotle (384–322 BC) can be found a profound disdain for manual labour and the crafts. He noted with approval that the better city-states would not admit artisans into their citizenship. Even a hyper-active inventor such as Archimedes was said to value his inventions more for their intellectual quality than for their practical utility and any benefit they might bring to his fellow citizens.

The Romans never much advanced beyond the Greek legacy of invention, despite impressive civil engineering works in the form of aqueducts, arenas, baths and basilicas. A real shortcoming in comparison with the classical Chinese was metallurgy. Wood was to remain the chief component of power-driven machinery, so that water mills needed constant repair and maintenance. In India a similar situation prevailed, although it has to be said that for both India and Iran the record is patchy. There is nothing, however, which suggests Chinese inventiveness was either independently equalled or in any way copied during classical times.

See ALEXANDRIA; ARCHIMEDES; CONFUCIUS: DAOISM; HAN DYNASTY; ROME; SLAVERY; WARFARE

*H. Hodges, *The Technology of the Ancient World* (New York, 1977); J. Needham, *Science and Civilization in China* (Cambridge, 1954 onwards).

**Ionian revolt** (499–494 BC) against Persian rule precipitated a major confrontation between the Greeks and the Persians, who invaded mainland Greece in 490 and 480–479 BC. The Greek cities situated on the seaboard of Asia Minor had been annexed by Persia following the defeat of Lydia in 546 BC. Unrest in Ionia, the coastal region facing the Aegean, came to a head in 499 BC when Aristagoras renounced his tyranny at Miletus and expelled other tyrants, who all had Persian support. Having taken the lead in the revolt, he went to mainland

Greece in order to secure military aid against the imminent Persian counter-attack. Because of the great distances involved in any campaign against the Persians, the conservative Spartans dismissed Aristagoras contemptuously. However, he had greater success at Athens and Eretria, who jointly promised a squadron of twenty-five warships. A very possible motive for Athenian willingness to send aid was the contact of their ex-tyrant Hippias with the Persian court: it was feared that the Persians might chose to back his restoration.

The rebels enjoyed initial success, burning in 498 BC the Persian stronghold of Sardis. But they lacked a unified plan, with the result that over the next four years the Persians recovered and methodically put down the rebellion. The defeat of a combined Greek fleet at Lade near Miletus, and then the capture of Miletus itself in 494 BC, effectively broke rebel resistance. The action at Lade revealed the deep divisions amongst the rebels. The fleet failed to fight as one, the Samian contingent hoisting sail and fleeing at the earliest opportunity. Whilst the Lesbians soon copied these tactics, the ships belonging to Chios and Miletus faced the enemy bravely, but they had no chance of winning, and so those vessels remaining afloat were obliged to conduct a fighting retreat. Though the Athenians and the Eretrians had withdrawn from the war well before the battle of Lade, the Persians remembered their early intervention. King

Darius I (521–486 BC) instructed a servant to constantly say: 'Do not forget the Athenians.' Aristagoras himself fled to avoid punishment, dying in Thrace before Darius launched his expedition against Athens and Eretria in 490 BC.

See ATHENS; DARIUS I; PERSIAN INVASIONS; TYRANTS

*A. R. Burn, *Persia and the Greeks: The Defence of the West, c. 546–479 BC* (London, 1962).

Jainism, a typically Indian faith, was more austere than Buddhism, the other major heterodox religion which branched from classical Hinduism. Its last, and twenty-fourth, saviour was Mahavira, a contemporary of the Buddha (*c.* 563–479 BC). Even though Mahavira's childhood was distinguished by miracles, he followed an ordinary path as a married man during the lifetime of his parents, who were devotees of Parsva, the twenty-third Jain saviour. They eventually chose to end their lives by the rite of fasting unto death. Afterwards Mahavira at the age of thirty-two distributed his personal possessions to the needy and began his own inner quest, an event Jain legend says was marked by an immediate heavenly response: the firmament glowed like a lake covered in lotus flowers, the air was filled with sounds of music, and gods descended to pay their respects to the arch-ascetic. For a time the names of Mahavira and Maskrin Gosala were linked together, possibly because they lived in the same religious community. But their views could not have been more opposed, and especially over the freedom of the will. Whereas Gosala argued that all beings would attain perfection in the course of time, albeit over a number of reincarnations, Mahavira asserted the

The Jain saviour Parsva, the immediate predecessor of Mahavira.

Jain belief that the individual soul had to secure its own escape through a sustained act of self-renunciation. And in contrast to the Buddha, too, Mahavira regarded the soul as physically bound and fettered by matter, so that the only way to gain repose at the top of the universe involved complete bodily disentanglement. A Jain monk even wore a veil over the mouth in case he accidentally swallowed an insect. Thus the Indian doctrine of non-violence reached its classical extreme.

Jainism was the only Indian philosophy to hold that the universe was eternal and uncreated. Hindu and Buddhist cosmology dealt in immense eras of time, but they were dwarfed by the Jain acknowledgement of infinity. Greek settlers in India and Afghanistan, following the campaigns of Alexander the Great, found Buddhism the most congenial belief. The conqueror's own troops were not a little baffled, on their return to Babylonia from India in 323 BC, when the ascetic Kalanos chose to burn himself alive. He was in all probability a Jain.

See BUDDHISM; GOSALA; HINDUISM; SCEPTICISM

*J. Jaini, Outlines of Jainism (Cambridge, 1940).

**Jews** were largely dispersed from their homeland by the Romans. A great deal of migration had taken place, however, before rebellions against Roman rule accelerated the exodus. From the arrival of Alexander the Great in 332 BC onwards, the Jews were uneasy about the imposition of foreign ways upon their traditional customs, and especially those connected with the Temple. The Seleucid dynasty (312–64 BC), one of the leading powers after the breakup of Alexander's empire, gave the Jews cause for anxiety, for the Greek culture which it sponsored enjoyed very considerable prestige and popularity. Antiochus IV (175–163 BC) seems to have been willing to heavily underwrite a programme of hellenization proposed by a group of pro-Greek Jews. But the Seleucid monarch's policy was far from altruistic, since he had his eye on the Temple treasury. The huge indemnity levied by the Romans, following the defeat of his predecessor Antiochus III in 190 or 189 BC at Magnesia, had saddled the dynasty with debt that was very difficult to service. A compliant Jewish upper class would offer Seleucid tax-collectors access to funds reserved for religious purposes. So a gymnasium was built on Temple hill, and crowds of young men, wearing broad-brimmed Macedonian hats, now flocked there to exercise with the enthusiasm of converts. Their desire to quit the cultural isolation imposed by strict Judaism was manifest in the efforts they made to disguise the fact of circumcision. In 171 BC Antiochus made his intentions absolutely clear: he wanted the Temple funds. Even hellenized Jews divided over this demand with the result that a revolt led by Judas Maccabaeus had the added dimension of a complicated civil war. To the surprise of almost all involved, the traditional Jews were victorious: by 142 BC the Seleucid garrison had been expelled for good from Jerusalem, and Judas' brother Simon was ruler and High Priest of Judaea. For the next eighty years the Jews enjoyed independence under a hereditary dynasty of High Priests.

A treaty made by Judas Maccabaeus with Rome in 161 BC was an early recognition of Judaean independence. Possibly this mutual defence pact did something to inhibit the Seleucid counterattack, but it is more likely that the task of reconquest was just too much. The rising power in the eastern Mediterranean was Rome and by 37 BC a Roman nominee such as Herod could be forced on the Jews. Herod the Great (37–4 BC) had fled to Rome when, in 40 BC, Parthian invaders had carried off as prisoner the last High Priest. The unpopularity of Herod's rule, and subsequent Roman administrative arrangements, culminated in the Jewish revolt of AD 66–70. It was ruthlessly put down by two future emperors, Vespasian (AD 69–79) and Titus (AD 79–81). In late AD 69 Vespasian entrusted its final phase to Titus, and in the following year, after a siege of four months, Jerusalem fell to his troops, who destroyed the Temple. Afterwards Judaea was simply a Roman province with its main garrison stationed at Jerusalem. Unrest reappeared in AD 115–118, as it did among Jewish communities in many parts of the empire, but the last straw for the Romans was Bar Cochba's rebellion of AD 132–135. So appalling was the devastation of Judaea that the emperor Hadrian (AD 117–138) forbade any Jewish settlement at Jerusalem. Once again it was an attack on Jewish ways which precipitated this last uprising, since Hadrian had forbidden the rites of both circumcision and castration throughout the empire. For Christians this law was of course not a problem. St Paul, a renegade Jew himself, had written to the Galatians about 'agitators' who insisted upon circumcision: he recommended that the 'mutilation' they desired so much be regarded as inappropriate as castration.

This final impetus to the diaspora effectively deprived the Jews of a homeland. Judaea was not emptied of all Jews but the permanent loss of Jerusalem made residence less important than before. Large communities already established abroad saw their numbers swell as the attractiveness of Judaea steadily diminished. One of the largest was at Alexandria, Alexander the Great's foundation in Egypt. The city was, under the Ptolemies (305–30 BC), the greatest centre of learning in the western classical world, a circumstance reflected in Jewish scholarship. There a translation of the Hebrew Bible into Greek was made. It is perhaps noteworthy that the prime motive for this project was an increasing inability on the part of Greek-speaking Alexandrian Jews to understand either Hebrew or Aramaic.

The fusion of Greek and Jewish thought had to await the work of the Jewish scholar Philo (20 BC – AD 50), a firm supporter of Roman rule. In AD 39 he led a deputation to Rome to protest at the relaxed attitude of the provincial authorities to pogroms. His idea of a ruler doing heavenly business on earth later proved influential in Christian thinking about the role of the Roman emperor. Bishop Eusebius (AD 260–340) was to extend this argument in order to justify the usurpation of Constantine, the first emperor to convert to Christianity. Constantine (AD 306–337) was convinced that restoring the unity of the Roman empire was his destiny: for Christians the vision of the cross he was supposed to have experienced in AD 312 served only to suggest that divine providence was involved too.

See ALEXANDRIA; EUSEBIUS; HADRIAN; HEROD; PHILO; PTOLEMIES; SELEUCIDS
*E. Bickerman, The Jews in the Greek Age (Cambridge, Mass., 1988); M. Goodman, The Ruling Class of Judaea: The Origins of the Jewish Revolt against Rome, AD 66–70 (Cambridge, 1987).

**Julian**, Roman emperor AD 361–363, was born at Constantinople in AD 332. Flavius Claudius Julianus was a committed pagan, and his attempt to revive pre-Christian religious beliefs earned him almost universal condemnation after his early death on campaign against the Sasanians. Possibly the insecurity of his childhood encouraged Julian's interest in the pagan classics: most of his family were butchered in the years immediately after the death of Constantine the Great (AD 306–337). He was only spared by Constantine's third son, Constantius II (AD 337–361), because of his extreme youth. Long periods of virtual house-arrest in Asia Minor gave Julian plenty of scope for study, and he secretly converted to a form of paganism associated with mysticism and magical practices. Yet his rejection of Christianity may not have been entirely a result of quiet introspection, for the affairs of the early church were in turmoil. Foreshadowing the later attitudes of eastern Roman, or Byzantine, emperors in religious affairs, Constantius was personally affronted when bishops failed to obey his commands. The problem the emperor posed for the western bishops, in particular, was that while he was Christian, he was, in their view, not orthodox. For Constantius followed Arius, whose heretical views had been condemned at the Council of Nicaea in AD 325, and held that Christ's essence 'was unlike that of the Father'. The bishops accepted that the emperor had the power to summon councils and to legislate to protect the church against pagans and heretics. What they objected to was Constantius' efforts to integrate the church with the state, with the resulting imperial intervention in ecclesiastical affairs, and most notably his dismissal of the Nicene Creed. The most determined opponent of the emperor was

Athanasius (AD 295–373), bishop of Alexandria, who suffered two exiles in the western provinces. Other bishops supporting Athanasius' commitment to the theological agreement concluded at Nicaea were also sent into exile.

Julian was also moved by natural beauty. 'From my childhood,' he recalled, 'a strange yearning for the rays of Helios, the sun god, sank deep into my soul; and from my earliest years my mind was so completely possessed by the light of heaven that not only did I desire to gaze intently at the sun, but whenever I went out at night, when the sky was clear and cloudless, I abandoned all else and devoted myself to the beauty of the heavens.' In Asia Minor Julian was initiated into several mystery cults, including those of Mithras, of Cybele and Attis, and of Hecate. A pagan party can be said to have formed around him, a group of philosophers, magicians and officials which earnestly wished for a programme of pagan restoration should Julian ever come to the throne.

Julian's chance for power came in AD 355, when Constantius appointed him as his junior partner in the west. He was sent there during invasions by the Franks and Alamanni. To the surprise of the imperial court, Julian won an important series of victories against the invaders and restored the Rhine frontier. It had been Constantius' intention on raising Julian to the rank of Caesar that he would act as a figurehead in the western provinces, carrying around the image of the emperor but leaving the civil and military administration in the hands of others. Now he faced a potential rival, since reports of Julian's popularity with the troops and the provincials were soon carried back to Constantinople, the effective capital. Constantius, therefore, decided to withdraw some of Julian's best legions and summon them back to his own army. But the soldiers at Lutetia (present-day Paris) refused to accept the order, and one evening in early AD 360 they surrounded the residence of Julian, proclaiming him Augustus. As this elevation had made him co-emperor with the vengeful Constantius, there was nothing he could do but prepare for war. In the event Julian succeeded peacefully to the throne because the emperor died of a fever in the autumn of AD 361. His arrival in Constantinople showed just how different a ruler Julian would be. He hated the pomp and circumstance of the new, Byzantine, style of the imperial court, and dismissed superfluous

The Roman emperor Julian dressed as a philosopher or a pagan priest.

cooks, barbers and other servants from the palace. His simpler tastes pleased his supporters, but many felt that an ascetic emperor diminished the majesty of the empire itself.

Having ruled out a war against the Goths on the Danube in favour of an attack on the Sasanians, Julian moved to Antioch in Syria as his base for the coming campaign in AD 362. Already he had issued an edict declaring temples open, and restored their lands and property which had been confiscated by Constantine. 'From all sides,' a contemporary noted, 'one could see columns returning to their place, some carried on ships, others on wagons.' But paganism needed more than buildings to rival Christianity and so he encouraged missionary activity, writing several texts for this purpose himself. At first Julian proclaimed the toleration of all religions. However, not only was the church deprived of many of its financial privileges, but in the religious disorders that followed, Christians were treated more harshly than pagans. Julian was especially incensed by the destruction of Apollo's temple by fire at Antioch, after the site had been purified by the clearing of human burials, including the relics of a Christian saint. In AD 363 he forbade Christians to teach classical literature in a shrewd attempt at breaking the link between the cultured urban upper classes upon whose support the empire depended and the church. But the order was never widely carried out, and a discouraged emperor marched the same year against Persia. Although the Sasanian king, Shapur I (AD 241–272), was sufficiently alarmed by the Roman preparations to offer negotiations, the opportunity to deal a decisive blow against such a troublesome enemy was too good to be passed over, and Julian left Antioch with a force of 65,000 men, the biggest army ever sent eastwards by Rome. But an effective scorched-earth policy caused the expedition to fail miserably. The historian Ammianus Marcellinus, an eyewitness, gives a graphic account of the sufferings of the retreat. The Romans could not live off the land, since the Persians had destroyed the crops, and they were constantly harried by surprise attacks. Julian himself fell in one such assault on the vanguard.

A council of senior officers chose then Jovian (AD 363–364) as the next emperor. This commander of the imperial guard protested that as a Christian he would be unable to lead a largely pagan army. 'We are all Christians,' the generals replied, and Jovian was reassured. The incident, however apocryphal, ended the pagan restoration, for once back in Roman territory Jovian announced the return of the empire to Christianity. The end of hostilities with the Sasanians was fortunate for Rome, because Jovian's successor, Valentinian (AD 364–375), was almost immediately plunged into a series of grave military emergencies on the northern frontiers.

*See* CHRISTIANITY; CONSTANTINE;

Constantinople; Rome; Sasanians; Shapur I; Valentinian

*G. W. Bowersock, *Julian the Apostate* (London, 1978); R. Browning, *The Emperor Julian* (London, 1975); Ammianus Marcellinus, *The Later Roman Empire, AD 354–378*, trans. by W. Hamilton (Harmondsworth, 1986).

**Justinian**, eastern Roman emperor AD 527–565, more than any other ruler, was responsible for shaping what today we call Byzantium, the Christian Greek civilization which survived through the Middle Ages. Arguably his contribution was as critical as that of Pericles (*c.* 495–429 BC) to classical Athens. For Justinian was an empire-builder, a law-giver, and a commissioner of great buildings such as Hagia Sophia. This great domed church in Istanbul still justifies the initial comment made by Justinian at the inauguration ceremony in AD 537: 'Glory to God who has deemed me worthy of accomplishing such a task!' Then the emperor added: 'O Solomon! I have beaten you!' Yet such projects, as well as his wars of reconquest in the western Mediterranean, were accomplished at a very high price: the neglect of the Balkan and Asian provinces. The most striking example of this was the sack of Antioch in AD 540. The Sasanian king Khusrau I (AD 531–579) used the vast spoils taken from this great city to build a new one near his own capital called 'Khusrau's superior Antioch'. He populated it entirely with war captives.

Mosaic of the eastern Roman emperor Justinian alongside Maximian, archbishop of Ravenna. From the church of San Vitale there: it dates from AD 547.

The best that Justinian could achieve on the eastern frontier was an uneasy truce with the Sasanians. Byzantine frontier garrisons put up a mediocre performance, except at Edessa, and so troops had to be rushed back from the west.

Justinian's western wars began with the recovery of Africa from the Vandals in AD 533–534. Italy was his next target, and by AD 540 all of the peninsula south of the Po was in Byzantine hands. A year later, however, there was a devastating outbreak of the plague: an enormous loss of life occurred, and Justinian himself almost died. The financial problems arising from the disaster undermined the army's morale because pay was often delayed. In his *Secret History*, Procopius relates how crushing taxation only caused rebellions that unpaid soldiers were not prepared to put down. In Italy the defeated Ostrogoths made a strong recovery and isolated Byzantine forces in a few strongpoints. Much of Byzantine Africa fell to the Moors, some troops deserted to them, and the remaining soldiers mutinied. In the early AD 550s renewed campaining recovered most of Italy and Africa, and added part of southern Spain, into which the Visigoths had been pushed by the Franks. Yet these reconquests were hard to hold. Within four years of Justinian's death in AD 565, Byzantine Spain was attacked by the Visigoths, Africa by the Moors, and Italy by the Lombards. All three were serious invasions, but the Lombards had most suc-cess, taking the north and most of the interior of Italy by AD 572. Within fifty years the empire of Justinian had largely gone: all that remained was Asia Minor, Syria, Egypt, Africa, with scraps of Thrace, Greece and Italy. The emperor Heraclius (AD 610–641) had great difficulty in defending these territories, and ominously in AD 633 the Arabs, newly converted to Islam, began their raids. In AD 636 Syria was lost, then in AD 640 Egypt was also overrun. It was hardly a compensation for the Byzatines that a year later Iran fell too. One eastern enemy had simply been replaced by another.

*See* GOTHS; ROME; SASANIANS; VANDALS
*J. Moorhead, *Justinian* (London, 1994); J. A. S. Evans, *The Age of Justinian* (London, 1996); Procopius, *The Secret History*, trans. by G. A. Williamson (Harmondsworth, 1966).

# K

Kaniska (AD 78–102) was the greatest of the Kushana rulers of India and Central Asia. Probably of Turkic extraction, the Kushanas were the most successful of the Central Asian invaders of India, the northern part of which they dominated from about AD 50 to 250. They had followed in the footsteps of the Scythian Sakas, and under Kaniska's energetic command put together a formidable empire. Its cosmopolitan nature is evident in the beautiful gold coins struck by Kaniska: Hindu, Buddhist, Zoroastrian, Mesopotamian, Greek and Roman deities are all represented, with Zoroastrian deities forming the largest group. The king himself seems to have been converted from Zoroastrianism to Buddhism by the famous poet-monk Ashvaghosa. Under his guidance Kaniska convened in the Punjab the Fourth Buddhist Council so as to reconcile the competing doctrines of the various sects. The great stupa (reliquary mound) he had built at present-day Peshawar was rated as an important contribution to the development of Buddhist monumental architecture. Apparently it was once 700 feet in height, an eastern wonder of the classical world.

Gold coin of the Kushana king Kaniska, who ruled over a cosmopolitan empire for nearly a quarter of a century.

But unlike Ashoka (268–232 BC), the earlier Mauryan convert to Buddhism, Kaniska did not lose his interest in warfare. It was he who completed the conquest of northern India, pushing Kushana arms far down the Ganges valley. Here Kaniska first encountered Ashvaghosa, who persuaded him to accept a sacred Buddhist relic instead of demanding an enormous indemnity from the defeated king of Pataliputra (modern Patna). Even though Buddhist tradition would seek to make this event the equivalent of Ashoka's shock over bloodshed after the Kalinga campaign, there is nothing in the historical record to suggest that Kaniska ever ceased to be primarily a war-leader. For he most probably died on campaign in Central Asia around AD 102: either the king was murdered by his own war-weary officers, or he fell in an engagement there with the Chinese. According to the Chinese records, a Kushana king had demanded a Han princess in marriage and was soundly defeated for his arrogance by General Ban Chao at Khotan in AD 90. Quite possibly Kaniska fell in a later battle in what the Chinese called the Western Regions. At stake was control of the highly lucrative silk trade, which the Kushanas succeeded in diverting through India via the Khyber pass. Shipments of silk then crossed the Arabian Sea to Characene, a kingdom at the head of the Persian Gulf. So profitable was this luxury item of commerce that Kaniska could afford to issue a gold coinage of his own. The Roman author Pliny the Younger complained that there was 'no year in which India does not attract 50 million of our coins'. The Kushanas were only too pleased to melt them down in order to reuse the precious metal.

After Kaniska's death his eldest son Vasiska came to the throne. His short reign of four years was followed by that of Huviska (AD 106–c. 140). During the period from Kaniska's succession in AD 78 till Huviska's death around AD 140, the Kushana empire was at the height of its authority. Its rule in northern India and Central Asia went unchallenged before the recovery of Iran under the Sasanian kings. It was the first Sasanian king, Ardashir I (AD 226–240), who effectively broke Kushana power by recovering control of the silk trade, a blow that encouraged Indian subjects to assert their independence.

*See* ASHOKA; BAN CHAO; BUDDHISM; KUSHANAS; SASANIANS; WESTERN REGIONS

*B. N. Puri, *India under the Kushanas* (Bombay, 1965).

**Kingship** for the Greeks came to be associated with despotism through Persian expansion westwards. The support given by Persian governors to compliant tyrants in the Greek cities of Asia Minor set the tone of the decisive encounter between the city-states of the Greek mainland and the invading Persians in 490 and 480–479 BC. For the historian Herodotus the Persian ruler was an absolute monarch who could tolerate no opposition to his will. Already he had characterized Cambyses (530–522 BC) as a ruthless despot with delusions of grandeur and suffering from a severe case of paranoia. Texts contemporary with Cambyses' conquest of Egypt, however, do not bear out Herodotus' image of a brutal foreign invader lacking any sensitivity to Egyptian customs. They indicate, on the contrary, that after Egypt was incorporated into the Persian empire in 525 BC, the local aristocracy was appointed to senior official positions. One remarkable inscription made by Udjahorresnet, who became chief physician, recounts how Cambyses at his request expelled foreign squatters at Sais from the temple of Neith, the mother of the sun god Re. 'His majesty commanded that offerings should be given to Neith, the Great One, the Mother of God, and to the great gods who are in Sais, as in previous times.' It is not impossible that Herodotus was reflecting later opinion of Persian rule, and especially resentment at the burden of taxation: Egyptian revolts were crushed in both 485 and 454 BC. An Athenian expeditionary force was even annihilated trying to aid the second rebellion.

But the view of Persian kingship found in Herodotus remained persuasive and was reinforced by later accounts of Alexander the Great's conquest of Persia. Darius III (336–330 BC), his opponent, is always cast as a weak-kneed coward. Overlooked is Darius' strategy of husbanding his military resources and trying to raise revolts against Alexander in his rear. That it took the Macedonian king twelve years of continuous fighting to emerge victorious is testimony to the remarkable solidity of the Persian empire. But it was just that: once Darius was murdered, Alexander could assume the role

of avenger of the legitimate Persian king and his rightful heir. As a hereditary ruler himself, this seemed a reasonable claim to make by right of conquest. The overlord of Greece was simply adding Persia to his own Macedonian realm. For the Greeks the conquest of Persia, therefore, made not the slightest difference in their attitude to kingship. Except for conservative Sparta, where a dual kingship of its own survived as part of an oligarchy, the Greek city-states were obliged to acknowledge with reluctance the royal pretensions of Alexander's generals, who carved out kingdoms for themselves after his death in 323 BC. One of the earliest to style himself king was Ptolemy (305–282 BC), who hijacked to Egypt the corpse of Alexander on the basis that an heir had responsibility for the funeral of a dead ruler. Possibly Ptolemy's own decision to associate himself with the divinity of the pharaohs was more palatable to the Macedonians than to the citizens of Greek city-states. On the death in 336 BC of Philip II, Alexander's father, the Macedonians had granted him divine honours. For them the ex-king was a descendant of the chief deity Zeus through the hero Heracles, their intermediary with the gods, and the obvious recipient of divine favour when judged by the standard of success. But it is doubtful whether the Ptolemies and the Seleucids could so easily have assumed divine honours had they not ruled peoples accustomed to such monarchic custom.

Coin of the first Macedonian ruler of Egypt, Alexander's general Ptolemy. The Ptolemies set the pattern for kingship in the eastern Mediterranean.

To the Persians kingship was an institution divinely ordained. The great god Ahura Mazda had set the king over the varied lands and peoples of the earth in order to maintain perfect order, without which only unhappiness would prevail. As the funerary inscription proclaims outside Darius' rock-cut tomb, 'Ahura Mazda when he saw the earth in turmoil, he bestowed it upon me, made me king . . . By the favour of Ahura Mazda I put it down in its place.' The success of Darius I (521–486 BC) in taking over the Achaemenid dynasty may have inspired his sense of destiny. His violent usurpation of the throne was hidden behind the bold assertion that his ancestors and those of Cyrus the Great (559–530 BC), the first Persian king, were descended from a certain Achaemenes. So effective was Darius' reign that the Achaemenids never lost their exclusive hold on the kingship

until the Macedonian conquest of Persia in 330 BC. The aims of subsequent rebels, with the exception of separatist Egypt, centred upon who should wield the god-given power of the King of Kings. Typical was the unsuccessful bid made by Cyrus the Younger in 401 BC to unseat his elder brother, Artaxerxes II. After the defeat and death of Cyrus in Babylon, his Greek mercenaries had to fight their way home, an amazing feat recorded by the Athenian author Xenophon (428–354 BC), one of the elected generals.

Even though India also accepted kings as part of the divine order, they were ranked beneath the brahmins, the hereditary Hindu priesthood. The difference between theory and practice was explained by the debasement of society in the so-called Kali age, the last of four in the present cycle of time. Whatever once had been the spiritual dignity of kingship was gone. Power in classical India abided only with the strong, the cunning, the daring, and the reckless. Specifically the downturn of virtue was said to have begun with the Nanda dynasty (546–322 BC), which destroyed the old aristocratic class and inaugurated professional warfare. The social upheaval which accompanied the establishment of the first large-scale Indian powers was reflected in the religious heterodoxy found in the teachings of the Buddha (c. 563–479 BC). He rejected the authority of the Vedas, the sacred texts of Hinduism, and proposed the idea of individual salvation by means of monastic self-discipline. Later his emphasis on personal endeavour was extended during the first century AD to salvation for all through a regime of worship and charitable service. The displacement of orthodoxy was just as clear in the belief of Candragupta (322–297 BC), the first Mauryan emperor, who is credited with ending his life as a Jain recluse. This ancient Indian faith had never been quite eradicated by the brahmins.

Political tradition in classical China took for granted strong central authority, embodied in the emperor as the Son of Heaven, once the Qin dynasty (221–207 BC) had destroyed feudalism. Prior to the imperial unification of China in 221 BC, a number of rival states boasted kings. Their quarrels, both internal and external, caused the destruction of the Warring States period (481–221 BC) and facilitated the rise of Qin as the sole royal house. The single-mindedness of Qin rulers stemmed in large measure from the tenets of Legalism, the first advocate of which was Shang Yang, a leading minister from 350 to 338 BC. Shang Yang's new law code strengthened the power of the throne at the expense of the aristocracy, and directed the energies of all subjects towards war. It is hardly surprising, therefore, that the First Emperor (221–210 BC) thought he could rule China by military means. The failure of this policy, and the political compromise favoured by the Han (202 BC – AD 220), the second imperial

dynasty, ensured that Chinese emperors were no longer despots, but it did not detract from the awe in which they were held. The very title itself contained the notion of divinity, or at least divine favour. Already an old and complex word, emperor had been used by Daoist thinkers as a means of elevating the semi-legendary figures they wished to claim as their own inspiration. They regarded the Yellow Emperor as the ancient sage from whom their teachings had descended. After giving his kingdom an orderliness previously unknown on earth, the Yellow Emperor, accompanied by officials and ladies, rose into the sky on the back of a dragon. The lure of immortality, as expressed in the elixir of life, was to fascinate the Chinese court, much to the benefit of cookery, medicine, and scientific method. No elixir could guarantee the duration of a dynasty, but the early acceptance of imperial unity as the only political possibility for China meant that it survived division and foreign conquest in contrast to other classical states.

Rome enjoyed no such consensus. The collapse of its republican order in the first century BC was not unconnected with militarism. The dictator Sulla (138–78 BC) tried a restoration, but his own use of soldiers served only to point up fundamental weaknesses. Attempts to de-politicize the army failed, even after the first Roman emperor, Augustus (31 BC – AD 14), defeated rival warlords to become sole ruler. In little more than half a century the accession was openly dependent upon the goodwill of the legions. Even then the fiction of Rome not having a military monarchy was still sustained, for in the absence of a civil service, unlike China, the emperors were obliged to co-operate with the Roman aristocracy in imperial administration. The emperor was the first citizen, never king, not, of course, that titles made much difference to the power he wielded between assassinations, rebellions, and usurpations.

See ADMINISTRATION; ALEXANDER THE GREAT; CAMBYSES; CANDRAGUPTA I; CYRUS THE GREAT; DARIUS I; NANDA DYNASTY; PERSIA; QIN DYNASTY; ROME; SHANG YANG; SPARTA

*J. M. Cook, *The Persian Empire* (London, 1983); A. Cotterell, *The First Emperor of China* (London, 1981); N. Hammond, *Philip of Macedon* (London, 1994); F. G. B. Millar, *The Emperor in the Roman World* (London, 1977).

**Kushanas** was the name given in India to the Central Asian invaders who controlled a great swathe of the subcontinent from about AD 50 to 250. They were known to the Chinese as the Da Yuezhi: in 138 BC the Han emperor Wu Di had dispatched the envoy Zhang Qian to find them in order to form an alliance against the Hunnish Xiongnu. Possibly of Turkic extraction, the Kushanas had moved westwards towards Central Asia around 175 BC, through Xiongnu pressure. Such movements frequently produced

a billiard-ball effect with one people impinging on another to send them moving ahead. One of these may have been the Scythian Sakas, who overcame the Greco-Bactrian kingdom (in present-day Afghanistan) about 140 BC. Less than a century later the Sakas had seized control of an area stretching from Taxila in northwestern India to Mathura in the Jumna valley. The last Greek king to have ruled here, Hermaeus, was deposed by the Saka chieftain Azes I about 55 BC. Little is known about the Sakas other than the names of their leaders. They were followed briefly by a number of Parthian rulers, before the arrival of the Kushanas around AD 50.

According to Chinese texts, the Da Yuezhi occupied the Oxus river valley, dispersed the Sakas still living there, and conquered the whole region up to the Hindu Kush. Unlike the Xiongnu, they were not just pastoral nomads and along the fertile Oxus many of them settled down to agriculture and trade. One of the five clans of the Da Yuezhi, the Kushanas, came to dominate the others, hence the Indian name for the whole people. The Greek alphabet was adopted for their script, while on the coins of King Kujula Kaphises around AD 25 were actually struck in Greek the titles 'great saviour' and 'king of kings'. His eldest son, Vima Kaphises (*c.* AD 64–70), extended Kushana control into northern India, where he may have penetrated as far as the Ganges valley. At Mathura, already an important cult centre, Vima was converted to the worship of Shiva: several of Vima's coins reveal the image of this Hindu deity.

Kaniska, the greatest of the Kushana kings, assumed power in AD 78 after some kind of interregnum. Whether there was a civil war or an external conflict, it is now impossible to tell, but Kaniska and his successors appear to have ruled with increased authority. The Kushana empire was at its height, as proved by archaeological finds throughout northern India; coinage began to be minted in gold, illustrated by divinities from a variety of pantheons; trade was enhanced by the diversion of caravans from China through the Khyber pass down to the Indus delta, whence their silk went by sea to Characene, a kingdom at the head of the Persian Gulf; and rulers took an active interest in religious matters. Though originally a follower of another faith, Kaniska became a convert to Buddhism and, like the earlier Mauryan emperor Ashoka (268–232 BC), he was concerned for the welfare of the monastic order. Under his patronage sacred texts were restored and the arts flourished, especially the so-called Gandharan school: this was a subtle blend of indigenous styles with Greek sculptural traditions, its representations of the Buddha striking Europeans as very familiar today. In order to bring some order to the doctrines of opposed Buddhist sects, Kaniska called a meeting in the Punjab, which later became known as the Fourth Buddhist Council. Repre-

sentatives of eighteen separate sects attended this distinguished gathering. Kaniska was guided by the Sanskrit poet Ashvaghosa, who had composed a full-length biography of the Buddha as well as other literary works of Buddhist interest. The compositions of this remarkable monk were to be translated into Chinese, once pilgrims such as Fa Xian carried texts home in AD 414.

Kaniska may have died fighting the Chinese in Central Asia, although an alternative account says that he was murdered by his own officers who were weary of continual campaigning. He was succeeded by his eldest son Vasiska (c. AD 102–106), then Huviska (AD 106–c. 140), whose name rather confusingly means 'the best' or 'the oldest'. Huviska's long reign indicates that the Kushana empire remained stable and prosperous. The last of its great kings was Vasudeva, who from his name, associated with the Hindu god Vishnu, shows an increasingly Indianized dynasty. During Vasudeva's reign (AD 140–176) there was a decline in the standard of coinage, possibly as a result of less profitable trade. The Sasanian kings of Iran had conquered some of the western Kushana provinces: they had in all probability seized control of the silk route from China. In the subsequent breakup of the Kushana empire from about AD 240 onwards, most of the territories within India were lost to the growing power of local rulers, and especially the Guptas. In Central Asia Kushana kings may have lingered on, however, as semi–independent vassals of the Sasanians. In AD 356 Shapur II was obliged to launch a campaign against one of them.

*See* ASHOKA; BACTRIA; BUDDHISM; GUPTA DYNASTY; KANISKA; SASANIANS; SCYTHIANS; XIONGNU; ZHANG QIAN

*B. N. Puri, *India under the Kushanas* (Bombay, 1965).

L

**Lao Zi**, or the 'Old Philosopher', was the founder of Daoism, the persistent challenger to Confucianism for intellectual supremacy in classical China. A native of Song, one of the oldest feudal states, Lao Zi was an older contemporary of Confucius (551–479 BC), and acted as keeper of the archives at the Zhou court in Luoyang. Access to records more ancient than anything available to Confucius in Lu may have persuaded Lao Zi of the falseness of traditions glorifying the feudal past. He became convinced that the causes of disorder in the country lay not in the shortcomings of feudal institutions but rather in the fact that they were themselves an unsatisfactory method of achieving order. Benevolence and righteousness, argued Lao Zi, usually acted as a mask for princely ambition. The book associated with his name, *The Way of Virtue*, sets the rivalry of feudal houses in a cosmic perspective. 'He who feels punctured must have been a bubble' has lost nothing of its cutting-edge in translation. Neither has 'Conduct your triumph like a funeral'.

What exercised Lao Zi's mind most was man's rootedness in Nature, an inner strength that made all men wiser than they knew. 'Knowledge studies others: wisdom is self-known.'

Lao Zi held that the artificial demands of feudal society had so disturbed the innate abilities of the people that instead of following the natural way of living, they were circumscribed through man-made codes of honour, love and duty. Most disliked of all by Lao Zi was the Confucian emphasis on the family as the cornerstone of society. For the Daoists believed that social evolution had taken a wrong turn with feudalism: their ideal was the primitive collectivist society that was supposed to have existed prior to the first kings. Reluctance to accept office or try to initiate reform sprang from the notion that things were best left alone. It was summed up in the concept of yieldingness. Daoist quietism was practised by a number of Lao Zi's followers, one of whom Zhuang Zi (350–275 BC), rejected the premiership of the huge southern state of Chu. As he succinctly commented: 'A thief steals a purse and is hanged, while another steals a state and becomes a prince.' In the turmoil of the Warring States period (481–221 BC), the only sensible policy for the sage was to live the life of a recluse.

Such an attitude was anathema to Confucian thinkers, who regarded service to the state as a moral obligation. The problem for the Daoists was that in classical times China had no popular institutions similar to those that arose in Greece for them to use in the furtherance of a fundamentally democratic philosophy. Withdrawal from service in government, or becoming a hermit, could never be more than a political protest. Lao Zi's own last protest was to do without a tomb, a deliberate display of indifference to the Confucian value placed on ancestor worship. It also indicates his interest in the elixir of life, a drug he may have finally journeyed westwards to find.

See CONFUCIUS; DAOISM; HUNDRED SCHOOLS; ZHUANG ZI

*A. Waley, *The Way and its Power: A Study of the Tao Teh Ching and its Place in Chinese Thought* (London, 1934); P. Carus, *The Canon of Reason and Virtue* (La Salle, Illinois, 1964).

**Legalism** was the school of philosophy which underpinned the Qin unification of China in 221 BC. Notwithstanding the superstition of the First Emperor (221–210 BC) and his

Daoist advisers, it was from the school of Law that his administration derived precepts for enforcing strict obedience. The fundamental idea of Legalism was standardization. At first connected with standard measures of weight, length and volume, it was later on extended to mean the general regulation imposed by an all-powerful ruler. Already apparent in the policies of Shang Yang (390–338 BC), Legalism claimed that the only model for conduct was the law of a state, which would determine punishments and rewards. Law thus became the regulator of all human action, replacing traditional notions of morality. This concept of a law devoid of any religious sanction was unique in a classical civilization.

A Qin standard weight. Regulation was the hallmark of Legalism, which provided the administrative philosophy for the unification of China under the First Emperor in 221 BC.

Shang Yang's ministry in Qin, from 350 till 338 BC, laid the foundation of that feudal state's triumph over its rivals at the end of the Warring States period

(481–221 BC). His new law code strengthened the throne's power by weakening the influence of the aristocracy, breaking up powerful clans, and freeing the peasantry from bondage. In place of customary ties Shang Yang substituted collective responsibility as a means of securing order. Groups of families were expected to control one another's behaviour. Those who did not denounce the guilty were cut in half at the waist, while those who denounced the guilty received the same award as if they had decapitated an enemy. For only 'the gate to riches and social status' under Legalism was situated on the battlefield. Nobles and merchants were dispossessed, so that the entire population could be organized for the benefit of the state's military power. 'If a state is strong and war is not waged,' said Shang Yang, 'the poison will be carried into its territory; rites and music and the parasitic functions will arise and dismemberment will be inevitable.' By poison the determined minister meant all the humane tradition of thought associated with the name of Confucius (551–479 BC). It is not, therefore, an accident that in 213 BC books should be burnt when Confucian scholars dared to express reservations about the harsh tendency of the First Emperor's policy. The destruction was nothing more than a thorough implementation of the Legalist idea of stupefying the mind of the people. Though Han Fei Zi (c. 280–233 BC), Shang Yang's greatest follower, was less extreme in stressing

war, he was just as firm on the dangers inherent in learning. 'In the state of an enlightened ruler,' commented Han Fei Zi, 'there is no literature written on bamboo strips, but the laws serve as the teaching. There are no sayings of ancient kings; magistrates act as teachers. And there is no valour through private swords; instead, courage will be shown by those who behead the enemy.'

Because Legalism took root so firmly in the comparatively backward state of Qin, the other feudal states tended to regard its extreme doctrines of social control as an aberration, even though its influence in strengthening the power of Qin could not be ignored. The heterodox Confucian philosopher Xun Zi (c. 320–235 BC) noted on a visit there the military and economic advantages enjoyed by its ruler, but deplored the reliance on naked force and terror. He was certain that, whatever short-term gains Qin might make, failure waited as its inevitable end. The same thought oppressed Li Si, the chief adviser of the First Emperor, when in 208 BC he was in the condemned cell. Out of favour with the Second Emperor (210–207 BC), Li Si lamented the impossibility of making plans for an unprincipled ruler. No one was allowed to point out the breaking-point which Legalist regulation had reached. Popular rebellion was already in the process of toppling the first imperial dynasty, but the Second Emperor simply executed messengers who brought bad news.

The Qin dynasty (221–207 BC) was doomed along with Legalism. In reaction to the unprecedented interference with everyday life, the Chinese ended totalitarian rule in the first nationwide revolt ever, and, through the compromise of the ensuing Han dynasty (202 BC – AD 220), sponsored a system of government that was founded upon a principle of responsibility for the whole country's welfare. Henceforth, no Chinese ruler could repeat the favourite utterance of the Roman emperor Caligula: 'Remember I can do anything to anyone.'

See CONFUCIUS; FIRST EMPEROR; HAN DYNASTY; HAN FEI ZI; LI SI; QIN; QIN DYNASTY; SHANG YANG; XUN ZI

★V. A. Rubin, *Individual State in Ancient China* (New York, 1976); J. J. L. Duyvendak, *The Book of Lord Shang: A Classic of Chinese Law* (London, 1928).

**Lepidus** (89–12 BC), the triumvir, was born into a well-established Roman family, although his father died as a disgraced outlaw in 77 BC through involvement with an abortive attempt to overthrow the constitutional arrangements made under Sulla's dictatorship (82–80 BC). These were dismantled during Lepidus' youth, however, as a new generation of leaders, including Cicero (106–43 BC), Pompey (106–48 BC), Crassus (112–53 BC) and Julius Caesar (100–44 BC), came to dominate Rome. Some of his father's well-intentioned proposals became law, but fundamental economic and social problems continued to threaten the republic. Lepidus threw in his lot with Caesar, acting on his behalf in Rome along with Mark Antony (83–30 BC). Once the civil war between Caesar and Pompey began in 49 BC he was compelled to actively support the anti-republican camp, since Caesar had no constitutional scruples. In 46 BC a victorious Caesar granted Lepidus a triumph at Rome for his governorship in north-eastern Spain. Although he saw little military action, he did play a role in keeping the peace in a land sympathetic to Pompey. It is likely that Caesar also chose to honour Lepidus for the sake of his family's reputation: the dictator for life needed as much support as he could get from the aristocracy. But Lepidus was not just an acceptable figure, for he succeeded in keeping the peace in Rome after Antony's miserable failure of 47 BC. When Caesar was assassinated in 44 BC by a group of senators, Lepidus may still have been responsible for law and order in the city, since he was conducting military drills in the suburbs at the time of the murder. The presence of his soldiers immediately put the conspirators on the defensive, even though at Cicero's urging the senate decided not to prosecute them. After Antony spoke at the funeral of Caesar, and displayed the dictator's blood-stained cloak, the populace went on the rampage and the conspirators fled.

Lepidus' moment had now come. He married his son to Antony's daughter, the usual way upper-class Romans cemented a political alliance, and with Caesar's great-nephew, Octavian (63 BC – AD 14), he formed the Second Triumvirate in 43 BC. According to the historian Plutarch, they 'divided the government as though it were a piece of property'. Initially given both Spain and Gaul, Lepidus lost ground in 42 BC when he remained behind to keep Italy under control, while Antony and Octavian gained prestige for their defeat of the conspirators' forces at Philippi in Macedonia. He was subsequently deprived of Spain and Gaul, but in 40 BC received Africa as a consolation prize. This, too, was taken by Octavian when in 36 BC Lepidus' legionaries refused to fight over the island of Sicily. Probably the office of chief priest saved his life, because Octavian was shrewd enough to realize that killing the holder of this life-long appointment would have caused consternation in Rome. Caesar had held it himself at the time of his assassination, a fact that Antony had exploited to the full during the funeral speech. So Lepidus lived on as an internal exile at Circeii (modern San Felice Circeo), south of Rome. His revenge was his longevity, for Octavian had been the emperor Augustus for many years before Lepidus died in 18 BC and left the chief priesthood vacant.

See AUGUSTUS; CAESAR; CICERO; CRASSUS; POMPEY; ROME
*R. D. Weigel, *Lepidus: The Tarnished Triumvir* (London, 1992).

**Li Ling** was a Chinese general unfortunate enough to be captured in 99 BC by the Xiongnu, probably the Huns who later invaded the Roman empire. Although success against these swift horsemen as a cavalry commander had brought about Li Ling's promotion, he was caught without adequate cavalry support on the steppe. His column of 5,000 infantrymen was surrounded by 30,000 mounted archers. Undaunted, Li Ling positioned his crossbowmen behind a wall of shields and spears so that their bolts could outrange the arrows shot from Xiongnu bows. The effect was devastating and Li Ling almost showed how properly armed foot-soldiers could defeat apparently invincible horse-archers. But without enough provisions and with crossbow bolts running low, he ordered his men to find their way back to the Great Wall as best they could. Only 400 soldiers reached the safety of its gateways, Li Ling himself being taken prisoner. This represented a double danger because a Chinese officer who surrendered to the Xiongnu not only placed his own life in enemy hands, but also put his whole family in danger of official punishment. When the Han emperor Wu Di (140–87 BC) heard of the surrender, he was furious that Li Ling had not died in battle. The historian Sima Qian wrote a memorial defending the general, saying that fighting had gone on as long as possible, but the emperor was encouraged by Sima Qian's enemies to regard this opinion unfavourably; the result was the charge of attempting to deceive the throne, a perfunctory trial, and castration. A year later, Wu Di recognized that he had been wrong in not dispatching relief to Li Ling, and sent for the general, but the latter would not return to China. As a result Li Ling's mother, wife and son were executed. The long struggle (138–91 BC) against the Xiongnu was eventually abandoned in the face of Chinese unrest. The Xiongnu raid of 87 BC, the year of Wu Di's death, was not followed up by a renewed offensive on the steppe. Instead of launching a punitive strike, the troops stationed along the Great Wall were merely set to strengthening its defences. However, relief was not to come from this bastion, for in 53 BC the Xiongnu became so divided that several major clans made peace with China.

*See* GREAT WALL; HAN WU DI; HUO QUBING; HUNS; SIMA QIAN; WARFARE; XIONGNU

★A. Waldron, *The Great Wall of China: From History to Myth* (Cambridge, 1990).

**Li Si** (died 208 BC) was the guiding spirit behind the imperial unification of China under the Qin dynasty. He advised King Zheng, the future First Emperor, who deployed his troops resolutely against one rival state after another, in the words of the historian Sima Qian 'as a silkworm devours a mulberry leaf'. In 247 BC Li Si left his home in southern China and sought service in Qin, the rising power in the north-west of the country. His teacher, the heterodox Confucian philosopher Xun Zi (*c.* 320–235 BC), warned him about the unbridled militarism of Qin, which 'victorious though it has been for four generations, yet it has lived in constant terror and apprehension lest the rest of the world should one day unite and trample it down'. But Li Si was keen to advance his official career, and he impressed King Zheng of Qin with his belligerent outlook. After the submission in 221 BC of Qi, the last independent Chinese state, Li Si was made Grand Councillor to the First Emperor, as Zheng styled himself.

Li Si's policies comprised a thorough-

Grand Councillor Li Si, holding his seal of office. More than any other advisor of the First Emperor, he was responsible for the sweeping changes which the first imperial government of China introduced.

going Legalism, a system of government as rigorous and oppressive as one introduced by the earlier Qin adviser, Shang Yang (390–338 BC). This minister had aimed through the coincidence of punishments and teachings to make sure that 'the gate to riches and noble status has its approach in soldiering: then, when the people hear of war, they congratulate each other and, whether at work or at rest, at times of drinking or eating, they will sing songs of war'. Opposition to such a brutal regime surfaced in 213 BC. That the chief critics were scholars of the Confucian persuasion only determined Li Si to stamp out this humane philosophy forever. All books were to be destroyed on pain of death, except those on medicine, agriculture and divination. Their public burning was intended to 'make the people ignorant' and to prevent the 'use of the past to discredit the present'. Li Si's exemption of works on divination was calculated, given the First Emperor's own obsession with the spirit world. Radical though Li Si's proposal was in its attempt to make knowledge an imperial monopoly, the proscription of books under Qin rulers was nothing new, Shang Yang having successfully destroyed copies of the *Book of Odes* and the *Book of History*, texts dealing with an ideal feudal past. The ultimate result was decisive, nonetheless. When a rebel army burned the imperial palace, the conflagration engulfed its library and in many cases reduced to ashes the sole surviving copies. The loss

caused a definite break in consciousness, for when, under the patronage of the ensuing Han dynasty (202 BC–AD 220), ancient texts were largely reconstructed from memory, the pre-imperial era of feudalism seemed remote.

But the so-called Burning of the Books in 213 BC did not silence the First Emperor's critics, and a year later over four hundred scholars were condemned to death. Crown Prince Fu Su was banished for recommending a less violent approach. When in 210 BC the First Emperor died on a tour of inspection, Li Si and the eunuch Zhao Gao (died 207 BC) hid the event long enough to secure their own positions through elevating to the throne Hu Hai, Fu Su's worthless younger brother. But the Second Emperor (210–207 BC) was never more than a puppet of the scheming Zhao Gao, although Li Si endeavoured to exercise some influence over policy. To curry favour with him the now isolated minister articulated an extreme Legalist point of view: the ruler himself was the reason for the existence of the state. 'The empire,' Li Si wrote, 'is to be used for a ruler's pleasures.'

The Second Emperor was never impressed with Li Si, however. For Zhao Gao made certain that Li Si always interrupted merrymaking and caused the ruler considerable annoyance. Yet Li Si's own attitude to power also contributed to his impotence, since he accepted the concentration of power in one person. Having helped to remove the competent Fu Su and elevate Hu Hai, he had put unlimited authority into degenerate hands. In the condemned cell, the hopeless position of the dynasty he served seems to have dawned on Li Si, when he lamented: 'For an unprincipled ruler, how can one make any plans?' After being tortured, Li Si and his son were publicly cut in half at the waist in 208 BC.

See FIRST EMPEROR; QIN DYNASTY; ZHAO GAO

*D. Bodd, *China's First Unifier: A Study of the Ch'in Dynasty as Seen in the Life of Li Ssu (c. 280 – 208 BC)* (Leiden, 1938); A. Cotterell, *The First Emperor of China* (London, 1981).

**Literature** is too vast an area of classical endeavour to offer here more than the barest outline: drama is treated separately. For the Greeks so much can be said to have derived from the poetry of Homer (ninth century BC) and Hesiod (seventh century BC), both in terms of religious ideas and concepts of heroism, that literature really began in Europe with their works. The *Iliad*, Homer's account of the Trojan War, and its sequel, the *Odyssey*, represented the epic standard to which a Roman poet such as Virgil (70–19 BC) still aspired to reach long after the age of heroes had passed. The Romans fondly believed that an important element among them came from Asia Minor, none other than Trojan refugees who escaped the sack of their city by the Greeks and followed Aeneas. This myth received classic restatement in Virgil's *Aeneid*, much to the contentment of Augustus, the first Roman emperor (31 BC – AD 14). But already Trojan ancestry had been cited by the Roman senate as a sufficient reason for granting protection to the Acarnanians, who were sorely harassed in 239 BC by the Aetolians: only the Acarnianians, Homer declares, held aloof from hostilities against Troy. Yet it is tempting to see in all this nothing less than a

A scene from Virgil's epic poem: Dido and Aeneas riding out to hunt. It comes from a mosaic found in Somerset.

Roman attempt to assert cultural parity with Greece. Just as the Romans had been overwhelmed by the range and interest of its mythology, so now the full impact of Greek literature was pointing up their own lesser achievement. There were no Roman counterparts of Simonides (died 468 BC) or Pindar (518–438 BC), two poets who excelled at celebrating great deeds. The former made his name in composing epitaphs, dirges and dedications for the Greeks who fell during the Persian invasions (490–479 BC), while the latter was famous for his songs in praise of athletic victories at the great national games. Both were professionals, willing to execute commissions for public performance from city-states and rich individuals.

Where the Romans came closest to Greek literature was perhaps in historical writing: the annals of Titus Livius, better known to us as Livy (59 BC – AD 17), and those of Cornelius Tacitus (AD 56–120) can be compared with the histories of Herodotus (484–425 BC) and Thucydides (455–400 BC). The context of composition was altogether different at Rome, where the early emperors made efforts to suppress subversive literary works. As a result, political dissent took refuge in the past. Even though Tacitus could not resist exacting posthumous revenge on rulers deemed hostile to his own senatorial class, his *Annals* and *Histories* afford by far the most penetrating political analysis to be written in Latin. More biographical were the writings of Gaius

Suetonius Tranquillus (AD 69–140), because he chose to place imperial achievements side by side with imperial vices. Suetonius is closer to the outstanding historical biographies of his Greek contemporary Plutarch (AD 50–120), although his concentration on human frailty as an explanation of political failure anticipates also a later Greek author, Procopius (born AD 500), whose *Secret History* is a thorough character-assassination of the emperor Justinian (AD 527–565).

The study of history was also a preoccupation of the classical Chinese. This antiquarian tendency can be traced to Confucius (551–479 BC), for whom the Early Zhou period (1027–771 BC) was almost a lost ideal. He claimed that his own teachings sought to 'follow Zhou' in establishing a moral code for 'all under Heaven', and insisted: 'I am a transmitter, not a creator. I believe in things old and love them.' Because society's rootedness in the past was always taken for granted in China it is hardly surprising that in the work of Sima Qian (145–*c.* 90 BC) we encounter the first attempt to write a history of the entire knowable past. The books which Chinese scholars most liked to read were the *Book of History*, ancient documents edited in the fourth century BC, the *Book of Odes*, an evocation of the feudalism so dear to Confucius, the *Book of Changes*, a collection of oracles, and the *Spring and Autumn Annals*, which cover the period from 770 to 481 BC. As in classical Greece, there was also a great

outpouring of philosophical speculation in China associated with the
schools of Confucianism, Daoism,
Legalism and Moism. Classical Chinese
prose, however, achieved its remarkable lucidity in the rationalism of
Wang Chong (AD 27–100), who was
the scourge of official extravagance.
From India, on the other hand, there
are few surviving historical narratives
or works of pure philosophy. Religion
appropriated epic poetry as well, the
100,000 verses of the *Mahabharata*
becoming a key Hindu text by the
Gupta period (AD 320–550). It also
absorbed popular story-telling through
the puranas, since their accounts of
mythological exploits were probably
less strictly religious than their present
form implies. Buddhism had its classical poets, too. Yet there was nonetheless a secular tradition in Indian
literature, which flourished primarily
in drama. Kalidasa, who wrote during
the period AD 350–450, was India's
greatest poet and dramatist of all time.

See CONFUCIUS; DRAMA; HERODOTUS:
SIMA QIAN; THUCYDIDES

*A. L. Basham, *A Cultural History of India*
(Oxford, 1975); M. R. Lefkowitz, *The
Lives of the Greek Poets* (London, 1981);
P. Levi, *Horace: A Life* (London, 1997);
K. Quinn, *Texts and Contexts: The Roman
Writers and Their Audience* (London, 1979);
*An Anthology of Chinese Literature*, ed. by C.
Birch (New York, 1965).

**Liu Bang** (247–195 BC) was the first
Chinese peasant to found an imperial
dynasty, the Han (202 BC – AD 220).
He won the complicated struggle
between insurgent leaders for the
honour of replacing the repressive
Qin dynasty (221–207 BC). Tradition
relates that in 209 BC, having lost
several convicts from a group he was
conducting to the capital, Liu Bang
released the others and placed himself at their head. While the popular
insurrection against Qin rule started as
an attempt to restore feudalism, the
old aristocracy soon showed itself
incapable of undertaking the task of
government and, faced with the
prospect of a protracted conflict, the
Chinese put their trust in the ordinary
men who had risen to prominence
during the course of the revolt.

Both the historians Sima Qian and
Ban Gu recall the remarkable physiog-
nomy of Liu Bang, his prominent nose,
dragon forehead, and the seventy-two
black moles on his left thigh, just as
they list the supernatural events surrounding his conception and early
manhood, but they cannot disguise the
historical fact of a peasant background.
Even before his final triumph over the
southern rebel leader and nobleman
Xiang Yu, Liu Bang revealed a peasant
distaste for the excessive ceremony
attached to learning. When some
scholars came to him in costume, he
snatched one of their elaborate hats and
urinated in it. But he was moderate in
comparison with Xiang Yu (233–
201 BC), a hard-bitten rebel leader
who thought nothing of boiling an
outspoken follower alive. The mild-

ness of Gaozu, as Liu Bang became known as the first Han emperor (202–195 BC), seems to have been genuine, a signal virtue in a very violent age, and it made his succession popular: people felt he would govern in their interests, unlike the absolute rulers of Qin. Gaozu neither aped aristocratic manners nor slackened his compassion for the peasantry, and his habit of squatting down, coupled with an earthy vocabulary, unsettled polite courtiers. But he knew the value of learned and cultivated advisers. To bring order to the daily life of his new palace at Chang'an, near the old Qin capital, he commissioned a new court ceremonial for his boisterous adherents. His only instruction to Chamberlain Lu Jia was 'Make it easy'.

Despite the brief Qin unification imposed by the First Emperor (221–210 BC), China remained a confederation of recently independent feudal states with still robust regional cultures. But Confucian standards and rituals together with inherited Qin administrative practice soon brought about a degree of cultural unity. By turning to scholars untarnished by the harsh policies of Legalism, Gaozu paved the way for the ultimate Confucianization of a bureaucratic empire. The transformation was a slow one because the first Han emperor settled for a political compromise after the oppression of the Qin dynasty. He allowed the restoration of certain feudal houses and granted fiefs to his own supporters and close relatives, but these diminished holdings were intertwined with districts controlled by imperial officials. In 154 BC use was made of a rebellion among these vassals to alter the laws of inheritance. Inherited land henceforth had to be divided between all sons in a family which hastened the breakdown of large units. Emperor Han Wu Di (140–87 BC) completed the dispossession of the old overpowerful aristocracy.

Internally the reign of Gaozu was an outstanding success. External relations, however, were much more problematic because of the pressure placed on the northern defences by the nomadic Xiongnu, probably the Huns who later invaded the Roman empire. In 200 BC Gaozu was lucky to escape capture at Pingcheng (near present-day Datong) after his forces numbering 300,000 men were surrounded by the mobile Xiongnu. The realization that these horse-archers could not be easily defeated in a set-piece battle beyond the line of the Great Wall led Gaozu to develop policies that sought to contain the threat they posed by a mixture of diplomacy and force. Essentially it meant the establishment of stable foreign relations through the payment of subsidies to unaggressive nomad rulers as well as the tolerance of international trade. The policy remained in operation till the 130s BC, when it was found that the cost of subsidy was no longer being balanced by a commensurate saving on military expenditure. Serious nomad raids had started once again.

*See* FIRST EMPEROR; HAN DYNASTY; LU JIA; QIN DYNASTY; XIANG YU; XIONGNU
\*M. Pirazzoti-t'Serstevens, *The Han Civilization of China* (Oxford, 1972).

**Liu Ying** (died AD 71) was the half-brother of the Han emperor Ming Di (AD 57–75). The ruler of a small dependent kingdom in the Huai river valley, Liu Ying has the distinction of being the first Chinese to be acknowledged as a worshipper of the Buddha. In AD 65 Ming Di issued an edict authorizing those who had committed crimes warranting the death penalty to redeem themselves by payment of a certain number of rolls of silk. Out of fear for his own position, Liu Ying took advantage of this offer of amnesty to present thirty rolls of yellow and white silk to the throne. Though senior officials believed otherwise, the emperor did not consider his half-brother guilty of any offence and, in addition to refusing to accept the ransom, declared that Liu Ying esteemed the teachings of Lao Zi and the Buddha. At this period Buddhism was regarded as a sect of Daoism, not unlike the contemporary position of Christianity and Judaism in the eastern provinces of the Roman empire.

In AD 70, however, the magical interests of Liu Ying in Daoism and Buddhism were denounced as treason. Apparently, because of a concern for favourable omens, he was accused of seeking independence from the empire. This seems most unlikely.

That Liu Ying surrounded himself with adepts as well as monks clearly shows that his goal was not an independent throne but longevity, even immortality. Ming Di received a strong official recommendation that his half-brother be executed for treason, but he refused the advice and altered the punishment to exile, with a great number of his courtiers, in the Yangzi river valley. On his arrival there, Liu Ying committed suicide. Thousands of his supporters were subsequently arrested: torture and trials continued until AD 77, when Ming Di's son and successor brought the persecution to a halt. But it would seem that the Buddhist community associated with Liu Ying had been allowed to continue in existence unharmed. A number of donations to its temple are recorded towards the end of the Han dynasty (202 BC – AD 220).

*See* BUDDHISM; HAN DYNASTY
\*E. Zurcher, *The Buddhist Conquest of China* (Leiden, 1959).

**Lu** was one of the oldest of the Warring States (481–221 BC). Situated in what is now Shandong province, the tiny state of Lu was the birthplace of two important philosophers, Confucius (551–479 BC) and Mo Zi (*c.* 468–376 BC). It was the philosophy of the former that ensured Lu's lasting fame, because the first Han emperor set the standard for court ceremonial around 200 BC by invoking the aid of the scholars of Lu and combining

Confucian ideas with the ceremonial of the Qin dynasty (221–207 BC), the first imperial house. It led in time to the triumph of Confucianism as the imperial ideology under Emperor Han Wu Di (140–87 BC), an event largely brought about by the teachings of Dong Zhongshu (c. 179–c. 104 BC). Lu, like the other Warring States, ceased to exist as an independent power when Qin forcibly unified China in 221 BC. A degree of self-rule was allowed under the Han dynasty (202 BC – AD 220), since the imperial administration initially comprised a dual system of commanderies and feudal holdings. But the diminished fiefs awarded to old families, supporters of the imperial house, and its own members were carefully intertwined with territories controlled by officials. A rebellion among the eastern domains in 154 BC upset the administrative balance, which subsequently tilted towards a purely bureaucratic state under strong central control. A king of Lu is reported to have been alive in the 80s BC. Apparently he halted the demolition of the house of Confucius, when workmen discovered hidden in a wall books and musical instruments. The tale, however, may be apocryphal because it was cited as proof of authenticity for certain Confucian texts. Few of the restored feudal states are known to have lasted for more than four generations under the Han emperors.

See CONFUCIUS; DONG ZHONGSHU; LIU BANG; MO ZI; SUN ZI; WARRING STATES

*H. H. Dubs, 'The Victory of Han Confucianism', *Journal of the American Oriental Society*, 58 (New Haven, 1938).

**Lu Jia** (died c. 160 BC) was one of the heroes of Confucian tradition. His rectitude under several Han emperors was regarded as something of a model for a Chinese minister, while his handling of the dynasty's founder was considered to be decisive. Gaozu, the first Han emperor (202–195 BC), was mild in comparison with his contemporaries, but a peasant background gave him a distaste for the excessive ceremony attached to learning. Prior to his accession, he once snatched an elaborate hat from a scholar's head and urinated into it. Hardly surprising, therefore, was Gaozu's considerable annoyance when Chamberlain Lu Jia kept quoting from the *Book of History*.

'I conquered the empire on horseback,' said Gaozu. 'What is the good of these quotations from books of old?' The Chamberlain replied: 'That is true, but Your Majesty will not be able to govern it on horseback. If Qin had governed with humanity and righteousness, if it had followed the precepts of the ancient sages, then Han would not have gained the empire.' At this the emperor blanched and said: 'Explain to me the reasons for the fall of Qin and the rise of Han, as well as what it was that won and lost kingdoms of old.' In obedience to Gaozu's wish, Lu Jia wrote a book about statecraft. When the emperor listened to his chamberlain reading aloud his book, he praised his ideas greatly.

This account of Gaozu's conversion to Confucian theories of government was a turning-point in Chinese intellectual history. It effectively ended the so-called Hundred Schools of philosophy, the competing systems of thought existing before the Qin unification of the country in 221 BC. Thereafter the developing philosophy of Confucius (551–479 BC) held sway, even though it was challenged during times of imperial crisis by both Daoist and Buddhist beliefs.

*See* CONFUCIUS; HAN DYNASTY; HUNDRED SCHOOLS; LIU BANG; QIN DYNASTY

*M. Pirazzoti-t'Serstevens, *The Han Civilization of China* (Oxford, 1972).

**Lucretius** (*c*.94–55BC) wrote the only philosophical poem of the classical era that has come down to us intact. Entitled *How Things Are*, it expounds the universe according to Epicurus, who in 307 BC had set up his austere community at Athens. Utterly different however is the impassioned expression of Titus Lucretius Carus, for left behind is the dryness of the Greek philosopher's prose in the rich sweep of his Latin verse. To his contemporary Cicero, no mean author himself, Lucretius' poetry was filled with 'flashes of genius'. Quite possibly a landowner from Pompeii, Lucretius may have picked up his ideas in the locality because the Syrian Epicurean

Philodemus (110–35 BC) lived at neighbouring Herculaneum. But whatever the immediate source, *How Things Are* does not hesitate to compare Epicurus with Hercules: the hero rid the world of terrible monsters, while the philosopher liberated mankind from the equal oppression of religion. Moving well beyond Epicurus' quiet belief in the gods, Lucretius places his own emphasis upon human will-power and reason alone. Hence his interest in the atomic theory as an explanation of natural phenomena when he wrote: 'All things move, all are changed by nature and compelled to alter. For one thing crumbles and grows faint and weak with age, another grows up and comes forth from contempt.' Rather like the Chinese rationalist Wang Chong (AD 27–100), Lucretius was concerned to free the mind from false and disturbing opinions. The macabre closing of his poem, a description of the aftermath of the plague which struck Athens in 429 BC, has suggested to some that Lucretius was very ill himself at the time. What is as likely is a poetical reminder of the fate which awaits everyone. Religion is said to offer no real succour in the face of death, whose terror can only be overcome through philosophical understanding. If anyone remains anxious over his body rotting in the grave or being burned on a pyre, then he must have some lingering belief in survival after death. As both the body and the soul perish together, Lucretius tells us, 'there is nothing to fear about dying'.

See EPICURUS; WANG CHONG

*D. R. Dudley, *Lucretius* (London, 1965); D. West, *The Imagery and Poetry of Lucretius* (Edinburgh, 1969).

**Lucullus** (117–56 BC) was underrated as a man of action in Rome because of his voluntary retirement in 59 BC to a life of refined luxury. Lucius Licinius Lucullus was Sulla's most reliable officer and he supported the reforms of this dictator (82–80 BC). In 74 BC he was given command against King Mithridates VI of Pontus, who was active once again in Asia Minor. Another Roman general already there had been outmanoeuvred and beaten by the time Lucullus arrived, and so he was not displeased when at Otroea (modern Iznik) a flame-like body fell from the sky between the Pontic and the Roman armies as they deployed for battle. Both sides, recognizing an evil omen, instantly withdrew. The reason for his willingness to forgo a major engagement was that Lucullus had already divined how best the war would be won. As the Pontic army was considerably larger than his own, he thought it prudent not to engage the enemy but simply to keep up a constant harassment. Lucullus' officers were less enthusiastic about his tactics, not least because they offered little booty in comparison with an immediate invasion of Pontus itself. But they gradually saw how Mithridates was squandering all his strength, while Lucullus expelled Pontic garrisons from the cities occupied in the earliest days of the war. The Roman commander also proceeded to levy ships from friends and allies in order to break Mithridates' mastery of the sea.

One night in 73 BC when Lucullus was encamped at Troy he dreamed that the goddess Aphrodite urged him to action, and a day or so later he won a victory at sea, off the island of Lemnos. This reverse persuaded Mithridates to withdraw his forces to Pontus, and there were some Roman officers who argued that hostilities should cease, but Lucullus was determined to finish the struggle once and for all. He pointed out that Mithridates had first challenged Rome in 88 BC and he would return to the attack sooner or later. Lucullus' army set off in pursuit of Mithridates, but not without complaints about a lack of booty.

Others were also annoyed at the moderation shown by Lucullus, when he eased the tax burden on cities involved in the First Mithridatic War (88–85 BC). He found that an extortionate interest rate had led to crippling debts, even though the entire indemnity imposed by Sulla had been paid twice over. So a maximum annual interest rate of 12 per cent was set, all interest in excess of the principal abolished, and a ceiling of one-fourth of any debtor's income fixed on the amount payable to a creditor. As a result, all debts were paid off within four years, an event which earned Lucullus deadly enemies in Rome among money-lenders, who financed aspiring politicians in return for rich pickings in the provinces. So it happened that Lucullus found himself in Pontus with a mutinous army, while his authority was being skilfully cut from under him at Rome.

Yet by late 70 BC he had forced Mithridates to abandon the core of his kingdom, and also captured Tigranocerta, the seat of his ally and son-in-law, King Tigranes I of Armenia. Tigranocerta was an artificial creation of Tigranes on an ancient site, and Lucullus returned its forcibly enrolled inhabitants to their homes. But this eastern advance of Roman arms was soon eclipsed by the appointment of Pompey (106–48 BC) first to suppress piracy, and then in 66 BC to make a general settlement of affairs in the east. Lucullus got a grudging triumph, for which he had to wait till 63 BC, but small thanks otherwise. In 60 BC he managed to embarrass Pompey in the senate by leading the opposition to ratification of his eastern arrangements and the settlement of his veterans. The move was a bad one, because a year later Pompey returned to the argument with two powerful allies, Licinius Crassus (112–53 BC) and Julius Caesar (100–44 BC). To achieve their political aims they had just formed a triumvirate, which by means of armed force effectively broke the power of the senate, and paved the way to one-man rule. Lucullus obviously understood that Rome, instead of being controlled by an oligarchy of aristocrats, was now in the power of three ambitious men.

He retired from public life and devoted himself to Epicurean pleasures, much to the disgust of his former friends in the senate. Progressively isolated from Roman society, yet willing to act as patron to Greek visitors and residents, Lucullus became the symbol of moral degeneracy. Because Romans judged a man's character by his public associates, Lucullus' disgust with contemporary politics only reinforced the impression of self-satisfied aloofness, with the result that eccentric sensualists were thereafter said to be 'leading the life of a Lucullus'.

*See* ARMENIA; CAESAR; EPICURUS; MITHRIDATES; ORACLES; POMPEY; ROME

\*A. Keaveney, *Lucullus: A Life* (London, 1992).

**Luoyang**, on a tributary of the Yellow river lower than Chang'an, was made the imperial capital of China by the first Later Han emperor Guangwu Di (AD 25–57). The enthronement in Luoyang did not put an end to the civil strife, following the usurpation of Wang Mang (AD 9–23). Eleven others claimed the right to occupy the dragon throne and, although by AD 27 the struggle began to go his way, the last pretender was removed only in AD 36 with the reconquest of Sichuan province. The ability of this part of the empire to resist for so long reflected a profound economic change. The transfer of the seat of imperial government from Chang'an to Luoyang was thus a tacit acknowledgement of the shift in the national centre of gravity. The Huai and Yangzi river valleys had overtaken the present-day province of Shaanxi, the old centre of Qin and Former Han power, as the most developed region in the empire. The temporary breakup of China during the Three Kingdoms period (AD 221–80) can be seen as a continuation of the same process in that the southern kingdoms of Shu and Wu were sufficiently strong to challenge for many years the northern state of Wei, the rump of the Han empire.

Luoyang was completed during the reign of the second Later Han emperor Ming Di (AD 57–75). More compact than Chang'an, Luoyang had a walled area of more than seven square miles. But its population, including extensive suburbs, was over half a million. Like other classical Chinese cities, it was approximately rectangular in shape and oriented on a north–south axis. Its streets formed a grid and around each ward were walls with gates for controlling the movement of people. At a certain hour the drum tower in the centre of the city signalled the closure of these gates for the night. Outside Luoyang's walls there was also a moat. The two walled palace compounds, located at the northern and southern ends of the city, served to reinforce the impression of imperial authority.

In the suburbs stood the brand new imperial university with some 30,000 students. Although this number represented an increase over the original institution in Chang'an, its purpose remained the same: the recruitment of officials for the civil service. Of all classical societies, China was most divided by literacy. The fundamental distinction was always between the educated gentry from whom officials were drawn and the peasants who could not read or write. The official ruling class, however, was neither entirely closed nor unchanging, especially in Later Han times because of the greater influence of large landowners.

The density of population was high in Luoyang, and even the wealthy had a rather restricted living area, though every courtyard, no matter how small, became something of a garden by the use of plants and small trees in pots. A sense of seclusion was preserved by house design, based on a central courtyard, often referred to as the 'well of Heaven'. Substantial family dwellings would be laid out around two or more courtyards. The richest inhabitants maintained a residence within the walled city as well as a mansion in the suburbs, where, among less built-up parts, were to be found official altars, shrines, parks and the imperial tombs.

Later Han Luoyang survived until AD 189, when, following the assassination of a general by the palace eunuchs, his troops sacked and looted the city for several weeks. The loss of the imperial library was almost as serious as the book-burning during the Qin dynasty (221–207 BC); Luoyang's ruin was so complete that the Wei dynasty (AD 220–265), the creation of another general's son, had to rebuild everything from the ground up with the exception of the rammed-earth city walls. Near the close of the classical era, in AD 311, the city was devastated once more, when the Xiongnu and other nomadic peoples were drawn into Chinese civil strife.

See CHANG'AN; HAN DYNASTY; THREE KINGDOMS; WEI DYNASTY

*M. Loewe, *Everyday Life in Early Imperial China* (London, 1968).

**Lysander** (died 395 BC) was the Spartan admiral responsible for the defeat of Athens in 404 BC at the end of the Peloponnesian War. He first defeated the Athenians in 407 BC off Notium on the coast of Asia Minor, but his friendship with Cyrus the Younger caused his replacement at the behest of the anti-Persian lobby, even though the Peloponnesian fleet relied on financial aid from Persia. The Athenian victory at Arginusae in 406 BC was followed by the cry for Lysander's recall, and as admiral once again he visited Sardis to seek further money from his friend Cyrus. The youthful Persian governor handed over a large sum, not least because his own dynastic plans required the support of a Greek army. Already Cyrus was in difficulty with the Persian court over his pretensions: he had executed two of his royal cousins, because they had refused to thrust their hands into their sleeves in the presence of Cyrus, a gesture of respect normally reserved just for the

Persian king. With Cyrus' new subsidy Lysander was able to pay the arrears in his crews' wages, and prepare for a confrontation with the Athenians. This took place in the Hellespont at Aegospotami in 405 BC. A surprise attack on this Athenian base caught many vessels on the beach without men or only partially manned. Over 170 Athenian triremes were swiftly destroyed or captured, and some 4,000 men taken prisoner. Afterwards he conducted a blockade of Piraeus, the port of Athens, till in 404 BC the Athenians surrendered.

Lysander was personally ambitious. Tradition recounts how he tried to alter the Spartan constitution to become king himself. He took advantage of his naval command to appoint his friends as oligarchs in cities liberated from Athens, and added garrisons under trusted governors where necessary. Sparta soon put a stop to this policy, however. To prevent Thebes from becoming too powerful in central Greece it withdrew support from the Thirty at Athens, a group of oligarchs set up by Lysander, and allowed the re-establishment of democracy. Though he was also recalled, Lysander did not abandon his hopes of power, and sponsored the election as Agesilaus (444–360 BC) as one of the two Spartan kings. But his protégé dropped him at the earliest opportunity, so that the disappointed commander had not really advanced his personal position at all by the time of his death on the battlefield in 395 BC. But his frustrated ambitions were never forgotten for the reason that, at Delphi, Lysander had commissioned from the booty taken at Aegospotami the so-called 'admiral's monument': it was immodestly made up of statues of the gods Zeus, Apollo and Poseidon, the goddess Artemis, Lysander himself, his soothsayer Agias, and Hermon, his steersman. The sea god Poseidon was actually shown crowning the victorious admiral.

See AGESILAUS; CYRUS THE YOUNGER; PELOPONNESIAN WAR

*D. Kagan, *The Fall of the Athenian Empire* (Ithaca, 1987); P. Krentz, *The Thirty at Athens* (Ithaca, 1982).

**Lysimachus** (360–281 BC), one of the close companions of Alexander the Great, assumed the title of king in 305 BC, the year Ptolemy in Egypt and Seleucus in Syria did the same. His father seems to have been a Thessalian Greek who migrated to Macedon. On Alexander's death in 323 BC Lysimachus was given Thrace to rule. By 284 BC he had built up a kingdom embracing not only Thrace, Macedon, Thessaly, but also a large part of Asia Minor. The natural stronghold of Pergamum, for instance, was in the hands of his lieutenant Philetaerus, who also guarded there a considerable amount of treasure. But just before Lysimachus' death in 281 BC on the battlefield, at Corupedium in Asia Minor, Philetaerus threw in his lot with the victor, Seleucus. The family of Philetaerus, however, eventually set

itself up as an independent dynasty, the Attalids.

The acquisition of Macedon and Thessaly in 285 BC made Lysimachus for a short time the strongest of all Alexander's successors in terms of manpower. But he was hated for the oppressiveness of his administration, and personally distracted by feuds. The most violent member of Lysimachus' family was his second wife Arsinoe, daughter of Ptolemy I (305–282 BC), who was most responsible for driving Philetaerus into the Seleucid camp. It was indeed the rising unpopularity of Lysimachus that persuaded Seleucus I (305–281 BC) to risk an engagement at Corupedium. Hardly anything is known about the course of the battle, except a story about Lysimachus' faithful dog. The animal is said to have guarded his body on the field and then jumped on his funeral pyre. But some members of Lysimachus' family tried to prevent the burial of his bones, until Seleucus forbade further strife and arranged for a proper interment in Thrace.

See ALEXANDER THE GREAT; ATTALIDS; PTOLEMIES; SELEUCUS I

*H. S. Lund, *Lysimachus: A Study in Early Hellenistic Kingship* (London, 1992)

# M

Ma Yuan (14 BC – AD 49), an accomplished Chinese general, was also instrumental in restoring the Han dynasty after the usurpation of Wang Mang (AD 9–23). On joining the side of the Han emperor Guangwu Di in AD 28, Ma Yuan commented with brutal frankness: 'In present times, it is not only the sovereign who selects his subjects. The subjects select their sovereign.'

Ma Yuan's family were powerful landowners in north-western China, although the execution of his great-grandfather for treason meant that the general was the first member to hold public office for two generations. Having served the usurper Wang Mang, like the overwhelming majority of officials, Ma Yuan switched to Guangwu Di's side in the complicated civil war at the start of the second half of the Han dynasty (202 BC – AD 220). He gave the new emperor loyal and effective service. As a governor in the far south, Ma Yuan found himself embroiled in a major rebellion in northern Vietnam, then part of the Chinese empire. With an army of 20,000 men he crushed the rebels in AD 40, and then set about improving the administration of the three Vietnamese commanderies. 'Wherever he passed,' it is recorded, 'Ma Yuan promptly established prefectures and districts to govern walled towns and their environs, and dug ditches to irrigate fields in order to sustain the people living in those places.' Garrisons were left to protect imperial officials, who were directly responsible for implementing the new regulations by which Ma Yuan bound the Vietnamese to the empire. Old customs henceforth had to operate within the confines of imperial edicts.

In AD 48 Ma Yuan volunteered to lead another expedition. Its task was to put down a rebellion amongst the non-Chinese people living on the south-western frontier. The hard campaign, however, dealt the general a double blow. During his absence from the capital a factional struggle caused the fall and disgrace of his relatives. His own death from fever while on active service then brought about his post-humous demotion. For six months Ma Yuan's widow did not dare to bury him in the ancestral plot. Emperor Guangwu Di refused to pardon Ma Yuan until AD 52, when at the family's request his youngest daughter was accepted into the harem of the heir apparent, the future emperor Ming Di (AD 57–75). With this prince's accession five years later the Ma family fortune at court was thus restored.

See HAN DYNASTY; VIETNAM

*W. Eberhard, *A History of China* (London, 1956); K. W. Taylor, *The Birth of Vietnam* (Berkeley, 1983).

**Macedon** comprised the first land-empire in Europe during the reign of Philip II, 359–336 BC. The origins of the Macedonian people he led to this achievement remain obscure, however. The few surviving words of their tongue do not show conclusively whether or not the Macedonians spoke Greek in early times. Later attempts to derive the name itself from Macedon, son of Zeus and Thyia, daughter of the Greek Noah Deucalion, are equally unconvincing. For Macedones also means 'highlanders', not a bad description for the inhabitants of such a rugged homeland. About 650 BC King Perdiccas brought the Macedonians out of their obscurity when he captured a lowland city and made it his capital. He called it Aegeae, or 'Goat-town', because of the abundance of goats. The historian Herodotus was certain that the royal house which Perdiccas founded, the Temenids, was of Greek origin. He writes that Perdiccas, along with his two brothers, had been exiled from Argos, the home of their ancestor Temenus. By the time the Persians first advanced into Europe around 510 BC, the Temenid house already controlled an extensive kingdom, to which was added a length of coastline in return for co-operation with the invaders. But Athens monopolized sea power after the defeat of the Persians in 479 BC, with the result that

A part of the Macedonian phalanx armed with long spears. Until the rise of Rome, this battle formation was unbeatable when combined with cavalry.

Macedon never had a free hand on the coast and was even challenged by the Athenians for control of the natural resources of nearby Thrace, especially its timber and gold.

A Macedonian king was elected by the citizen body, the Macedonians of military age. Although there were disputes over the succession, it was always a question of which Temenid to elect, with no outsiders ever coming near to the throne until after the death of Alexander the Great in 323 BC. Then the struggle for supremacy between his generals caused the last members of the Temenid line to be put to death. Alexander's own posthumous son by the Bactrian princess Roxane was murdered in 311 BC on the orders of Cassander (*c.* 358–297 BC), who later had himself declared as the king of Macedon. The sheer extent of the lands these experienced soldiers battled over was enough to shift the focus of power from Macedon. Alexander's father had built an effective European empire, but he died before he could lead an expedition against the Persians. His military reforms, however, gave his son the means to become the greatest conqueror of classical times. The struggle for the succession eventually left Macedon as one of three eastern Mediterranean states – the others were Ptolemaic Egypt and Seleucid Asia. A fourth contestant arose in Epirus under King Pyrrhus of the Molossians, but during the 280s BC he was drawn into a fruitless contest with the Romans for the control of southern Italy. In the second century BC another power also arose in Asia Minor with the support of Rome: it was the Attalid kingdom of Pergamum which eventually became the Roman province of Asia.

The last Macedonian dynasty derived not from Cassander though, but from Demetrius, son of Antigonus. Demetrius was acclaimed king of Macedon in 294 BC, yet the Antigonid dynasty was not secured until the reign of his own son, Antigonus Gonatas, who dealt with an incursion of Gauls, winning a much-publicized victory in 278 BC at Lysimachia. Within two years he was king of Macedon and Thessaly. In 272 BC Gonatas defeated Pyrrhus in the Peloponnese, where the Epirote king died from head injuries caused by a tile thrown from an Argive roof. A decade later he defeated the Greek states and ruled henceforth through their puppet governments. His dynasty, the Antigonids, lasted till 168 BC.

Perseus, the last king of Macedon. The final eclipse of the phalanx occurred at Pydna in 168 BC, when the Romans slew 20,000 Macedonians.

Antigonid Macedon was encircled by enemies and constantly at war, whether with rebellious Greek states, other dynasties, the Balkan tribes, or Rome. Its wars with the first two were inconclusive, although these campaigns helped to maintain the supply of slaves. Balkan opponents often inflicted heavy losses, especially the Dardanians in 229 BC. But the long conflict with the Romans proved terminal. At Cynoscephalae in 197 BC the Romans outmanoeuvred the Macedonian phalanx, and assaulted it from the rear and the sides. The sarissa, the huge pike introduced by Philip II, proved useless at close quarters against the sword and better defensive armour of the Roman legionary. Confronted by the most militaristic of all classical states in Rome, Macedon could do no more than lick its wounds and await the final reckoning, which was delivered at Pydna in 168 BC by the legionaries of Aemilius Paullus (228–160 BC). Some 20,000 Macedonians fell, the 3,000 men of King Perseus' own guard fighting to the last. Perseus later gave himself up to grace the victor's march of triumph at Rome and die under harsh conditions of captivity. Macedon was partitioned into four self-governing republics for twenty years, till a fruitless rebellion caused the Romans to annex it as a single province.

See ALEXANDER THE GREAT; ATTALIDS; CASSANDER; DEMETRIUS I; PHILIP II; PTOLEMIES; PYRRHUS; ROME; SELEUCIDS

*E. N. Borza, *In the Shadow of Olympus: The Emergence of Macedon* (Princeton, 1990); N. G. L. Hammond, *A History of Macedonia (vol. 1): Historical Geography and Prehistory* (Oxford, 1972); N. G. L. Hammond and G. T. Griffith, *A History of Macedonia (vol. 2): 550–336 BC* (Oxford, 1969); N. G. L. Hammond and F. W. Walbank, *A History of Macedonia (vol. 3): 336–167 BC* (Oxford, 1988).

**Mandate of Heaven** was an ancient Chinese notion that became part of imperial ideology during the Han dynasty (202 BC – AD 220). Said to have been first formulated by Mencius (371–288 BC), the heavenly mandate to rule was transformed by another follower of Confucius, Dong Zhongshu (c. 179–c. 104 BC), into an explanation of dynastic change. Dong Zhongshu maintained that an emperor's position was granted by Heaven: divine disapproval of imperfect government would manifest itself both in celestial portents and popular rebellion. Prior to his usurpation of the throne in AD 9, Wang Mang arranged for a number of omens to point to an imminent shift in the mandate. They were interpreted by means of the Five Elements – wood, fire, earth, metal and water. Diviners proclaimed that fire, the element belonging to the Han dynasty, which Wang Mang interrupted from AD 9 until 23, was in steep decline and a new imperial house associated with earth could be expected to assume power shortly. This proved to be Wang

Mang's brief Xin dynasty.

Imperial authority was always understood in classical China to derive from two distinct sources: the qualities inherent in the emperor and the powers delegated to him by Heaven. Only if his ability matched the task of ruling the empire would heavenly support be forthcoming. Because Confucian theory exulted virtue as the key quality required in a ruler, and held that government existed for the sake of those who were governed, the heavenly mandate provided an effective vehicle for reminding the throne of its responsibilities. An emperor was expected to listen to unpalatable advice because it was a minister's duty to warn him if he was in danger of forfeiting heavenly approval. A tradition of remonstrance unique in classical courts thus evolved in China.

See DONG ZHONGSHU; HAN DYNASTY; MENCIUS ; ORACLES; WANG MANG

*Hsiao Kung-chuan, *A History of Chinese Political Thought: From the Beginnings to the Sixth Century AD* (Princeton, 1979); R. T. Ames, *The Art of Rulership: A Study in Ancient Chinese Political Thought* (Honolulu, 1983).

**Manichaeism** was a gnostic belief first expounded by Mani (AD 216–277). Born near present-day Basra in southern Iraq, he grew up as a member of an ascetic Christian sect which had communities on both sides of the Perso-Roman frontier. It accepted the Gospel of Matthew only, and an emphasis placed upon baptism involved spending much time in purificatory ablutions. It was believed that there were two primary natures, male and female, to which all creation was related: thus vegetables belonged to the male, but weeds to the female. Keen gardeners, the sect members were able to make their community at Basra self-supporting, and its meals sacramental occasions. But this closed world was not exempt from the changes being wrought in Iran by the new Sasanian dynasty (AD 226–651), which was inflicting impressive defeats on Rome. The year of Mani's rejection of the sect, AD 240, witnessed a successful campaign in northern Mesopotamia, and the crowning by the Sasanian king Ardashir I (AD 226–240) of his son, Shapur I (AD 241–272) as the heir-presumptive. 'Coming to me,' Mani later told his followers, 'the Heavenly Twin chose me, judged me fit for him, separated me by drawing me away from the midst of the sect in which I was reared.' The breaking away was as abrupt as Augustine's a century and a half afterwards, when the future saint, moving in the opposite spiritual direction, suddenly abandoned Manichaeism for Christianity.

Mani travelled eastwards to the Sasanian provinces in India so as to study Buddhism. He also went westwards as an envoy of Shapur to the Romans. The focus of his mission, however, was the Sasanian court, where for much of his life he was protected by the monarch from the

Zoroastrian priesthood, and especially the mullah-like Kartir. This prelate eventually persuaded King Bahram I (AD 273–276) to execute Mani. For Mani's appropriation of the names of the Zoroastrian deities for his own religious purposes caused the Zoroastrian clergy to regard him as a very dangerous heretic. Just as galling to them was his use of its dualism to develop the notion of a struggle between good and evil in every person. According to Mani, the body was destined to destruction unlike the soul, which alone through knowledge could discover eternal freedom. Hence, the vigour with which he rejected the Christian belief in the resurrection of the body. 'Good is refined little by little and goes up,' Mani asserted. Such soul-searching was a parallel of the theological debate then dividing Christianity in the eastern Mediterranean. It could indeed be said that Mani was a systematizer as well as a prophet. More than anyone else in classical times he came to appreciate how much Christianity, Zoroastrianism and Buddhism had in common. In a very real sense Manichaeism was an attempt to incorporate in a single system the religious experience of South and West Asia. Missionaries are known to have been active between AD 244 and 262 in the Roman empire, where converts were swiftly made. It was rather odd that pagan magistrates were to find themselves cast as umpires during the bitter contests between the followers of Christ and Mani. In the Roman province of Africa from AD 373 to 382 even Augustine preferred the austere teachings of Manichaeism to contemporary Christianity.

*See* AUGUSTINE; CHRISTIANITY; GNOSTICISM; ROME; SASANIANS; SHAPUR I; ZOROASTRIANISM

*F. C. Burkitt, *The Religion of the Manichees* (Cambridge, 1925); S. N. C. Lieu, *Manicheism in the Later Roman Empire and Medieval China* (Manchester, 1985).

**Manu** is credited with the authorship of an important Hindu code, now dated to the second or third century AD. Whether or not a historical compiler by that name existed then, it is impossible to know. The name refers to the Indian Noah, one of the forefathers of mankind. The Hindu deity Vishnu is believed to have saved Manu from the flood, and later on provided him with a wife.

After the collapse of the Mauryan (322–183 BC) and Sunga (183– 72 BC) dynasties, there was a period of uncertainty which led to a renewed interest in traditional ways. With northern India under the control of Central Asian conquerors, like the Kushanas (*c.* AD 50–250), native lawgivers felt it their duty to codify them for the benefit of future generations. A contemporary resurgence of Sanskrit must have supported this endeavour as well as prepared cultural conditions for the classical splendour of the Gupta era (AD 320–550). Though little known at the time, Manu's code was to be profoundly influential on the future development of Hindu society. For it set the pattern of orthodoxy, in particular the division of society into four main classes: priests, warriors, artisans and peasants. Originally serfs, the peasants were, by Gupta times, predominantly smallholders, farmers in possession of modest plots of land. Their task, Manu reaffirms, was divinely ordained service of the three higher classes. Concern is also expressed over any confusion between the duties of peasants and artisans, in all probability because the latter had risen in wealth via trade. 'Should these two classes swerve from their obligations, they will throw the whole world into confusion.' Harsh though Manu is on the peasants, he does concede certain rights to slaves. An Indian master was forbidden to strike a slave other than on the back, in contrast to the absolute authority enjoyed by his Roman counterpart. Most of those enslaved in classical India had fallen into servitude through debt.

Below the peasantry were the outcasts, the so-called untouchables. Their origins remain a matter of controversy, although the most likely explanation would be the descendants of aboriginal tribesmen. The first precisely datable reference to the practice of untouchability comes from the writings of the Chinese pilgrim Fa Xian, who travelled to India between AD 399 and 414 in search of Buddhist scriptures. He was bewildered that, 'if they enter a town or market, these outcasts sound a piece of wood in order to separate themselves'. Both Jain and Hindu texts describe untouchables as the meanest men on earth, unlucky to see and evil to touch. One records how 16,000 brahmins, or priests, lost status because they unknowingly took food which had been polluted by contact with the leavings of a single outcast's meal. Even some Buddhist texts mention this severe taboo, despite the Buddha's own rejection of the system of hereditary classes. A man's position, he maintained, is determined not by birth but by worth, by conduct, and by character rather than by descent. Hence the Buddhist view that government should promote the welfare of all those who live in a state, including animals. Manu was much less concerned about non-violence, however. He wanted the state to remain strictly hierarchical and unchanging. All had to fulfil social obligations before seeking individual salvation. Asceticism should be practised only in old age, and not in youth like the itinerant Buddha.

*See* BUDDHISM; JAINISM; GUPTA DYNASTY; KUSHANAS; MAURYAN DYNASTY; SLAVERY; SUNGA DYNASTY
★J. L. Brockington, *The Sacred Thread: Hinduism in its Continuity and Diversity* (Edinburgh, 1981).

**Marius** (157–86 BC) was a 'new man' like the elder Cato (234–149 BC) and Cicero (106–43 BC) because he lacked consuls among his ancestors. Less concerned with tradition than Cato, Gaius

Marius was willing to further his own political career with the popular support of the assembly, a new factor in the politics of Rome since the upheaval accompanying the reforms of the Gracchi (133 and 123–121 BC). Marius first came to notice in Spain at Numantia, where in 134 BC he served with great distinction under Scipio Aemilianus (185–129 BC). Back in Rome, however, he attracted the hostility of many senators who feared his growing prestige. But they could not prevent his election as consul in 107 BC, when the assembly pointedly chose to ignore the senate's wishes. Marius was elected to this supreme military office in order to speed up the war in north Africa against Jugurtha, the usurper of Numidia. This kingdom had come within the Roman sphere of influence after the destruction of Carthage in 146 BC, and the annexation of Africa (approximately present-day Tunisia). To recruit soldiers quickly, Marius ignored the usual property qualifications for military service and called up impoverished volunteers on an unprecedented scale. Popular though this move undoubtedly was with the urban poor, it introduced a dangerous military dimension into Roman politics because volunteer and conscript soldiers alike gradually began to look to their generals to use their own power to gain them rewards. On arrival in Numidia, Marius enjoyed some swift successes but he could not entirely crush enemy resistance. Only a trap laid by his lieutenant Sulla

(138–78 BC) brought about the end of the war through the capture of Jugurtha, who was executed in early 104 BC after Marius' triumph at Rome.

This bust of Marius captures his roughness, his warlike character. He inflicted shattering casualties on the invading German peoples, the Teutones and Cimbri.

Almost as difficult to deal with were the incursions of two separate German peoples, the Cimbri and Teutones. The threat they posed to Italy secured Marius' election as consul every year from 104 to 101 BC. Overpopulation in their native Jutland seems to have propelled these formidable peoples on a devastating foray through the Celtic lands of Spain and France, before in 102 BC they threatened Italy. That year Marius caught the Teutones at Aquae Sextiae (present-day Aix) in the south of France. With the aid of the native Ligurians (Roman allies since their conquest by Aemilius Paullus in 181 BC), Marius' well-trained legionaries routed the Teutones in a very bloody engagement made worse by the involvement of their womenfolk. So angered were they by the disorderly retreat of the Teuton warriors, the historian Plutarch tells us, that 'the women came out against them, armed with swords and axes and making a horrible shrieking, falling upon both pursuers and the pursued – the former their enemies, the latter as men who had betrayed them'. It was the turn of the Cimbri in 101 BC to suffer annihilation in the upper Po valley. Yet despite similar scenes of self-destruction more than 60,000 prisoners were still taken.

Rewards for Marius' veterans were first proposed in 103 BC by the allotment of land in Africa to those who had served in the Numidian war. Three years later more land was to be made available in the provinces for veterans of the German campaigns. These and other proposals received strong support from the veterans and were forced through the assembly by violent means. In the growing disorder Marius was compelled to side with the senate, which was only too pleased to block every single proposal. Possibly a disillusioned Marius retired to his luxury country villa at Baiae, near Naples. Plutarch simply says he quit soldiering on the grounds of ill health. But in 88 BC his jealousy at the rising reputa-

tion of Sulla made Marius attempt to replace him as commander of the forces about to be dispatched against Mithridates VI of Pontus in northern Asia Minor. This war (88–85 BC) was the first of several against that monarch, extending over more than two decades. Sulla was not to be so readily pushed aside, and he took the unprecedented step of marching his troops on the capital, which fell without a blow. After enacting some constitutional measures which foreshadowed those of his dictatorship, Sulla left for the east. Marius returned after his brief flight to the safety of Africa, took revenge on his enemies, and was elected consul once again in 86 BC, but he died soon afterwards.

See GRACCHI; MITHRIDATES; PAULLUS; ROME; SULLA

*T. F. Carney, *A Biography of Gaius Marius* (Chicago, 1970).

**Mauryan dynasty** (322–183 BC) was founded in northern India by Candragupta (322–297 BC). It was the first to control extensive territory, coming eventually to dominate nearly the entire subcontinent. Centred on the old state of Magadha, in the lower Ganges valley, which Candragupta seized in 322 BC, the Mauryan empire gradually expanded its frontiers at the expense of smaller neighbours by means of a combination of diplomacy and arms. Candragupta was fortunate to have in his chief minister, Canakya, an adviser of great quality. To his authorship is credited the *Arthasastra*, India's earliest study of statecraft. The skill of Canakya is evident in the good relations established with the Seleucids following the peace treaty of 303 BC. Seleucus I (305–281 BC) had inherited Alexander the Great's Asian conquests, and two years earlier he had endeavoured to reassert his authority in northwestern India, where Candragupta filled the political vacuum left after the Macedonian withdrawal westwards. Defeat obliged Seleucus to cede Aria, Arachosia and Paropamisadae (essentially modern Afghanistan and western Pakistan) to Candragupta in return for 500 war elephants. A marriage alliance was also arranged, but it is unlikely that his son and successor, Bindusara (297–272 BC), had a Macedonian mother. To the Seleucids Bindusara was known as Amitrochrates, perhaps a Greek translation of his Sanskrit nickname 'slayer of foes'. By the time Bindusara was succeeded by Ashoka (268–232 BC), Mauryan power was irresistible in India. The succession was not smooth, however. Buddhist tradition relates how Ashoka executed all his brothers to gain the throne, with the possible exception of Tissa, a younger one. But the conversion of Ashoka to the Buddhist faith ranks in importance, for Asia, with the conversion of the Roman emperor Constantine in the 320s AD to Christianity, for Europe. His imperial patronage lifted what had begun as a doctrine of exacting spiritual exercises to the position of a prosperous and popular religion. Ashoka's embrace of the gentle teachings of the Buddha was brought about by the unprecedented slaughter of the Kalinga campaign in 261–260 BC. This part of present-day Orissa was conquered at such cost that the emperor seems to have been stricken with remorse. As a result, Ashoka turned to Buddhism for comfort and soon became a zealot, although he chose not to dismember the Mauryan empire. On the contrary, he assumed that it was his destiny to become the first Buddhist ruler, and spread the teachings of the faith. In place of hunting, Ashoka instituted the pious custom of imperial pilgrimages to the holy places of Buddhist legend. His initial guide was the monk Upagupta, the saint who had converted him.

It is not impossible that the magnitude of the Mauryan empire was connected with Ashoka's propagation of Buddhism. Rather like the First Emperor of China in 221 BC, Ashoka found himself without any effective rivals politically. And he ruled over an even more heterogeneous empire without any unifying set of beliefs. Buddhism thus seemed to provide an answer to both his personal anxieties and national disunity. Ashoka is said to have supported 64,000 monks, and had built countless stupas (reliquary mounds), besides erecting the columns on which he announced the new faith. Yet the readiness of Ashoka to adopt what were non-orthodox teachings was not out of line with Mauryan dynastic tradition. Neither his grandfather nor his father had been loyal to brahmanical orthodoxy. Candragupta had abdicated in order to die as a Jain recluse, while Bindusara ignored spiritual concerns altogether by espousing the determinism of the heterodox Ajivikas. Ashoka's greatest contribution to religion was sending a Buddhist mission to Sri Lanka, where today the oldest scriptures are to be found. One of the missionaries was Mahinda, the emperor's own son, who may have taken with him a branch of the tree under which the Buddha attained enlightenment. It is claimed to survive there, although the parent tree in India was cut down in later centuries by an anti-Buddhist fanatic.

After Ashoka's death in 232 BC, the Mauryan empire suffered a period of disunity which was ended around 223 BC by Samprati, who may have been a grandson of Ashoka. If so, then he repeated his grandfather's usurpation by using as his base Ujjain, in present-day Madhya Pradesh. Jain texts regard Samprati as a powerful ruler, treating him as a patron of Jainism almost in the same way that Buddhist texts treat Ashoka. In reality, however, the empire had already begun to disintegrate. In the north-west the weakening of the Seleucid grip on its outlying territories had led to the emergence of an independent Bactria. Under its second dynasty, founded by Euthydemus about 235 BC, Greco-Bactrian armies came to threaten Mauryan control, which was effectively ended before 190 BC. Expeditions under

Euthydemus' energetic son, Demetrius I (200–190 BC), penetrated into the Ganges as well as the Indus valleys. The steady disintegration of the Mauryan empire gave the Greeks a second chance of domination in India, which they took in the Punjab and what is now Pakistan. One of the most famous rulers of the Indo-Greek kingdoms there was Menander, whose capital between 160 and 130 BC was at Peshawar. That Menander seems to have abdicated in order to devote his final years to Buddhism served only to endear him to his Indian subjects. The last Mauryan emperor, Brhadratha, did not have such an opportunity because he had been assassinated around 183 BC by his general Pusyamitra, the founder of the Sunga dynasty.

*See* ALEXANDER THE GREAT; ASHOKA; BACTRIA; BINDUSARA; BUDDHISM; CANAKYA; MENANDER; SELEUCUS I
★K. A. Nilakanta Sastri, *The Age of the Nandas and Mauryas* (Banaras, 1952); R. Thapar, *Asoka and the Decline of the Mauryas* (Oxford, 1961); W. Narain, *The Indo-Greeks* (Oxford, 1957).

**Mausolus**, the ruler of Caria from 377 to 353 BC, has given us the word mausoleum. His kingdom in south-western Asia Minor lay within the Persian empire, but local administrations were allowed considerable freedom provided they promptly collected taxes and rendered military aid. Mausolus is said to have moved his capital from the interior to the coastal city of

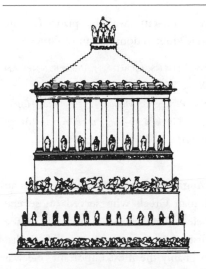

Reconstruction of the famous Mausoleum at Halicarnassus.

Halicarnassus (modern Bodrum). It was his sister and wife, Artemisia, who completed the Greek-inspired tomb, the Mausoleum, between 353 and 351 BC. It measured 120 feet by 100 feet at the base, rising to nearly 140 feet in height. Famous Greek sculptors were employed to carve the numerous human and animal statues which adorned its sides. One of the so-called seven wonders of the ancient world, the colossal monument has now completely disappeared, except for its rock-cut foundations and a litter of broken columns. Surviving fragments of sculpture indicate the magnificence of the original construction, something the Ptolemies (305–30 BC) were soon to imitate in their public buildings in Egypt.

*See* PERSIA; PTOLEMIES

*J. Hornblower, *Mausolus* (Oxford, 1982).

**Megara** was a city-state wedged uncomfortably between the territories of Athens and Corinth. A part of its northern border touched upon Plataea, a Boeotian power allied to Athens. Perhaps its small size was the stimulus for colonization, with early settlements founded at Megara Hyblaea in Sicily, Heraclea Pontica on the Black Sea, and in the Propontis no less than four at Byzantium, Selymbria, Chalcedon and Astacus. Shortage of land certainly led the Megarians to an early experiment in what was termed 'unbridled democracy'. Having thrown out the tyrant Theagenes, the historian Plutarch relates, they were soon carried away with freedom to the extent that 'the poor would enter the homes of the rich and demand to be wined and dined lavishly. And if they were not satisfied, they would ransack everything. At last they passed a law which required the interest formerly collected by their creditors to be paid back.' It antedates Solon's law of 594 BC in Athens by at least a decade. The appointment of Solon as a mediator between rich and poor also reflected conditions of mounting debt, usurious practices, and harsh persecution of defaulting debtors.

Neither in Megara nor in Athens is it clear whether outstanding debts were totally abolished and foreclosed property returned to the original owners. What seems to have been achieved by the Megarian democrats is an end to accelerating debts and some redistribution of land. This was apparently the work of the citizen assembly. Its foreign policy, however, lost the island of Salamis. Solon drove the Megarians away and reinstated Athenian settlers. One tradition states that Salamis was Solon's birthplace, so that his parents were evidently among the refugees of the Megarian seizure sometime before 600 BC. This reverse coupled with continued pressure on the better-off brought about a coup. The philosopher Aristotle (384–322 BC) noted how expulsions turned 'the exiles into a formidable force, and they returned and defeated the democrats and established an oligarchy'. Megara may have tried democracy again in the 460s BC, when it became a bone of contention between Corinth and Athens. Or the oligarchy could have received assurances from the Athenians that an alliance would involve no interference with the domestic affairs of Megara. Whatever the arrangements made, Megara quit the Peloponnesian League and allied itself to Athens. The alliance lasted until 446 BC, when Megara changed sides and threw in its lot with Sparta again. Although there was little the Athenians could do at the time, the desertion deeply offended them, with the result that there was general support in 432 BC when Pericles introduced the Megarian decree. Its denial of trade to the Megarians was intended to starve them into submission. By the outbreak of the Peloponnesian War in the ensuing year the embargo was causing distress. The defeat of Athens in 404 BC, at its end, was a relief for Megara, which largely kept clear of all inter-city warfare prior to the Macedonian domination of Greece.

See ATHENS; CORINTH; PELOPONNESIAN WAR; PERICLES; SOLON

*R. P. Legon, *Megara: The Political History of a Greek City-State to 336 BC* (Ithaca, 1981).

**Megasthenes** (*c.* 350–290 BC) was an Ionian Greek who served on several Seleucid embassies to Candragupta, the first Mauryan emperor of India. Arguably the most important one was the first in 302 BC, which followed an agreement about frontiers. In return for ceding to Candragupta the lands of Aria, Arachosia and Paropamisadae (essentially the present-day Iran-Pakistan border), Seleucus I (305–281 BC) was given 500 war elephants. Two years later in Asia Minor these great animals carried all before them at the battle of Ipsus (modern Sipsin). Their decisive intervention did more than defeat Antigonus (382–301 BC), for victory over this would-be successor to Alexander the Great confirmed the division of his vast spear-won realm into separate kingdoms. Luckily for the Ptolemies (305–30 BC) in Egypt and the Antigonids (294–168 BC) in Macedon, Seleucus did not acquire crossbows as well. The most lethal of classical weapons, the crossbow was to stay in China for another millennium.

As a result of his visits to northern India between 302 and 291 BC, Megasthenes wrote the best and most comprehensive account of India known to the classical west. Particularly surprising to Megasthenes, coming from a world in which slavery was commonplace, was the apparent absence of slaves in Mauryan India. 'It is a remarkable thing,' he wrote, 'that all Indians are free, and no Indian at all is a slave.' Though the evidence is somewhat slender, there would appear to have been some slavery under the Mauryan dynasty, including the enlightened reign of Ashoka (268–232 BC). The main cause of enslavement then was debt. Numbers remained low in India throughout the classical and early medieval periods, at least until the arrival of Muslim armies in the subcontinent from the eighth century AD onwards. According to Megasthenes, the reason for the ban on slavery was the teaching of the ancient Indian sages which held: 'Those who have learned neither to domineer over others nor to subject themselves to others will enjoy a manner of life best suited to all circumstances.' The very different notions of wisdom prevalent in India had already been noted by the Greeks, and contributed to the shaping of sceptical thought. Pyrrhon of Elis (*c.* 365–270 BC), the founder of Greek scepticism, had travelled to India as part of Alexander's train.

*See* MAURYAN DYNASTY; SCEPTICISM; SELEUCIDS; SLAVERY; WARFARE

*M. Cary and E. M. Warmington, *The Ancient Explorers* (London, 1929); J. S. Romm, *The Edges of the Earth in Ancient Thought: Geography, Exploration and Fiction* (Princeton, 1992).

**Menander** was the greatest king of the Indo-Greeks, who ruled between 160 and 130 BC a kingdom focused near modern Peshawar in Pakistan. He was the son-in-law of the Bactrian ruler Demetrius I, on whose behalf he launched attacks on northern Indian states. The collapse of the Mauryan dynasty around 183 BC gave the Greek settlers of Bactria an opportunity to enlarge their sphere of influence. The last Mauryan king had been assassinated by a general named Pusyamitra. Buddhist tradition depicts him as a terrible persecutor, but this adverse account of his usurpation may owe something to the fact that Pusyamitra ended a dynasty under which Buddhism had flourished. Menander was certainly attracted to the faith himself, although the Buddhists living in northwestern India probably rallied to the Greeks as a matter of policy. He led an expedition into the Ganges valley as far as the old Mauryan capital of Pataliputra, without annexing any territory there to his own kingdom.

The Indo-Greek king Menander, who is said to have become a Buddhist.

Menander actually features as a convert in one Buddhist text. It opens with an idyllic description of his capital, where the monk Nagasena expounds the major concepts of Buddhism to the eager Greek king. At the close of the work Milinda, as Menander is called, becomes a lay Buddhist and, after entrusting the throne to his son like native Indian rulers, he embraces the faith fully as a monk. An alternative ending has the king acknowledge a longing to join the Buddhist community of monks, but regret that political considerations rule it out. Archaeological testimony of Greek interest in Indian religion is evident at Vidisha (in present-day Madhya Pradesh), where a stone memorial pillar stands dedicated to Krishna. It was erected by a Greek ambassador around 100 BC.

The Greeks in Bactria and India, entirely cut off from the Greco-Roman world, flourished down to the mid-first century BC, when invaders from Central Asia finally extinguished their independence.

See BACTRIA; MAURYAN DYNASTY
*W. W. Narain, *The Indo-Greeks* (Oxford, 1957); G. Woodcock, *The Greeks in India* (Oxford, 1966).

**Mencius** (371–288 BC) was the greatest follower of Confucius prior to the Han dynasty, when Dong Zhongshu (c. 179–c. 104 BC) recast the older philosopher's ideas in a mould that remained the standard form down till modern times. A native of Zhou, a tiny feudal state in present-day Shandong province, Mencius, like Confucius (551–479 BC), was a great student of history and shared his master's admiration for Tan, the duke of Zhou. This learned aristocrat acted as regent during the minority of the second Zhou king sometime after 1027 BC. Very well acquainted with the ways of the deposed Shang dynasty from his many

A renowned incident in the early life of Mencius. When he told his mother he had completed his education, she cut through her cloth to reveal his stupidity. Neither his learning nor her weaving had been properly completed.

years as a young man at the Shang court, Tan was able to unite the nobility, draw up new laws, establish a central bureaucracy, organize schools throughout the realm, and also show proper respect for the fallen house by arranging for the continuation of ancestral sacrifices. His most conciliatory gesture was finding employment for Shang officials, a precedent that during subsequent changes in dynasty freed scholar-bureaucrats from slavish devotion to any particular lineage.

Recalling the wise programme of Tan during the turmoil of the Warring States period (481–221 BC), Mencius said that he wished 'to rectify men's hearts, and put an end to perverse doctrines; to oppose one-sided actions and put away licentious expressions, so as to carry on the work of the sages'. In particular, he was concerned to deal with the growth of Moist and Legalist ideas. The resolute face Mencius presented to the authoritarian trend in contemporary philosophy came from his own belief in the natural goodness of mankind. 'A benevolent man,' he said, 'extends his love from those he loves to those he does not love. A ruthless man extends his ruthlessness from those he does not love to those he loves.' The archetypal filial son, Mencius was always the upholder of the family against the encroaching state. To a disciple who once asked about the source of ill-conduct, he remarked: 'A trail through the mountains, if used, becomes a path in a short time, but, if unused, becomes blocked

by grass in an equally short time. So a heart can become overgrown.'

Though he held office under a number of rulers, Mencius spent most of his life teaching, like Confucius before him. But his ideas were more practical, more concerned with political economy. For Mencius the ideal was the so-called 'well-field system', which may have existed at the time of Tan. He argued that such a system of land tenure ought to be revived in order to alleviate the plight of the peasant-farmer, whose accumulating debts forced him to sell out and become either a tenant or share-cropper. The well-field system was supposed to have contained nine squares of land; the central square belonged to the ruler, and the remaining eight were each cultivated by a family. If this arrangement were to be revived in the countryside, Mencius believed, then near towns and cities instead of cultivating the ruler's plot people could pay a tenth part of their own produce and render military service. Such co-operation, however, was understood to depend on the quality of government in a state, not least because Mencius extended Confucius' concept of righteous opposition to injustice into the right of the people to take up arms against wicked rulers. Whenever a ruler lost the goodwill of his subjects and resorted to oppression, the heavenly mandate to rule was said to have been withdrawn and the ruler's replacement by a more suitable candidate justified. It was perfectly practicable for Mencius to argue the case for open rebellion: offensive weapons from the Warring States period onwards were always superior, the crossbow ruling out an armoured domination by royal or imperial troops. Mao Zedong was the communist leader who fully appreciated the revolutionary dynamic inherent in the agrarian revolts which punctuated Chinese history. Hence the attention paid after 1949 to the rebellion of Chen Sheng, the earliest documented leader of the peasant uprising which culminated in the overthrow of Qin (221–207 BC), the first imperial house.

See CONFUCIUS; DONG ZHONGSHU; HUNDRED SCHOOLS; LEGALISM; MANDATE OF HEAVEN; MO ZI.

*C. Lau, *Mencius* (Harmondsworth, 1970).

**Meng Tian** (died 210 BC) came from a family which had served the Qin state for generations as military leaders. It was hardly surprising, therefore, that Meng Tian was made commander-in-chief of the imperial forces in 221 BC, the year in which the last independent feudal state of Qi surrendered to Qin. Its final defeat confirmed the position of the Qin king as the unopposed ruler of the Chinese people, and to mark the great event of unification he adopted the new title of First Emperor. By promoting Meng Tian to the rank of Prefect of the Capital, the First Emperor (221–210 BC) was putting him on a par with his closest adviser, Grand Councillor Li Si (died 208 BC). It was an elevation that would cost

Meng Tian his life in the conspiracy hatched by Li Si and the eunuch Zhao Gao after the First Emperor's sudden death in 210 BC. But the enormous task Meng Tian was set – strengthening of the northern defences – kept him away from the court for almost all of the reign. First, a very hard-fought campaign cleared from the Ordos, an expanse of semi-desert enclosed by the great northern loop of the Yellow river, the most determined nomadic peoples encountered by the classical Chinese, the Xiongnu. Probably the Huns who later invaded the Roman empire, the Xiongnu used the Ordos as a starting-point of attacks in a number of directions. Then, secondly, he built along the northern frontier 'a Great Wall, constructing its defiles and passes in accordance with the configuration of the terrain. It ran,' the historian Sima Qian wrote, 'for a distance of more than ten thousand li. For ten years Meng Tian overawed the Xiongnu.'

Politics began to catch up with the energetic general in 212 BC, however. For his protests against the repressive policies of Li Si, the heir apparent Fu Su was banished to the Great Wall to oversee its completion. When the scheming minister finally eliminated Fu Su in 210 BC, Meng Tian was also arrested on suspicion of disloyalty to the Second Emperor, whom Li Si and Zhao Gao had just installed on the throne. Although the Second Emperor (210–207 BC) was inclined to release the general from prison, Zhao Gao worked on his fears and an order for his execution was given. Apart from his own personal ambitions for power, the eunuch had a grudge against the Meng family: Meng Tian's younger brother had been obliged to bring charges against Zhao Gao, for which he would have been condemned to death without the First Emperor's intervention. So it happened, according to Sima Qian, that Meng Tian accepted the condemnation. He is supposed to have said: 'I have a crime for which to die. I have made walls and ditches over ten thousand li. In this distance it is impossible not to have cut through the veins of the earth. This is my crime.'

See FIRST EMPEROR; GREAT WALL; LI SI; ZHAO GAO

*D. Bodde, *Statesman, Patriot, and General in Ancient China: Three Shih Chi Biographies of the Ch'in Dynasty* (New Haven, 1940).

**Miltiades** (c. 550–489 BC), an Athenian nobleman, was sent around 524 BC by the tyrant Hippias to consolidate the Athenian position in the Hellespont, the vital route by which vessels carrying Black Sea corn sailed to Athens. He ruled over the Thracian inhabitants of the Gallipoli peninsula, and encouraged Athenian settlement of its coastal cities. During the European campaign in 513 BC of the Persian king Darius I, Miltiades urged the other eastern Greeks in the Persian army to rebel on news of a Scythian victory. Although he had to flee Darius' wrath, his own position in the Hellespont was not per-manently weakened. Possibly his marriage to the daughter of a Thracian king afforded some protection, for he was restored to power by 496 BC. The Thracian princess bore him a son, Cimon (510–450 BC), who was to have a notable career as a general and statesman at Athens.

Miltiades took advantage of the Ionian revolt (499–494 BC) to seize the strategically situated islands of Lemnos and Imbros. So as to prevent them from becoming bases for the Persian navy, he presented both islands to the Athenians, who immediately dispatched settlers. On the collapse of the Ionian revolt, Miltiades fled from the victorious Persians and returned to Athens with four ships. There his associations with the deposed tyranny, and his own autocratic mode of government overseas, led to a trial for behaving in the manner of a tyrant. To the annoyance of his political enemies, Miltiades was not only acquitted but, in 490 BC, became one of the elected generals then charged with defending Athens against a Persian expeditionary force, even though the ex-tyrant Hippias was known to be advising its commanders. He persuaded the Athenian assembly that the Persians must be met wherever they chose to land, with the result that the citizen army was ready as soon as news arrived of a landing at Marathon, on the northern coast of Attica. The Athenians were there joined by their longstanding allies, the Plataeans. Together they were supposed to contain the Persian invaders, while the Spartans marched up in support from the Peloponnese. However, Miltiades made up his mind to attack, carried his fellow generals with him, and engaged when the heavily-armed Persian cavalry was not in position.

Eleven thousand bronze-clad Greeks charged, at the double, a bigger body of infantry which they hit with a single, staggering blow. 'When the Persians saw them coming at such a pace,' noted the historian Herodotus, 'they got ready to receive them, convinced that the Athenians were possessed with a frenzy of self-destruction. They were so few in number, and had no support from cavalry and archers. That was how the Persians saw it; but when the two armies closed together, then the Athenians fought superbly.' The Persian infantrymen, who were superior in archery, sent a terrible barrage of arrows at their attackers: once through this fire, the Greeks had the advantage, for the Persians were virtually without armour. When the routed Persians finally succeeded in escaping seawards, they left 6,000 dead on the shore. The Athenian fallen, 192 citizens in total, were afterwards cremated and their bones buried on the battlefield: a mound marks the place today.

The victory failed, nonetheless, to save Miltiades' political career. His absence from Athens during 489 BC was a mistake especially as it involved an unsuccessful attack on the island of Paros. It was used by his opponents to organize the city-body against him, in part by playing on fears of another tyranny. On his return to the city he was accused of 'deceiving the people', found guilty, and fined 50 talents, a very large sum of money. His son Cimon eventually paid the fine: Miltiades himself died of a wound received on Paros shortly after the trial.

See HIPPIAS; PERSIAN INVASIONS
*Herodotus, The Histories, trans. by A. De Sélincourt (Harmondsworth, 1954); H. T. Wade-Gery, Essays in Greek History (Oxford, 1966).

**Mithridates** was the name of six kings of Pontus, an Iranian state in northern Asia Minor. A mountainous yet fertile kingdom, Pontus derived its wealth from the iron it exported to the Greco-Roman world. The most famous king was Mithridates VI the Great (120–63 BC), who continued the warlike policies of his predecessors so vigorously that he turned the Black Sea into a Pontic lake. Deeply influenced by the example of Alexander the Great (356–323 BC), Mithridates led his Iranian or Iranized people in three wars against Rome, whose interests in Asia Minor clashed with those of Pontus. A settled resentment towards the Romans dated from the refusal of the senate to honour a territorial promise made to Mithridates' father in recognition of his help in putting down a revolt in Pergamum. It had broken out in 133 BC on the bequest of this kingdom to Rome. After the rebellion was crushed and Roman rule established,

Pontus received Phrygia as a reward until in 116 BC the senate decided that it should be added to the province of Asia, as Pergamum was then called. Conflicts with Rome's puppet-kings in Asia Minor led to a Roman ultimatum, which Mithridates dared to reject, the first eastern ruler to show defiance since King Perseus of Macedon in 170 BC. The so-called First Mithridatic War lasted from 88 to 85 BC.

King Mithridates VI of Pontus, the most persistent enemy of Rome.

Mithridates put his trust in his large and well-trained army as well as a powerful fleet. Anti-Roman sentiment also provided a number of valuable allies, for many Greek cities including Athens contributed to his initial success on land and sea. The attraction of the Pontic king for the Greeks and Macedonians lay in the fact that he offered them their only chance to break loose from the hated domination of Rome. In the province of Asia he symbolically ended Roman greed by forcing a captured official to drink molten gold. Another 80,000 Roman and Italian settlers followed him to the grave. Legends about Mithridates have much to do with his skilful use of propaganda: he was said to be a reincarnation of Alexander, immune to murderous attempts on his life, with an ability to outrun and outfight wild beasts. The Roman counterattack had recovered Athens by 86 BC, in spite of a spirited defence under Mithridates' Greek general Archelaus. But the urgent political preoccupations of Sulla (138–78 BC), the Roman commander, meant that a major offensive in Asia Minor could not be contemplated, and in 85 BC peace was agreed at Dardanus near Troy. Although Mithridates was obliged to evacuate all his conquered territories and pay an indemnity, the terms were mild for a Roman agreement, since Pontus was recognized as a friend and ally of Rome; punishment for the war fell on the rebellious cities in the form of pillage and reparations. This abandonment was not forgotten when Pontic forces returned to the attack fifteen years later in the Third Mithridatic War (74–66 BC). In this final clash with Rome – a very minor conflict had occurred in 84 BC – Mithridates did not enjoy much foreign support, except from the Ciclician pirates who were worried by growing Roman power at sea. Pontic forces were finally mastered through the generalship of Lucullus (117–56 BC). In three short years this underrated soldier and statesman broke Mithridates' power and that of his ally and son-in-law Tigranes of Armenia, only for Pompey (106–48 BC) to reap all the credit shortly afterwards. Mithridates fled to the Crimea, where in despair he committed suicide, leaving Pompey to make a general settlement of affairs in the east. The Pontic king had to get a companion to dispatch him when he found that he was immune to the strongest poisons, a last embarrassing instance of his amazing capacity for self-preservation.

See ATTALIDS; LUCULLUS; POMPEY; ROME; SULLA

*B. C. McGing, *The Foreign Policy of Mithridates VI Eupator, King of Pontus* (Leiden, 1986).

**Mo Zi** (*c.* 468–376 BC) remains an enigmatic philosopher despite efforts by later Chinese scholars to shed light on his life and thought. Hated by the followers of Confucius (551–479 BC), especially Xun Zi (*c.* 320–235 BC), Mo Zi advocated frugality, social uniformity and simple burial rites. He had become disillusioned with the practice of Confucianism because so many Confucianists settled for comfortable careers as advisers on ritual. Turning away from this emphasis on ceremony, Mo Zi argued that before the development of feudalism society had managed to run on 'good faith'. His belief in the power of love led him to tour the feudal states so as to get their warlike rulers to forswear aggressive policies. On one occasion he is said to have persuaded

the huge southern state of Chu to disband an expedition against tiny Song. Quite possibly Mo Zi headed a philosophical school in Lu, the state in which Confucius had been born. If this was the case, then his doctrine of universal love should be seen as a polemic against the peculiar Confucian emphasis on the family as the basic social unit. That this challenge in traditionalist Lu really hurt can be seen in the later comment of Mencius (371–288 BC), the greatest follower of Confucius. 'By preaching affection for all,' Mencius said, 'Mo Zi repudiated the family.' The followers of Mo Zi seem to have been practical men. Many were artisans skilled in the art of military defence, and so the support they gave to beleaguered rulers was appreciated. Above all Moists responded to the plight of those caught up in the turmoil of the Warring States period (481–221 BC). They did not restrict their sympathy to family, clan, or even native place.

Another point of disagreement between Confucius and Mo Zi concerned the spirit world. Whereas the spirits were respected but kept at arm's length by Confucius, Mo Zi made them the guardians of justice. 'If the fact that spirits reward the worthy and punish the evil can be made the cornerstone of policy in a state,' commented Mo Zi, 'it will provide a means to bring order to the state and benefit to the people.' The later disappearance of Mo Zi's ideas under the Han emperors (202 BC – AD 220) may have been a result of the affluence then enjoyed by educated men. Stable political conditions led to a growing sophistication which, with the triumph of Confucianism, had much less interest in the spirit world. This was appropriated instead by Daoism, the enduring opponent of Confucian ideology and, until the arrival of Buddhism, its most subtle challenger.

See CONFUCIUS; DAOISM; HUNDRED SCHOOLS; MENCIUS; XUN ZI
*V. A. Rubin, *Individual and State in Ancient China* (New York, 1976); B. Watson, *The Basic Writings of Mo Tzu, Hsun Tzu and Han Fei Tzu* (New York, 1967).

**Mount Li** is the site of the mausoleum of the First Emperor of China, who died in 210 BC. Situated 25 miles east of the modern city of Xi'an, in Shaanxi province, archaeologists were alerted to the richness of its finds when villagers, digging a series of wells in 1974, chanced upon a large pit filled with life-sized terracotta warriors. Some 3,200 foot-soldiers, as well as twelve charioteers, are estimated to be deployed as an infantry regiment in this pit. Other pits discovered near the tumulus contain terracotta cavalrymen and charioteers, with their horses, as well as senior officers; and bronze chariots. Although there are signs of mass-production methods having been used for the bodies of the terracotta warriors, each head is a personal portrait, as so far archaeologists have not found two faces which are the same. Unlike

stereotyped funerary statues, these soldiers are patently modelled on living men. Quite possibly the First Emperor wished to celebrate the unification of China in showing the varying physical features of its inhabitants.

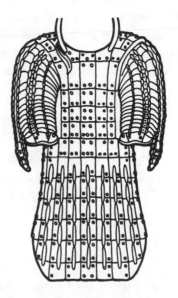

Detail of the iron armour worn by the terracotta army buried at Mount Li. This belonged to a charioteer.

Nearly 700,000 convicts are known to have laboured at Mount Li between 221 and 209 BC. According to the historian Sima Qian, 'they dug through three underground streams; they poured molten copper for the outer coffin; and they filled the burial chamber with models of palaces, towers and official buildings, as well as fine utensils, precious stones and rarities. Artisans were ordered to fix automatic crossbows so that grave robbers would be slain. The waterways of the empire, the Yellow and Yangzi rivers, and even the great ocean itself were represented by mercury and were able to flow mechanically. Above, the heavenly constellations were depicted, while below lay a representation of the earth. Lamps using whale oil were installed to burn for a long time.'

The elaborate preparations made by the First Emperor for the afterlife were unprecedented in classical China, although he institutionalized imperial grave sacrifice by erecting the first permanent funerary temple next to a tomb. Apart from guards and servants raised in the neighbourhood, a number of the emperor's concubines were usually drafted as warders of the grave and its garden. In the case of the First Emperor, however, we cannot be sure of the identity of his funeral attendants, since the Second Emperor (210–207 BC) buried his father's childless concubines with him. That Mount Li should be so grand is hardly surprising: the First Emperor was sole ruler of China and most anxious about personal immortality. During his eleven-year reign huge sums were also spent on vain attempts at making contact with the immortals in order to obtain the elixir of life. The First Emperor's dread of dying derived in part from the three attempted assassinations he survived, but there is little doubt how Daoist magic also encouraged both his hopes and fears.

See DAOISM; FIRST EMPEROR

★A. Cotterell, *The First Emperor of China* (London, 1981).

**Music** was accorded, except possibly in Rome, the highest esteem by classical civilizations. For the Greeks it was an integral part of life and an essential feature of religion and literature. The great religious festivals had competitions in which poetry was sung, whether epic, lyric, or the choruses in tragedy and comedy. So potent was the influence of music believed to be that the legendary Greek poet and musician Orpheus was able to descend into the realm of the dead and draw 'iron tears' from Hades, its implacable ruler. The musical instrument which Orpheus played so effectively was the lyre, a simple harp with strings supported by two symmetrically carved horns. The oracular god Apollo, possibly the father of Orpheus, was known as 'the god of the golden lyre'. Lyric poets were thus performers who accompanied themselves with the lyre.

The shamanism of Orpheus, whose playing could move not only animals and plants but even rocks and the elements, is also found in Chinese traditions about classical music. 'The fine notes being in relation,' one Chinese text reads, 'follow the numbers by which the world is made,' implying that experience of perfect music transports the auditor to a unique level of understanding. For Confucius (551–479 BC) music was very significant indeed. So affected was he by the music of Qi, one of the oldest feudal states, that for three months 'he did not know the taste of meat'. Because Confucius sought an inner harmony of mind and a balanced expression of emotion, the discipline involved in playing a musical instrument or singing greatly appealed to him. He was well aware, however, that there was music which encouraged frivolity, lewdness and violence, and he roundly condemned such pieces as being unworthy of the cultivated man. The favourite instrument of such a person would have been the zither, which could have as many as twenty-five silk strings. Even though the Greek philosopher Aristotle (384–322 BC) acknowledged the effect that rhythms and melodies had on the soul, he argued for all types of music as a means of relaxation.

A Chinese zither, which could have two dozen silk strings.

The different scales used by Chinese and Indian musicians belonged to traditions quite distinct from classical Europe, although the extraordinary variety of musical types found in India must have something to do with foreign invasion as well as its own heterogeneous culture. Classical Indian music had an elaborate musical theory and literature well before Gupta times (AD 320–550). One ruler on the Deccan has recorded in a cave at Udayagiri (near present-day Bhuaneshwar in Madya Pradesh) that he had reintroduced sixty-four arts of song, dance and instrumental music which had been prohibited under the Mauryas (322–183 BC). Music always remained important for worship in India, but Indian cities were centres of musical experiment and development along secular lines, in particular for dramatic performance.

Little is known about classical Iranian music. It seems likely that the Parthians and the Sasanians shared the Chinese delight in drums, however. At Carrhae, in northern Mesopotamia, the Romans were demoralized as much by Parthian drums as the poor generalship of Crassus (112–53 BC). Music was, of course, commonplace on the battlefield, the terror of their Greek opponents for long being the sound of the pipes that accompanied the steady advance of the Spartan phalanx. The requirement to keep this close-packed body of infantrymen from losing cohesion caused the Spartans to practise movement to music. Classical Chinese armies, on the other hand, responded to orders transmitted by means of gongs, drums, banners and flags.

See ARISTOTLE; CONFUCIUS

*W. D. Anderson, *Music and Musicians in Ancient Greece* (Ithaca, 1994); G. Comotti, *Music in Greek and Roman Culture* (Baltimore, 1989); H. A. Popley, *The Music of India* (Calcutta, 1950).

**Nanda dynasty** (546–322 BC) escaped possible destruction in 326 BC when the Macedonian soldiers in Alexander the Great's army refused to march further east. It did not long enjoy a respite, however, because four years later another native house, the Mauryan, took its place. Despite being overshadowed by the splendour of this successor, the Nanda dynasty was the first to rule over an extensive state in India. Its founder may have been Bimbisara (546–494 BC), who built a fortress on the lower Ganges (modern Bihar). Later the site developed into Pataliputra, the greatest city in Magadha. Here the first Mauryan emperor Candragupta (322–297 BC) was to receive in 302 BC Megasthenes, the ambassador of Seleucus I.

The Nandas gradually put together a large state covering most of the mid and lower Ganges river valley. They were inspired in their ambitions by the Persians, who annexed north-western India in the late sixth century BC. Two Persian provinces were established there: one in the north comprising Gandhara and Satagu (present-day northern Pakistan), and the other the lower Indus valley in the south (southern Pakistan and part of India). Their governors, though subject to the commands of the Persian king, exercised considerable powers including the minting of coins. As elsewhere in the empire, the administration was assisted by local rulers who accepted Persian overlordship. So determined were the Nanda kings in their imitation of the Persians that they became synonymous with violence, chroniclers blaming them for inaugurating the present age of the world, the Kali. It is supposed to be a time riven with quarrels, dissension, wars, and strife. Particularly belligerent was Ajatasatru, whose long reign (probably between 494 and 462 BC) witnessed a major expansion of the Nanda kingdom. Buddhist texts place Ajatastru's death a quarter century after that of the Buddha at the hands of his own son, Udayabhadra, who entirely rebuilt Pataliputra (modern Patna).

The Nandas were still in control of

the Ganges valley when in the summer of 326 BC the Macedonians refused to invade it. Once Alexander the Great himself realized that he was nowhere near to 'the end of India', and that the size of the Nanda army made it a formidable foe, there was nothing he could do but order a fighting withdrawal. The historian Arrian relates the joy felt by the Macedonians at this decision: 'They came to Alexander's tent and called down every blessing upon him for allowing them to prevail – the only defeat he had ever suffered.'

*See* ALEXANDER THE GREAT; CANDRA-GUPTA; MAURYAN DYNASTY

★K. A. Nilakanta Sastri, *The Age of the Nandas and Mauryas* (Banaras, 1952).

**Nero**, Roman emperor AD 54–68, was born in AD 37. He was the adopted son of the fourth emperor Claudius (AD 41–54); his mother, Agrippina, was the sister of the third emperor Caligula (AD 37–41), and Claudius' fourth wife. The education of the young Nero was entrusted to the Stoic author Seneca the Younger (4 BC – AD 65). But Agrippina prohibited Nero from learning philosophy, which she regarded as a hindrance to political authority. Her son was rather to learn how to conduct himself as emperor, a task in which his teacher signally failed to exercise a moderating influence.

Since Nero was not yet seventeen on Claudius' death, the empire was at first largely governed by Agrippina (AD 15–59). Within eighteen months

of his accession, though, Nero asserted his independence from his mother, who was transferred to a residence outside the imperial palace. Already he

On this coin, minted in AD 54, Agrippina is given equal prominence with the young emperor. The inscription reads 'Agrippina Augusta, wife of the deified Claudius, mother of Nero'.

had secured his position by killing Britannicus, Claudius' son by his first wife Messalina. It is not impossible that Agrippina intended to back Britannicus in the event of her own son getting out of control. But she had already lost the power struggle, for Nero removed her personal detachment of the Praetorian Guard. The loyalty of this élite corps of troops to the young emperor was by no means absolute, because its commander had to warn him that he could not ask them to dispose of Agrippina. She was eventually executed in southern Italy on Nero's orders: he told the senate that his mother had sent an assassin to the palace, so frustrated were her ambitions for power. The historian Tacitus, however, records Agrippina's realism. 'When she asked astrologers about the baby Nero,' he tells us, 'they told her that he would become emperor but kill his mother. Her response was to express a willingness to accept such a death, provided her son ruled as an emperor.' Agrippina's body was cremated on her dining couch, so as to disguise the brutality of her murder. Then her ashes, which under happier circumstances would have been stored next to her ancestors in the imperial mausoleum in Rome, were given a casual burial by her slaves. During Nero's reign there was never a proper burial, nor was the plot marked in any way at all.

Not long after Agrippina's death, Nero gained a ruthless adviser in Tigellinus (died AD 69), a Sicilian who acted as the emperor's evil genius. He kept a tight grip over the armed forces in Rome, cowed senatorial opposition by a revival of the treason laws, and encouraged the emperor to pursue his abiding passions: chariot racing, music, poetry, and sex. Nero divorced and executed his wife Octavia, Claudius' daughter, and married his mistress Poppaea, who in AD 63 bore him a short-lived daughter. But Nero's habits proved expensive, since they encompassed vast building programmes and lavish spectacles. Initially it was only the tax-payers in the provinces who suffered. In newly conquered southern Britain, imperial agents were so efficient in the collection of taxes that they raised the Iceni to rebellion under the leadership of Boudicca. This warlike queen overwhelmed the provincial capital at present-day Colchester, and also sacked London and Verulamium (modern St Albans). The rebellion was put down with such ferocity in AD 60 that a more conciliatory governor had to be sent from Rome in order to settle the province. If Nero's endless demand for tax revenue was not enough to make his reign unpopular, the great fire in Rome of January AD 64 united sentiment against him at the very heart of the empire. His indifference to the sufferings of the populace were neatly encapsulated in the story about Nero playing the lyre while Rome burned.

There can be no doubt that the emperor was worried about the extent of the damage, not least because of the attempt to blame the Christians for starting the fire. But Nero only compounded the disaster by embarking upon a grandiose reconstruction programme for his own benefit, a new palace which was built on land belonging to many senatorial families. To fund what became known as the Golden House, he ordered the confiscation of temple treasures in the provinces. In late AD 66 the forcible removal of money from the temple treasury in Jerusalem sparked off a serious rebellion against Roman authority, which was not put down till AD 70. Unconcerned by signs of discontent, Nero found pleasure in his new palace, where he said that at last he could live comfortably. Opposition to his rule, however, emerged during a tour of Greece in AD 67: no amount of prizes for his poetry could disguise an increasingly uneasy imperial administration. Handing out death sentences to his army commanders was a policy hardly calculated to impress their troops, even though Tacitus says the legions 'were late in abandoning Nero'. Dynastic loyalty still remained strong, despite the obvious signs of Nero's own loss of any grip on political reality. The emperor had only been persuaded to return from Greece in AD 68 by news of open hostility at Rome. It was soon matched by a legionary uprising in Gaul; worse still, the legions from Germany involved in crushing the rebels also refused to acknowledge the authority of Nero. The crisis might have passed if the emperor had acted with resolution, but illness had removed Tigellinus from the scene, and the new Praetorian prefect, Nymphidius Sabinus, prompted his men to abandon their allegiance. Even then, the German horse guard refused to support the senate, which condemned Nero to be flogged to death. This special bodyguard had been raised in the 50s BC by Julius Caesar, and its loyalty to the Julio-Claudian dynasty was fearsome. On the assassination of Caligula in AD 41, the Germans had gone on the rampage. For some unknown reason, however, the horse guard handed over its commander, a gladiator favoured by Nero, to the populace: he was crushed to death under the torn-down statues of the emperor. Nero cut his own throat. Galba, declared the next emperor by the senate, unfairly cashiered the Germans as betrayers of Nero, and paid the price a year later. There were no Germans to defend him against the Praetorian Guard.

See BOUDICCA; CALIGULA; CLAUDIUS; GALBA; ROME

*J. Elsner and J. Masters, *Reflections of Nero* (London, 1994); M. T. Griffin, *Nero: The End of a Dynasty* (London, 1984); A. A. Barrett, *Agrippina: Mother of Nero* (London, 1996); Tacitus, *The Annals of Imperial Rome*, trans. by M. Grant (Harmondsworth, 1956).

A brass coin of the Roman emperor Nero, showing on the reverse side the Temple of Janus. This issue celebrated one of the rare moments of peace for Rome during which its doors were closed.

**Nicias** (*c.* 470–413 BC) was the Athenian general blamed for the failure of the great expedition sent against Syracuse. On 27 August 413 BC an eclipse of the moon caused Nicias to countermand the order for the besieging force to sail away from the city and save itself. Since the Spartan Gylippus had assumed command of the Syracusan defences, the fortunes of the Athenians had gone from bad to worse. While disease as well as despondency gnawed away at the expedition's strength, the enemy was growing daily stronger and more confident, so that the only hope was a retreat to a new base at a distance from Syracuse. But Nicias took the eclipse to be a divine warning, and the opportunity to move was lost. The Syracusans first sank his ships, then captured his forces during an overland march. Nicias was taken prisoner and executed, against the wishes of Gylippus. The Athenian survivors were enslaved, thousands of them dying in the quarries of Syracuse. Athens never recovered from the loss of what the historian Thucydides termed 'the costliest and most splendid fleet that had sailed from a single city with a Greek force up to that time'.

But it has to be recognized that Nicias' view of the eclipse was shared by his fellow Athenians. They remembered how adverse omens had been ignored prior to the expedition's sailing two years earlier, including the mutilation of stone pillars dedicated to the god Hermes throughout Athens. In the light of the difficulties encountered at Syracuse they also believed that they should not make the same mistake again by undertaking a voyage after a divine warning. Yet a less pious man than Nicias might have put such an apparently unfavourable omen to good use: a dark night would have helped cover the Athenian departure. An earlier leader, Pericles (*c.* 495–429 BC), had reassured his men during an eclipse of the sun by conducting a simple experiment that illustrated the natural origin of the phenomenon. The real problem was that Nicias had been persuaded only with great difficulty that withdrawal was necessary, so that he regarded the eclipse as divine confirmation of his original judgement. He was also aware of the likely reaction of the Athenian assembly to failure: trial and execution was the usual fate of ineffective commanders.

The choice of Nicias as one of the three commanders of the Sicilian expedition was not unconnected with the popular belief that his piety went far to explain his consistent success as a general. Even the attempt he made to prevent the expedition being launched, when in 415 BC he told the assembly a massive force was needed, backfired: the advice was accepted at face value, and he found himself one of the commanders along with Alcibiades and Lamachus. His reputation as a moderate served only to reinforce the impression of good sense in balancing the enthusiasm of Alcibiades (*c.* 450–404 BC), the headstrong, young kinsman of Pericles. For Nicias had already done a similar thing with the populist leader Cleon (died 422 BC), and for good measure concluded with Sparta a peace in 421 BC that ended the first round of hostilities in the Peloponnesian War. Thus it came about, after Alcibiades' flight from charges of sacrilege, that the reluctant Nicias was left to conquer Syracuse and extend Athenian influence in Sicily.

*See* ALCIBIADES; ATHENS; CLEON; PELOPONNESIAN WAR; SICILIAN EXPEDITION; SYRACUSE

*D. Kagan, *The Peace of Nicias and the Sicilian Expedition* (Ithaca, 1981).

# O

Olympia in Elis, a state in the north-eastern Peloponnese, was the chief sanctuary of Zeus, the supreme deity of the classical Greeks. There was housed in the main temple a 70-foot-high statue of Zeus enthroned, one of the so-called seven wonders of the ancient world. 'The statue,' a visitor tells us, 'is made of ivory and gold and is of such size that although the temple itself is very large, the sculptor Phidias may be criticized for not having appreciated the correct proportions. He has shown Zeus seated, but with the head almost touching the ceiling, so that we have the impression that if Zeus moved to stand up, he would unroof the temple.' The shrine became a focus for pilgrimage for the whole Greek world and no city was ever built on the site, which every four years held a festival in honour of the god which reached a climax in the famous Olympic Games. The games were held regularly from 776 BC till AD 261. In late Roman times the emperor Theodosius I (AD 379–395) outlawed non-Christian cults and shut all temples. The conversion of one of the buildings at Olympia into a church thus made it impossible for any more pagan games to take place. Already the sacred site had become rundown, but the Olympian temples were not immediately destroyed.

In the spring of an Olympic year, three heralds set out from Olympia to visit every place where Greeks lived, proclaiming a period of holy truce

The great statue of Zeus in the temple of Olympia.

during the forthcoming games. The competitors, and their trainers, were required to arrive in Elis at least one month beforehand and to train under the supervision of judges. Worshippers and spectators were allowed only to attend the festival itself. The first event of the Olympic Games was the most expensive, the chariot-race in the Hippodrome, a large, rectangular space next to the Stadium used for athletic contests. Some of the odes of Pindar (518–438 BC), the Boeotian poet, were written in celebration of winners of the chariot-race. One was commissioned by Hieron, tyrant of Sicilian Gela, when in 470 BC his entry won the chariot-race. The charioteers, and the jockeys in the horse race, got little attention in contrast to the adulation heaped upon their Roman and Byzantine counterparts. Other events included throwing the discus and javelin, the long jump, wrestling, boxing, and running. A famous wrestler was Milo of Croton, who won the boys' wrestling at Olympia in 540 BC, and the senior event at five successive Olympiads between 532 and 516 BC. He also enjoyed the distinction of saving the life of Pythagoras, when in Croton he held up a column of a collapsing building so that the philosopher and his followers could escape. However, Milo shunned the pankration, a lethal mixture of judo, wrestling and boxing. The travel writer Pausanias tells of a contest between two bruisers which ended in a dead man being declared the winner. The winner was

strangled but, just before drawing his last breath, he made his opponent submit by breaking his toes. The final Olympic event was a race in full armour, later reduced to helmet and shield. Its place at the end may have been intended as a reminder that power had shifted in Greek city-states from horse-riding aristocrats to ranks of armoured infantrymen, the citizen-soldiers.

See LITERATURE; WARFARE

*L. Drees, *Olympia: Gods, Artists and Athletes* (London, 1968); M. I. Finley and H. W. Pleket, *The Olympic Games: The First Thousand Years* (London, 1976).

The damage to this wrestler's face is witness to the toughness of the Olympic Games.

**Oracles**, and omens, received widespread attention in the classical world. For the Greeks an oracle was the response of a god to a question asked him by a worshipper. Oracular shrines, such as the famous one dedicated to Apollo at Delphi, acted as the mouthpieces of the gods, offering direct comment on human action. They might be consulted by individuals as well as city-states. An ambiguous response given at Delphi to a question about war cost the Lydian king Croesus his throne in 546 BC. Not all oracles were obtained from such famous shrines, however. Ordinary people appealed to oracle-mongers for a preview of the future, even an interpretation of sacred law. Before every engagement diviners likewise searched for a clue to the outcome of the fighting. So at Plataea in 479 BC, the pious Spartans stoically stood their ground under a hail of Persian arrows, refusing to advance till there were favourable omens. In desperation the Spartan king Pausanias, the historian Herodotus informs us, 'turned his eyes to the temple of Hera and called upon the goddess for aid, praying that the Greeks would not be robbed of their hope of victory. Then, while the words were still upon his lips, their Tegean allies sprang forward to lead the attack, and a moment later the sacrificial victims promised success. At this, the Spartans, too, at last advanced.'

Omens, of course, were subject to manipulation, just as oracles could be readily interpreted to suit a desired outcome. The Roman general Lucullus was pleased in 73 BC to interpret unfavourably an omen in order to avoid an engagement against the forces of the Pontic king Mithridates VI (120–63 BC), which were considerably larger than his own. The battle lines were already drawn when a fiery body fell from the sky between the two armies. Earlier Marius (157–86 BC), another Roman commander, chose to exploit the utterances of a Syrian prophetess called Martha during his campaign against the German Cimbri. 'Usually she was carried along in a litter,' the historian Plutarch recounts, 'but when she attended the sacrifices she used to wear a double purple robe fastened with a buckle and carried a little spear with ribbons and garlands on it. The theatrical nature of this performance made many people wonder whether, in making a show of this woman, Marius really believed in her himself or was only playing a part and pretending to do so.'

Two methods of divination used in classical China were reading the cracks on scorched tortoise-shell and the alignment of shaken stalks.

The importance of favourable signs should not be underestimated, however. The Chinese usurper Wang Mang (AD 9–23) fabricated a number of omens to justify his seizure of power. One omen was reported after another: the discovery of inscribed stones, a stone ox, the spontaneous opening up of a well, and last but not least, a dream in which a heavenly messenger appeared. The general drift was clear: there was in progress one of the periodic changes of the five elements, which revealed the timeliness of Wang Mang, whose element was earth, replacing the fire belonging to the Han dynasty. Following his deposition, the restorers of the Han evoked similar omens to ridicule Wang Mang's pretensions.

See CROESUS; LUCULLUS; MARIUS; PERSIAN INVASIONS; SPARTA; WANG MANG
*W. Burkert, *Greek Religion* (Oxford, 1985); R. M. Ogilvie, *The Romans and their Gods in the Age of Augustus* (London, 1979).

A sherd used in an ostracism at Athens.

**Ostracism** was a temporary banishment from Athens, the city-state with the most developed democracy of all in classical Greece. First of all, there had to be a vote in the citizen-assembly as to whether an ostracism should be considered. Then for the ostracism procedure itself to be valid at least 6,000 Athenian citizens had to cast a vote, in the form of an inscribed potshed, against the politician whom they wished to have exiled for ten years. The candidate with the most votes won this reverse election, as did the democratic leader Themistocles (*c.* 528–462 BC) when he fell from favour in 472 BC. Even though the Athenians were reminded by Aeschylus that same year of the contribution Themistocles had made to the defence of Greece in his play *The Persians*, the assembly still chose to banish him. That the play was financed by Pericles (*c.* 495–429 BC), a relative of Themistocles, suggests it was part of a wider discussion about foreign policy. One famous instance of a bungled ostracism occurred in 417 BC. Then the extreme democrat Alcibiades (*c.* 450–404 BC) and the moderate Nicias (*c.* 470–413 BC) collaborated to turn the vote against Hyperbolus, who, the historian Thucydides tells us, was 'ostracized, not for fear of his power or prestige, but because he was such a wretched character and a disgrace to the city'. Afterwards ostracism was never used again at Athens. Its origin seems to have been the constitutional reforms of Cleisthenes in 508 BC, shortly after the fall of the tyrant Hippias. For the Athenians preferred to put their trust in the citizen-body rather than in individuals.

See ATHENS; CLEISTHENES; HIPPIAS; THEMISTOCLES; TYRANTS
*C. G. Starr, *The Birth of Athenian Democracy: The Assembly in the Fifth Century BC* (Oxford, 1990).

**Parthians** were one of the most persistent enemies of Rome, having in 53 BC inflicted upon Crassus a disastrous defeat at Carrhae, in northern Mesopotamia. This colleague of Julius Caesar (100–44 BC) was killed and 10,000 men taken prisoner, along with their legionary standards. The Parthian army was essentially an armoured cavalry force, a deadly host of lancers and mounted archers. It used the mobility of the horse to attack where an enemy was weak and to break off contact where strong. Such a tactical withdrawal was not understood by the Romans, who suffered a number of reverses against the Parthians by mistaking the manoeuvre as an admission of defeat. Detachments of Roman soldiers would pursue an apparently beaten foe only to become surrounded and beaten in turn. The readiness of the Parthians to flee suggests a nomadic ancestry, which the historian Plutarch seems to confirm when he says at Carrhae that they 'still wore their long hair bunched up over their foreheads in the Scythian fashion in order to make themselves look more formidable'. The extent of the Roman defeat in this engagement owed much to the Parthian commander-in-chief, Suren, then in his late twenties. Plutarch relates how Suren abandoned his original plan to charge the Romans with lances on seeing 'the depth of the walls of shields'. He pretended to fall back in disorder, but 'actually succeeded in surrounding the hollow square in which the Romans were marching before Crassus realized what was happening'. The Parthians then 'spread out and began to shoot their arrows

King Arsaces I of Parthia. Minted in 209 BC, the year in which he came to terms with the Seleucid ruler Antiochus III.

from all sides. There was no attempt at accurate marksmanship, since the Romans were so densely crowded together that it was impossible to miss the target even if one wished to do so. They merely kept shooting with their powerful bows, curved so as to give the maximum impetus to the arrows, and the blows fell continuously and heavily on the Romans.' The arrival of camel trains loaded with extra ammunition meant there could be no relief from the arrows, 'which pierced readily armour and shields alike'.

The result of Carrhae was that the Parthians acquired an instant fame for their prowess as cavalrymen. The mismanagement of the campaign was largely overlooked: Crassus was an ageing politician without any credentials as a commander. It was fortunate for Rome that internal wrangling among the Parthians prevented any exploitation of the victory. Similar domestic political feuding stopped them from taking advantage of another Roman defeat in 36 BC, when Antony (82–30 BC) found himself as weak as Crassus in cavalry. Once again the support promised by the Armenians in this arm failed to materialize. Cleopatra (69–30 BC) had to provide Antony's broken force with food, clothing and pay after its painful retreat to Syria.

Armenia was a bone of contention between Rome and Parthia, after they both took over territories previously belonging to the Seleucids (312–64 BC). This Macedonian dynasty had been squeezed in the west by the Romans and in the east by the Parthians. The new border between them ran through northern Mesopotamia, a location in which the friendship or the hostility of Armenia could prove critical. At this period the homeland of the Armenians lay not in the Caucasus, but near the headwaters of the Tigris. Their political importance developed under the Artaxiad dynasty, named after Artaxias (190–159 BC), a friend of the celebrated Carthaginian general Hannibal. Under a descendant of Artaxias, Tigranes the Great (95–56 BC), Armenia possessed a short-lived empire in Mesopotamia and Syria. Its fundamental weakness was exposed by Roman arms in the 70s BC under the command of Lucullus. Rome's attitude towards Armenia varied according to the threat posed to its eastern provinces by the Parthians. As long as its rulers were anti-Parthian, there was no need for military intervention but, in the event of a Parthian thrust westwards, Rome expected Armenia to actively support the legions with cavalry units. In AD 54 a crisis arose when the throne of Armenia was claimed by the brother of the Parthian king. By AD 59 the Armenian capital, Tigranocerta, was in Roman hands: a year later the emperor Nero (AD 54–68) installed as ruler Tigranes V, the offspring of a client-king of Cappadocia: and, in AD 66, this new king was formally crowned in Rome, having successfully beaten off a Parthian invasion. Although the emperor Trajan (AD 98–117) decided to make Armenia a Roman province in AD 115, the subsequent rationalization of the eastern frontier saw the restoration of another anti-Parthian king.

Parthian sculpture from Hatra, north-western Iraq. It was probably a votive offering.

Throughout these years the Parthians struggled to maintain their contest with the Romans. Trajan's soldiers captured the Parthian capital of Ctesiphon in AD 114, the first of several Roman penetrations of Mesopotamia. Considering their military strength, the weakness of the Parthians must be put down to dis-

unity. Fierce feuds were typical as well as sudden executions. Suren, the victor of Carrhae, was swiftly murdered on the orders of King Orodes II (56–38 BC). It would appear, therefore, that the Parthians never managed to shake off nomadic ways. They were Iranians, like the Persians who invaded Greece in 490 and 480–479 BC, and the Sasanians, who later challenged both Rome and Constantinople from AD 226 to 651. But during their own supremacy (171 BC – AD 226), the Parthians conspicuously failed under the Arsacid dynasty to establish anything approaching a centralized realm. Outlying areas even dared to send embassies to Rome. The old Persian title of 'king of kings' was dropped after AD 89, possibly in recognition of the looser political arrangements which prevailed. The pattern of rivalry can be traced almost from the beginning of Parthia, with its kings mounting repressive campaigns against Parthian aristocrats. A hegemony rather than an empire, Parthia swiftly lost territory to separatist movements to the east as well as the south. Most notable were Hyrcania, its original homeland near the Caspian Sea, and Characene, a trading kingdom established at the head of the Persian Gulf. A Chinese embassy was turned back in AD 97 at Characene, where Parthian influence seems to have revived. It is believed that the Han dynasty in China was trying to make direct contact with Rome so as to overcome problems with the Parthians, who sought to impose very heavy customs duties on the silk trade. In northern India the Kushana empire (AD 50–250) had already responded to Parthian greed by diverting caravans from China through the Khyber pass down to the Indus delta, whence the silk went by sea to Characene.

The Chinese envoys obviously followed this route westwards. Apart from the imposition of customs duties, political uncertainties in Parthia may also have affected the safety of caravans travelling all the way overland. East-west trade was big business, with a massive export of Roman gold eastwards to pay for silk, perfume, spices, medicine, and sugar cane. 'In exchange for trifles,' complained the Roman author Pliny the Younger, 'our money is sent to foreign lands and even to our enemies.' The huge trade imbalance was probably one of the reasons for Trajan's attack on Parthia in AD 114. Despite this invasion, and difficulties over trade, the Parthians held on to power till AD 226. Increasing internal divisions and a steadily debased coinage, however, were the signs of serious decline. In AD 197–198 the emperor Septimius Severus (AD 193–211) punished the Parthians for becoming involved in the civil war which he had won to gain power. Even though Ctesiphon fell once again to the Romans, any annexation of Mesopotamia was still found to be impracticable. Yet the end of Parthia was already in sight, as widespread unrest turned into an outright rebellion: by AD 220 it had broken what remained of royal authority. King Artabanus V (AD 213–226) was unable to cope with Ardashir, whose revolt was centred in modern Fars, southern Iran. Ardashir defeated and killed the king in AD 226, after which the remaining Parthian forces fled to the mountains, where Artabanus' son continued the struggle for a few years. Eventually captured, he was executed in Ctesiphon, now the capital of a new Iranian power, the Sasanians.

See ANTONY; ARMENIA; CRASSUS; HAN DYNASTY; KUSHANAS; PERSIA; ROME; SASANIANS; SELEUCIDS; SUREN; TRAJAN
*M. A. R. Colledge, *The Parthians* (London, 1967); N. C. Debevoise, *A Political History of Parthia* (Chicago, 1938); Plutarch, *The Fall of the Roman Republic*, trans. by R. Warner (Harmondsworth, 1958).

**Pataliputra** (modern Patna) was the first capital of an Indian empire. Occupying a site of strategic importance in Magadha (present-day Bihar), Pataliputra stood on a high bank of the Ganges and when the river was in flood during the monsoons, the city looked like an island in the midst of flooded plains. From the outset it had the added advantage of promixity to Magadha's rich supply of metals. The first dynasty of consequence to fortify Pataliputra was the Nanda (546–322 BC), whose imperial pretensions were stimulated by the Persian occupation of north-western India under Darius I (521–486 BC). Its heyday most probably occurred under the subsequent Mauryan dynasty (322–183 BC), although the later Gupta dynasty (AD 320–550) endeavoured to restore the city to its former glory. Many Mauryan buildings were still in existence at the start of Gupta rule: one of them, the palace built by Ashoka (268–232 BC), was even standing when the Chinese pilgrim Fa Xian stayed in the city almost a century later.

*See* GUPTA DYNASTY; MAURYAN DYNASTY; NANDA DYNASTY

**Paullus** (228–160 BC) was the Roman conqueror of the Macedonians. Lucius Aemilius Paullus Macedonicus was the son of a consul who fell in 216 BC at Cannae, the worst defeat ever suffered by the Romans. A memory of this Carthaginian triumph probably came to mind in 181 BC, when he found himself surrounded by the Ligurians, a fierce people occupying north-western Italy and the south of France as far as the Rhône valley. Assuming that messengers sent to Rome for reinforcements had perished, Aemilius Paullus inspired his troops with a stirring speech and then led them to crush the Ligurians. His victory must have been great because it ended a war originally started in 238 BC. He razed the walls of Ligurian cities and confiscated all pirate vessels, long the scourge of merchant ships passing along the Ligurian coast. Rather than exterminate or enslave the Ligurians, Aemilius Paullus allowed them to survive as a buffer state between Italy and Rome's most hated enemies, the Gauls.

Believed to be the head of Aemilius Paullus. It was discovered at Athens, where a victory monument is known to have been erected.

Little is known about Aemilius Paullus' life between this successful campaign and his election once again as consul in 168 BC. Under King Perseus (179–168 BC) the Macedonians were preparing to make their final stand against Rome, and the senate was very relieved indeed when Aemilius Paullus accepted the command against them. The historian Livy relates how the new commander warned his fellow citizens about the adverse effect on morale of idle speculation. 'In clubs and at dinner parties,' he said, 'there are strategists who take armies into Macedon ... And they do not just lay down the law about what should be done; when anything has been done contrary to their views they accuse the consul as if he were standing in the dock! Such talk is a handicap to those on active service.'

Having offered to pay himself the expenses of anyone who might wish to come and give advice on campaign, Aemilius Paullus crossed to Greece and shook up the Roman army stationed there in a similar manner. After Paullus dismissed his first parade, Livy tells us, 'his hearers in general, including veterans, admitted that they had felt like raw recruits, learning for the first time how matters should be conducted on active service. And it was not only in talk like this that they displayed the approval with which they had listened to the consul's words; there was an immediate result in action as well. Before long there was not one idle man to be seen in the whole camp.'

Although there can be no doubt of Livy's desire to present Aemilius Paullus as the embodiment of Rome's greatness, the thoroughness of preparations that he made for the encounter at Pydna were really necessary, since the Macedonian phalanx remained irresistible when fought in close order. Above all Roman success would depend upon flexibility, the exploitation of opportunities in the battle itself: courage and skill in hand-to-hand combat was required from every legionary. In Greek and Macedonian armies, each soldier was one of thousands constituting a closely packed phalanx of spearmen whose military effectiveness depended on everyone moving together in unison; any wish to show off individual courage at the expense of maintaining the battle line was frowned upon. The battle line of the republican Roman legion was much more open, and the individual soldier had more scope to use offensive weapons, as the Macedonians found to their horror once the action began.

Livy reports that 'the consul led the first legion into battle. The men were impressed by the prestige of his office, the fame of the man himself, and even more his age; for though he was over sixty he kept taking on duties of men in the prime of life, undertaking far more than his share of toil and danger.' The tactics of Aemilius Paullus worked for the 'cause of victory because there were many scattered engagements which turned the Macedonian phalanx into an unwieldy mass of spears, before its final collapse as a formation'. Of the enemy 20,000 were slain, 6,000 taken prisoner, and another 5,000 fled the battlefield. Roman losses were put at less than 100 men. The clemency shown by Aemilius Paullus to the defeated Macedonians is cited by Livy as a sign of nobleness, just as his subsequent tour of Greece is presented as no more than a connoisseur's indulgence. Glossed over is punishment meted out in 167 BC to Epirus, an old enemy of Rome and a Macedonian ally: after a period of pillage and rape, 150,000 Epirotes were sold into slavery. Nor is it made clear how the victor of Pydna confiscated wholesale Greek statues and paintings to adorn public buildings at Rome. He did leave, however, a statue of himself at the sanctuary of Delphi, and asked the Athenians to erect another victory monument. And the attempt by Livy, and other historians, to praise the care taken of the booty, much to the disappointment of his own troops, as an example of Roman rectitude cannot disguise the fear Aemilius Paullus had of a senate investigation, like the one which engulfed the Scipios after the defeat of the Seleucid ruler Antiochus III in 190 or 189 BC. But there is no doubt that his lack of personal interest in spoils was unusual, and remarkable for that reason. The amount of booty was not inconsiderable because it enabled the senate to abolish the unpopular property tax, introduced as an emergency source of state revenue during the wars against Carthage. The only object Aemilius Paullus coveted was the Macedonian king's library, which he appropriated for himself and his sons. One of them who fought with him at Pydna, Scipio Aemilius (185–129 BC), was very keen on Greek learning: he had been adopted as a Scipio in order to cement an alliance between the two noble families. While in Greece this young soldier became friends with the historian Polybius.

See MACEDON; ROME; SCIPIOS

*Livy, *Rome and the Mediterranean*, trans. by H. Bettenson (Harmondsworth, 1976); Polybius, *The Rise of the Roman Empire*, trans. by I. Scott-Kilvert (Harmondsworth, 1979); W. Reiter, *Aemilius Paullus: Conqueror of Greece* (London, 1988).

**Pausanias** (died *c.* 469 BC) was the commander of the Greek army at the battle of Plataea in 479 BC. He was the son of the Spartan king Cleombrotus. The crushing victory at Plataea over the invading Persians seems to have turned Pausanias' head. The subsequent naval campaign which Pausanias led was marked by arrogant behaviour so offensive to his Greek allies that the Spartans were eventually obliged to recall him. The historian Thucydides relates how the 'Ionians and states who had just been liberated from Persian domination . . . had approached the Athenians, asking them, since they were their own kinsmen, to take them under their protection and, if Pausanias continued to act in a dictatorial manner, not to permit it'. Even before Pausanias' departure it was apparent to them that Athens was more likely than Sparta to offer effective protection from Persia. Once they had rejected the successor Sparta proposed to Pausanias in 478 BC, the way was open for the respected Athenian general Aristides (*c.* 525–467 BC) to organize mutual defence under the auspices of the Delian League.

Pausanias was found guilty in Sparta of enough charges to deprive him of further command. Indeed, Thucydides tells us, from this time onwards 'the Spartans came to fear that when they sent their commanders overseas they would become corrupted'. A precursor of Lysander (died 395 BC), the ambitious victor of the Peloponnesian War, Pausanias was able to maintain himself till 470 BC in Asia Minor, possibly with Persian support. On his return home that year Pausanias was accused of fomenting unrest, however. He starved to death outside the temple in which he sought sanctuary. His last breath was drawn there because the Spartan authorities had had him removed: they were not prepared to defile sacred ground with his corpse.

*See* ARISTIDES; DELIAN LEAGUE; LYSANDER; PERSIAN INVASIONS

*R. Meiggs, *The Athenian Empire* (Oxford, 1972).

**Pausanias** lived and wrote between AD 120 and 180 a *Guidebook to Greece*, a work that could well be called the Baedeker for classical Greece. During most of this time the Mediterranean world was at peace under Roman rule. The emperor Hadrian (AD 117–138) had forsworn the policy of annexation pushed by his predecessor, Trajan (AD 98–117), to the limits of the empire's resources. Instead of expansion, there was consolidation and the construction of fixed defences such as Hadrian's Wall along the northern frontier of Britain. Except for the Jewish revolt of AD 132–135 in Palestine, the Romans engaged only in minor campaigns until in AD 162–166 the Parthians had to be faced on the eastern frontier. They won a great victory but the legionaries carried home a plague that devastated the empire's population.

A Greek born in Asia Minor, Pausanias was able to take personal advantage of the Roman peace and travel widely. But his abiding interest was Greece, which he could not help resenting was no longer free. Though his *Guidebook* also makes plain a dislike for Macedon, Greece's oppressor before Rome, Pausanias pointedly ends his narrative in 146 BC, the year the Romans destroyed Corinth and made their domination permanent. The value of the *Guidebook* is its thoroughness and accuracy, notwithstanding numerous mythological digressions. In the late 1870s Heinrich Schliemann, the discoverer of Troy, used Pausanias' description of Mycenae to locate the grave of Agamemnon, the legendary leader of the Greek expedition against the Trojans. According to Pausanias, at the ancient site of Mycenae 'parts of the wall are still preserved as well as the gate over which the lion stands. In the ruin there is ... the tomb of Agamemnon, one of Eurymedon the charioteer, and one of Teledamus and Pelops – for they say Cassandra gave birth to these twins and that while they were still infants Aegisthus killed them with their parents – and one of Electra. Clytemnestra and Aegisthus were buried a little outside the wall, for they were not deemed worthy of burial in it, where Agamemnon lies and those who were murdered with him.'

*See* ATHENS; HADRIAN; HADRIAN'S WALL; JEWS; MACEDON; ROME; SPARTA; TRAJAN

*J. G. Frazer, *Pausanias' Description of Greece* (London, 1898); C. Habicht, *Pausanias' Guide to Ancient Greece* (Berkeley, 1985).

**Peloponnesian League** was the most enduring political organization in classical Greece. Strictly speaking, it was not really a league, nor was it altogether Peloponnesian. It included states to the north of the Isthmus of Corinth, and relationships among its members were very loose. Rather a periodic alliance for the purposes of war, the modern name of the Peloponnesian League fits less well than what the Greeks called it: 'The Lacedaemonians and their allies'. For the league was first and foremost a device by which Sparta guaranteed the security of the Peloponnese. It evolved through a series of treaties negotiated by Sparta with other states, and by 525 BC excluded only Achaea and Argos. Each treaty effectively confirmed Spartan hegemony by passing control of foreign policy to the league. Fear of Argos, Sparta's traditional rival, and fear of popular unrest caused the oligarchies in charge of most Peloponnesian states to become league members. Spartan intervention against tyrants, even at Athens in 510 BC, was always undertaken in the interests of oligarchic government. Unlike the Delian League later established in the Aegean by Athens, the Peloponnesian League collected no tribute and in consequence lacked a treasury capable of sustaining a prolonged conflict. During the great Persian invasion of Greece in 480–479 BC it served, however, as the nucleus of a coalition of states that defeated on both land and sea a previously unbeaten enemy.

Custom required Sparta to consult the league assembly before demanding support from the allies, who were required by oath to accept a majority vote. It seems unlikely that Sparta ever needed to vote itself in order to secure a desired result, such was the influence derived from the reputation of its army, at least till the defeat suffered in 371 BC at the hands of the Thebans in Leuctra. Few meetings of the league assembly are recorded. As none could take place unless Sparta called them, it is apparent that they were held only when found to be useful or necessary to the Spartans. In 432 BC, prior to the declaration of war against Athens, an assembly of league members simply had to occur. The subsequent Peloponnesian War (431–404 BC) resulted from a belief on the part of Sparta and its allies that Athens had become a serious threat to them. When no league war was in progress, members were free to carry on separate wars even with other members. In 423 BC, for instance, the Spartans chose not to intervene in a conflict between Tegea and Mantinea, even though there was only a truce in operation with Athens.

On its surrender in 404 BC Athens was forced to accept a treaty with Sparta promising complete obedience on questions of war and peace. A year later the Spartans and their allies marched against Athens because it was judged to have broken this treaty. Corinth and Thebes refused to participate in the campaign, as they did in 400 BC in an invasion of Elis, a state in the north-western Peloponnese. By 395 BC the Spartans were at war with the Corinthians and the Thebans, both long-standing allies. Though the Spartan king Agesilaus (444–360 BC) at first held the initiative, the balance of power was already shifting towards the Thebans, whose greatest general Epaminondas (died 362 BC) led several expeditions against Sparta, destroying the Peloponnesian League.

See AGESILAUS; ARGOS; DELIAN LEAGUE; EPAMINONDAS; SPARTA

*D. Kagan, *The Outbreak of the Peloponnesian War* (Ithaca, 1969); G. L. Huxley, *Early Sparta* (Cambridge, Mass., 1962); W. G. Forrest, *A History of Sparta* (London, 1968).

**Peloponnesian War** (431–404 BC), between rival blocs headed by Sparta and Athens, marked the end of brief campaigns in which heavily armed infantrymen clashed on conveniently sited plains. All expected a short war; no city-state was ready for the full twenty-seven years that it took to bring the conflict to a conclusion. They failed to foresee the dislocation such a war would bring to classical Greece: the corrosive violence, the decline of moral standards, social unrest and economic stagnation, as well as a chronic political instability after the Spartan victory that was a gift to Philip II (359–336 BC), the ambitious king of Macedon.

The length of the struggle was due in part to the strengths and weaknesses of each side: Sparta was all-powerful on land, while Athens ruled the waves. The Spartans might invade Attica, but as long as the Athenians were willing to evacuate the countryside and stay within the Long Walls, connecting the city with the port of Piraeus, there was a stalemate. Grain from the Black Sea could be brought in to feed the population taking refuge there. Not even a visitation of the plague in 429 BC was enough to weaken Athens, although it carried off its notable leader Pericles (c. 495–429 BC) and a quarter of the citizens. For the Spartans the position was particularly frustrating, for their allies in the Peloponnesian League were not used to anything other than swift victories. Worse still, two brilliant Athenian strokes brought the conflict home to Sparta. The capture of Pylos, on the south-western coast of the Peloponnese, offered a rallying-point for Messenian helots, the servile slaves upon which Sparta depended. In 425 BC the demagogue Cleon turned this operation into an unprecedented victory when he captured 120 Spartans on the nearby island of Sphacteria. His fellow general Demosthenes was an expert in fighting on rugged terrain, and the successful strategy followed was doubtless of his making.

The surrender of so many Spartan citizens was, according to the historian Thucydides, 'the most unexpected event of the war'. Sparta considered the reverse so serious that repeated embassies were sent to Athens in order to secure the release of the prisoners.

But by threatening to kill them if Attica was ever invaded again, the Athenians had a scope for a second stroke at Sparta without any real risk. So a base for more raids was established on the island of Cythera, off the southern coast of the Peloponnese. The Spartans, however, were saved by Brasidas, a commander of unusual enterprise and courage. He led an expedition northwards and took the very important Athenian colony of Amphipolis in Thrace: Cleon fell in 422 BC trying to recover it, and the philosopher Socrates (469–399 BC) only saved himself by a hasty retreat. Though Brasidas also died of wounds, the Athenians were ready to discuss terms, and a fifty-year treaty between the two sides was agreed in 421 BC; it was called the Peace of Nicias after the Athenian general who more than any other brought the treaty into being.

However, it proved impossible to carry out the terms of the treaty, and war-parties in both Athens and Sparta kept tension high. Among the Athenians, the most forceful advocate of anti-Spartan measures was the nobleman Alcibiades (c. 450–404 BC), a kinsman of Pericles. Arguably the Athenians should have stuck to a peaceful line, not least because all could see that the Spartans had not won the war. But at the insistence of Alcibiades, the Athenians concluded an alliance with Argos and other enemies of Sparta in 420 BC. Two years later the Spartans narrowly defeated these city-states at the battle of Mantinea, to

which Athens half-heartedly contributed 1,000 infantrymen and some cavalry. The formal peace between Spartan and Athens somehow endured this crisis, but the Spartan victory meant that never again would the Athenians be able to risk a land battle. Instead, once again at Alcibiades' urging, Athens made the error of embarking in 415 BC on an expedition against Syracuse, possibly with the intention of acquiring a Sicilian empire.

Things went wrong with the expedition to Sicily from the very start. Unfavourable omens cast a shadow over its departure from Athens. And rather than face trial for sacrilege, in connection with one of them, Alcibiades fled into exile and persuaded the Spartans to lend a hand to Syracuse, since it was a colony of its ally Corinth. In Italy and Sicily the sheer size of the expeditionary force had already frightened off friendly city-states, with the result that few of the allies the Athenians expected to join them actually did so. Perhaps most unfortunate of all was the effect of Alcibiades' flight on the direction of the expedition, for it left cautious Nicias (c. 470–413 BC) as the senior general. Under his command the mistaken adventure turned into an utter disaster. The original expedition, and a subsequent reinforcement, was lost by 413 BC: half the forces of Athens perished along with the fleet. 'Only a few of the many,' commented the historian Thucydides, 'came back home.'

The final phase of the Peloponnesian War began when on the recommendation of Alcibiades the Spartans planted in 413 BC a fortress at Decelea to permanently dominate Attica, the Athenian countryside. Shortly afterwards the renegade moved to Asia Minor as an adviser to one of its Persian governors. Yet, as Thucydides pointed out, the Athenians still remained very difficult to overcome. For 'even after their defeat in Sicily, where they lost most of their ships as well as their men, and factional strife had already broken out in Athens, they nevertheless held out for ten more years, not only against their previous enemies and the Sicilians who joined them and most of their allies, who rebelled against them, but also later against Cyrus, son of the Persian king, who provided money to the Peloponnesians for a navy. Nor did they give in before they destroyed themselves by falling upon one another because of private quarrels.' There were two short periods of political reaction (in 411 BC and 404 BC), but more damaging to the war-effort was the general suspicion in Athens. The oligarchy of 411 BC was overthrown by the fleet and army stationed at Samos. They also recalled Alcibiades, who won a number of naval actions in the Hellespont, the route by which critical Black Sea corn supplies sailed to Athens. Yet victories at sea could only postpone defeat, once the Spartans properly co-ordinated their efforts with the Persians. The Spartan admiral Lysander (died 395 BC) gradually

gained the upper hand on what previously had been an Athenian preserve, for his naval victories culminated in the capture of the bulk of the Athenian fleet at Aegospotami in 405 BC. No longer able to protect its corn ships, Athens had no choice but to surrender a year later. A brief oligarchy, the notorious Thirty, ruled until in early 403 BC the Spartans allowed the restoration of the Athenian democracy. Power politics dictated this gesture of friendship, for Sparta wished to use Athens as a check on growing Theban power in central Greece.

*See* ALCIBIADES; ATHENS; CLEON; LYSANDER; NICIAS; ORACLES; PERICLES; PHILIP II; SICILIAN EXPEDITION; SPARTA; THEBES; THUCYDIDES; WARFARE
★Thucydides, *The Peloponnesian War*, trans. by R. Warner (Harmondsworth, 1954); D. Kagan, *The Outbreak of the Peloponnesian War* (Ithaca, 1969), *The Archidamian War* (Ithaca, 1974), *The Peace of Nicias and the Sicilian Expedition* (Ithaca, 1981), and *The Fall of the Athenian Empire* (Ithaca, 1987).

**Pericles** (*c.* 495–429 BC) was, in the judgement of the historian Thucydides, Athens' greatest leader. 'During the whole period of peace-time when Pericles was at the head of affairs the state was wisely led and firmly guarded, and it was under him that Athens was at her greatest. And when the war against Sparta broke out, he alone accurately estimated what the power of Athens was. He survived the outbreak of hostilities for two years and six months, and after his death his fore-sight with regard to the war became even more evident. For Pericles said that Athens would be victorious if she bided her time and took care of her navy, if she avoided trying to add to her empire, and if she did nothing to risk the safety of the city itself. But his successors did the exact opposite, and in matters which apparently had no connection with the war personal ambition and profit led to policies which were bad for the Athenians themselves and for their allies.'

Related to the reformer Cleisthenes, Pericles was instrumental in develop-ing Athens' democratic constitution. While the rest of the classical world continued to be characterized by hier-archical societies, democracy in Athens was carried as far as it would go before modern times. Although soon limited to adult males of native parentage, Athenian citizenship granted full and active participation in every decision of the state without regard to wealth or status, despite the continued influence of noble families such as Pericles' own relations on his mother's side, the Alcmaeonids. Unlike Rome, where nobles could be identified by their pur-ple-edged togas, Athenian aristocrats were accorded no special privileges and suspicion of misconduct was subject to punishment by ostracism. Pericles was almost unique in avoiding this ten-year banishment which the assembly could impose on a leader who seemed too ambitious for the safety of the state. Public office was even decided by lot,

with one exception, the ten chosen to command the army and navy each year. No citizen ever suggested that military officials should be appointed on grounds other than merit. Pericles was elected to an almost continuous generalship from 455 BC onwards.

The Athenian leader Pericles. Even his popularity could not save him from payment of a fine in 429 BC.

According to the historian Plutarch, Pericles became leader of the democra-tic party shortly after the ostracism in 461 BC of Cimon, leader of the aristo-crats. That same year Ephialtes was stabbed to death in the night by an unknown assassin, because Ephialtes and Pericles had stripped the aristo-cratic members of the Aeropagus council of their powers, and asserted the supremacy of the citizen-assembly. Little else is known, however, about Pericles' initial outlook as leader, even though he must have backed the build-ing of the so-called Long Walls:

constructed between 461 and 456 BC, these defences joined the city to its port, Piraeus, four miles away. During the Peloponnesian War (431–404 BC) they turned Athens into an island on land, as the rural population of Attica sought protection from the Spartans inside the fortications, where they were sustained by provisions brought by sea. The Spartans forced a defeated Athens to dismantle the Long Walls in 404 BC.

About 450 BC Pericles himself introduced a law imposing a much stricter definition of Athenian citizenship. Before this, children of an Athenian father and a foreign mother were legitimate Athenian citizens; the new law required that both be Athenian. The purposes of the new law are unclear, but its effect was to emphasize the exclusive value of citizenship in Athens. The Athenian assembly also gave itself the entitlement to use the surplus funds of the Delian League, in order to rebuild the temples on the acropolis; this led to the construction of the Parthenon, probably the most expensive Greek temple ever erected. What had begun on Delos in 478–477 BC as a mutual self-defence organization against Persia was now an undisguised Athenian empire. It is possible that the destruction of the expedition to Egypt hastened the transformation from league to empire. A tempting target because of its corn and treasure, the rebellious Persian province of Egypt was supported by a fleet of over 200 ships, previously on

campaign in Cyprus. Eventually the Persians were obliged to exert themselves and launch a major offensive against the Egyptian rebels, whom they defeated in battle. The Athenian and allied forces were soon besieged on an island in the Nile. They held out for almost eighteen months, but in 454 BC the entire Greek force was destroyed, and Egypt was restored to Persian control. The psychological impact of the disaster was even more damaging than the unprecedented loss of men and ships. It ended Athens' uninterrupted series of victories over Persia, caused unrest amongst its Aegean allies, and forced a curtailment of Athenian efforts against Sparta on mainland Greece. Immediately the treasury of the Delian League was removed from the island of Delos to Athens for safe-keeping.

Pericles' peace of 446–445 BC with the Spartans had one important consequence, however. It meant that Sparta recognized the existence of an Athenian empire. A grave danger in the division of the Greek world into two mutually suspicious blocs was political instability in either Sparta or Athens. As long as their leaders could minimize friction the peace would last, as it did till 431 BC. For Pericles these years of peace with Sparta gave him the ideal opportunity to strengthen the empire, develop democracy, and adorn Athens with public buildings. In the late 440s BC the Athenians tightened their control of the empire by imposing the use of Athenian weights, measures and coins, closing down local mints and so depriving subject-allies of a traditional symbol of independence. They also tightened the rules for the collection of tribute, requiring that the trials of those accused of default be held in Athens. States that rebelled were suppressed by swift military action. In 440–439 BC Pericles sailed to Samos with forty ships and replaced a rebellious oligarchy with a democracy, a move which kept the Samians loyal to Athens throughout the worst years of the Peloponnesian War. Only they refused to surrender to the Spartan admiral Lysander on the collapse of the Athenian empire, and even slaughtered aristocrats who desired to yield to the Spartans. The Athenians were so grateful that they passed a remarkable law granting the Samians Athenian citizenship even while they retained their autonomy.

Another means of securing Athenian authority overseas was the planting of colonies, a policy favoured by Pericles. They were sent out to the Aegean island of Imbros, Chalcis and Eretria on Euboea, Thurii in southern Italy, Amphipolis in Thrace, and Colophon, Erythrae and Hestiaea in Asia Minor. 'Of all his campaigns,' Plutarch tells us, 'it was the expedition to the Chersonese which was most gratefully remembered, since it proved the salvation of the Greeks who lived there. Pericles not only brought with him 1,000 Athenian colonists and so provided the cities there with strength and vigour, but he also secured the neck of the isthmus against Thracian attack

with a fortified line stretching from sea to sea.' This area, the present-day Gallipoli peninsula, was vital to Athens because through it came the grain transports from the Ukraine on which its large population depended. That the final defeat of the Athenian navy occurred in 405 BC here at Aegospotami should come as no surprise. It was the lifeline for the fortified island Athens had become, hemmed in as it was by Spartan land forces.

Because Pericles turned Athens into such a strong imperial power he made a conflict with Sparta inevitable. Even Thucydides, the great admirer of Pericles, had to admit that it was 'the growth of Athenian influence which frightened the Spartans and forced them to war'. Two incidents involving Corinth and Athens were later cited as pretexts for the outbreak of hostilities. The first concerned the Athenians giving aid to Corcyra (modern Corfu), a rebellious colony of Corinth. And then another Corinthian colony, Potidaea in the Chalcidice, left the Athenian empire in 432 BC with the promise of Spartan support. The Megarians also complained of a trade embargo, instituted by Pericles the same year. Taken together, the complaints of Corinth and Megara were thought sufficient to justify a Spartan declaration of war. Few Greeks then believed that Athens could survive for more than a year or two of traditional warfare against the Spartans and their allies but, as Pericles realized, the Peloponnesian War would be an unusual conflict between land-based and sea-based powers. His strategy was to reject battle on land and abandon the Attic countryside to Spartan devastation, forcing the Spartans to adopt siege warfare in which they had little skill. Meanwhile, the Athenian navy would launch a series of commando raids on the coast of the Peloponnese. This strategy would continue until a frustrated enemy was prepared to make peace. It worked, even after a visitation of the plague carried off in 429 BC Pericles and thousands of others crowded inside the Long Walls. Stalemate meant Athenian survival, for the Spartans had to win to maintain their hegemony. But later on a kinsmen of Pericles, Alcibiades (*c.* 450–404 BC), persuaded the Athenian assembly to undertake an expedition to Sicily, which ended in 413 BC as a more serious disaster than the earlier Egyptian one. And thereafter the war tilted in favour of a Persia-backed Sparta. By selling the freedom of the Greek cities in Asia Minor, the Spartans obtained money from the Persians to build up a fleet capable of challenging a diminished Athens at sea.

*See* ALCIBIADES; ATHENS; CLEISTHENES; EGYPT; EPHIALTES; PELOPONNESIAN WAR; PERSIA; SPARTA

*D. Kagan, *Pericles of Athens and the Birth of Democracy* (London, 1990); Plutarch, *The Rise and Fall of Athens: Nine Greek Lives*, trans. by I. Scott-Kilvert (Harmondsworth, 1960); Thucydides, *The Peloponnesian War*, trans. by R. Warner (Harmondsworth, 1954).

A Persian nobleman, one of the many who attended upon the King of Kings at Persepolis.

**Persepolis** was the Greek name for Parsa, the residence of the Achaemenid kings, the rulers of the Persian empire. One of the great sites of the classical world, Persepolis was built between 520 and 450 BC to display the splendour of an empire which for the first time incorporated the whole of West Asia, parts of Europe, Egypt and northwestern India. The monumental complex of structures stood on an artificial platform covering 33 acres. Nearby were substantial houses belonging to courtiers and high officials, while at Nash-i-Rustam, six miles distant, the royal cemetery comprised a series of rock-cut tombs. There two bas-reliefs also celebrate the later triumphs of the Sasanians, the final Iranian dynasty (AD 226–651) prior to the Islamic conquest. The extent of Achaemenid dominion is still visible today in the carvings of tribute delegations on the stairway to the great hall at Persepolis: included are Medes, Susians, Armenians, Aryans, Babylonians, Lydians, Arachosians, Sogdians, Cappadocians, Egyptians, Scythians, Ionian Greeks, Parthians, Gandarans, Bactrians, Sagartians, Chorasmians, Indians, Skudrians, Arabians, Drangianians, Lybians and Ethiopians. Disaster struck Persepolis shortly after Alexander the Great arrived at the beginning of 330 BC. Continued hostility from the Persian nobility to his claim to have replaced the last Achaemenid as King of Kings persuaded him to obliterate this symbol of Persian power. What he could not bend to his wishes, Alexander chose to break. He let his troops go on the rampage during a day of plunder. The official treasury he reserved for himself, however.

See ALEXANDER THE GREAT; PERSIA

*D. N. Wilber, *Persepolis: The Archaeology of Parsa, Seat of the Persian Kings* (Princeton, 1989); E. F. Smidt, *Persepolis* (Chicago, 1953–70).

**Persia** was the name given by the Greeks to the vast empire which Cyrus the Great (559–530 BC) had founded. Amazingly, it was put together within the space of a single generation through a series of conquests that followed one another with a rapidity matched later only by those of Alexander the Great (356–323 BC), at Persia's own downfall. The earliest and greatest imperial power ever to be based on Iran, Persia was later imitated by two other Iranian empires of the Parthians (171 BC – AD 226) and the Sasanians (AD 226–651), both implacable enemies of the Romans. No contemporary classical state could rival the authority of Iran under the Achaemenids, the name of the Persian royal family. Cyrus the Great claimed descent from Achaemenes, in all probability Hakhamanish, who was said to have been brought up by an eagle. Around 700 BC Achaemenes established the Persians in Persis, what is now the modern Iranian province of Fars. At this early period Fars was still under the domination of the Medes, Iranian cousins settled to the north with their capital at Ecbatana. They appear more prominently in ancient West Asian records, and especially those found in Assyrian archives, so it is likely that Achaemenes' dynasty began as their client kings. In 550 BC, however, Cyrus rose in revolt, defeated the Median army and captured his overlord, King Astyages. Cyrus did not harm Astyages in any way, indeed he treated him favourably; but the defeat ended the power of the Medes, who thereafter served as shock-troops in the Persian army. At the battle of Thermopylae in 480 BC, when the Spartan king Leonidas for a few days defied the might of the Persian expeditionary force to Greece, the Persian king used the Medes for the initial assault. King Xerxes, according to the historian Herodotus, 'put the Medes in front of all the other peoples, either because he preferred them by reason of their courage or because he desired to destroy them in a body; for the Medes still retained a proud spirit, the supremacy which their ancestors had exercised having only recently been overthrown.' The Medes charged, to break like waves against the Spartan shield-wall, and 'in spite of heavy losses they refused to be easily repulsed'.

Cyrus' victory over the Medes provided the Persians with the additional manpower they needed to embark on an unprecedented series of conquests. Misjudging the situation, the Lydian king Croesus (560–546 BC) seized the opportunity of the Median collapse to advance eastwards. He had been encouraged in this action by the Delphic Oracle, which informed him, with typical ambiguity, that if he crossed the River Halys he would destroy a great empire. It turned out to be his own. In 546 BC the Lydian capital Sardis fell, and Croesus committed suicide rather than risk less generous treatment than Astyages had received. Between 546 and 539 BC Cyrus systematically reduced to obedience the Greek cities along the coast of Asia Minor.

Babylonia, too, was affected by Cyrus' defeat of the Medes and the Lydians, with whom the Babylonians were then allied. The Old Testament records the downfall of Babylon and the return of the Jews to their homeland, after fifty years of exile. While the Babylonian ruler Nabonidus was away in Arabia, his son Belshazzar was left to govern Babylon, where a powerful priesthood smarted with discontent. At a splendid feast given by Belshazzar

mysterious writing appeared on the palace wall. The prophet Daniel alone was able to read the message, which told of the kingdom's imminent conquest by the Persians. So it came about that in late 539 BC Cyrus made a ceremonial state entry into the city of Babylon without a blow being struck, and the following year his own son Cambyses was installed as governor. The last decade of his life Cyrus spent organizing the great and heterogeneous empire he had acquired. Unlike their Assyrian and Babylonian predecessors, the Persians exhibited little interest in imposing uniform values or a bureaucracy over the vast empire they conquered. Most local traditions were left intact, as long as they could be made to support Persian hegemony. Hence, the famous generosity shown to the Jews, which was probably paralleled elsewhere. Cyrus was killed in 530 BC on the eastern frontier, where he carried Persian arms into Central Asia. Cyrus' own modest tomb at Pasargadae was probably the handiwork of Ionian Greek stonemasons: its eclectic simplicity says a great deal about the character of this notable conqueror. His son Cambyses (530–522 BC) continued expanding the Persian empire through the conquest of Egypt in 525 BC. As with Babylon, the Persians adopted a policy of tolerance towards Egyptian traditions and the pharaoh might well have been installed as a client king, if he had chosen to co-operate. In 552 BC, while Cambyses was still seeing to the settlement of Egypt, a rebellion broke out in Media, led by a man who claimed to be the ruler's younger brother. Cambyses hurriedly set out, but died in unexplained circumstances on his way through Syria. The rebellion was put down by Darius I (521–486 BC), son of Hystaspes, who belonged to a branch of the Achaemenid family, and had actually been serving on Cambyses' staff in Egypt. Suspicion points to Darius as a regicide and usurper himself, however. For a public sense of outrage at the royal murder is reflected in the numerous revolts which broke out on Darius' succession.

It took Darius just over a year to cope with massive uprisings in Iran, Babylon, Armenia and Central Asia. His achievement in putting them down in a series of set battles, followed up by the public execution of the ringleaders and their supporters, remains astonishing. From the great rock inscription he had cut at Behistun (present-day Fars) it is clear that Darius survived only because several powerful Persian nobles remained loyal to him throughout. For the convulsion of 522–521 BC revealed the deep political divisions in Persian society, doubtless a direct result of such rapid and unprecedented expansion. Possibly as a means of asserting his own authority afterwards, Darius continued to extend the imperial frontiers: he conquered north-western India, some of the Aegean islands, and Thrace. This forward policy was interrupted, however, by the Ionian revolt (499–494 BC),

when many of the Greek cities of Asia Minor were encouraged to rebel by a Persian reverse suffered at the hands of the Scythians. The Greek rebels even succeeded in burning the Persian stronghold of Sardis before a swift counterattack turned the struggle into a bitterly fought campaign on land and sea. What was to have been in 490 BC the final campaign against the rebellious Greeks was a punitive attack on Eretria and Athens, two mainland Greek city-states which had become embroiled with the Persians. Even though the Eretrians were carried away into captivity (they were resettled near the royal city of Susa), the Athenians at the battle of Marathon decisively defeated the Persians, who were then intent on restoring the Athenian ex-tyrant Hippias (527–510 BC) as a client ruler. The death of Darius in 486 BC did not mean an end to Greco-Persian antagonism for the reason that his son, Xerxes I (486–465 BC), was also determined to extend the imperial frontier westwards. Just how far we cannot tell. Herodotus tells us that a Persian naval intelligence mission was sent out to survey the coasts and harbours, not only of mainland Greece, but also of southern Italy.

In 480–479 BC Xerxes tried, and failed, to force mainland Greece to acknowledge Persian power. Some Greeks did bind themselves to Persia, most notably Thessaly and Thebes; but others, such as Sparta and Athens, refused. From the perspective of Persia's Aegean interests, extending a measure of control to the European shore was logical. The importance of this strategy is signalled by the fact that the Persian king himself led the expedition, by sea and land, to try to bring the Greeks to heel. After initial Persian successes, the Greeks won a critical engagement at Salamis in 480 BC. Appalled, Xerxes could only watch the destruction of his navy, seated on a golden throne high above the straits in which the action took place. Yet he did not forget to reward those who had fought well. 'Whenever he saw any of his own captains perform a worthy exploit,' Herodotus relates, 'Xerxes enquired concerning him; and the man's name was taken down by his scribes, together with the names of his father and his city.' This system of reward for service certainly worked, as shown in the heroism of the Carian queen Artemesia. Upon the active co-operation of such local powerholders, whether Persian or otherwise, imperial strength ultimately relied.

Although Xerxes left a substantial army behind in Greece, the Persian king returned to Asia in order to forestall would-be rebels making any use of news of this crushing defeat. At Plataea, in central Greece, the Persian expeditionary force was also defeated on land, and in the same year of 479 BC the Athenians began their drive to free Greek cities everywhere from Persian control. The Persian invasion of the mainland was the turning-point in Greco-Persian relations. Thereafter the Persians were content to employ gold rather than troops to influence Greek affairs. Gold coins stamped with the Persian king carrying a bow were found to be effective in stimulating internecine Greek rivalries. Referring to the strength they gave to the Thebans, the Spartan king Agesilaus (444–360 BC) was to say that he had been obliged to withdraw from Asia Minor because of the cunning distribution of 10,000 'archers'.

In 465 BC, Xerxes and his crown

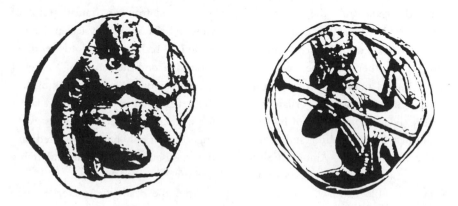

Two Persian 'archers'. Such gold coins outmanoeuvred the Spartan king Agesilaus in Asia Minor.

prince, Darius, were murdered in a palace plot. Like the earlier death of Cambyses, the events are obscure, a circumstance suggesting the complicity of Artaxerxes I (465–425 BC), a younger son. During his reign there was pressure on the western frontier, as Athens turned an anti-Persian maritime league into a powerful empire of its own. But in Egypt the Athenians lost in 454 BC an entire fleet, when they were crushed along with their allies, the rebellious Egyptians. New fortified garrison-points were also set up to strengthen Persia's coastal defences in Cyprus and Syria, other targets of the Athenians. By 450 BC there was tacit agreement concerning spheres of influence between Athens and Persia. It lasted down till the Peloponnesian War (431–404 BC), the final struggle for supremacy between Sparta and Athens. In its final stage Persian gold was used by the Spartans in order to challenge and overcome the Athenians at sea.

The Persian succession was not troubled again till the reign of Artaxerxes II (404–359 BC), the grandson of Artaxerxes I. Once again, a younger brother, by the name of Cyrus, nursed ambitions for the throne and gathered a group of Persian supporters, aided by troops from his area of command in Asia Minor and a force of Greek mercenaries. Among the latter was the Athenian soldier-author Xenophon (428–354 BC), who has left an account of the rebellion and, after its failure, the march of the Greeks home-

wards. The insurgents almost reached Babylon, where they were defeated at the battle of Cunaxa in 401 BC. The victorious Artaxerxes was to be one of the most enduring Persian kings, but apart from Cyrus' early challenge little else is known about him. Surviving royal inscriptions tell us more about religious developments than the administration of a great empire, which seems to have remained in the hands of a tiny group, drawn exclusively from the highest levels of the Persian aristocracy. Although the ruler was still regarded as the favourite of Ahura Mazda, the chief Iranian god, special help was believed to derive from two other deities as well: Mithra, Ahura Mazda's son, who was associated with the light that preceded the sun when it rose, and the goddess Anahita, the source of all the rivers and streams in the world. Deeply rooted in Iranian religion was the belief in the extreme sanctity of both pure light and fresh water. Like other divinized elements of the material world, all waters were understood from an Iranian point of view to be at once a physical entity and a divine reality. Herodotus entirely misunderstood the action of Xerxes at the Hellespont. The Persian king had the sea flogged with a hundred lashes for wrecking his bridge of boats: royal anger was simply being translated into the chastisement of an unhelpful, living divinity.

After the death of Artaxerxes II in 359 BC, there was another succession struggle before one of his sons took the throne as Artaxerxes III (359–338 BC). The major achievement of his reign was the reconquest of Egypt in 343 BC, but significantly the fifty-year-or-so rebellion was ended only through the use of large numbers of Greek mercenaries. Growing Persian dependence on hired soldiers was shortly to excite the ambitions of two Macedonian kings, Philip II (359–336 BC) and his son, Alexander the Great. It must have encouraged these warrior-kings, too, that in 338 BC Artaxerxes and most of his family died in a veritable bloodbath, masterminded by the eunuch Bagoas. Bagoas then installed the sole surviving young son of Artaxerxes on the throne for two years, before switching his allegiance to a member of a collateral branch of the Achaemenid family. Once firmly established as Darius III (336–330 BC), however, the last Persian king had Bagoas executed. Darius III's reputation has suffered badly as the victim of Alexander the Great (356–323 BC). To the Greeks and Romans the Macedonian conquest of Persia was a world-shaking event. Overlooked in the excitement of the narrative of Alexander's campaigns is the twelve years of continuous fighting which it took to subdue the Persian empire. The Persian nobility was slow to accept defeat, as were other local rulers. Following the murder of Darius in 330 BC, Alexander was able to cast himself in the role of avenger of a Persian king and his rightful heir, but he still had to fight every inch of the way, taking province after province in the east by force, before he could claim to have won Asia by the spear.

See ALEXANDER THE GREAT; ATHENS; CAMBYSES; CYRUS THE GREAT; CYRUS THE YOUNGER; DARIUS I; EGYPT; IONIAN REVOLT; PARTHIANS; PERSIAN INVASIONS; SASANIANS; XENOPHON

*J. M. Cook, The Persian Empire (London, 1983); P. Green, M. A. Dandamaev and V. G. Lukonin, The Culture and Social Institutions of Ancient Iran (Cambridge, 1989); J. Wiesehöfer, Ancient Persia (London, 1996).

**Persian invasions** of Greece occurred in 490 BC as well as 480–479 BC. Their unexpected, apparently miraculous repulse became the 'great event' of Greek history, which portrayed the war as the defeat of an overwhelming barbarian host content to live under a despotic king. Actual events were not quite so simple: many Greeks fought alongside the Persian invaders, while others openly sympathized.

Behind the heroic confrontation lay a desire on the part of the Persian king Darius I (521–486 BC) to consolidate his frontiers. As in the distant east in India, he wanted in the far west to secure the borders of his enormous realm. So in the Aegean, several islands including Samos were brought under Persian control, and in 512 BC an expedition crossed the Hellespont into Thrace. An abortive campaign north of the River Danube against the Scythians was most likely part of a strategy to contain the nomad peoples who troubled the Persians the length of their long, northern frontier. But the Persians were more taken aback when in 499 BC the Greek cities in Ionia rebelled. This Ionian revolt was doomed, given the lack of a unified plan, the strength available to the Persians, and the inadequate response from the city-states of mainland Greece. Only two of these, Athens and Eretria, sent ships to Asia Minor. Although in 498 BC the rebels burned the Persian stronghold of Sardis, the powerful Persian counterattack extinguished the revolt within four years. A final act of punishment aimed first at Eretria, then Athens, even brought Persian invaders to Greece in 490 BC.

According to the historian Herodotus, Darius was thinking at this time of the possibility of a general advance into the Mediterranean. For Persian officers had already conducted a recon-naissance of the coasts of Greece and Italy. Without doubt the Persian king intended to subdue Athens and Eretria as a first step towards the conquest of all Greece. Most of the island states accepted the demand for submission, including the strong naval power of Aegina; many states on the mainland also promised obedience, but Sparta and Athens were among those who refused. The submission of the Aeginetans worried both and, at the request of Athens, the Spartan king Cleomenes I intervened to take hostages; ten prominent citizens were held against the possibility of the Persians using the island of Aegina as a naval base. This action caused the bitter enmity between Cleomenes (519–490 BC) and his co-monarch Demaratus (510–491 BC) to flare into public row, which was ended with Demaratus seeking refuge in the Persian court.

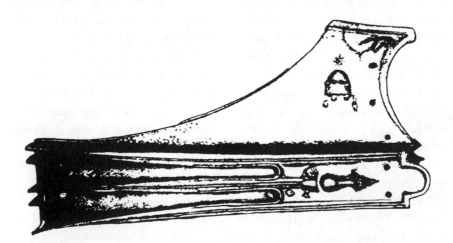

Bronze rams like this one gave the Greeks victory at Salamis in 480 BC. This ship's ram was recovered near Cyprus.

Relations, never entirely good, between the Spartans and the Athenians were improved by the Persian threat. But the Persians moved so swiftly that by the arrival of the Spartans, who were delayed through a religious festival, the first invasion was over. After taking Eretria by treachery, and deporting its population as slaves, the Persian commanders Datis and Artaphernes were, Herodotus tells us, 'guided to Marathon by Hippias', the exiled Athenian tyrant. The landing-place on the northern coast of Attica was chosen as 'the most suitable for deploying cavalry', the arm in which the Persians excelled. In response the Athenians marched northwards under the command of Miltiades (c. 550–489 BC) and other elected generals. Carrying his fellow commanders with him, Miltiades immediately engaged when the heavily armed Persian cavalry were not in position. Once through a barrage of arrows, the Athenian and allied Plataean foot-soldiers had the advantage because the Persian infantry wore very little body armour. According to the dramatist Aeschylus (525–456 BC), who took part in the battle at Marathon, the thrusting spear overcame the bow. Six thousand Persians lay dead on the battlefield for a loss of under 200 Greeks. After this defeat the Persian ships gathered up the remnant of Datis and Artaphernes' force and sailed round Attica to Athens; but, making no further attempt to land, they then withdrew.

Darius decided that a more co-ordinated attack was required to settle the troublesome Greek frontier, but he died in 486 BC before preparations were complete. Against this renewed threat Themistocles (c. 528–462 BC), the leader of the democratic party at Athens, was the moving spirit behind the build-up of Greek resistance. In 483 BC he persuaded the Athenian assembly to use the lucky strike of a rich vein of silver at the state mines at Laurium to build a new fleet of triremes. By 480 BC 200 of these oar-propelled warships were in service. According to Herodotus, this decision 'saved Greece by making Athens a maritime power'.

That the Greeks now faced a determined foe in Darius' son, Xerxes, there could be little doubt. Rebellions in Egypt and Babylon had been harshly put down, and King Xerxes I (486–465 BC) also decided to lead the second invasion of Greece himself. The enormous expeditionary force left Sardis in 481 BC, crossing over to Europe on two pontoon bridges secured to the seabed of the Hellespont. Estimates put the number of combatants at between 300,000 and 400,000 men, as well as the sailors and marines of 800 or more vessels in the Persian navy. A conference of Greek states held at Corinth endeavoured to organize a defence using the mountain ranges of Thessaly and the pass at Thermopylae in central Greece. On Xerxes' coming in 480 BC, however, the defenders found that they had insufficient forces to hold Thessaly, and instead the Spartan king Leonidas attempted to halt the Persians at Thermopylae. But the king and his small army were betrayed, and fought bravely to the last man.

Meanwhile the Persian navy shadowed the expeditionary force, and suffered a small reverse at Artemisium, north of the island of Euboea. But the Greek ships which took part in the action were not able to prevent its sailing southwards in support of Xerxes. No further resistance was offered in central Greece, Thebes took the Persians' side, and Athens now lay at the mercy of the invader. On Themistocles' recommendation, the bulk of the population was evacuated to the nearby island of Salamis. He argued that the oracle received from Delphi about the Athenians putting their trust in a wooden wall referred to the newly built ships and not the improvised defences of the acropolis. In early September Xerxes occupied Athens, slaying its stubborn defenders, and concentrated his navy off Salamis. It was Themistocles' plan to lure the Persian ships into the straits there, so that in the narrow waters the enemy's numerical advantage would be greatly reduced. And, when the Persians took the bait, everything turned to the Greek advantage. Seated on a golden throne, Xerxes could only observe in impotent fury as his navy suffered a stunning defeat. According to the historian Plutarch, three noble Persian prisoners-of-war were offered to the

god Dionysus by the Athenians in return for success that day. The Greeks were in a state of acute alarm and it is not impossible that Themistocles had to tolerate some blood-letting.

An Athenian war memorial. The goddess Athena reads a list of those Athenians who fell fighting the Persians.

However apocryphal this story of human sacrifice, the victory at Salamis wrested the initiative from the Persians. Fear of renewed unrest at the news of this reverse caused the Persian king to hurry home, but he left Mardonius with a force of 300,000 to continue the invasion after the winter. The combined Greek army under the command of the Spartan general Pausanias overcame him at Plataea in the summer of 479 BC. Victory was won after a hard-fought engagement in which the Persian cavalry was well deployed, and the Greek infantry showed a surprising lack of cohesion. But the Persians had lost their chance of conquest, for the Greeks went over to the attack in the same year. A naval victory off Mycale liberated the Greek cities of Asia Minor from Persian rule. But after 477 BC, however, Sparta declined to continue with the counter-offensive: Athens was quick to fill the vacuum left by the lack of Spartan leadership, and instead of allowing the eastern Greeks to resume full independence, it established at Delos an alliance based on Athenian maritime supremacy. Over time this anti-Persian organization evolved into the Athenian empire.

Even though the myth of Persian invincibility was shattered, the failure of the two invasions of Greece did not weaken the Achaemenids, as the Persian royal house was called after its legendary founder, Achaemenes. Nor can the subsequent assassinations in 465 BC of Xerxes and his heir-apparent, Darius, be seen as of any real consequence. For the new Persian king Artaxerxes I (465–425 BC) was able to secure a satisfactory peace with the Greeks in the 440s BC.

See ATHENS; CLEOMENES; MILTIADES; ORACLES; PERSIA; PLATAEA; SACRIFICE; THEBES; THEMISTOCLES; THERMOPYLAE; WARFARE

*A. R. Burn, *Persia and the Greeks: The Defence of the West, c. 546–478 BC* (London, 1962); J. M. Cook, *The Persian Empire* (London, 1983); Herodotus, *The Histories*, trans. by A. de Sélincourt (Harmondsworth, 1954).

**Philip II**, king of Macedon 359–336 BC, established the first land-empire in Europe. Instead of imposing democratic governments and settlements of its own citizens like Athens, or oligarchies and governors backed by garrisons like Sparta, Philip left subject peoples to run their own internal affairs once he had conquered them. They were also expected to see to their own defence, besides supplying soldiers to fight in his armed forces. And the cities which he founded never consisted of Macedonian settlers alone. It was a daring policy in the volatile Balkans. His treatment of defeated Greek city-states was equally light-handed after his victory at Chaeronea in 338 BC over the Thebans and the Athenians. He persuaded them to substitute for their internecine warfare a collective security agreement, as well as a crusade against Persia. Only stubborn Sparta remained outside these arrangements, reduced to no more than an irritant to its Peloponnesian neighbours. Philip conspicuously followed the principle of the Theban general Epaminondas (killed 362 BC), who had said 'that anyone who desired to lead the Greeks should preserve by generosity what they had gained by military prowess'.

Except in the Chalcidice, an area still largely populated by Greeks from previously independent city-states, there was little slavery in the Macedonian kingdom, nor the disdain for manual labour and military service so evident in contemporary Athens. Other than

Philip II, the architect of Macedon's rise as a world power. His assassination in 336 BC allowed Alexander to assume leadership of the war against Persia.

the Macedonians, whose function was military, the population was engaged in farming, manufacture and commerce. The king and the Macedonian army acted as the government; for they decided all matters of foreign policy and enacted laws. Strong though reverence was for the Temenid royal house, the Macedonian king always ruled by persuasion, never force. In 326 BC Philip's son, Alexander the Great, had to bow to the will of the assembly of the Macedonians, when he discovered in India that there was an unwillingness to advance farther east. The young king avoided a public humiliation only by announcing a decision to turn back

on military grounds.

Philip's rise to the position of the most powerful European leader was in large measure due to his own diplomatic and military genius. It was his reform of the Macedonian army along Theban lines, his successful incorporation of Balkan tribes within his kingdom, and his deft exploitation of inter-state rivalry in Greece that gave Philip ultimate victory. The Athenian statesman Demosthenes (384–322 BC) was wrong to say he only won by trickery and bribery. An affable man, the behaviour of the Macedonian king belied Greek propaganda about any barbarian despotism. For he appointed as Alexander's tutor the philosopher Aristotle (384–322 BC), a staunch supporter of the city-state. Thus Philip's assassination at the age of forty-six in 336 BC came as a shock, on the eve of the joint Macedonian and Greek invasion of Persia.

*See* ALEXANDER THE GREAT; DEMOSTHENES; EPAMINONDAS; SACRED WARS; SLAVERY; WARFARE

*N. Hammond, *Philip of Macedon* (London, 1994); M. B. Hatzopoulous and L. D. Loukopoulos, *Philip of Macedon* (London, 1981); G. L. Cawkwell, *Philip of Macedon* (London, 1978).

**Philo** (20 BC – AD 50) was an Alexandrian Jew, whose influence on the local development of Christianity was enormous. The Christian saint and scholar Clement (AD 150–215) can be said to have brought to fruition Philo's view that religion and philosophy were utterly compatible. Philo recounts: 'There was a time, when I devoted all my waking hours to philosophy and contemplation ... I seemed to be standing on a watch-tower, looking down at the rest of humanity as it scurried after its inconsequential tasks. But the serenity was not to last; I entered politics. Ever since that choice was thrust upon me, I felt as though I was pushed off that watch-tower into a sea of troubles. Then just when I think I am about to drown, the waves become calm, and I have the sensation of floating above the waters, once more in the sunlight. . . . In these periods of peace I study the law of Moses and explain its meaning to those few who are not satisfied with surface understanding and yearn for the truth in all its depth.'

The metaphor of the tower and sea, the famous lighthouse and harbour of Alexandria, was consciously chosen by Philo to express his appreciation for the stimulating city in which he lived. Heir to the whole tradition of Greek philosophy through the conspicuous patronage of learning shown by the Ptolemies, who ruled Egypt from there between 305 and 30 BC, Alexandria was also the most important settlement of the Jewish diaspora. During Philo's lifetime the Jews were a majority of the population in two of the five districts into which the city was divided, and there were Jews resident elsewhere in the city. Very few possessed Alexandrian citizenship but the Jewish community was allowed a council of

its own. Scholarly Jews had already immersed themselves in Greek learning prior to Philo's use of it to interpret holy writ. Like St Paul, Philo aspired to mystical experience and he used the ideas of the philosopher Plato as a means of understanding divine action. From later Stoic notions he also formulated the idea of a ruler doing heavenly business on earth. Philo himself felt that this ideal was fulfilled by Augustus who in 31 BC had brought peace to the war-torn Mediterranean world and laid the foundations of the Roman empire. It was to prove incredibly attractive to Christians; for the idea provided a means by which they could eventually identify with Rome. Later still it formed the basis of the Byzantine theory of kingship.

Philo's loyalty to the Roman empire was unshaken by the pogrom of AD 38 in Alexandria. He led a delegation to Rome, where the emperor Caligula (AD 37–41) was at the time pressing his desire to be worshipped as a living god. Caligula decided to have a large gilded statue of himself erected in Jerusalem, but the Roman governor delayed the project in order to avoid Jewish unrest. Philo was neither discouraged by Caligula's indifference to his delegation, nor was he unduly dismayed by the expressed desire to be recognized as a deity. Relief was not long coming to the Alexandrian Jews in the more practical approach of Claudius, who became emperor on Caligula's assassination. Claudius (AD 41–54) reversed the imperial policy of demanding

299

divine honours during an emperor's lifetime, and in Alexandria he restored peace between the Jews and the rest of the population.

See ALEXANDRIA; CALIGULA; CHRISTIANITY; CLAUDIUS; CLEMENT

★S. Sandmel, *Philo of Alexandria: An Introduction* (Oxford, 1979); D. L. Sly, *Philo's Alexandria* (London, 1996).

**Pisistratus** (died 527 BC) was the first tyrant at Athens, seizing power in 561 BC through a bodyguard foolishly voted him by the assembly. It is ironic that Pisistratus' mother was related to the reformer Solon, who warned that 'a city's ruin comes from great men, and the people in their folly fall into the slavery of a ruler'. Though no democrat like the later Cleisthenes, Solon had been concerned to replace the exclusiveness of aristocratic rule in 594 BC. What he correctly foresaw were the dangers his new constitution faced from the contemporary vogue for tyranny. The historian Herodotus informs us of the ruse Pisistratus used to become tyrant: 'He cut himself and his mules about the body and then drove his cart into the market square, and pretended that he had escaped from his enemies who had tried to kill him as he was driving out of the city. Then, relying on the reputation he had won during his command of the expedition against neighbouring Megara, he asked the people to give him a guard. The Athenians, taken in by the trick, consented to a number of club-bearers. With their assistance Pisistratus captured the acropolis, and from that moment made himself master of Athens. He was no revolutionary, but governed the country in an orderly and excellent manner, without changing the laws or disturbing the existing magistracies.'

However, the aristocrats tired of the tyranny after five years and Pisistratus was driven into exile. He might well have remained out of power had his opponents not been so at odds with each other. But one faction invited Pisistratus to return, which he did ostensibly in the company of Athena. A countrywoman, dressed in a suit of armour, drove a chariot to Athens in order to impersonate the goddess. Even Herodotus found it hard to credit the event. 'Of all the Greeks,' he commented, 'the Athenians are allowed to be the most intelligent: yet it was at their expense that this ridiculous trick was played.' It seems to have backfired, for Pisistratus was soon an exile once more. When he finally returned for good in 546 BC, the tyrant no longer placed his trust in trickery but came with a force of mercenaries. Until his death from natural causes in 527 BC Pisistratus ruled Athens without real difficulty. His long rule effectively weakened the influence of the aristocrats over their followers, a necessary precondition for the democratic reforms of the fifth century BC. The second and last tyrant at Athens was Pisistratus' eldest son Hippias, who ruled from 527 to 510 BC.

See HIPPIAS; SOLON; TYRANNY

*A. Andrewes, *The Greek Tyrants* (London, 1956).

**Plataea**, a small city-state with fewer than 1,000 citizens in southern part of Boeotia, received Athenian aid when threatened by the Thebans in 519 BC. Grateful Plataeans fought alongside the Athenians in 490 BC at Marathon, where the first Persian invasion of mainland Greece was repulsed. They also joined the Athenian fleet in 480 BC, after the Persians sacked both Plataea and Athens. Near to the ruined site of Plataea the Greeks under the command of the Spartan general Pausanias decisively defeated this second Persian expedition in 479 BC. The Plataeans rebuilt their city but, on the outbreak of war between Sparta and Athens in 431 BC, they found themselves again under Theban attack. Plataea's democratic government had always resisted incorporation in the Boeotian League dominated by oligarchic Thebes, and hostilities offered the chance to settle this old score. Though the night-attack of the Thebans failed, this surprise move against a loyal Athenian ally constituted the first action of the Peloponnesian War (431– 404 BC).

The Athenians evacuated all the women, children and old men from Plataea as soon as the Thebans withdrew. Then a garrison of 480 men as well as 110 women as cooks was left to hold the well-sited city. It resisted bravely until in 427 BC the Spartans joined in the siege. The historian Thucydides says that 'the hostile attitude of the Spartans in the whole matter of Plataea was chiefly on account of the Thebans, for the Spartans thought that the Thebans would be useful to them in the war just then beginning'. Publicly the Spartans declared that tiny Plataea was assisting Athens in maintaining an empire at the expense of the freedom of other Greeks. Shortage of supplies eventually compelled the defenders of Plataea to surrender, although not before half of them had escaped to safety. The surrendered garrison was promised a fair trial, but the only question asked by the Spartan judges was what good service had the Plataeans done to the Spartans. Shocked by this deception, the Plataeans protested that against the Persians they had rendered good service to all the Greeks, unlike the Thebans who had been Persian allies. This argument, though embarrassing to the Spartans, was of no avail: 200 Plataeans and twenty-five Athenians were put to death.

Even though they knew that they could not have risked a battle on land to save Plataea, the cruel fate suffered by its garrison shamed the Athenians, and so they granted the surviving Plataeans the almost unique privilege of Athenian citizenship. This enfranchisement was still in force in 386 BC, when the Spartans restored Plataea as a city-state in order to thwart the Thebans. After another destruction in

373 BC, and a second period of desolation, the Macedonians finally resettled Plataea on a permanent basis. Its old enemy Thebes had been utterly destroyed in 335 BC as a punishment for rebelling against Alexander the Great. Thebes never recovered its strength and so Plataea survived unmolested into Roman times.

*See* ATHENS; MACEDON; PELOPONNESIAN WAR; PERSIAN INVASIONS; SPARTA; THEBES

★Thucydides, *The Peloponnesian War*, trans. by R. Warner (Harmondsworth, 1954).

**Plato** (429–347 BC), undoubtedly the greatest Greek thinker, was born into a wealthy Athenian family, unlike his mentor Socrates, who was the son of a sculptor and a midwife. He derived his hatred of democracy from the execution in 399 BC of Socrates on a charge of impiety. For the next decade Plato lived abroad, visiting the Sicilian tyrant Dionysius I at Syracuse. On his return home in 385 BC he established the Academy, over which he presided for the remainder of his life. Its name came from an olive grove sacred to the hero Academus, on the outskirts of Athens. The philosophical school was intended to provide an education for future statesmen, rather like the one Confucius (551–479 BC) had already set up in China for would-be ministers. The curriculum Plato favoured was in all likelihood similar to that described in his most substantial work, the *Republic*, which outlines an ideal society: subjects taught included mathematics, political theory and dialectics. Astronomy was also an early interest of the Academy, but later purely philosophical concerns became dominant.

The influence of Socrates on Plato was profound, although he did not follow his mentor's example of rejecting the written word in favour of personal encounter. But Plato never quite lost a Socratic suspicion of writing, despite the remarkable range of his own style. He even expounded most of his ideas in a form previously associated with entertainment; namely, the dialogue. In the early dialogues the dominant figure is indeed Socrates, but as Plato's own thought developed it becomes plain that the figure of Socrates serves merely to voice the writer's ideas. And the late dialogues concentrate on issues which Socrates chose to ignore, such as cosmology and rhetoric. How far Plato moved from the individualistic outlook of Socrates can be seen in his treatment of society. He is prepared to consider the historical context seriously and approach ethics from a wider viewpoint than that of the individual, no matter the urgency of such a person for justice. In *Laws*, Plato's longest and perhaps last dialogue, extremes of depotism and freedom are both condemned, in a vision of a small city-state kept in harmony by traditional religion. The other great philosopher of the age, Aristotle (384–322 BC), agreed wholeheartedly that the first care of a state was to its gods.

See ARISTOTLE; ATHENS; SOCRATES

*I. M. Crombie, *An Examination of Plato's Doctrines* (London, 1962–3); J. E. Raven, *Plato's Thought in the Making* (Cambridge, 1965).

**Polycarp**, the wealthy bishop of Smyrna, was martyred in either AD 155 or 165 at the age of eighty-six. His violent death, of which we possess a graphic record, illustrates the strength and weakness of early Christianity, its undoubted heroism and narrowness of vision. A staunch defender of Christian orthodoxy as well as a respected member of the local community, Polycarp was executed following the arrest and condemnation of several of his own flock. The hue and cry for Polycarp started when the crowd in the amphitheatre cried for his blood. At first he was induced to flee to one country estate, then on to another. Officials followed him to the first, where they routinely tortured two slaves to learn of his whereabouts. They arrested him late at night, and the next morning Polycarp was taken for interrogation in the amphitheatre, where his own words were nearly drowned by such cries as: 'This is the teacher of Asia, the father of the Christians, and the destroyer of our gods.' Nothing except a public recantation could have saved him from immediate death, and this action Polycarp refused to make. It is evident from the record that the Roman magistrate was aware of the irregularity of trying a citizen who had been the victim of an illegal search. He showed embarrassment in his questioning, avoiding any hint of an accusation of Christianity and even pretending to be ignorant of Polycarp's religious beliefs, in the hope that the defendant himself would be tricked into confessing to being a Christian. The truth did come out, at which the judge revealed considerable anxiety about the attitude of the spectators. They called out for Polycarp to be devoured by a lion, but this was ignored on the grounds that the wild-beast season was over, with the result that instead the old bishop was burnt alive.

The Jews were especially zealous in preparing the fire. Confronted by the threat posed by Christianity, the established religions made common cause against the newcomers. The odium which had once been the lot of the Jews in Asia Minor now fell on the Christians. But for the Christian community Polycarp's martyrdom was a parallel of the fate suffered by Christ. Neither had set out to defy the Roman authorities, which interestingly took a dim view of the Smyrna persecution. A surviving document reprimands the local officials for stirring up trouble for those they accused of atheism, ignoring the fact that the gods were certainly able to deal with such people without any help. It also blames them for losing their heads over earthquakes, and of allowing official searches to be carried out for Christians against imperial policy. In the interests of public order, the conservative emperor Antoninus Pius (AD 138–161) was concerned to limit the number of occasions on which those who refused to acknowledge the imperial cult could be actively persecuted. Possibly the Romans had recognized the potential danger in so readily making martyrs. For very different to Polycarp had been the attitude of Ignatius, bishop of Antioch, who positively welcomed his death in AD 108 at the Colosseum in Rome. 'Chained as I am to half a score of bestial soldiers, who only grow more insolent the more bribes they are given,' he said, 'how I look forward to the real lions that have been prepared for me!' No threat worried him other than the loss of salvation. 'Fire, cross, beast-fighting, hacking and quartering, splintering of bone and mangling of limb, even the pulverizing of my whole body – let every horrid and diabolical torment come upon me, provided only that I can win my way to Jesus Christ!'

*See* ANTONINE DYNASTY; CHRISTIANITY
G. W. Bowersock, *Martyrdom and Rome* (Cambridge,1995).

**Pompeii**, situated five miles southeast of Vesuvius, is one of the most famous archaeological sites in Europe. For the hundreds of thousands of people who visit this Roman city each year are able to walk through streets that were preserved by the eruption of AD 79. They can identify public squares, private houses, bars, brothels, theatres, the amphitheatre, which is the earliest known permanent structure for such events as gladiatorial contests, and even the plaster casts of the dead.

Originally Pompeii was founded by the Etruscans, and Italian peoples formed the majority of the population, until, as a punishment for siding against Rome in the so-called Social War (91–87 BC), the Roman dictator Sulla imposed a colony of his veterans. The settlement of a large number of soldiers alongside the Pompeians caused a certain amount of conflict. Argument seems to have been focused on the city's own administrative arrangements, although there is no evidence to show that the new settlers monopolized public office. Possibly disagreement was stimulated by the taking over of land for the construction of new buildings: town hall, treasury, prison, theatre and amphitheatre. But Pompeii quickly became a prosperous centre for industry and trade based on small-scale workshop production. It made a distinct red pottery which has been discovered in places as distant as Greece, Africa, Germany and Britain. Some of these storage jars may have been used to transport fish sauce. The Romans regarded fish as a luxury and high prices were paid for both fresh fish, eels, and shellfish, as well as fish products. The older Cato had already complained in the second century BC how a bullock cost less than a barrel of salted fish.

In AD 62 an earthquake struck Pompeii, which was close to the epicentre. Other towns were affected, including nearby Herculaneum, which was another Etruscan foundation. Parts

A Roman bar. One of the low-life haunts of Pompeii.

of Pompeii were never repaired before the eruption of Vesuvius in AD 79 overwhelmed the city as well as Herculaneum. The younger Pliny (AD 61–112) has left us a description of the event, which he observed from a distance. Pliny's uncle died in an effort to evacuate people by sea. 'On Vesuvius,' he wrote to his friend the historian Tacitus, 'broad sheets of fire and leaping flames blazed at several points.' Then came black clouds, falling pumice-stones, fumes and a thick layer of ash, besides several lava flows. Even 'the sea appeared to have shrunk, as if withdrawn by the tremors of the earth.'

*See* ETRUSCANS; ROME; SULLA

★W. Jongman, *The Economy and Society of Pompeii* (Amsterdam, 1988); R. Lawrence, *Roman Pompeii: Space and Society* (London, 1994).

**Pompey** the Great (106–48 BC) helped Sulla (137–78 BC) become dictator in 82 BC by raising soldiers from his own estates at Picenum, south of modern Ancona. After destroying Sulla's enemies in Sicily and Africa, he was grudgingly allowed a triumph in Rome, probably in 80 BC, the year before the dictator stepped down. The rather unorthodox career of Gnaeus Pompeius Magnus, favoured at one point by the senate, then at another not, reveals the basic unease of this soldier with the business of politics. His strained relations with Crassus (112–53 BC), the richest man in Rome, had to be publicly healed in 70 BC at a meeting of the assembly, shortly after they had combined to defeat the massive slave uprising under Spartacus.

Gnaeus Pompeius Magnus, Pompey the Great, the chief rival of Julius Caesar.

Pompey's opportunity to match the wealth of his rival soon came in an unprecedented command against pirates, especially in the eastern Mediterranean where they were giving aid to the Pontic ruler Mithridates VI, an old enemy of Rome. Against the wishes of the senate, he was in 67 BC given authority over all islands and coastlines, the power to raise funds and recruit troops, and the command of an army of 120,000 men. Then, to the greater distress of the senators, in 66 BC Pompey was also authorized to make a general settlement of the east, following Roman successes there against Mithridates under the generalship of Lucullus (117–56 BC). Having virtually ended the war, Lucullus was less than delighted by Pompey's new position and, according to the historian Plutarch, they exchanged harsh words when they met. 'Pompey accused Lucullus of being too fond of money,' he tells us, 'while Lucullus accused Pompey of being too fond of power. Their friends had some difficulty in parting them.' But this exchange was somewhat wide of the mark, because Lucullus had actually undermined his own position by curbing extortion among Roman tax-collectors in Asia Minor, and Pompey was about to exhibit a notable interest in money himself.

In 63 BC Mithridates committed suicide, leaving Pompey with a free hand militarily and politically. He founded colonies, some of which were settled by ex-pirates; created the new provinces of Bithynia and Pontus, Cilicia and Syria; and established a buffer zone of client kingdoms, including Colchis, Paphlagonia, Armenia, Commagene and Judaea.

Pompey's decision to annex Syria meant the end of a kingdom established by the Macedonian general Seleucus in 312 BC. Lucullus had approved the accession of Antiochus XIII in 69 BC, but Pompey scornfully told the supplicant monarch that he did not deserve a throne if he could not defend himself. Though it gave him pleasure to overturn Lucullus' decision, there can be little doubt that the Seleucids then offered a poor defence against the rising power of Parthia. For Pompey, of course, the annexation provided yet another opportunity to acquire wealth. He returned to Rome a multimillionaire, a financial equal of Crassus, the man who said that no one could call himself rich unless he was in a position to support a legion out of his own income. Pompey's settlement was unique: for one man, invested with supreme powers, had redrawn the political map without any supervision. It anticipated the authority later exercised by Augustus, the first Roman emperor (31 BC–AD 14). The senate was unwilling to ratify the settlement, in part because of the speeches of Lucullus, but in 60 BC Pompey joined forces with Crassus and Julius Caesar (100–44 BC) in an unofficial coalition to get his way. Their blatant use of force revealed how Rome, instead of being controlled by an oligarchy of nobles, was now in the power of three ambitious men. Caesar had asked Cicero (106–43 BC) to join them, but to his credit he refused. The decision effectively marginalized him, since the combination of Pompey's popularity, Crassus' connections and Caesar's acumen proved irresistible. Their so-called triumvirate survived the departure of Caesar in 58 BC to Gaul, where he embarked on its conquest. In Rome his interests were served by street gangs belonging to Publius Clodius until in 52 BC this popularist was killed in a brawl with Pompey's supporters. The event provoked a riot in which the senate house was burnt down. Three years before the triumvirate had been renewed, but after Crassus died in 53 BC, on a campaign against the Parthians, relations between Caesar and Pompey broke down. Pompey found himself a favourite of the senators, who passed legislation aimed against Caesar. The civil war that ensued cost Pompey his life and Rome its republic.

When Caesar invaded Italy in early 49 BC, Pompey chose not to face him, but instead staged a skilful withdrawal across the Adriatic and began to mobilize his forces in the Balkans. Thus Italy fell without a blow to Caesar, who entered Rome and seized the contents of the treasury. Having dealt with forces sympathetic to Pompey in Spain, Caesar moved east in 48 BC to discover his opponent encamped at Dyrrhacium (modern Durazzo in Albania). After suffering a reverse there, Caesar marched to Thessaly and Pompey followed to Pharsalus, where his army was routed. A fugitive Pompey was murdered in Egypt by a centurion who had served under him during the pirate war. 'Not long afterwards,' the historian Plutarch writes, 'Caesar arrived. When one of the Egyptians was sent to him with Pompey's head, he turned away from him with loathing, as from an assassin.'

*See* CAESAR; CICERO; CRASSUS; ROME; SELEUCIDS; SPARTACUS

⋆P. A. L. Greenhalgh, *Pompey: The Roman Alexander* (London, 1980); R. Syme, *The Roman Revolution* (Oxford,1939); Plutarch, *Fall of the Roman Republic*, trans. by R. Warner (Harmondsworth, 1958).

**Population** figures are difficult to calculate in classical times, though for taxation purposes censuses were carried out by both the Romans and the Chinese. For classical Greece it is Athens which provides the most complete picture. On the eve of the Peloponnesian War in 431 BC the total population of Attica, the territory of the Athenian city-state, was around 300,000. Of these inhabitants some 60,000 were enslaved: they were all foreigners, and in the main Thracians employed in the state silver-mines at Laurium. Although in 404 BC, at the end of the Peloponnesian War, the Athenians were forced to surrender to the Spartans, the victors found within thirty years that an acute manpower shortage had undermined their own strength. The population of Sparta seems to have fallen dramatically, so that by 369 BC the number of citizens capable of bearing arms was barely 1,000. To meet a Theban-led attack on

Sparta itself, King Agesilaus (444–360 BC) resorted to calling up 6,000 helots to strengthen defences. Not all of these armed slaves stood their ground, however, and the very number of the new recruits inspired terror within the Spartan ranks. The ultimate victor in Greece was Macedon, which under Philip II (359–336 BC) enlarged its armed forces by incorporating whole peoples into the realm. Yet the combined population of Macedon and its Greek allies was tiny in comparison with the Persian empire, which Alexander the Great conquered between 334 and 324 BC. Realization of the even greater populousness of India was one of the reasons for the Macedonians refusing to advance further eastwards, into the lower Ganges valley. News had been received of the huge armies and gigantic war elephants belonging to its rulers, the Nanda dynasty (546–322 BC).

A census taken in AD 2 gave China a total population of just under 58 million, making the Han emperors the rulers of the greatest number of people in the classical world. Another census of AD 140 showed a decrease of nearly 8 million, which may be explained by a number of factors: natural disasters, famine, large-scale migration southwards, and a less efficient count not unconnected with tax evasion by increasingly powerful landowners. Twice the Yellow river had shifted its course, killing many peasant-farmers and driving others from the populous northern plains. The population of

the Roman empire is estimated at 54 million in AD 14, Rome itself having about a million inhabitants. High mortality rates and conditions of life in the city necessitated a continuous high level of migration, a steady stream of people coming from the cities of the eastern Mediterranean. The free population of Alexandria, the second largest city in the Roman empire, probably topped 300,000.

See AGESILAUS; ATHENS; HAN DYNASTY; NANDA DYNASTY; ROME; SPARTA

*M. I. Finley, *Economy and Society in Ancient Greece* (London, 1981); P. Garnsey and R. Saller, *The Roman Empire: Economy, Society and Culture* (London, 1987).

**Porus** was an Indian ruler who met Alexander the Great in battle near the Hydaspes river in the spring of 326 BC. The action was complicated because the river (the Jhelum, a tributary of the Indus) had a swift and turbulent current: the Himalayan snows were melting and the rains were starting. A night crossing surprised Porus, but his considerable army stood firm against the Macedonian attack. His forces were deployed in the so-called garuda battle formation. Its object of placing 200 elephants in front of the line was to scare away the Macedonian cavalry, which was standing in a compact body. Both wings of Porus' army were protected by chariots and cavalry, while an infantry screen was thrown around the elephants to deal with skirmishers. But the unexpected mobility of Alexander's troops decided the outcome of the engagement. Porus' chariots and horse proved ineffectual, once the infantry came into contact, and his prized war elephants were disabled by removing their mahouts. The exceptionally long Macedonian spear was also invaluable at close quarters. Indian losses were put at 25,000, whereas Alexander's casualties were less than 100 of his infantry and just over 200 cavalrymen.

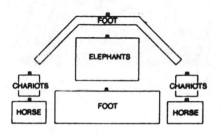

The battle-formation adopted by King Porus at Hydapses river.

The personal bravery of Porus deeply impressed Alexander, however. 'Throughout the action,' the historian Arrian tells us, 'Porus had proved himself a man indeed, not only as a commander but as a soldier of the truest courage. When he saw his cavalry cut to pieces, most of his infantry dead, and his elephants killed or roaming about the battlefield, his behaviour was very different from that of the Persian king Darius: unlike Darius, he did not lead the scramble to escape, but so long as a single unit of his men held together, fought bravely on.' When Porus was finally persuaded to meet Alexander,

such was his noble bearing that Porus was restored to his throne by the Macedonian king. After the battle Alexander also founded two cities, Nicaea and Bucephala. The latter was named in memory of his own charger Bucephalus or 'Oxhead', which had recently died of old age and exhaustion. Only Alexander had ever succeeded in riding him. So impressed was his father, King Philip II, by this feat that he said: 'My boy, seek a kingdom to match yourself. Macedon is not large enough to hold you.'

It was the Macedonians in Alexander's army who ultimately decided the limits of his conquests. Within months of the victory at Hydaspes river they refused to advance farther eastwards, where their next major opponent would have been the Nanda dynasty (546–322 BC). Disillusion gripped the Macedonians, who were suffering from exhaustion and the effects of seventy days of continuous rain; for they felt they had been misled and the promised end of Asia was nowhere in sight. It has to be said that Alexander himself was baffled by the sheer size of India. According to his tutor, the philosopher Aristotle (384–322 BC), the sub-continent was no more than a small peninsula pointing eastwards into the great ocean which encircled the world. Even though he still wanted to advance into the Ganges valley, Alexander recognized that this was now impossible and he decided to turn back, much to the delight of the Macedonians.

*See* ALEXANDER THE GREAT; WARFARE
*Arrian, *The Campaigns of Alexander the Great*, trans. by A. de Sélincourt (Harmondsworth, 1958); G. T. Date, *The Art of War in Ancient India* (Bombay, 1929).

**Ptolemies** ruled Egypt from 305 BC, following the collapse of Alexander the Great's empire, until the suicide of Cleopatra in 30 BC, when the kingdom became another Roman province. The Macedonian dynasty known as the Ptolemies was founded by Ptolemy I (305–282 BC). A close companion of Alexander and a distinguished general, he was born about 367 BC and became the governor of Egypt in 323 BC. Ptolemy's dynastic ambitions were clear from the start: he quickly annexed Cyrenaica (most of modern Libya) and kidnapped Alexander's body. Macedonian custom decreed that a ruler had the duty of burying his predecessor. Instead of allowing the burial to take place in the royal graveyard at Aegeae, the Macedonian capital, Ptolemy kept the body of the great conqueror on permanent display in a gold coffin at Alexandria. In fact it was Alexander's last wish to be interred at nearby Siwah, the Libyan oasis where an oracle first addressed him as 'the son of Zeus Ammon'. Ptolemy issued coins with a divine portrait of Alexander, and later ones showing himself as a favourite of Zeus as well. Another religious move that Ptolemy made to legitimize his position was the cult of Serapis, a Greco-Egyptian deity who

Serapis was the state god of Ptolemaic Egypt. A healer, he was held to be superior to fate and a power in the underworld too.

was meant to unite the polyglot non-Egyptian ruling élite of Alexandria and other major cities. Possibly derived from worship of the Apis Bull at Memphis, this syncretic god was regarded as a healer, and numerous miracles made his cult very popular. The Serapeum in Alexandria eventually drew pilgrims from the whole of the eastern Mediterranean: it survived till the reign of the Roman emperor Theodosius I (AD 379–395), who congratulated the Christians on its destruction at the instigation of the local patriarch.

Under the Ptolemies Egypt was treated rather like a private estate. The king drew profits from commercial monopolies and spent the extensive revenues on learning, mercenaries, and courtly extravagance. From the start of the kingdom there was a monopoly on coinage: merchants bringing foreign coins from abroad had to exchange them for Ptolemaic currency, or have them restruck at the royal mint. Once again, the motive for the unusually closed currency system appears to have been profit. The only sphere of life in which the native Egyptians retained any control was religion. In their relationship with temples and their priesthoods the Ptolemies adopted a cautious policy, appreciating the need to establish an understanding with this most cherished feature of Egyptian life. Prior to moving Alexander's remains to Alexandria, Ptolemy I at Memphis had even given the former king a pharaoh's funeral. An early attempt to employ Egyptians in an administrative capacity proved unsuccessful, and it was not till 217 BC that they were recruited in large numbers to the Ptolemaic army. It was Ptolemy IV's (217–205 BC) victory over the Seleucid ruler Antiochus III at Raphia the same year that

changed the situation: the victory was only won with the help of native troops. Quite possibly their use awakened within the Egyptian population a sense of its own power, for rebellion soon occurred. Discontent was not new, but a great belligerence towards authority was characteristic of the remainder of Ptolemaic rule. Adoption of the pharaonic cult never really reconciled Egypt to its Macedonian masters.

The last Ptolemy, Cleopatra VII, was the first one to learn the Egyptian language (she was fluent in nine, but interestingly not Latin), and from the very beginning of her reign in 51 BC she took part in native religious festivals. Following a short period of civil upheaval, the Roman general Julius Caesar reinstated Cleopatra as joint ruler with her eleven-year-old brother Ptolemy XIV in 47 BC. She was Caesar's guest in Rome at the time of his assassination in 44 BC, but she quickly returned to Egypt, killed her brother, and had her four-year-old son

Ptolemy IV and his sister-wife Arsinoe, whose marriage followed pharaonic custom.

Caesarion declared co-ruler. Ptolemy Caesar (Caesarion's official name) was most probably the son of Julius Caesar. Cleopatra's later involvement with Mark Antony (82–30 BC) destroyed the Ptolemaic dynasty and led to Rome's annexation of Egypt.

*See* ALEXANDER THE GREAT; ANTONY; CAESAR; CLEOPATRA; COINAGE; EGYPT; MACEDON; ROME; SELEUCIDS

*P. Green, *Alexander to Actium: The Hellenistic Age* (London, 1990); H. I. Bell, *Egypt from Alexander the Great to the Arab Conquest* (Oxford, 1948); D. J. Thompson, *Memphis under the Ptolemies* (Princeton, 1988).

**Pyrrhus** (319–272 BC) was the most famous of the Molossian kings of Epirus (today most of modern Albania and north-western Greece). He had twice suffered exile before his hold on the kingdom was secured in the 290s BC. Southern Illyria was soon annexed to Epirus, along with border areas of Macedon. In 288 BC he combined with Lysimachus (360–281 BC), the ruler of Thrace, to drive Demetrius from Macedon. During one of his exiles Pyrrhus had served Demetrius (336–283 BC) and his father Antigonus. The historian Plutarch tells us that he fought 'at the great battle of Ipsus, in which all the kings who had succeeded Alexander the Great took part. He was only eighteen at the time, but he routed the contingent that was opposed to him and distinguished himself brilliantly in the fighting.'

Demetrius' own impetuosity had cost Antigonus his life and the battle, which effectively confirmed the division of Alexander's far-flung conquests between his generals. However, Pyrrhus did not immediately turn against Demetrius, whose extravagant behaviour tended to alienate friend and foe alike. Wily Ptolemy I (305–282 BC), the king of Egypt, recognized the natural abilities of Pyrrhus as a soldier and gave him the encouragement he needed to become independent. It suited Ptolemy to have a powerful ally on the doorstep of Macedon. What few realized in 288 BC was just how unpopular Demetrius was with the war-weary Macedonians. For Demetrius' support crumbled with appalling speed; his forces were swiftly defeated by Pyrrhus and he went abroad, where he died as an indulged but confined house-guest of Seleucus I (305–281 BC), the Asian ruler. According to Plutarch, the invasion did 'not fill the Macedonians with anger or hatred against Pyrrhus . . . because all those who resisted it and witnessed his exploits talked endlessly about him and marvelled at his courage. They compared his appearance and the speed and vigour of his movements with those of Alexander the Great. The other kings, they said, could only imitate Alexander in superficial details, with their scarlet cloaks, the bodyguards, the angle at which they held their heads, or the lofty tone of their speech: it was Pyrrhus alone who could remind them of him in arms and action.'

After an indecisive war with Lysimachus in 283 BC, Pyrrhus responded to a request for aid against Rome by the Greek city-state of Tarentum (present-day Taranto). Epirote ties with southern Italy were long-standing, and in 280 BC Pyrrhus landed with a force of 20,000 infantrymen, 3,000 cavalry, 2,000 archers, 500 slingers, and twenty elephants. The ensuing battle at Heraclea, west of Tarentum, was the first encounter ever between the Romans and a veteran Greek army led by a Greek ruler. The Roman legions stood up well to Pyrrhus' phalanx, which proved somewhat unwieldy. But his elephants routed the Roman cavalry and then charged the flank of the legionaries, putting them to flight.

Another engagement a year later at Asculum, in northern Apulia, also resulted in a heavy loss of life on both sides; hence, a Pyrrhic victory for a costly defeat of an enemy. Failing to end the war against Rome satisfactorily, Pyrrhus turned his attention to Sicily, where he combined with the Greek cities there to defeat the Carthaginians. Again, there was no lasting result from his military successes, and so Italy beckoned once more. The Romans, however, had learned from their defeats and, no longer at the mercy of the elephants, they forced Pyrrhus to return home in 275 BC. The historian Polybius explained the Roman victory in terms of enduring adversity and profiting from bitter experience. 'In the first place,' he tells us, 'once the Romans had grown accustomed to suffering great losses at the hands of the

Gauls, there was no more terrifying event than this which they need expect either to undergo or fear. Secondly, by the time that they had to meet Pyrrhus they came to the contest like trained and seasoned athletes in military operations. They were able to crush the aggressive spirit of the Gauls while there was still time to do so; then, having disposed of this threat, they could give their undivided attention first to the war with Pyrrhus for the possession of Italy, and later to the war with Carthage for the possession of Sicily.'

King Pyrrhus of Epirus. He was knocked unconscious by a tile thrown by an old woman from a rooftop in Argos, then decapitated by a Macedonian soldier.

Two years after his evacuation of Italy Pyrrhus was killed in street fighting at Argos, during a campaign aimed at dominating the Peloponnese. He was undoubtedly a clever tactician and a brave commander, but he lacked persistence and any grasp of long-term strategy. The Romans always took the longer view and for that reason in 272 BC the Tarentines bowed to the inevitable and accepted the alliance that was proposed to them.

See ALEXANDER THE GREAT; ANTIGONUS; DEMETRIUS; LYSIMACHUS; MACEDON; PTOLEMIES; ROME; SELEUCIDS; WARFARE

*E. S. Green, *The Hellenistic World and the Coming of Rome* (Berkeley, 1984); N.G.L. Hammond, *Epirus* (Oxford, 1967); Plutarch, *The Age of Alexander*, trans. by I. Scott-Kilvert (Harmondsworth, 1973); Polybius, *The Rise of the Roman Empire*, trans. by I. Scott-Kilvert (Harmondsworth, 1979).

**Pythagoras** left the island of Samos in 531 BC, perhaps to escape the tyranny of Polycrates (546–522 BC), and settled at Croton in southern Italy. Like his follower Empedocles (*c.* 492–433 BC), Pythagoras was an enigmatic figure, a mixture of philosopher and priest. He wore an imposing costume, including a gold crown, a white robe, and trousers. 'Indeed,' the commentator Diogenes Laertius tells us, 'his bearing is said to have been most dignified, and his disciples held the opinion about him that he was Apollo come down from the far north. There is a story that once, when he was undressed, his thigh was seen to be of gold.' Pythagoras was also in the habit of referring to the poems of

Orpheus, whose cult was emerging in classical Greece as a mystery faith. This peace-loving poet was credited with the idea of the immortal soul being trapped in the body: later his worshippers would employ dietary restrictions and ritual practices to free it from the contamination of the body. A series of reincarnations, it was hoped, might then liberate the soul altogether.

Pythagoras may have extended the idea of reincarnation to encompass animals and plants. He believed that, by reverently contemplating the order inherent in the world, man could become progressively purified until he eventually escaped from the cycle of rebirth and attained immortality. His mystical interest in mathematics and music appeared to disclose a unifying structure for all phenomena in the universe. According to the account of Diogenes Laertius, Pythagoras claimed 'the soul is divided into three parts, intelligence, reason, and passion. Intelligence and passion are possessed by other animals as well, but reason by man alone. The seat of the soul extends from the heart to the brain; the part of it which is in the heart is passion, while the parts located in the brain are reason and intelligence. The senses are distillations of these. Reason is immortal, all else mortal . . . When the soul is cast upon the earth, it wanders in the air like the body.'

At an unknown date the Crotoniates tired of the Pythagoreans and the philosopher was lucky to escape to nearby Metapontum, where he died in peace. Over 400 of his male and female followers lost their lives in the bloody expulsion. The movement, however, did not entirely disappear after Pythagoras' death, in part because it chimed with a growing concern for personal salvation, and in part for the reason that his vision of cosmic order provided later thinkers with a planetary system into which the earth could be satisfactorily fitted.

*See* EMPEDOCLES

★G. S. Kirk, J. E. Raven and M. Scholfield, *The Presocratic Philosophers* (Cambridge, 1983).

# Q

Qin existed as a small state or feudal principality long before one of its kings united China under the so-called Qin dynasty (221–207 BC). Although its foundation is traditionally ascribed to 897 BC, the effective emergence of this north-western state dates from after 771 BC. Following a nomad attack on their capital of Hao, in the Wei river valley, the Zhou kings moved eastwards to Luoyang and left the local Qin chieftain to defend the abandoned capital. With the benefit of hindsight, a chronicler wrote of this 'unwise act' that 'the very duties ennobled Qin was called upon to perform inevitably developed his ambition, for the military skills of his people were improved by constant struggles against raiders along the western frontier'. But there was little the weakened Zhou dynasty could do but quit such a dangerous area. In 707 BC its reduced authority as the supreme feudal house became transparent to all when a humiliating defeat was inflicted upon royal forces by a tiny territory previously under Zhou suzerainty. During the Warring States period (481–221 BC), Qin was but one of seven major states which fought for supremacy with scant regard to their nominal overlord, the Zhou monarch.

Model of a grain silo from a Qin grave. Irrigation gave Qin an advantage over the other feudal states.

That Qin triumphed in this long contest can be attributed to a number of factors. First, the military emphasis in its society allowed a Legalist minister such as Shang Yang to easily introduce authoritarian reforms during the fourth century BC, which greatly enhanced the power of the Qin ruler. A second advantage was a reliable agricultural surplus based on unusually large-scale irrigation schemes. The most famous project was the Chengkuo canal, completed in 246 BC: it turned the Qin homeland into the first key economic area, a place where agricultural productivity and facilities for transport allowed a supply of grain-tax so superior to that of other places, that the ruler who controlled it could control all China. A final factor to be taken into account when considering the triumph of Qin in 221 BC must be the character of Zheng, the First Emperor. His determination was the engine that drove the Qin juggernaut, carefully steered though it was by his chief minister Li Si (died 208 BC). As even the unsympathetic historian Sima Qian admitted, the First Emperor was efficient and hard working. He handled 'one hundred pounds of reports daily', and he undertook frequent tours of the empire. Yet there was nothing in this supreme ruler's personality to mitigate against the harshness of Legalism, and after his death the Chinese people rose and overthrew the Qin dynasty. Its successor, the Han (202 BC – AD 220), kept the capital in the north-west till in AD 25 it was moved to Luoyang. This transfer of the seat of imperial government from Chang'an was a tacit recognition of the shift in the national centre of gravity. The Huai and the Yangzi river valleys had overtaken the old Qin heartland as the most developed region in the empire. The temporary breakup of China during the Three Kingdoms period (AD 222–280) can be seen as a continuation of the same process in that the southern states of Shu and Wu were sufficiently strong to challenge for many years the northern state of Wei, the rump of the Han empire.

See CHENG KUO; CHU; FIRST EMPEROR; LI SI; QIN DYNASTY; SHANG YANG; WARRING STATES

*Ch'ao-ting Chi, *Key Economic Areas in Chinese History, as Revealed in the Development of Public Works for Water-Control* (London, 1936).

**Qin dynasty** (221–207 BC) unified China for the first time. As the first imperial house, the Qin set the pattern for future emperors albeit on an extreme scale.

In 221 BC, the year in which the state of Qin finally triumphed over all its rivals, the problem of feudalism was immediately solved by enforced migration. Feudal holdings were abolished and the nobles compelled to take up residence in the western provinces, away from their supporters. This radical move for the rest of China was by no means novel in Qin itself: there the reforms of Shang Yang in the fourth century BC had already had the effect of detaching status from birth. War was made the only avenue for the acquisition, and maintenance, of any position in the social hierarchy. The resulting success on the battlefield was undoubtedly the reason for the Qin ruler's enthronement as the First Emperor. His soldiers wore no helmets and discarded their body armour before

317

joining the fray, a chronicler comments, 'with untold ferocity'.

Although the Qin dynasty was of short duration, such was the energy and determination of the First Emperor (221–210 BC) that this period represents a turning point in the history of Chinese civilization. The bureaucratic type of government developed under centralized Qin rule became the model for future Chinese political organization, lasting till modern times. For the First Emperor, on the advice of his chief minister Li Si (died 208 BC), issued a stream of edicts intended to control his subjects, harness their strength, and exploit natural resources in order to strengthen and enrich the state. In his drive for uniformity he became the greatest destroyer of the classical era. Lacking a degree of economic integration, the Qin empire was held together solely by military power. Once the nobles had been removed from their lands, garrisons were placed at strategic points, joined by a national network of roads and canals. To protect the northern frontier against the Xiongnu, most probably the Huns who later invaded the Roman empire, the First Emperor in 214 BC ordered the construction of the Great Wall. Peasant farmers received greater rights over their land, but became liable to taxes, labour on public works, and military service. Merchants, the special target of discrimation, were sent as conscripts to the frontiers, where many agricultural colonies were set up. Standardization was hastened through the introduction of common weights and measures, coinage, axle wheels, and written script.

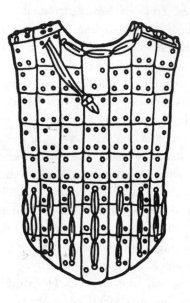

Detail of infantry armour from the terracotta army buried at Mount Li. Notice on the right a toggle to facilitate swift removal.

When the First Emperor in 213 BC discovered that these innovations drew criticism from the scholar-gentry, he ordered that all schools of philosophy were to be shut and books were to be burnt, except for the writings of the authoritarian Legalists and useful works on medicine, agriculture and divination. A year later a purge of Confucian scholars occurred, despite protest from the crown prince, Fu Su. But his objection did nothing, according to the historian Sima Qian, to stem the influence at court of 'alchemists who wasted millions without obtaining the elixir of life'. For the First Emperor was deeply concerned about his own mortality and tried to make direct contact with the immortals. His immense burial complex at Mount Li can be seen as part of the same anxiety. Court intrigue on the First Emperor's sudden death at the age of fifty in 210 BC was abetted by the secrecy imposed upon his movements by Daoist adepts. As a result Fu Su was obliged to commit suicide, while Li Si and the eunuch Zhao Gao installed as the Second Emperor his worthless younger brother Hu Hai. By 207 BC Zhao Gao had disposed of both Li Si and the Second Emperor, but his own attempt to usurp the throne failed, so that the First Emperor's nephew Zi Ying assumed power. The young ruler chose to eschew an imperial title, however. But this tacit recognition of the independence of the states overcome by his uncle was not enough to save the situation, as China was already engulfed in a nationwide rebellion. Sima Qian noted how 'Zi Ying sat on the throne for only forty-six days. In early February 206 BC a rebel army under Liu Bang arrived at the capital. Ministers and princes forgot their duties and surrendered to the rebels. As a consequence, Zi Ying, accompanied by his wife and sons, bound his neck with a silken cord and made his submission . . . Thereupon Liu Bang took charge of the Qin king and his capital, sealing up the treasures and palaces . . . More than a month later Xiang Yu arrived with the main rebel army of 400,000 men. Then Zi Ying was

beheaded along with all the other members of the imperial clan. There was wholesale massacre as palaces and houses were looted and fired. The burning lasted till the third month. Thus it was that the Qin empire was lost.'

From the title of this dynasty it is more than likely our word for China was derived. The Greeks remained ignorant of China, notwithstanding Alexander the Great's expedition to India in 327–325 BC. For the Romans the Chinese were simply Seres, no more than a reference to silk.

*See* DAOISM; FIRST EMPEROR; GREAT WALL; LI SI; LIU BANG; MOUNT LI; ZHAO GAO

*A. Cotterell, *The First Emperor of China* (London, 1981).

# R

**Religion** was perhaps the most diverse feature of the whole classical world. Of its various religious traditions, if Christianity is excluded as a very late development in the Roman empire, only two reveal any continuity with modern times: those belonging to India and China.

An early Roman coin of around 220 BC showing the two heads of Janus, who was connected with the fortunes of war. He was an ancient Italian deity adopted by the Romans.

The Zoroastrian faith of Iran has virtually disappeared, while the ancient beliefs of the Greeks and Romans survive now only in folklore. For very different to that of modern Europe was the religious outlook of classical Greece and Rome. There was neither a taught doctrine nor a creed to which believers were required to subscribe. A Greek or a Roman was free to think what he liked about the gods; what mattered was what religious action he performed. As a consequence, heresy and religious persecution were in principle impossible, although this did not prevent individuals from being condemned for impiety. A Greek city-state such as Athens regarded impiety as an absence of respect for the beliefs and rituals shared by its inhabitants. The most famous Athenian to be condemned was the philosopher Socrates, who in 399 BC drank poison for corrupting the young, undermining belief in the city gods, and introducing new deities. The trial and death of Socrates were all the more spectacular for being so rare, since Greek city-states were willing to tolerate unbelief, as long as it did not give rise to acts of impiety. The accusation of impiety may well have been included to sway the jury, while the real reason for the attack was Socrates' influence on the minds of young men, which was held to be subversive because of his own association with an anti-democratic faction at Athens.

An altar on a coin struck during the reign of the first Roman emperor Augustus, who was very concerned to maintain traditional piety.

Piety for the Greeks and the Romans was never the expression of intimacy between man and god. This dimension of belief had to await the advent of the so-called mystery religions and Christianity. Even though the former drew upon older cults with secret initiation ceremonies, such as the Greek corn goddess Demeter and the ecstasy god Dionysus, their real strength lay in a promise of individual salvation during a period of political impotence for the city-state. The larger powers in the Mediterranean, such as Antigonid Macedon, Seleucid Asia, Ptolemaic Egypt and, even more, the incipient empire of Rome, had reduced local power and local pieties to little more than provincialism. Instead

of finding satisfaction any longer in a community's worship of the gods, many people began to favour inward-looking cults and philosophies, such as Epicureanism. Followers of the Iranian-inspired mystery cult of the sun god Mithras actually shared in a sacramental meal akin to the Christian eucharist. A late ruler like the Roman emperor Julian (AD 361–363) installed a Mithraeum in one of his palaces and underwent a rebirth by means of ritual washing in the blood of a sacrificed bull. Julian's personal belief in Mithras, however, had hardly anything in common with the dualistic, militant Mithraism of the Roman soldier and the man in the street, not least because, like Christianity, Mithraism drew its adherents from practically every walk of life. At a Mithraeum in Ostia, Rome's seaport, of the twenty-one names identified, four were slaves, and the others were freedmen. An unusual aspect of Roman religious attitudes was a willingness to embrace foreign cults, notwithstanding continuing problems over more extravagant rites. The transfer of Cybele, the Phrygian mother goddess, to Rome in 205 BC soon caused anxiety. The Romans were shocked by her rites, whose wild dances culminated in bloody self-flagellation and self-injury. Initiates unmanned themselves in imitation of Attis, Cybele's castrated, killed, and resurrected lover.

Today the legacy of the strict dualism of Zoroastrianism can be found in India amongst the Parsees, fugitives from the Muslim conquest of Iran. Only the beliefs of this small community can claim linear descent from classical Persian religion. Except for ruined fire temples, no material trace remains of a once-powerful faith. Without the Avesta, the holy book of Zoroastrianism, we would have almost no idea about the most rigorous of all classical religions. For under the Sasanian kings (AD 226–651) there was a systematic attempt by the Zoroastrian clergy to impose doctrinal orthodoxy. The bloody persecution was directed against unbelievers as well as heterodox believers, the prophet Mani in AD 277 suffering execution. Such religious power could never have been exercised by a priesthood in the Greco-Roman world, because religion was always looked upon as being the property of the people as a whole. Its fundamentally democratic power was evident in sortition. Even a conservative philosopher such as Plato (429–347 BC) could argue that in choosing a priest each year the best method was to 'leave it to the god himself to express his wishes, and allow him to guide the luck of the draw'. An idea like this would have entirely baffled classical India, which possessed in the brahmins a hereditary class of religious specialists and guardians of traditional lore.

Although the social position of the brahmins was for a time effectively challenged by the teachings of the Buddha (*c.* 563–479 BC), the new religion of Buddhism was a spent force in India by the Gupta period (AD 320–

550). Its greatest influence was about to be felt abroad in China, Korea and Japan, just as Christianity had a lasting impact only outside the country of its birth. One reason for the reassertion of what is known today as Hinduism was the Indian tendency in matters of faith to separate personal enlightenment from religious observance. Once Buddhism ceased to be the way of the solitary seeker of truth, and turned itself into an established church, its eventual coalescence with traditional belief was inevitable. The Buddha was even absorbed as an incarnation of Vishnu, one of the most important Hindu gods. In classical India the significant religious figure was always the outsider, the saint. He was the one for whom everything was holy. According to one Hindu legend, an ascetic once slept with his feet on the lingam, a post sacred to the god Shiva. A brahmin saw this desecration and rebuked him fiercely. The ascetic said he was sorry and asked for his feet to be placed where there was not a sacred post. Angered, the brahmin seized the ankles of the ascetic, but wherever he swung them a lingam sprang from the ground. Thereupon the brahmin reverently bowed to the reposing saint and went on his way.

Prior to the arrival of Buddhism in the first century AD, China was isolated from the beliefs and ideas of other classical civilizations. Indeed, so late was the arrival of this new faith that its advocates found the conversion of the Chinese very hard going, little headway being made until the chaotic years following the fall of the Han dynasty in AD 220. The civil disturbances which ensued not only put the Chinese empire into temporary eclipse but also undermined the Confucian orthodoxy upon which imperial power rested. Confucianism, with its insistence upon man as the measure of all things, had become the dominant belief. Its key ritual concerned ancestor worship, a rite unique to the Chinese. Ancestor worship had been transformed by Confucius (551–479 BC) into the focus of a moral code in which proper social relations were clearly defined: the loyalty a minister owed to a prince was the same as that owed to a father by a son. This stress on submissiveness and loyalty was one of the features of Confucianism which made it so suited to a bureaucratic state, once the harsh tenets of Legalism had been discredited with the overthrow of the oppressive Qin dynasty (c. 221–207 BC). The emphasis placed by Legalist thinkers, such as Shang Yang (390–338 BC) and Han Fei Zi (c. 280–233 BC), on the need to organize society for the benefit of the state had led to a reliance on excessive punishment. Opposed to both Confucianism and Legalism was Daoism, the indigenous religion of personal salvation. For Daoism drew strength from shamanism as well as quietist philosophy. That its founder, Lao Zi (born 604 BC), had no known grave indicates a total indifference to the Confucian preoccupation with the family and the rituals of ancestor worship. However, Confucius himself was purely practical in his attitude to religion. 'I stand in awe of the spirits,' he told his followers, 'but keep them at a distance.'

*See* BUDDHISM; CHRISTIANITY; CONFUCIUS; DAOISM; EPICURUS; GUPTA DYNASTY; HAN DYNASTY; JULIAN; LEGALISM; MANI; ORACLES; PERSIA; PLATO; ROME; SHANG YANG; SOCRATES; ZOROASTRIANISM

Followers of Confucius mourning at the philosopher's grave. Because of his teaching ancestor worship became the focus of classical Chinese religion.

*W. Burkert, *Greek Religion* (Oxford, 1985); M. Loewe, *Chinese Ideas of Life and Death: Faith, Myth and Reason in the Han Period* (London, 1982); W. M. Malandra, *An Introduction to Ancient Iranian Religion* (Minneapolis, 1983); L. H. Martin, *Hellenistic Religions: An Introduction* (Oxford, 1987); R. M. Ogilvie, *The Romans and their Gods in the Age of Augustus* (London, 1979); H. Zimmer, *The Philosophies of India* (Princeton, 1969).

The sun god Helios, the patron of Rhodes, whose bronze statue was regarded as one of the seven wonders of the world.

**Rhodes** revolted in 411 BC, with Spartan support, from the Athenian empire. Although this change of allegiance did not bring about autonomy, it led to an event that laid the foundation of its future independence; for in 407 BC the city-states of Lindus, Ialysus and Camirus combined as a single political entity, with a capital at the north of the island called Rhodes. On the death of Alexander the Great in 323 BC, the Rhodians were strong enough to expel a Macedonian garrison and go it alone. In the ensuing

struggle for power amongst Alexander's generals they refused to help Antigonus against Ptolemy, so that for a year in 305–304 BC Antigonus' son Demetrius (336–283 BC) besieged the capital city. The attacking force comprised a fleet of 370 ships and 40,000 infantry, as well as an unknown number of cavalrymen. A census in Rhodes showed the defenders numbered 6,000 citizens and 1,000 resident aliens of military age. They were supported, however, throughout the siege by the rest of the population. Attacks were repulsed on both the city's harbour and landward walls, before 2,000 mercenaries arrived from Ptolemy in Egypt to stiffen the defences. One of the assault machines built by Demetrius was 150 feet high, armoured, and divided into nine storeys equipped with catapults that fired through shutters. In spite of such a determined effort Demetrius was unable to capture Rhodes, and he received instructions from his father to obtain the best possible terms and break off the operation. It was agreed, as the Rhodians always wanted, that they would assist Antigonus against all except Ptolemy, whose navy could badly injure their commerce. Because of the unprecedented siege Demetrius became known as 'the besieger'. His generous abandonment of all his siege engines at Rhodes led to an even more notable commemoration of the event, since with the money raised from their sale the Rhodians erected a colossal bronze statue to their patron deity, the sun god

Helios. It was later recognized as one of the seven wonders of the ancient world. Rhodian independence lasted till the enforced alliance with Rome in 168 BC. The unfavourable terms were imposed as a punishment for the ambivalent attitude of Rhodes to Perseus, the last king of Macedon whom the Romans had just defeated at Pydna. Gradually the island turned into little more than a museum state within the Roman empire. Even before the extinction of the Roman republic, Rhodes along with Athens had become a stopping place on the Greek grand tour. In 78 BC Cicero (106–43 BC) had studied oratory there under Posidonius, and Pompey (106–48 BC) stopped off twice between campaigns to meet the famous orator. So impressed was Posidonius with the famous Roman general that he wrote a history of his eastern wars. Rhodes' most distinguished resident was Tiberius, the future Roman emperor, who chose to retire there in 6 BC following a deterioration in his relations with Augustus, the first emperor (31 BC – AD 14).

See ANTIGONUS; CICERO; POMPEY; PTOLEMIES; TIBERIUS
*R. M. Berthold, *Rhodes in the Hellenistic World* (Ithaca, 1984).

**Rome** was the most aggressive of all classical states. Its rise from an Italian city-state to dominate the whole Mediterranean world represents a spectacular example of energy and determination matched only by the Qin unification of China in 221 BC. As the historian Livy could write with pride, the Romans were like 'no other people in the world'. But their achievement was to prove less enduring than the Chinese; because in the fifth century AD the western provinces of the Latin-speaking empire, and the city of Rome itself, passed under barbarian control, and a diminished Greek-speaking eastern empire, later known as Byzantium, struggled on till the fall of Constantinople to Muslim arms in 1485.

The foundation myth of Rome. This fourth century AD mosaic of Romulus and Remus with a she-wolf was found in Yorkshire.

In explaining the origins and early growth of their city the Romans deployed a variety of myths, the most famous of which were the arrival of the Trojan fugitive Aeneas and the foundation of the city itself by his descendant Romulus. But part of early Rome also belonged to the Etruscans, a neighbouring people who were organized into a number of powerful city-states. By 510 BC Rome was also a major power, with a large stretch of territory under its protection. Within a few years the last Etruscan king was expelled, and a republic established. The expulsion was not accompanied by any movement against the sizeable Etruscan population of Rome, suggesting that it resulted from the same political frustrations that had just toppled Hippias, the last tyrant of Athens. Unlike the Athenians, though, the Romans did not turn their republic into a thorough-going democracy, as the continuous contest for public office by a small group of noble families, such as the Scipios, soon stamped the constitution with an oligarchic character. It was their ambitions and jealousies, complicated by bitter feuds between the rich and the poor, which finally led to the dictatorships of Sulla (138–78 BC) and Julius Caesar (100–44 BC), and under the emperor Augustus (31 BC–AD 14) the restoration of a disguised monarchy. In the Twelve Tables of 451 BC, however, the ordinary people did succeed in establishing a written law code. It was a concession no aristocrat could refuse, because they bore the brunt of the fighting which steadily enlarged the republic's territory, first in Italy, then overseas. But the story was not one of unremitting Roman success. There were major defeats by the Samnites at the battle of the Caudine Forks in 321 BC and by the Epirote ruler Pyrrhus (319–272 BC), who tried to protect the Greek cities of southern Italy and Sicily; and there were the recurrent raids of the Gauls, beginning

with the famous sack of Rome in 390 BC. But Roman persistence won through these setbacks and expansion brought increased manpower because, unless defeated enemies were enslaved, they were either incorporated directly into the state as citizens or forced to become subject allies. At the same time Roman power was consolidated by the establishment of colonies at key points in conquered territory.

Penetration of the southern part of Italy brought Rome not only into direct contact with Greek cities here and in Sicily but also threatened the interests of Carthage, the great Phoenician city in present-day Tunisia. The sophistication of the Greeks inspired the Romans to emulate their cultural achievements and by 200 BC a Latin translation of the *Odyssey* had appeared along with the first history of Rome. Drama was launched through adaptation of the comic works of the Athenian playwright Menander, although Plautus (*c.* 254–184 BC) and Terence (*c.* 185–159 BC) invested their comedies with a specifically original Roman quality. And despite his criticism of the demoralizing influence of Greek learning, the elder Cato (234–149 BC) was one of the first to introduce the full technique of Greek oratory into Roman public life. An even greater impact was made by the Greeks on Roman religion, which had a parallel pantheon. Roman gods were identified with their Greek counterparts and acquired their myths and forms. Rooted as it was in a peasant sense of supernatural control over the natural processes, Roman religion had been slow to conceive of deities anthropomorphically. Its initial pantheon, and especially the triad of Jupiter, Juno and Minerva, was largely Etruscan in inspiration.

The assertiveness of the Carthaginians, on the other hand, soon precipitated an intense struggle for hegemony of the western Mediterranean, which was ended at Cato's insistence only by the deliberate destruction of Carthage in 146 BC. His embassy there in 153 BC was enough to convince him that a resurgent foe could still threaten Rome, and in 149 BC the Third Punic War was declared. To understand this anxiety, even obsession on the part of Cato, it is necessary to recall the ordeal of Hannibal's invasion of Italy during the Second Punic War (218–201 BC). This Carthaginian general had marched with a force of 40,000 men and thirty-seven elephants from Spain, crossing the Alps in late 218 BC. Having been driven out of Sicily at the end of the First Punic War (264–241 BC), and losing Sardinia as well to Rome shortly afterwards, Carthage diverted its energies to the creation of a land empire in Spain, and it was the mineral and man-power resources thus acquired that emboldened Hannibal (246–182 BC) to attack one of Rome's Spanish allies and renew the struggle. Hannibal inflicted three major defeats on the Romans, including the worst ever suffered in 216 BC at Cannae in southern

Italy. There he encircled two armies and slew 80,000 men. Weakened by the defection of many of their allies in Italy, the Romans fell back on a strategy of attrition, designed to reduce the insurgents and prevent them from giving aid to Hannibal. The Carthaginians were also helped by being able to open a second front when they secured the alliance of the Macedonians, who like the Epirots under Pyrrhus before them, were worried by Roman expansion into the Greek world. But Hannibal was fighting far from home, without the possibility of either regular supplies or reinforcements, and the Romans slowly but surely penned him into the south of the Italian peninsula. After Scipio Africanus (236–184 BC) had exploited Roman supremacy at sea to land an invasion force in Africa in 204 BC, Hannibal was finally recalled; but even he was unable to prevent a Carthaginian defeat at Zama in 202 BC, as well as the imposition of humiliating

Coin issued in Spain by Scipio Africanus after his capture in 209 BC of New Carthage, modern Cartagena.

peace terms that effectively ended Carthage's role as a major power.

The consequences of the Second Punic War were not only the extension of Roman power to Spain and southern France but also to Greece. Rome had a score to settle and at Cynoscephalae in 197 BC the Macedonians were heavily defeated. This campaign was swiftly followed by a confrontation with the Seleucid ruler Antiochus III (223–187 BC). With his defeat in 190 or 189 BC at Magnesia, Rome thus became dominant in the Aegean and much of Asia Minor. The Macedonians made one final attempt to stem the tide of Roman influence; they went down at Pydna in 168 BC at a cost of 20,000 casualties, and within twenty years Macedon was a Roman province, to be followed by the rest of Greece in 146 BC. What distinguished the Romans from their enemies was a capacity for virtually constant warfare. The long contest with Carthage had transformed the Roman army from an essentially part-time force of farmers into a quasi-professional organization in which it was not uncommon for men to serve abroad for years on end. And no one was allowed to hold a political office at Rome before they had completed ten annual military campaigns. The expansion arising from this glorification of conquest did not stop with the annexation of the Greek mainland. Roman control was progressively extended over Asia Minor, Africa, Spain, Syria, Libya, Egypt, and France. In his ten-year conquest of

Gaul, as the latter was then called, Julius Caesar enslaved one million Gallic prisoners, a bag indicating how profitable successful wars really were. Though he was obliged to march on Rome in 49 BC, and inaugurate the civil war that destroyed the republic, Caesar's long absence on campaign was not a political handicap when it gained him immense wealth, an opportunity to describe his own military exploits, and the undying loyalty of his troops.

But the republican empire was acquired at a very high price, not least because the economic and political problems it threw up combined to undermine its democratic institutions. The immediate issue that fuelled civil dissension was the plight of non-Roman Italians who did not enjoy the privileges of Roman citizenship but had to carry many of the burdens, and were increasingly evicted from their own lands either to make way for veterans or for the big estates of the aristocracy. The scale of the problem is difficult to assess, but agrarian reform had already caused bloodshed in Rome. Two aristocratic reformers, the brothers Tiberius and Gaius Gracchus, had been elected by the ordinary citizens in order to resettle the landless on illegally held public property, land belonging to the state by right of conquest. The senate, the council of former holders of public office and the stronghold of the large landowners, opposed all their reforms. Tiberius was surprised and killed by senators in 133 BC, while his younger brother met a similar end in 121 BC, after proposing a more radical solution to Rome's problems. Gaius wanted to found colonies for poor citizens, provide state-subsidized grain for those resident in Rome, and break the senatorial monopoly over the courts. His chief opponent, the historian Plutarch records, 'was the first consul who arrogated to himself the powers of a dictator, and who condemned to death without trial three thousand Roman citizens, among them Fulvius Flaccus and Gaius Gracchus, the one a consul who had celebrated a triumph, and the other the foremost man of his age in virtue and reputation'. The land question was not solved by the so-called Social War between the Romans and the Italians (91–87 BC), after which the principle that the Italians should be entitled to Roman citizenship was conceded; the solution was a huge extension of settlements for veterans, Italians and others, outside Italy, something only Julius Caesar and Augustus were ready to pursue.

Motivated though they were by genuine democratic principles, the Gracchi revealed that the urban poor, whether former slaves or free born, now offered a new constituency for political ambition. One beneficiary was the humbler soldier Gaius Marius (157–86 BC), who received command against the north African leader Jugurtha in 107 BC, despite opposition from the senate. In order to recruit troops for the war, Marius ignored the property qualification for service in the citizen-army and called up landless volunteers on a huge scale. Jugurtha was captured in 104 BC through an act of treachery arranged by Marius' lieutenant Sulla, but afterwards Marius destroyed in turn two marauding German tribes, the Cimbri and the Teutones. A harbinger of the military dictators to come, Marius used his troops politically in Rome until he himself fled to Africa in 88 BC as Sulla marched on the city. The aristocratic Sulla was anxious to secure his own position and ensure that the senate retained its political power. His own military appointment against King Mithridates VI of Pontus had been overturned by the assembly in an unprecedented move. It took nearly five years for Sulla to drive Mithridates back to Pontus, on the southern shore of the Black Sea; by which time Rome had fallen into the hands of his political enemies. Returning to Italy in 83 BC, the outlawed Sulla seized power and wiped out his enemies, whose estates

Coin issued in 82 BC by the dictator Sulla. It shows him in a chariot being crowned by Victory.

he gave to his veterans. After serving as dictator 'for the reform of the constitution', he retired from public office in 79 BC, and died in the ensuing year.

Sulla's attempt to put the clock back failed to resolve political conflict in Rome, but he set the pattern for the final collapse of the republic. Intense rivalry between two generals, Julius Caesar and Pompey (106–48 BC), brought about another civil war after the death of Crassus, on an ill-fated attack on the Parthians in 53 BC. Reputedly the richest man in the Roman world, Licinius Crassus had been part of an informal triumvirate with Caesar and Pompey that ran Rome in all but name. Caesar's victory in 48 BC over Pompey at Pharsalus in Greece made him supreme, and he duly became dictator for life. There is evidence that he intended to assume the status of king and god, prior to his assassination by senators in early 44 BC. Their cry of 'freedom from tyranny' was a cover for preserving their own power and privileges. It made no difference to Octavian (63 BC – AD 14), the future emperor Augustus: his driving ambition first destroyed Caesar's murderers in 42 BC, and then at Actium, off the north-western coast of Greece, removed Mark Antony (82–30 BC) and Cleopatra (69–30 BC), the last opponents to his sole rule.

With the constitutional settlement of 27 BC Augustus (as Octavian was henceforth called after a title bestowed on him by the senate) laid the foundations of an imperial system of government that gave the Mediterranean world peace for two and a half centuries. Essentially this was a monarchy modified so as to make it acceptable to republican traditions. Thus Augustus was not referred to as the ruler but 'the first citizen'. His power, nonetheless, was like that of a king in that it rested on hereditary loyalty, especially of the army, to himself, his family, and his descendants, whether by birth or the common Roman practice of adoption. And Augustus' personality was publicized through the so-called imperial cult, a complex of ceremonies making use of the forms of religion to express and instil loyalty to the first citizen. In theory, at least, the powers which Augustus enjoyed had been bestowed upon him by the senate, the sole surviving republican institution.

An unequivocal statement of the first Roman emperor's power. The title Augustus is accompanied by laurel branches.

By his death in AD 14, Augustus had turned the army into a professional force, extended the imperial frontiers, and reorganized the administration of the whole empire. At Rome for the first time there was a police force, fire brigade and organization for flood control. Literature also responded to the Augustan peace, most notably in the epic poetry of Virgil (70–19 BC) and the history of Livy (59 BC – AD 17). The admiration of Livy for Brutus and Cassius, the assassins of Julius Caesar, did not prevent Augustus from being on friendly terms with the historian, whom he teased for his republican sympathies. Yet the poet Ovid (43 BC – AD 17) did rouse the emperor's anger, and he suffered banishment to Tomis (modern Constanta) on the Black Sea. How anti-Augustan Ovid actually was prior to his exile in AD 8 is difficult to judge. The poet was irreverent towards Augustus' moral line because it was too solemn a target to miss. Ovid's mistake was probably no more than reminding Augustus of the ineffectiveness of his campaign against contemporary social failings. In 2 BC he had had to banish his only child, Julia, from Rome because of her scandalous behaviour. A gloomy and disappointed emperor did not need a fashionable poet to rub salt into his wounded pride: his angry reaction surprised the aristocracy as much as Ovid. But then Roman society never knew quite where it stood in the early years of the empire. The poet Horace (65–8 BC) alone seems to have grasped Augustus' attitude to freedom of speech, when in a brief history of Latin literature he praised the curbing of excessive licence through legislation. Yet this should not be seen as greatly increased censorship, if only because in Rome the tradition of free speech associated with Athens never existed. For the Roman state was always concerned with every public utterance, whether the speaker was a poet or a politician.

Under Tiberius (AD 14–37), Augustus' chosen successor, the atmosphere was soured by a large number of treason trials. After he retired to Capri in AD 26, Rome was left in the hands of Sejanus (died AD 31), the commander of the only regular troops in Italy, the Praetorian Guard. The result was a complete breakdown of relations between the elderly emperor and his chief subjects, with results fatal to numerous senators and eventually to ambitious Sejanus himself. Tiberius survived, hated but in power; his successor Caligula (AD 37–41) did not escape assassination, however. Caligula seems to have aimed at ruling openly as a king rather than as first citizen like Augustus. He came close to recognition as a god in his own lifetime as well. On Caligula's death the senate debated whether to restore the republic, but the praetorians proclaimed his uncle Claudius (AD 41–54). Even though the undignified and unhealthy fifty-one-year-old was a figure of fun, the reign of Claudius was not without its own triumphs, including the conquest of southern Britain between AD 43 and 47. When Claudius died suddenly in AD 54, it was believed that his fourth wife Agrippina, Caligula's sister, had poisoned him in order to elevate Nero, her son by a previous marriage. At all events, Nero (AD 54–68), with the help of his tutor, the younger Seneca (4 BC–AD 65), and the praetorians, succeeded peacefully to the imperial throne. In the first years of Nero's rule Agrippina was the effective ruler, but after her execution in AD 59, Nero was able to fully indulge his extravagant tastes. Public appearances as a charioteer and singer cost the emperor the respect of the aristocracy, but his position was really undermined by the growing insecurity of provincial governors and army commanders, who were tempted to revolt. One of these was the seventy-year-old Galba: his troops in Spain hailed him as emperor, and this was confirmed by the senate. Deserted by the praetorians, outlawed by the senate, and abandoned by all but a few followers, Nero finally cut his own throat.

The Julio-Claudian dynasty was now extinct, and dynastic loyalty ceased to restrain the army. Three emperors – Galba, Otho and Vitellius – were proclaimed by their troops before a fourth, Vespasian (AD 69–79), ended the civil wars and founded a new dynasty, the Flavian. As the historian Tacitus commented, the events of AD 68 and 69 showed that emperors could be made outside Italy as long as they commanded enough military support. The third and last Flavian emperor, Domitian (AD 81–96), was assassinated and replaced by the senator Nerva (AD 96–98), who could maintain power only by adopting Trajan, the commander of the armies stationed in Upper Germany. Trajan (AD 99–117) and his own adopted successor, Hadrian (AD 117–138), were both great soldiers, but credit is due to the latter for rationalizing the imperial frontiers. Hadrian evacuated recently conquered Mesopotamia, built a wall across Britain, and improved the discipline of the legions. He also opened the central administration in Rome to those who had not first held a military commission. The stability of the empire depended in large measure upon the goodwill of the local ruling classes who bore the brunt of provincial administration. Much of the business of imperial government was conducted by means of internal diplomacy, wherein cities sent delegations and letters to governors and ultimately to the emperor himself. The pro-Roman Jewish philosopher Philo (20 BC–AD 50) had headed such a

Under the emperor Trajan the frontiers of the Roman empire reached their widest extent.

delegation to Caligula after a pogrom in Alexandria. Only through such diplomacy could powerful people hope to retain their privileges and prestige, and also, if they wished, to advance beyond purely provincial significance to become senators or imperial officials – possibly even emperors. That revolts against Rome were relatively uncommon indicates the social advantages that the powerful provincial families enjoyed under Roman rule.

The Antonine dynasty (AD 138–192) is often referred to as the golden age of the Roman empire, an image perhaps reinforced by the writings of the Stoic emperor Marcus Aurelius (AD 161–180). It is often overlooked how he was obliged to spend the greater part of his reign defending the northern frontier against German tribesmen. In the devastated frontier provinces Marcus Aurelius settled many of these intruders, a policy that later emperors were to follow at their cost. Internally the granting of Roman citizenship to numerous individuals and communities in the provinces did much to bind the empire together, but the upper classes still enjoyed a special status which protected them from horrific punishments like crucifixion or being thrown to the beasts. Commodus, Marcus Aurelius' wayward son, was assassinated in AD 192 when these well-placed Romans judged the usefulness of the Antonine dynasty was ended. Despite the following Severan dynasty (AD 193–235)

extending citizenship to all inhabitants other than slaves, power had already shifted to the army. For in these much tougher times Rome's survival depended entirely upon a military monarchy. Between the fall of the Severans in AD 235 and the accession of Diocletian in AD 284 twenty-two commanders endeavoured to rule the empire and deal with repeated foreign invasions. That Aurelian (AD 270–275) had to construct a 12-mile wall around Rome, in spite of his own successes against the invading Germans, indicates how insecure the late Roman empire had become. It was given a renewed lease of life by the reforms of Diocletian (AD 284–305), but the price was the establishment of an autocracy that Constantine the Great's conversion to Christianity in the 320s AD did nothing to lessen. Perhaps the other great event of his reign, after the Christianization of the empire, was the foundation of a second capital at Constantinople (modern Istanbul). It

The emperor Diocletian presided over the complete reorganisation of Rome's defences, for which he had to levy enormous taxes.

marked the shift of the political centre of gravity to the Greek-speaking eastern provinces, where the empire's economic and cultural centre had long been.

Apart from an abortive attempt by Julian (AD 361–363) to turn the clock back to pagan times, the rise of Christianity continued unchecked. Even the barbarians who were about to overrun the western provinces of the empire were Christians, although some of them, like the Vandals, were followers of Arius' heretical doctrines. The final century up to the deposition of Romulus Augustulus (AD 475–476) was marked by progressive disintegration in the west, whose growing insecurity led in AD 404 to the removal by Honorius (AD 395–423) of the imperial government from Rome to the safety of marsh-girt Ravenna: in the east, on the contrary, Constantinople was gradually transformed into a new Christian Greek civilization which was to last right through the Middle Ages. A final attempt was made by the eastern Roman emperor Justinian (AD 527–565) to reconquer the western Mediterranean provinces, but within a decade of his death most of the gains were lost again. What Constantinople, or by now Byzantium, had to recognize was the permanent presence there of German settlers. Yet such had been the depth of the man-power crisis facing Rome by the end of the fourth century AD that its army was already largely German. The Romanized Vandal general Stilicho

(died AD 408), appointed guardian of the young emperor Honorius in AD 395, was a potent symbol of German power. One explanation of the barbarian triumph in the west was offered by Salvianus, a presbyter at Marseilles till his death in AD 470. He attributed it to the increasing domination of Roman society by a rich and powerful minority: either the great landowners who could muster large numbers of dependents for their own defence, or the military leaders who had become landowners themselves. According to Salvianus, 'many people chose to seek Roman humanity among the barbarians, because they could no longer support barbarian inhumanity among the Romans'.

See ANTONINE DYNASTY; ANTONY; AUGUSTUS; AURELIAN; CAESAR; CALIGULA; CARTHAGE; CATO; CHRISTIANITY; CICERO; CLAUDIUS; CONSTANTINE; CRASSUS; DIOCLETIAN; ETRUSCANS; FLAVIAN DYNASTY; GALBA; GAULS; GOTHS; HADRIAN; HANNIBAL; HONORIUS; JULIAN; JUSTINIAN; LEPIDUS; LUCULLUS; MACEDON; MARIUS; NERO; PAULLUS; PYRRHUS; POMPEY; ROMULUS AUGUSTULUS; SCIPIOS; SENECA; SEVERAN DYNASTY; SPARTACUS; SULLA; THEODOSIUS I AND II; TIBERIUS; TRAJAN; TWELVE TABLES; VALENTINIAN
*M. Grant, *History of Rome* (London, 1978).

**Romulus Augustulus** was the last Roman emperor in the west, AD 475–476. After the death of the western emperor Honorius in AD 423 a period of steep decline began at Ravenna, where the imperial court sheltered nervously behind protective marshes. What real power there was in the west belonged to the military leaders, who were invariably Romanized Germans. For the various German peoples who were settled in the western provinces, either by arrangment like the Visigoths in south-western Gaul or by conquest like the Vandals in Africa, had effectively declared their independence. The Vandal king Gaiseric (died AD 477) probably did more than anyone else to undermine Roman power in these years. In AD 429 he moved his people from Spain to Africa, where a decade later he occupied Carthage and gained control of most of Italy's grain supply. In AD 431 and 441 Gaiseric defeated attempts by the eastern emperor Theodosius II (AD 408–450) to curb Vandal power, although Sicily was denied his grasp, unlike Sardinia and Corsica. Rome itself suffered so thorough a sack in AD 455 that the Vandals became synonymous with wanton destruction. Then, as earlier, the government at Ravenna proved powerless. When in AD 452 Atilla led the Huns into Italy, it was a pope who had negotiated his withdrawal.

Imperial edicts issued in AD 440 and 443 served only to underline the manpower crisis afflicting Rome. The army had long ceased to offer an attractive career, with the result that it now consisted almost entirely of Germans.

Whole units were also formed on tribal lines, since the policy of spreading recruits among existing ones had ended with the disintegration of the legions, recklessly used up in continuous civil strife. Commanders, often backed by barbarian kings, raised and deposed a string of emperors at Ravenna, some of whom were never recognized by Constantinople. The young Romulus Augustulus was placed on the throne by his father Orestes, a soldier from the Danube frontier. Emperor Julius Nepos (AD 474–475) had fled by sea from Ravenna on the approach of Orestes' soldiers, who disliked this eastern nominee. But Orestes controlled Italy for less than a year, because some of the troops stationed there mutinied over a demand for land. Only in Italy had Germans not been given land in return for military service. They did not insist on receiving two-thirds, in line with Honorius' settlement of the Visigoths in south-western Gaul in AD 418, but instead said they would be content with one-third. Apparently Orestes had promised land in return for support against Julius Nepos, then changed his mind after his son's elevation. A German officer by the name of Odoacer led the rebellion in which Orestes lost his life.

'Then not long after Romulus Augustulus had been dethroned,' the chronicler Cassiodorus noted, 'Odoacer was made king and remained in his kingdom for thirteen years.' Although he immediately sent the imperial insignia to Constantinople,

Odoacer's claim to power in Italy was never really recognized by the eastern emperors, for in AD 488 the Ostrogoths were dispatched against him from the Balkans. Quite possibly Constantinople was as concerned to remove the Ostrogoths from its territory as toppling the upstart Odoacer. In the event it only installed a powerful Ostrogothic kingdom in Italy, which later the eastern emperor Justinian (AD 527–565) had to fight very hard to overcome.

See ATTILA; GOTHS; HONORIUS; JUSTINIAN; ROME; VANDALS

*J. B. Bury, *History of the Later Roman Empire from the Death of Theodosius I to the Death of Justinian* (New York, 1958).

**Sacred Band**, a select formation of the Theban army, was never beaten until the battle of Chaeronea in 338 BC. It won fame on the battlefield at Leuctra, when in 371 BC a Spartan force for the first time met defeat. With numerically superior forces, the Spartans and their Peloponnesian allies might have won an engagement of the traditional type. But instead of deploying his phalanx of armoured infantrymen in a usual line of equal depth, Epaminondas (died 362 BC) concentrated his entire battle-hardened Theban contingent directly opposite the Spartans, ranking them at least 50 shields deep and some 75 wide. The Theban formation, deep but narrow, actually thrust out of the Boeotian line in a point. The Sacred Band, commanded by Epaminondas' fellow general Pelopidas (died 364 BC), was stationed at the very front. Their impact was increased by a cavalry action which disordered the Spartan line at the start of the infantry charge. When Pelopidas saw the confusion amongst the Spartans, he ordered the

Sacred Band to attack on the run. Epaminondas immediately followed with the striking column, and the battle soon turned into a rout. Under this unexpected pressure, the Spartans broke and ran, leaving behind 400 of their number dead. The Boeotian

The monument set up at the battlefield of Chaeronea to commemorate the destruction of the Sacred Band in 338 BC.

forces led by Epaminondas and Pelopidas had shattered the legend of Spartan invincibility. Hardly surprising, therefore, was the prestige enjoyed by the Sacred Band after the battle.

Yet the Sacred Band seems to have been well known for another reason. The unit's morale was associated with uncommonly strong bonds among its members, who comprised 150 homosexual couples. Throughout classical Greece there is evidence that homosexual friendships were a contributory factor to bravery on the battlefield, but it remains something of a mystery that the Sacred Band should have been a Theban unit rather than a Spartan one. At Sparta, unlike Thebes, the separation of the sexes at an early age resulted in overtly homosexual relationships being a feature of barrack life. Formed seven years before the engagement at Leuctra, the Sacred Band was turned into a crack force by Pelopidas, who recognized the value of such shock troops. He kept them together as a unit, which was quartered on the Theban acropolis. Their intensive training, and that of the Theban army in general, certainly impressed the future Macedon king Philip II (359–336 BC): he spent three years as a hostage at Thebes. It was indeed Philip's own military reforms that led to the Sacred Band's annihilation at Chaeronea. The unit was marked down as a target by the Macedonians in order to break the power of Thebes, once and for all. Its members were wiped out to a man, and even Philip

was struck by the sight of the huddled mass of their paired corpses. The historian Plutarch says that the king wept and exclaimed: 'A curse on those who imagine that these men ever did or suffered anything shameful!'

See EPAMINONDAS; PHILIP II; SPARTA; THEBES; WARFARE

★V. D. Hanson, *The Western Way of War: Infantry Battle in Classical Greece* (London, 1989); Plutarch, *The Age of Alexander*, trans. by I. Scott-Kilvert (Harmondsworth, 1973).

**Sacred wars** occurred three times in Greece. They derived their name from the Delphic Amphictiony, which declared war on city-states for acts of sacrilege against Apollo. Amphictionies, or 'dwellers round about', were leagues connected with temples and the maintenance of their cults, such as the oracle of Apollo at Delphi. The most infamous of the sacred wars was the last, which began in earnest with the seizure of the temple treasure by Philomelus in 355 BC. This Phocian commander used the money to hire 10,000 mercenaries and defy other members of the league, especially Thessaly and Thebes. Not all league members opposed Phocis: Athens and Sparta were its allies, while Achaea remained neutral. Philomelus was killed in battle, but his successor Onomarchus twice defeated Philip of Macedon (359–336 BC), who had been invited by the Thessalians to join the conflict. Before Athenian forces were able to reach Onomarchus in 352 BC, however, Philip won a third engagement in Thessaly. The Macedonians entered the fray wearing laurel wreaths as warriors of Apollo. Six thousand Phocians and mercenaries fell alongside Onomarchus, and another 3,000 were taken prisoner. All of the prisoners were put to death by drowning, a traditional punishment for sacrilege. Philip used this stunning victory to reconstitute the Thessalian League, and bind it as an ally to his growing kingdom.

See ATHENS; DELPHI; PHILIP II; SPARTA; THEBES; THESSALY; WARFARE

*H. W. Parke and D. E. W. Wormell, *The Delphic Oracle* (Oxford, 1956).

**Sacrifice** The philosopher Plato (429–347 BC) spoke for the Greeks and the Romans when he said that a sacrifice was a gift to the gods. As their religions managed to do without a theology which insisted upon a set of beliefs, the act of sacrifice was the universal form of worship. Providing a man performed the proper acts in the proper way he could expect to satisfy the gods and obtain their favour. Thus it came about that every undertaking of consequence possessed its appropriate ritual. During times of war the Greeks, for instance, always marched with flocks of sheep and goats, so that animal sacrifices could be performed before crossing a border, choosing a line of advance, building an encampment, or attacking a town. On the battlefield

itself, when the sides were drawn up and facing each other, a final sacrifice was made in front of the battle-line. Prior to the Greek victory over the invading Persians at Plataea in 479 BC, the Spartans would not advance until a favourable sacrifice had been made, even though many of them were being killed and wounded by Persian arrows. After a victory it was usual practice to use the arms and armour of the enemy dead as a thank-offering to the gods who had given assistance. An earlier defeat of the Persians at Marathon in 490 BC was acknowledged by the Athenians to be due to the goat god Pan. This pastoral deity had the power to inspire fear, utter panic in both men and animals.

A Greek soldier sacrifices a goat. Animals were always taken on campaign for such a purpose.

Human sacrifice was never widely practised by the Greeks, although in the third century BC a historian wrote that at one time they always killed a man before going into battle. The most famous example, the Athenian sacrifice of three Persian prisoners in 480 BC

339

before the decisive naval engagement at Salamis, was in all likelihood unhistorical, which is not to say human sacrifice could not have happened. For there is no doubt that Alexander the Great (356–323 BC) deliberately killed those suspected of his father's assassination next to his tomb as a form of sacrifice. The Persians whom Alexander went on to conquer did on occasion sacrifice men, if the historian Herodotus is to be believed. Earlier in 480 BC, he tells us, the Persians captured a Greek ship and 'picking the best-looking of the fighting men on board, took him forward and cut his throat, thinking, no doubt, that the sacrifice of their first handsome Greek prisoner would benefit their cause'. Again it seems an unlikely action for the Persians, whose policy was to endorse the animal sacrifice common at temples throughout their empire. One Babylonian temple kept 7,000 head of cattle and 150,000 head of smaller livestock for this purpose. Although the perpetrators could have been Phoenician sailors serving in the Persian fleet, the adult sacrifice does not square with their notorious preference for child victims. At Carthage, the great Phoenician colony in present-day Tunisia, archaeologists have uncovered thousands of urns containing the remains of small children burnt alive in sacrifices to the goddess Tanit. Yet the Romans were not themselves immune from the tension and hysteria that prompts human sacrifice. Following the disastrous defeat inflicted upon

them by the Carthaginian general Hannibal in 216 BC at Cannae, the Roman populace insisted that two Greeks and two Gauls be buried alive. Two Vestal Virgins, who were discovered to have broken their vows, also lost their lives. The last recorded execution of an errant Vestal Virgin dates from the reign of the emperor Domitian (AD 81–96).

A Carthaginian priest prepares to sacrifice a child. According to Christian commentators, the sacrifice of children survived in Africa well into the Roman era.

But it was in the amphitheatre, according to a Christian convert such as Tertullian (AD 160–240), that most human sacrifices occurred. There gladiators fought in honour of the dead, the earliest public contest having been staged at the funeral of a prominent citizen on the eve of Rome's first war with Carthage (264–241 BC). The competitiveness of Roman public life meant that each gladiatorial contest had to improve on the one before; in 65 BC the senate stopped Julius Caesar from courting popularity by presenting 320 pairs of gladiators, ostensibly in memory of his aunt. Yet there is no real evidence to show that the Romans thought that human sacrifice was appropriate for funerals. It has even been argued that, instead of seeing gladiatorial combat as a public display of killing, they regarded it as a demonstration of the power to overcome death. Through valour one gladiator survived, and sometimes the loser might win back his life, too, by satisfying the audience that he had fought courageously. Such an interpretation would not be at odds with the determined outlook of Rome, the most militaristic of classical states. It is true that the younger Seneca (4 BC – AD 65) regarded the gladiatorial contests with distaste, but this attitude was not really humanitarian; rather, a sophisticated Roman was showing his lack of interest in all spectacles suited to people of simple tastes. An irony of history is the fact that Christians were introduced once again into amphitheatres in AD 303, after the emperor Diocletian was convinced that sacrifices conducted on his orders were being disturbed by the presence of Christians. However, he tried initially to avoid bloodshed, appreciating the danger of making Christian martyrs, that potent symbol of human self-sacrifice in the late classical Mediterranean.

Opposed to all blood sacrifices were

Pythagoreans, a Greco-Roman sect. These followers of the philosopher Pythagoras (died *c*. 485 BC) set their

A defeated gladiator awaits the death-blow; the hand on the left, however, signals that he will be granted his life.

face against the eating of meat and took nourishment from honey and cereals, the foods that they sacrificed to the gods. Their belief in reincarnation, almost certainly in animals, may have exerted the same influence on diet that it did in India, the home of classical non-violence. In spite of the war-torn times, or perhaps because of them, Indians held that the first principle of the saint and sage was non-killing. For both Jain and Buddhist believers there could be no question about the seriousness of this principle. If a Jain monk, for instance, inadvertently swallowed a morsel of meat while eating the food that he had collected in his alms-bowl during his daily begging-round, then his soul was automatically tarnished. A Buddhist monk would be held guilty only if he knew the animal had been expressly killed for him. Should he merely happen to receive some scraps along with the rice that he was offered, he could swallow these with the rest of the dish without becoming polluted. For the Buddhist notion of progress to purity, self-detachment and final enlightenment rested upon moral watchfulness over one's own feelings and inclinations. According to Hindu tradition, people were sacrificed in pre-classical times. Horse sacrifice seems to have satisfied classical rulers, the Gupta emperor Samudragupta (AD 335–376) celebrating his successful campaigns with the solemn rite of a horse sacrifice. After running wild for a year, the horse was slaughtered sacrificially with the most elaborate rites. Its royal owner had

Here offerings of food and wine are being placed in front of a shrine before the start of ancestor worship in China.

demonstrated that he could send herds to graze as he pleased, for the horse had roamed the world itself.

In China sacrifice was connected primarily with ancestor worship and involved the preparation of cooked food. A legacy of human sacrifice lingered into classical times, however. The Second Emperor in 210 BC added to his father's burial at Mount Li (near present-day Xian) the childless members of the imperial harem and the artisans responsible for the construction of the tomb. The event was unusual enough to be specially noted in the account of the Qin dynasty (221–207 BC). For the humanitarianism of Confucius' teachings had already made cruelty and violence into the actions of the unworthy man. In the first century BC a Han prince was posthumously punished for forcing slave musicians to follow him into death: his lands were confiscated and his son disinherited by imperial edict.

See ALEXANDER THE GREAT; CARTHAGE; CHRISTIANITY; CONFUCIUS; GUPTA DYNASTY; HANNIBAL; PERSIA; PERSIAN INVASIONS; PYTHAGORAS; QIN DYNASTY; ROME
*R. August, Cruelty and Civilization: The Roman Games (London, 1972); D. D. Hughes, Human Sacrifice in Ancient Greece (London, 1991).

**Samos** rose to fame in Greece under the tyranny of Polycrates (535–522 BC). The Aegean island had always maintained a navy, but Polycrates increased its size to 150 vessels, with 1,000 archers on board. 'All his campaigns were a success,' remarked the historian Herodotus, 'his every venture was a success.' One of his allies, the Egyptian ruler Amasis, had warned Polycrates that the continuous good fortune he enjoyed would provoke the anger of the gods, and he advised him to divest himself of the thing he valued most. Therefore, in a ceremony at sea the tyrant cast overboard his magnificent signet ring, an emerald set in gold. But it happened a week afterwards that a big fish presented to Polycrates by one of his subjects was discovered to contain the same ring. When he told this to Amasis, his ally replied that anyone whose luck held even to the extent of recovering what he deliberately threw away must be destined to die a miserable death. He also ended his pact with him. In 524 BC Polycrates' luck held and he beat off an attack by the Spartans and the Corinthians, but a year later he was lured by promises of financial support for his schemes to dominate the Aegean Sea to Sardis, when the Persian governor Oroetes put him to death.

The story of Polycrates' ring fascinated the Greeks, who grudgingly admitted the achievements of his tyranny. Besides his naval exploits, he was responsible for three of the greatest feats of construction: an aqueduct driven a mile through solid rock; a half-mile-long mole which ran into 20 fathoms of water; and the largest temple in Greece. Subsequent tyrants performed less well, although they maintained better relations with Persia. During the Ionian revolt of 499–494 BC the Samians briefly deposed the tyrant Aiakes, but he regained his position and ensured that they fought on the Persian side during Xerxes' invasion of Greece in 480–479 BC. At this time he was succeeded by Theomestor, whom Herodotus says 'was invested by the Persians with the lordship of Samos' for his naval services at the battle of Salamis. But it seems likely that Theomester was tyrant sometime earlier than this. His reign was unstable, as he endeavoured to publicly acknowledge Persian authority while privately coming to terms with the Greek city-states on the mainland. At the battle of Mycale, on the coast of Asia Minor opposite the island of Samos, the Samians were disarmed by the Persians once fighting was imminent, evidently because their loyalty had become suspect. After the Greek victory at Mycale in 479 BC an allied council was held on Samos, which was enrolled in the anti-Persian league that later developed into the Athenian empire.

The Samian fleet was a welcome addition to Athens, the prime mover to liberate the Greeks of Asia Minor from Persian rule. Though Samos revolted unsuccessfully from Athens in 440 BC, the relationship between the Athenians and the Samians was close once democracy took root on the island. During the oligarchic reaction in Athens of 411 BC, at the height of the

Peloponnesian War, Samos was the stronghold of democracy. For their noted loyalty the Samians were made Athenian citizens in 405 BC, but a Spartan victory a year later ended this unusual arrangement. In the fourth century BC Samos was eclipsed by nearby Rhodes as a naval power.

*See* DELIAN LEAGUE; RHODES; XERXES
★G. Shipley, *A History of Samos, 800–188 BC* (Oxford, 1987).

The Sasanian king hunting. Like the Parthians, the Sasanians excelled at mobile warfare and prized the bow and lance above all other weapons.

**Sasanians** (AD 226–651) were the third Iranian dynasty of classical times. The first were Achaemenids, the rulers of the Persian empire from 559 to 330 BC, while the second were the Parthian Arsacids (171 BC – AD 226), the enemies of Rome. Revival under the Parthians and later the Sasanians says something for the resilience of the Iranian people, and their culture as a whole, after a century and a half of Greco-Macedonian rule. For following the overthrow of Persia by Alexander the Great (356–323 BC), the Iranians remained a subject people till the Parthians asserted their independence and pushed the Seleucid dynasty (312–64 BC) westwards. Beginning around 171 BC, the Arsacid kings established a power in what is today north-eastern Iran that the Seleucids could never suppress. Thus pressed by the Parthians in the east and the Romans in the west, the Seleucid kingdom contracted upon Syria, which in 64 BC Pompey (106–48 BC) eventually annexed for Rome. The immediate consequence of this annexation was conflict on its eastern frontier between the Romans and the Parthians, a settled animosity which the Sasanians were only too ready to sustain. It came indeed as a rude shock to Rome, after a series of successful attacks on Parthia, that a new and more powerful Iranian dynasty had appeared in AD 226.

Originating in Fars, the southern part of present-day Iran, the new Sasanian dynasty soon caused deep pessimism at Rome. 'Here was a great source of fear to us,' wrote the contemporary historian Cassius Dio, 'menacing not only Syria, but threatening to regain everything occupied by the ancient Persians, all the lands of Asia to the Aegean Sea. For so formidable does the Sasanian king seem to our eastern legions that some are liable to go over to him, and others are unwilling to fight at all.' This king was Ardashir I (AD 226–240), the first Sasanian ruler. The dynasty's name was derived from Sasan, Ardashir's father: he had died shortly after the birth of the future king. From the outset of his reign, Ardashir set about recovering all the territories traditionally under Iranian control, although he does not seem to have had quite the ambition in the eastern Mediterranean that Cassius Dio believed. What he did insist upon was the removal of Roman troops from northern Mesopotamia, where outlying defensive positions existed for the protection of Syria and Asia Minor. Emperor Severus Alexander (AD 222–235) turned down this demand and initially his campaigns against Ardashir were effective. But German pressure on the Danube obliged the Roman emperor to accept a stalemate on the eastern frontier, something an impressive triumph at Rome in AD 233 was meant to hide. Severus Alexander's death at the hands of the mutinous Danube legions two years later provided the Sasanians with much more than an opportunity to recover northern Mesopotamia, because the assassination inaugurated nearly half a century of military anarchy for the Roman empire. So determined were the legionaries to have emperors to their liking that their squabbles raised and pulled on over twenty rulers. Although the Roman recovery can be dated to Aurelian's reign (AD 270–275), even this energetic commander

could not avoid the assassin's knife. He was killed by one of his staff officers on the way to Syria, from where he intended to campaign in northern Mesopotamia against the Sasanians.

Shapur I, the Sasanian king whom the Romans feared most.

Aurelian doubtless intended to rebuild Rome's shattered prestige on the eastern frontier. Unprecedented reverses had been suffered there in battles against Ardashir's son, Shapur I (AD 241–272). The rock carvings commissioned by Shapur at Nash-i-Rustam, near ancient Persepolis, celebrate above all else his victories over the Romans. Immense figures of Shapur and his horse tower above the Roman emperor Philip I (AD 244–249), who hastens to plead for peace on his knees. Of Arab extraction, Philip seems to have disposed of his youthful predecessor, Gordian III (AD 238–244), while on campaign in northern Mesopotamia: his first act as emperor was to conclude an unfavourable agreement with the Sasanians. The

345

second Roman emperor shown at Nash-i-Rustam is the wretched Valerian (AD 253–260), who was captured near Edessa (present-day Urfa in Turkey). Shapur has seized the two raised arms of Valerian, one of whose hands is hidden in his sleeve as a token of respect and submission. Controversy still surrounds Valerian's capture in AD 260. He may have been tricked into a parley with an inadequate escort, or he may have decided to take refuge with the Sasanians to flee his own mutinous army. Afterwards on public occasions Shapur used the imperial prisoner as a footstool when mounting his horse. The Sasanian inscription recounts how, during Shapur's third war against Rome, there 'occurred beyond Carrhae and Edessa a great battle in which Valerianus Caesar was taken captive. Afterwards the provinces of Syria, Cilicia and Cappadocia were burned, devasted, and conquered.' As many as thirty-six cities fell to the Sasanians, who led home over 70,000 prisoners.

Yet this dramatic success did not lead to permanent Sasanian control over the region. Possibly Shapur's real interests lay in Fars, where ambitious projects were underway, including the gigantic carved reliefs already mentioned. The Sasanian king may also have been influenced by the radical teachings of Mani (AD 216–277), a prophet who was born into an ascetic Christian community. Mani's advocacy of worldly withdrawal infuriated the Zoroastrian priesthood, and culminated in the prophet's own execution, but he enjoyed the protection of a sympathetic Shapur till AD 272. The prelate Kartir was particularly incensed by Mani's appropriation of the names of Zoroastrian deities for his own religious purposes. Although as much a systematizer of Buddhist, Christian and Zoroastrian beliefs as a prophet, the dualistic account of the universe propounded by Mani was too close to Sasanian official orthodoxy for comfort, and so Kartir singled out Manichees as the special enemies of Zoroastrianism. But quite unique in the classical world as a whole was the right claimed by Sasanian kings to impose a systematic orthodoxy. Shapur's father had been the first to shed the blood of heretics, a circumstance which makes the relaxed out-

Bahram I (AD 273-276). It was during Bahram's brief reign that the chief prelate, Kartir, assumed the right to control many of the affairs of state by his religious pronouncements.

look of Shapur himself all the more remarkable. Inscriptions dating from the reigns of Bahram I (AD 273–276) and Bahram II (AD 276–279) boast of Kartir's repressive actions against Jews, Christians, Manichees, Buddhists and Hindus.

The short reigns of kings after Shapur indicate the power of the aristocracy, a persistent feature of Iranian politics. Often the nobles were instrumental in establishing their own preferred candidates on the throne. One of them was Bahram I, who was not directly in line for the succession. It was during his reign that the chief prelate, Kartir, assumed the right to control many of the affairs of state by his religious pronouncements. Mullah-like, Kartir pursued the enemies of Zoroastrianism, and within the faith itself promoted fire-worship. 'Images are destroyed,' he made plain, 'because in them dwell demons.' This iconoclasm prefigured the controversy over icons in Constantinople during the eighth century AD, when volcanic activity was thought to be the result of divine anger over idolatrous images. Sasanian coins nearly always show a fire altar on the reverse side, but following Kartir's replacement of cult images with sacred fires Zoroastrianism became almost synonymous with fire worship. Every aspect of official life was related to fire. But religious orthodoxy could not secure victory against the Romans, to whom the Sasanians ceded much of northern Mesopotamia. The usurpation of Narseh (AD 293–302) appears to be connected with this military crisis, brought about by enemy thrusts deep into Sasanian territory.

Narseh had to accept the terms dictated by the Roman emperor Diocletian (AD 284–305), making the Tigris the frontier between the two empires. A Roman advance 'across the Tigris' led in AD 387 to the permanent partition of Armenia as well.

By this time though, the Sasanian dynasty was firmly in the hands of one of its greatest kings, Shapur II (AD 309–379). It was very unfortunate because the founding of Constantinople as a new Christian capital for the Roman empire in AD 330 caused the two great powers to renew hostilities in earnest. Already a Christian state, Armenia was seen by Shapur as both a Roman ally and a religious foe. It was attacked on several occasions, along with the eastern provinces of the Roman empire. The great counter-attack launched by the pagan emperor Julian (AD 361–363) was intended to be a decisive blow in this long-running struggle. At the head of 65,000 men, Julian penetrated deep into Mesopotamia and in AD 363 won an engagement outside Ctesiphon. However, he did not feel able to attack the capital city, and instead withdrew, in order to join forces with reinforcements coming up behind him. Gloom overtook the Romans, the historian Ammianus Marcellinus tells us, once the main Sasanian army approached under Shapur. Its 'presence was betrayed by the bright gleam of close-fitting mail', scale armour apparently invented by the Parthians. Continually harassed by the Sasanians, the Romans limped back to Syria without Julian: he died of a wound received in a cavalry skirmish, a tactic in which Shapur's soldiers excelled.

Although after the death of Shapur, in AD 379, the Sasanians were still preoccupied with the threat posed by the eastern Roman emperors, they had other enemies to worry about as well. The Huns were active on the eastern frontier, prior to their assaults on Gupta India. King Peroz (AD 457–484) had to leave his son Kavadh as a hostage with the Huns, and pay a ransom for his own release, when he was defeated by them in AD 469. Kavadh's own reign (AD 488–531) was even interrupted by a period of voluntary exile with the Huns, after he had failed to deal with determined opposition from both the nobility and Zoroastrian clergy. Order was only properly restored by Khusrau I (AD 531–579), a younger son of Kavadh. This monarch always kept three empty thrones ready near his own: one for the emperor of China, one for the eastern Roman emperor, and one for the king of the Khazars, should they choose to visit him. The arrangement reveals the foreign powers which the Sasanians recognized as their equals. The Gupta dynasty (AD 320–550) had long since ceased to count on the international stage. But the maintenance of the thrones had nothing to do with peaceful coexistence, since Khusrau was happy to raid Syria for the sake of plunder, notwithstanding a fifty-year peace agreed with the eastern Roman

emperor Justinian (AD 527–565).

The Byzantines, as it is usual to call the eastern Romans after the barbarian conquest of the western provinces, made under the emperor Maurice (AD 582–602) a concerted effort to contain Sasanian attacks. In order to deal with foreign invasions generally, Maurice united political and military authority in the provinces in the hands of a single official. Thus began for Byzantium the militarization of the provincial administration, a process which came to comprehend its whole empire. So effective were Maurice's measures that Khusrau II (AD 591–628) sought military assistance against rebellious nobles, who tried to bar him from the throne. Envoys sent to beg Maurice for help are recorded as arguing for mutual respect between great powers. 'It is impossible,' they said, 'for a single monarchy to embrace the innumerable cares of the universe, with one mind's rudder to direct a creation as great as that over which the sun watches. For it is never possible to aspire to the unity of divine rule, and to approach an order corresponding to its completeness.' The Byzantines backed Khusrau, gaining territory in the Caucasus as a reward, so that peaceful relations might have prevailed had not Maurice been assassinated during a military mutiny, caused by a policy of severe financial retrenchment. The Sasanian king used his sponsor's death as an excuse to reopen hostilities. By AD 619 he had overrun Asia Minor, Syria and Egypt, an expansion equivalent to that predicted nearly four centuries earlier by Cassius Dio. Even the True Cross was carried away from Jerusalem as booty, too. For a moment it looked as if the Byzantines were lost, with a Sasanian army stationed on the eastern shore of the Bosporus, massive infiltration by Slavs and Bulgars in the Balkans, and a Lombard invasion of Italy. In Heraclius (AD 610–641), however, they found an emperor worthy of the crisis. He not only kept his nerve, but also drew upon ecclesiastical treasure to rebuild his army, before conducting between AD 622 and 628 a series of gruelling campaigns against Khusrau. The long war has been described as the first crusade of the medieval world. It was accompanied by feverish religious enthusiasm and hatred on the Christian side, which spilled over into attacks on Zoroastrian fire temples in revenge for the desecration of Jerusalem.

By AD 629 the Sasanians were ready to sue for peace. A shaken dynasty relinquished all claims to recently conquered territory, and then endured a series of assassinations that fatally weakened its resolve to resist Arab invaders in AD 641. The Islamic onslaught immediately struck both Byzantium and Sasanid Persia: it was soon to reach Visigothic Spain in the west and northern India in the east. In AD 751 the Arab defeat of a Chinese army on the Talas river (in present-day Turkestan) wrested Central Asia from the Chinese sphere of influence and added large parts of it to the Muslim world. The establishment of an Islamic empire thus marked the final termination of the classical times.

See ALEXANDER THE GREAT; ARDASHIR I; ARMENIA; AURELIAN; CHRISTIANITY; CONSTANTINOPLE; HUNS; JULIAN; JUSTINIAN; MANICHAEISM; PARTHIANS; PERSIA; POMPEY; SHAPUR I; ZOROASTRIANISM

*J. Wiesehöfer, Ancient Persia (London, 1996).

**Scepticism** was a Greek school of philosophy started by Pyrrhon of Elis (c. 365–270 BC). He had taken part in Alexander the Great's expedition to Asia and may have been influenced by forms of asceticism which he met in India. The asceticism of Pyrrhon's school had much in common with the views of the Academy in Athens under Arcesilaus (315–241 BC) and the object of its teaching was close to that of Epicurus (341–270 BC); that is, to secure tranquillity of mind. However, Pyrrhon adopted an extreme form of scepticism, holding that judgement should be suspended because of the unreliability of the senses. After his return from India, he lived in a manner consistent with the view that 'no single thing is in itself more than another'. The commentator Diogenes Laertius also relates how Pyrrhon's friends had to protect the philosopher from carts, precipices and dogs. When asked by one of them on his deathbed if he were still alive, Pyrrhon is supposed to have replied that he was not sure. Such

The tomb of Lucius Cornelius Scipio Barbatus. The Scipios were unusual in favouring burial rather than cremation.

imperturbability could not, of course, produce a body of thought and Plato's famous Academy went into decline through adopting a sceptical approach. 'According to some,' notes Diogenes Laertius, 'one result of Arcesilaus suspending judgement on all matters was that he never so much as wrote a book.' Pyrrhon was more fortunate in having Sextus Empiricus record around AD 200 the main doctrines of Scepticism. A doctor and philosopher himself, Sextus Empiricus dismisses at once the idea of Sceptics acknowledging a number of beliefs consistent with a school of philosophy. 'But if you count as a school a persuasion which, to all appearances, coheres with some notion of how it is possible to live correctly,' he wrote, 'then we can say Sceptics do belong to a school. For we coherently follow, to all appearances, a notion which shows us a life in conformity with traditional customs and the law and persuasions and our own feelings.'

See EPICURUS; PLATO

*A A. Long, *Hellenistic Philosophy: Stoics, Epicureans, Sceptics* (London, 1974); Sextus Empiricus, *Outlines of Scepticism*, trans. by J. Annas and J. Barnes (Cambridge, 1994).

**Scipios** were typical of the narrowness of the Roman ruling class in the middle period of the republic, approximately 300–150 BC. This family held no less than twenty-three consulships, the highest public office. The oldest tomb in the family cemetery at Rome belongs to Scipio Barbatus, consul in 298 BC; its inscription records his military exploits against the Samnites, who in 321 BC had inflicted a major defeat on the Romans at the battle of the Caudine Forks. Scipio Barbatus' son, consul in 259 BC, enjoyed mixed success attacking Carthaginian bases on Corsica and Sardinia. His grandsons, both consuls during the Second Punic War (218–201 BC) suffered defeats at the hands of the Carthaginians in Spain. But family honour was more than redeemed by his great-grandson, Scipio Africanus (236–184 BC), the victor over the Carthaginian general Hannibal in 202 BC at the battle of Zama. Scipio Africanus' first taste of fighting against the wily Hannibal (246–182 BC) was at Cannae, where in 216 BC he rallied the survivors of the worst defeat ever to be suffered by the Romans. Later he was sent to Spain, where he followed his late father's offensive strategy, and won a decisive victory in 206 BC at Ilipa, near present-day Seville. Here Scipio Africanus (his full name was Publius Cornelius Scipio Africanus Major) copied Carthaginian tactics, strengthening his flanks so as to encircle the enemy. By the end of the year Carthage was entirely excluded from the Iberian peninsula. As consul in 205 BC Scipio Africanus' plan of invading Africa while Hannibal was still in Italy was opposed by his political enemies in the senate, but he won the issue and, after training his troops in Sicily, crossed to Carthaginian territory in 204 BC. As planned, successes in Africa brought Hannibal home to defeat at Zama in 202 BC and a peace which finished off Carthage as a major Mediterranean power.

Scipio Africanus was consul for a second time in 194 BC, when he vainly argued that Greece should not be completely evacuated of Roman troops, after their defeat of pro-Carthaginian Macedon, lest the Seleucid ruler Antiochus III (223–187 BC) decided to invade it. This monarch already held Thrace and a fugitive Hannibal was urging him to take offensive action. Encouragement from a number of Greek states did lead to a Seleucid invasion, but for the first time in 190 BC a Roman army crossed into Asia to deal with Antiochus on his own territory. It was commanded by Scipio Asiaticus (Lucius Cornelius Scipio Asiaticus), the brother of Scipio Africanus, who came along as a member of his staff. The Scipios could muster no more than 30,000 men against an enemy army of 75,000; but the Seleucid troops were a mixed lot and, after the recent defeat of the Macedonians at Cynoscephalae (197 BC), Antiochus knew the potential of Roman legionaries. However, a negotiated settlement could not be agreed and a battle took place at Magnesia in 190 or 189 BC. Despite a powerful cavalry charge and a heroic stand by the infantry, the Seleucid army finally broke, its stampeding elephants adding greatly to the rout. Another of Scipio Barbatus' descendants had forcibly demonstrated the power of Rome, and in the process materially enlarged the family coffers. Senatorial opponents demanded to see the accounts for the campaign; an inquiry was established to discover the whereabouts of the war indemnity paid by King Antiochus. It seemed particularly outrageous to the elder Cato (234–149 BC) that Scipio Asiaticus brought back from Asia Minor the first bronze couches, bed-covers, ornate tables, and singing girls ever to be seen in Rome. And Cato's moral condemnation prevailed, for not long afterwards, he drove both the Scipios out of public life.

Yet the career of Scipio Africanus was a turning-point in Roman politics. He was not one of the previously anonymous consuls who with little fuss defeated Rome's enemies; instead, he was the first general to be known by the name of the country he had over-come, Africanus; just as his very greedy brother was called Asiaticus. Much to the annoyance of Cato neither Scipio was afraid to take personal pleasure in display, an un-Roman habit that he blamed on their fascination for all things Greek.

The last great Scipio was also edu-cated by Greek tutors and became patron of the historian Polybius, who was brought to Italy from Greece as a hostage in 168 BC. Publius Cornelius Scipio Aemilianus Africanus Numan-tinus (185–129 BC) was not a direct descendant of Scipio Barbatus, but the adopted grandson of Scipio Africanus. His father was Aemilius Paullus, the victor over the Macedonians at Pydna in 168 BC. Scipio Aemilianus fought there under his command, and after-wards in Greece became friends with Polybius. At the end of the Third Punic War (149–146 BC), he stood with the historian and watched as his own troops burnt Carthage to the ground. The reputation he had gained as a junior officer early in the conflict caused his unprecedented election to the consulship at the age of only twenty-eight; special legislation was required to avoid disqualification because of his youthfulness. In 134 BC he was elected consul once again and sent to northern Spain, where Roman troops were also making slow progress with the siege of Numantia, a city long defiant of Rome. On his triumphal return to Rome, Scipio Aemilianus took the lead among the senators opposing the agrarian reforms of the Gracchi brothers, Tiberius and Gaius. This stance cost him much popular support and, on his death in 129 BC, there were even rumours that angry Romans had murdered him.

See CARTHAGE; GRACCHI; HANNIBAL; PAULLUS; ROME; SELEUCIDS

*A. E. Astin, Scipio Aemilianus (Oxford, 1967); H. H. Scullard, Scipio Africanus: Soldier and Politician (London, 1970).

**Scythians** was the name given by the Greeks to Central Asian peoples living to the north of the Black Sea. They traded with the Greek coastal cities, exchanging wheat and furs for pottery, wine and jewellery. Expert mounted archers, the Scythians pushed south-wards in the late sixth century BC until Persian arms drove them in Asia from what is today eastern Turkey, and in

Europe back across the Danube. In 512 BC, however, the Persian king Darius I suffered a defeat while on campaign north of the Danube. The historian Herodotus tells us that 'the Scythians, realizing how they were unable to cope with Darius in a straight fight, sent off messengers to their neighbours, whose chieftains had already met and were forming plans to deal with the Persian threat'. This combined force obliged Darius to withdraw in some disorder. But the Persian king had already decisively beaten the Sakas, the name given in India to the Scythians still inhabiting Central Asia. These Scythians invaded north-western India in the first century BC, and briefly ruled there. More successful invaders were the Kushanas, who came to control a great swathe of northern India as well as Central Asia between AD 50 and 250.

Greek ambivalence towards the Scythians is very evident in comedies, where they are always portrayed as drunks, and in the reception given earlier by the Athenians in 590 BC to the Scythian philosopher Anacharsis. This man became so celebrated that he was regarded as one of the seven sages. At Athens, too, Scythian archers were employed as guardians of law and order.

*See* DARIUS I; KUSHANAS

*R. Rolle, *The World of the Scythians* (London, 1989).

**Seleucids** ruled an extensive state in Asia from 312 BC till Roman and Parthian arms in the second century BC reduced it effectively to the area of modern Syria. But from the start Seleucid power was in retreat in both the east and the west. At both extremities separate kingdoms arose, carved out of the unwieldy dominions of Alexander the Great. The first Seleucid king, the Macedonian nobleman Seleucus I (305–281 BC), had already ceded north-western India and other eastern borderlands to Candragupta, the aggressive Indian ruler, while his son Antiochus I (281–261 BC) was forced to recognize the independence of Pergamum in Asia Minor. Inspired by the example of Attalus I (241–197 BC), who first took the royal title in 230 BC and gave his name to the dynasty, Attalid Pergamum was to develop, eventually with Roman support, into a kingdom of almost equal status with Antigonid Macedon, Seleucid Asia and Ptolemaic Egypt. By

Seleucus' son, Antiochus I, encouraged immigration from Europe like his father, by granting land and founding cities in a conscious policy of colonization.

the 230s BC a Greek named Diodotus had also claimed independence in Bactria from Seleucus II (246–225 BC). This isolated kingdom, in Central Asia, survived till around 50 BC, when it was overrun by nomadic peoples including the Sakas and the Kushanas.

In many ways the Seleucid realm in Asia provides a striking contrast to Ptolemaic Egypt. It encompassed very different territories at different times, since its frontiers fluctuated violently. To Babylonia, his original holding, Seleucus had added by 304 BC the eastern conquests of Alexander, with the notable exception of India. In the early third century BC he and his son Antiochus acquired most of Syria, Mesopotamia and Asia Minor, but by the middle of that century everything east of the Caspian Sea had been lost, either through revolt or defeat by the Parthians. Although in 200 BC Antiochus III took Palestine from the Ptolemies, after his crushing defeat by the Romans at the battle of Magnesia in 190 or 189 BC he had to relinquish everything west of the Taurus mountains. Whatever its frontiers at any particular time, however, the Seleucid kingdom was very different from Egypt in the variety of the peoples and cultures which it embraced. The Seleucids could draw upon the administrative procedures of the Persian empire, of which their realm was the successor: but any unity had to be imposed by the Seleucid army, a composite force of Macedonian, Greek and Asian professionals.

Quite typical was the action of Antiochus III the Great (223–187 BC) after his defeat by the Romans. He

Although he campaigned successfully against the Ptolemies and on his eastern frontier, Antiochus III discovered in 190 and 189 BC that his army was no match for Rome's legions.

went to Babylon, a cuneiform inscription relates, and with his wife and sons sacrificed at the great temple of Marduk. 'That day,' the local priesthood was pleased to note, 'King Antiochus entered Esangil and prostrated himself.' Following sacrifices to other deities given worship there, 'he went, in the afternoon, out of Babylon to Seleucia on Tigris, the royal city'. The elaborate ceremonies indicate that the Seleucid control was undiminished by the defeat at Magnesia. Not until the Parthians conquered Babylonia in the reign of Antiochus VII (138–129 BC) would the Greek and non-Greek cities of the region be lost. Even though the freedom granted to these numerous cities was largely illusory, as they were subject to royal taxation, many of them were issuing coinage.

One city that gave the Seleucids

considerable problems was Jerusalem, where there was an intense conflict between hellenized and traditional Jews. According to I Maccabees, the pro-Greek group went to Antiochus IV (175–163 BC) and received authority to introduce non-Jewish laws and customs. They built a sports stadium in the gentile style in the city. Somehow they removed their marks of circumcision and repudiated the holy covenant. They intermarried with gentiles, 'and abandoned themselves to evil ways'. The subsequent revolt against this hellenization was led by Judas Maccabeus and his brothers Jonathan and Simon, who between 167 and 141 BC frustrated four Seleucid attempts to subdue Judaea. Concessions wrung from Demetrius II (145–125 BC), prior to his capture by the Parthians in 139 BC, left Simon not only as the secular ruler of Jerusalem, but also hereditary High Priest of Israel. Apart from his decade of captivity, Demetrius was threatened by pretenders and indeed was finally murdered by one of them. The Seleucids staggered through other crises till in 64 BC the Roman general Pompey (106–48 BC) ended the dynasty. He bluntly told the last Seleucid king that he did not deserve a throne, since he could not defend it himself: he had been acclaimed by no more than the people of Antioch. Thus Pompey did away with the Seleucid dynasty, for the good political reason that it was simply too weak to be of any conceivable use to Rome as a client kingdom. Syria thus became another

Roman province, and a bastion in the defence system against the aggressive Parthians.

*See* ALEXANDER THE GREAT; ANTIOCHUS III; ATTALIDS; MACEDON; PARTHIANS; POMPEY; PTOLEMIES; ROME; SELEUCUS I

*S. Sherwin-White and A. Kuhrt, *From Samarkhand to Sardis: A New Approach to the Seleucid Empire* (London, 1993); P. Green, *Alexander to Actium: The Hellenistic Age* (London, 1990); B. Bar-Kochva, *The Seleucid Army: Organization and Tactics in the Great Campaigns* (Cambridge, 1976).

**Seleucus I** (305–281 BC) founded the Seleucid dynasty in Asia. Born in 358 BC, he was one of Alexander the Great's lesser generals, although in 326 BC he commanded a wing of the infantry at the battle of the Hydaspes river, and was in the thick of the fighting against the war elephants belonging to the Indian ruler Porus. This experience may have left a very strong impression on Seleucus, because in 303 BC he was to cede north-western India to Candragupta, founder of the powerful native Mauryan dynasty, in return for 500 of these great animals. In Asia Minor they gave him revenge on Antigonus at the battle of Ipsus (modern Sispin) two years later; this senior Macedonian general had temporarily deprived Seleucus in 316 BC of Babylon, his share of Alexander's empire after the death of the great conqueror. Though Antigonus endeavoured to stop its break-up into separate realms, there was no clear successor whom the powerful generals could serve, for the posthumous son of Alexander was still a child and survived only till 310 BC. As a result, there was almost continuous warfare down to Antigonus' death in 301 BC. Loot at this period comprised not only land and captured treasure, but also surrendered soldiers. After the fighting at Ipsus, the forces of Antigonus were split equally between Lysimachus (360–281 BC) and Seleucus himself, although about 10,000 men escaped to Greece with Antigonus' son Demetrius. These Greek, Macedonian and Asian veterans, whose common tongue was Greek, were a key asset, not least because planted in cities throughout Seleucus' kingdom they provided the means of keeping down and exploiting the native peasantry.

Seleucus was pre-eminently a colonizer by urban settlement. His eastern capital, Seleucia on Tigris, reveals something of his philosophy. Across

Coin of Seleucus I minted in Bactria, one of his eastern possessions. Unlike other senior Macedonians, he remained faithful to his Asian wife after Alexander's death: she was in fact a Bactrian.

the river, connected by a bridge, was the eastern suburb of Apamea. It was named after his Bactrian wife, whom he had married in 324 BC at Alexander's behest. This marriage lasted, unlike others between Macedonians and Asian brides, and Apama was the mother of Seleucus' eldest son and successor Antiochus I. In his western capital of Seleucia in Pieria, on the Syrian coast, Seleucus kept his second wife, Stratonice, the daughter of Demetrius. This marriage took place after Apama's death around 298 BC. The Macedonian-Iranian mixture of blood in his veins may have helped to make Antiochus acceptable as a ruler to his Asian subjects, after Seleucus' assassination in 281 BC. It did not, however, prevent Antiochus from coveting his stepmother, and in 292 BC Seleucus handed her over to his son along with the eastern provinces. Tradition says that Antiochus became so ill with his desire for Stratonice that Seleucus was persuaded by the court doctor to give her up in order to preserve his son's sanity.

Seleucus was struck down in Europe, while trying to capture Macedon, the best recruiting ground for soldiers. So died, according to the historian Arrian, 'the greatest king of those who had succeeded Alexander', being of 'the most royal mind, and ruling over the greatest extent of territory, next to Alexander himself'. Shortly afterwards, in 278 BC, Antiochus made peace with the Macedonian king, his brother-in-law Antigonus Gonatas

(276–239 BC). Thereafter Antigonid Macedon and Seleucid Asia remained on friendly terms, their common enemy being Ptolemaic Egypt. But warfare gradually became less intense as it had to be financed out of taxation, the accumulated treasure of the Persians being by then exhausted.

*See* ALEXANDER THE GREAT; ANTI-GONUS; DEMETRIUS; MACEDON; PORUS; PTOLEMIES; SELEUCIDS

*J. D. Grainger, *Seleukos Nikator: Constructing a Hellenistic Kingdom* (London, 1990); P. Green, *Alexander to Actium: The Hellenistic Age* (London, 1990).

**Seneca** the Younger (4 BC – AD 65) was born in southern Spain. Descended from Italian stock, his father had amassed a considerable fortune either as an official or a trader. He also established a reputation for himself as an author. Lucius Annaeus Seneca found that he had inherited these liter-

Seneca was obliged to commit suicide on the order of the emperor Nero, his ex-pupil, in AD 65.

ary interests when brought to Rome as a boy by an aunt. He was not without a business sense, however. His money-lending activities later helped to stir up the Iceni to revolt under Boudicca in southern Britain.

Because of his poor health, Seneca was probably less exposed to the rigour of a Roman education than his upper-class contemporaries, with the result that he seems to have developed a view of a benevolent universe: something he was to come to doubt as Nero's tutor, then his adviser. Disappointment and anger are evident in all his dark and powerful tragedies. Nothing seems to limit the cruelty that men and women can visit upon one another. Seneca makes the estranged Medea comment: 'Horror, we know, is real. The rest is a dream, pretence, or a children's story we cannot ever quite abandon.' Seneca's own first brush with danger occurred during the reign of Caligula (AD 37–41). The emperor had reached the conclusion, after a severe illness, that he was divine. As a result, he was annoyed when presiding in the senate to realize that Seneca spoke almost as well as himself. Caligula would have put Seneca to death except for the suggestion of one of his courtiers that his consumption would kill him anyway.

Banished by Claudius, Caligula's successor, in AD 41 to Corsica, Seneca had time to pursue his literary and philosophical studies. During his eight years of exile he perfected his famous epigrammatic style while writing a number of important works. One of them, *On Anger*, is a show-piece of late Stoic argument. It was addressed to his elder brother, the same Gallio who in AD 52 at Corinth refused to consider the case put by the Jews against St Paul. Lucius Annaeus Gallio held further governorships before his brother's ruin forced him to commit suicide too.

In AD 49 Seneca received an offer he could not refuse. Agrippina, Claudius' fourth wife, recalled him to become tutor to her twelve-year-old son Nero, the heir-apparent. Doubtless Seneca had the example of Aristotle in mind when he returned to Rome: that Greek philosopher had as his pupil in 343 BC none other than Alexander the Great. For almost a decade Seneca exercised an influence over Nero, who succeeded to the throne in AD 54. Once rid of his determined mother, however, Nero's behaviour became unpredictable and dangerous. In AD 62 Seneca requested permission to retire, was refused, but nevertheless withdrew from the court and moved from Rome. Accused three years later of complicity in a conspiracy, he felt that he had no option but to obey the emperor's command and commit suicide.

Another member of Nero's court who met the same fate was Petronius, the so-called arbiter of imperial taste. But historian Tacitus could have not taken greater pains to contrast the two deaths. Whereas the suicide of Seneca evoked the philosophical calm of Socrates in Athens, Petronius spent his last hours listening to friends 'not dis-coursing on the immortality of the soul, or on the precepts of the philoso-phers, but reciting light lyrics and impromptu verses'. In his will, so far from following the convention of flat-tering the emperor to ensure the safety of his relations, Petronius cynically documented Nero's vices, mentioning the names of his male and female part-ners and the novel forms of sex which he practised with each one. Having sealed the will with his signet-ring, he sent it straight to the court. Tacitus adds how 'Nero could not imagine how his nocturnal ingenuities were known so well.'

*See* BOUDICCA; CALIGULA; CLAUDIUS; LITERATURE; NERO; ROME; STOICISM
★M. T. Griffin, *Seneca: A Philosopher in Politics* (Oxford, 1976); Seneca, *Letters from a Stoic*, trans. by R. Campbell (Harmonds-worth, 1969); Petronius, *The Satyricon*, trans. by P. C. Walsh (Oxford, 1996).

**Severan dynasty** ruled at Rome from AD 193 to 235. It followed a brief period of confusion brought about by the assassination of the last Antonine emperor, Commodus (AD 180–192), the worthless son of the philosopher-emperor Marcus Aurelius (AD 161–180). His successor in AD 193 for three months was Pertinax, the city prefect, until the financial retrenchment neces-sitated by Commodus' extravagance cost him the support of the Praetorian Guard, the only regular military unit stationed in Rome. Its members killed him in March, and then sold the throne at an auction to Didius Julianus, a rich senator. The historian Dio Cassius relates how 'both the city and the whole empire were auctioned off. The sellers were the ones who had slain their previous emperor, and the would-be buyers were the late emperor's father-in-law, Titus Flavius Sulpicianus, and Didius Julianus.' Although the commander of the praetorians was himself soon removed, Didius Julianus found that he had more serious rivals in the provinces, where the legions had proclaimed two of their commanders emperor: Septimius Severus on the Danube frontier and Pescennius Niger in Syria. Negotiations with Septimius Severus came to nothing, and the senators had

Septimius Severus, Rome's first African emperor. Erected at the veteran colony of Cuicul, modern Djemila in Algeria.

Didius Julianus killed after a nine-week reign, just before troops arrived from the north. Within four years Septimius

Severus had eliminated all his rivals and declared his eldest son Caracalla his heir.

The civil war was reminiscent of the strife of AD 68–69, the so-called year of the four emperors, but it lasted longer and proved far more damaging to the empire. Thereafter Rome was hard-pressed by its enemies and there was a severe, although temporary, collapse after the Severan dynasty. It might be said that the work of reconstruction achieved during Septimius Severus' reign (AD 193–211) was frittered away by his lesser successors. Born in AD 145 at Lepcis Magna in Tripolitania, Lucius Septimius Severus probably had some Carthaginian blood in his veins. His family moved to Italy and quickly rose to high office. The future emperor was governor of Sicily before in AD 190 moving northwards to Upper Pannonia. On arrival in Rome he disbanded the entire Praetorian Guard, replacing it with a force twice the size drawn from the legions, and especially those on the Danube frontier. Septimius Severus is said to have cursed the praetorians and ordered them out of the city for ever. The new imperial guard was in reality an expansion of the old German horse guard, first raised by Julius Caesar during the conquest of Gaul (58–50 BC). Now it entirely replaced the Italian praetorians, much to the annoyance of the inhabitants of Rome. Dio Cassius tells us that members of this provincial force were 'clod-hoppers to look at, boorish to listen to, and most dreadful to talk to'. But, unlike the greedy praetorians, they were faithful and knew how to fight. The guard moved into a new fortress on the edge of Rome upon its return from a successful invasion of Parthia (AD 197–199). Since the Parthians had given aid to his rival Pescennius Niger, and raided Roman territory, Septimius Severus was moved to capture their capital Ctesiphon and reassert his authority in the east. Even though he did not attempt to repeat Trajan's annexation of Mesopotamia in AD 115, the blow dealt to Parthia was serious enough to open the way to a change of dynasty in Iran. For the Sasanians (AD 226–651) were about to seize control and become a greater threat to Roman security.

The tougher times facing Rome caused Septimius Severus to favour a new military aristocracy. Army service was soon an increasingly attractive prelude to an official career, a feature of Roman society that did much to revive its traditional militarism. On his deathbed in Eburacum (modern York) the emperor summed up the situation perfectly in his advice to his sons: 'Be on good terms with one another, be generous to the soldiers, and don't give a damn for anyone else!' Yet Septimius Severus made a very bad mistake in insisting that both his sons, Caracalla and Geta, must succeed him, given his knowledge of their rivalry and faults. Caracalla was not only hot-tempered and cruel, but he also pointedly refused to listen to his father's counsellors. Almost his first action was the elimina-

tion of Geta in AD 211, who was cut down in their mother's arms. Some 20,000 of Geta's supporters were to follow him to the grave. Most of Caracalla's reign (AD 211–217) was spent in vain campaigning on the eastern frontier, where at the age of twenty-nine he was assassinated. Only one event makes his reign memorable, the conferring of citizenship on all the inhabitants of the empire other than slaves. Possibly enacted for financial reasons, the measure acknowledged the final breakdown of Roman and Italian exclusiveness. The prompter of his assassination, and his successor from AD 217 to 218, was Marcus Opellius Macrinus, a former gladiator, huntsman and courier. This Mauretanian officer seems to have acted through fear that Caracalla might be intending to put him to death. His own end came in a battle near Antioch against rebellious legionaries supporting the fourteen-year-old Elagabalus, Septimius Severus' nephew. Varius Avitus Bassianus reigned from AD 218 till 222 as Elagabalus because this religious title took precedence over the emperor's other names. He was the hereditary priest of the sun god El-Gabal at Emesa (present-day Homs) in Syria. At Rome Elagabalus' own religious and sexual interests were notorious, despite misguided efforts by his mother to link together Syrian and Italian beliefs. He was married to a Vestal Virgin, an act of outright sacrilege in Roman eyes. As offensive was the status to which he raised the cult of the sun god, making it superior to that of Jupiter himself. It also did not help that at the sun god's festival on midsummer day the emperor celebrated the event by running backwards, facing an image of the deity carried in a splendid chariot. But Elagabalus' attitude to sex was perhaps the most baffling of all, for he was a pathic. Even though homosexuality never achieved the prominence in Rome that it did in Greece, there was tolerance for emperors who exhibited an interest in young men, like Hadrian (AD 117–138). Where bewilderment and revulsion set in was the discovery that Elagabalus expected his pages and slaves to service him.

The antics of the young emperor were ended by another assassination.

One of the oddest Roman emperors was Elagabalus, whose favourite 'husband' was a Carian slave named Hierocles.

So his cousin Severus Alexander (AD 222–235) succeeded to the throne and was dominated first by his grandmother, then by his mother. Trouble on the northern and eastern frontiers eventually brought the Severan dynasty down. In AD 231 the twenty-two-year-old emperor and his mother, Julia Mamaea, left Rome to meet an attack on Syria by Ardashir I (AD 226–240), the founder of the Sasanian dynasty. This Iranian ruler had requested in vain that the Romans evacuate lands in northern Mesopotamia captured from the Parthians. Heavy losses on both sides ended in stalemate, a situation the emperor and his mother probably wished to avoid in another struggle against the Germans. But they badly misjudged the temper of the soldiers stationed on the Danube and were executed for an attempt to buy the invaders off. In AD 235, therefore, the legions there declared as emperor their own senior officer, Maximinus, a man of Danubian or Thracian extraction. He may even have been a Goth.

With Maximinus I's brief reign (AD 235–238) began a half-century of extreme internal instability and repeated foreign invasions. Over twenty emperors tried to salvage the empire before first Diocletian (AD 284–305) and then Constantine the Great (AD 306–337) restored order. These two emperors, however, owed much to the earlier efforts of Aurelian (AD 270–275), who was the son of poor Danubian parents.

*See* ANTONINE DYNASTY; ARDASHIR I; AURELIAN; CONSTANTINE; DIOCLETIAN; GOTHS; HADRIAN; PARTHIANS; ROME; SASANIANS

*A. Birley, *Septimius Severus: The African Emperor* (London, 1996).

**Shang Yang** (390–338 BC) was the foremost exponent of Legalism, the totalitarian philosophy that the Chinese ultimately rejected in the first nationwide revolt against the Qin dynasty (221–207 BC). The subsequent compromise under the Han emperors (202 BC–AD 220) saw the triumph of Confucianism as the official ideology, even though something of the administrative approach of Legalism still lingered in the imperial civil service.

In his copious writings, Shang Yang recorded the argument he used to persuade the ruler of Qin state to adopt his reform programme in 350 BC. It concerned the sanctity of customary law. Whereas the conservative counsellors at court urged the following of established practice in all things, Shang Yang recommended a complete break with past customs. 'A wise man,' he said, 'creates laws, a worthless man is controlled by them; a man of talent reforms rites, but a worthless man is enslaved by them. With a man who is controlled by laws, it is useless to discuss change; with a man who is enslaved by rites, it is useless to discuss reform. Let your Highness not hesitate.' So it was that Shang Yang became chief minister of Qin and set

this feudal state on a path that ultimately led to victory over all its rivals. This was the period of the Warring States (481–221 BC), when the feudal powers were engaged in constant warfare with each other. Already the notional overlord of all China, the Zhou king, was reduced to a ceremonial role in a tiny domain surrounding Luoyang. Yet even the strongest states were threatened by rebellion and war, a situation which Shang Yang's reforms aimed to rectify for Qin.

Shang Yang's dedication, his subservience to the ruler's wishes, almost bordered on the fanatical. When the crown prince transgressed one of the new laws, Shang Yang demanded that he be punished like everyone else. The widespread complaints over his measures and edicts compelled the reformer to stand firm on the issue, even though he recognized that the person of the heir apparent could not be harmed. Therefore, the Qin ruler agreed that the prince's guardian should be downgraded and that the face of the prince's tutor be tattoed, presumably on the grounds that these unfortunate nobles were held responsible for the prince's misbehaviour. It is said that from the following day onwards all the people of Qin obeyed the laws. Yet this fanaticism brought Shang Yang to his own undoing. Unloved, and feared by the nobility and the people alike, he was safe only as long as his patron reigned. After the accession of the crown prince in 338 BC, Shang Yang's enemies swiftly accused him of sedition and officers were sent to arrest him. The fleeing minister at first sought refuge in an obscure inn but the inn-keeper, ignorant of his identity, informed him that under the laws of Lord Shang he dared not admit a man without a permit for fear of punishment. When he was apprehended, Shang Yang's own punishment was to be torn limb from limb by chariots – as an example to the disloyal. The historian Sima Qian felt that 'the bad end the minister finally came to in Qin was hardly more than he deserved'.

Yet even Sima Qian had to admit the far-reaching effects of Shang Yang's reforms. 'Nothing lost on the road was picked up and pocketed, the hills were free of bandits, every household prospered, men fought bravely on the battlefield but avoided quarrels at home, and good government existed in both towns and villages.' But the purpose of this transformation was military supremacy, as the key activities of Shang Yang's totalitarian state were agriculture and war. For he held that the law had to make it worse for someone to be arrested by the police than enter the fray. And the fall of Shang Yang did not lead to any abolition of his reforms, for Qin rulers were not unaware of the political and military advantages of centralized power, a disciplined bureaucracy, and a strong army.

Argument continues over Shang Yang's role in the development of Legalism. On one hand, it is argued that he was the founder of the school of Law; on the other, there is a view that sees Shen Buhai (c. 400–337 BC) as being instrumental in developing the technique of controlling and testing the abilities of officials, an innovation of critical importance in the Legalist approach to government.

See HAN DYNASTY; LEGALISM; QIN; QIN DYNASTY; SHEN BUHAI; ZHOU DYNASTY
*Kung-chuan Hsiao, A History of Chinese Political Thought. Volume One: From the Beginnings to the Sixth Century AD (Princeton, 1979); J. J. L. Duyvendak, The Book of Lord Shang: A Classic of Chinese Law (London, 1928); V. A. Rubin, Individual and State in Ancient China (New York, 1976).

**Shapur I**, the second Sasanian king AD 241–272, continued with spectacular success the aggressive policy of his father, Ardashir I (AD 226–240), against Rome. Taking full advantage of the military anarchy which afflicted the Roman empire after the collapse of the Severan dynasty in AD 235, Shapur launched three invasions of its eastern provinces, capturing the great Syrian city of Antioch twice. Thousands of people were transplanted to new settlements within Sasanian territory. One distinguished prisoner was none other than the Roman emperor Valerian (AD 253–260), who suffered an ignominious defeat near Edessa (present-day Urfa) in Turkey. The hapless Valerian spent the rest of his life acting as a footstool for the Sasanian king

Rome at bay. This rock-cut scene at Nash-i-Rustam shows Shapur seizing Valerian, while another Roman emperor, Philip, kneels before his horse.

when he mounted his horse. That the Romans did not permanently lose control of Syria may have had as much to do with Sasanian restraint as military recovery. For it seems that Shapur was interested in plunder, not in land for settlement. His victories were aimed at clearing the Romans out of northern Mesopotamia, keeping the Armenians within the Sasanian sphere of influence, and providing his forces with an adequate supply of booty. In the AD 260s Shapur acquiesced in an independent Palmyra (modern Tadmor in Syria). An oasis-city on the caravan route from Syria to Babylon, Palmyra also seized the opportunity provided by Roman weakness to establish a brief trading empire. Even though the Palmyrenes harassed Sasanian forces operating in Syria, and encouraged them to leave the devastated province, Shapur was quite indifferent to Queen Zenobia's further expansion into Asia Minor and Egypt. Possibly he saw this brief episode as an aspect of Roman political turmoil, which in a sense it was. For once the emperor Aurelian (AD 270–275) decided to march against Palmyra, the city was easily brought back in AD 273 under Roman rule. Shapur's successor, Bahram I (AD 273–276), avoided a confrontation with this determined emperor because Aurelian was struck down by an assassin two years later, en route to a campaign once again in northern Mesopotamia.

See ARDASHIR I; ARMENIA; AURELIAN; ROME; SASANIANS; SEVERAN DYNASTY
*F. Millar, *The Roman Near East, 31 BC–AD 337* (Cambridge, Mass., 1993).

**Shen Buhai** (*c.* 400–337 BC) was a man of humble origin who served as chief minister of the feudal state of Han for fifteen years with such vigour that its ruler was untroubled by any enemy. Though reputed to be a Daoist, Shen Buhai's administration paralleled the Legalist methods used in Qin by Shang Yang (390–338 BC). At this troubled period in China there was a new spirit of government abroad, a quest for efficiency without regard to traditional morality. Fragmentary though his surviving writings are, Shen Buhai exhibits a concern for correctness in the running of a bureaucratic state. The later Legalist philosopher Han Fei Zi (*c.* 280–233 BC) summarized his theory of government as appointing officials according to ability, demanding that they perform the duties of office, examining the worth of all ministers, and keeping control of justice. While Shen Buhai stressed the position of the ruler, he advocated the use of neither naked power nor harsh punishments unlike the full-blooded Legalist Shang Yang, his contemporary and adviser to rival Qin. In Han the ruler was expected to govern firmly and hold his officials responsible for their actions. Yet strictness in the application of punishments during Shen Buhai's administration still remained chilling. When on one occasion the ruler of Han got drunk and fell asleep in a cold place, the crown-keeper put a coat over him. Coming to, the monarch asked who had covered him, and being informed, punished the coat-keeper but put the crown-keeper to death, on the principle that stepping outside the duties of office was worse than negligence.

Han Fei Zi, who quoted this judgement with approval, pointed out that 'Shen Buhai advocated methods and Shang Yang advocated law'. But he added that 'with respect to law and methods, the two both failed to achieve perfection'. According to Han Fei Zi a combination of strict supervision and pitiless punishment was required for the security of a state.

*See* HAN FEI ZI; LEGALISM; SHANG YANG
★Kung-chuan Hsiao, *A History of Chinese Political Thought. Volume One: From the Beginnings to the Sixth Century AD* (Princeton, 1979).

**Sicels** was the name given by Greek settlers to the indigenous inhabitants of Sicily. They were supposed to have crossed to the island from the Italian mainland. Other early peoples were the Sicans, said to be of Iberian origin, and the Elymi, the descendants of the Trojans. In the fifth century BC the Sicels briefly became a force in Sicilian politics, but after the Syracusan defeat of the Athenian expedition in 413 BC, they fell increasingly under Greek sway. Dionysius I of Syracuse brought most of the interior of the island under his control. Enslaved Sicels doubtless participated in the revolts which convulsed Sicily in both 135–132 BC and 104–100 BC. These arose from the conditions of slaves on large wheat-growing estates, which the Romans had introduced following the annexation of the island in 211 BC.

See DIONYSIUS I; ROME; SICILY; SLAVERY; SYRACUSE
*M. I. Finley, *Ancient Sicily* (London, 1979).

**Sicilian expedition** of 415–413 BC was instrumental in causing Athens to lose the Peloponnesian War (431–404 BC). Even though this disastrous adventure did not cripple totally the Athenians, the extent of their losses encouraged rebellion amongst subject allies and roused the Spartans to a final effort against them. The historian Thucydides regarded the Sicilian defeat as the worst of 'the many blunders' the Athenians committed after the death of Pericles in 429 BC.

The specific reason for intervention in Sicily was an appeal for help by one of Athens' allies, the city of Segesta, in a war against the neighbouring city of Selinus, and its protector Syracuse. This request in 415 BC revived long-standing Athenian ambitions over the island. Pericles' kinsman Alcibiades (c. 450–404 BC) was strongly in favour of intervention, while the respected general Nicias (c. 470–413 BC) counselled caution. In order to dampen the enthusiasm of the Athenian assembly, Nicias said that only a very large expedition could hope for success and was astounded when it voted for Alcibiades, Lamachus and himself to command such an armada. These three commanders were given no other objective than the succour of Athens' allies, but there was an expectation of new additions to the Athenian empire.

From the outset the Sicilian expedition was unlucky. Omens pointed to an unsatisfactory outcome. An unidentified man climbed onto the altar of the Twelve Gods, believed to be sited on the navel of the city of Athens, and castrated himself with a stone. News also came from Delphi that a golden offering dedicated there to the bravery of the Athenians during the Persian invasions of mainland Greece had been pecked to pieces by ravens. Worst of all, one night unknown persons disfigured the statues of Hermes which stood on square pillars all over Athens. As Hermes was the god of travellers, the mutilation of his statues was plainly a warning against the imminent expedition to Sicily. Thucydides wrote that the Athenians 'took the matter seriously', and an investigation was started. At that very moment, in the charged atmosphere of the city, Alcibiades was accused of an act of sacrilege quite unconnected with the desecration of Hermes' statues. Alcibiades demanded a trial before the expedition sailed, confident of an acquittal, but his political opponents persuaded the assembly to leave the charge untried till the war was over. Their ploy was revealed for what it was in Sicily, when a ship soon arrived to bring back for trial Alcibiades and others accused of sacrilege, including the mysterious insult to Hermes. Had

Alcibiades declined to return to Athens, it is possible that the expedition would have mutinied, but he chose to give his captors the slip on the way home and offer his services to Sparta instead.

The result was a serious setback for the Athenians. The members of the Sicilian expedition were troubled that Alcibiades' departure left its direction in the hands of the reluctant Nicias, since Lamachus had little influence over strategy. They became even more concerned when at the suggestion of Alcibiades the Spartans dispatched in 414 BC the experienced campaigner Gylippus to help organize Syracuse's defence. That year Lamachus was killed and Nicias left in sole command. Since the Athenians were unable to force the surrender of the Syracusans through battle, the struggle settled down to a siege of Syracuse. Counter-walls built on the orders of Gylippus eventually thwarted the attackers, who, despite a large reinforcement from Athens in 413 BC, found they had lost the initiative.

One of the commanders of the second Athenian armada was Demosthenes, the inspiration for the famous victory over the Spartans at Sphacteria in 425 BC. Appreciating the gravity of the situation at Syracuse, he urged withdrawal after the failure of a final attack. But Nicias refused to abandon the siege, although the expedition was now close to defeat. Most likely the ailing Nicias feared the wrath of his fellow citizens if he returned to Athens

with nothing to show for the vast amount of money spent. Also his own piety seems to have convinced Nicias of the possibility of divine favour, no matter the difficulties then facing the Athenians. In the end, he had to agree to an overland retreat which ended in death and enslavement: Nicias and Demosthenes lost contact with each other and were defeated separately. In spite of assurances which were given when they surrendered, both were executed. The remainder of the captives, more than 7,000 of them, were perhaps not as fortunate as their generals, for they were condemned to toil in the stone quarries of Syracuse. Some Athenians who managed to return home owed their release to an ability to recite the verses of the dramatist Euripides, since the Syracusans were mad about his poetry.

According to Thucydides, the Sicilian expedition was the greatest single action of the Peloponnesian War. For 'it was the most glorious for those who won and the most disastrous for those who lost. Because the losers were beaten in every possible manner; they met total destruction – their army and their ships were destroyed – and only a few of many returned.'

*See* ALCIBIADES; NICIAS; ORACLES; PELOPONNESIAN WAR; PERICLES; SYRACUSE

*D. Kagan, *The Peace of Nicias and the Sicilian Expedition* (Ithaca, 1981); Thucydides, *The Peloponnesian War*, trans. by R. Warner (Harmondsworth, 1954).

Bronze cauldron with ram's heads, sixth century BC. Excavated at the Greek colony of Leontini in eastern Sicily.

**Sicily** and Magna Graecia (southern Italy) were both settled by large numbers of Greeks before 550 BC, thus becoming for several centuries a western extension of the Greek world. Even following their take-over by Rome, at the end of the Second Punic War (218–201 BC), the Greek language remained dominant in many areas. The Greek cities in Sicily were more successful than those in southern Italy because the Sicels, the indigenous islanders, were relatively weak and inclined to live in peace with the new settlements. Wars were frequent, however, with the Carthaginian cities at the western end of the island.

In 480 BC, the same year the Greeks blunted the Persian invasion of their homeland at the sea-battle of Salamis, the Greek inhabitants of Sicily thwarted at Himera on the northern coast of the island a full-scale attack under the Carthaginian leader Hamilcar. The historian Herodotus underlines the importance of the victory by exaggerating the Carthaginian strength to 300,000 men. During the engagement, he tells us, 'Hamilcar remained in camp trying to obtain a favourable omen from sacrifices, burning whole carcasses on an immense fire; and at last, seeing, as he poured wine upon the sacrificial victims, that his army was giving way, he leapt into the flames and was burnt to nothing.' It is not impossible that the Carthaginian invasion was a result of Persian diplomacy. Critical in the defeat of the Carthaginians was the contribution made by Syracuse, the greatest Greek city in the western Mediterranean. It had been founded in 734 BC on an outstanding harbour site, at the eastern end of the island.

In 415–413 BC, with military advice from Sparta, the Syracusans were strong enough to defeat the great expedition which Athens dispatched against them. But this costly failure to add Sicily to the Athenian empire disturbed the political balance at Syracuse and allowed the return of tyranny. Dionysius I (430–367 BC) ruled the city for thirty years and became the most powerful Greek of his times. He dominated Sicily and southern Italy, despite reverses at the hands of the Carthaginians. Only the intervention of the Corinthian general Timoleon (died 334 BC) rid the island of tyranny and encouraged a fresh wave of Greek immigration. And he also kept the Carthaginians at bay through the organization of a mutual defence system among the Greek city-states.

But serious decline is evident in the 270s BC. Then the assistance of the Epirote ruler Pyrrhus (319–272 BC) was required in dealing with the Carthaginians. He almost expelled them from Sicily, but broke off the campaign and returned his troops to Italy in order to continue his war against the Romans. The failure of Pyrrhus to halt the southward expansion of Rome sealed the fate of Sicily, which was annexed in 211 BC after the siege of Syracuse. Its citizens had dared to flirt with the Carthaginians during Hannibal's invasion of Italy, a lapse of friendship the Romans could never forgive. Under the republic Sicily developed into one of Rome's most important granaries. On its large wheat-growing estates broke out two major slave revolts, in 140 and 104 BC. The attention paid by the rebels in the second uprising to procuring an adequate supply of arms and food meant that the Romans lost control of the island for over five years. Athenion, the rebel leader, used some of his followers as troops and kept others in their customary occupations, so as to feed his kingdom. This Sicilian slave, who dressed like a monarch, may have held a management position before killing his master and freeing his fellow slaves. Yet the inevitable outcome of the revolts here, as well as southern Italy, taught the slaves the futility of contemplating mass rebellions; their protests were better made along safer avenues of resistance that did not attract the might of the Roman army. So it was that Sicily remained for the rest of the classical era a mixture of large estates, villages and decaying cities.

See CARTHAGE; DIONYSIUS I; PERSIAN INVASIONS; PYRRHUS; ROME; SICELS; SICILIAN EXPEDITION; SLAVERY; SYRACUSE; TIMOLEON

*A. G. Dunbabin, *The Western Greeks* (Oxford, 1948); M. I. Finley, *Ancient Sicily* (London, 1979).

**Sicyon** was a Greek city-state on the Corinthian Gulf originally founded by Argos. The Sicyonians effectively asserted their independence from the Argives under a tyranny. A late tyrant named Cleisthenes (600–570 BC) made strenuous efforts to downgrade the historical link. He tried to eclipse the local cult of Adrastus, a legendary Argive king who was buried at Sicyon. After receiving a dusty answer about exhuming the ruler's remains from the oracle at Delphi, Cleisthenes brought from Thebes the bones of Melanippus, who was Adrastus' bitterest enemy, having slain his brother and his son-in-law in a conflict recorded in Aeschylus' play *Seven Against Thebes*. On the battlefield the tyrant was less successful against the Argives, even though the philosopher Aristotle (384–322 BC) reports his reign well for 'treating the Sicyonians with moderation and adhering to the laws'. The tyranny was ended by the Spartans in the 550s BC, when Sicyon became an oligarchy and a loyal member of the Peloponnesian League. During the period of Macedonian and Roman domination the city survived as a famous centre of art, its most celebrated son being Lysippus the sculptor.

See PELOPONNESIAN LEAGUE; TYRANTS

*A. Griffin, *Sikyon* (Oxford, 1982).

**Sima Qian** (145–*c*. 79 BC) was to China what the historians Herodotus and Thucydides combined were to Greece. His *Records of the Grand Historian* brings the history of China from the legendary enthronement in 2697 BC of the Yellow Emperor, the earliest mortal ruler, down to his own times and the hectic reign of the Han emperor Wu Di (140–87 BC). Eschewing supernatural explanation, Sima Qian believed the accession of the Yellow Emperor was the result of his military successes against warlike tribesmen.

Except for a chapter on Wu Di himself, the whole of Sima Qian's text is virtually intact, in marked contrast to the works of his Greco-Roman con-

temporaries such as Polybius and Livy. The missing chapter may be explained by the historian's humiliation in 99 BC.

Classical China's greatest historian, Sima Qian, who was castrated in 99 BC by the Han emperor Wu Di.

That year an expedition under the command of Li Ling, an experienced field commander, was overwhelmed by the nomadic Xiongnu, probably the Huns who later invaded the Roman empire. A memorial about the nomad war written by Sima Qian, who knew Li Ling personally, was misunderstood by the throne and manipulated by his opponents at court; the result was the charge of attempting to deceive the emperor, a perfunctory trial, and castration. According to classical Chinese custom, a gentleman was expected to commit suicide before allowing himself to be dragged off to prison for investigation, which entailed torture until the accused confessed. Alternatively, a heavy fine could be paid to commute the punishment. Sima Qian chose to suffer himself rather than impoverish his relations, because he desperately wanted to finish his history. Whether or not the emperor considered him too learned a man to execute, or whether Sima Qian himself requested the shameful punishment of castration in preference to death, is unknown. Afterwards Wu Di made him a palace secretary, a position of great honour that could only be filled by a eunuch, since it involved admission to the inner palace where the imperial women lived.

No doubt the hostility the historian harboured against the emperor for his unjust treatment was poured out in the missing chapter. Elsewhere in his account of Wu Di's reign a certain bias can be detected. Yet Sima Qian makes apparent his admiration for the Han administration which he served as Grand Historian, an appointment he had inherited from his father Sima Tan in 110 BC. The later years of the Zhou dynasty (1027–256 BC) he dismissed largely as a sham. Its feudalism, which was characterized by ceremonial, meant nothing during the Warring States period (481–221 BC). The Qin dynasty (221–207 BC), by contrast, was a rude intrusion that failed to hold China together because it relied on the philosophy of Legalism, a harsh code that the subsequent Han dynasty wisely rejected in 202 BC. The triumph of Confucianism under the Han emperors (Wu Di's own Legalist tendencies aside) was thus a welcome return to the early years of the Zhou, an ideal age.

It has been suggested that either Wu Di himself or a later emperor suppressed Sima Qian's missing chapter. There is in fact no evidence either way. Court historians were usually protected by the convention that only they were allowed to read what they had written. As each document was composed, it was deposited in an iron-bound chest, which remained locked until the dynasty ceased to rule. Then the chest would be opened and the documents edited into a 'veritable record'. When an emperor once asked about the possibility of examining documents before they were deposited, he was respectfully reminded that judgement must lay with posterity. For the historian remarked: 'My duty in office is to uphold the brush, so how can I not record both good and bad points?'

See HAN DYNASTY; HAN WU DI; LI LING
*B. Watson, *Records of the Grand Historian* (New York, 1961).

**Sima Yan** was a Chinese warlord who established in the kingdom of Wei the Western Jin dynasty (AD 265–316). He styled himself Wu Di, or 'warrior ruler', and presided over the defeat in AD 280 of Wu, the last of the Three Kingdoms. Wei had already annexed its other rival Shu seventeen years earlier. During Sima Yan's reign (AD 265–289) China was reunited and prosperous, with no external enemies threatening any of its long borders. Measures introduced to bring about a general disarmament, after the civil strife of the Three Kingdoms period (AD 221–280), and to regenerate the rural economy, including a reduction of labour due on public projects, led to a marked rise in the population. Additional people in the northern provinces also included the Xiongnu, probably the Huns who later invaded the Roman empire. Large numbers of nomad allies were settled inside the northern frontier as part of a more conciliatory foreign policy. That these people posed an internal threat was not really recognized, although care was always taken to disperse the largest tribes into smaller groups, each under the supervision of a Chinese official. Periods of civil strife were the most dangerous as opposing sides were tempted to call upon friendly tribesmen for aid. This occurred after Sima Yan's death in AD 289, when his relatives fought each other for power. The result was the loss of the northern provinces, and the establishment of a diminished Eastern Jin dynasty in AD 317 at Nanjing.

Sima Yan himself must bear some responsibility for this disaster, since in order to protect himself from palace coups he made the fatal error of allowing twenty-seven sons and near relations to govern separate territories. Their forces were certainly available to support the emperor in the capital at times of crisis, but the growth of provincial power tended to weaken central government, encourage family conflict, and offer the nomads their chance of decisive intervention.

See THREE KINGDOMS; CAO CAO; WEI DYNASTY

*W. Eberhard, *A History of China* (London, 1956).

**Skandagupta**, the fifth or sixth Gupta emperor (AD 455–467), was the last ruler to control an extensive territory in classical India. As a prince he had already been sent against a very threatening enemy, the Hunas, known in Europe as the White Huns. Their migrations in India had a similar impact on the Gupta empire to that suffered by Rome at the hands of their cousins under Attila (AD 434–453): they accelerated its break-up. One inscription says that the Hunas had 'great resources in men and money', and that during his campaign against them 'to restore the fallen fortunes of his family', Skandagupta passed a whole night on the bare ground. Another tells of the 'heroism by the strength of his arms', which was 'an antidote against hostile kings, who were so many serpents, lifting up their hoods in pride and arrogance'. Both inscriptions, dating from shortly after AD 455, indicate the immense relief felt by 'happy men, even down to the children' at the accession of a warrior-emperor. What Skandagupta achieved so brilliantly on the battlefield was the temporary repulse of the Hunas, who were to force their way into northern India five years later. He could do no more than postpone the inevitable, since semi-autonomous governors of distant provinces were only too pleased to exploit Hunas pressure for their own ends. Inscriptions from the final years of Skandagupta's reign give the impression of security and wealth, but the situation was in fact becoming desperate for the Gupta dynasty. After AD 460 the Hunas were left unchallenged in the Punjab, and by about AD 495 they had captured large parts of north India. Thereafter only Magadha, the Gupta heartland, remained loyal for a half-century. By the AD 570s all trace of the Guptas had vanished.

*See* GUPTA DYNASTY
*S. K. Maity, *The Imperial Guptas and their Times* (Delhi, 1975).

**Slavery**, although common to all classical civilizations, was most in evidence among the Romans. Their highly developed sense of property succeeded in turning slaves into little more than pieces of equipment which happened to be alive. Slaves possessed virtually no rights, and slave-owners were expected to keep them in this state of servitude. A law passed in 2 BC strictly regulated the number of slaves a slave-owner was allowed to set free at will. With several million resident slaves, as much as 15 per cent of the population in Italy, it is not surprising that Augustus, the first Roman emperor (31 BC – AD 14), was concerned about irresponsible manumission. The great slave revolts of the recent past, and especially the one led by the Thracian gladiator Spartacus (died 71 BC), still haunted Rome and

made the authorities very concerned about the maintenance of public order. Roman dependence on slaves is apparent by the second century BC.

A captive German mother and her distressed son. The Roman soldier regarded the taking of slaves as a regular form of booty.

One reason for slavery becoming so widespread in Italy then was undoubtedly the plentiful supply of war captives. Whenever a campaign was launched, or a province annexed, Roman legionaries brought home as booty large numbers of prisoners. On occasions a victorious general might be directed by the senate to sell a whole people into slavery. This happened in 167 BC to Aemilius Paullus, a year after his final defeat of the Macedonians at Pydna. He sold 150,000 Epirotes as a punishment for not fighting on the Roman side. The only relief enjoyed by slaves living in Rome occurred during the festival of Saturn each

December. Then slaves ate at the master's table and every household distinction between free men and slaves was suspended: slaves ordered others to wait upon them and addressed their masters without the usual respect. To avoid this annual celebration of Saturn's golden age, Cicero (106–43 BC) always fled to the countryside for the day. As the chief exponent of Roman belief in property, privilege and power, he had given voice in Latin to the Greek view of the inevitability of slavery. Though his own treatment of slaves was humane, Cicero's deepest instincts were affronted when two slaves he had freed chose to leave his household. He even thought of compelling their return by neglecting to register the manumission.

Greek acceptance of slavery as a fact of life finds expression in the *Politics* of Aristotle (384–322 BC). Yet even this attempt to argue that it was part of the natural order of things is hardly convincing, as Aristotle had to concede that too many were enslaved by accident, through warfare, shipwreck or kidnapping. Opponents might point out how slavery was unjust, but they seem to have also acknowledged that it was inevitable. Quite possibly the massive enslavement of non-Greeks lay at the root of this attitude: the number of Thracian slaves, for instance, working at the Athenian silver mines at Laurium before 413 BC was greater than the total population of some of the smaller Greek city-states. For all these city-states were slave societies. It is some-

what ironic, therefore, that the Greeks should have been so concerned about freedom in their opposition to Persia when citizens' lives depended upon the exploitation of people they owned. In Persia itself slavery was never economically important. Although there was a feeling that one should not really enslave free Greeks, slaves formed a regular part of war booty in classical Greece. At Athens slaves could never testify in court unless they had been tortured; the idea was that they were inherently untrustworthy and would lie unless they gave their testimony under pain. Only the Macedonians preferred to manage without a large number of slaves. In Europe they did not reduce those they conquered to serfdom or slavery, although in 335 BC Alexander the Great acquiesced in a decision to destroy Thebes, by razing the city, selling its inhabitants as slaves, and outlawing Theban exiles from Greece. In Asia, however, he consistently spared defeated opponents, his anger being reserved for the Greek mercenaries in Persian service. But Alexander's successors were hard-bitten generals and they had no such scruples over running their own kingdoms. Hence the amazement in 302 BC of Megasthenes, a Greek ambassador to the court of the Indian ruler Candragupta, on discovering that 'no Indian at all is a slave'.

Apparently under the Mauryan dynasty, including the reign of conscience-stricken Ashoka (268–232 BC), there were slaves. The main cause of enslavement here, as in China, was debt. Most slaves were employed in domestic service, agriculture, or the army. They were never segregated, or deprived of the right to own property and earn wages. Megasthenes was sure that the apparent absence of slavery was due to the teaching of the Indian sages which held: 'Those who have learned neither to domineer over others nor subject themselves to others will enjoy a manner of life best suited to all circumstances.' By the time the Chinese pilgrim Fa Xian arrived in India around AD 400 looking for Buddhist scriptures, however, the social position of the lowest class, the peasants, had considerably improved. Under the Guptas (AD 320–550) they also branched into trade and industry, along with those still enslaved. Both were better off than the so-called untouchables, people entirely excluded from the class system. That accidental contact with an untouchable would cause pollution, and necessitate ritual ablutions, left Fa Xian utterly bewildered. What in fact this Buddhist pilgrim encountered in Gupta India was nothing less than the re-emergence of orthodoxy in a form much closer to modern Hinduism, a view of society already outlined in the second-century AD lawbook of Manu.

Before the arrival of the Buddhist faith in China there was an attempt to abolish slavery altogether. The usurper Wang Mang (AD 9–23) drew upon the humane tenets of Confucianism when he forbade the buying and selling of human beings. Slaves already possessed civil rights and could not be killed at will: Wang Mang had no hesitation in ordering his middle son to commit suicide for such a crime. In AD 17, nonetheless, he was forced to draw back from outright abolition, and instead impose a stiff annual tax on each slave owned. Thus slavery survived in China, but an efficient metallurgy was combined with irrigation to boost agricultural production to such an extent that rural slavery was unnecessary. And the Chinese were also more than willing to redeem foreign captives as part of border diplomacy. The majority of slaves remained therefore native-born Chinese who had fallen into debt. Very poor families with no means of supporting their children would sell them as slaves. This was recognized by law and sometimes even encouraged by the imperial government during a famine or civil disturbance. In 205 BC the future Han emperor Gaozu decreed that people living in the environs of the capital might sell their children and emigrate southwards in search of food. Four years later, when his dynasty was secure and the empire at peace, another edict was issued to free those persons who had sold themselves into slavery so as to avoid starvation. In AD 44 there were some 100,000 government slaves, the majority of whom were engaged in looking after livestock. Only convicts are mentioned as working in iron mining and manufacture. Convicts, unlike slaves, were sentenced to servitude for a definite period of time. Compulsory labour on public works provided the manpower necessary for large-scale water-conservancy projects, grain transportation, even the constant repair of the Great Wall. Chinese officials frequently complained about the uselessness of government slaves who 'idle with folded hands', in contrast to the hard-working peasants.

It was once thought that Christianity, rather like Confucianism, was an important factor in the manumission of slaves. Between AD 315 and 323 the first Roman emperor to be baptized, Constantine the Great, banned crucifixion and branding the face as punishments, though these improvements may not have been much solace while slaves could still be forced to drink boiling oil or molten lead. Yet neither the imperial convert nor his bishops were morally outraged by the institution of slavery itself. Christians accepted it as a normal part of life throughout the Roman empire. A well-born lady such as Melania could renounce the world in AD 375 and free the 8,000 slaves working on her Spanish estates without having any impact at all on clerical attitudes. Not even the reminder that human beings were created 'in the image of God', a point made around the same time by Gregory of Nyssa, caused serious reflection. For St Augustine (AD 354–430) the relations between master and slave were divinely ordained, as those between husband and wife. Becoming a Christian did not excuse a slave from his or her duties.

See ARISTOTLE; CICERO; MANU; SPARTACUS; WANG MANG
*K. Bradley, *Slavery and Society at Rome* (Cambridge, 1994); D. R. Chanana, *Slavery in Ancient India* (Delhi, 1960); M. I. Finley, *Classical Slavery* (London, 1987); C. M. Wilbur, *Slavery in China during the Former Han Dynasty, 206 BC–AD 25* (Chicago, 1943).

**Socrates** (469–399 BC), the best-known Greek philosopher, was condemned to death by his fellow Athenians for denying the city gods, introducing strange deities, and misleading young men with his ideas. His refusal to suggest the counter-penalty of exile, which the jury would doubtless have preferred to impose, and the calm he displayed in the condemned cell, was a personal demonstration of the capacity of reasoned argument to free the mind from fear. For Socrates held, according to his most distinguished follower Plato, that his immortal soul would be unaffected by

Socrates was condemned to death by the Athenians in 399 BC.

hemlock, the poison he was obliged to drink.

Because Socrates did not leave behind any philosophical writings we have to rely in large measure on the dialogues written by Plato (429–347 BC), whose stature as an original thinker was second to none in classical Greece. How far he invented, or, less unkindly, reinterpreted the ideas of his elder contemporary remains a matter of heated debate today. What is transparent, however, is the impact that Socrates' relentless cross-questioning had on the minds of those who met him. His razor-like ability to expose pretensions to wisdom by cutting through to the ill-founded assumptions on which they rested was probably bound to cause conflict, if the subject under discussion was religion. For him knowledge was something possessing supreme power and authority: it alone was the source of wisdom. Thus Socrates' outlook presented a challenge to the very concept of Athenian democracy, which operated on the principle that only the citizen-body had the right to determine who should be worshipped and in what manner. By calling for the death penalty, the prosecution was underlining the fact that his behaviour was subversive of democracy and contemptuous of popular belief. That Socrates also chose at his trial to antagonize the jury by suggesting that his punishment should be free meals at state expense for the rest of his life just hardened opinion against him.

See ATHENS; PLATO; RELIGION

*B. S. Gower and M. C. Stokes, *Socratic Questions: New Essays on the Philosophy of Socrates and its Significance* (London, 1991); R. Garland, *Introducing New Gods: The Politics of Athenian Religion* (London, 1992); R. Parker, *Athenian Religion: A History* (Oxford, 1996).

**Solon** and Draco were the Athenian lawgivers. It was Draco who in 620 BC published the first Athenian law code, a concession made by the ruling aristocracy following Cylon's failed bid at tyranny. After this ambitious Athenian noble had won a footrace at Olympia in 640 BC, he married the daughter of the Megarian tyrant Theagenes, who lent him soldiers for the attempted coup. Draco's code was superseded by that of Solon, except for the law of homicide, which remained the basis of classical Athenian practice.

Solon was recognized as an important leader as a result of the recapture of the island of Salamis from Megara. Appointed in 594 BC as a mediator between the poor and the rich, Solon cancelled excessive debts, bought citizens out of slavery, and prohibited all future loans on the security of the person. The abolition of slavery for debt guaranteed the personal freedom of the humblest citizen; it crystallized as well the concept of fundamental, inalienable civil rights without which citizenship would be rendered valueless. Solon himself considered this measure his most significant reform, and he steadily refused any redistribution of land owned by the aristocracy, as had happened at Megara a few years earlier. A free peasantry was Solon's ideal, and indeed, throughout the classical period that Athens was a city-state, it was smallholders who comprised the majority of its citizen body.

Now eligible for the highest offices of state were larger farmers, the so-called 500-bushel men. Through one of these annual posts, the archonship, they could gain entry to the peerage, the Council of the Areopagus, whose life members oversaw the direction of state affairs. Named after Ares' hill, a craggy knoll hard by the acropolis, the council originally advised the king in his capacity of war leader, priest and judge, but with the decline and disappearance of the monarchy the aristocratic councillors were left virtually in charge of the government. The next two classes, the knights, and the yokemen, were eligible for minor offices and the new council of 400, which Solon set up. As the minimum income qualification was not high, most citizens would have served as armed infantrymen, or hoplites. At first the knights, as lesser nobles, may have had precedence over the yokemen, though the latter were able to stand for election as archons from 456 BC onwards. The lowest class of citizens with less than 200 measures of produce a year were restricted to the assembly.

The opening of politics to men of substance marked the end of the nobility's stranglehold on government, though not its dominance. Although Athens had taken the first steps along the path to a democratic system of government, Solon intended that the new council should act as a counterweight to the assembly; along with the Council of the Areopagus he saw it as one of the two anchors securing the ship of state, so that it would 'pitch less in the surf and make the people less turbulent'. Its middle-class members had the task of preparing legislation to be voted upon by the general assembly of citizens. But the calming effect they were supposed to have exercised over debate failed to stop the assembly granting a bodyguard in 561 BC to Pisistratus, who used it to set himself up as tyrant. Solon's reforms may not have prevented Athens, like many other Greek city-states, undergoing a period of tyranny, but he was later revered as one of the founders of its democracy.

See ATHENS; MEGARA; TYRANTS

*W. G. Forrest, *The Emergence of Greek Democracy* (London, 1966); O. Murray, *Early Greece* (London, 1993).

**Spain** had already been colonized by Phoenicians and Greeks prior to the start of the classical era in Europe. According to the historian Thucydides, the Phoenicians had been using promontories and islets off Sicily for trade with the natives until the arrival of the Greeks in the eighth century BC drove them to the western end of the island. It is now recognized that the

Greeks, and not the Phoenicians, were the first to settle in Sicily. The Phoenicians had sailed farther west to the Iberian peninsula, and then used the profits made from its silver to found colonies in the central Mediterranean. Carthage, the implacable enemy of Rome, was initially no more than an anchorage and place of supply for Phoenician ships plying the whole length of the Mediterranean Sea. The foundation date for Gadir (present-day Cadiz) has been put as early as 1100 BC. There is a tradition that the Phoenician city of Tyre had to send out three expeditions before locating Gadir as the site of its chief colony overseas. Outside the Pillars of Melqart, as the Phoenicians first named the Straits of Gibraltar, Gadir served as an entrepot for vessels trading north-wards to Britain and southwards along the African coast.

Rivalry between Carthage and Rome, which lasted from 264 till 146 BC, drew Spain into the political affairs of the classical world. Having lost Sicily and Sardinia to the Romans by 238 BC, the Carthaginians turned their attention to Spain in order to achieve direct control over its mineral resources and to create there an army capable of matching the Roman legions. This policy was especially dear to Hannibal (246–182 BC), who rejected Rome's threats against expansion in the Iberian peninsula, two-thirds of which was already under Carthaginian control. Hannibal led his new army from Spain, crossed the Alps, and ravaged Italy.

On the surrender of Carthage in 201 BC Rome held only the southern coast of Spain, and this remained the extent of Roman territory for another half-century. At first, the Romans had apparently no grand design for extending their control: rather their campaigns comprised a random hunt for peoples to fight and booty to take home. The whole of the peninsula was not conquered till the reign of the first emperor Augustus (31 BC – AD 14), but there was steady penetration as Rome came to appreciate its mineral and agricultural wealth. Three provinces came into existence: Tarraconensis (today northern and eastern Spain), Baetica (southern Spain), and Lusitania (most of present-day Portugal). Later Terraconensis was reduced in size to make

The West Asian goddess Astarte, eighth century BC. Discovery of this statuette is witness to the very early arrival of the Phoenicians in Spain.

two more provinces, Gallaecia and Carthaginensis. The prosperity of all five provinces was hard hit during the movements of barbarian peoples under the western emperor Honorius (AD 395–423), when Visigoths and Vandals crossed the Pyrenees. The latter moved on in AD 429 to Africa, leaving Spain in Visigothic hands till the eastern Roman emperor Justinian (AD 527–565) briefly reclaimed a coastal strip.

See CARTHAGE; HANNIBAL; HONORIUS; JUSTINIAN; ROME

*M. E. Aubet, *The Phoenicians in the West: Politics, Colonies and Trade* (Cambridge, 1993); L. A. Curchin, *Roman Spain: Conquest and Assimilation* (London, 1991).

**Sparta** was once the most powerful of the classical Greek city-states. Yet any idea that Sparta was a city with splendid monuments like Athens would be quite wrong. For as Thucydides, the narrator of the long war between these two rivals, wrote in wonder: 'If Sparta was deserted, and only its temples and its ground plan left, future generations would never believe that its power had matched its reputation . . . without any urban unity, made up as it is of distinct villages in the old style, its effect would be trivial.' The singular lack of fortification always amazed visitors in an age when inter-state rivalries were inevitably settled through warfare. Their absence stemmed from the confidence felt by the Spartans in their own military prowess, a legacy tradi-

tionally ascribed to the reforms of Lycurgus sometime before 600 BC. Possibly as a result of his work Sparta ended up with a distinctive constitution and socio-military institutions. Spartan youth was dedicated from the age of seven years to a regime of training and obedience which produced the most disciplined and feared army in Greece.

Small bronze statue of a Spartan soldier showing tresses. At Thermopylae the Spartans quietly dressed their hair before resisting the Persians.

This unique concentration upon military preparation was made possible by the exploitation of the helots, state-owned slaves who toiled in the fields. Helots comprised dishonoured ex-citizens, prisoners of war, and the conquered population of Laconia; their numbers had been dramatically increased by the annexation of Messenia around 715 BC. Anxiety about the helots rising in revolt haunted the Spartans, who periodically declared war on them. There was even an official death squad which killed rural slaves thought to be dangerous. Recruited from young Spartans, this squad may have been a survival of an early warrior initiation rite, although the philosopher Aristotle (384–322 BC) credits Lycurgus with its introduction. Emphasis on war led the Spartans to expose at birth unhealthy or deformed boys; the future king Agesilaus may have been spared because his lameness was not severe, or his royal blood was revered above others. His father was, nevertheless, fined for marrying a short woman who produced 'not kings but kinglets'. Poor Agesilaus was also unusually short for a Spartan.

The constitution of Sparta was oligarchic. Power lay with a small board of annually elected magistrates, the ephors or 'overseers', as well as the two hereditary and co-equal kings. One of them belonged to the Agiad house, the other to the Eurypontid; both traced their lineage back to the hero Heracles. Sparta was unique in the survival of the monarchy, and doubly unique in having a dual one. Elsewhere the collapse of kingship was followed by aristocratic rule. But in some city-states, such as Athens, Corinth, Sicyon and Samos, a tyrant seized power and ruled arbitrarily. Their rule was rarely long-lasting, except in Sicily, and Sparta was itself instrumental in suppressing tyranny in Greece. But however oligarchic Sparta may have been, all important matters were referred to the citizen assembly: its decisions, however, were usually guided by proposals received from a council of twenty-eight elders, on which the two kings sat as well. The council really needed to consult the assembly only when more than one course of action was suggested.

Sparta secured its position by means of the Peloponnesian League, a set of alliances which obliged most of the city-states in the Peloponnese to accept its leadership. Originally this league may have grown from Sparta's struggle against Argos, once the deployer of a powerful army. According to Aristotle, it was Pheidon, the tyrant of Argos, who first perceived the value of standardized weapons and regular training for infantrymen. By the reign of King Cleomenes I (c. 519–490 BC), Sparta was recognized as the strongest state in Greece. He pursued an adventurous foreign policy and in 510 BC invaded Attica, bringing down the Pisistratid tyranny at Athens. But the oligarchy he attempted to impose there failed despite Spartan military intervention, and the Athenians embarked upon their own notable experiment with democracy.

To Sparta went general command of the patriotic struggle in 480–479 BC against the invading Persians. At Thermopylae King Leonidas, brother and successor of Cleomenes, made a heroic stand with 300 Spartans, to the utter amazement of the Persian king Xerxes (486–465 BC). He fell with his men, fulfilling the oracle given to Sparta by Delphi at the outset of the war that either their land would be laid waste or a Spartan king killed. After the

Persians had been driven out of Greece in the ensuing year Sparta dithered, leaving Athens to continue operations against them at sea. As a result the Athenians built up a maritime empire to rival, and eventually fight, the Peloponnesian League in a long war which lasted on and off from 431 to 404 BC. Defeat of Athens left Sparta unmatched, but once again it did not know how to handle victory. King Agesilaus (444–360 BC) failed to make headway against the Persians in Asia Minor, while in Greece the Spartan resort to force was successfully met by the Thebans under Epaminondas at the battle of Leuctra in 371 BC.

Thereafter Sparta was a shadow of its former self. Messenia was liberated and other Peloponnesian states lost their fear of Spartan arms. Demography and the deadening system of military training were the causes of the collapse. 'The Spartans,' Aristotle said, 'are stable enough in the field but are less effective when they have gained a victory. They do not appreciate leisure and never engage in any kind of pursuit higher than war . . . Those like the Spartans, who specialize in one and ignore the other in their education, turn men into machines.' In the final century of Sparta's separate existence, prior to its defeat by Rome in 195 BC, several attempts were made to break this narrow mould, but it was already too late for the Greek city-state.

See AGESILAUS; ATHENS; CLEOMENES; PELOPONNESIAN LEAGUE; PELOPON-NESIAN WAR; PERSIAN INVASIONS; THEBES; THERMOPYLAE; TYRANTS; WARFARE

*W. G. Forrest, *A History of Sparta* (London, 1968); J. T. Hooker, *The Ancient Spartans* (London, 1980); N. M. Kennell, *The Gymnasium of Virtue: Education and Culture in Ancient Sparta* (London, 1995); Thucydides, *The Peloponnesian War*, trans. by R. Warner (Harmondsworth, 1954).

**Spartacus** (died 71 BC) was the leader of a major slave revolt in southern Italy. With the growing dependence of the Romans on slavery, the uprisings from 140 BC onwards were to be anticipated. Starting in the west, with outbreaks on the island of Sicily (140–132 and 104–101 BC) among its population of nearly one million slaves, and spreading to the east, they convulsed the Mediterranean world for several generations, before slowly dying away. The most terrifying revolt was led by the Thracian gladiator named Spartacus, who between 73 and 71 BC routed five Roman armies and dominated the southern Italian peninsula. According to the historian Plutarch, unnecessary cruelty at a gladiatorial school in Capua triggered the rebellion. 'Less than a hundred gladiators escaped, armed with choppers and spits they had seized from the kitchens. But on the road,' Plutarch relates, 'they came across some waggons which were carrying arms for gladiators to another city, and they took these weapons for their own use. Then they occupied a strong position on Mount Vesuvius, and elected Spartacus as their leader.' He was said to have been brought as a prisoner of war to Rome, while his followers were mainly Gauls, Germans, or other Thracians who had been acquired through the regular slave trade. After a force of 3,000 soldiers sent from Rome was easily routed in a surprise attack, the rebellious slaves 'were joined by herdsmen and shepherds of those parts, all sturdy men and fast on their feet. Some of these they armed as infantrymen and made use of others as scouts and light troops.' Two further Roman forces met the same fate, and the geographical base of the rebellion widened considerably. 'But these successes,' Plutarch tells us, 'did not make Spartacus lose his head. He realized then he could not defy the power of Rome forever.' An attempt to escape northwards was abandoned, even though more defeats were inflicted on the Romans, and in the winter of 72–71 BC the rebels found themselves trapped in the toe of Italy, and unable to cross to Sicily. Crassus (112–53 BC) had brought against them an army of 40,000 men, and reinforcements were on the way from Spain and the Balkans. Spartacus was obliged to break out and accept battle on unfavourable terms. The inevitable result was total defeat; Spartacus died on the battlefield with most of his followers, while 6,000 taken alive were later crucified along the Appian Way.

This terrible punishment was intended as an example to any other slaves who might be contemplating rebellion. It indicates a denial of any human rights for slaves: to the Romans they were merely property. The continued expansion of Rome overseas maintained the inflow of barbarian slaves to the end of the first century AD, but already replacements were having to be found from within the frontiers, a condition that ultimately brought about a lesser dependence on servile labour. The Greco-Roman experience was, therefore, very different from the situation in classical China, where an efficient metallurgy combined with irrigation to such an extent that rural slavery was in large measure unnecessary.

See SICILY; SLAVERY; STOICISM

*K. R. Bradley, *Slavery and Rebellion in the Roman World, 140–70 BC* (London, 1989).

**Stoicism**, a Greco-Roman school of philosophy which originated at the beginning of the third century BC, was influential down to the conversion of the Roman empire to Christianity in the fourth century AD. What is perhaps the most fascinating aspect of the Stoic school is the complete transformation it underwent: it changed from a radical doctrine in the time of its founder, Zeno of Citium (335–263 BC), to little more than a justification of Roman rule. It does indeed seem odd that Roman aristocrats should have been attracted to a philosophy with such a political heritage, even if some members of that school were trying so hard

The founder of Stoicism, Zeno of Citium, arrived in Athens around 310 BC.

to discard its radicalism.

Zeno, who came to Athens from his native Cyprus around 310 BC, characterized all forms of subordination as unjust, a notion that had appeal to city-states then suffering from Macedonian dominance. 'The people of Athens,' the commentator Diogenes Laertius tells us, 'held Zeno in high honour, as is proved by their depositing with him the keys of the city walls, and their honouring him with a golden crown and a bronze statue . . . Antigonus also favoured him, and whenever he came to Athens would hear him lecture and often invited him to his court.' Encapsulated here is the political dilemma facing classical Greece at this period: a once-powerful city-state had become no more than a cultural centre attractive to rulers of large states such as Antigonus Gonatas, king of Macedon from 276 till 239 BC. Zeno himself

refused the royal invitation, but sent one of his followers instead. He preferred to stay in the Stoa, the Athenian painted hall from which his school of philosophy took its name.

In resisting the imperialism of Macedon the Stoic idea of unjust subordination was used by a Spartan king to rally the impoverished countrymen of the Peloponnese. Proclaiming a return to the Sparta of Lycurgus, Cleomenes III (235–219 BC) cancelled debts, redistributed land and admitted to the citizen body dependent allies as well as foreign residents. The violent reaction these sweeping measures met elsewhere in southern Greece arose as much from the coherence Stoicism gave to his programme as sheer disbelief over revolution ever breaking out in oligarchic Sparta. Backed by the Ptolemaic kingdom of Egypt, Cleomenes succeeded in gaining control of all the Peloponnese except the Achaean League, which enjoyed Macedonian support. In 222 BC, however, he was forced to stake everything on a battle at Sellasia, eight miles north of Sparta. His forces were defeated by a largely Macedonian army, and Cleomenes fled with all his family to Alexandria. But refuge there had little to offer the former reformer and in 219 BC he perished in an abortive attempt to raise the Alexandrian poor against Ptolemy IV, the Macedonian king of Egypt.

What Cleomenes had drawn upon in Sparta was the idea that non-citizens should be taken into account and not simply ignored. Whereas a philosopher such as Aristotle (384–322 BC) saw the city-state only as the sum of its citizens, the early Stoics included all the people living in the same place and governed by the same law. Possibly the fact that the first three heads of the Stoic school – Zeno, Cleanthes (331–232 BC) and Chrysippus (280–207 BC) – were not Athenian citizens encouraged such a broader outlook, which also entailed an unusual interest in the position of slaves. Zeno had condemned slavery in a general assault on contemporary society, which in itself was no more than a hierarchy of slavery with chattel slaves at the very bottom. 'Among the wise,' he said, 'all are treated as equal, but among the bad all relationships are based on self-interest.'

In Rome it is hardly surprising that Stoicism interested the Gracchi brothers, the elder of whom consulted Blossius, a Stoic philosopher from Cumae in southern Italy. Although the murder of Tiberius Gracchus in 133 BC marked the end of upper-class solidarity in Roman politics, the ordinary citizens were not to derive much benefit themselves, in part because this disintegration opened the way for military adventurers. As important though was a split within the ranks of the Stoic school, which in 129 BC gave its headship to Panaetius (185–109 BC). This Rhodian philosopher was a close associate of Scipio Aemilianus (184–129 BC), a most determined opponent of Gracchan agrarian reform. Later Cicero (106–43 BC) was to deploy the

conservative ideas of Panaetius for his *On Moral Obligations*, a work on the nature of duty which consistently upholds the regime of property, privilege and power. A late Stoic, like the younger Seneca (4 BC–AD 65), had to console himself with the thought that, since the freedom of the wise was the only type that possessed any moral significance, it was the only one that mattered, so there was little point in examining anything besides moral subordination. It may have been some consolation to him when his ex-pupil, the emperor Nero, forced Seneca to commit suicide.

*See* ARISTOTLE; ATHENS; GRACCHI
★A. Erskine, *The Hellenistic Stoa: Political Thought and Action* (London, 1990); A. A. Long, *Hellenistic Philosophy: Stoics, Epicureans, Sceptics* (London, 1974).


**Sulla** (138–78 BC) was a member of an old but not very prominent Roman family. He managed to combine as a young man 'a dissolute way of life', much to the amazement of the historian Plutarch, with 'winning a good name for himself on military campaigns'. It was his ingenuity that ended the war against the Numidian usurper Jugurtha, whom Sulla captured with the help of treacherous relatives. Rivalry with Marius (157–86 BC), his commander in Africa, may have stemmed from Sulla's belief that he never received proper credit for this scheme. Marius came to dislike him thoroughly and in 88 BC he emerged from retirement in order to replace Sulla as commander of the forces about to be sent against Pontus, in northern Asia Minor. Sulla refused to accept this, and he marched his troops on the capital, which fell without a blow. Marius fled to Africa.

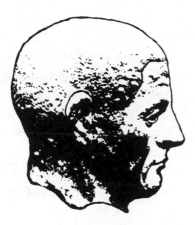

Lucius Cornelius Sulla Felix, dictator of Rome 82–80 BC.

After enacting some constitutional measures which foreshadowed his dictatorship, Sulla left for the war against the Pontic king Mithridates VI. This conflict, which lasted till 85 BC, was the first of three wars to spread over more than two decades. Most of the fighting in the First Mithridatic War occurred in Greece, where in 86 BC Sulla sacked Athens after a siege. Its inhabitants had unwisely thrown their lot in with Mithridates, and were saved from total slaughter or enslavement only by the pleas of Athenian exiles in Sulla's retinue. In the ensuing year Sulla crossed to Asia Minor but, instead of continuing the fight, he negotiated a

peace with Mithridates. The mild terms were dictated by the fact that he could no longer afford to be absent from a Rome dominated by his political enemies.

An outlawed Sulla openly rebelled and invaded Italy in 83 BC. He was joined by Crassus and Pompey, later members of the triumvirate formed by Julius Caesar (100–44 BC). A bitter civil war ended in early 81 BC with Sulla undisputed leader at Rome. He killed his opponents, gave their lands to thousands of his retired legionaries, and embarked on a programme of constitutional reconstruction. For himself he chose the obsolete position of dictator, an office of almost unlimited powers that was supposed to be occupied for only six months at a time. Sulla used this powerful position to reshape the state, enhancing the role of the senate but placing restraints on the authority of chief office-holders. On the one hand, his reforms sought to end the popular disorder fomented by Marius' supporters; on the other, he was determined that no one should imitate his own use of military force. It was an impossible aim. An ailing Sulla died in 78 BC, shortly after stepping down as dictator. Plutarch recounts how he burst an internal ulcer by shouting too loudly when he had a corrupt official strangled in front of him. Lucius Cornelius Sulla Felix's epitaph indeed announced with some satisfaction that he had not been outdone by any of his friends in doing good or by his enemies in doing harm.

See ATHENS; CAESAR; CRASSUS; MARIUS; MITHRIDATES; POMPEY; ROME
*Plutarch, *Fall of the Roman Republic*, trans. by P. Warner (Harmondsworth, 1958); E. Badian, *Lucius Sulla: The Deadly Reformer* (Sydney, 1970); A. Keaveney, *Sulla: The Last Republican* (London, 1982).

**Sun Zi** is credited with composition of the *Art of War*, the oldest known military treatise in the world. The handbook used by Chinese generals from the Warring States period (481–221 BC) onwards, its cardinal principle is the overcoming of an enemy with the minimum of conflict. This realism stemmed from Sun Zi's own appreciation of logistics, and their burdensome cost. 'When all your weapons are dulled and morale is weakened, all your strength exhausted and your treasure spent, other rulers will take advantage of your distress. Then no adviser, however clever, will be able to save your state.'

Though the identity of Sun Zi has long been the subject of debate, his name is usually associated with Wu Qi (430–381 BC), a native of Wei state. Having migrated eastwards to Lu, Wu Qi became a recognized expert in warfare, and received there a military command on the outbreak of hostilities between the states of Lu and Qi. Initially the ruler of Lu hesitated over the appointment of Wu Qi, because the strategist's wife hailed from Qi. The issue of loyalty was settled by her execution. Wu Qi said he could find another wife more readily than an opportunity to direct a campaign. This cold-blooded killing can stand as a symbol of the Warring States period. Despite the exhortation in the *Art of War* to avoid unnecessary fighting and bloodshed, a ruthlessness on the battlefield could no longer be disguised: 'blood for the drums' ceased to be the occasional sacrifice of a handful of prisoners after the fight when, in 260 BC at Chang Ping, the Qin generals ordered the wholesale slaughter of the Zhao captives.

In 387 BC Wu Qi fell from favour in Lu and sought refuge in the vast southern state of Chu. There he became chief minister and reorganized the administration and army, but not with the extreme rigour which Shang Yang later used to reform Qin. The policies ultimately responsible for the new aggression evident at Chang Ping were those of Shang Yang, who introduced his reforms shortly after 350 BC. A new spirit of government, a quest for efficiency without regard to traditional morality, already permeated several of the Warring States, but none of them adopted as enthusiastically as Qin the harsh tenets of Legalism. Like Shang Yang, Wu Qi did not long survive his master's death.

As a commander Wu Qi was severe, but he gained the affection of his troops by sharing every hardship with them. Even though the *Art of War* almost certainly dates from after his death, it is quite possible that the work represents a distillation of his military theory.

What Sun Zi, or Wu Qi, did was to document the professionalization of command. Because the core of contending armies consisted of highly trained and well-equipped regular soldiers, rulers were anxious not to waste in unprofitable engagements such a major investment: thus their growing tendency to entrust military affairs to professional commanders. The *Art of War* was translated into French in 1782, and is said to have been admired by Napoleon.

*See* CHU; LU; QIN; SHANG YANG; WARRING STATES
*S. G. Griffith, *Sun Tzu: The Art of War* (Oxford, 1963); L. Giles, *Sun Tzu on the Art of War* (London, 1911).

**Sunga dynasty** (183–72 BC) was founded by Pusyamitra, a general in the service of the last Mauryan emperor Brhadratha. A coup eliminated Brhadratha in 183 BC and transferred power in Magadha (modern Bihar) to the new dynasty. Pusyamitra may have had the army's support for a more aggressive policy towards intruding Greco-Bactrian forces. Certainly the outgoing Mauryan dynasty had lost all hope of containing the growing threat in the north-west, something which Pusyamitra's numerous campaigns there were designed to meet. Sunga rulers were in fact almost constantly at war, and during the second half of the second century BC the whole of the Ganges valley formed the core of their not unextensive territories. But frontiers fluctuated in the north-west under growing Greco-Bactrian pressure and in the south-east from a revived kingdom of Kalinga, part of present-day Orissa. Buddhist texts portray Pusyamitra as a persecutor of the faith. Quite likely there was deep resentment at his overthrow of the first Buddhist dynasty, since there is no evidence of persecution. The Sunga period did see a revival of brahminical influence and the beginnings of Krishna-worship, but there was also royal patronage of Buddhist centres such as Sanchi in present-day Madhya Pradesh. Perhaps it is telling, however, that a Greek inscription from nearby Vidisha, erected by a Greek ambassador around 100 BC, refers to Krishna and not the Buddha.

The Sunga kingdom was overthrown around 72 BC in a similar manner to its predecessor. A powerful courtier by the name of Vasudeva seized power and proclaimed the Kanvas house. Little is known of the half-century it ruled in Magadha. Invaders from Central Asia ended its days of power, along with the independence of other north Indian states, including the few enclaves of Indo-Greek rule. First the Scythian Sakas arrived, then the Kushanas, the most successful of several Central Asian invaders.

*See* BUDDHISM; KUSHANAS; MAURYAN DYNASTY

**Suren** (*c.* 80–52 BC) was an outstanding Parthian general, who was killed on the orders of King Orodes II (56–38 BC) shortly after his crushing defeat of the Romans at Carrhae, in northern Mesopotamia. This summary execution was not untypical of the feuding that bedevilled Parthian politics. Time and again the Parthians were incapable of exploiting major victories because of chronic internal wrangles. As little documentary evidence survives about individual Parthians, the account of Suren given in the historian Plutarch's life of Crassus (112–53 BC) is invaluable. Suren was the scion of one of the seven great Parthian families. 'In wealth, birth, and in the honour paid to him,' Plutarch tells us, 'he ranked next after the king; in courage and ability he was the foremost Parthian of his lifetime; and in stature and looks he had no equal. When he travelled about the country on his own affairs he was always accompanied by a baggage train of 1,000 camels; 200 wagons transported his harem; 1,000 armoured cavalry and still more mounted archers formed his escort. He had, as an ancient privilege of his family, the right to be the first to set the crown on the head of the Parthian monarch at the coronation. And when this particular King Orodes had been deposed, it was Suren who restored him to the throne.' So it was against this very young commander, possessed of 'the highest reputation' for careful planning and intelligence, that the ageing Roman politician Crassus found himself fighting in 53 BC.

Crassus' ambition to emulate the eastern conquests of Alexander the Great was one of the oddest manifestations of warlord politics at the end of the Roman republic. But then he felt himself to be in direct competition with the military reputations of Caesar (100–44 BC) and Pompey (106–48 BC). Despite his immense wealth, Crassus could only hope to win greater prestige than either of them on the battlefield. According to Plutarch, Suren was able to win because his opponent was 'easy to deceive, first because he was proud and over-confident, and secondly because he was shattered by reverses'. What is perfectly clear at Carrhae is that the Parthians inflicted losses and broke the morale of a larger Roman force. Possibly the bulk of the Parthian cavalry involved in the action had been trained by Suren himself, because the great Parthian families led their own followers in the service of the king. The failure to move towards a centralized kingdom with a standing army explains the Parthian failure to follow up victories effectively. The ruler's distrust of the great families was responsible for the marked reluctance shown over mustering a sizeable army. On the Roman advance Orodes did not have enough troops at hand for an immediate reaction. In 54 BC Crassus was able to cross the Euphrates, capture and garrison several cities and return to winter quarters in Syria, before any significant Parthian force was gathered to oppose him. It may well be that Suren was expected to deal with the invasion on his own.

Orodes seems to have occupied Armenia so as to prevent its king rendering Rome any military assistance. Although this disposition may at first appear eccentric, the blow against the Armenians was shrewd, not least because Crassus expected to receive a much-needed boost to his own cavalry from them. The Armenian absence in 53 BC was to prove decisive once the Roman army had been lured onto ground suited to the cavalry tactics of the Parthians.

For the Parthian army was essentially a cavalry force. Its tactics exploited the mobility of the horse, with swift advances and withdrawals. Suren is said to have commanded an army of 10,000 mounted archers and 1,000 mail-clad lancers, who co-operated well with each other. In direct contrast to the Parthians, the 40,000 Romans were armoured foot-soldiers, equipped for close fighting: they carried a shield and spear, which was thrown, before closing with a short sword. Plutarch relates how Suren abandoned his original plan to charge this infantry force with lances on seeing 'the depth of the walls of shields'. He decided to take advantage of the Roman weakness in cavalry instead: the legionaries soon discovered themselves surrounded by mounted archers, who rode round in Red Indian fashion, pouring into them a deadly hail of arrows from every side. 'The Romans endured all this so long as they had hopes that once the Parthians had used up their arrows, they would either break off the engagement or come to

close quarters,' reports Plutarch. 'But when they realized that a large number of camels loaded with arrows was standing by and that those who had first surrounded them were getting fresh supplies of ammunition from the camels, then Crassus saw no end to it and began to lose heart.' During a lull in the engagement overnight, the would-be Alexander sank into a state of utter despair, with the result that a demoralized army attempted next morning a ragged retreat. Crassus was killed during an abortive parley, and his scattered troops were subsequently hunted down by the Parthians. Of the original Roman force which Crassus commanded, hardly a quarter escaped, for 20,000 were slain and 10,000 were made prisoner.

Plutarch gives details of the fate of a couple of hundred legionaries under a certain Vargontius. Separated from the main body of the army while it was still dark, 'this force was surrounded by the Parthians on a small hill and, fighting back against its attackers, was entirely destroyed, except for twenty men. These tried to force their way through the enemy with drawn swords and the Parthians, admiring their courage, opened their ranks and let them march quietly away.' So complete a victory made Suren the most powerful man in Parthia. Possibly in his excitement he earned the enmity of Orodes, to whom he had sent Crassus' head. Plutarch's account of the antics of Suren immediately after the battle cannot be accepted at face-value, but they probably record some kind of unwarranted display. Apparently Suren pretended that Crassus was still alive in order to stage a mock triumph of his own. He may also have insulted the king's forebears. Suren's execution, however, was part and parcel of Parthian politics, Orodes being strangled by one of his own sons some years later.

See CRASSUS; PARTHIANS; ROME; WARFARE

*Plutarch, *Fall of the Roman Republic*, trans. by R. Warner (Harmondsworth, 1958).

**Syracuse**, on the east coast of Sicily, was founded around 733 BC by Corinth, the strongly maritime city on the Isthmus in central Greece. Its aristocratic constitution was punctuated by tyrannies down to the Athenian siege of 415–413 BC, after which democracy briefly flourished. But renewed conflict with Carthage, however, gave Dionysius I the opportunity to establish a tyranny in 406 BC, which lasted until the expulsion of his son Dionysius II by the Corinthian general Timoleon in 344 BC. Timoleon went on to overthrow tyrannies in other Sicilian cities and also defeat the Carthaginians. But the moderate oligarchy he set up in Syracuse was replaced by tyranny within twenty years, and this was the form of government until just before the Roman sack in 211 BC. For the assassination of Hieronymus, the last tyrant, had left Syracuse dangerously in the hands of pro-Carthaginian aristocratic leaders.

A coin struck in Syracuse to celebrate the utter defeat of the Carthaginians in 480 BC.

Deeply troubled in Italy by the campaigns of the Carthaginian general Hannibal (246–182 BC), the Romans were in no mood to let Syracuse defect to the enemy camp. An army was dispatched to the city, where a swift assault was expected to provide victory. 'But here the Romans failed to reckon with the talents of Archimedes or to foresee that in some cases the genius of one man is far more effective than superiority in numbers.' Thus the historian Polybius introduces the remarkable weapons devised by the mathematician and inventor Archimedes, including skilful defensive works, powerful catapults, anti-scaling devices, and small anti-personnel catapults which fired iron darts. Calling off the initial assault, one of the Roman commanders said how 'Archimedes uses my ships to ladle water into his wine-cups', so badly damaged was the fleet. Even though Archimedes' scientific genius baffled the Romans, in the end Syracuse was betrayed. The gates

were opened, the city sacked, and
Archimedes killed. Henceforth Sicily
was a Roman province, and its administrators bled it even whiter than its
home-grown tyrants had done. As the
island's chief city Syracuse bore the
brunt of this exploitation, especially
under Gaius Verres. This notorious
Roman governor was successfully
prosecuted by Cicero in 70 BC.

*See* CARTHAGE; CICERO; DIONYSIUS I;
ROME; TIMOLEON
*M. I. Finley, *Ancient Sicily* (London,
1979).

**Thebes** was the leading city of Boeotia in central Greece. Its hostility to Athens dates from 519 BC, when a Theban attack on the border city of Plataea was only just thwarted through Athenian aid. As a punishment for siding with the Persians during Xerxes' invasion of Greece in 480–479 BC, Thebes lost its predominant position in the Boeotian confederacy. But the long Peloponnesian War (431–404 BC) gave it a chance to recover at the expense of its smaller neighbours, the territory of Plataea being absorbed in 427 BC. After the defeat of Athens in 404 BC, the Spartans tried to impose their will throughout Greece, even placing a garrison in the Theban citadel in 382 BC. King Agesilaus (444–360 BC) of Sparta also supported four years later a commander who unsuccessfully tried to repeat the trick by seizing at night the Piraeus, the port of Athens. In response to this blatant provocation, Athens and Thebes drew together with other states to resist Spartan aggression. Yet despite their common fear of Sparta, they had essen-tially different interests: Theban concerns centred on the mainland, while Athens as a commercial state looked to the sea. So by 375 BC Thebes revived the Boeotian confederacy and introduced military reforms to overcome the Spartans on the battlefield. Ably commanded by two of their generals, Epaminondas and Pelopidas, the Thebans exploded the myth of Spartan invincibility at Leuctra in 371 BC. The knockout blow was delivered by the Sacred Band, an élite infantry force of 150 homosexual couples led by Pelopidas (died 364 BC). Its attack in column broke the Spartan battle-line.

Afterwards Epaminondas took an army into the Peloponnese and permanently injured the Spartan war machine by liberating the Messenian helots, state-owned slaves. But his own death there at the battle of Mantineia in 362 BC marked the end of Theban importance outside Boeotia itself. Fear of Philip II of Macedon later brought Thebes and Athens into an active alliance once again, until at Chaeronea in 338 BC their forces were beaten by the improved tactics of the Macedonians. Philip is said to have wept at the sight of the fallen Sacred Band, lying together as paired corpses. But pity for these brave men did not prevent his son Alexander the Great from destroying Thebes four years later, after a brief revolt. The new Macedonian king was careful, however, to let the Greek states determine the sentence of destruction, and the selling of its 30,000 inhabitants as slaves.

See AGESILAUS; ALEXANDER THE GREAT; EPAMINONDAS; PHILIP II; SACRED BAND; WARFARE

*R. J. Buck, *Boiotia and the Boiotian Leagues, 432–372 BC* (Edmonton, 1994); J. Buckler, *The Theban Hegemony, 371–362 BC* (Cambridge, Mass., 1980).

**Themistocles** (*c.* 528–462 BC) had the foresight to persuade the Athenians that their salvation against the Persians lay in a powerful fleet. On his recommendation in 483 BC the Athenian assembly voted to devote the profits from a newly discovered vein of silver at the state mines in Laurium to the construction of 200 warships. As the historian Herodotus remarked, this decision 'saved Greece by forcing Athens to become a maritime power'.

Themistocles had taken over the leadership of the democratic party in 493 BC. Intense rivalry with the aristocratic party, even after the fall and death of Miltiades in 489 BC, was marked by numerous attempts at ostracism, which Themistocles survived. There is no doubt that he had gained control of Cleisthenes' political

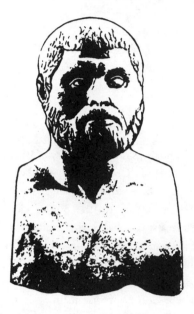

Themistocles was the architect of Greek naval supremacy, a critical factor in the defence of the Greek mainland against the Persians.

following. The moderate democratic reforms which in 508 BC Cleisthenes used to reduce the importance of local influence and aristocratic control of religious shrines had made citizens living in and around Athens a powerful voice in the assembly; they also encouraged these poorer Athenians to be lukewarm towards the policies of the great landowning families unless they coincided with their own wishes. Themistocles' naval programme won their approval, and his own use of ostracism removed all his political enemies from the scene. The ascendancy of Themistocles might have lasted a very long time, and the power of the aristocrats, whose leaders languished in exile, might have been permanently reduced were it not for the invasion of the Greek mainland in 480–479 BC by the Persian king Xerxes. A recall of exiles weakened Themistocles' position, even though he was honoured as author of the naval victory at Salamis in 480 BC, and allowed the son of Miltiades, Cimon (510–450 BC), to rally the aristocratic party. The energetic campaigning of Cimon after the repulse of the Persians made him a formidable political rival to Themistocles, who in 471 BC was eventually ostracized himself. The democrats, however, later recovered under the leadership of Ephialtes (died 461 BC), and then Pericles (c. 495–429 BC), ushering in what the historian Plutarch called 'a thoroughgoing democracy'.

Themistocles was remembered, therefore, for his defence of Athens against the Persians rather than the advancement of the democratic cause. In the face of an overland invasion the city of Athens was indefensible. Only the Peloponnese seemed to offer a safe refuge for the Greeks, since fighting on its narrow isthmus reduced the advantage in numbers enjoyed by the Persians. But removal of the Athenian population behind the line of this defence was out of the question. Themistocles proposed instead an evacuation to the nearby island of Salamis, which could be protected by the new fleet which had just been completed on his recommendation. Such a move meant the abandonment of the city's temples and shrines, a price for political survival that very many Athenians found to be far too high. An oracle delivered at Delphi about protection coming from 'a wooden wall' was interpreted variously as the doors of the acropolis and the warships. Because the naval victory at Salamis in 480 BC was won, like the Athenian success at Marathon a decade earlier, against superior odds, the unexpected outcome was similarly attributed to supernatural agency. All the historical evidence, however, clearly points to Themistocles' daring interpretation of the Delphic utterance to mean nothing else but his Salamis strategy. He staked everything on seapower to save Athens. And few victories have ever depended more upon the intelligence and resolve of one man. Weeks before the battle it was nearly decided not to face the Persians at sea. Themistocles let a bribe of 30 talents pass to the Spartan admiral in order to prevent his dispersal of the Greek fleet at Artemisium, where the Persians were first encountered. On the night before the battle the Greek fleet almost abandoned the Athenians on Salamis by withdrawing to the Peloponnese. Themistocles stopped this from happening through a message carried by a slave to the Persians: it told them to blockade the Greek fleet lest the withdrawal take place. Minutes before the battle began Themistocles steadied

Greek nerves and exhorted the fighting men from all contingents to win the day. A disputed passage in Plutarch says that he was even prevailed upon by the Athenians to sacrifice three Persian prisoners to the god Dionysus just as the fighting got underway. Though revolted by the deed, Themistocles is said to have tolerated it because his fellow citizens were convinced of the need by a seer named Euphrantides, who claimed that human sacrifice alone would ensure a Greek victory.

It is somewhat ironic that the single-minded victor of Salamis should have spent his final years living under Persian rule. But after his banishment from Athens in 471 BC Themistocles annoyed the Spartans by taking up residence with the Argives, their traditional enemies in the Peloponnese. Forced to flee to Persia, he was well received by King Artaxerxes I and given 200 talents, that amount being the price set for his capture. He died in 462 BC as the governor of the Greek city of Magnesia in Asia Minor – it is rumoured from a draught of poison which he had taken in order to avoid helping the Persians against Cimon, the Athenian general then engaged in establishing the supremacy of the Delian League.

See ATHENS; CIMON; CLEISTHENES; DELIAN LEAGUE; MILTIADES; ORACLES; PERSIAN INVASIONS; SPARTA

*F. J. Frost, *Plutarch's Themistocles: A Historical Commentary* (Princeton, 1980); R. J. Lenardon, *The Saga of Themistocles* (London, 1978); A. J. Podlecki, *The Life of Themistocles* (Montreal, 1975); Plutarch, *The Rise and Fall of Athens: Nine Greek Lives*, trans. by I. Scott-Kilvert (Harmondsworth, 1960).

**Theodosius I** the Great, Roman emperor AD 379–395, hailed from Spain, where his father held a senior military position. The future emperor served in AD 368 on his father's staff during the reconquest of Britain, after a brief period of invasion and rebellion. Though hardly critical to the imperial defences, the turmoil on the island was not untypical of the situation along most of the northern frontier, as barbarian attack alternated with unrest among Roman commanders. Theodosius was to discover in the late AD 380s, after his successful conclusion

Theodosius I with a halo. Conversion to Christianity did not lessen imperial authority but, rather, gave it divine sanction.

of the war against the Visigoths, that usurpers could quickly threaten the integrity of the empire by depleting its scarce military resources.

Rome was at this time suffering from a severe manpower crisis, not entirely connected with a decline in the general population. Imperial edicts repeatedly point to the obstruction of army recruiters by the wealthy landowning classes. This was particularly troublesome in the older Mediterranean provinces, where villa-based agriculture still flourished with the labour of slaves and semi-dependent workers. Another problem for the authorities was the growing unattractiveness of military service, and the extent to which individuals would go to avoid conscription. An imperial edict even cites 'the disgraceful amputation of the fingers to evade the use of arms'. Added to the shortage of recruits was the struggle to pay those who joined the army, a further symptom of imperial decline. The burden of taxation caused widespread complaint, appeal and flight. Civil unrest and government oppression certainly provided adherents for would-be usurpers, since the lowest orders of society are known to have rallied to several of them, including Magnus Maximus. This rebellious commander from Britain overran Gaul in AD 383 and secured Theodosius' initial recognition. But when in AD 387 he suddenly invaded Italy, Theodosius skilfully deployed German and Hunnish troops to destroy him. The emperor won, but only

through fielding an army that was largely non-Roman.

Recruitment of barbarians settled within the imperial frontiers, or living beyond them, was not a new policy. Foreign captives had often long been spared death or years of slavery in return for their enlistment. There were set procedures for the recruitment, training, and stationing of such troops in order to ensure their loyalty and the stability of the regular units they joined. Where the practice differed under Theodosius was in its sheer extent, for as a result of the disastrous defeat of the emperor Valens in AD 378 by the Visigoths at Adrianople (modern Edirne in Bulgaria), the Roman army was seriously under-strength. And after he had dealt with this unexpected reverse, Theodosius had still to settle the surrendered Visigoths within the empire, and so he chose to enlist many of them in his own forces. As one contemporary noted with satisfaction: 'The emperor entered the city of Constantinople as a victor, and made a treaty with Athanaric, the king of the Goths, in order that he might not exhaust the small body of Roman troops by continual campaigning. Athanaric, however, died immediately after reaching Constantinople. Upon the death of their king, all the Gothic tribes, on seeing the bravery and kindness of Theodosius, submitted to Roman rule.'

The young emperor Gratian (AD 367–383), Valens' nephew, had called Theodosius out of retirement and appointed him co-emperor of 'Thrace and the East'. Priority was given to Thrace because there the Visigoths remained unsubdued. Hard fighting brought about the peace agreed with Athanaric in AD 381, but it was novel in one important respect: for the first time, Rome was obliged to accept as an ally a whole barbarian people, settled on land within the empire and yet living under its own laws and ruler. Similar agreements with other German tribes helped to fill the gap in civilian and military manpower in the frontier provinces and to turn armed attacks into peaceful invasions. But there were dangers: Theodosius' army now consisted largely of Germans, and so did the armies of western usurpers challenging him for the throne. The limits of Roman power were thus becoming increasingly clear. Rather like the situation in classical China during the Western Jin dynasty (AD 265–316), civil wars were extremely dangerous once barbarian tribesmen joined opposing sides. Just as their involvement led to the temporary loss of the northern provinces of China in AD 317, so it was in the Roman west that German peoples were soon to cause the final collapse of imperial control.

Apart from restoring the northern frontier, albeit with barbarian assistance, Theodosius was termed 'the Great' as much for his efforts on behalf of Christianity as anything else. At an early point in his reign, during a grave illness, he had requested baptism.

Thereafter his orthodoxy was never in question, even though Ambrose (AD 339–397), bishop of Milan, publicly humbled the emperor on at least two occasions. By refusing communion in AD 388 and again in 390, Ambrose compelled Theodosius to leave unpunished a fellow bishop who had destroyed a synagogue, and to undergo penance for allowing soldiers to riot in Thessalonica. These two historic victories of church over state set the scene for the anti-pagan programme Theodosius espoused. The Olympic Games were suppressed in AD 393, and two years later riots by zealous Christians in Alexandria could only be contained through ordering soldiers to assist in the destruction of its temples. An incidental victim was the enormous library founded by the Ptolemies (305–30 BC). Pagan commentators later blamed his religious policy for the downfall of Rome, but, when in early AD 395 Theodosius died, the empire was at peace for the first time in many years. He bequeathed it to his two sons, Arcadius (AD 395–408) and Honorius (AD 395–423), to reign in the east and west respectively. The Roman empire remained divided until Justinian's reconquest of Italy in the mid-sixth century brought a part of the west briefly back under eastern, or Byzantine, control.

See ALEXANDRIA; GOTHS; HONORIUS; JUSTINIAN; ROME

★S. Williams and G. Friell, *Theodosius: The Empire at Bay* (London, 1994).

**Theodosius II**, Roman emperor in the east AD 408–450, was the grandson of Theodosius I (AD 379–395), the last ruler of a united empire. Whereas Roman authority in the western provinces failed to survive the great migrations of the fifth century, and in late AD 476 the last emperor there, Romulus Augustulus, was deposed by an army mutiny, in the east a new Christian civilization was being shaped which lasted right through the Middle Ages. It is usually termed Byzantine in order to distinguish its distinctively Greek character. The new landward defences built at Constantinople in AD 413 were not breached till 1204; here occurred no equivalent of the sackings of Rome, by the Visigoths in AD 410 and the Vandals in AD 455. Within the eastern capital public higher education was reorganized in AD 425, reflecting the gradual process by which the official language of the eastern provinces was changing from Latin to Greek. This state-sponsored revival of learning drew the aristocracy and the imperial government together, unlike in the west, where local centres of power came into existence through the accommodations made by the great landowners with the new German rulers. For that reason the eastern church accepted a close association with the state, in contrast to the western church which had to preserve its independence in order to deal with a multiplicity of new states.

Occasional military intervention was tried with mixed success in the affairs of the west. In AD 431 an eastern army was sent to Africa to attack the Vandals, and a decade later Sicily was occupied to prevent it falling into Vandal hands. Anxious to forestall such a counter-attack by sea the Vandal king Gaiseric had seized Sardinia and Corsica with a powerful fleet. Its vessels dominated the western Mediterranean till the eastern emperor Justinian (AD 527–565) sought to reconquer the lost maritime provinces.

In the east the ravages of the Huns, the implacable foe of the Romans and Germans alike, were contained through the payment of tribute and the strengthening of city defences. It was fortunate for Theodosius that Attila (AD 434–453) lost interest in raiding the eastern provinces and turned his attention to the feebler west. When he died in AD 450, Theodosius had achieved the longest reign in the whole course of Roman history: forty-two years as sole emperor of the east.

See ATTILA; ROMULUS AUGUSTULUS; CHRISTIANITY; JUSTINIAN; THEODOSIUS I; VANDALS

*J. B. Bury, *History of the Later Roman Empire from the Death of Theodosius I to the Death of Justinian* (New York, 1958).

**Theramenes** (died 403 BC) was a victim of the Thirty, a tyrannous oligarchy established by the Spartan admiral Lysander, following the defeat of Athens in the Peloponnesian War (431–404 BC). A moderate figure in Athenian politics, Theramenes found himself involved in two oligarchic reactions: first in 411 BC, then again in 404 BC. Both events arose from the strains placed on democratic government as a result of the long and bitter struggle between Athens and Sparta. The first oligarchy, the Four Hundred, originated in the fleet at Samos in 412 BC. The idea took root when the exiled leader Alcibiades (*c.* 450–404 BC) claimed that a change of government at Athens would cause the Persian king to end his financial support of Sparta. Envoys were sent to Athens and an oligarchic coup was staged in an atmosphere of terror. Having discarded Alcibiades and ended negotiations unsuccessfully with Persia, the oligarchs may have tried to end the war with Sparta by surrendering the city of Athens. With most of the Athenian forces overseas, the Spartans were naturally suspicious of the Four Hundred, who were increasingly dominated by extremists. That the oligarchs were not perceived as the real Athenian government is shown by the arrival on Samos of a delegation from the Argive democracy. There sometime in 411 BC Thrasybulus (died 388 BC) founded in opposition to the Four Hundred, a democratic state based on the Athenian fleet, and recalled Alcibiades from banishment.

Meanwhile in Athens, Theramenes tried to rally the moderate oligarchs. The historian Thucydides says the line of Theramenes was that 'he feared not only Alcibiades and his men at Samos but also those who have been sending embassies to Sparta, lest they do harm to the state without consulting the majority'. He and his supporters 'did not go so far as to suggest getting rid of the oligarchy altogether', but they maintained that the government should be set up on 'a wider basis'. Cynical though Thucydides is about Theramenes' motive, there is evidence of real consistency in his outlook. Xenophon, whose own history covers the period from 411 BC till 362 BC, is in no doubt that Theramenes 'never altered his view that the best constitution is that which is in the hands of those who can serve the state with horse and shield'. That is to say the well-to-do, not a tiny group of privileged oligarchs. He paid with his life in 403 BC for expressing similar sentiments. In 411 BC, however, Theramenes had better luck and the Four Hundred were deposed. The oligarchs made the mistake of assembling a large body of men to strengthen fortifications at Piraeus. They thus had time to discuss their situation and call for a wider franchise. When a full restoration of democracy occurred in 410 BC, Theramenes was on active service in the Hellespont, where a notable naval victory had been won at Cyzicus. It restored Athenian morale and induced the Spartans to sue for peace.

After the naval engagement at Arginusae in 406 BC, Theramenes escaped blame for leaving survivors from twelve wrecked ships to drown. He commanded a single vessel. The unjust decision by the assembly to

execute six of the victorious commanders, and reject peace overtures
from the Spartans, sealed Athens'
defeat. Within two years Theramenes
was negotiating surrender terms with
the Spartan admiral Lysander. After
Athens surrendered he was appointed
as one of the Thirty, but was soon
killed by his fellow oligarchs. His chief
opponent was the violently pro-
Spartan Critias, who fell himself shortly
after Theramenes' death fighting
democratic forces led by Thrasybulus.

*See* ALCIBIADES; ATHENS; LYSANDER;
PELOPONNESIAN WAR; SPARTA;
THRASYBULUS

★D. Kagan, *The Fall of the Athenian Empire*
(Ithaca, 1987).

King Leonidas of Sparta, who led the heroic
stand at Thermopylae.

**Thermopylae**, meaning 'hot gates'
from its sulphur springs, was a narrow
pass between mountains and sea providing the only practical route from the
north into central Greece. There in
480 BC King Leonidas of Sparta faced a
Persian army 400,000 strong with less
than 7,000 infantrymen. King Xerxes
of Persia (486–465 BC) could not credit
reports that the 300 Spartans with
Leonidas calmly exercised and combed
their hair before the unequal battle.
The exiled Spartan king Demaratus
told Xerxes, however, that 'they
always dressed their hair whenever
they were about to put their lives at
risk'. To Xerxes' horror the Greek line
held firm as Demaratus predicted,
inflicting dreadful casualties on his best
troops. Encirclement via a mountain
track seemed the answer, but then
Leonidas merely sent southwards the
bulk of his troops while covering their
retreat with the Spartans and some
Boeotians. Still the Persians were
forced to engage in deadly fighting
at close quarters until the last Greek
fell. Of the Spartans the historian
Herodotus recounts how 'they resisted
to the last, with their swords, if they
had them, and, if not, with their hands
and teeth, until the Persians . . . finally
overwhelmed them'. So it was that the
prophecy of the Delphic oracle was
fulfilled: either the land of Sparta
would be laid waste or a Spartan king
be killed. Though Thermopylae was
hailed as a heroic feat of Greek arms,
the victory gave the Persians control of
central Greece, including Thebes. The
Athenians escaped destruction immediately afterwards only by taking refuge
on the island of Salamis.

See PERSIAN INVASIONS
*A. R. Burn, *Persia and the Greeks: The Defence of the West, c. 546–478 BC* (London, 1962).

**Thessaly**, in northern Greece, comprises a great plain almost completely surrounded by mountains. Prior to coming under Macedonian control in 352 BC, it was ruled by a landed aristocracy, from whose ranks a chief magistrate would only be appointed in an emergency. In the 370s BC Jason, tyrant of Pherae, was appointed to this post and built up considerable power. Jason allied himself to the Thebans, who summoned him to Leuctra in 371 BC, immediately after their unprecedented defeat of the Spartans. With ambitions of his own in central Greece, Jason welcomed the opportunity to investigate the novel situation in person. Quickly gathering his mercenaries, he marched into Boeotia, where at Leuctra he found the Spartans thoroughly beaten in their camp. He rejected the suggestion of the Theban general Epaminondas (died 362 BC) for a joint assault on the Spartan position, in part because such an attack would prove bloody, and in part because he had no desire to strengthen Thebes' new power. Instead, Jason negotiated a truce between the belligerents which allowed the defeated Spartans to go home. On his own way back to Thessaly he seized a couple of cities in order to protect its borders against his now powerful ally. But his plans were interrupted in 370 BC when assassins struck him down.

Thessalian disunity following Jason's death offered the Thebans the possibility of extending their authority northwards, at least till another tyrant of Perae by the name of Alexander (369–358 BC) rose to prominence. The nephew of Jason, Alexander struggled to resist this advance as well as reduce the whole of Thessaly to obedience. In 364 BC at Cynoscephalae the Thebans inflicted a heavy defeat on Alexander, although the victorious Theban general Pelopidas was killed in the action. Afterwards the Thebans heaped around Pelopidas' body the spoils taken from the Thessalians, while they sheared their horses' manes and cut their own hair as signs of mourning. The treaty that Alexander was compelled to agree with Thebes represented the low point of his tyranny, but the Thebans took no real interest in Thessalian affairs again. Alexander met the same end as his uncle in 358 BC, and then the Thessalians returned to their traditional rivalries without outside interference till 352 BC, when Philip II of Macedon intervened in a so-called Sacred War against Phocis. This involved the Thessalians and Philip exploited his victory to reconstitute a Thessalian League, but subject to Macedonian leadership. Both Philip and his son, Alexander the Great (356–323 BC), made extensive use of Thessalian cavalry in their many campaigns. From 196 BC Thessaly enjoyed a period of independence till its incorporation in

148 BC as part of the Roman province of Macedonia.

See EPAMINONDAS; MACEDON; THEBES; TYRANTS; ROME; SACRED WARS; WARFARE

*H. D. Westlake, *Thessaly in the Fourth Century BC* (London, 1935).

**Thrace**, situated north of the Aegean and west of the Black Sea, was inhabited by a hardy people whom the Greeks considered backward. Respect was given to the military prowess of the tribes living in the Thracian mountains, although most contact was with the more peaceful farmers living along the coasts. But even these could prove to be formidable opponents, and in the late 440s BC Pericles needed to reassert Athenian authority in the Chersonese (now the Gallipoli peninsula). He drove off Thracian raiders, built a fortified line across the neck of the isthmus, and strengthened the Greek cities with 1,000 Athenian settlers. This part of Thrace was vital to Athens because its grain convoys from the Ukraine passed close by. Athenian influence was first established there by the tyrant Pisistratus (died 527 BC), from whom it eventually passed to Miltiades, the future victor of the battle of Marathon in 490 BC. Marriage to a Thracian princess may have helped to secure his position, but Persian pressure drove Miltiades back to Athens with his wife and young son, Cimon (510–450 BC). Another part of Thrace the Athenians found very attractive

was the Strymon valley, where in 465 BC they planted the colony of Amphipolis in order to exploit the local sources of gold, silver and timber. This was captured in 424 BC by the Spartan general Brasidas.

Slavery always seems to have been associated with Thrace. There were two methods of supply. One was captives, the victims of war or piracy. The second was through purchase, again sometimes as a result of inter-tribal wars. The historian Herodotus also tells us, however, that 'the Thracians carry on an export trade in their own children'. It is impossible to calculate how many Thracians there were in the 60,000 slaves thought to be owned by Athenians in the late fifth century BC. Thrace remained involved in the slave trade after its conquest in the late 350s BC by Macedon. As late as AD 376 there is reference to slaving activities by the Roman army. The most infamous slave the Romans ever obtained from Thrace was the gladiator Spartacus, who between 73 and 71 BC routed five Roman armies and dominated southern Italy. After the final defeat of the Macedonians at Pydna in 168 BC, western Thrace had been incorporated into the Roman province of Macedonia, while the rest of the region remained under Thracian kings friendly to Rome down to the creation of a separate province of Thrace in AD 48. Although the Romans encouraged urban development, the region never possessed many cities. Near one of them, Adrianople, the Roman emperor Valens was overwhelmed in AD 378 by the Visigoths and their allies. Two-thirds of the Roman force fell in the battle, and the emperor's body was never recovered. A subsequent agreement allowed the Visigoths to settle in northern Thrace.

See ATHENS; GOTHS; MACEDON; MILTIADES; PERICLES; SLAVERY; SPARTACUS

*S. Casson, *Macedonia, Thrace and Illyria* (London, 1926).

**Thrasybulus** (died 388 BC) was responsible for restoring democracy at Athens following its defeat by Sparta in the Peloponnesian War (431–404 BC). This was the second occasion on which he had been obliged to rally democratic forces against reaction. The first occurred in 411 BC. Then Thrasybulus, along with the fleet at Samos, effectively resisted the oligarchy of the Four Hundred in Athens. After the recall of the exiled Alcibiades (c. 450–404 BC), the moderate oligarch Theramenes (died 403 BC) worked very closely with Thrasybulus. The two men served as generals in the Hellespont and, together with Alcibiades, they won the naval engagement at Cyzicus in 410 BC. After another successful engagement at Arginsuae, four years later, they were acquitted together of any blame for the drownings in the ensuing storm.

The Thirty, a second oligarchy established at Athens later by the Spartan admiral Lysander in 404 BC, banished Thrasybulus and executed Theramenes. Theramenes had stayed in the city, become a member of the Thirty, and endeavoured to moderate its rule. But he failed to repeat the constitutional transformation of 411 BC, and it was Thrasybulus who returned from exile to overthrow the oligarchy by force of arms. In 403 BC he seized the Piraeus and defeated contingents sent against him. The murderer of Theramenes, the violently pro-Spartan oligarch Critias, fell in the fighting. Afterwards democracy was restored to Athens. 'Oaths,' the historian Xenophon tells us, 'were sworn that there should be an amnesty for all that had happened in the past, and to this day everyone lives together as fellow-citizens and the people abide by the oaths which they had sworn.'

The unity of purpose resulting from the moderate approach of Thrasybulus in 403 BC served the Athenians well. They were able to rebuild their city walls and their fleet. In 389 BC Thrasybulus sailed through the Aegean and drew some of Athens' old allies into a new maritime league. He was killed at Aspendus in Pamphylia, when his camp was surprised by local inhabitants enraged at Athenian pillage.

See ATHENS; LYSANDER; PELOPONNESIAN WAR; SPARTA; THERAMENES
*D. Kagan, *The Fall of the Athenian Empire* (Ithaca, 1987); B. S. Strauss, *Athens after the Peloponnesian War* (London, 1986).

**Three Kingdoms** period (AD 221–280) in China arose from the deposition in AD 220 of the last Han emperor by Cao Pi, son of the infamous warlord Cao Cao. Determined to secure his own position, Cao Pi (AD 186–226) declared himself to be the first emperor of a new dynasty, the Wei (AD 220–265). Even though Chinese historians traced the line of legitimacy through the Wei, ignoring Cao Cao's rivals, the fact remains that China was divided following the end of the Han dynasty. For two other warlords swiftly declared themselves emperors. In the south-west of China (in present-day Sichuan province) the Shu, or Shu Han, dynasty was founded by Liu Bei, who claimed to be connected with the deposed imperial house; while in the south, along the lower Yangzi river valley, Sun Quan styled himself the imperial Wu.

That China could fragment for over half a century of sustained rivalry indicates more than a break-down of the imperial system, weakened though that undoubtedly was by factionalism. Beneath the warlord struggle lay a profound economic transformation. The national centre of gravity was shifting southwards, as the Huai and Yangzi river valleys overtook the productivity of the northern provinces, and especially present-day Shaanxi province, the old dynastic centre of the Qin (221–207 BC) and the early period of the Han (202 BC – AD 9). The shift of economic power was already evident during the usurpation of Wang Mang (AD 9–23), who moved the capital to Luoyang. Whilst census figures, too,

underline the growing prosperity of the southern provinces, the majority of the population still resided in north China. Against the 30 million people living in Wei, 12 million lived in Wu and another 8 million in Shu.

In the struggle between these three powers the population differences eventually told. Shu's aggressiveness, in particular, could not be readily maintained, despite the military genius of Zhuge Liang (AD 181–234). His ability to master apparently insoluble problems has made him something of a legend. On one occasion Zhuge Liang saved Shu after its army had collapsed during an invasion of Wei, by means of a ruse. He ordered the gates of the city into which the defeated soldiers had fled to be thrown open, while conspicuously on the undefended battlements he strummed a lute. So at odds with the military situation was the joy of the music that the anxious Wei commander decided to withdraw in case a

General Zhuge Liang, the inventor of the wheelbarrow. It was used to transport military supplies.

trap was being set. Another example of Zhuge Liang's ingenuity was the invention of the wheelbarrow, or 'wooden ox', which allowed the transport of military supplies over the mountainous terrain separating Shu and Wei.

Shu fell to Wei in AD 263. At this time the Sima family had come to dominate the latter state, although the last Wei emperor was not forced to abdicate until AD 265. That year Sima Yan became the first Western Jin emperor. Under his direction Wei reunified China by overthrowing in AD 280 the surviving southern state of Wu. What facilitated this final triumph was a greater concentration on agriculture and water transport as a means of strengthening military power. Extra manpower also came from foreign peoples who were allowed to settle in large numbers within the Great Wall. This policy of barbarian settlement was to have the same dire consequences it had for the western provinces of the Roman empire. But by waging a war of economic attrition, alongside an orthodox military campaign, the Western Jin (AD 265–316) was able to emerge victorious.

See CAO CAO; GREAT WALL; HAN DYNASTY; SIMA YAN; WESTERN JIN DYNASTY

*W. Eberhard, *A History of China* (London, 1950).

**Thucydides** (455–400 BC) was the historian of the Peloponnesian War, the long and bitter struggle between Sparta and Athens which engulfed classical Greece between 431 and 404 BC. An Athenian aristocrat and a supporter of Pericles (*c.* 495–429 BC), Thucydides was blamed in 424 BC for the loss of the important colony of Amphipolis in Thrace. He was in command of the Athenian fleet there, but failed to move quickly enough to prevent the Spartan commander Brasidas (*c.* 472–422 BC) from taking the colony's surrender. The Athenians were annoyed by the loss and brought Thucydides to trial, sending him into an exile that lasted for the rest of the war. His accuser, in all likelihood, was Cleon, the dominant Athenian politician after Pericles: this advocate of more energetic military activities was to die in 422 BC at Amphipolis, vainly attempting its recovery. Even though Thucydides does not comment directly on his sentence, his history lays the blame on the Athenian general responsible for holding the colony. 'If he could have held on for one more day we would have thwarted Brasidas, but he did not. My quickness and foresight saved Eion,' wrote Thucydides, referring to a city nearby on the coast. The truth was that Brasidas surprised the Athenians by a sudden march. That they were unprepared for this move, and the moderate terms offered to the composite population of Amphipolis, the history virtually admits. Hence the difficulty Thucydides must have faced at his trial.

Although Thucydides does not mention the historian Herodotus

(484–425 BC) by name, we know that he attended one of the readings Herodotus gave of his account of the Persian invasion of Greece when resident in Athens. Thucydides was moved to tears, but his own writings were very different from those of Herodotus. He was more aware of the shortcomings of oral evidence and, possibly because accurate information was so hard to find about events years before the outbreak of hostilities, his history concentrates on events of his own lifetime. Another difference between the two historians is the way in which Thucydides selected his material. He saw it as a historian's duty to make up the reader's mind for him; and the simplest way of achieving that is to leave out, as far as possible, alternative versions of events. It might be said that he was giving his own version of the Peloponnesian War down to 411 BC, where his narrative breaks off. But Thucydides always insisted that he had cross-checked his sources wherever possible. After his death in 400 BC the unpublished history was brought to public attention by Xenophon (428–354 BC), who also continued a narrative of events down till the 360s BC, the heyday of Thebes.

*See* HERODOTUS; XENOPHON

*S. Hornblower, *Thucydides* (London, 1987); S. Usher, *The Historians of Greece and Rome* (London, 1969).

**Tiberius**, Roman emperor AD 14–37, was born in 42 BC. The mother of

Tiberius Claudius Nero was Livia, whom the future emperor Augustus married in 39 BC. Her long and successful second marriage allowed Livia (58 BC–AD 29) to exercise considerable political influence during the reigns of Augustus (31 BC–AD 14) and her son Tiberius. It was even said that Tiberius retired to Capri in AD 26 chiefly to be away from her.

The second Roman emperor Tiberius, a man of ability but chronic uncertainty.

Tiberius was a loyal and competent assistant to Augustus, whose wayward daughter Julia he suffered for many years as a wife. Not the first choice as Augustus' successor, but the only surviving candidate, Tiberius had his constitutional powers put on terms of equality with Augustus in AD 13. 'When Augustus died a year later,' the historian Tacitus tells us, 'Tiberius was given the password of the Praetorian Guard. He already had the trappings of a court, too, such as personal bodyguards and men-at-arms. When he moved about Rome, he had soldiers to escort him. He sent letters to armies as though he were already emperor. He only showed signs of hesitation when he addressed the senate.'

Though the senate confirmed his appointment as the first citizen, the Roman euphemism for monarch, Tiberius' relationship with the senators left a good deal to be desired. Tacitus relates how his suspicious nature caused Tiberius to 'twist every word, every gesture into some criminal significance'. It was a weakness exploited by Sejanus, to whom he entrusted the praetorians, the only regular troops stationed in Italy. This astute commander concentrated the formation in Rome, a move that left him all-powerful once Tiberius retired from the capital himself. Trials multiplied, as Sejanus used new treason laws to get rid of his enemies. But he was executed in turn in AD 31, when a plot of his came to light aimed at removing Tiberius' designated successor, Caligula. Six years later a thoroughly disillusioned Tiberius died in his seventy-eighth year. But according to Tacitus, his passing was not entirely peaceful. For Caligula (AD 37–41) had begun his reign, when a report arrived that 'Tiberius had recovered his speech and sight, and was asking for food after his fainting-fit . . . Caligula was stupefied . . . but Sejanus' successor, Macro, ordered the old man to be smothered with a heap of bed-clothes and left alone.'

See AUGUSTUS; CALIGULA; ROME

*B. Levick, *Tiberius the Politician* (London, 1976); Tacitus, *The Annals of Imperial Rome*, trans. by M. Grant (Harmondsworth, 1956).

**Timoleon** (died 334 BC) was a middle-aged Corinthian general who around 344 BC expelled the tyrant Dionysius II from Syracuse. The aristocrats of this Sicilian city had asked Corinth for assistance, for that Greek state had sent out the first settlers there. Against all the odds, Timoleon succeeded in reviving the Greek cities of Sicily. He overthrew tyrants, encouraged federation, and dealt effectively with the Carthaginians. Thousands of new colonists arrived from Greece as a result of his intervention, which was effective for about twenty years. Then the old Sicilian tendency to tyranny reasserted its influence, especially at Syracuse. Timoleon relinquished office there around 336 BC because of blindness. He was given a splendid funeral two years later as the saviour of Sicily. The historian Polybius, however, felt that Timoleon had received too much praise for his achievements, and ruefully noted that the general 'had sought fame in a mere saucer of a place such as Sicily'.

See SYRACUSE

*R. J. A. Talbert, *Timoleon and the Revival of Greek Sicily* (Cambridge, 1974).

**Tissaphernes** (died 395 BC), governor at Sardis from 413 BC, was largely responsible for Persian policy towards the Greeks at a critical point in the Peloponnesian War (431–404 BC). Tissaphernes had been appointed after assisting Darius II (424–405 BC) in putting down the rebellion of the previous governor, Pissuthnes. This challenge was particularly worrying for the Persian king because, whereas he was only an illegitimate usurper himself, Pissuthnes was the grandson of Darius I (521–486 BC) and an experienced governor with an army which included many Greek mercenaries. A combination of bribes and force destroyed the rebels and gave Darius II an opportunity to regain control of Ionia, since in the same year that Pissuthnes was killed the Athenians suffered the loss of their Sicilian expedition. For the first time a Spartan victory over Athens seemed possible, with Persian subsidies for a navy. The Persian governors in Asia Minor were under pressure to collect tribute from Greek cities, but as long as the Athenians controlled the waters of the Aegean this was not easy to achieve. In order to remove Athens' hold over these cities, therefore, Tissaphernes made an alliance with the Spartans, most likely through the support of the Athenian exile Alcibiades, who was then resident at Sparta. For in 412 BC Alcibiades sailed into the Aegean with a Spartan admiral and encouraged many Ionian cities to revolt from Athens. Fearing for his safety, the exile then transferred his allegiance to Persia and moved to Sardis, where Tissaphernes appointed

Alcibiades (c. 450–404 BC) his adviser. Apparently he advised there should be no great hurry to end the war between Sparta and Athens, but it is quite possible that the Persians were content to let both sides exhaust themselves.

A coin with a portrait of Tissaphernes, sworn enemy of Cyrus the Younger. Minted in Sardis around 400 BC.

After Alcibiades' recall home, Tissaphernes may have considered switching his subsidy from Sparta, but he was no more impressed by the Four Hundred, oligarchs who had seized power at Athens in 411 BC, than he was by the revival of its naval fortunes a year later at Cyzicus, in the Hellespont. Already Tissaphernes had not enough scope for manoeuvre, and in 408 BC he was relegated to Caria, a less important posting. His replacement as senior Persian governor was none other than Cyrus (423–401 BC), the second son of Darius II. When the Spartans complained about Tissaphernes' lack of support, the historian Xenophon tells us, Cyrus said he had been sent by his father to prosecute the

war energetically. Cyrus' close working relationship with the Spartan admiral Lysander was undoubtedly a factor
in the Athenian defeat of 404 BC. But
Tissaphernes got his personal revenge
in 401 BC, when Cyrus tried with the
aid of Greek mercenaries to depose his
elder brother, Artaxerxes II (404–
359 BC). A participant in the battle of
Cunaxa north of Babylon, Xenophon
records how Tissaphernes led a cavalry
charge that reached Cyrus' camp.
Although the undefeated Greeks lost
not a single man, the death of Cyrus
left them without a purpose deep
inside the Persian empire. They were
undaunted when Tissaphernes killed
their commanders at a parley, and
marched homewards via the Black Sea.
He left the so-called Ten Thousand to
continue their march and returned to
the western frontier, where Sparta for a
time endeavoured to keep the Persians
out of Ionia. After a defeat in 395 BC
at Sardis, Tissaphernes was unable to
stop the Spartan king Agesilaus from
moving freely through Persian territory and, annoyed by this affront to his
authority, Artaxerxes II turned against
his governor. Tissaphernes was seized
as he was taking a bath, and executed.
In less than a decade, however, Sparta
was obliged to accept Persian rule over
the Greek cities in Asia Minor.

See AGESILAUS; ALCIBIADES; ATHENS;
CYRUS THE YOUNGER; LYSANDER;
PELOPONNESIAN WAR; PERSIA
*J. M. Cook, *The Persian Empire* (London,
1983); Xenophon, *A History of My Times*,
trans. by R. Warner (Harmondsworth,
1966).

**Trajan**, Roman emperor AD 98–117,
belonged to an Italian family settled in
south-western Spain. Marcus Ulpius
Trajanus was governor of Upper
Germany in AD 97 when he learned of
his adoption by Nerva (AD 96–98), the
stop-gap emperor swiftly installed on
Domitian's assassination. The choice
was popular with the Roman army, the
effective basis of imperial power. On
Nerva's death the forty-five-year-old
Trajan succeeded to the throne without difficulty, duly arranging for divinity to be conferred on his adoptive
father.

From the start of his reign, Trajan
acted with decision. He revived the
imperial guard, the famous German
horsemen first raised by Julius Caesar
in the 50s BC. It once again acted as a
personal bodyguard and as a crack
fighting unit. Trajan also set up a military secret service with the aim of gathering intelligence about those opposed
to his regime. But these measures
aimed at protecting the emperor's
person were a preliminary to what he
believed to be his life's work, the emu-
lation of his hero Julius Caesar's foreign
conquests. So Trajan annexed Arabia
Petraea and conquered Dacia (present-
day Romania) as well as Mesopotamia.
The Roman empire now reached its
widest extent, and the army topped
400,000 regulars. There were 180,000
legionaries and 220,000 auxiliaries

recruited in the provinces; the latter were incorporated in the armed forces in order to make use of local specialist skills. In Arabia, for instance, Nabataean cavalry familiar with its arid borderlands supplemented the single legion stationed in the new province. Yet the thirty legions at the core of the Roman army were no longer predominantly Italian; they consisted mostly of provincial volunteers. The conquest of Mesopotamia was the most easterly advance made by Rome in a calculated attempt to cripple Parthia, or at least break its stranglehold over trade with India and China. Though the Parthian capital Ctesiphon fell and Roman troops reached the Persian Gulf, Trajan soon found holding onto Mesopotamia was far from easy. A rebellion had to be crushed almost at once, and Jewish revolts which followed in Palestine, Cyrenaica and Egypt soon made an extended eastern frontier untenable. By the year of his death, Trajan had even stopped trying to consolidate his Parthian conquests, and it was left to his successor, Hadrian (AD 117–138), to order the complete evacuation of Mesopotamia.

The enormous booty from his wars, like the half-million slaves taken in Dacia, enabled Trajan to initiate vast public works, including a new forum and shopping centre at Rome. It also gave him scope for relief measures aimed at poor children. Taxation was eased in the provinces, a move which gained Trajan the accolade of being the first of five 'good emperors'. The stroke which killed him in Asia Minor in AD 117 did not disable the imperial administration, even though rumour claimed that Hadrian was never formally adopted. For Trajan's reign ushered in a sequence of emperors – Hadrian (AD 117–138), Antonius Pius (AD 138–161), Marcus Aurelius (AD 161–180) and Lucius Verus (AD 161–169) – who were later looked upon as occupying an imperial golden age, which ended when the last of the Antonines, Commodus, was assassinated in AD 192: this son of Marcus Aurelius believed he was an incarnation of the legendary hero Heracles, and decided to become a gladiator. The subsequent dynasty, the Severan, was founded by Septimius Severus (AD 193–211), who hailed from Lepcis Magna in Africa.

Coin struck in celebration of Trajan's eastern conquests. The emperor is shown presenting a king to Parthia.

See ANTONINE DYNASTY; ARABIA; HADRIAN; PARTHIA; SEVERAN DYNASTY
*J. Bennett, *Trajan. Optimus Princeps. A Life and Times* (London, 1997).

**Twelve Tables** comprised the earliest Roman code of laws, published in 451 BC. They were formulated by a commission of ten under the chairmanship of a noble by the name of Appius Claudius. He seems to have appreciated that the bitter antagonism existing between rich and poor citizens needed a legal framework to resolve disputes. Unrest was fuelled by famine, disease, and almost continuous warfare, all of which bore down hardest on those least able to protect themselves. Their demand for a written law was a first attempt to break the monopoly of the aristocracy over the administration of justice. The contribution of Appius Claudius to what was in effect the starting-point of Roman law is hard to estimate, because he was later regarded as a legendary example of official corruption. His own assassination, or enforced suicide, may have become entangled with the myth of Virginia, the Roman maiden after whom a magistrate lusted. According to this story, Appius Claudius even dared to use his official powers to have the girl handed over to him as a slave. At the last moment her father stabbed Virginia through the heart, declaring that her death was less painful to endure than her dishonour. The populace rose to support him and checks were placed on magistrates' powers. Like the story of the earlier rape of Lucretia by the eldest son of Rome's last Etruscan ruler, the sexual violence which threatened Virginia brought about significant constitutional change.

*See* ROME

*A. Watson, *Rome of the Twelve Tables* (Princeton, 1975).

**Tyrants** in the Greek world rarely succeeded in establishing long-term dynasties. Derived from a word of non-Greek origin, a tyrant was a ruler whose position was unconstitutional, and usually obtained by force of arms. The Lydian usurper Gyges would appear to be the first person the Greeks called a tyrant: in 685 BC, as a member of the royal bodyguard, he murdered the Lydian king Kandaules, married his widow and usurped the throne. By the time Polycrates seized power on the Greek island of Samos, in 535 BC, the word tyrant had become a term of abuse. This is what the Athenian reformer Solon meant when he said: 'A city's ruin comes from great men, and the people in their folly fall into the slavery of a ruler.' One king who exceeded the bounds of royal authority to become a tyrant was Pheidon of Argos. But this semi-legendary figure was unlike most tyrants, who simply grabbed power in a crisis. For short periods of time tyrannies were established at Sicyon, Corinth, Megara and Athens, but they had nearly all passed away by the beginning of the fifth century BC. In Asia Minor, however, tyrants tended to survive as clients of the Persians. And a late flowering of tyranny occurred on the island of Sicily, where Dionysius managed to have himself awarded unprecedented powers by the Syracusans sometime after 406 BC. They were intended to assist Dionysius in dealing with the Carthaginians, but he used them to establish a military dictatorship instead.

See DIONYSIUS; HIPPIAS; IONIAN REVOLT; PISISTRATUS; SAMOS; SICYON

*A. Andrewes, *The Greek Tyrants* (London, 1956).

# V

**Valentinian**, Roman emperor AD 364–375, was proclaimed by the troops at Nicaea after the death of Jovian (AD 363–364). His predecessor had with difficulty extricated the army from Mesopotamia after the expedition launched by Julian (AD 361–363) failed. A humiliating treaty with the Sasanians may have hurt Roman pride, but the

Co-emperor and brother of Valentinian, the unfortunate Valens fell fighting the Visigoths at Adrianople in AD 378.

long period of peace that ensued in the east enabled the empire to face a new German challenge with mixed success.

Flavius Valentinianus, and his younger brother Flavius Julius Valens (AD 364–378) whom he appointed co-emperor in the east, were soon plunged into a series of grave military emergencies. The Alamanni crossed the Rhine, the Anglo-Saxons and the Picts raided Britain, and the Sarmatians struck across the Danube. Almost continuous campaigning was necessary before Valentinian expelled them all in AD 375. His own death that year resulted from a burst blood-vessel, so enraged was he at the insolence of some German envoys. Valentinian's sixteen-year-old son Gratian (AD 367–383) succeeded him. Meanwhile in the east pressure was building up on the lower Danube frontier, over which Valens had authority. The Visigoths were being rolled forward by the Huns, and they demanded to be allowed to settle within the imperial borders. Barbarians had been settled in the past, with the result that they were a feature of frontier society and served alongside the Romans. Very different were the frontier provinces now from the situation that prevailed during Constantine's reign (AD 306–337). Civilians had left in great numbers and those who remained were enmeshed in a highly militarized world. In AD 375 the Roman army could operate with little regard for civilian values. Large areas behind the frontier could be left to fend for themselves for long periods of time. But never before had an emperor admitted a whole barbarian people, and Valens at first hesitated over the decision. Then he agreed to the settlement of the Visigoths, disarmed and under Roman supervision. 'They were,' noted the historian Ammianus Marcellinus, 'a countless multitude.' For Valens they represented new military recruits and substitution payments the provincials would contribute to the imperial treasury to have the Visigoths fight on their behalf.

The settlement soon went wrong, however. The Visigoths were beyond Rome's ability to feed and process. Friction turned in AD 377 into revolt, and Valens was compelled to march against them. The following summer at Adrianople (modern Edirne in Bulgaria) the Romans were utterly defeated, thousands falling along with the emperor, whose body was never recovered. 'Barely a third of the army escaped,' reports Ammianus Marcellinus. The Balkans were entirely at the mercy of the Visigoths, who made peace and settled down there as allies of Theodosius I (AD 379–395) only after six years of hard-fought campaigning.

See Goths; Huns; Julian; Theodosius I

*J. Matthews, *The Roman Empire of Ammianus* (London, 1989); Ammianus Marcellinus, *The Later Roman Empire, AD 354–378*, trans. by W. Hamilton (Harmondsworth, 1986).

**Vandals**, along with other starving German peoples, crossed the frozen Rhine at Mogontiacum (present-day Mainz) on the last day of AD 406. The invaders quickly took Durocorturum, Samarobriva and Nemetacum (modern Rheims, Amiens and Arras respectively). Whole areas of Gaul were devastated, before in AD 409 the Vandals and their allies moved into Spain. Relatives of the western Roman emperor Honorius (AD 395–423) had raised local forces to block the passes in the Pyrenees, but they attracted the attention of usurpers in Gaul and were soon annihilated. It is not unlikely that one of these dissident Roman generals allowed the Vandals to occupy north-western Spain in order to induce them to stop their plundering. Also such an agreement would have allowed him to withdraw the modest garrison of regular Roman troops from the peninsula for use in the complicated civil war then being fought out in Gaul.

The Vandals may even have become a Roman ally on a similar basis to the settlement of the Visigoths in south-western Gaul in AD 418. Because a year afterwards they were settled with some kind of imperial approval in

Baetica, the southernmost and richest Spanish province. But a decade later King Gaiseric (died AD 477) transported over 50,000 Vandals across the Pillars of Hercules, seeking a new homeland in Africa. This move was of grave concern to Ravenna, now the seat of the western imperial government, because the provinces around Carthage represented one of the empire's major sources of grain. It might have been a source of worry, too, that the Vandals had been encouraged to go to Africa by a would-be usurper, as the historian Procopius later claimed. At first the Vandals were granted the right of residence in Mauretania, well to the west of Carthage, but Gaiseric was not satisfied with this land and by AD 439 he had conquered north Africa as far as Tripolitania. Counterattacks by western and eastern Roman armies failed to dislodge the Vandals, who built up a powerful fleet and seized Sardinia and Corsica. In AD 441 an eastern force occupied Sicily so as to prevent it from falling to Gaiseric, by far the most troublesome of the barbarian kings. In AD 455 he captured and pillaged Rome, afterwards harassing the Italian coast with a fleet of sixty ships. These warlike activities earned the Vandals a dubious reputation, about which it is not easy to reach a balanced view today because their Arianism caused a conflict with orthodox Christians that ensured all testimony is strongly anti-Vandal. And there was a greater flight of wealthy landowners from Africa

than Gaul, another factor dwelt upon by contemporary chroniclers. The smallness of the Vandal population, however, meant that existing Roman legal and administrative traditions had to be retained in order to prevent a collapse of the economy. Prior to the eastern Roman reconquest of Africa in AD 533–534 there is even a reference to the regular shipment of grain to Constantinople, possibly as a form of tribute. If nothing else, it shows a desire on the part of the Vandals to participate in international trade. Evidence also points to the return of those who fled Africa, or their heirs, and to compensation being paid for the loss of ancestral lands.

General Belisarius commanded the expedition sent by the eastern emperor Justinian (AD 527–565) against the Vandals. According to Procopius, who served on the general's staff during the campaign, their defeat within a few months was stunning: he wondered whether such a campaign had ever occurred before. With 10,000 infantry and 5,000 cavalry, Belisarius caught the last Vandal king, Gelimer (AD 530–534), quite unprepared. The bulk of the Vandal army was in Sardinia, putting down a rebellion which had probably been encouraged by Justinian. Belisarius soon captured Carthage and, entering Gelimer's palace, he sat on his throne and ate the lunch already prepared for the Vandal king. In AD 534 Gelimer was forced to admit defeat, and Belisarius sent him as a prisoner to Constantinople along with the loot taken from Rome eighty years earlier. Surprisingly, Africa, unlike other eastern Roman or Byzantine conquests in the west, did not prove hard to hold. In his *Secret History* Procopius places the blame for the loss of reconquered Italy and Spain firmly on Justinian, whose grandiose schemes resulted in 'an outbreak of revolts that led to widespread destruction'.

*See* AFRICA; CHRISTIANITY; GAUL; HONORIUS; JUSTINIAN; SPAIN

*M. Todd, *Everyday Life of the Barbarians: Goths, Franks, and Vandals* (London, 1972); Procopius, *The Secret History*, trans. by G. A. Williamson (Harmondsworth, 1966).

Vercingetorix, king of the Arverni, from a Roman coin.

**Vercingetorix** (died 46 BC) led a general rebellion of the Gauls against Rome in 52 BC. News of Caesar's political difficulties with Pompey (106–48 BC) encouraged the uprising, which represented a last, desperate bid to regain independence. According to Caesar's own account, the Gauls said that 'it was better to be killed in battle

than fail to recover their ancient glory in war and the freedom they had inherited from their ancestors'. The lead was taken by Vercingetorix in what today is the Auvergne: his people, the Arverni, had once held sway over the whole of south-western Gaul and his father, Caesar relates, 'had been killed by his fellow tribesmen because he wanted to become king'. Using scorched-earth tactics and avoiding a pitched battle, the Gauls outmanoeuvred the Roman army till at Alesia, 30 miles north-west of modern Dijon, they were besieged in a strong defensive position. All efforts to relieve Alesia having failed, Vercingetorix bowed to the inevitable and surrendered. Caesar held some tribesmen as hostages, but the majority of the prisoners were distributed as booty among his army. Vercingetorix survived till two years before Caesar's own violent death; he was executed in Rome after a splendid triumph in 46 BC.

*See* CAESAR

*H. Hubert, *The Greatness and Decline of the Celts* (London, 1987); Julius Caesar, *The Battle for Gaul*, trans. by A. and P. Wiseman (London, 1980).

**Vietnam** was incorporated into the Chinese empire during the Han dynasty (202 BC – AD 220). Prior to its conquest in 111 BC southern China itself was called Nan Yueh, from which the modern name of Vietnam derives. Notionally annexed by the earlier Qin dynasty around 213 BC, Nan Yueh was treated as semi-dependent till internal strife compelled the Han emperor Wu Di (140–87 BC) to send forces southwards. Nine commanderies were set up to administer the conquered territory, which included what today is northern Vietnam. The three Vietnamese commanderies were Jiozhi, Jiuzhen and Rinan, whose southernmost boundary reached as far as present-day Hué. At first Chinese policy was to uphold the local chieftains, the so-called Lac lords. Legend claims that these earliest rulers descended from Lac Long Quan, the Lac dragon-lord, who came from the sea, subdued evil spirits, taught the Vietnamese how to grow rice and wear clothes, and offered to return if they were ever in distress. This they were when a Chinese ruler, finding the land without a king, claimed it himself. When the Vietnamese people cried out to Lac Long Quan for deliverance from the foreign ruler, he returned as promised: he captured Au Co, the wife of the intruder, and took her to a mountain. Failing to retrieve his wife, the Chinese king quit Vietnam in despair. But the sons Au Co bore the dragon-lord became the first Lac lords.

The closeness of the Vietnamese relationship to classical China is evident in this foundation myth, although credit for civilization and independence goes to the local culture-hero. It is likely that the Lac lord's maritime inheritance was the mythical background to the introduction of water into rice-fields and the consequent increase in production. Chinese records indicate that strenuous efforts were made to switch from hunting and fishing to the cultivation of rice, with the aid of iron implements. As junior officials within the Han administration, the Lac lords would have been expected to encourage agriculture. Their co-operation was also necessary for the sinicization that accompanied this fundamental shift in economic activity. This transformation was not unopposed, however. In AD 40 two aristocratic sisters, Trung Trac and Trung Nhi, led a major rebellion. General Ma Yuan, with an army of 20,000 Chinese troops, overcame the rebels and promptly set about strengthening the administration of the Vietnamese commanderies. 'Wherever he passed,' a Chinese chronicler reports, 'he established prefectures and districts to govern walled-towns and their environs, and dug ditches to irrigate the fields in order to sustain the people living in those places.' Garrisons were also left to protect imperial officials, who were directly responsible for implementing the regulations by which Ma Yuan bound the Vietnamese to the Chinese empire. Thus the Vietnamese came more and more under Chinese influence, many intermarrying with the flood of immigrants from China.

The legacy of Ma Yuan was full Chinese administration. The beheading of the Trung sisters in AD 42 showed how far the independence of Vietnam had declined since the days of the mythical Au Co. But the influence of China penetrated no further south than Hué, until an independent Vietnam started expanding in that direction at the expense of the Indianized kingdom of Champa. This loosely organized state first attacked the commandery of Rinan in AD 399. That Ma Yuan's settlement was effective in northern Vietnam can be seen from the brick-built tombs excavated in the Red river valley. These traditional Chinese graves, the epitome of ancestor worship, served the needs of the great provincial families who arose during the Three Kingdoms period (AD 221–280). Their fortified houses controlled the countryside, offering security to indigenous peasants as well as employment to immigrant scholars, and in times of disorder they acted as bastions of Chinese authority. But the Vietnamese language survived and local magnates spoke it alongside the official Chinese tongue. Vietnam shared in the population growth of the southern provinces, and had certainly passed the one million mark. It remained a quiet provincial backwater till the sixth century AD, when the first of a series of rebellions broke out. They failed to secure Vietnamese independence for another three centuries, however.

See HAN DYNASTY; MA YUAN; QIN DYNASTY

*K. W. Taylor, *The Birth of Vietnam* (Berkeley, 1983).

# W

**Wang Chong** (AD 27–100) was the outspoken rationalist of the final centuries of the Han dynasty (202 BC– AD 220). He lived through the restoration and consolidation of Chinese imperial authority following the brief usurpation of Wang Mang (AD 9–23), but he was sceptical about the easy intellectual assumptions of his contemporaries at this time of marked prosperity. Retiring from the civil service in AD 88, Wang Chong chose a life of rural solitude, an old tradition for disillusioned scholars. 'Living in poverty,' he remarked, 'my ambition did not flag. I read ancient writings in plenty, and listen with delight to curious conversations. The books of this age and the common views make me uneasy. Dwelling in voluntary seclusion, I examine and appraise the true and the false.'

Hatred of the false and the preposterous was undoubtedly the driving force behind his voluminous writings. Wang Chong's scepticism was especially aroused by divination. He protested that omens taken from shells and stalks could not reasonably be said to reflect the heavenly will. Such a belief assumed that supernatural forces were willing to interfere in human affairs for good or ill: Wang Chong saw no evidence to support such a proposition. Likewise the regular eclipses of

Wang Chong chose rural solitude in order to pursue his own philosophical studies.

the sun and moon had nothing to do with government. 'A hundred such strange occurrences or a thousand calamities all share a natural explanation; they are not something that the ruler or the government could bring about.' Thus Dong Zhongshu's (c. 179–c. 104 BC) theory of cosmic interaction was in the opinion of Wang Chong nothing more than an attempt to bolster Confucian social distinctions. Established conventions and custom were sufficient to ensure the maintenance of society. Probably Wang Chong was himself aware of the strikingly modern ideas of the contemporary Infinite Empty Space school, which saw the heavens as 'empty and void of substance . . . and having no bounds. The sun, the moon, and the company of stars float in empty space, moving or standing still. All are condensed vapour.' Yet he also accepted that at birth the stars could exercise influence on an individual's destiny. It has been suggested that Wang Chong was pushed into this explanation of fortune by a desire to avoid entanglement with the arbitrary powers then ascribed to deities and spirits. At least the stars were regular in their motions.

Astrology was at this time spreading to the people from its former restricted function at the courts of the rulers. Wang Chong fully recognized both its status and involvement with scientific advance. He would not have been surprised that shortly after his own death the Director of Astrology, Zhang Heng, would invent the first practical seismograph. Nor would he have been taken aback by this official's assertion in AD 133 that a particularly severe earthquake indicated heavenly disapproval of eunuch power in the imperial balance. Another object of Wang Chong's scepticism was the spirit world. Against contemporary anxiety about ghosts, he argued that there was no proof of anything surviving the corruption of the body. He pointed out the scarceness of supposed sightings. If indeed the dead could become spirits and be observed, then instead of appearing in ones or twos, there would be ghosts thronging the roads in great numbers.

*See* DONG ZHONGSHU; ORACLES; ZHANG HENG

*Kung-chuan Hsiao, *A History of Chinese Political Thought. Volume One: From the Beginnings to the Sixth Century AD* (Princeton, 1979); J. Needham, *Science and Civilisation in China. Volume Two: The History of Scientific Thought* (Cambridge, 1956); M. Loewe, *Chinese Ideas of Life and Death: Faith, Myth and Reason in the Han Period (202 BC–AD 220)*, (London, 1982).

**Wang Mang** (33 BC–AD 23) formally usurped the Chinese throne in AD 9. He was the nephew of a consort of the Han emperor Yuan Di (49–33 BC) and became a powerful figure at court during the period when his aunt assumed power on behalf of the child-emperor Ping Di (1 BC–AD 6). Then Wang Mang was appointed as commander-in-chief of the armed forces with full authority over the civil administration. Determined to prevent rival families of consorts from challenging his position, Wang Mang degraded the previous emperor's surviving empresses, and even desecrated their families' tombs. The sudden death of the fourteen-year-old emperor in AD 6 was blamed on Wang Mang, but he seems an unlikely poisoner. With the young man already married to his own daughter, his position as the power behind the throne was hardly threatened by any future birth of an imperial heir who would be his grandson. Dowager Empress Wang moved swiftly to declare Wang Mang regent: the two-year-old great-great-grandson of Emperor Han Xuan Di (74–49 BC) was designated as heir-apparent. Within three months, however, the regent had changed his title to acting emperor. The ease with which Wang Mang suppressed rebellions raised by discontented members of the imperial clan, and the acceptance of his government by practically all officials, was undoubtedly the turning point of his career, for it appeared that the Han dynasty had lost the heavenly mandate to rule.

Fabrication of omens, such as the discovery of a bronze casket with a favourable inscription, set the scene for Wang Mang's usurpation in AD 9. Then he declared Han rule finished, and ascended the throne himself, calling his dynasty the Xin, or 'New'. The young Han prince he had displaced was not killed, and was later married to

one of his granddaughters. Had Wang Mang founded a successful dynasty, then Chinese historians would have regarded him as the legitimate ruler and detailed with sympathy the policies of his reign. But with the collapse of his administration and his violent death in AD 23, Wang Mang automatically became a usurper who was blamed for a whole series of bungled decisions.

His reign was a time of severe economic crisis. At the centre of the reforms Wang Mang introduced to tackle it was a redistribution of land aimed at curbing the power of substantial landowners and relieving peasant distress. The process of land concentration may have helped to feed a growing urban population, but the advent of speculation in the countryside offered nothing to smaller farmers. A bad harvest, higher taxation, official corruption, an imperial requisition, rebellion, a nomad incursion – any of these events spelt debt and ruin to the peasant who lacked financial reserves. So the buying and selling of land was banned by Wang Mang, and small families in possession of large estates were forced to surrender part of their holdings for reallocation to those who had none. Government loans at low interest were offered to poor peasants for the purchase of tools and seed, the finance for this regeneration of the countryside coming from state monopolies over salt, iron, alcohol and gold. More rigorous in operating these sources of imperial revenue, Wang Mang sought to extend the measures for price stabilization also first introduced by the Han emperor Wu Di in 110 BC. Added to foodstuffs were the items commonly used in the making of clothes, like silk cloth, thread and wadding.

Another reform of Wang Mang was the restriction placed on slavery. The measure mainly affected wealthy families that kept domestic slaves. The lowest group in society, the enslaved were never a really significant feature of classical China, unlike the Greco-Roman world. Although he was obliged to abandon an outright ban on the buying and selling of slaves, and instead substitute a stiff annual tax, Wang Mang did much to improve the lot of the servile. He had no hesitation, for instance, in ordering his middle son to commit suicide for having murdered a slave.

Wang Mang's fall was triggered by the effects of a prolonged drought. That it coincided with large-scale operations against the Hunnish Xiongnu only made matters worse in the northern provinces, which rose in two great peasant rebellions: the 'Red Eyebrows' in present-day Shandong province, and the 'Green Woodsmen' in neighbouring Hubei. The success of the 'Green Woodsmen' in repulsing an imperial expedition gave encouragement to anti-Wang movements elsewhere, with the result that in AD 23 the severed head of the usurping Xin emperor was stoned by the crowd.

See HAN DYNASTY; MANDATE OF HEAVEN; ORACLES; SLAVERY

*M. Loewe, *Crisis and Conflict in Han China* (London, 1974).

**Warfare** was at times endemic during the classical era. China was rightly termed the Warring States prior to imperial unification in 221 BC; rivalry between the successor kingdoms of Alexander the Great's empire – Antigonid Macedon, Seleucid Asia and Ptolemaic Egypt – kept the eastern Mediterranean in turmoil during the third and second centuries BC; India endured both foreign invasion and internecine conflict between the Mauryan (322–183 BC) and the Gupta dynasties (AD 320–550); and Rome was almost constantly at war during the late republic (200–31 BC), while afterwards its imperial forces were confronted on the northern frontier by German tribesmen and in the east by the Parthians (171 BC–AD 226) and the Sasanians (AD 226–651).

In the classic encounter in Europe, however, the Athenians and their Plataean allies in 490 BC defeated at Marathon a Persian expeditionary force. To the amazement of the invaders, the Greeks charged without any support from cavalry or archers. The Persian reaction was that these infantrymen were insane, until the disciplined tactics of the Greeks told in hand-to-hand fighting. According to the dramatist Aeschylus (525–456 BC), who took part in the battle, the thrusting spear overcame the bow. Although some of the Persians had body armour of scales sewn on leather jerkins, the majority were lightly attired for the more mobile warfare practised in West Asia: the Greeks, in contrast, wore bronze helmets, corslets and greaves. They were also protected by a large round shield made of wood and reinforced by bronze, the so-called hoplon, from which footsoldiers took their name of hoplites. Once through the terrible barrage of enemy arrows, therefore, the Athenians and the Plataeans had the advantage, for the Persians were, in comparison with the hoplites, virtually unprotected.

The equipment of the Greek infantryman, the hoplite: helmet, corslet, shield and sword. Only the spear and greaves are missing.

Because hoplite equipment cost a great deal, the development of the phalanx, the close-packed body of infantry in which hoplites deployed, cannot be regarded as the democratization of Greek armies. Only the highly trained Spartans received state aid for armour, a fact which ensured in most city-states that poor citizens were obliged to fight as light-armed auxiliaries on land, or pull an oar at sea. A phalanx was never less than four ranks deep, so that an engagement between two tended to be a slow process of attrition and required a steady nerve – no mean test for the part-time citizen-soldier. What appears to have happened when the battle lines met was a pushing match, as ranks to the rear of each phalanx put their bodies into the hollows of their shields and forced those ahead constantly onward. The key to success was to remain in rank, and to preserve the cohesive protection offered by the line of shields. Heavy casualties only occurred when the shield-wall fell apart. It has been plausibly argued that the set-piece encounter of phalanxes was designed to minimize the death-toll. Annihilation of entire armies was rare in classical Greece, as uniform body armour ensured protection from repeated attacks. Not until the composite armies pioneered by the Macedonians became the norm would heavy casualties be suffered by huge phalanxes at the hands of cavalry, elephants and missile-throwers. From a safe distance, for example, slingers hurled deadly shot, which might even be inscribed with insults. For warfare between Greek city-states was essentially an extension of the sheep-raid. Gaining agricultural supplies by raiding was an alternative to farming, a way of making up deficiencies in one's own supplies. A counter-raid might then lead to a battle, if opposed in strength. Since those who farmed the land were the ones most directly interested in defence, phalanxes were largely composed of farmers. According to the philosopher Aristotle (384–322 BC), 'there was a law in some communities that those who live right next to the border should not take part in the debates about going to war with neighbours, on the grounds that their own private interests prevent them from giving good counsel'.

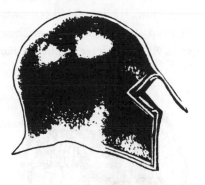

The so-called Corinthian helmet, beaten from a single piece of bronze. It gave the head full protection, but also rendered the wearer temporarily deaf.

Sparta and Athens, the two powers that emerged dominant from the Persian attack 480–479 BC on Greece, were unrepresentative. Their struggle for hegemony in the Peloponnesian War (431–404 BC) was as unusual as it was unexpectedly long. The Athenians were exceptional in having a large reserve of cash, the accumulated tribute from a maritime empire, while the mass rural slavery supporting the Spartans left these hardened professionals free to drill and campaign without any concern for agriculture. Indeed, for over a century after Marathon the battlefields of Greece belonged to the Spartans, whose phalanx advanced at a steady and unnerving pace to the accompaniment of pipes. Though for a Spartan there could be no question of retreat, standing firm was eventually to prove inadequate in the face of new tactics. At Leuctra, in central Greece, the Theban generals Epaminondas (died 362 BC) and Pelopidas (died 364 BC) ended Spartan invincibility by the skilful use of cavalry and a mass of hoplites fifty shields deep on the left of their phalanx. The striking column slammed into the Spartan line, which was unable to push it back. The deaths of the two generals in action soon ended the run of Theban victories, but no single Greek state could reach such a height of military power that it could permanently subjugate the others. The result was a stalemate prior to the rise of Macedon, whose future king Philip II (359–336 BC), the father of Alexander the Great (356–323 BC), was a hostage in Thebes shortly after Leuctra. The tactical lessons he learned there undoubtedly influenced the military reforms he sponsored on ascending the throne. For the Macedonian conquest of Greece and Persia was achieved by means of flexible deployment of horse and foot, although the core of the army remained a phalanx armed with a huge pike, the sarissa.

The eastward advance of the Macedonians was halted in 326 BC by anxiety over the size of the Indian army belonging to the Nanda dynasts of the Ganges valley. Awaiting Alexander were reportedly 200,000 infantry, 20,000 cavalry, 4,000 elephants, and 2,000 chariots. What the weary Macedonians preferred not to face was one of the earliest professional armies in classical India. Hindu tradition regards the Nandas (546–322 BC) as marking a decisive downturn in Indian history. As destroyers of the old aristocratic class, they inaugurated an era in which, for the most part, rulers were low-born and unrighteous. The demotion of the hereditary warrior-class implies the end of heroic battles, an event in China that can be dated to the fifth century BC eclipse of the chariot-archer by the crossbowman. Candragupta (322–297 BC), the first Mauryan emperor, regularly fielded 600,000 infantry, 30,000 cavalry, and 9,000 elephants. War in India had clearly become a professional concern. For the successors of Alexander, victory on the battlefield was no less important. Lacking the traditional legitimacy of the city-state, these self-acclaimed kings were entirely dependent on military power. Hence the initial advantage enjoyed by Seleucus I (305–281 BC) with his elephant corps. In return for ceding Aria, Arachosia and Paropamisadae (the areas round modern Herat, Kandahar and Kabul respectively) to Candragupta, Seleucus received in 303 BC a gift of 500 war elephants. Two years later in Asia Minor these great animals executed a decisive manoeuvre at the battle of Ipsus (present-day Sipsin) and confirmed the division of Alexander's vast spear-won realm between his generals. The elephants prevented enemy cavalry from attacking the exposed phalanx. Luckily for the Ptolemies in Egypt and the Antigonids in Macedon, the Seleucids did not acquire the crossbow as well. This Chinese invention was to remain in East Asia for another millennium. Its eventual adoption in medieval Europe proved an even more startling event than the elephant charge. In 1139 all those who employed the 'diabolical machine' against Christians were anathematized.

A coin minted by Hannibal to pay his troops in Italy. Elephants were only absent from the battlefields of China.

The increased scale of fighting that arose in the Mediterranean as a consequence of the rivalry between Greco-Macedonian monarchs became even more pronounced with the growth of Roman power. Of all classical powers Rome was distinguished by its capacity for virtually constant warfare: its sole rival would be the Chinese state of Qin. At Cynoscephalae in 197 BC the legions ended the supremacy of the phalanx, when the outmanoeuvred Macedonians were assaulted from the flanks and rear as well. The sarissa proved useless at close quarters against the sword and better defensive armour of the Roman legionary. Macedon's final defeat, however, was brought about in 168 BC at Pydna, when Rome forced war upon its last king, Perseus (179–168 BC). There the sixty-year-old consul Aemilius Paullus slaughtered 20,000 Macedonians, the 3,000 men of the royal guard fighting to the last. Perseus later gave himself up to grace the victor's march of triumph at Rome and die under harsh conditions in captivity.

Thus the military-minded Romans came to dominate the Mediterranean world. Paullus' victory satisfied a desire for glory which was the supreme value of the Roman aristocracy. 'No one could hold a public office at Rome,' the historian Polybius tells us, 'before he had completed ten campaigns.' Besides military prowess, there was also an economic motive behind the war-policy. Hugh areas of land came into Roman hands, as did enormous quantities of plunder; millions of people were enslaved; tribute poured in; and the activities of officials and businessmen exacted large profits wherever the legions went.

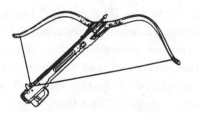

The Chinese crossbow, the most effective of classical weapons.

The Roman preoccupation with warfare is evident in the implacable nature of Mars, a war god with none of the capriciousness of the Greek Ares. Neither of them, however, have anything in common with Guan Di, the Confucian god of war, who sought to prevent conflict in China. It is indeed a paradox that the classical Chinese possessed in the crossbow the most effective weapon of all, yet they chose to subordinate under the Han dynasty (202 BC – AD 220) the military arm to the control of civilian officials. But then the Chinese emperor was only supposed to attain his ends through benevolence, so force was never easy to glorify because its use necessarily represented an admission of failure. Possibly the violence and oppression of the Qin, after its triumph in 221 BC over all the other feudal states, was a factor in this unprecedented development. But even in the writings of Sun Zi (430–381 BC), the earliest military theorist in the world, we find a concentration on the social and psychological aspects of warfare. Weaponry is hardly mentioned, and the best victory is said to be the one achieved without any fighting taking place. Even though Chinese armies easily outnumbered Roman ones, they were rarely interested in envelopment and massacre. Manpower shortages eventually forced a change in Roman tactics, so that the recruitment of foreign captives became a regular method of maintaining the strength of garrisons along the imperial frontiers. Other methods of swelling

427

the ranks with men from outside the empire were voluntary recruitment or conscription as a result of a treaty. These recruits were split into small contingents and mixed with existing units. One Sasanian officer who surrendered to the emperor Julian in AD 363 later rose to high rank. Yet the Roman army was already a very heterogeneous force. Even its famous battle-cry, which rose from a murmur to an awesome roar in a long crescendo, was itself of German origin. After the disastrous defeat at Adrianople (modern Edirne in Bulgaria) in AD 378, the Romans were dependent on Gothic recruits, a circumstance which eventually led to the loss of the western provinces. From Constantinople a diminished Roman state fought on to become Byzantium. It held at bay the Sasanian rulers of Iran, although an attempt to reconquer the western Mediterranean under the emperor Justinian (AD 527–565) proved to be as ill judged as it was ruinous.

See ALEXANDER THE GREAT; ATHENS; CANDRAGUPTA; EPAMINONDAS; GOTHS; JUSTINIAN; PAULLUS; PERSIAN INVASIONS; QIN DYNASTY; ROME; SELEUCIDS; SPARTA; SUN ZI; THEBES

*B. Bar-Kochva, The Seleucid Army (Cambridge, 1976); G. T. Date, The Art of War in Ancient India (Bombay, 1929); A. Ferrill, The Fall of the Roman Empire: The Military Explanation (London, 1986); A. K. Goldsworthy, The Roman Army at War, 100 BC–AD 200 (Oxford, 1996); V. D. Hanson, The Western Way of War: Infantry Battle in Classical Greece (London, 1989); W. V. Harris, War and Imperialism in Republican Rome, 327–70 BC (Oxford, 1979); W. K. Pritchett, The Greek State at War (Berkeley, 1971 onwards); W. Treadgold, Byzantium and its Army, 284–1081 (Stanford, 1995); Sun Zi, The Art of War, trans. by S. G. Griffith (Oxford, 1963).

**Warring States** period (481–221 BC) witnessed an unprecedented bout of internecine conflict among the feudal powers which constituted the Middle Kingdom, as China was then called. That this rivalry also gave rise to the oldest surviving military treatise in the world is a sign of the intense contemporary preoccupation with armed solutions to the problem of political instability. Because war was of such vital importance to a state, Sun Zi wrote his Art of War as a systematic guide for feudal rulers in much the same way as philosophers offered advice on administration and justice. But in spite of the belligerence of the times, the Art of War makes plain how an engagement on the battlefield is only one part of warfare and not the preferred part. The aim of the skilled strategist is rather the overcoming of an opponent without the clash of arms. For Sun Zi's restraint derives from an appreciation of logistics, and their burdensome cost. 'Operations inevitably require the expenditure of 1,000 pieces of silver a day . . . And, if a campaign is protracted, the resources of a state will prove unequal to the strain.'

Seven major states fought for supremacy during the Warring States period: Qi, Yan, Zhao, Han, Wei, Qin and Chu. The main contenders were Qin, situated in the north-west, and the southern state of Chu. The final campaign between them did not occur until 223 BC. That year the veteran Qin general Wang Qian took a leaf out of the *Art of War* and lulled the Chu army into a mood of over-confidence, and then launched an attack at the moment its discipline was loose and its alertness lost. The crushing victory paved the way for unification of China in 221 BC and the foundation of the Qin dynasty.

*See* CHU; QIN; QIN DYNASTY; SUN ZI
★S. G. Griffith, *Art of War* (Oxford, 1963); J. I. Crump, *Chan-kuo T'se* (Oxford, 1979).

**Wei dynasty** (AD 220–265) was founded by Cao Pi, the son of the infamous Chinese warlord Cao Cao. On his father's death in AD 220, Cao Pi (AD 186–226) quickly moved to strengthen his own position in north China. Having taken over the offices and titles held by Cao Cao, he cut short the mourning expected of a filial son and went on a festive tour of the southern part of his domain. This was the politically sensitive frontier because two prominent families in the south and south-west refused to accept the dominant position enjoyed by the Cao. In order to assert his superiority over both of them, Cao Pi forced the last Han emperor to abdicate in his favour. An obliging courtier had already revealed an omen some seven years old which predicted this transfer of the heavenly mandate to rule.

The result was a declaration by the Sun family in the lower Yangzi river valley that it ruled as the imperial Wu, while at present-day Chengdu the Liu, a branch of the imperial Han clan, set itself up as the Shu dynasty. Although Chinese historians came to regard the Wei dynasty as legitimate, it never ruled the whole of China. The period of struggle between Wei, Wu and Shu was called the Three Kingdoms. It was ended in AD 280 by the Western Jin dynasty (AD 265–316), which had toppled the Wei house fourteen years earlier. The first Western Jin emperor, Sima Yan, was another northern general in the mould of Cao Cao, but he outdid him by briefly achieving the reunification of China.

*See* CAO CAO; HAN DYNASTY; ORACLES; THREE KINGDOMS; SIMA YAN; MANDATE OF HEAVEN
★W. Eberhard, *A History of China* (London, 1956).

**Western Jin dynasty** (AD 265–316) was the last imperial house of the classical era in China. It was founded by a northern warlord by the name of Sima Yan, whose father had dominated the previous Wei dynasty (AD 220–265) for a number of years. Like the founder of the Wei house before him, Sima

Yan staged an elaborate abdication and enthronment ceremony to mark the transfer of the heavenly mandate to rule. Because he had come to the throne with the aid of his extraordinarily large and ramified family, Sima Yan rewarded nearly thirty of their number with semi-independent territories. The idea behind this development of provincial power was the protection of the throne from the kind of palace coup he had organized himself. While the enfeoffed princes could rally their forces to the dynasty whenever a military crisis occurred, there was nothing to stop them quarrelling amongst themselves once Sima Yan's firm grip was removed from the tiller of state. This is exactly what happened after the death of Sima Yan in AD 289. In little more than a decade the Western Jin dynasty was racked by internal conflict. Factions at court used assassination to remove rivals. Provincial princes began to vie for power, negotiating for support from foreign allies settled within the imperial frontiers. In AD 304, however, the Hunnish Xiongnu decided to rise up in their own interest rather than that of a Chinese warlord. By AD 311 they had sacked the capital, Luoyang, and taken the nominal emperor prisoner; then in AD 316 the last Western Jin emperor was captured at Chang'an, and the whole of north China passed into foreign control. The remnant of Sima Yan's house fled southwards and at Nanjing established the Eastern Jin dynasty (AD 317–420).

By AD 325 some 60 per cent of the Chinese upper classes had moved south as well. Attempts by the Hunnish Xiongnu and the Tartar Xianbei to follow proved abortive. In AD 383 the Eastern Jin army managed to halt at Feishui, the southernmost nomadic thrust from the steppe, thus confirming the independence of the Chinese settled south of the Huai river valley. The line of partition was the northern boundary of the wet-rice growing area, country unsuited to cavalry. But the remarkable victory at Feishui over an infantry force of 600,000 supported by 270,000 cavalry could not avert the division of China for almost three centuries.

See MANDATE OF HEAVEN; SIMA YAN; WEI DYNASTY; XIONGNU

★W. Eberhard, *A History of China* (London, 1956).

**Western Regions**, so-named by the classical Chinese because they lay beyond the western end of the Great Wall, were first formed into a protectorate around 100 BC. The interest of the Han emperor Wu Di (140–87 BC) had been aroused in Central Asia by reports of large horses there. His envoy Zhang Qian passed this valuable piece of information to the throne in 126 BC, on his return from a mission to the Da Yuezhi, the enemies of the Hunnish Xiongnu. Wu Di recognized at once how these mounts could be used to carry heavily armed men against the Xiongnu, who rode the smaller Mongolian pony. The subsequent expansion of Chinese influence into the Western Regions was thus a direct result of conflict with nomadic peoples living next to the Great Wall. In search of allies and horses, Chinese forces pressed westwards, reaching Kashgar in 101 BC. There they discovered enough horses for stud purposes, and shortly afterwards a protectorate was declared over the whole of the Tarim basin. As long as China kept the upper hand over the Xiongnu, its oasis states remained friendly and helpful. But the maintenance of influence in such a distant sphere involved a heavy outlay of resources, for a system of earthen defences had to be built well to the west of Dunhuang. 'Those who were submissive,' a chronicler noted of the Western Regions, 'from the very beginning received gifts and official seals as an imperial favour, but those who surrendered after a fight were punished. Agricultural garrisons were set up in fertile places and post-stations established on the main highways. Messengers and merchants travelled freely, and commerce flourished' on what later became known as the Silk Road.

The Chinese grip over the Western Regions relaxed during the dynastic troubles that culminated in the usurpation of Wang Mang (AD 9–23). But following the restoration of the Han dynasty in AD 25, the Chinese were able to reassert their influence because of the different relations they enjoyed for many years with the Xiongnu. Once this nomadic people split

into two mutually antagonistic groups China could employ one of them to contain the other. Until AD 150 the balance of power on the steppe favoured China, and the domination of Central Asia by the two empires of the Han and the Kushanas guaranteed the safety of caravans along the Silk Road. A famous Chinese general involved in this reassertion of authority was Ban Chao, the brother of the historian Ban Gu. He was protector-general of the Western Regions till AD 100, shortly before he died in retirement. During his tenure of office Ban Chao had to deal not only with nomad–raiders and restive local rulers but also, in AD 90, with the Kushanas, who had seized power in north-western India. After defeating this powerful Da Yuezhi people, Ban Chao advanced as far as the eastern shores of the Caspian, the closest a Chinese army ever got to the Roman empire. Contact between China and Rome was never direct in the classical era, notwithstanding the supposed Roman embassy of Marcus Aurelius. Its members in AD 166 were presumably merchants from Roman Syria, who pretended an official role for their own personal advantage. Silk, however, freely passed through the Western Regions on its way to Rome. The Chinese seem to have been aware of the potential value of exported surplus silk, which they also knew passed through the hands of the Parthians. The revival of Xiongnu power after AD 150 meant that Chinese influence declined in Central Asia, although caravans still passed through the Western Regions laden with luxury items of trade.

*See* BAN CHAO; GREAT WALL; XIONGNU; ZHANG QIAN

★Ying-shih Yu, *Trade and Expansion in Han China: A Study of the Sino-Barbarian Economic Relations* (Berkeley, 1967).

**Women** found themselves in a subordinate position throughout the classical world. In some societies, however, their comparative freedom was quite remarkable, as at Sparta. For the Spartans were unique in insisting upon a public education for their womenfolk. This education included physical exercise, and Spartan girls were the only Greek females who are known to have stripped naked for athletics, like Greek males. The emphasis on fitness was bound up with Sparta's preoccupation with war: all Spartan men were educated to become warriors, and the women's principal task was to give birth to warriors. The semi-legendary reformer Lycurgus, usually dated to the seventh century BC, was also said to have denied the right of a man to sleep with his wife as he chose, insisting that infrequent sexual relations were more likely to produce vigorous offspring. But the military decline of Sparta, according to the philosopher Aristotle (384–322 BC), was partly due to the wealth of its women. A husband's continual absence as a warrior, eating and sleeping in a barracks with other men, and going away for lengthy campaigns,

had affected family relationships and women's status. Spartan men seem to have deferred to their wives and let them intervene in public affairs to an extent unknown elsewhere in classical Greece. Although they were as usual denied citizenship, Spartan women could own property and amass private fortunes, something unheard of in Athens. There young girls were destined, as at Sparta, for marriage and motherhood, although marriage arrangements tended to be made by their male relations with an eye to both economic and political advantages. Marriage to relatives was attractive especially among wealthier families, since the burden of paying for Athens' military adventures fell heaviest upon them. They were required not only to command a warship but also to fit it out and even to supplement the state pay of the rowers. Before the disastrous expedition to Sicily (414–413 BC), one wealthy citizen was always appointed for each ship in the fleet, but soon afterwards two were needed to share the expense. Men of sufficient wealth to perform military service for the state were becoming scarce well before the end of the Peloponnesian War (431–404 BC).

In Athens the ideal was for a girl of fourteen years of age to marry a man around thirty. The necessity that the bride be a virgin, coupled with the classical Greek view that young girls were lustful, made early marriage desirable. Late marriage for Athenian men can be attributed to their duty to serve as soldiers or sailors for ten years. In the event of a divorce, which might be initiated by either party, the children always remained in the father's house, since they had been born to perpetuate his line. Even though they undertook important religious duties, Athenian women spent their lives running the home, where they had their own quarters. One prominent woman was the hereditary priestess of Athena, who in 480 BC supported the decision to evacuate Athens in the face of the Persian threat by reporting that the goddess' sacred snake had already left the acropolis. Another deity important to Athenian women was Dionysus, god of vegetation, wine and ecstasy. We cannot be certain that they attended plays performed at his twice-yearly festivals, but they participated in other aspects of the god's worship, if surviving scenes from painted vases are regarded as reliable testimony.

The scope for independent action enjoyed by Spartan women, while

Ideal womanhood, third century BC Italy. Roman women were often very wealthy in their own right.

their husbands were away at war for long periods of time, anticipated the liberty gained by Roman wives. Dominated though Rome was by a military culture which elevated masculinity, its reliance on women to bear legitimate heirs tended to give them an altogether unintended status. Women were allowed to own property in their own right, since the rules of inheritance treated male and female claimants equally. As a result some aristocratic widows found themselves in control of great wealth. And their education seems to have been sufficient for them to be able to hold their own in a male-dominated society. Perhaps the greatest conflict between two women in Rome was that between Octavia, the sister of the first Roman emperor Augustus (31 BC – AD 14), and Cleopatra, the last Macedonian ruler of Egypt. Their point of dispute was Mark Antony (82–30 BC), who eventually chose to stay with Cleopatra because she delivered him an heir. It should be recalled, too, that Antony's marriage to Octavia in 40 BC had been part of a peace agreement signed with her brother. In 37 BC Antony had abandoned her for Cleopatra, who promptly produced a son. Not until 32 BC did a formal divorce occur and provide the future emperor with an excuse to resume hostilities. Until then, Octavia was still able to present herself as Antony's wife, because his relationship with Cleopatra was not recognized by Roman law, the Egyptian queen lacking any rights as a non-Roman.

In classical Persia high-born women also exercised an influence on affairs of state. Members of the Achaemenid

Octavia, second wife of Antony and rival of Cleopatra. After Antony's death she brought up all his children.

royal family possessed their own estates, and documents survive showing their active involvement in management: letters relate to the shipment of grain, wine and animals to palaces from distant land-holdings. The only limits on the extent of the authority exercised by the Persian king's mother, for instance, were set by the monarch himself. She had no formal power, but, like other royal women, she used the economic independence that her position gave her to further her own ends. Aristocratic women seem to have exercised similar roles in the upper reaches of Persian society. That the Persian king maintained a harem, however, complicated palace life and encouraged intrigue. In 465 BC the would-be conqueror of Greece, Xerxes, perished in a palace intrigue. For that reason the account of Persia found in the Greek historian Heredotus often portrays women as threatening the existing order. A parallel anxiety may have led to a lowering of the status of women in India during the first and second centuries AD. The law code of Manu accepted child-marriage as normal practice, thereby accentuating the difference between boys and girls. Young Hindu men were expected to remain celibate during a period of education which prepared them for adult life, but young women entirely bypassed such instruction in order to become wives and mothers.

Humility was also the expected pattern of behaviour for women in China, since they were naturally held to be inferior to men. Its most famous woman, Ban Zhao (died *c.* AD 120), sister of the historian Ban Gu, based her *Lessons for Women* on this principle. 'Yin and yang,' she wrote, 'are not of the same nature; men and women behave differently. Rigidity is the virtue of the yang; yielding is the function of the yin. Strength is the glory of men; weakness is women's quality. Thus it is that the way of obedience is the proper behaviour for a woman.' Subordination was shown in women's deference to their fathers when they were children, their husbands when they were married, and their sons when they were widowed. The ideal age for a girl to marry was fifteen, but wedlock could not be countenanced between persons of the same surname, lest the couple have a common ancestor. This taboo originated during the

Warring States period (481–221 BC), when social upheaval gave rise to family names, and its influence has not entirely disappeared among modern Chinese. There were seven grounds for divorcing a wife: namely, disobedience to parents-in-law, barrenness, adultery, jealousy, incurable disease, loquacity and theft. It should be noted, however, that a man could have only one wife. Concubines were never regarded as full members of the family and the status of a concubine was always inferior to that of a wife. Unfortunately for women, Ban Zhao's recommendation that they should receive the same classical education that she had enjoyed was generally ignored. Because of her Confucian learning she was able to complete her brother's history of the earlier part of the Han dynasty (202 BC – AD 9) and Wang Mang's usurpation (AD 9–23). Her *Lessons for Women* arose from Ban Zhao's appointment as tutor to a Han empress and her ladies-in-waiting.

*See* ATHENS; BAN ZHAO; MANU; PERSIA; ROME

*M. Brosius, *Women in Ancient Persia, 559–331 BC* (Oxford, 1996); S. B. Pomeroy, *Goddesses, Whores, Wives and Slaves: Women in the Classical World* (London, 1975); N. L. Swann, *Pan Chao: Foremost Woman Scholar of China* (New York, 1932).

**Xenophon** (428–354 BC) was born of a comparatively wealthy Athenian family, but his involvement with the oligarchic reaction of 404 BC led him to live abroad. After the surrender of Athens at the end of the Peloponnesian War (431–404 BC) the Spartan admiral Lysander installed a repressive regime known as the Thirty. Somewhat naïvely Xenophon accepted their rule as a necessary prelude to the introduction of a franchise limited to property-holders. Born of a generation hardened to violent death, he does not seem to have been unduly worried by the suggestion that the Spartan garrison backing the tyrannous oligarchy should be paid from the money belonging to murdered rich alien residents. But the execution in 403 BC of Theramenes, who typically opposed this confiscation, did trouble Xenophon, because in his *History of My Times* he later wrote that 'the Thirty had come to regard him as an obstacle in the way of their complete liberty to do as they pleased'. No longer under any illusion about the nature of the regime he sup-

ported, Xenophon may have taken the opportunity to switch sides when Thrasybulus (died 388 BC) organized a democratic counterattack from Thebes. There is no evidence to show that Xenophon suffered persecution under the restored democracy, and indeed he is credited with bringing Thucydides' unpublished *History of the Peloponnesian War* to public notice. Possibly he had begun to write his own history, which picks up the narrative exactly where Thucydides' breaks off.

Against the strong advice of the philosopher Socrates (469–399 BC), Xenophon went to Asia Minor and joined at Sardis the Greek mercenary army of Cyrus, the second son of the Persian king Darius II. The monarch had died in 405 BC, leaving four sons, of whom the first two disputed the throne. Artaxerxes II, the eldest, succeeded, but Cyrus claimed the better right because he had been born while his father was reigning. Xenophon's account of the campaign, entitled the *March Up-country* or the *Persian Expedition*, presents Cyrus as a model leader and not the ambitious rebel he undoubtedly was. Written in the 370s BC, while Xenophon was living near Olympia, the *March Up-country* relates how the Ten Thousand, the name by which the Greek contingent was known, reluctantly marched to Babylon and almost gave Cyrus victory in 401 BC at the battle of Cunaxa. But Cyrus fell and the Persians rallied under Tissaphernes, the previous governor of Sardis. Tissaphernes (died 395 BC) later lured the Greek commanders into a trap and killed all of them. Undaunted, the Ten Thousand elected new leaders, one of whom was Xenophon, and set off northwards towards the Black Sea. They fought a passageway through the bitterly cold mountains until a great cheer went up at the sight of the sea. Returning to the Aegean coast, the mercenary force came into favour with the Spartans, who until 394 BC were trying under King Agesilaus to end Persian domination there. Xenophon was employed by Sparta as a general, and his friendship with Agesilaus (444–360 BC) dates from this period. Once again, the exiled Athenian showed his preference for oligarchic rule by admiration of this energetic but unsuccessful monarch. A participant in 394 BC at the battle of Coronea, Xenophon has to admit that Agesilaus 'did not adopt the safest plan [of action, but] crashed into the Thebans front to front. So with shield pressed against shield they struggled, killed and were killed.'

Allowed to stay in Sparta, and then presented by the Spartans with an estate near Olympia, Xenophon settled down to life as an author. Besides his historical writings, he dealt with such subjects as horsemanship, hunting and estate management. His *Education of Cyrus*, an imaginary biography of the first Persian king, could be described as the first Greek novel.

*See* AGESILAUS; CYRUS THE YOUNGER; SPARTA; THERAMENES; THRASYBULUS; TISSAPHERNES

*Xenophon, *A History of My Times*, trans. by R. Warner (Harmondsworth, 1966); Xenophon, *The Persian Expedition*, trans. by R. Warner (Bristol, 1981); J. K. Anderson, *Xenophon* (London, 1974).

**Xiang Yu** (233–201 BC) was a leading rebel commander in the bitter struggle to overthrow the Qin dynasty (221–207 BC), the first Chinese imperial house. He was a noble of the former state of Chu and his uncle, Xiang Liang, was the son of a famous Chu general. Early in 208 BC the uncle and the nephew staged an uprising in what today is the city of Suzhou, in the lower Yangzi river valley, and then led a force of 8,000 men northwards. Learning of the death of Chen Sheng, the first rebel leader against Qin domination, they installed the grandson of a former Chu ruler as king. As the so-called 'Avenging Army of Chu' advanced other rebel groups joined forces with it, including the one led by Liu Bang, the future first emperor of the Han dynasty (202 BC – AD 220).

Tactics were agreed among the

rebels, although Xiang Yu was already looked upon as the most influential commander. Apart from his birth, Xiang Yu had a powerful physical presence: he was seven feet in height and, according to the historian Sima Qian, he was 'so strong he could lift a bronze cauldron unaided'. While Liu Bang was sent westwards to take the war to the Qin heartland, Xiang Yu grew over-confident of his military position and unwisely risked a pitched battle at Dingtao, in modern Shandong province. His uncle fell and his forces were routed. Only Xiang Yu's courage and determination rallied the rebels, whom he steadied through a display of confidence. He 'sank all his boats, smashed the cooking pots and vessels, and set fire to his huts, to make clear to his followers that they must fight to the death, for he had no intention of retreating'. A series of engagements designed to relieve besieged rebel cities wrested the initiative from the imperial army and persuaded its commander, Zhang Han (died 206 BC), that the time was ripe for negotiations with the rebels. Zhang Han's loss of nerve was not unconnected with a reprimand he had just received from the Second Emperor for not achieving victory. The power behind the throne, the eunuch Zhao Gao, had pointedly refused to acknowledge Zhang Han's difficulties when he sent a special envoy to the capital. 'With tears streaming from his eyes', therefore, the Qin general joined the rebellion in 207 BC. But his troops were not well

received as many of the rebels had previously suffered at Qin hands when working on public works, such as the Great Wall. So restive did Zhang Han's army become that Xiang Yu ordered a surprise attack one night, putting 200,000 men to the sword. The massacre ended Qin military power.

Meanwhile Liu Bang had broken into the Wei river valley and threatened the Qin capital. The deaths of both the Second Emperor and Zhao Gao had left the First Emperor's nephew, Zi Ying, to face the wrath of the rebels. He surrendered at the beginning of 206 BC to Liu Bang, who sealed the treasures and palaces. On the arrival of Xiang Yu a month or so later an orgy of killing and looting took place. The violence appalled Liu Bang, but there was nothing he could do to stop the devastation or the subsequent division of the empire between the rebel leaders. Later in 203 BC he upbraided Xiang Yu for the misbehaviour: 'You desecrated the tomb of the First Emperor and you appropriated the wealth of Qin for your private use. You also executed Zi Ying, the king of Qin, who had already submitted.' What made this arrogance on the part of Xiang Yu more than Liu Bang could stomach was the breaking of the agreement by the rebels that he should receive Qin as a reward for capturing the capital. The struggle between Xiang Yu and Liu Bang lasted from late 206 to 202 BC. Seizure of the Qin heartland gave Liu Bang the edge, for he could draw on the agricultural resources of his stronghold, unlike Xiang Yu who was constantly beset by problems of supply. Never defeated on the battlefield, Xiang Yu discovered to his horror that he had frittered away his strength in unimportant quarrels. He died fleeing with a small detachment of cavalry, all that was left of 'The Avenging Army of Chu'.

*See* CHEN SHENG; GREAT WALL; LIU BANG; QIN DYNASTY; ZHANG HAN; ZHAO GAO

*A. Cotterell, *The First Emperor of China* (London, 1981).

**Xiongnu** were a permanent thorn in the side of classical China. Probably the Huns who later invaded the Roman empire, the Xiongnu compelled the Chinese to develop the line of northern defences which in 214 BC the First Emperor connected to form the Great Wall. The nomad threat was, according to Confucius (551–479 BC), first contained by an early feudal ruler, whose energetic campaigns along the northern frontier gave Chinese civilization scope to evolve in its own distinct manner. 'But for him,' Confucius remarked, 'we should now button our clothes down the side and wear our hair down the back.'

Different tactics were tried to deal with nomad incursions, the worst of which were invariably launched by the aggressive Xiongnu, but by the Han dynasty (202 BC – AD 220) it was recognized that a mix of peaceful and warlike measures were required. A stable frontier was usually secured by payment of subsidies to friendly nomad kings and the tolerance of international trade. Punitive expeditions were rare outside the reign of Han Wu Di (140–87 BC) for the good reason that defence in depth when combined with playing one tribe off against another tended to minimize conflict. Divisions within the Xiongnu, who never numbered over 3 million, were often the main cause of peace. To encourage disunity amongst the nomads Wu Di sent Zhang Qian as an envoy to Central Asia, where he noticed horses larger than the ponies used by the Xiongnu. These 'western' mounts later enabled the Chinese to inflict unprecedented defeats on the Xiongnu with armoured cavalry. But it was another of Wu Di's commanders, Li Ling, who came closest to removing the nomad threat altogether: he almost showed how the crossbow could master cavalry-archers.

During the first century AD a hostile split between the northern and the

A ceremonial broach with a nomad design. Han emperors presented such gifts of silver to Xiongnu chieftains in order to buy peace along the northern frontier.

southern Xiongnu produced a long period of peace for the Chinese empire. Diplomatic relations between China and the friendly southern Xiongnu settled down into a regular routine. A senior official with a sizeable staff and some troops was the Chinese representative at the court of the southern Xiongnu leader. A son of this nomad king stayed as hostage at the imperial court in Luoyang. At the end of each year, Xiongnu envoys and a Chinese official escorted a new hostage to Luoyang, while the old hostage was conducted back to his father. The two delegations met on the way so as to be sure that both sides honoured the agreement. Expensive gifts were also sent to the Xiongnu ruler with his returning son. The Chinese were usually content to leave the Xiongnu to their own quarrels, but in AD 89 a joint southern Xiongnu-Chinese expedition crossed the Gobi to rout the northern Xiongnu. The recovery of the northern Xiongnu, however, led to the later settlement of the southern Xiongnu within the imperial boundaries. It was here that their descendants rose in AD 304 against the Western Jin dynasty (AD 265–316). Because the Western Jin emperors were unable to cope with barbarian allies drawn into a protracted civil war, north China was lost and the classical era came to an end.

See GREAT WALL; HAN WU DI; LI LING; ZHANG QIAN

*Ying-shih Yu, *Trade and Expansion in Han China: A Study of the Structure of Sino-Barbarian Relations* (Berkeley, 1967); T. J. Barfield, *The Perilous Frontier: Nomadic Empires and China, 221 BC to AD 1757* (Oxford, 1989).

**Xun Zi**, also known as Xun Kuang (*c.* 320–235 BC) hailed from the northern state of Zhao. He travelled widely and taught his heterodox brand of Confucian philosophy in the eastern state of Qi. He also held official posts in Chu, the great southern state centred on the Yangzi river valley. Even though he died prior to the final collapse of the feudal states and the imperial unification in 221 BC under the Qin dynasty, Xun Zi recognized the depth of the social crisis through which classical China was passing. He was not unaware of the military imperative behind the growing ascendancy of Qin. He noted how its inhabitants feared officials, shunned humanizing rites and ceremonies, and showed no interest in music or literature. 'These simple and unsophisticated people can only gain benefits from their superiors by achieving distinction in battle. And rewards increase to keep pace with achievement; thus a man who returns from battle with five enemy heads is made the master of five families in the neighbourhood.' This single-minded dedication achieved ultimate victory at a heavy price. As the philosopher Aristotle wisely remarked of Sparta's miserable failure in Greece after the defeat of Athens in 404 BC, an exclusively military training was no preparation for peace and, in the last resort, was itself a cause of eventual defeat by Thebes. The Spartans 'do not appreciate leisure and never engage in any kind of pursuit higher than war . . . Those like the Spartans who specialize in one and ignore the other in their education turn men into machines.'

After a visit to Qin around 264 BC, Xun Zi had already reached the same opinion. The disdain shown for propriety, the social cement of a civilized state, condemned Qin to ultimate disaster. 'Stout armour and sharp weapons are not enough to assure victory; high walls and deep moats are not enough to assure safety; stern commands and numerous punishments are not enough to assure authority. What proceeds by the way of ritual will advance; what proceeds by any other way will fail.' Like Mencius (371–288 BC), Xun Zi believed that only a virtuous ruler could unify the feudal states. 'A petty man using petty methods,' he wrote, 'can seize a small state and hold it without much strength. But China is great and, unless a man is a sage, he cannot take possession of it.'

Xun Zi's emphasis on rites in the service of a strict social hierarchy and rigorous moral training derived from his heterodox notion about the evil nature of mankind. In the thought of Confucius there had been less stress placed on the necessity of political control for the reason that the decay of feudalism was not so advanced as in Xun Zi's lifetime. Whereas Confucius felt benevolence was the key virtue of a ruler, Xun Zi took the view that the people really needed guidance through family upbringing and state education. For Xun Zi the spiritual realm was irrelevant, and superstitious practices devised to obtain heavenly favours such as rain were a sham. 'They are done,' he wrote, 'merely for ornaments. Hence the cultivated man regards them as ornamental, but the people regard them as supernatural.' As rites and ceremonies were necessary for the maintenance of civilized society though, it was prudent to follow the practice of 'ancient kings who established rituals in order to curb disorder, to train man's desires, and to provide their satisfaction.' This combination of morality and scepticism was to form an important undercurrent in Chinese classical thought, its most notable spokesman being Wang Chong (AD 27–100). A scourge of official corruption, Wang Chong was a thoroughgoing rationalist. Xun Zi's own reputation, on the other hand, suffered from the animosity later directed at two of his students, Han Fei Zi (c. 280–233 BC) and Li Si (died 208 BC). They were both closely associated with the harsh and oppressive Qin dynasty (221–207 BC).

See CONFUCIUS; HAN FEI ZI; HUNDRED SCHOOLS; LI SI; MENCIUS; QIN DYNASTY; WANG CHONG; WARRING STATES
*H. H. Dubs, *Hsuntze: The Moulder of Ancient Confucianism* (London, 1927).

# Z

Zhang Han (died 206 BC) was a renowned Qin general. Although in 208 BC he heavily defeated the main rebel army at Dingtao (in modern Shandong province), Zhang Han could not permanently hold back the first nationwide revolt in Chinese history. So incensed were ordinary people about the harshness of life under the Qin, the first imperial house, that they rallied behind the various rebel leaders who arose from 209 BC onwards. Despite sharp the reverse at Dingtao, the southern aristocrat Xiang Yu rallied the rebels and forced Zhang Han to desert the Second Emperor's cause in 207 BC. The decision, however, was brought about as much by court intrigue as rebel strength, not least because the eunuch Zhao Gao manipulated the emperor for his own personal ends. Even so Qin was severely pressed prior to Zhang Han's desertion, for his army was recruited in part from the convicts labouring on the First Emperor's tomb at Mount Li. But the switch of sides suited neither Zhang Han nor his men, most of whom were Qin reservists. Because the rebels had themselves previously suffered as conscripted labourers on public works, they treated the recent converts to the rebellion badly. To prevent more trouble Xiang Yu launched a secret night attack and massacred the Qin soldiers. Zhang Han committed suicide in 206 BC, shortly after Liu Bang overran the Qin heartland.

See LIU BANG; QIN DYNASTY; XIANG YU; ZHAO GAO

*A. B. Cotterell, *The First Emperor of China* (London, 1981).

Zhang Heng (AD 78–139) was the inventor of the first practical seismograph. A talented poet and calligrapher, Zhang Heng was Director of Astrology at Luoyang when around AD 130 he devised his famous 'earthquake weathercock'. Although it could not furnish a scientific explanation for earthquakes, the seismograph gave the Chinese emperor immediate notice of a disaster and its direction from the capital. The

Confucian theory of the heavenly mandate to rule made the throne sensitive to the interpretation of natural phenomena. This explains the political importance of the observatory which Zhang Heng ran. In AD 133 he used his position to declare that a particularly severe earthquake indicated heavenly disapproval of eunuch power in the imperial palace. His memorial called for the restoration of authority to the place where it belonged, the emperor's own person as the Son of Heaven.

The profound sense of mystery that Zhang Heng obviously retained in the universe as an astrologer-scientist puts into perspective the scepticism of a philosopher such as Wang Chong (AD 27–100). Like the Roman philosopher and poet Lucretius (94–55 BC), Wang Chong was concerned to liberate the mind from false and disturbing opinions. But his attack on the absurdities of official ideology was largely ignored until after the disaster of AD 316; Confucian orthodoxy went unchallenged prior to the loss of the northern provinces to the Tartars that year. Thereafter Daoism, and newly arrived Buddhism, provided consolation for a partitioned China.

*See* BUDDHISM; DAOISM; INVENTIONS; LUCRETIUS; WANG CHONG

*J. Needham, *Science and Civilization in China. Volume Three: Mathematics and the Sciences of the Heavens and the Earth* (Cambridge, 1959).

**Zhang Qian** was a Chinese envoy around whom legend later gathered. It is certain, however, that the Han emperor Wu Di (140–87 BC) sent him on two embassies to Central Asia, and a third one southwards in order to find another route to India via modern Burma. His first embassy in 138 BC was caused by renewed border problems with the Xiongnu, probably the Huns who later invaded the Roman empire. After the Chinese defeat by the Xiongnu in 200 BC at Pingcheng, where the first Han emperor Gaozu was lucky to escape capture, a new defensive arrangement was tried on the northern frontier. It involved the establishment of friendly relations with nomad rulers, to whom subsidies were paid, and the tolerance of international trade. One reason for the Chinese acceptance of an armed truce with the nomad peoples of the steppe was the unity achieved by the Xiongnu, through the rise of a supreme ruler. There was no scope for playing one tribal group off against another.

But the new arrangement was not a lasting success. Hostilities continued while it was in effect and, by the accession of Wu Di in 140 BC, it was accepted that conciliation would have to be abandoned. The annual gifts of silk, wine, rice and silver were no longer being balanced by any saving on military expenditure. In 138 BC Zhang Qian was dispatched westwards to stir up the enemies of the Xiongnu in Central Asia. In spite of being held prisoner by the Xiongnu for a decade, Zhang Qian eventually located the Da

Yuehzi far removed from China. They were not, however, pastoralists even in their original home, from which they had been driven westwards by the Xiongnu. Thus the fertile valleys of Bactria provided a perfect place for their farms, and they were uninterested in an active alliance with the Chinese. Later one of the five clans of the Da Yeuhzi, the Kushanas, came to dominate the others, hence the name generally used for this people. And in the first century AD the Kushanas went on to gain control of north-western India.

What impressed Zhang Qian most about his visit to Bactria was the extent of settlement. We can still catch something of the amazement of the envoy when he returned to Chang'an, the Chinese capital, in 126 BC and reported that in what is today Afghanistan there were 'cities, mansions, and houses as in China'. Zhang Qian did not appreciate that Bactria had been very recently part of the Greco-Macedonian world. Yet no cultural exchange occurred: China became aware of other civilizations, but the only foreign influence during the classical period was to come from India in the form of Buddhism. Specific things brought back by Zhang Qian were the grape-vine, the walnut and the hemp plant.

Energetic campaigning on the steppe, especially by the Chinese general Huo Qubing (141–117 BC) who adopted the mobile tactics of the Xiongnu, had reduced the nomad threat to some extent during Zhang

Qian's absence, but there remained a problem over mounts. The small Mongolian pony was unsuitable for an armoured rider, and so Wu Di was very interested in the large horses Zhang Qian had noticed in the 'Western Regions', as the Chinese termed Central Asia. So in 115 BC the envoy was sent out again on a mission to its horse-breeding peoples. As a result one of the chieftains living near Lake Balkhash, in modern Kazakhstan, asked for the hand of a Chinese princess and sent a thousand horses as a bethrothal present. The chieftain was given Liu Xijun, a princess of the royal blood, who in 110 BC set off with a large retinue for the distant land. It was not long, however, before Wu Di tired of indirect contacts and in 101 BC, after a three-year campaign, Chinese forces succeeded in securing enough horses for stud purposes. The 'Western Regions' were declared a Chinese protectorate, although the city-states based on its oases vacillated between the Xiongnu and China according to which side pressed them hardest. Yet Zhang Qian's two embassies, and the subsequent military operation, had disturbed the old balance of nomad power and this in itself weakened the Xiongnu.

Zhang Qian seems to have been sent on a final embassy southwards. His report on Bactria revealed the presence there of goods made in Sichuan province, suggesting the existence of a trade route to India through Burma. Zhang Qian's undated journey came to nothing, even though it provided material for legends about his discovery of the source of the Yellow river. Its waters were said to flow from Heaven and be a continuation of the Milky Way. For his intrepid service Zhang Qian was ennobled by the emperor.

See BACTRIA; HAN WU DI; HUO QUBING; WESTERN REGIONS; XIONGNU
*T. J. Barfield, *The Perilous Frontier: Nomadic Empires and China, 221 BC to AD 1757* (Oxford, 1989); Ying-shih Yu, *Trade and Expansion in Han China: A Study in the Structure of Sino-Barbarian Economic Relations* (Berkeley, 1967).

**Zhao Gao** (died 207 BC) was a powerful eunuch who served both the First and Second Emperors of China. His scheming did much to hasten the collapse of the Qin dynasty (221–207 BC), the first imperial house. He conspired with Grand Councillor Li Si to deny the succession to the heir apparent Fu Su in 210 BC, and issued a false edict in favour of Hu Hai, the worthless second son. The opportunity for the deception occurred through the First Emperor's sudden death in present-day Shandong province. The event was kept secret until Zhao Gao and Li Si had secured their own positions: both feared the anger of Prince Fu Su, whose exile from the court they engineered several years before. Another victim of their plot was the commander-in-chief of the imperial forces, Meng Tian (died 210 BC). At one stroke, therefore, the most able member of the imperial family and the most vigorous general were lost to a dynasty already facing a wave of popular discontent. That the imperial forces were not then concentrated together, but were dispersed in garrisons all over China, also played in rebel hands. Some of these troops, led by their commanders, even revolted.

The Second Emperor, however, was the creature of Zhao Gao. He was persuaded not only to execute messengers who brought unfavourable military tidings, but in 208 BC he also agreed to Li Si's execution. Bidding for supreme power himself, Zhao Gao forced the Second Emperor to commit suicide in the ensuing year, but a chronicler stated how 'no official would accept his usurpation, and when he entered the audience chamber, three persons offered him harm. Realizing that Heaven had refused to grant him the empire, and that the officials as a whole would not co-operate with his wishes, he summoned the nephew of the First Emperor and reluctantly handed over the imperial seal.' While this was the only occasion on which a eunuch tried to usurp the Chinese throne, Zhao Gao was a prophetic figure as eunuchs tended to assume great power when an emperor was weak, or a child. Towards the end of the Han dynasty (202 BC – AD 220) palace eunuchs were actually employed by rulers against powerful consort families, till they became a dangerous faction in their own right. Zhao Gao met his own end at the hands of a fellow eunuch.

See FIRST EMPEROR; MENG TIAN; QIN DYNASTY
*A. Cotterell, *The First Emperor of China* (London, 1981).

**Zhou dynasty** (1027–256 BC) is divided into two parts: Early Zhou (1027–771 BC) and Later Zhou (770–256 BC). Largely feudal relics by the advent of the classical era in China, Later Zhou kings were restricted to a religious role on an impoverished domain surrounding the city of Luoyang. Archaeological finds of ritual bronzes indicate the growth of independent centres of power, as their dedicatory inscriptions no longer refer to the Zhou monarch but proclaim the names of the great lords for whom they were made.

During the Warring States period (481–221 BC) these rulers took for themselves the title of king. Two of them, the kings of Qin and Chu, even toyed with the title of emperor. This ancient word contained the notion of divinity, or at least divine favour: it was eventually incorporated into the imperial title, for in 221 BC the ruler of Qin became the First Sovereign Qin Emperor.

See QIN DYNASTY; WARRING STATES
*A. Cotterell, *China: A History* (London, 1990).

**Zhuang Zi** (350–275 BC) was the most distinguished follower of Lao Zi, the founder of Daoism. He was born at a time of intense struggle in China. The battles fought by the warring feudal states were of a size unmatched elsewhere in the classical world. There was an intensification of warfare right down to the country's unification under the Qin in 221 BC and the civil war following the overthrow of this oppressive dynasty. In all this turmoil the only sensible policy, according to Zhuang Zi, was to live the life of a recluse.

Hence the famous event recorded of Zhuang Zi's life was his rejection of the premiership of Chu, the huge southern state centred upon the Yangzi valley. Envoys from the Chu court found the philosopher fishing. Intent on what he was doing, Zhuang Zi listened without turning his head. At last he said: 'I understand that there is in the capital a sacred tortoise which has been dead for three thousand years. And that the ruler keeps this tortoise carefully enclosed in a chest in the ancestral temple. Now would this tortoise prefer to be dead but honoured, or alive and wagging its tail in the mud?' The high officials answered that it would rather be alive and wagging its tail in the mud. 'Clear off, then!' shouted Zhuang Zi. 'I'll also wag my tail in the mud here.'

Such an attitude was anathema to Confucian thinkers, who regarded service to the state as a moral obligation. The problem for Daoists was that in classical times China had no popular institutions similar to those which appeared in Greece: there was nothing for them to use in the furtherance of a practical democratic philosophy. Withdrawal from service in government could never be more than a political protest, although it is arguable that the self-centredness of Daoism, and its essentially reflective nature, ruled out any serious competition with Confucianism in public affairs. Daoism flourished best during the periods of national degeneration and harsh government.

Zhuang Zi's contribution to Daoist thought was increased scepticism about the efficacy of government and a stronger affirmation of the value of the individual. 'There is no such thing,' he said, 'as letting mankind alone; there has never been such a thing as governing mankind. Letting alone arises from a fear of perverting natural goodness, but, since this cannot be perverted, what need is there for government?' Zhuang Zi held that the individual had to find a way of living without doing violence to an inner strength that was naturally attuned to the universe. 'Those who understand the way of life devote no attention to things which life cannot accomplish. Those who understand the way of destiny devote no attention to things over which knowledge has no control.' Thus the Daoist sage was always humble and, interestingly in Chinese tradition, often regarded as a fool when recognized at all. For Zhuang Zi 'lived without leaving any traces; he engaged in activities that were not recorded for posterity'.

See CONFUCIUS; DAOISM; HUNDRED SCHOOLS; LAO ZI

*H.A. Giles, *Chuang Tzu: Taoist Philosopher and Mystic* (London, 1989); Hsiao Kung-chuan, *A History of Chinese Political Thought. Volume One: From the Beginnings to the Sixth Century AD* (Princeton, 1979).

**Zoroastrianism** is the classical Iranian belief associated with the prophet Zoroaster, or Zarathustra (*c.* 628–551 BC). Like the Buddha and Christ, he had the vision of transforming his inherited religion into a new faith. Though today only relatively small numbers of his followers survive in India, the Zoroastrian faith was once the official religion of three Persian empires: under the Achaemenids (559–330 BC), the Parthian Arsacids (171 BC – AD 226), and the Sasanians

The prophet Zoroaster.

(AD 226–651). Probably trained by choice as a priest, Zoroaster had a passionately personal relationship with

Ahura Mazdah, the supreme Iranian deity. Fire was the symbol of truth which Ahura Mazdah had bestowed on his worshippers, and so it is hardly surprising that a fully developed Zoroastrianism under the Sasanians should have elevated fire worship above all else. Then the iconoclasm of the Zoroastrian clergy interestingly anticipated the eighth-century AD Byzantine controversy over icons, when volcanic activity was thought by many Christians to be the result of divine anger over idolatrous images. Yet although Ahura Mazdah was regarded as the creator god concerned with truth, he stood at the head of a large pantheon, which included his opposite, Angra Mainya, the spirit of destruction. 'In the beginning,' said Zoroaster, 'the twin spirits were known as the good one and the other evil, in thought, word, and deed. Between them the wise chose rightly, not so fools. And when these spirits met they established life and death so that in the end the followers of deceit should meet the worst existence, but the followers of truth with the wise lord, Ahura Mazdah.'

It is now impossible to gauge what balance Cyrus the Great (559–530 BC), the founder of the first Persian empire, personally held between traditional Iranian polytheism and Zoroaster's teaching about the supremacy of Ahura Mazdah. His dynasty, the Achaemenids, was relaxed over religious matters in comparison with later Iranian dynasties, and especially the Sasanians. But its empire included so many different traditions that the only practical policy was to accept the continuation of existing worship, whether this involved Egyptian, Semitic or Indian deities. Such an inclusive attitude of mind was typical of the early classical age, except in remote China. In his own religious outlook Alexander the Great (356–323 BC) saw himself as Cyrus' true heir, willingly associating himself with the gods of the peoples he had conquered, with a single exception: Zoroastrianism. For the surviving West Asian texts, as distinct from Greek sources, record the execution of Zoroastrian priests and the destruction of fire temples. Possibly in this alien persecution are to be found the roots of later religious intolerance.

During the classical period the Sasanians were unique in systematically attempting to impose a religious orthodoxy. From the start of the dynasty in AD 226, Sasanian kings (with one notable exception, Shapur I) strove to distance themselves from the less rigorous outlook of their predecessors, the Parthians. The very first monarch, Ardashir I (AD 226–241), claimed the right to suppress heterodox traditions that had been freely incorporated in the Avesta, the holy book of Zoroastrianism. A letter from the chief prelate Tansar asserts that Ardashir was justified in shedding blood because of doctrinal errors. During the reigns of Bahram I (AD 273–276) and Bahram II (AD 276–279) another leading member of the clergy, Kartir, extended the persecution beyond the Zoroastrian faithful. Apart from having the prophet Mani executed in AD 277, he hounded Jews, Christians, Manichees, Buddhists and Hindus. Additionally, Kartir first assumed the right to control many of the affairs of state by his religious pronouncements.

See ALEXANDER THE GREAT; ARDASHIR; BUDDHISM; CHRISTIANITY; MANICHAE-ISM; PARTHIANS; PERSIA; SASANIANS

*W. W. Malandra, *An Introduction to Ancient Iranian Religion* (Minneapolis, 1983); J. H. Moulton, *Early Zoroastrianism* (London, 1913).

# CHRONOLOGY

WEST     MEDITERRANEAN     EAST

**600 BC –**

Solon asked to mediate between the rich and the poor at Athens 594

Pisistratus becomes tyrant of Athens 561

Pythagoras settles at Croton 531

Persians conquer Egypt 525
Tyrant Polycrates killed by Oroetes 523

Expulsion of Etruscan kings from Rome c.510

Persians campaign in Thrace 512
Hippias expelled from Athens 510
Cleisthenes' democratic reforms at Athens 508
Aeginetans raid coast of Attica 506

Treaty agreed between Carthage and Rome 507–506

**500 BC –**

Ionian revolt 499–494
Spartans defeat Argives at Sepeia 494
Persian invasions of Greece 490 and 480–479
Delian League formed 478–477

Defensive alliance between Rome and the Latins 493
Birth of Empedocles at Acragas c.492
Carthaginians defeated by the Greeks at Himera 480

Cimon ostracized from Athens 461

Athenian fleet lost in Egyptian revolt 454
Building of the Parthenon started 447

Twelve Tables, first written law code for Rome 451
Pericles sponsors panhellenic foundation of Thurii, where Herodotus settles 443

The Peloponnesian War begins 431
Death of Pericles 429
Spartan defeat at Sphacteria 425
Death of Cleon at Amphipolis 424
Oligarchic reaction at Athens 411
Athens surrenders to Sparta: Long Walls and fleet destroyed 404
Theramenes killed by the Thirty, a Sparta-backed oligarchy 403

Sicilian Expedition 415–413
Dionysius I seizes power at Syracuse 405

**400 BC –**

| WEST | MEDITERRANEAN | EAST |
|---|---|---|
| **400 BC —** | | |
| Rome sacked by the Gauls 390 | | Athenians execute Socrates 399 |
| Plato visits Syracuse 387 | | Death of Lysander 395 |
| | | Thrasybulus rebuilds Athenian naval power 389 |
| | | Plato founds the Academy at Athens 385 |
| | | Thebans defeat Spartans at Leuctra 371 |
| | | Messenia freed by the Thebans 369 |
| | | Death of Epaminondas at Mantineia 362 |
| Timoleon overthrows tyrants in Sicily 345 | | Aristotle appointed as Alexander's tutor 343 |
| Rome becomes predominant in Latium 338 | | Macedon defeats Thebes and Athens at Chaeronea 338 |
| | | Assassination of Philip II of Macedon 336 |
| | | Destruction of Thebes 334 |
| | | Alexander visits oracle of Siwah in Libyan desert 331 |
| Samnites defeat Romans at Caudine Forks 321 | | |
| | | Zeno of Citium arrives at Athens 310 |
| | | Epicurus settles in Athens 307 |
| | | Ptolemy becomes king of Egypt 305 |
| **300 BC —** | | Demetrius becomes king of Macedon 294 |
| Pyrrhus invades Italy at the request of Tarentum 280 | | Seleucus I assassinated shortly after his defeat of Lysimachus 281 |
| Pyrrhus wins costly victory over the Romans at Asculum 279 | | Gauls invade Macedon and Greece 279 |
| Pyrrhus evacuates Italy 275 | | Antigonus Gonatas becomes king of Macedon 276 |
| Carthage and Rome go to war, and first gladiatorial show at Rome 264 | | Death of Pyrrhus at Argos 272 |
| | | Cleanthes succeeds Zeno as head of the Stoa 263 |
| Romans occupy Sardinia and Corsica 238 | | |
| Hannibal besieges Saguntum, an ally of Rome in Spain 219 | | King Cleomenes III of Sparta defeated at Sellasia 222 |
| Disastrous Roman defeat at Cannae 216 | | Egyptian troops give Ptolemies victory over Seleucids at Raphia 217 |
| Romans sack Syracuse, killing Archimedes: Sicily annexed 211 | | Alliance between Macedon and Carthage against Rome 215 |
| First Roman possessions in Spain 206 | | |
| Hannibal recalled from Italy, and defeated at Zama 202 | | |
| Carthage turned into a Roman satellite 201 | | |
| **200 BC —** | | |

WEST      MEDITERRANEAN      EAST

**200 BC –**

Romans defeat Macedonians at Cynoscephalae 197

The elder Cato becomes censor at Rome 184
Romans campaign in Spain 181

Romans end Macedonian independence at Pydna 168
Senate orders Aemilius Paullus to enslave Epirotes 167

The historian Polybius brought to Rome as a hostage 167
Death of the Roman playwright Terence 159

Romans destroy Corinth and annex Greece 146

Romans destroy Carthage and annex Africa 146
The Stoic philosopher Panaetius becomes a close associate of Scipio Aemilianus 144
Failure of land reforms at Rome 133 and 123–121

Marius enlists poorest Romans to fight against Jugurtha, the usurper of Numidia 107
Teutones and Cimbri destroyed by Marius 102–101
Birth of Julius Caesar 100
Birth of Lucretius c.94

**100 BC –**

Athens, under a restored democracy, joins Mithridates VI of Pontus against Rome 88
Sulla sacks Athens 86
Cicero in Athens and Rhodes 79

Rivalry between Marius and Sulla leads to first military coup at Rome 88
Sulla becomes dictator at Rome 82
Spartacus leads slave revolt in southern Italy 73–71
Pompey given special command against pirates 67
Cicero executes Catiline 62
First triumvirate formed between Pompey, Crassus and Caesar 60
Caesar begins Gallic campaign 59

Caesar defeats Pompey at Pharsalus in Thessaly 48
Caesar in Alexandria 48–47
Battle of Philippi 42

Rebellion of Vercingetorix in Gaul 52
Assassination of Julius Caesar; Octavian declared his heir 44
Second triumvirate formed between Antony, Octavian and Lepidus 43

Antony and Cleopatra defeated at Actium 31
End of Ptolemaic rule in Egypt 30

Senate formally acknowledges supremacy of Octavian, the first Roman emperor Augustus 27

**BC –**

| WEST | MEDITERRANEAN | EAST |
|---|---|---|
| | | Illyrian revolt 6–9 |
| Loss of three legions in Germany 9 | | |
| Death of Augustus, the first Roman emperor 14 | | |
| Fall and execution of Sejanus 31 | | |
| Death of Tiberius 37 | | |
| | | Philo leads Jewish delegation from Alexandria to Rome 39 |
| Assassination of his successor Caligula 41 | | |
| Southern Britain annexed by Claudius 43 | | |
| Claudius poisoned by Agrippina, whose son Nero succeeds him 54 | | |
| Rebellion of Boudicca 60–61 | | |
| Great fire at Rome blamed on Christians 64 | | |
| | | Jews rise in revolt 66 |
| | | Nero tours Greece, having prizes awarded for his poetry to himself everywhere 67 |
| Suicide of Nero ends first imperial dynasty at Rome 68 | | |
| Vespasian becomes emperor with support of his troops 69 | | |
| Eruption of Vesuvius 79 | | |
| Dedication of the Colosseum 80 | | |
| Assassination of Domitian, Vespasian's younger son 96 | | |
| Accession of Trajan 98 | | |
| | | Trajan annexes Dacia and Arabia 105–106, then campaigns against the Parthians, annexing Mesopotamia 113–117 |
| Accession of Hadrian 117 | | |
| Hadrian visits Britain 121–122 | | |
| | | Gnosticism flourishes at Alexandria 130–180 |
| | | Jewish revolt of Bar Cochba 132–135 |
| Accession of Antoninus Pius 138 | | |
| Frontier in Britain advanced into Scotland 142 | | |
| | | Polycarp martyred at Smyrna 155 or 165 |
| Accession of Marcus Aurelius 161 | | |
| | | Roman campaign against Parthia 162–166 |
| Campaigns of Marcus Aurelius against the Germans 167–180 | | |
| Death of Marcus Aurelius and accession of his son Commodus 180 | | |
| Assassination of Commodus 192 | | |
| Accession of Septimius Severus, the first Roman emperor from Africa 193 | | |
| | | Septimius Severus campaigns against the Partians, capturing Ctesiphon 197–199 |

AD –

AD 100 –

AD 200 –

| WEST | MEDITERRANEAN | EAST |
|---|---|---|
| | | Clement flees from persecution of Christians in Alexandria 202 |
| Assassination in 235 of Alexander, last Severan emperor, followed by a long period of military anarchy and foreign invasion | | Ardashir I takes over Parthian empire becoming first Sasanian ruler 226 |
| Decius persecutes Christians 250–251 | | Sasanians sack Antioch 256<br>Valerian captured by Sasanians 260<br>Last Olympic Games held 261<br>Palmyra overruns eastern Roman provinces 267–272<br>Major Gothic inroads in Thrace and Greece 268 |
| Aurelian forced to build defences for Rome 270 | | Aurelian suppresses Palmyra 270 |
| Accession of Diocletian and his reform of the empire 284 | | Peace agreement with Sasanians 288 |
| Constantine hailed as emperor by troops at York 306 | | Retirement of Diocletian and Maximian 305 |
| Constantine first acknowledges Christianity 312 | | Council of Nicaea 325<br>Constantine founds Constantinople as Christian capital of Roman empire 330 |
| Baptism and death of Constantine 337 | | |
| Accession of Julian, who withdraws privileges given to the church by Constantine 360<br>Accession of Valentinian I and his brother Valens 364<br>Campaigns against the Alemanni on the Rhine 365–375<br>Death of Valentinian I 375 | | Julian killed in battle against the Sasanians 363<br>Visigoths given permission to settle south of Danube 376<br>Visigoths defeat and kill Valens at Adrianople 378<br>Theodosius I finally settles Visigoths as Roman allies 382 |
| Theodosius prohibits pagan rituals 391–392<br>Western Roman emperor Honorius under Stilicho's control 395 | | Honorius' brother, Arcadius, rules in the east 395 |

AD 200 –

AD 300 –

AD 400 –

| | WEST | MEDITERRANEAN | EAST |
|---|---|---|---|
| AD 400 – | Honorius flees to Ravenna 404<br>Massive German crossing of the Rhine 406<br>Visigothic leader Alaric sacks Rome 410<br>Visigoths allowed to settle in south-western France 418 | | Landward defences of Constantinople strengthened 413<br>Theodosius II sponsors learning at Constantinople 425 |
| | Vandals cross to Africa 429<br>Death of St Augustine during Vandal siege of Hippo 430 | | Death of Theodosius II, who achieved the longest reign of any Roman emperor 450 |
| | Defeat of the Huns on the Catalaunian Fields in Gaul 451<br>Death of Attila, king of the Huns 453<br>Vandals sack Rome 455 | | |
| | Deposition of Romulus Augustulus, last western Roman emperor: Odoacer becomes first barbarian king of Italy 476 | Ostrogoths set out for Italy 488 | |
| | Ostrogoths overthrow Odoacer by 493 and establish their own kingdom in Italy. | | |
| AD 500 – | Beliarius recaptures Africa from Vandals 533–534<br>Eastern Roman army recovers much of Italy by 540 | Accession of Justinian 527<br>Dedication of Hagia Sophia 537<br>Sasanians under Khusrau I sack Antioch 540 | |
| | Most eastern Roman gains lost after 570: Visigoths capture Spain and the Lombards take nearly all of Italy | Death of Justinian 565 | Accession of Maurice, who reorganizes Byzantium's defences 582<br>Maurice backs Khusrau II as Sasanian king 591 |
| AD 600 – | | | |

| | WEST ASIA | INDIA | CHINA |
|---|---|---|---|
| **600 BC –** | Death of Zoroaster 551<br>Cyrus overthrows the Medes 550<br>Croesus of Lydia defeated by Cyrus who also subdues the Greek cities of Ionia 546<br>Peaceful surrender of Babylon 539<br><br>Death of Cyrus in Central Asia 530<br><br>Accession of Darius I amid widespread rebellions 521 | Birth of the Buddha 563<br><br>King Bimbisara founds Nanda dynasty 546<br><br><br>The Jain saviour Mahavira dies c. 528<br>Persians annex north-western India 518 | Birth of Confucius 551 |
| **500 BC –** | Ionian revolt 499–494<br><br>Persians dispatch expeditions against mainland Greece 490 and 480–479, and against Egyptian rebels 485 and 459–454<br>Death of Darius I 486<br><br>Xerxes assassinated 465<br>Peace agreed between Persia and Athens 449 | Nanda expansion under Ajatasatru, 494–462 | Warring States period begins 481<br>Death of Confucius 479<br>Birth of Mo Zi 468 |
| **400 BC –** | After failure of Athenian expedition to Sicily, Persia switches sides and backs Sparta with gold 413<br>Spartans back Cyrus the Younger in his bid for the Persian throne 401 | | Birth of Shen Buhai 400 |

| WEST ASIA | INDIA | CHINA |
| --- | --- | --- |
| | | |
| 400 BC — | | |
| King Agesilaus of Sparta abandons war against Persia in Asia Minor 394 | | Birth of Mencius 372 |
| | | |
| Accession of Darius III 336 | | Shang Yang introduces his Legalist reforms in Qin 350s |
| Battle at Granicus river opens Asian campaign of Alexander 334 | | Birth of Zhuang Zi 350 |
| Final Persian defeat at Gaugamela 331 | | |
| Persepolis fired on Alexander's orders 330 | Invasion of Alexander 327–325 | Dismemberment of Shang Yang 338 |
| Alexander campaigns in Bactria 328 | Candragupta founds Mauryan dynasty 322 | |
| Death of Alexander at Babylon 323 | | |
| | Seleucus I cedes Indian possessions to | Qin annexes modern Sichuan 316 |
| Seleucus I founds dynasty 305 | Candragupta and acquires 500 war | |
| Battle of Ipsus confirms the break-up | elephants 303 | |
| of Alexander's vast kingdom 301 | | |
| | Abdication of Candragupta to become | |
| 300 BC — | Jain recluse 297 | |
| Demetrius surrenders to Seleucus 285 | | |
| | | |
| Gauls (Galatians) enter Asia Minor 278 | Accession of Ashoka 268 | |
| | Kalinga conflict and conversion of Ashoka | Last Zhou king deposed by Qin 256 |
| Bactria asserts its independence 250 | to Buddhism 260 | Chengkuo canal opened 246 |
| | | |
| Seleucids forced to recognize | | Death of Han Fei Zi 233 |
| independence of Pergamum c. 230 | Unrest in Mauryan empire 232–223 | Chu defeated by Qin 223 |
| | | Unification of China 221 |
| | | Great Wall begun 214 |
| Antiochus III campaigns in Parthia and | | First Emperor burns the books 213 |
| Bactria 212–206 | | Death of First Emperor 210 |
| | | Execution of Li Si 208 |
| | | Collapse of Qin dynasty 207 |
| | Greco–Bactrian attacks weaken Mauryan | Official start of Han dynasty 202 |
| Palestine taken by Seleucids from | authority after 200 | |
| Ptolemies 200 | | |
| 200 BC — | | |

459

| | WEST ASIA | INDIA | CHINA |
|---|---|---|---|
| 200 BC – | First independent state of Armenia under Artaxias 190<br>Romans defeat Antiochus III at Magnesia 190 or 189 | Last Mauryan king, Brhadratha, deposed by Pusyamitra, founder of Sunga dynasty 185–72 | Birth of Dong Zhongshu 179 |
| | | Menander rules from near modern Peshawar and shows sympathy for Buddhism 160–130 | Rebellion by eastern vassals 154 |
| | Parthians conquer Babylon 141 | | Accession of Han Wu Di 140<br>Mission of Zhang Qian to find the Da Yuezhi in Central Asia 138 |
| | Attalus III dies and bequeaths his kingdom to Rome 133<br>Seleucid bid to recapture Mesopotamia fails 130 | | State monopoly declared over iron and salt industries 119<br>Death of Huo Qubing 117 |
| 100 BC – | Sulla concludes peace with Mithridates VI of Pontus 85 | Vasudeva overthrows the last Sunga king and founds Kanva dynasty c.72 | North Korea and north Vietnam annexed, as well as a protectorate declared over Tarim basin 109–101<br>Capture of Li Ling and castration of Sima Qian 99 |
| | Suicide of Mithridates 65<br>Pompey ends Seleucid dynasty and annexes Syria 64<br>Romans under Crassus defeated by Parthians at Carrhae 53 | Scythian Sakas invade India c.50<br>Last Greek king, Gondophares, dethroned 46 | Death of Han Wu Di 87<br>Debate on the iron and salt industries 81 |
| BC – | Parthians return captured legionary standards to Augustus and make peace 2 | | Birth of Wang Mang 33 |

| | WEST ASIA | INDIA | CHINA |
|---|---|---|---|
| **AD –** | | | Usurpation of Wang Mang 9–23<br>Long struggle to restore the Han dynasty 25–36 |
| | | | Chinese authority restored by Ma Yuan in Vietnam 40–42 |
| | Romans intervene to block Parthian candidate for Armenian throne 54–60 | Kushanas found their empire 50 | |
| | | Vima Kaphises extends its influence into Ganges valley 64–70 | Ban Chao reasserts Chinese control over Tarim basin 70 |
| | Political chaos in Parthia 70–110 | Accession of Kaniska 78<br>Later he converts to Buddhism and convenes the Fourth Buddhist Council | |
| | Chinese embassy to Rome turned back by Parthians 97 | | |
| **AD 100 –** | | Kaniska dies on campaign 102<br>Accession of Huviska 106, a ruler noted for his fine coinage | Death of Wang Chong 100<br>Manufacture of paper announced 105 |
| | Trajan captures the Parthian capital, Ctesiphon 114<br>Hadrian evacuates Mesopotamia 117 | | Death of inventor Zhang Heng 139 |
| | | Accession of Vasudeva, last effective Kushana ruler 140 | |
| | Romans campaign against the Parthians and place a garrison at Dura 162–166 | | Civil strife among the Xiongnu takes pressure off northern frontier till 150 |
| | | | Death of An Shihkao c. 168 |
| | | | Widespread peasant rebellion 180s |
| **AD 200 –** | Septimius Severus punishes Parthians for joining in Roman civil war, Ctesiphon sacked once again 197–199 | | Cao Cao assumes control of imperial government 196 |

| | WEST ASIA | INDIA | CHINA |
|---|---|---|---|
| AD 200 – | Parthian decline after 210 leads to change of dynasty | Lawbook of Manu compiled c. 200 | Deposition of last Han emperor 220<br>Wei dynasty 220–265<br>Three Kingdoms period 221–280 |
| | Ardashir I founds Sasanian dynasty 226 | Sasanian pressure under Ardashir I in Central Asia 226–240 | Death of Zhuge Liang 235 |
| | Accession of Shapur I 241<br>Shapur defeats Romans and dominates Armenia 244 | Collapse of Kushana empire c.240 | |
| | Shapur returns home with 70,000 Roman prisoners, as well as Valerian 260 | | Western Jin dynasty 265–316 |
| | Death of Shapur I 272<br>Execution of Mani 277 | Accession of Ghatotkachagupta, earliest known Gupta king 280 | Death of Sima Yan 289 |
| AD 300 – | Armenia becomes first Christian state sometime before 301 | | Xiongnu sack Luoyang 311<br>Loss of northern provinces to Xiongnu and Xianbei 316 |
| | Under Shapur II, 309–379, the Sasanian state acquires a centralized bureaucracy | Gupta dynasty firmly founded in imitation of Mauryans 320<br>Samudragupta extends Gupta power greatly 335–375 | |
| | Julian fails to capture Ctesiphon, and dies during retreat 363 | Accession of Candragupta II c.377 | Southern China saved from Tartar Xianbei conquest at Feishui 383 |
| AD 400 – | | Arrival of the Chinese monk Fa Xian, in search of Buddhist scriptures 399 | |

| | WEST ASIA | INDIA | CHINA |
|---|---|---|---|
| AD 400 – | | Accession of Kumaragupta I c. 412<br>Fa Xian returns to China via Sri Lanka and Sumatra 414 | Death of Hui Yuan, the Chinese<br>St. Augustine 416 |
| | Accession of Peroz 457 | First invasion by Hunas, Hunnish tribesmen 454<br>Hunas temporarily held in check by Skandagupta 455–467 | |
| | Peroz forced to pay a ransom for his own release from Huns 469 | Accession of Buddhagupta c.477 | |
| AD 500 – | Accession of Khusrau I 531 | | |
| | Sasanians sack Antioch 540 | End of Gupta dynasty through a combination of internal weakness and Hunas pressure c.550 | |
| | The Huns defeated by Khusrau I 562 | | |
| AD 600 – | Khusrau II seeks military aid from the Byzantine emperor Maurice against rebellions nobles. In return the Byzantines receive territory in the Caucasus 590s | | |

# MAPS

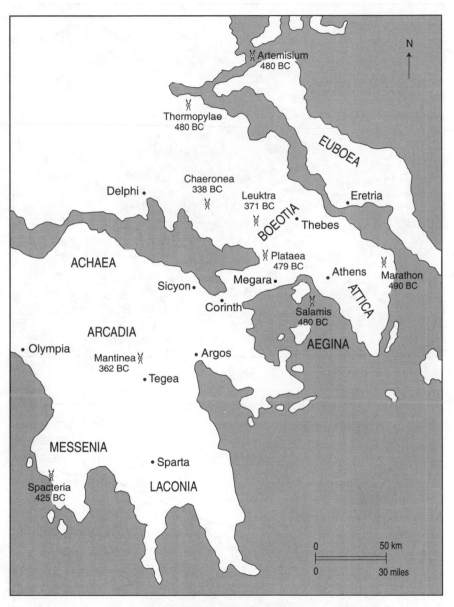

Central Greece and the Peloponnese

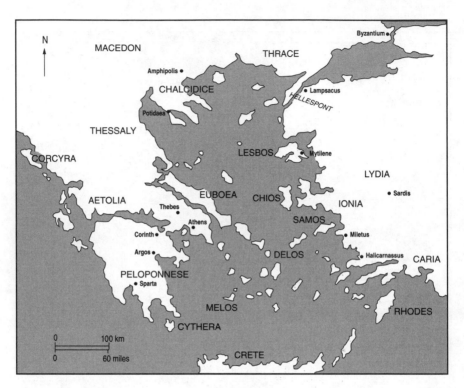

The Aegean

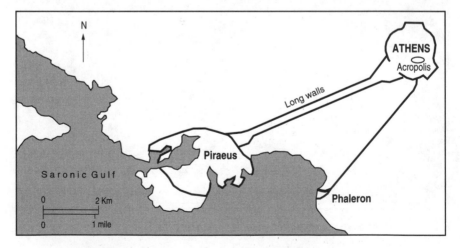

The landward defences which transformed classical Athens into an island

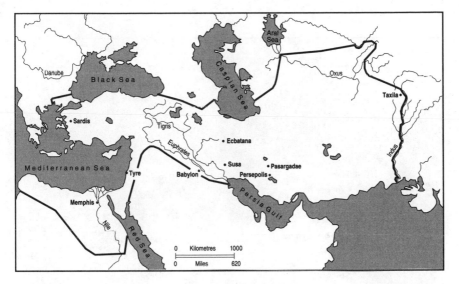

The Persian empire (500 BC)

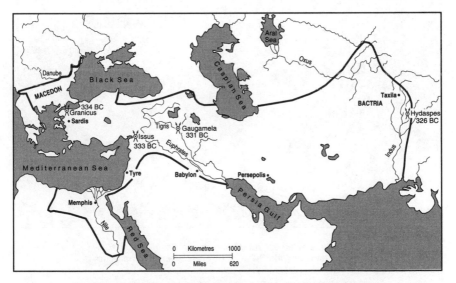

The Macedonian empire on the death of Alexander the Great (323 BC)

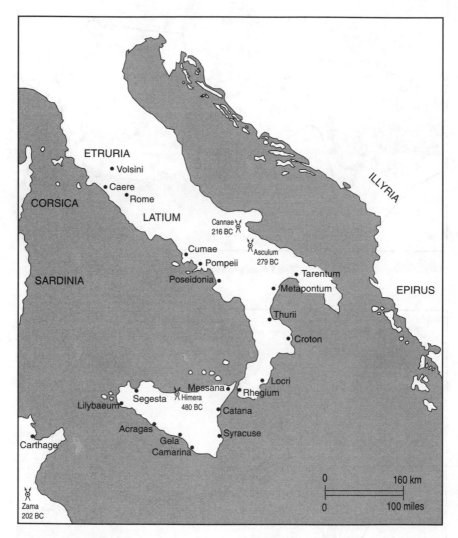

The powers of the central Mediterranean: Etruria, Carthage,
Epirus, Rome and the Greek cities of Sicily and southern Italy

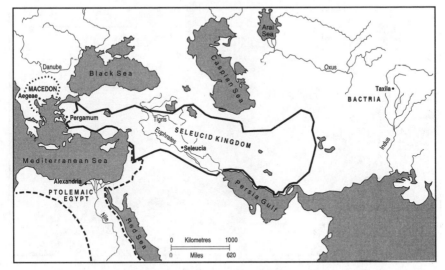

Successor powers to the Macedonian empire: Antigonid Macedon, Seleucid Asia,
Ptolemaic Egypt around 240 BC

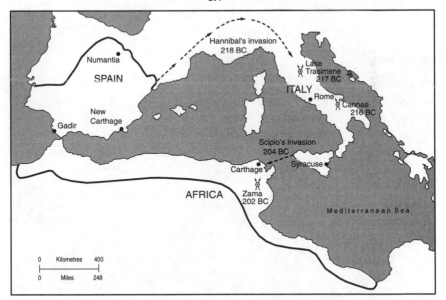

The Carthaginian empire on the outbreak of the second war against Rome, 218 BC

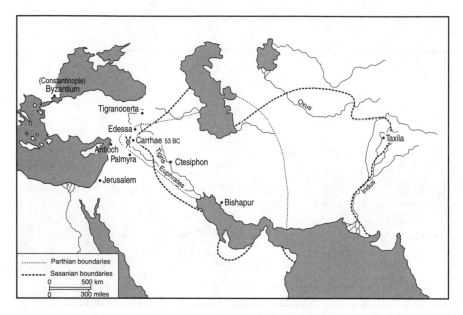

The Parthian (171 BC–AD 226) and Sasanian (AD 226–651) empires

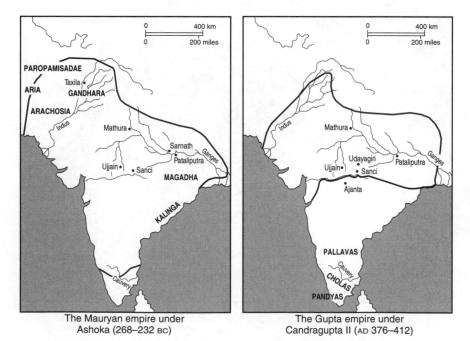

The Mauryan empire under
Ashoka (268–232 BC)

The Gupta empire under
Candragupta II (AD 376–412)

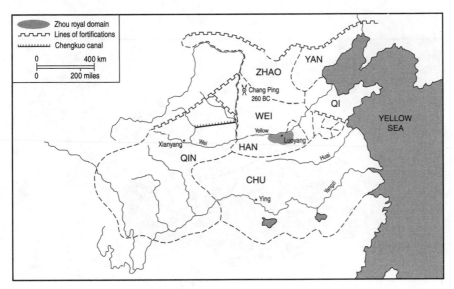

The Warring States of China (481–221 BC)

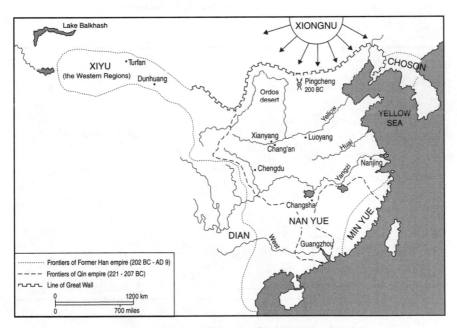

Imperial unification of China: the Qin (221–207 BC) and
Han empires (202 BC – AD 220)

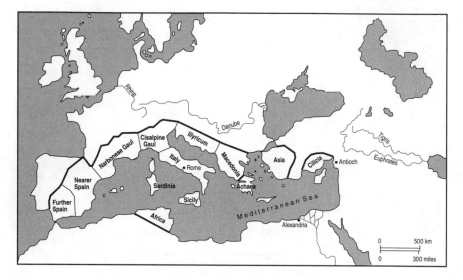

The provinces of late republican Rome (100 BC)

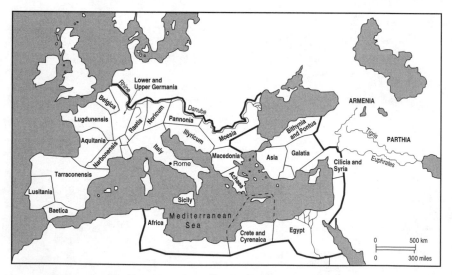

The Roman empire on the death of Augustus (AD 14)

474

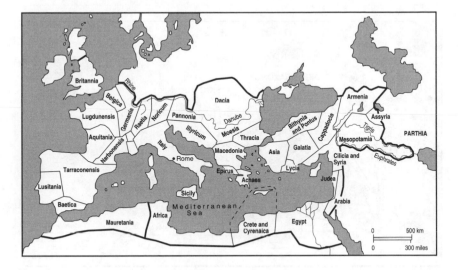

The Roman empire on the death of Trajan (AD 117)

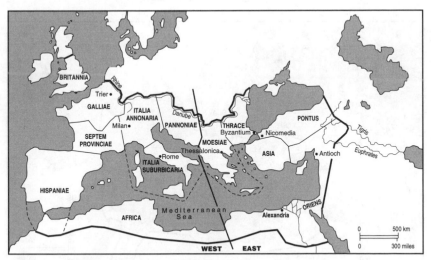

The administrative dioceses introduced by the Roman emperor Diocletian (AD 284–305)

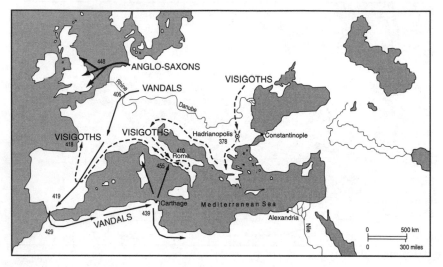

The routes taken by just three barbarian invaders, the Vandals, Visigoths and Anglo-Saxons, in the fifth century AD

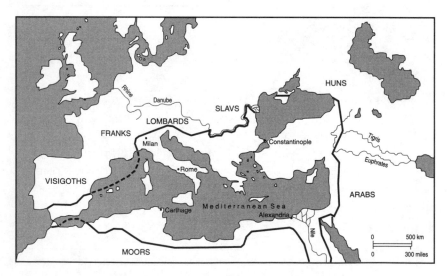

Eastern Roman empire on the death of Justinian (AD 565)

**Index of names and subjects which are not titles of entries in the dictionary**

Academy (school) *see* PLATO

Accius (playwright) *see* DRAMA

Achaemenids (dynasty) *see* PERSIA

Actium (battle) *see* ANTONY

Adrianople (battle) *see* GOTHS

Aegosopotami (battle) *see* LYSANDER

Aeneas (hero) *see* LITERATURE

Aeschylus (playwright) *see* DRAMA

Ajivikas (sect) *see* GOSALA

Agrippina (mother) *see* NERO

Ai Khanum (city) *see* BACTRIA

Alaric (king) *see* HONORIUS

Alexander of Pherae (tyrant) *see* THESSALY

Amasis (pharaoh) *see* EGYPT

Ambrose (bishop) *see* THEODOSIUS I

Amphictionies (leagues) *see* SACRED WARS

Amphipolis (city) *see* CLEON

Amrakardava (general) *see* CANDRAGUPTA II

Anacharsis (philosopher) *see* SCYTHIANS

Anaximander (philosopher) *see* INVENTIONS

Ancestor worship (Chinese) *see* RELIGION

Antigonids (dynasty) *see* MACEDON

Antiochus I (king) *see* SELEUCIDS

Antoninus Pius (emperor) *see* ANTONINE DYNASTY

Antony (hermit) *see* EGYPT

Arataphernes (general) *see* PERSIAN INVASIONS

Arcadius (emperor) *see* HONORIUS

Archonship (office) *see* SOLON

Areopagus (council) *see* SOLON *and* EPHIALTES

Arginusae (battle) *see* THERAMENES

Aristagoras (tyrant) *see* IONIAN REVOLT

Aristophanes (playwright) *see* DRAMA

Arius (heretic) *see* CONSTANTINE

Arsacids (dynasty) *see* PARTHIANS

Artaxerxes I (king) *see* PERSIA

Artaxerxes II (king)*see* PERSIA

Artaxerxes III (king) *see* PERSIA

Artaxias (king) *see* ARMENIA

Asculum (battle) *see* PYRRHUS

Ashvaghosa (poet) *see* KUSHANAS

Assembly (legislature) *see* ATHENS

Astyages (king) *see* CYRUS THE GREAT

Athanaric (king) *see* THEODOSIUS I

Athanasius (bishop) *see* JULIAN

Athaulf (king) *see* HONORIUS

Athenion (rebel) *see* SICILY

Atrebates (people) *see* CARATACUS

Attalus I (king) *see* ATTALIDS

Attalus III (king) *see* ATTALIDS

Aurelius, Marcus (emperor) *see* ANTONINE DYNASTY

Azes I (king) *see* KUSHANAS


Babylon (kingdom) *see* PERSIA

Bahram I (king) *see* SASANIANS

Bahram II (king) *see* SASANIANS

Bar Cochba (rebel) *see* JEWS

Basilides (gnostic) *see* GNOSTICISM

Belisarius (general) *see* VANDALS

Belshazzar (prince) *see* PERSIA

Bharata (critic) *see* DRAMA

Bhasa (playwright) *see* DRAMA

Blossius (philosopher) *see* STOICISM

Bogoas (eunuch) *see* PERSIA

Brasidas (general) *see* CLEON

Brhadratha (emperor) *see* MAURYAN DYNASTY

Burgundians (people) *see* GOTHS

Burma *see* GUPTA DYNASTY

Burning of the books *see* LI SI


Cambodia *see* GUPTA DYNASTY

Cao Pi (emperor) *see* WEI DYNASTY

Caracalla (emperor) *see* SEVERAN DYNASTY

Carrhae (battle) *see* CRASSUS *and* SUREN

Catalaunian Fields (battle) *see* GOTHS

Catuvellauni (people) *see* CARATACUS

Caudine Forks (battle) *see* ROME

Celts (people) *see* GALATIANS *and* GAULS

Chaeronea (battle) *see* PHILIP I

Chang Ping (battle) *see* SUN ZI

Characene (kingdom) *see* PARTHIANS

Chengkuo canal *see* CHENG KUO

Chrysippus (philosopher) *see* STOICISM

Cimbri (people) *see* MARIUS

Cleanthes (philosopher) *see* STOICISM

Cleisthenes (tyrant) *see* SICYON

Cleombrotus (king) *see* EPAMINONDAS

Cleomenes III (king) *see* STOICISM

Clodius (politician) *see* CICERO

Commodus (emperor) *see* ANTONINE DYNASTY

Constantine (usurper) *see* HONORIUS

Constantius (emperor) *see* DIOCLETIAN

Corcyra (city-state) *see* PERICLES

Coronea (battle) *see* AGESILAUS

Corupedium (battle) *see* LYSIMACHUS

Critias (oligarch) *see* THRASYBULUS

Crossbow *see* WARFARE

Cunaxa (battle) *see* CYRUS THE YOUNGER

Cybele (deity) *see* RELIGION

Cylon (would-be tyrant) *see* SOLON

Cynoscephalae (battle) *see* MACEDON

Cyprian (bishop) *see* AFRICA

Cyzicus (battle) *see* THERAMENES


Dacia (province) *see* TRAJAN

Damocles (courtier) *see* DIONYSIUS

Daniel (prophet) *see* PERSIA

Darius III (king) *see* PERSIA

Datis (general) *see* PERSIAN INVASIONS

Decius (emperor) *see* CHRISTIANITY

Demaratus (king) *see* THERMOPYLAE

Demetrius I (king) *see* BACTRIA

Demetrius II (king) *see* SELEUCIDS

Democracy *see* ATHENS

Democritus (philosopher) *see* EPICURUS

Demosthenes (general) *see* SICILIAN EXPEDITION

Didius Julianus (emperor) *see* SEVERAN DYNASTY

Dingtao (battle) *see* XIANG YU

Diodotus I (king) *see* BACTRIA

Diogenes (philosopher) *see* CYNICISM

Dionysius II (tyrant) *see* SYRACUSE

Domitian (emperor) *see* FLAVIAN DYNASTY

Donatists (heretics) *see* AUGUSTINE

Draco (lawgiver) *see* SOLON

Elagabalus (emperor) *see* SEVERAN DYNASTY

Ephors (magistrates) *see* SPARTA

Erastosthenes (scientist) *see* INVENTIONS

Eretria (city-state) *see* IONIAN REVOLT

Euclid (mathematician) *see* ARCHIMEDES

Euripides (playwright) *see* DRAMA

Euthydeus (king) *see* ANTIOCHUS III

Fa Hu (translator) *see* BUDDHISM

Feishui (battle) *see* WESTERN JIN DYNASTY

Former Han *see* HAN DYNASTY

Four Hundred (oligarchy) *see* THERAMENES

Franks (people) *see* GOTHS

Gadir (city) *see* SPAIN

Gaiseric (king) *see* VANDALS

Gaius (emperor) *see* CALIGULA

Galatia (province) *see* GALATIANS

Galen (doctor) *see* INVENTIONS

Galerius (emperor) *see* DIOCLETIAN

Galla Placidia (sister) *see* HONORIUS

Gelimer (king) *see* VANDALS

Geta (emperor) *see* SEVERAN DYNASTY

Gladiators *see* SACRIFICE

Gordian III (emperor) *see* SASANIANS

Gratian (emperor) *see* VALENTINIAN

Greek League *see* CORINTH

Gyges (tyrant) *see* TYRANTS

Gylippus (general) *see* SICILIAN EXPEDITION

Han Gaozu (emperor) *see* LIU BANG

Han (state) *see* CHENG KUO

Hegesistratus (tyrant) *see* HIPPIAS

Heraclitus (philosopher) *see* ANAXAGORAS

Heraclius (emperor) *see* SASANIANS

Hermaeus (king) *see* KUSHANAS

Hesiod (poet) *see* LITERATURE

Himera (battle) *see* SICILY

Hippocrates (doctor) *see* INVENTIONS

Homer (poet) *see* LITERATURE

Hoplite (footsoldier) *see* WARFARE

Hua Tuo (doctor) *see* INVENTIONS

Hui Yuan (abbot) *see* BUDDHISM

Huviska (king) *see* KUSHANAS

Hysiae (battle) *see* ARGOS

Iceni (people) *see* BOUDICCA

Ignatius (martyr) *see* POLYCARP

Ilipa (battle) *see* SCIPIOS

Indonesia *see* GUPTA DYNASTY

Isocrates (orator) *see* ATHENS

Ipsus (battle) *see* DEMETRIUS

Ireland *see* GAULS

Japan *see* CHOSON

Jason of Pherae (tyrant) *see* THESSALY

Jovian (emperor) *see* JULIAN

Judaea (kingdom) *see* HEROD

Jugurtha (usurper) *see* MARIUS

Julia (wife) *see* TIBERIUS


Kanvas (dynasty) *see* SUNGA DYNASTY

Kartir (prelate) *see* SASANIANS

Kavadh (king) *see* SASANIANS

Khusrau I (king) *see* SASANIANS

Khusrau II (king) *see* SASANIANS

Koguryo (kingdom) *see* CHOSON

Korea *see* CHOSON

Kumaraguta I (emperor) *see* GUPTA
DYNASTY


Lade (battle) *see* IONIAN REVOLT

Later Han *see* HAN DYNASTY

Leo (pope) *see* ATTILA

Leonidas (king) *see* THERMOPYLAE

Leuctra (battle) *see* EPAMINONDAS

Licinius (emperor) *see*
CONSTANTINE

Livy (historian) *see* LITERATURE

Lolang (commandery) *see* CHOSON

Long Walls (Athens) *see* PERICLES

Lyceum (school) *see* ARISTOTLE

Lycurgus (reformer) *see* SPARTA

Lydia (kingdom) *see* CROESUS


Maccabeus (rebel) *see* SELEUCIDS *and*
JEWS

Macrinus (emperor) *see* SEVERAN
DYNASTY

Magna Graecia *see* SICILY

Magnus Maximus (usurper) *see*
THEODOSIUS I

Magnesia (battle) *see* ANTIOCHUS III

Magnetism *see* INVENTIONS

Manetho (author) *see* BEROSSUS

Mani (prophet) *see* MANICHAEISM

Marathon (battle) *see* PERSIAN
INVASIONS

Marcian (emperor) *see* GOTHS

Mardonius (general) *see* PERSIAN
INVASIONS

Martyrdom *see* POLYCARP

Maurice (emperor) *see* SASANIANS

Maxentius (emperor) *see*
CONSTANTINE

Maximian (emperor) *see* DIOCLETIAN

Maximinus (emperor) *see* SEVERAN
DYNASTY

Medes (people) *see* PERSIA

Medicine *see* INVENTIONS

Megarian decree *see* MEGARA

Menander (playwright) *see* DRAMA

Meng Tian (general) *see* GREAT
WALL

Milo (wrestler) *see* OLYMPIA

Mithras (deity) *see* RELIGION

Mulvian bridge (battle) *see*
CONSTANTINE

Mycale (battle) *see* PERSIAN
INVASIONS

Mysteries *see* RELIGION

Mystery religions *see* RELIGION


Nagasena (monk) *see* MENANDER

Nabonidus (king) *see* PERSIA

Narseh (king) *see* SASANIANS

Nekhtharehbe (pharoah) *see* EGYPT

Nepos (emperor) *see* ROMULUS
AUGUSTULUS

Nerva (emperor) *see* FLAVIAN
DYNASTY

New comedy *see* DRAMA

Notion (battle) *see* ALCIBIADES

Numidia (kingdom) *see* MARIUS

Octavian *see* AUGUSTUS

Odoacer (king) *see* ROMULUS
AUGUSTULUS

Oligarchy *see* PELOPONNESIAN
LEAGUE *and* ROME

Omens *see* ORACLES

Orodes II (king) *see* SUREN

Orestes (general) *see* ROMULUS
AUGUSTULUS

Orpheus (poet) *see* PYTHAGORAS

Otho (emperor) *see* GALBA


Palmyra (state) *see* AURELIAN

Panaetius (philosopher) *see* STOICISM

Paper-making *see* INVENTIONS

Parmenides (philosopher) *see*
EMPEDOCLES

Pasargadae (city) *see* ARCHITECTURE

Paul (saint) *see* CHRISTIANITY

Perdiccas (king) *see* MACEDON

Pergamum (kingdom) *see* ATTALIDS

Periander (tyrant) *see* CORINTH

Peroz (king) *see* SASANIANS

Perpetua (martyr) *see* AFRICA

Pertinax (emperor) *see* SEVERAN
DYNASTY

Pescennius (general) *see* SEVERAN
DYNASTY

Petra (city) *see* ARABIA

Petronius (author) *see* SENECA

Phalanx (formation) *see* WARFARE

Pharos (lighthouse) *see* ALEXANDRIA

Pharsalus (battle) *see* POMPEY

Pheidon (tyrant) *see* ARGOS

Phidias (sculptor) *see* ART

Philippi (battle) *see* ANTONY

Philodemus (philosopher) *see*
EPICURUS

Phrynichus (playwright) *see* DRAMA

Picts (people) *see* DIOCLETIAN

Pindar (poet) *see* LITERATURE

Pingcheng (battle) *see* ZHANG QIAN

Plataea (battle) *see* PERSIAN
INVASIONS

Plautus (playwright) *see* DRAMA

Plutarch (historian) *see* LITERATURE

Polycrates (tyrant) *see* SAMOS

Polybius (historian) *see* ACHAEAN
LEAGUE

Pontus (kingdom) *see* MITHRIDATES

Posidonius (orator) *see* RHODES

Potidaea (city-state) *see* PERICLES

Praetorians (guards) *see* CLAUDIUS *and*
TIBERIUS

Procopius (historian) *see* LITERATURE

Protagoras (philosopher) *see* ATHENS

Ptolemy I (king) *see* PTOLEMIES

Punic Wars (against Rome) *see*
CARTHAGE

Pusyamitra (king) *see* SUNGA
DYNASTY

Pyrrhon (philosopher) *see* SCEPTICISM

Pythia (priestess) *see* DELPHI


Qi (state) *see* WARRING STATES


Ramagupta (emperor) *see* GUPTA
DYNASTY

Raphia (battle) *see* PTOLEMIES

Red cliffs (battle) *see* CAO CAO

Roxane (wife) *see* ALEXANDER

Rudrasena III (king) *see*
CANDRAGUPTA II

Ruler cult *see* KINGSHIP


Saguntum (city-state) *see* HANNIBAL

Sakas (people) *see* SCYTHIANS

Salamis (battle) *see* PERSIAN
INVASIONS

Salvianus (presbyter) *see* ROME

Samprati (emperor) *see* MAURYAN
DYNASTY

Samudragupta (emperor) *see* GUPTA
DYNASTY

Sarissa (pike) *see* WARFARE

Science *see* INVENTIONS

Scipio Aemilianus *see* SCIPIOS

Scipio Africanus *see* SCIPIOS

Scipio Asiaticus *see* SCIPIOS

Scipio Barbatus *see* SCIPIOS

Sejanus (commander) *see* TIBERIUS

Seleucus II (king) *see* SELEUCIDS

Sellasia (battle) *see* STOICISM

Sepeia (battle) *see* CLEOMENES I

Serapis (deity) *see* PTOLEMIES

Severus Alexander (emperor) *see*
SEVERAN DYNASTY

Shapur II (king) *see* SASANIANS

Silk Road *see* WESTERN REGIONS

Silures (people) *see* CARATACUS

Simon Magus (Gnostic) *see*
GNOSTICISM

Simonides (poet) *see* LITERATURE

Sophists (philosophers) *see* ATHENS

Sophocles (playwright) *see* DRAMA

Steel-making *see* INVENTIONS

Stilicho (general) *see* HONORIUS

Suetonius (historian) *see* LITERATURE

Susa (city) *see* DARIUS I


Tacitus (historian) *see* LITERATURE

Tanit (deity) *see* SACRIFICE

Taxila (city) *see* ASHOKA

Temenids (dynasty) *see* MACEDON

Ten Thousand (expedition) *see*
XENOPHON

Teutones (people) *see* MARIUS

Terence (playwright) *see* DRAMA

Tertullian (presbyter) *see* AFRICA

Thales (philosopher) *see* INVENTIONS

Theagenes (tyrant) *see* MEGARA

Theodoric (king) *see* GOTHS

Thirty (oligarchy) *see* THRASYBULUS

Tigranes (king) *see* ARMENIA

Tigranocerta (capital) *see* ARMENIA

Tissa (prince) *see* ASHOKA

Titus (emperor) *see* FLAVIAN
DYNASTY

Transport *see* INVENTIONS

Trinovantes (people) *see* BOUDICCA

Trittyes (divisions) *see* CLEISTHENES

Triumvirates *see* CAESAR *and*
ANTONY

Trojan War *see* LITERATURE


Udjahorresnet (official) *see* EGYPT

Ugo (king) *see* CHOSON


Valens (emperor) *see* VALENTINIAN

Valerian (emperor) *see* AURELIAN

Vasiska (king) *see* KUSHANAS

Vasudeva (king) *see* KUSHANAS

Verica (king) *see* CARATACUS

Verus (emperor) *see* ANTONINE
DYNASTY

Vespasian (emperor) *see* FLAVIAN
DYNASTY

Vima Kaphises (king) *see* KUSHANAS

Virasena Saba (minister) *see*
CANDRAGUPTA II

Virgil (poet) *see* LITERATURE

Vitellius (emperor) *see* GALBA


Wang Qian (general) *see* WARRING
STATES

Wei (state) *see* WARRING STATES

Wiman (king) *see* CHOSON


Xanthippus (general) *see* CARTHAGE

Xianbei (Tartars) *see* GREAT WALL

ARTHUR COTTERELL was born in Berkshire in 1942. He was educated at Ashmead School, Reading, and St. John's College, Cambridge. Now Principal of Kingston College of Further Education in Surrey, he combines a career in education and training after school with an extensive interest in other civilizations, many of them ancient. His published works include *The Minoan World, A Dictionary of World Mythology, The First Emperor of China,* and *China: A Concise Cultural History.* He has also written a general history of East Asia, an area in which he is well traveled. He is also editor of the new *Penguin Encyclopaedia of Classical Civilisations.* He is married, with one son, and lives in Surrey.